Katherine A. [Loop] Hannon

Author: Katherine A. Loop

Master Books Creative Team:

Editor: Craig Froman

Design: Jennifer Bauer

Cover Design: Diana Bogardus

Copy Editors:
Judy Lewis

Willow Meek

Curriculum Review:
Kristen Pratt
Laura Welch
Diana Bogardus

First printing: March 2016
Sixth printing: March 2021

Master Books®, P.O. Box 726, Green Forest, AR 72638
Master Books® is a division of the New Leaf Publishing Group, Inc.

ISBN: 978-0-89051-906-6
ISBN: 978-1-61458-490-2 (digital)
Library of Congress Number: 2015937807

Some sections are heavily adapted with permission from Katherine Loop, *Revealing Arithmetic: Math Concepts from a Biblical Worldview* (Fairfax, VA: Christian Perspective, 2010).

Printed in the United States of America

Please visit our website for other great titles:
www.masterbooks.com

Acknowledgments

I don't believe you would be holding this curriculum in your hands today if it were not for some very special people. It's with much appreciation that I'd like to acknowledge and thank

my mom (Cris Loop) for being my right-hand helper throughout this project, solving hundreds of math problems and painstakingly working with me to make the material understandable.

my dad (Bob Loop) for his overall support (and specifically for all his input into the statistics and probability sections).

my brother Brian Loop for putting up with math questions at all hours of the day and helping me think through concepts and flow.

my cousin Hannah and my aunt Marie Ferreira for testing the initial draft, thereby giving me a weekly deadline and providing invaluable feedback.

Joy Dubbs for being my technical sounding board on so many concepts, for reading drafts for me, and for never tiring of a math question.

Abbey Ryan for reading the material, cheering me onward, and reminding me why I was writing this.

the graphic designer, Jennifer Bauer, for laboriously formatting the material and patiently dealing with my changes.

my editor, Craig Froman, for always having an understanding and encouraging word.

the rest of the team at Master Books for believing in the project and moving it into publication.

everyone else who has prayed for and supported me during this project in one way or another.

Above all, I'd like to thank the Lord, without whom all our labors are in vain.

Have You Completed Book 1?

The book you're holding in your hands builds on the foundational concepts covered in Book 1 of *Principles of Mathematics: Biblical Worldview Curriculum.*

Book 1 covers the core principles of arithmetic and geometry (along with some statistics), while Book 2 builds on those principles as it introduces the core principles of algebra, probability, and trigonometry (along with more statistics).

In Book 1, students learned to find the height of a tree without leaving the ground, use negative numbers to describe the force on objects, explore historical multiplication methods, apply math to music, and much more! In Book 2, students will build on that knowledge so they'll be prepared to understand and see the purpose of algebra and other upper math courses. From exploring genetics to force to sequences in music, they'll continue seeing how math truly is a real-life tool we can use to explore God's creation and serve Him.

About the Author

Katherine Loop is a homeschool graduate from northern Virginia. Understanding the biblical worldview in math made a tremendous difference in her life and started her on a journey of researching and sharing on the topic. For over a decade now, she's been researching, writing, and speaking on math, along with other topics. Her books on math and a biblical worldview have been used by various Christian colleges, homeschool groups, and individuals.

Website and Blog: www.ChristianPerspective.net
(Check out the free e-newsletter.)

About This Curriculum

This is Book 2 of a two-book math course designed to give students a firm mathematical foundation, both academically and spiritually. Not only does the curriculum build mathematical thinking and problem-solving skills, it also shows students how a biblical worldview affects our approach to math's various concepts. Students learn to see math, not as an academic exercise, but as a way of exploring and describing consistencies God created and sustains. The worldview is not just an addition to the curriculum, but is the starting point. Science, history, and real life are integrated throughout.

How Does a Biblical Worldview Apply to Math . . . and Why Does It Matter?

Please see Lesson 1.1 for a brief introduction to how a biblical worldview applies to math and why it matters.

Who Is This Curriculum For?

This curriculum is aimed at grades 6–8, fitting into most math approaches the year or two years prior to starting high school algebra. If following traditional grade levels, Book 1 should be completed in grade 6 or 7, and Book 2 (the book in your hands) in grade 7 or 8.

The curriculum also works well for high school students looking to firm up math's foundational concepts and grasp how a biblical worldview applies to math. High school students may want to follow the alternate accelerated schedule provided in the *Teacher Guide* and complete each year of the program in a semester, or use the material alongside a high school course.

Where Do I Go Upon Completion?

Upon completion of Book 1, students will be ready to move on to Book 2. Upon completion of both years, students should be prepared to begin or return to any high school algebra course.

Are There Any Prerequisites?

Book 1: Students should have a **basic knowledge of arithmetic** (basic arithmetic will be reviewed, but at a fast pace and while teaching problem-solving skills and a biblical worldview of math) and **sufficient mental development** to think through the concepts and examples given. Typically, anyone in 6th grade or higher should be prepared to begin.

Teacher Guide

Book 2: It is strongly recommended that students complete Book 1 before beginning Book 2, as math builds on itself, and the principles of arithmetic and geometry are essential for understanding the principles covered in Book 2. Before beginning Book 2, students need to be comfortable with basic math skills (including rounding and working with decimals), fractions, unit conversion, negative numbers, geometry formulas (finding perimeter, area, and volume), and exponents; they also need to have problem-solving skills.

What Are the Curriculum's Components?

The curriculum consists of the ***Student Textbook*** and the ***Teacher Guide***. The *Student Textbook* contains the lessons, and the *Teacher Guide* contains all the worksheets, quizzes, and tests, along with an Answer Key and suggested schedule.

How Do I Use This Curriculum?

General Structure — This curriculum is designed to be self-taught, so students should be able to read the material and complete assignments on their own, with a parent or teacher available for questions. If teaching in a classroom, the text can serve as the basis for the teacher's presentations. This *Student Textbook* is divided into chapters and then into lessons. The number system used to label the lessons expresses this order. The first lesson is labeled 1.1 because it is Chapter 1, Lesson 1.

Worksheets, Quizzes, and Tests — The accompanying *Teacher Guide* includes worksheets, quizzes, and tests to go along with the material in this book, along with a suggested schedule and answer key.

Answer Key — A complete Answer Key is located in the *Teacher Guide*.

Schedule — A suggested schedule for completing the material in one year, along with an accelerated one-semester schedule, is located in the *Teacher Guide*.

[CONTENTS]

Preface

In Book 1 of *Principles of Mathematics*, we explored together the core concepts of arithmetic and geometry, seeing how math's very existence declares God's praises, and how it serves as a real-life tool. While in that book we looked mainly *backwards* at aspects of math with which you were probably already familiar, in this course we'll be looking *ahead* at concepts into which you'll dig into more depth in future math courses. As we do, we'll see that all of these new concepts, like the ones we looked at in the last book, work because of God's faithfulness and are tools we can use to serve Him.

Researching for this second book has been a fun yet stretching process for me, as it has forced me to revisit many concepts that I saw as meaningless when I first learned them. The more I continued to learn and research, though, the more amazed I grew at how useful different concepts are in describing the intricacies of God's creation. I've joked that you know you're writing a math curriculum when you begin to "see" math everywhere...which for me was quite a switch.

You see, I didn't grow up loving math or seeing it as a way of describing God's creation. As I mentioned in the preface to Book 1, while I was good at math, I viewed it as a subject of rules to be memorized, applied, and forgotten. It wasn't until I read *Mathematics: Is God Silent?* by James D. Nickel as a senior in high school that I realized that math wasn't neutral or confined to a textbook—it was a way of describing God's creation that loudly proclaimed the Creator's praises.

Seeing the biblical worldview in math was transformational for me—so much so that I wanted to share it with everyone I could. It led to more than a decade of research on the topic, several books on teaching math from a biblical worldview, and lastly this curriculum series.

It's been such a joy to hear from users of Book 1 and my previous books about how they have blessed them. Hearing that one mom found her child reading extra lessons on her own, watching students' eyes light up at conventions when they realize math really is more than apparently meaningless bookwork, finding out that a biblical worldview of math encouraged a mom to overcome her fears of the subject, and listening as a longtime teacher shared how excited she was to finally know how to teach math biblically has warmed my heart.

My earnest hope and prayer is that God will use this curriculum as well to bless readers. While the curriculum is labeled for junior high, it really applies to anyone of any age who wants to really "get" what math is all about from a biblical worldview. Whatever you're age and mathematical leaning (or lack thereof), I hope you'll find the material friendly and helpful. I hope you will find it a fascinating journey of discovery, helping you discover God's handiwork in math. Above all, I hope you'll leave encouraged that God can be trusted completely.

Writing this curriculum has been quite a journey for me, both in exploring math to a deeper level and of watching God faithfully provide. There were times I never thought the curriculum would actually reach completion, but it has. The acknowledgements don't begin to describe how blessed I was to be supported by a lot of talented people who were willing to let me hound them with questions, read countless drafts, work with me on refining and formatting concepts, check changes, and pray for and encourage me.

May the One who holds all creation together by the Word of His power (Hebrews 1:3) be honored and glorified in every page.

By God's Grace,

Katherine Loop

[CHAPTER 1]

The Big Picture

1.1 Overview of Mathematics

You probably learned to write numbers and count at a young age. At some point, you mastered the basic operations: addition, subtraction, multiplication, and division. Then came fractions, ratios, and percentages. Along the way, you learned to recognize different shapes, measure them, and find their perimeter, area, and volume.

86%

$1 + 1 = 2$

$8 - 2 = 6$

928.32

$88 \div 2 = 44$

$5\frac{1}{2} + 10\frac{1}{2} = 16$

We've become so familiar with math that it's easy to lose sight of math's purpose. What does 1 + 1 = 2 really mean? Why does 1 + 1 equal 2? Why do we have fractions, ratios, and percentages? What's the purpose of exploring shapes?

Before we jump into new concepts, we are going to pause and look at math's overall purpose — at the "big picture," so to speak. First, though, we need to talk about worldviews, as our worldview determines how we see both the "big picture" and the details of mathematics.

Worldview Matters

Whether we realize it or not, our perspective on any area of life is determined by what is called a worldview. In *Understanding the Times*, David Noebel (founder of Summit Ministries) defines a worldview this way: "A worldview is like a pair of glasses — it is something through which you view everything. And the fact is,

everyone has a worldview, a way he or she looks at the world."[1] In other words, a worldview is a set of truths (or falsehoods we believe to be true) through which we interpret life.

As we look at the "big picture" of math and study math together, we'll be seeking to start with the Bible — God's revealed Word to man — as our source of truth, using it as the "glasses" through which we look at math. We'll discover that the Bible gives us solid answers to where math originated, why math is possible, what we should expect as we use math, and how we should use math. With that in mind, let's begin looking at the "big picture" of math.

Where Did Math Originate?

Have you ever stopped to think about where math originated? How did we get math? Did men invent it? Has it just always been there?

To understand *where* math came from, we have to first consider *what* math really is. Is math just a collection of facts in a textbook? While it may feel that way at times, math is hardly confined to a textbook. The main reason math is such an essential subject is because it applies outside of a textbook.

Take a moment to think about how many times you see numbers each day. Price tags, exit signs, clocks, calendars, addresses, expiration dates, nutritional data, Bible verses, speed-limit signs, rulers, radio dials, TV remotes, thermometers, store hours — we see numbers all the time.

Every occupation utilizes math to some degree or another. Scheduling airplane flights, generating computer graphics, managing businesses, designing bridges and buildings, laying out roads, producing digital sounds — all of these tasks require math. Even non-mathematical fields employ math. Artists deal with proportions, musicians work with a musical notation based on fractions, airplane pilots compute a weight and balance to make sure their plane will handle the cargo, veterinarians have to know how much medicine to give — math proves useful on the job, whatever that job might be.

Math is also used behind the scenes to develop or produce the technology and resources we use on a daily basis. Computers, cars, ovens, medical treatments, airplanes, cell phones, toys, GPS units — name something you use, and chances are math helped in developing or producing it. Pick a topic from science class — be it the distance to the stars or how an atom works — and most likely math has been used in its exploration.

Departures 17:59

DESTINATION	BOARDING TIME	GATE	STATUS
DUBAI	17:35	15	FINAL CALL
SYDNEY	17:50	04	BOARDING
SYDNEY	18:05	16	BOARDING IN 5 MINS
DUBAI	18:10	02	BOARDING IN 10 MINS
BUENOS AIRES	18:25	07	BOARDING IN 25 MINS
RAROTONGA	18:35	01	BOARDING IN 35 MINS
LOS ANGELES	18:35	06	BOARDING IN 35 MINS
SAN FRANCISCO	18:50		BOARDING IN 50 MINS

All that to say, math is clearly more than a textbook exercise. **Math** is a way of describing the quantities and consistencies all around us — quantities and consistencies the Bible tells us the triune God created and sustains.

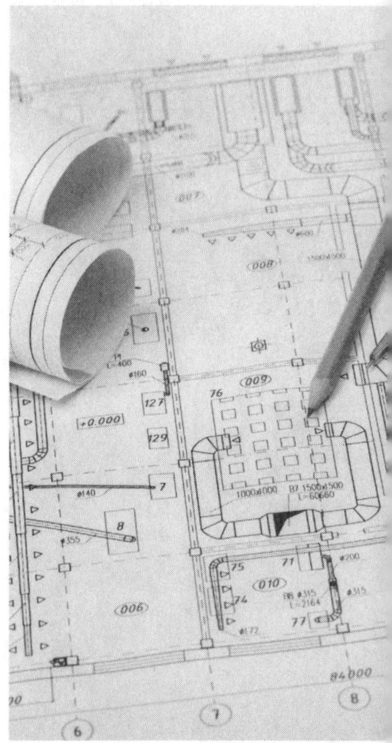

> *In the beginning God created the heaven and the earth. And the earth was without form, and void; and darkness was upon the face of the deep. And the Spirit of God moved upon the face of the waters (Genesis 1:1–2).*
>
> *In the beginning was the Word, and the Word was with God, and the Word was God. The same was in the beginning with God. All things were made by him; and without him was not any thing made that was made. . . . And the Word was made flesh, and dwelt among us, (and we beheld his glory, the glory as of the only begotten of the Father,) full of grace and truth (John 1:1–3, 14).*
>
> *Jesus answered them. . . . I and my Father are one (John 10:25, 30).*
>
> *For by him [Jesus] were all things created, that are in heaven, and that are in earth, visible and invisible, whether they be thrones, or dominions, or principalities, or powers: all things were created by him, and for him: And he is before all things, and by him all things consist (Colossians 1:16–17).*
>
> *[referring to Jesus] . . . upholding all things by the word of his power . . . (Hebrews 1:3).*

In other words, while men (using their God-given abilities) have developed the different symbols and techniques used in math over the years, the underlying principles those symbols and techniques describe are principles God created and sustains. In fact, as we'll see next, it's God's faithfulness that makes math possible.

Ignoring the Question

The fundamental question of why math works is one that has baffled secular philosophers for years, as it doesn't make sense apart from a biblical worldview. Consider this quote: "Some of the most abstruse concepts of mathematics have an uncanny way of becoming essential tools in physics. Many physicists have been so impressed by the usefulness of mathematics that they have attributed to it almost mystical power. . . . In this article I shall not attempt any deep philosophical discussion of the reasons why mathematics supplies so much power to physics. . . . The vast majority of working scientists, myself included, find comfort in the words of the French mathematician Henri Lebesgue: 'In my opinion a mathematician, in so far as he is a mathematician, need not preoccupy himself with philosophy.'"[2] In other words, this scientist is saying that he's going to avoid the fundamental question of why math works and just use it. As Christians, we don't have to ignore the question — the Bible gives us an answer.

Why Is Math Possible?

People who love math often say they love it because it's always predictable. You can count on 1 + 1 to equal 2. There's no subjectivity to math — it works the way it does.

Why is this? Again, the Bible gives us the answer. In Jeremiah 33:25, God tells us that He is keeping His covenant with the "ordinances" of heaven and earth.

> *Thus saith the LORD; If my covenant be not with day and night, and if I have not appointed the ordinances of heaven and earth;*

Day in and day out, our faithful, consistent Creator is holding all things together in such a predictable and reliable way that we can use math to describe it. Math is reliable *because* God is reliable. In fact, God uses the "ordinances" of heaven and earth to remind the Israelites that He'll be that reliable to His covenant with them.

> *Then will I cast away the seed of Jacob and David my servant, so that I will not take any of his seed to be rulers over the seed of Abraham, Isaac, and Jacob: for I will cause their captivity to return, and have mercy on them (Jeremiah 33:26).*

Water Droplets and Addition

It's important to note that when we say the universe is consistent, we don't mean that it all operates exactly the same way. For example, one water droplet plus another water droplet does *not* equal two water droplets — instead, they merge to form one larger droplet. The apparent contradiction in how liquids combine reminds us that, no matter how well we think we have things figured out, God's laws and universe are more complex than we can imagine. God has different, though equally consistent, principles for governing liquids at the visible level than He does solids.

Note, though, that while we visibly see one larger droplet instead of two, that is not what occurs on the atomic level. At the atomic level, the starting atoms plus the final atoms add together following the rules of regular addition — if we started with 1 atom and added 1 more atom, the ending larger droplet would have 2 atoms.

Men have often sought to make either experience or man's intellect the foundation for the underlying truth in math. Yet neither of these foundations hold up to scrutiny. Raindrops baffle those who would say truth in math is determined solely intellectually,[3] as it's experience that tells us one raindrop plus another equals a larger one. Yet experience can't be the source of truth either, as we use concepts in math we've never experienced (such as infinite numbers). In a biblical worldview, though, we have a solid answer for why we're able to learn both experientially and intellectually — God both created the world and gave us the ability to explore it.

The Bible also gives us a reason for understanding why we're able to discern and record the orderly world God created. It tells us God created man in His image and gave man dominion over the earth.

> *And God said, Let us make man in our image, after our likeness: and let them have dominion over the fish of the sea, and over the fowl of the air, and over the cattle, and over all the earth, and over every creeping thing that creepeth upon the earth. So God created man in his own image, in the image of God created he him; male and female created he them (Genesis 1:26–27).*

Thus we're capable of exploring the universe and developing different symbols and techniques to describe it.

What Should We Expect as We Use Math?

Not only does the Bible give us principles that explain where math came from and why it works, but it also helps us know what to expect as we use math to describe the quantities and consistencies around us. The Bible tells us that God created a perfect world, but sin marred that world.

> *And God saw every thing that he had made, and, behold, it was very good. . . . (Genesis 1:31)*

> *Wherefore, as by one man sin entered into the world, and death by sin; and so death passed upon all men, for that all have sinned: (Romans 5:12).*

Thus we should expect to find evidence of design (pointing us to the wisdom and care of the Creator), yet at the same time a world marred from that perfect order (reminding us of the Fall). And guess what? That is exactly what we find.

For a simple example, we can observe that cats have four legs. Math helps us describe this aspect of the design God placed in cats. Yet if you were to look at enough cats, you'd eventually find a cat that was missing a leg, as we live in a fallen world.

How Should We Use Math?

The Bible tells us to do all that we do in the name of Jesus and with thanksgiving to God.

> *And whatsoever ye do in word or deed, do all in the name of the Lord Jesus, giving thanks to God and the Father by him (Colossians 3:17).*

Notice that this verse doesn't say, "and whatsoever ye do *but math.*" It says "and whatsoever ye do." Math is not exempted. Within math, as in every other area of life, we have an opportunity to depend on and praise God. We can also use math, along with other skills we learn, to help us in the tasks God has given us to do.

Term Time
Here are a few terms we'll use extensively as we explore the principles of mathematics together. Be sure to familiarize yourself with them before we get started.

Expression — An expression is "a collection of symbols that jointly express a quantity."[4] For example, 4 + 5 is an expression — 4, 5, and + are a collection of symbols that together express the quantity 9.

Equation — An equation is "a statement that the values of two mathematical expressions are equal (indicated by the sign =)."[5]

Simplify — When we refer to simplifying an expression or equation, we mean to express it as simply as possible. For example, 5 + 6 simplifies to 11.

Keeping Perspective

Wow — that's quite an amazing "big picture," isn't it? Think about it for a minute. Every time you use math and see that it works it's reminding you that you can trust God. Math's an exploration of God's handiwork — a tool we can use to explore His creation while worshiping the Creator.

I hope you're excited about digging deeper into math this year. As we do, we'll see over and over again how math helps us describe the quantities and consistencies God created and sustains. We'll learn how to use concepts outside a textbook, applying what we learn to help us with the tasks God's given us to do. Above all, we'll reflect on what a faithful, wise, infinite Creator we serve — a Creator worthy of all our trust.

1.2 The Language of Mathematics — Symbols and Conventions

Before we jump into the details of math, we're going to take the rest of this chapter to continue building the "big picture." In this lesson, we're going to look at the language side of mathematics.

Many aspects of math can be thought of as a language system. Mathematical symbols, notations, and conventions are like a language system to communicate about the quantities and consistencies God created and sustains.

Symbols

For years, you've been using symbols to **name** quantities. For example, you might use "5" to represent five cups of flour, five inches, or five additional CDs. You've also used symbols to **identify** (the numbers in a telephone number identify a specific telephone line) and to **order** (such as the 5th most popular song of the year).

You've also used symbols such as – (minus), + (plus), x (times), ÷ (division), = (equals), and ≠ (does not equal) for years. These symbols make it simpler to write and solve equations. (After all, can you imagine having to write "plus" every time you want to show the addition of two numbers instead of writing "+"?)

As we did in Book 1, we'll be representing multiplication different ways. All four methods shown here are legitimate ways of representing 4 times 5.

4 x 5 4 • 5 4(5) (4)5

Note: A number written next to a set of parentheses means to multiply that number by whatever is inside the parentheses. For example, 4(5) means to multiply 5 by 4.

It's important to understand that the symbols with which we're familiar are but *one way* of describing God's creation. There are others! The chart shows some of the different ways a single quantity has been represented. Again, the symbols we use are merely part of a language system to describe the quantities and consistencies God created and sustains.

Different Symbols That Have Been Used to Express a Single Quantity[5]

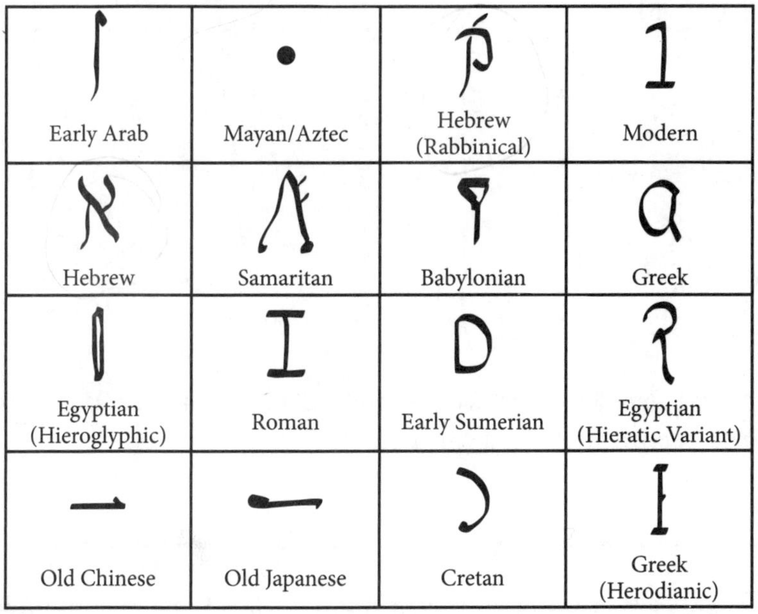

Early Arab	Mayan/Aztec	Hebrew (Rabbinical)	Modern
Hebrew	Samaritan	Babylonian	Greek
Egyptian (Hieroglyphic)	Roman	Early Sumerian	Egyptian (Hieratic Variant)
Old Chinese	Old Japanese	Cretan	Greek (Herodianic)

Math, Adam, and the Animals

Much as Adam used names back in the Garden of Eden to describe the animals, we use names like "three" and symbols like "3" to describe various aspects of God's creation. Much as Adam named the animals while in the Creator's presence, through Jesus we can again use math while fellowshipping with the Creator.

Notations

Place value, fractions, decimals, percents, exponents, etc. — these are all notations (a "series or system of written symbols used to represent numbers, amounts, or elements . . ."[7]) that help us represent amounts. Since we covered all of these notations thoroughly in Book 1, they all should already be familiar to you. We'll encounter them again as we explore math together.

It's worth a quick reminder, though, that our decimal system (the notation we typically use to represent quantities) is a place-value system (a system in which the place, or location, of a symbol determines its value) based on 10. Each place to the left is worth 10 times the previous place, and each place to the right is worth $\frac{1}{10}$ of the previous place. The decimal point separates the whole numbers from the partial ones.

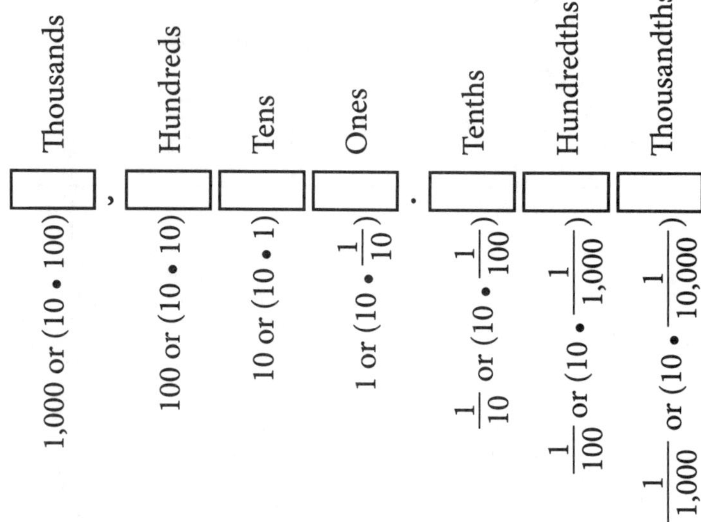

The rules you've learned for performing operations on whole and decimal numbers help keep track of place value automatically.

Conventions

Conventions are agreed-upon protocols or rules that aid us in communication.

All conventions apply within a context. Some conventions may only be followed for a specific situation or industry. Other conventions are followed throughout our typical number system.

One important convention that applies throughout our typical number system is the order of operations. The **order of operations** is an agreed-upon order in which to read mathematical symbols and notations.

While the order of operations applies throughout our typical number system, it's possible to follow a different convention. In fact, some calculators and computer programming languages have/do. Every convention applies within a context!

The Order of Operations

1) Solve anything within parentheses first, using the following order (which is the same order we'll follow outside of parentheses too):
   a) Simplify exponents and roots, from left to right.*
   b) Multiply or divide, from left to right.
   c) Add or subtract, from left to right.
2) Next, simplify exponents and roots, from left to right.*
3) Now multiply or divide, from left to right.
4) Last, add or subtract, from left to right.

**There will not be any exponents or roots in your problems until they are reviewed in Lesson 1.5 (exponents) and Lesson 17.1 (roots).*

The order of operations helps us know what's meant by an expression. For example, consider 4 + 12 ÷ 2. What does this equal? Do we need to divide 12 by 2, and then add 4, in which case we would get 10, or do we need to add the 4 and 12 and then divide the sum (16) by 2, in which case we would get 8?

The order of operations makes it clear the order in which we should complete the operations. We divide first, and then add.

$$4 + 12 \div 2$$
$$4 + \quad 6 = 10$$

But if there had been parentheses involved, we would have solved whatever was inside the parentheses first.

$$(4 + 12) \div 2$$
$$16 \quad \div 2 = 8$$

Did you know?
Years ago, other methods, such as a line above or below numbers, were used to indicate groupings instead of parentheses. An example is shown below.

$\overline{4 + 5} \bullet 3$
instead of
$(4 + 5) \bullet 3$

Parentheses are just a convention used to show groupings.

Parentheses and Assumed Groupings

Even though the first point in the order of operations is listed as "solve anything within parentheses first," the principle is to **solve groupings first**.

If we saw $2\overline{)5 + 6 + 9}$, we'd know that we need to add the numbers underneath the division sign before completing the division. Although there aren't parentheses, it's a clearly understood grouping. The *sum* of 5 + 6 + 9 is the number we need to divide. The first point of the order of operations is to deal with grouped numbers first. Parentheses are just a common convention used to show groupings.

Keeping Perspective

Much of studying math is similar to learning a language — we learn the symbols, notations, and conventions we've adopted to help us describe God's creation. While it's easy to get lost in the language side of math, remember that the purpose of a language is to communicate . . . and the purpose of the many symbols, notations, and conventions you'll encounter in math is to communicate about the quantities and consistencies God created and sustains.

1.3 The Consistency of Mathematics — Operations and Properties

Math symbols, notations, and conventions are useful because they help us describe the underlying consistencies all around us — consistencies God created and sustains. Let's do a quick "big picture" review of the consistency of mathematics.

Operations and Properties

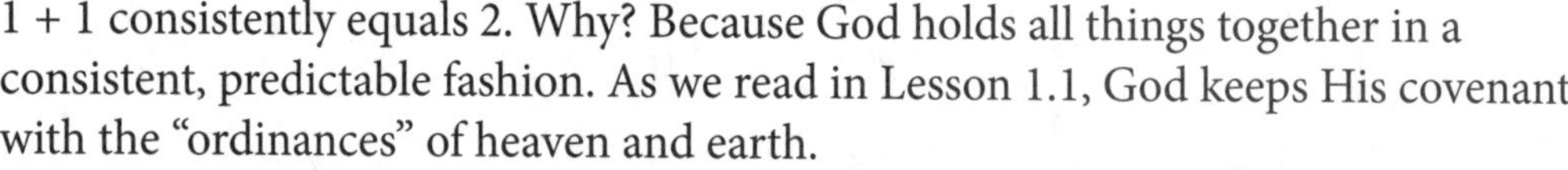

1 + 1 consistently equals 2. Why? Because God holds all things together in a consistent, predictable fashion. As we read in Lesson 1.1, God keeps His covenant with the "ordinances" of heaven and earth.

> *Thus saith the LORD; If my covenant be not with day and night, and if I have not appointed the ordinances of heaven and earth; Then will I cast away the seed of Jacob and David my servant, so that I will not take any of his seed to be rulers over the seed of Abraham, Isaac, and Jacob: for I will cause their captivity to return, and have mercy on them (Jeremiah 33:25–26).*

God's faithfulness enables us to memorize addition, subtraction, multiplication, and division facts, as well as to use **algorithms**, or step-by-step methods, to solve problems we don't have memorized. Algorithms work because of the underlying consistency God created and sustains. While there are many different algorithms we could use to add, subtract, multiply, and divide, the ones traditionally taught are shown below. We saw in Book 1 how each of these algorithms helps us break down problems we don't have memorized into problems we do, keeping track of place value for us.

Traditional Addition, Subtraction, Multiplication, and Division Algorithms

$$\begin{array}{r} {}^{1} \\ 12 \\ +19 \\ \hline 31 \end{array} \qquad \begin{array}{r} {}^{1}\,{}^{1} \\ \not{2}4 \\ -\ \ 9 \\ \hline 15 \end{array} \qquad \begin{array}{r} \not{1} \\ 12 \\ \times 29 \\ \hline 108 \\ +240 \\ \hline 348 \end{array} \qquad \begin{array}{r} 24 \\ 2\overline{)48} \\ -4 \\ \hline 08 \\ -8 \\ \hline 0 \end{array}$$

God's faithfulness also allows us to make observations about the properties of operations and apply those properties to other situations. A **property** is a characteristic that holds true in every situation. Basically, a property is a way of expressing a truth about the ordinances God created and sustains. Take a moment to review these properties we covered in Book 1, as we'll be applying them over and over again in this book too.

Commutative Property of Addition and Multiplication

Order doesn't matter.

Addition	Multiplication
$1 + 2 = 2 + 1$	$2 \bullet 3 = 3 \bullet 2$
$3 = 3$	$6 = 6$

Associative Property of Addition and Multiplication

Grouping doesn't matter.

Addition	Multiplication
$(1+2) + 3 = 1 + (2+3)$	$(2 \bullet 3) \bullet 4 = 2 \bullet (3 \bullet 4)$
$3 + 3 = 1 + 5$	$6 \bullet 4 = 2 \bullet 12$
$6 = 6$	$24 = 24$

Identity Property of Multiplication

Multiplying by 1 doesn't change the value.

$$2 \bullet 1 = 2$$

Note: It follows that dividing by 1 doesn't change the value of a number either,[8] *as division simply reverses multiplication. 2 • 1 equals 2, and 2 ÷ 1 equals 2.*

Test the properties we're reviewing today with any objects you have around the house. For example, add quantities with different groupings — the grouping won't matter. Again, these properties describe what happens in real life. Properties are a way of expressing truths about the ordinances God created and sustains.

Identity Property of Addition

Adding 0 doesn't change the value.

$$2 + 0 = 2$$

The Distributive Property of Multiplication

If you distribute multiplication among addends and then add those results together, you'll get the same result as if you first did the addition and then multiplied by the sum.

$2(3 + 4)$	$2(3 + 4)$
	$2(3) + 2(4)$
$2(7) = 14$	$6 + 8 = 14$
14 total	**14 total**

Note: It doesn't matter which side of the parentheses the multiplier is on. The following would also hold true:

(3 + 4)2	(3 + 4)2
	(3)2 + (4)2
(7)2 = 14	6 + 8 = 14
14 total	**14 total**

Worldview Matters

Take a look at this typical property presentation:

> *A property describes the way something is. We can't change properties. We are stuck with properties because they are what they are.*[9]

Let's reword this to convey a biblical worldview instead.

> *A property describes the way God has chosen to govern an aspect of His creation. We can't change properties because we can't change God. We are stuck with properties because God is who He is and He is going to govern creation the way He has decided to govern creation whether or not it's popular with us.*

Do you see the different message conveyed? One leaves us looking at properties . . . the other lifts our eyes to the One holding properties together.

As you study math or any other subject, filter what you read through a biblical worldview, giving God the glory for His creation.

Keeping Perspective

Every time you solve a math problem, you're relying on the underlying consistency present in math. And every time you see that math still operates consistently, it's testifying that God is still on His throne, faithfully holding all things together.

For ever, O LORD, thy word is settled in heaven (Psalm 119:89).

1.4 The Usefulness of Mathematics — Problem Solving

Since we live in a consistent universe held together by a consistent, faithful God, and since math helps us describe those consistencies, we should expect math to prove quite useful outside of a textbook. In fact, Walter W. Sawyer compares math to a chest of tools.

> *"Mathematics is like a chest of tools: Before studing the tools in detail, a good workman should know the object of each, when it is used, how it is used, what it is used for." — Walter W. Sawyer*[10]

Before studying the tools in details, a good workman should know the object of each, when it is used, how it is used, what it is used for.[11]

I love that analogy. Tools come in all sorts of shapes and sizes. Some are intuitive; others require practice to use effectively. Each one, though, serves a useful purpose. As we study math together, we're going to discover how the various aspects of math are like tools. Each one, serves a useful purpose. And as with actual tools, sometimes it takes multiple mathematical tools to get a job done.

Problem-Solving Steps

In order to help you learn to see and use math as a practical tool, we'll be including a good deal of problem-solving practice throughout this course. These problems will give you practice in applying the tools you learn. When you encounter a word problem (or a real-life problem), here are some helpful steps to follow:

1. Define — Write out the information you know and the information you need to find.

2. Plan — Think through how you can find the information you need to find — it may take more than one step. Here's where you need to look at the information you know and see how it relates to the information you need to find. Can you find the information you're seeking by addition? Subtraction? Multiplication? Division? A combination? It's often helpful to use words or symbols to write out equations showing how the information you know relates to the information you're trying to find.

3. Solve — Here's where you do the math.

4. Check — Does the answer make sense?

This example was taken from an early 1900s math book[11]—prices have gone up since then!

Example: The average yield of a certain field is 36 bushels of corn per acre. By putting in an average of 2 days per acre more time cultivating the crop, the farmer is able to increase the yield to 54 bushels per acre. If corn is worth 45 cents per bushel, how much per day does he earn for his extra work?

1. Define — Let's look at the information we've been given.

original average yield = 36 bu

increased average yield = 54 bu

increase in time = 2 days

sales price = \$0.45

earnings per additional day = ?

2. Plan — We want to find the earnings per additional day. These earnings will be the increase in total dollars the farmer receives for the additional corn (i.e., the increase in earnings) divided by the increased time.

earnings per additional day = *increase in earnings* ÷ *increase in time*

We know the increase in time is 2 days. But how much more do we make for that increased time? That is, what's our increase in earnings? To find that, we have to first figure out how many more bushels we're getting. Multiplying the increase in bushels by the sales price at which we sell those bushels will tell us the increase in earnings.

increase in number of bushels = original average yield – increased average yield

increase in earnings = increase in number of bushels • sales price

Notice how it will take a few steps, but we can find the information we need to find from the information we were given.

3. Solve — Let's use the values we've been given to execute our plan.

increase in number bushels = 54 bu – 36 bu = 18 bu

increase in earnings = 18 • $0.45 = $8.10

earnings per additional day = $8.10 ÷ 2 = $4.05

4. Check — $4.05 seems to be a reasonable answer considering that we have 18 bushels more to sell, each one sells for about a half a dollar, and it took 2 extra days worth of work. (We rounded and mentally estimated to see that $4.05 seemed reasonable.) If we were uncertain of our math or got an answer that seemed unreasonable, we could go back and check our math using the reverse operation too.

Checking our subtraction with addition:

18 bu + 36 bu = 54 bu

Checking our multiplication with division:

$8.10 ÷ 18 = $0.45

Checking our division with multiplication:

$4.05 • 2 = $8.10

You don't necessarily need to write out every step in the word problem — they're listed here to walk you through the process. You'll often be able to define, plan, and check mentally, only writing down the actual solving step. However, it's important to be familiar with the process of

defining (thinking about what you know),

planning (figuring out how to find what you need to know),

solving (doing the math), and

checking (making sure your answer makes sense).

It's also important to note that **you can use letters to stand for the different numbers in a word problem rather than words.** For example, in the example, we could have written *b* instead of "increase in number of bushels," *x* instead of "increase in earnings," and so forth.

Keeping Perspective

As we continue looking at the principles of mathematics together, we're going to look at how the concepts we learn serve useful purposes. We'll also include opportunities for you to learn to use those tools yourself in a useful way — after all, a tool doesn't do much good if you don't know how to use it. Since math applies in every occupation, knowing how to use it can help you with whatever tasks God assigns you, whether at home or on the job.

1.5 Overview of Geometry

As we saw in Book 1, math helps us describe and explore the shapes all around us. Without going into too much detail, let's take a "big picture" review of the branch of math known as geometry.

Understanding Geometry

Geo means "earth" and *metron* means "measure," so *geometry* actually means "earth measure." Both directly and indirectly, geometry helps us "measure the earth."

Naming Shapes

Shape names give us a handy way to refer to shapes with specific properties. While we won't review all the shape names we covered back in Book 1 here, you'll review some of them on Worksheet 1.5. (All worksheets are located in the *Teacher Guide*.)

rectangle

hexagon

triangle

Measuring Shapes

We often find ourselves measuring different aspects of shapes. Let's do a quick review of units of measure, perimeter, area, and volume, all of which we looked at thoroughly in Book 1.

First, though, let's talk for a minute about formulas. We use formulas to help us find perimeter, area, and volume. As we discussed in Book 1, a **formula** is "a mathematical relationship or rule expressed in symbols."[12] For example, the area of a rectangle always equals the length times the width. We can express this as a formula like this:

$$A = \ell \bullet w$$

Here we've used the symbols A, ℓ, and w to stand for the area, length, and width of a rectangle.

It's worth noting that formulas rely on consistency. If real-life shapes constantly morphed from one shape into another like Silly Putty, we wouldn't be able to represent mathematically how the area related to the length and width (at least not with it meaning anything outside of a textbook). Once again, wherever we use math, we find it pointing us to our faithful, consistent Creator and Sustainer.

Formulas describe all sorts of different mathematical relationships, not just those within geometry. For example, if you make an hourly wage, then the mathematical relationship between the hours you work and the money you make a day at that job could be written as a formula.

$$\textit{money made per day} = \textit{hourly wage} \bullet \textit{number of hours worked}$$
$$m = w \bullet h$$

Be sure to take some time to review the geometry formulas we covered in Book 1 (you'll find them in the appendix at the back of this book, as well as in the reference sheets you were given from the *Teacher Guide).*

Units of Measure

To measure, we need a standard against which to measure. There are many different **units of measure** we could use to measure (inches, feet, meters, cubic feet, gallons, etc.). We use abbreviations to express units (in, ft, m, ft^3, gal, etc.).

Remember to always include the unit of measure (which we'll often refer to as simply the **unit**) in problems where one is given. For example, if a problem has you add 2 in and 7 in, give your answer as 9 in, not 9.

Perimeter

The **perimeter** is the distance around a closed shape. Knowing how to find the perimeter of various shapes helps us figure out how much edging to buy for a garden (or crown molding for a room), the fencing needed to enclose a yard, the distance around a basketball court, etc.

Example: Find the perimeter of the raised rectangular garden bed shown if its length is 8 ft and its width is 3.25 ft.

The perimeter of a rectangle equals 2 times the length plus 2 times the width.

$$P = 2 \bullet \ell + 2 \bullet w$$

Knowing this, we only need to substitute the values for length and width to find the perimeter.

$$P = 2 \bullet \mathbf{8\ ft} + 2 \bullet \mathbf{3.25\ ft}$$

$$P = \mathbf{16\ ft} + \mathbf{6.5\ ft}$$

$$P = \mathbf{22.5\ ft}$$

Area

Area is the space a two-dimensional shape encloses. Finding the area helps us find the carpet needed to cover the floor of a room, the paint needed to paint the walls of a room, the amount of grass needed to cover a yard, etc.

We measure area in square units — that is, units that are 1 unit wide by 1 unit long. In other words, a square inch is a square with 1-inch sides, a square foot is a square with 1-foot sides, and a square yard is a yard with 1-yard sides.

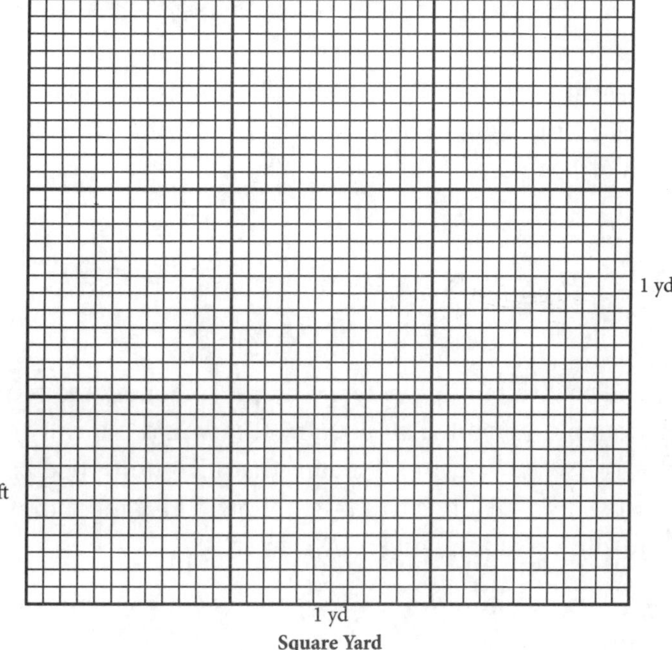

Square Inch

Square Foot (1 ft by 1 ft, or 12 in by 12 in)

Square Yard (1 yd by 1 yd, or 3 ft by 3 ft, or 36 in by 36 in)

We typically use exponents to represent squared units. For example, an area of 60 square feet would be written like this: 60 ft^2. The superscript ^{2} is an **exponent** — a shorthand way of representing repeated multiplication. In 60 ft^2, the ft^2 means that ft is multiplied by itself ($ft^2 = ft \cdot ft$).

Notice that the area is in ft^2. If we do the math correctly, area will be in square units. Here, we multiplied 8 ft by 3.25 ft . . . which gave us 26 ft • ft . . . which we wrote as 26 ft^2.

Example: Find the area of the raised rectangular garden bed shown if its length is 8 ft and its width is 3.25 ft.

The area of a rectangle equals the length times the width.

$A = l \cdot w$

Knowing this, we've only to substitute the values for length and width to find the area.

$A = \mathbf{8\ ft \cdot 3.25\ ft}$

$A = \mathbf{26\ ft^2}$

Volume

Volume is the term used to describe the space inside a *three-dimensional*, or *solid*, object. Finding the volume helps us figure out such real-life problems as how much space a shipping container encloses, how much dirt a raised garden requires, and how much water a pool can hold.

We measure volume in cubic units — that is, units that are 1 unit wide by 1 unit long by 1 unit high. In other words, a *cubic* inch is a *cube* with a width, height, and length of 1 inch.

1 Cubic Unit

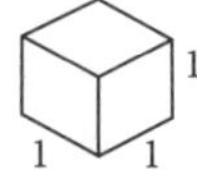

Exponents can be used with numbers as well as units. 6^2 is a shorthand way of writing 6 • 6 — that is, 6 multiplied by itself. For a review of exponents, look back at Lesson 16.1 in Book 1, or ahead at Lesson 15.1 in this book.

As with squared units, we typically use exponents to represent cubic units. For example, a volume of 60 cubic feet would typically be written like this: 60 ft^3. The superscript ^{3} next to ft means that ft is multiplied by itself three times ($ft^3 = ft \cdot ft \cdot ft$). Notice from the following example that when finding the volume, we do end up multiplying ft by ft by ft.

Example: Find the volume of the raised rectangular garden bed shown if its length is 8 ft and its width is 3.25 ft and its height is 1 ft.

We know the volume of a rectangular prism equals the area of the base times the height.

$V = B \bullet h$

And since the base is a rectangle, we can find the area of our base by multiplying the length times the width. Knowing this, we only need to substitute the values to find the volume.

$V = \mathbf{8\ ft \bullet 3.25\ ft \bullet 1\ ft}$

$V = \mathbf{26\ ft^3}$

Keeping Perspective

Since geometry helps us measure the shapes all around us, it's a very useful application of math. While we won't be exploring geometry as much in this course as we did in Book 1, we will add a few additional tools to our "measure shapes" toolbox, as well as discover some ways geometric "tools" help us explore other aspects of God's creation too.

1.6 Chapter Synopsis

I hope our "big picture" look at math has you excited about studying it this year. Usually the chapter synopsis will include a review of the main points or some tidbit from history or science. However, since this entire chapter was review, I'll simply end with a reminder that math is an exciting exploration of God's handiwork and a useful tool we can use to serve Him.

[CHAPTER 2]

Mastering Fractions and Negative Numbers

2.1 Fractions as Division

Before we jump into new material, we need to make sure we've mastered the basic notations and skills we covered in Book 1. While we won't review everything we covered there, two particular mathematical "tools" — fractions and negative numbers — are worth revisiting, as they may still be newer to you than some of the other tools, and they are both tools we'll be using over and over again. We'll start our review of them by looking at fractions.

Understanding Fractions

The word "fraction" is used many different ways in our English language, which can lead to lots of confusion.

The word can be used to describe a *partial quantity*, no matter how it's represented. In this sense, both $\frac{1}{6}$, 0.17, and 17% are all fractions, as they all represent a part of a whole.

More commonly, though, people associate the word fraction with *a specific notation* that compares parts to the whole. The top number — what we call the **numerator** — tells us how many parts of the whole we're considering, while the bottom number — called the **denominator** — tells us how many parts are in a whole. In this sense, we think of $\frac{1}{6}$ as 1 part out of 6 parts to a whole.

$$\frac{1}{6}$$

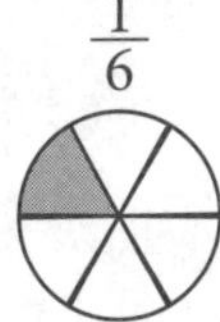

1 part; 6 parts to a whole

If at any point in our review of fractions you need more information or clarification, see Chapters 5 and 6 of Book 1.

What many people don't realize, though, is that **fractions can also be thought of as *a division problem*.** For example, $\frac{1}{6}$ is another way of writing $1 \div 6$. Notice that this division results in getting 1 part out of 6 parts to a whole.

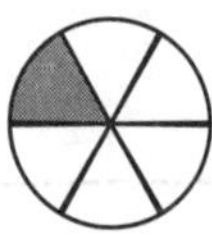

$$1 \text{ pie} \div 6 \text{ pieces} = \frac{1}{6}$$

Likewise, $\frac{1}{3}$ represents 1 divided by 3 . . . which results in getting 1 part, with 3 parts to a whole.

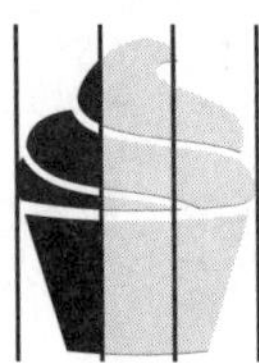

$$1 \div 3 = \frac{1}{3}, \text{ or } 0.33$$

And 4 wholes divided by 3 would leave us with 4 parts out of 3 parts to a whole, or $1\frac{1}{3}$.

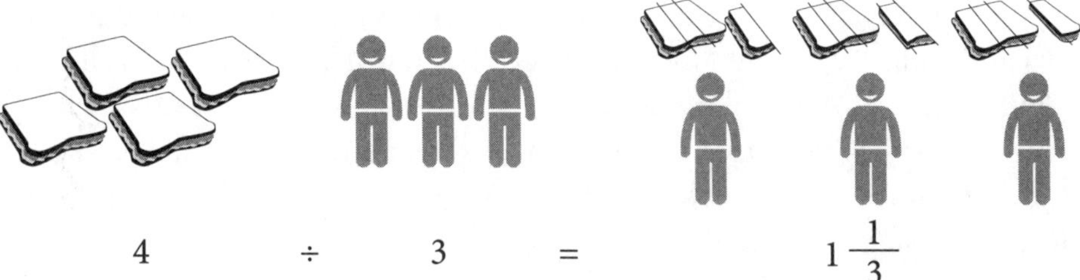

$$4 \div 3 = \frac{4}{3} = 1\frac{1}{3}, \text{ or } 1.33$$

Note that viewing fractions as division makes it incredibly easy to convert from a fraction to a decimal. Just complete the division!

Example: Express $\frac{3}{4}$ as a decimal.

$$\frac{3}{4} = 3 \div 4 = 0.75$$

Mixed Number Reminder

A **mixed number** is a whole number and a fraction combined. For example, $2\frac{1}{2}$ is a mixed number.

Improper fractions are fractions in which the numerator is equal to or greater than the denominator (such as $\frac{5}{2}$); **proper fractions** are fractions in which the numerator is less than the denominator (such as $\frac{1}{2}$).

It's easier to convert improper fractions to either mixed numbers or decimals: simply complete some or all of the division.

Example: Express $\frac{5}{4}$ as a mixed number.

$$\begin{array}{r} 1 \\ 4\overline{)5} \\ -\underline{4} \\ 1 \end{array}$$

5 divided by 4 equals 1, with a remainder of 1 that we still need to divide by 4. We can express this as $1\frac{1}{4}$.

Example: Express $\frac{5}{4}$ as a decimal.

$$\begin{array}{r} 1.25 \\ 4\overline{)5.00} \\ -\underline{4} \\ 10 \\ -\underline{8} \\ 20 \\ -\underline{20} \\ 0 \end{array}$$

Improper fractions are often easier to work with than mixed numbers. So you'll sometimes need to rewrite a mixed number as an improper fraction. You can do this by multiplying the whole number portion by the denominator, and then adding that product to the numerator and using the sum as your new numerator. This works because it's really re-expressing the whole number as a division by the denominator.

Example: Express $1\frac{1}{4}$ as an improper fraction.

Multiply the whole number by the denominator:

$1\frac{1}{4}$

$1 \bullet 4 = 4$

Add that product to the numerator:

$$\frac{\mathbf{4} + 1}{4} = \frac{5}{4}$$

$1\frac{1}{4}$ can be rewritten as $\frac{5}{4}$.

Keeping Perspective

Fractions are an example of men using their God-given abilities to find different notations to express God's creation. Why do we need different notations? Because God created a complex, incredible universe, and it takes a lot of different notations to begin to describe it!

One of the beauties of fractions is that we can use them **to represent division.** In fact, we'll frequently use the fraction line instead of the division symbol in this course. This will prepare you for algebra and other upper math courses where the fraction line replaces the division sign. While it might be harder at first, the fraction line proves a simpler way of showing division once you get used to it.

2.2 Factoring and Simplifying Fractions

For more information on factoring and simplifying fractions, see Lessons 5.3–5.5 and 6.3 in Book 1.

It's time now for a quick review of how to factor and simplify fractions. We know from the identity property of multiplication (which is a way of describing how God causes multiplication to work) that **multiplying by 1 doesn't change the value of a number** . . . and neither does dividing by 1. Thus we can find equivalent fractions (i.e., fractions that represent the same quantity) by multiplying or dividing by fractions worth 1.

$$\frac{2}{12} \div \frac{2}{2} = \frac{1}{6}$$

$\frac{2}{2}$ is worth 1, as any number divided by itself equals 1. By dividing $\frac{2}{12}$ by $\frac{2}{2}$, we are dividing the fraction by a fraction worth 1, which does not change its value. Both $\frac{2}{12}$ and $\frac{1}{6}$ represent the same value.

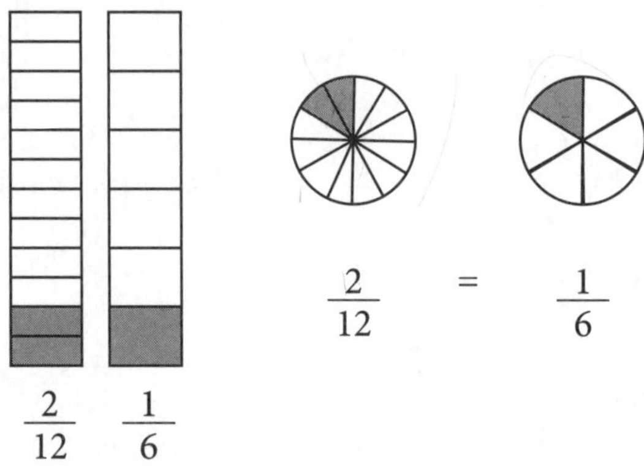

How do we know what number to divide the numerator and the denominator by to simplify a fraction as much as possible? Well, sometimes it's obvious; when it's not, factoring can help us. Since factoring also helps us understand numbers better and will aid you in upper-level math, let's briefly review it.

While the definition of whole numbers varies (some definitions include 0), we'll define it as a way of describing non-fractional quantities of 1 and greater.

Factoring is what we call the process of looking at a number as a product and seeing what non-fractional numbers could be multiplied to make that product (i.e., what are the number's **factors**). When we factor, it's helpful to find the **prime factors** — the factors that are a whole number greater than 1 that cannot be evenly divided by any whole number except by themselves and 1.

By finding the prime factors of the numerator and the denominator, we can figure out what is the greatest number by which we could divide both the numerator and the denominator, thereby simplifying the fraction as much as possible.

Example: Simplify $\frac{42}{78}$

Now, it's not instantly obvious what number to divide $\frac{42}{78}$ by in order to simplify it. However, looking at the prime factors of 42 and 78 will make it obvious.

```
     42                78
     ^                 ^
  2 • 21            2 • 39
       ^                 ^
     7 • 3             3 • 13
```

Prime factors of 42: 2, 3, 7

Prime factors of 78: 2, 3, 13

Notice that 2 and 3 are the only two prime factors both 42 and 78 share; we would call their product (6, as 2 • 3 equals 6) the **greatest common factor** of 42 and 78. This tells us that 6 is the greatest number we could divide both the numerator and denominator of $\frac{42}{78}$ by. Thus if we divide $\frac{42}{78}$ by $\frac{6}{6}$, we'll have simplified the fraction as much as possible.

$$\frac{42}{78} \div \frac{6}{6} = \frac{7}{13}$$

Simplifying in One Step

It's common to complete some of the simplification of fractions in our heads. For example, rather than writing this:

$$\frac{42}{78} \div \frac{6}{6} = \frac{7}{13}$$

We could write this:

$$\frac{\overset{7}{\cancel{42}}}{\underset{13}{\cancel{78}}} = \frac{7}{13}$$

In the second case, we divided both 42 and 78 by 6 in our head.

Fractions and Units

Often, we'll need to simplify fractions that include units of measure. For example, if we want to divide 60 ft by 10 ft, we'd have this fraction:

$$\frac{60\ \mathit{ft}}{10\ \mathit{ft}}$$

Notice that we have ft in both the numerator and the denominator. We can divide both the numerator and the denominator by 10 ft.

$$\frac{60\ \mathit{ft}}{10\ \mathit{ft}} \div \frac{10\ \mathit{ft}}{10\ \mathit{ft}} = \frac{6}{1} = 6$$

Notice that we could have done all the division in our head, simplifying the fraction in a single step.

$$\frac{\overset{6}{\cancel{60}}\ \cancel{\mathit{ft}}}{\underset{1}{\cancel{10}}\ \cancel{\mathit{ft}}} = 6$$

Simplifying Square and Cubed Units Reminder

We can simplify fractions containing square and cubic units too.

$$\frac{60\ \text{ft}^2}{10\ \text{ft}} = 6\ \text{ft} \qquad \frac{60\ \text{ft}^3}{10\ \text{ft}} = 6\ \text{ft}^2$$

It's easiest to see the simplification in the examples above if we don't use exponents but instead write out ft^2 as ft • ft and ft^3 as ft • ft • ft.

$$\frac{\overset{6}{\cancel{60}}\ \cancel{\text{ft}} \bullet \text{ft}}{\underset{1}{\cancel{10}}\ \cancel{\text{ft}}} = 6\ \text{ft} \qquad \frac{\overset{6}{\cancel{60}}\ \cancel{\text{ft}} \bullet \text{ft} \bullet \text{ft}}{\underset{1}{\cancel{10}}\ \cancel{\text{ft}}} = 6\ \text{ft}^2$$

Keeping Perspective

Hopefully, nothing we covered in this lesson was new. We're simply reviewing some principles we'll be building on as we continue our mathematical explorations.

2.3 Operations with Fractions

While you've probably been solving problems with fractions for years, let's take a lesson to review the basics and make sure you've mastered how to work with fractions.

Reviewing Adding and Subtracting Fractions and Mixed Numbers

Before adding or subtracting fractions, remember to rewrite the fractions so the denominators are the same (otherwise, you won't be adding or subtracting parts of, or divisions by, the same quantity).

Example: If you have $\frac{2}{3}$ yd and $\frac{1}{6}$ yd of fabric, how many yards of fabric do you have altogether?

+

$\frac{2}{3}$ yd $\frac{1}{6}$ yd

Rewrite $\frac{2}{3}$ yd so it has the same denominator as $\frac{1}{6}$ yd:

$\frac{2}{3}\text{ yd} \bullet \frac{2}{2} = \frac{4}{6}\text{ yd}$

We can now add the fractions.

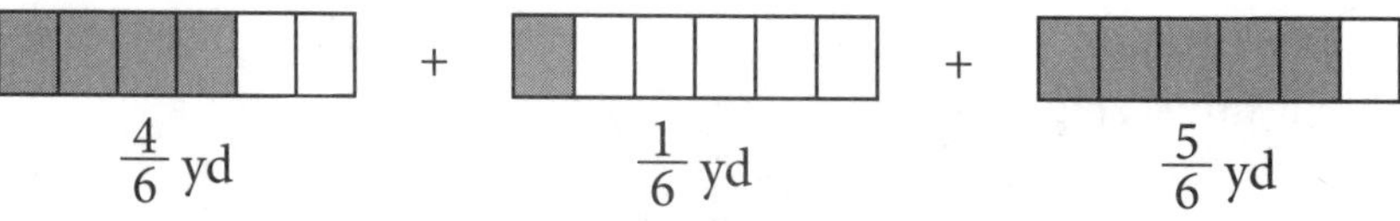

$\frac{4}{6}$ yd $\frac{1}{6}$ yd $\frac{5}{6}$ yd

Notice that in the example above we included the unit of measure (yards, which abbreviates to yd) in our answer — again, always include the unit when one is given.

Example: If you have $\frac{2}{3}$ yd of fabric and use $\frac{1}{6}$ yd, how many yards do you have left?

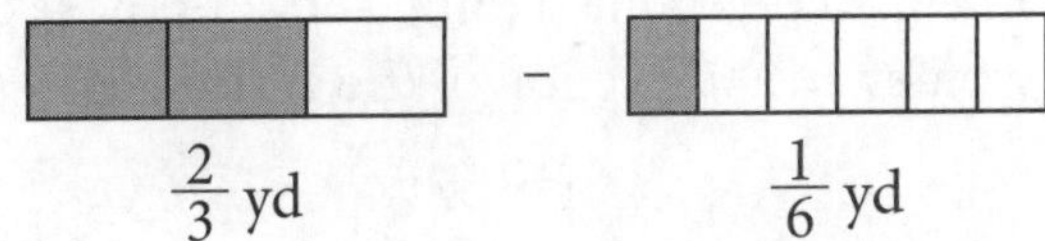

$\frac{2}{3}$ yd　　　$\frac{1}{6}$ yd

Rewrite $\frac{2}{3}$ yd so it has the same denominator as $\frac{1}{6}$ yd:

$\frac{2}{3}\text{ yd} \cdot \frac{2}{2} = \frac{4}{6}\text{ yd}$

We can now subtract the fractions.

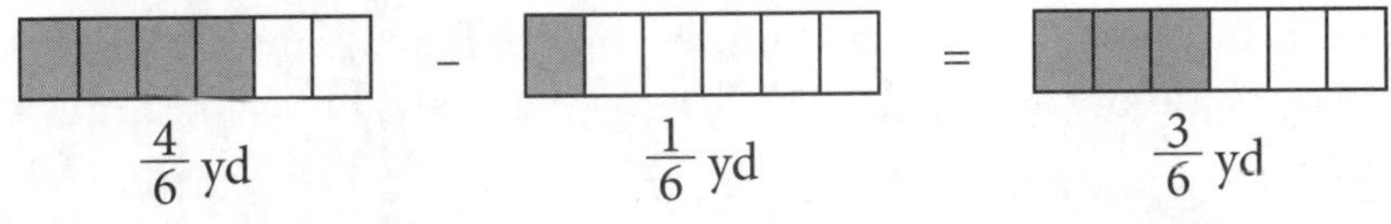

$\frac{4}{6}$ yd　　　$\frac{1}{6}$ yd　　　$\frac{3}{6}$ yd

which simplifies to

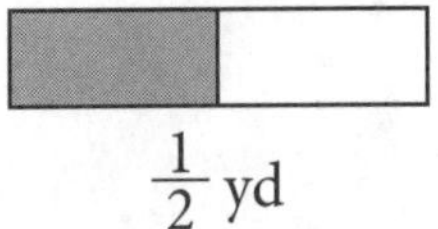

$\frac{1}{2}$ yd

To **add or subtract mixed numbers**, simply rewrite the mixed number as an improper fraction, and then add or subtract as you would proper fractions.

Example: If you have $1\frac{1}{4}$ yards of fabric and use $\frac{1}{2}$ a yard, how many yards do you have left?

$1\frac{1}{4}$ yd　　　$\frac{1}{2}$ yd

Rewrite $1\frac{1}{4}$ as an improper fraction:

$1\frac{1}{4}\text{ yd} = \frac{5}{4}\text{ yd}$

Rewrite $\frac{1}{2}$ so it has the same denominator as $\frac{5}{4}$:

$\frac{1}{2}\text{ yd} \cdot \frac{2}{2} = \frac{2}{4}\text{ yd}$

We can now complete the subtraction.

$\frac{5}{4}$ yd　　　$\frac{2}{4}$ yd　　　$\frac{3}{4}$ yd

You could also add or subtract the whole number portion and the fractional portion of a mixed number separately. For example, $4\frac{3}{8} - \frac{1}{8}$ equals $4\frac{2}{8}$. However, be careful when you do, as it's easy to make mistakes this way on less obvious problems, especially when subtracting a fraction that's greater than the fractional part of the mixed number we're subtracting it from. In general, convert mixed numbers to improper fractions.

Multiplying and Dividing Fractions and Mixed Numbers Reminder

To **multiply fractions**, simply multiply the numerators and the denominators together.

Example: $\frac{2}{3} \bullet \frac{5}{8}$

Example Meaning: If $\frac{2}{3}$ of the women surveyed liked pink, and $\frac{5}{8}$ of those who participated in the survey were women, what fraction of the entire group surveyed were women who liked pink?

$$\frac{2}{3} \bullet \frac{5}{8} = \frac{10}{24}, \text{ which simplifies to } \frac{5}{12}$$

Term Reminder

The **multiplicative inverse** is a name used to describe the **number that, when multiplied by another number, equals 1**. Some people also call it the **reciprocal** of a number, or, so long as the context is clear, simply the **inverse.**

$\frac{8}{1}$ (or just 8) is the inverse of $\frac{1}{8}$ *and* $\frac{1}{8}$ is the inverse of $\frac{8}{1}$ (or just 8)

$$8 \bullet \frac{1}{8} = \frac{8}{8} = 1 \qquad \frac{1}{8} \bullet 8 = \frac{8}{8} = 1$$

$\frac{2}{3}$ is the inverse of $\frac{3}{2}$ *and* $\frac{3}{2}$ is the inverse of $\frac{2}{3}$

$$\frac{2}{3} \bullet \frac{3}{2} = \frac{6}{6} = 1 \qquad \frac{3}{2} \bullet \frac{2}{3} = \frac{6}{6} = 1$$

As we mentioned in Book 1, we could divide fractions another way...only inverting and multiplying is usually simpler.

To **divide by a fraction**, we invert the divisor (i.e., take the multiplicative inverse of the divisor) and multiply. This "rule" is a shortcut to help us quickly find the answer.

Example: $\frac{2}{3} \div \frac{5}{7}$

Example Meaning: How many times does $\frac{5}{7}$ fit inside $\frac{2}{3}$?

We can complete the division by inverting the divisor ($\frac{5}{7}$) and multiplying.

$$\frac{2}{3} \div \frac{5}{7} = \frac{2}{3} \bullet \frac{7}{5} = \frac{14}{15}$$

Using a Fraction to Represent the Division

Since the fraction line represents division, we could represent $\frac{2}{3} \div \frac{5}{7}$ like this: $\frac{\frac{2}{3}}{\frac{5}{7}}$. Remember, you can think of the fraction line as a division symbol.

$$\frac{\frac{2}{3}}{\frac{5}{7}} = \frac{2}{3} \div \frac{5}{7} = \frac{2}{3} \bullet \frac{7}{5} = \frac{14}{15}$$

To **multiply or divide by a mixed number**, convert to an improper fraction and then multiply or divide. You could also multiply a mixed number without converting using the distributive property, but you'll avoid errors and save time by simply converting to an improper fraction and then multiplying or dividing.

These methods all work because they accurately describe the real-life principles God created and holds together.

Simplifying while Multiplying

You can save some steps by simplifying a fraction as you multiply. When you simplify as you go, you're essentially dividing by a fraction worth one, just as you would be if you did the simplification at the end.

Simplifying as you go:

$$\frac{\overset{1}{\cancel{2}}}{3} \bullet \frac{5}{\underset{4}{\cancel{8}}} = \frac{5}{12}$$

Simplifying at the end:

$$\frac{2}{3} \bullet \frac{5}{8} = \frac{10}{24}$$

$$\frac{10}{24} \div \frac{2}{2} = \frac{5}{12}$$

Keeping Perspective

The rules about how to add, subtract, multiply, and divide fractions help us make sure that we're accurately describing the real-life consistencies God created and sustains. Since fractions prove a useful notation, it's important to make sure you are familiar with working with them.

2.4 Negative Numbers

Now that we've reviewed fractions, let's also make sure we've mastered negative numbers. **Negative numbers** are a useful way of indicating the *opposite of* a positive quantity. Whether it's money owed, distance in an opposite direction, or temperature less than zero, negative numbers are useful tools.

$5 we owe

−$5

$5 we have

+$5

5 ft in the opposite direction

−5 feet

5 ft in the positive direction

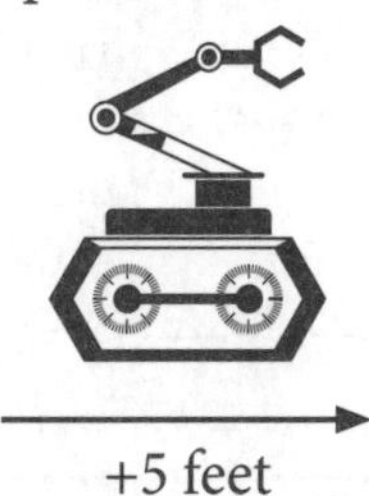

+5 feet

Negative and positive numbers are perhaps easiest to define and picture on a **number line.** A number line is a pictorial aid to help us view how numbers relate to each other.

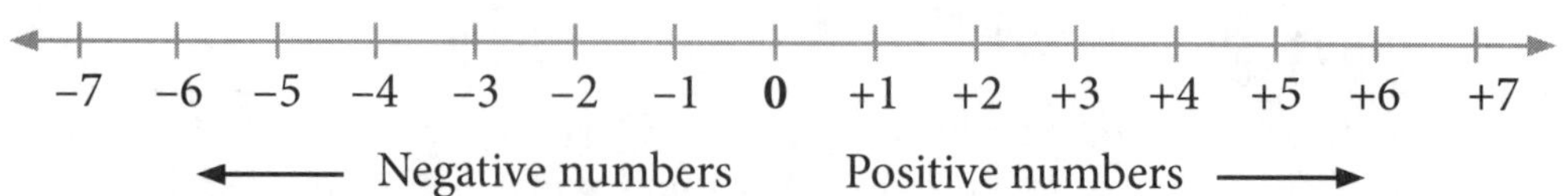

We call numbers to the right of 0 on the number line *positive numbers*, and those to the left *negative numbers*. The negative numbers are the exact same as the positive ones, except they're going in the *opposite direction*. Negative numbers are indicated by a negative sign (−); positive numbers are indicated by a positive sign (+), although most of the time we don't bother putting the plus sign in front of a positive number. Think of a negative sign (−) as meaning *the opposite of*; −4 indicates *the opposite of* 4, or 4 in the *negative* direction.

Negative and positive numbers are simply another convention to help us describe how quantities relate to one another.

Different Types of Numbers

It's often helpful to refer to numbers as a group, or set. A set is simply a collection (i.e., a group). The chart recaps some common names used to categorize numbers into sets based on specific characteristics. Much as we could categorize clothes different ways (by color, type, purpose, etc.), we can (and do) categorize numbers different ways. These names help us easily refer to numbers with certain characteristics.

Rational Numbers
Rational numbers can be expressed as a ratio (i.e., division) of one integer to another.
{..., $-\frac{1}{2}$, −1, −0.3, 0, $\frac{1}{2}$, 0.75, 1, ...}

Integers
Non-fractional numbers. {..., −1, 0, 1, ...}

Even {−4, −2, 0, 2, 4, ...}
Integers that can be divided by 2.

Odd {−3, −1, 1, 3, ...}
Integers that cannot be divided by 2.

Whole (Natural or Counting) Numbers {1, 2, ...}
Integers 1 and greater. (Some definitions include 0.)

Prime Numbers
Whole numbers that can't be evenly divided by any whole number but themselves and 1.
The prime numbers under 100 are 2, 3, 5, 7, 11, 13, 17, 19, 23, 29, 31, 37, 41, 43, 47, 53, 59, 61, 67, 71, 73, 79, 83, 89, and 97.

Irrational Numbers

Example: π (3.14159265...) Irrational numbers have decimal digits that go on and on for infinity without ever repeating. They cannot be expressed as a ratio (i.e., division) of one integer to another.

Getting to 0 — Additive Inverse

What happens if we subtract 4 candies from a pile of 4 candies? Obviously, we end up with 0 candies.

4 and –4 are what we call the additive inverse of each other. An **additive inverse** is a fancy name to describe the number that, added to a number, equals 0.

$$4 + -4 = 0$$

Sounds pretty obvious, doesn't it? And it is. Yet we'll use this obvious relationship frequently as we continue our math explorations.

Subtraction as Addition

We saw in Book 1 (Lesson 10.2) that we can look at subtraction as addition of a negative number. Both 4 – 3 = 1 (i.e., taking 3 away) and 4 + –3 = 1 (i.e., adding *the opposite of* 3) mean to move over 3 to the left (the negative side).

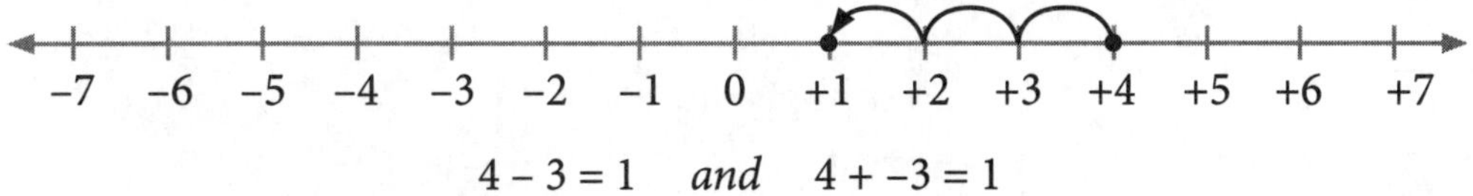

$$4 - 3 = 1 \quad \textit{and} \quad 4 + -3 = 1$$

Train yourself to think of subtraction as addition of a negative number. Viewing subtraction as addition helps us solve problems, as it allows us to apply the properties of addition. After all, subtraction itself is not commutative or associative. The order in which we subtract matters. Notice how we get a different answer when solving 8 – 4 – 2 if we subtract the 4 from the 8 first versus if we subtract the 2 from the 4 first.

Correct

Subtracting the 4 from the 8 first:

8 – 4 – 2
4 – 2 = 2

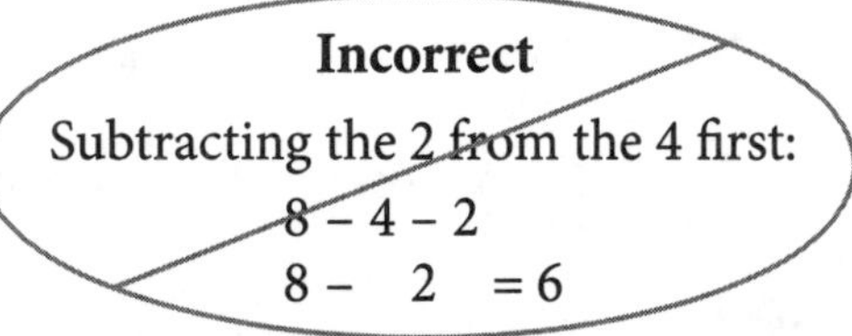
Incorrect

Subtracting the 2 from the 4 first:

8 – 4 – 2
8 – 2 = 6

We know that 2 is the correct answer to 8 – 4 – 2 because it's the answer we obtain when we follow the order of operations and subtract from left to right.

Note, though, that if we think of subtraction as an addition of negative numbers, then the order no longer matters *because the negative sign moves with the number.* Below, we get 2 no matter which order we follow; after all, we're now dealing with addition, and addition is associative and commutative.

Correct	**Correct**
Adding –4 to 8 first:	Adding –2 to –4 first:
8 + –4 + –2	8 + –4 + –2
4 + –2 = 2	8 + –6 = 2

Addition — whether of positive or of negative numbers — is associative and commutative. Turning a subtraction problem into an addition problem by **viewing the subtraction as an addition of a negative number allows for the use of the associative and commutative properties of addition.**

Working with Negative Numbers

The key principle to remember when working with negative numbers is to think of each negative sign as meaning ***the opposite of***. Each negative sign means to take the additive inverse, or opposite, of the number.

The first negative sign makes the number negative (i.e., *the opposite of* the number). The second makes the opposite of that, which is positive. Then another makes the opposite of that, which is negative again. Then positive, etc.

We can see this visually on number lines.

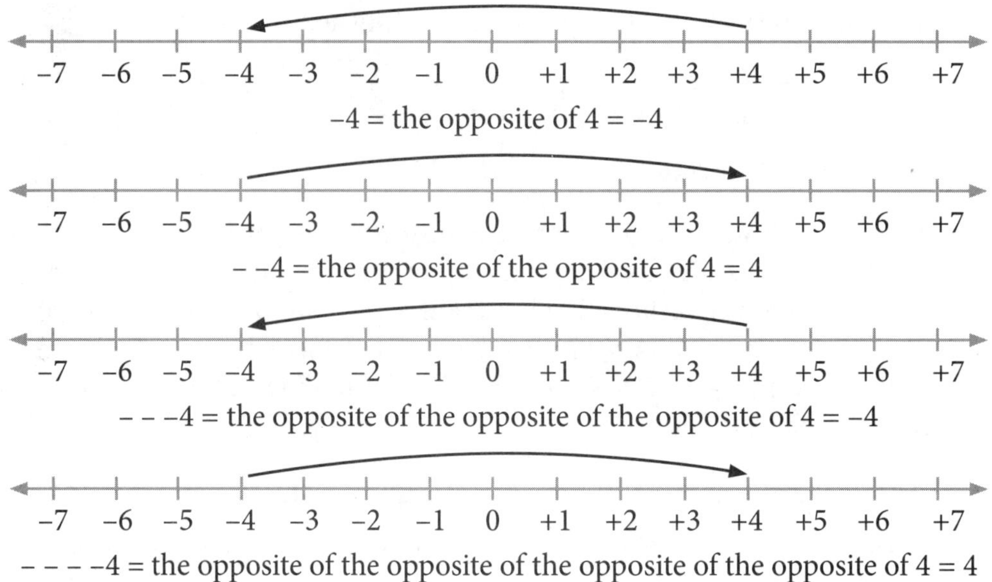

You can easily figure out whether the final number is a negative or positive by saying "negative, positive, negative, positive..." as you read off the negative signs. If you end with a negative, the answer is negative; if you end with a positive, the answer is positive.

<table>
<tr>
<td>Adding</td>
<td>
Add negative numbers the same way you would subtract: move that many numbers over in the negative direction.

Example: 2 + –4

This means 2 plus the opposite of 4.

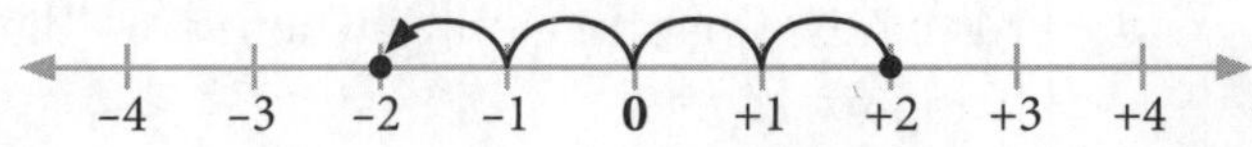

We start at 2, and move 4 in the negative direction.

2 + –4 = –2
</td>
</tr>
<tr>
<td>Subtracting</td>
<td>
View each negative sign as the opposite of. Two consecutive negative signs in front of a number make a positive (the opposite of a negative is a positive), three a negative, four a positive, etc.

Example: 8 – –4

Let's start by inserting a plus sign for clarity. After all, we can look at subtraction as the addition of a negative number.

8 + – –4

We know that – –4 means the opposite of the opposite of 4, so this means 8 plus the opposite of the opposite of 4, or 8 + 4!

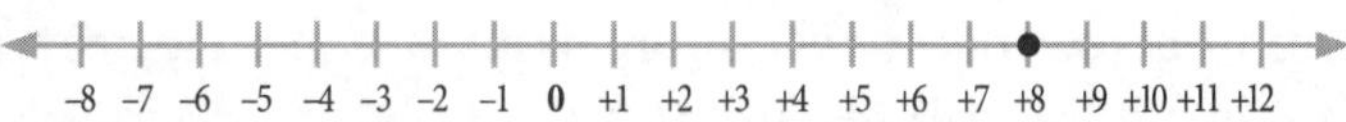

We start at +8.

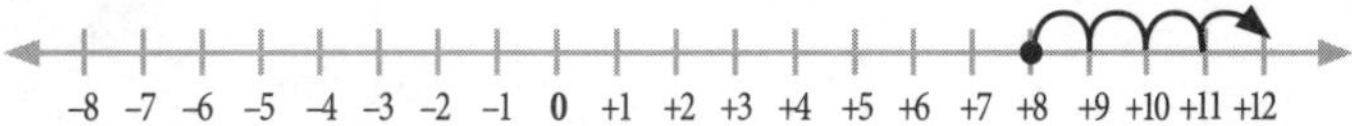

We add – –4, or positive 4.

8 + – –4 = 12

Example: 8 – – – 4

Again, let's insert a plus sign for clarity.

8 + – – –4

This time, we have three negative signs. This means the opposite of the opposite of the opposite of 4, which simplifies to negative 4, giving us 8 + –4.

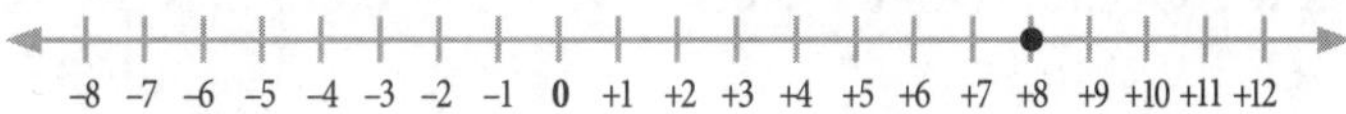

We start at +8.

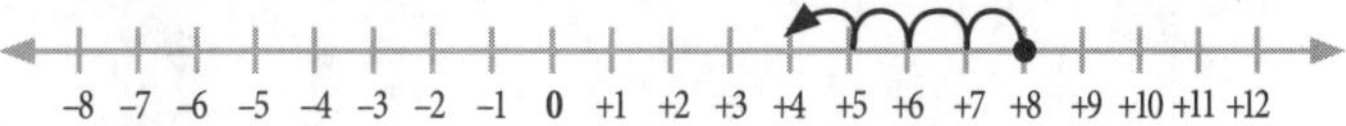

We add – – –4, or –4.

8 + – – –4 = 4
</td>
</tr>
</table>

We could tell that – – –4 means –4 by reading off the negative signs: "negative, positive, negative." We ended on negative, so the answer will be negative.

Multiplying	Each negative sign means *the opposite of*, so one negative sign involved in the multiplication gives a negative answer, two a positive, and so forth. $-4 \bullet -2 = 8$ $-4 \bullet 2 = -8$ $4 \bullet -2 = -8$ Note how this still applies when more than two numbers are being multiplied. $-4 \bullet -2 \bullet -1 = -8$ $-4 \bullet -2 \bullet 1 = 8$
Dividing	Again, each negative sign means *the opposite of*, so one negative sign involved in the division gives a negative answer, two a positive, and so forth. $8 \div -2 = -4$ $-8 \div 2 = -4$ $-8 \div -2 = 4$ Note that fraction lines can be thought of as division. $\frac{8}{-2} = -4$ $\frac{-8}{2} = -4$ $\frac{-8}{-2} = 4$

Keeping Perspective

As you review the rules of working with negative numbers, don't lose sight of the big picture in the details. We have rules about how to work with negative numbers so that we can more easily use them as real-life tools. We can rely on quantities to add, subtract, multiply, and divide consistently because we can rely on God to govern all things consistently.

2.5 Latitude and Longitude

While we're reviewing negative numbers, let's take a look at a couple of fun applications we didn't have time for in Book 1. These applications are examples of how negative numbers help us describe God's creation.

Consider the task of describing specific locations on earth. Where exactly is Brasília (the capital of Brazil in South America). . . and Brazzaville (the capital of Congo in Africa)? How far apart are the two cities? If you're in the middle of the Atlantic Ocean, where exactly are you in comparison? Which way do you need to travel?

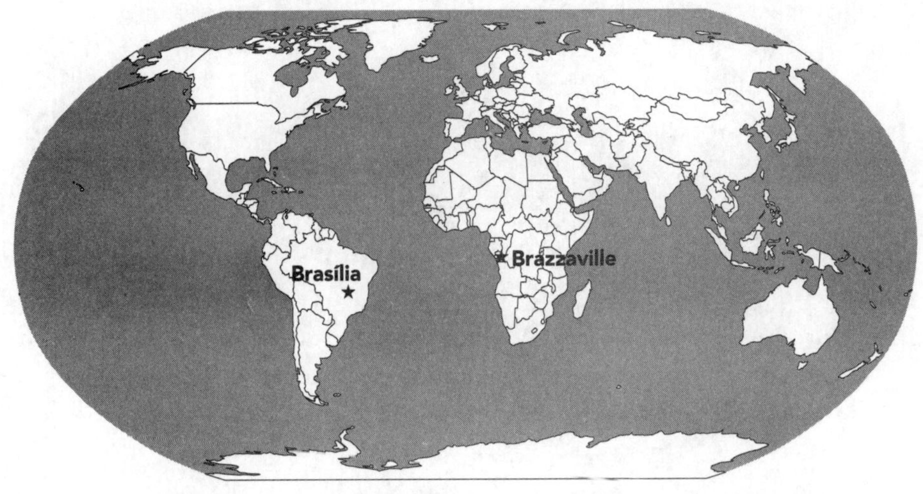

We need a way to refer to specific locations on earth. And we have one! Join me in looking now at latitude and longitude.

Latitude

We use an imaginary line called the **equator** to divide the earth in half horizontally.

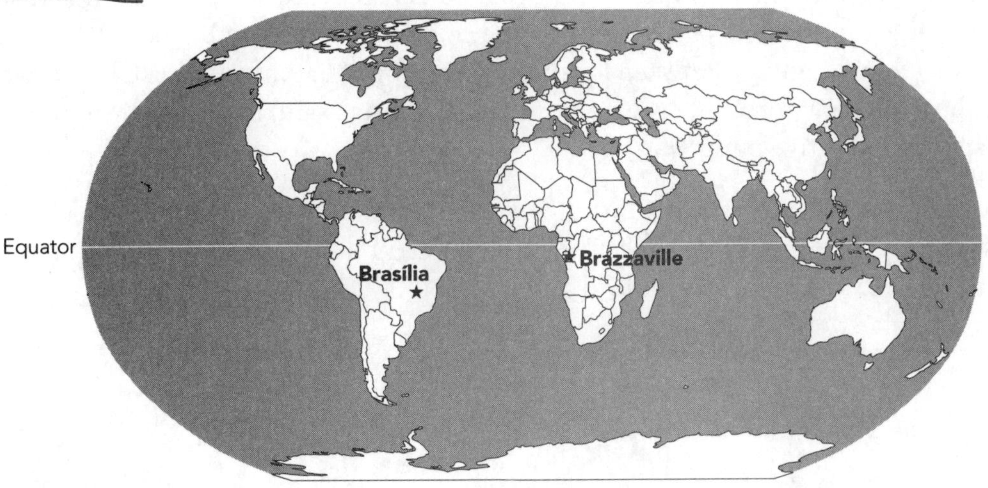

We then mark distances by how they relate to the equator, picturing additional imaginary parallel lines called **lines of latitude** as dividing the earth.

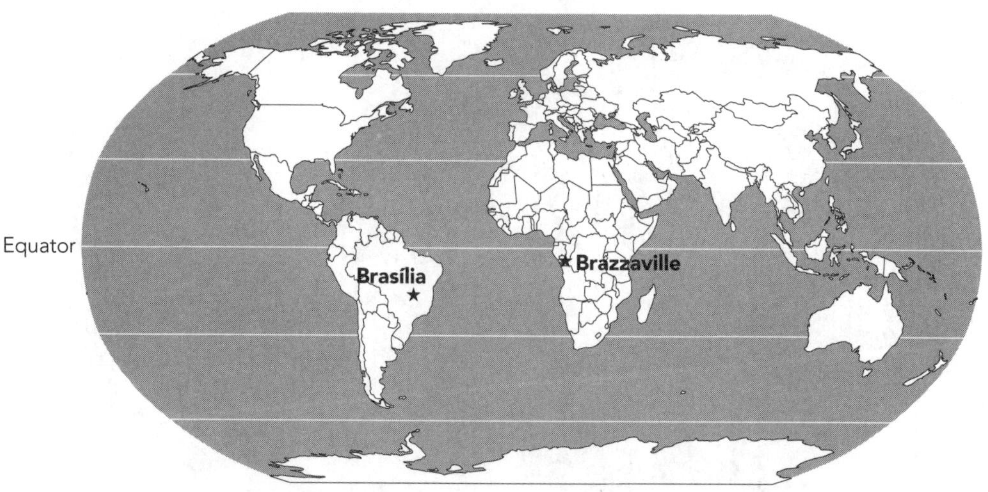

The earth is spherical.

Notice that we've used the word "line" to describe the equator. While you may be used to thinking of a line as a "breadthless length,"[1] we view a line as a great circle in spherical geometry. (The earth is spherical in shape, so spherical geometry helps us describe locations on its surface.)

We measure the distance of latitudes from the equator in degrees, breaking up the distance from the equator to either pole into 90 degrees (i.e., 90°), and then further into minutes and seconds. Any point on the equator is considered to be at 0° latitude. To differentiate between locations above the equator from those *below*, we use the words north/south, or use a positive or negative sign. (See, I told you we'd be applying negative numbers!)

For example, a location that's 30° south of the equator would be referred to as having a latitude of 30° S *or* –30°, while a location 30° north of the equator would be referred to as having a latitude of 30° N *or* +30°.

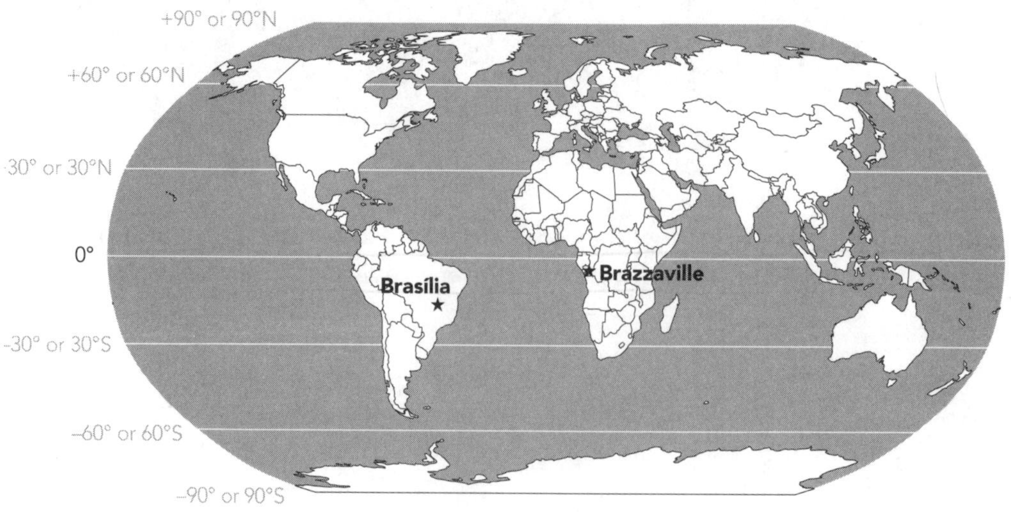

Longitude

Much as the equator serves as a reference point for horizontal locations, we use an imaginary line called the **prime meridian** as a vertical reference.

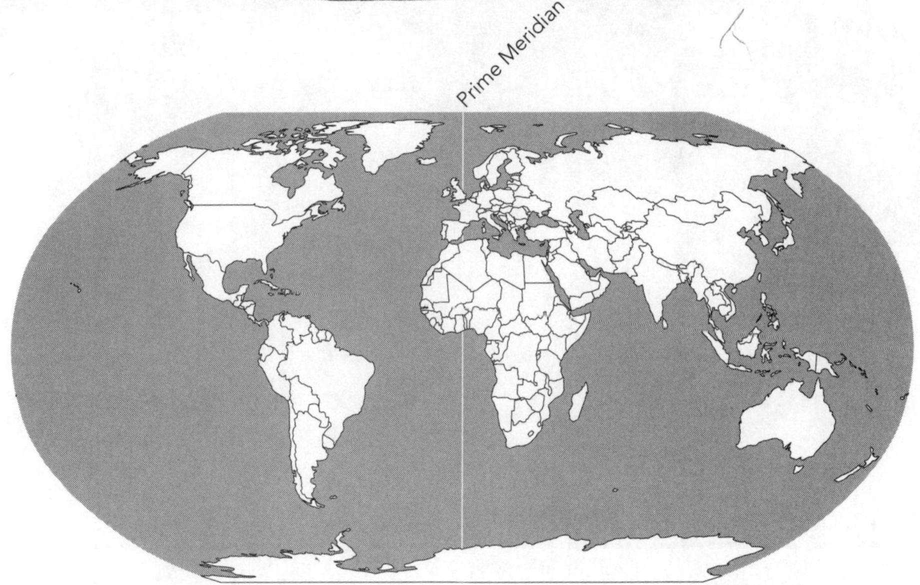

We then mark distances by how they relate to the prime meridian, viewing these as being additional imaginary parallel lines called **lines of longitude**.

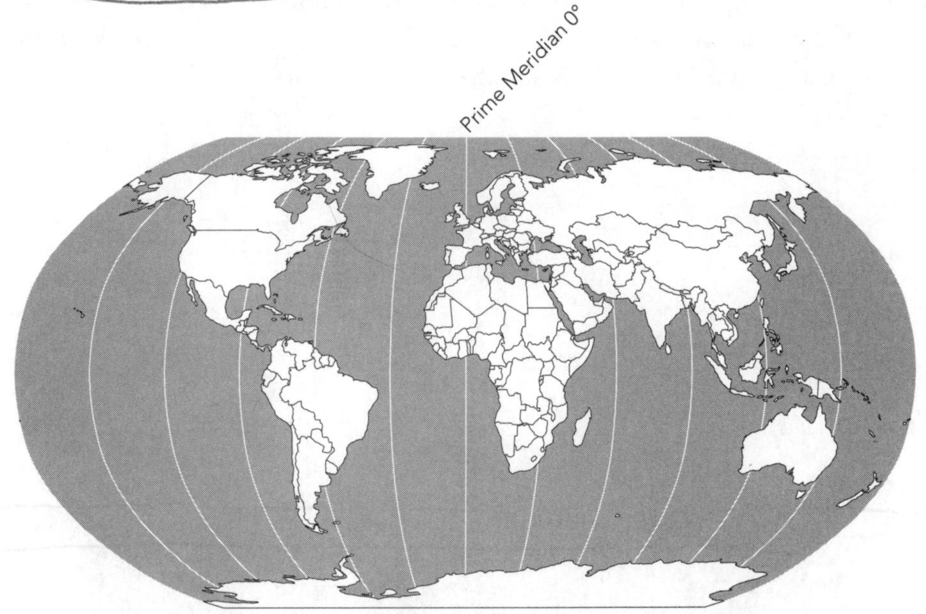

The prime meridian marks 0° longitude. We then measure the distance of longitudes from the prime meridian. To differentiate between locations to the *right* of the prime meridian from those to its *left*, we use the words east/west, or put a positive or negative sign. (Again, notice the use of negative numbers!)

For example, a location that's 30° west of the prime meridian would be referred to as having a longitude of 30° W *or* –30°, while a location 30° east of the prime meridian would be referred to as having a longitude of 30° E *or* +30°.

–180° or 180°W
–160° or 160°W
–120° or 120°W
–90° or 90°W
–60° or 60°W
–30° or 30°W
0°
+30° or 30°E
+60° or 60°E
+90° or 90°E
+120° or 120°E
+150° or 150°E
+180° or 180°E

Using Longitude and Latitude to Describe Locations[2]

Every location on earth has both a longitude and a latitude. By listing these values, we can easily describe a city's location.

Let's see this in action with two cities: Brasília (the capital of Brazil in South America) and Brazzaville (the capital of Congo in Africa). Brasília has a latitude of –15.78° and a longitude of –47.93°. Brazzaville has a latitude of –4.27° and a longitude of +15.28°.

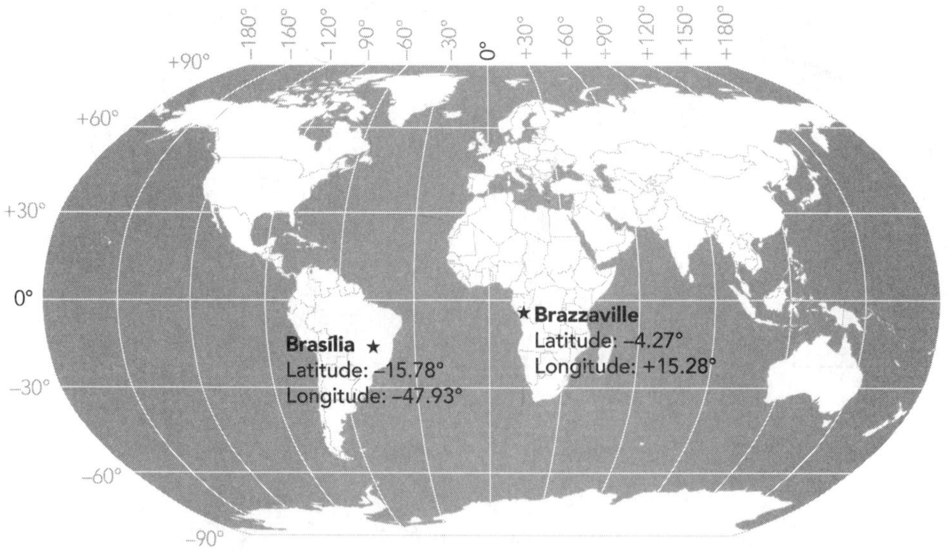

The latitude and longitude values give us a way of describing these cities' exact locations. We can also use these values to compare their locations. To understand how, though, we first have to review absolute value.

Reviewing Absolute Value

The **absolute value** is the fancy name for the value of a quantity regardless of whether it's positive or negative (i.e., its distance from 0). The absolute value of both +5 and –5 is 5. It doesn't matter if we mean 5 to the right or 5 to the left of the 0 on the number line. Both are 5 away from 0.

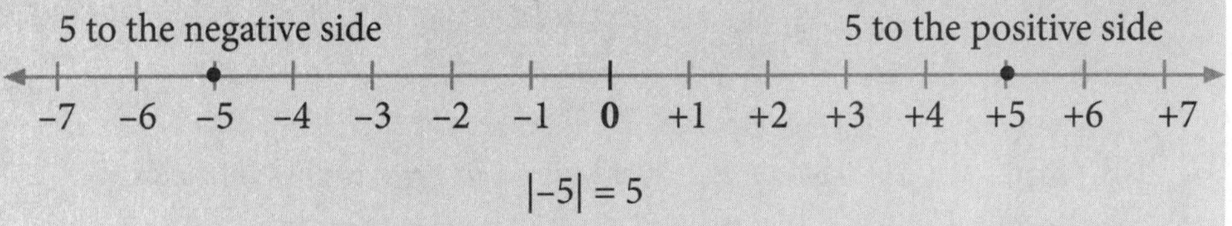

$|-5| = 5$

The absolute value of negative 5 equals 5.

$|+5|$ or $|5| = 5$

The absolute value of positive 5 or the absolute value of 5 equals 5.

Using Longitude and Latitude to Compare Locations

If all we care about is the distance between the latitude or longitude of two locations (not the direction), we find the absolute value of the difference between them.

For example, if one city is at a latitude of +5 and another of –5, we'd find the distance between them by finding the absolute value of the difference between +5 and –5. We do this by subtracting one from the other, and then taking the absolute value.

Subtracting to find the difference: $5 - -5 = 5 + 5 = 10$

Taking the absolute value: $|10| = 10$

Since we're taking the absolute value in the end anyway, we could subtract either location from the other. We'll get the same answer in the end.

Subtracting to find the distance: $-5 - 5 = -10$

Taking the absolute value: $|-10| = 10$

So if one city is at a latitude of +5 and another at a latitude of –5, the distance between them is 10 degrees of latitude. This can easily be seen on a number line.

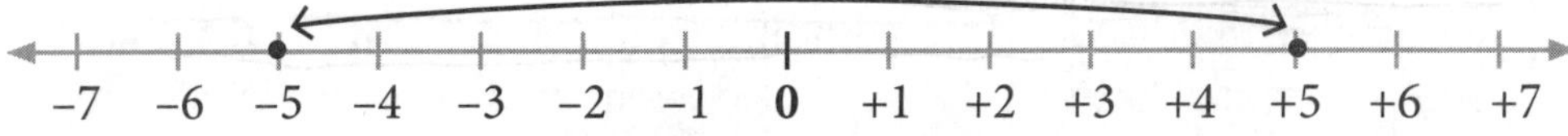

The distance between +5 and –5 is 10.

Now, that was a simple example. Let's take a look at one with some more realistic numbers. In fact, let's look at the difference in longitude between Brasília and Brazzaville. Note that we can use this same approach to find the latitude between two cities.

Example: What is the difference in longitude between Brasília (–47.93°) and Brazzaville (+15.28°)?

To find the answer, we need to subtract one longitude from the other (i.e., find the difference between them), and then take the absolute value of that difference.

$$-47.93° - +15.28° = -63.21°$$

$$|-63.21°| = 63.21°$$

Note: We could also have found the same answer by subtracting –47.93° from +15.28°.

$$15.28° - -47.93° = 63.21°$$

$$|63.21°| = 63.21°$$

No matter how we find it, there's a 63.21° difference in longitude between these two cities.

Keeping Perspective

Math helps us describe locations on the earth's surface. **Longitude** and **latitude** are an example of negative numbers and absolute value in action — of men, using their God-given abilities to describe God's creation (in this case, locations on the earth).

2.6 Time Zones

Time zones are another example of using math to describe the movement of the sun (and the passage of time) that God put in place. As we explore time zones, we'll again find ourselves applying both negative numbers and absolute value.

Understanding Time Zones

Time zones are based on longitude lines. The prime meridian is in the middle of the time zone we refer to as **Prime Meridian Coordinated Universal Time (UTC)**. Every location within this "zone" (a 15° width of longitude) has the same time. We then represent all other time zones based on *how they relate to UTC time*, using positive numbers to show time zones that are ahead of that time, and negative numbers to show time zones that are behind UTC time.

Every 15° longitude to the east of the UTC time zone a new time zone begins that is an additional hour ahead, while every 15° longitude to the west of the UTC time zone a new time zone begins that is an additional hour behind. When it's 11 a.m. in the UTC time zone, it's 10 a.m. in the zone to its west, and 12 p.m. (noon) in the zone to its east. In this way, it's noon in each zone at approximately the time the sun is directly overhead in that zone.

STANDARD TIME ZONES OF THE WORLD

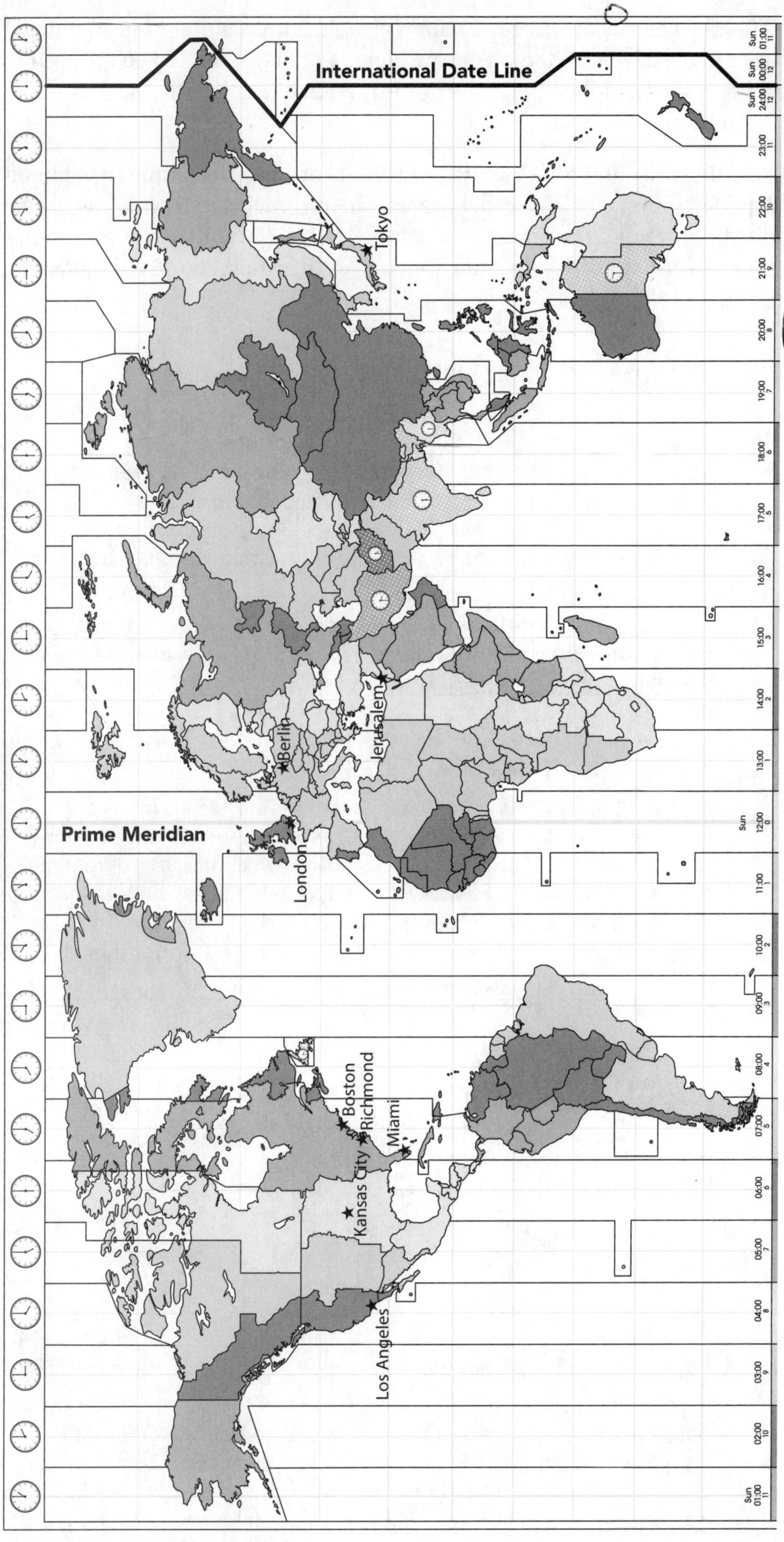

International Date Line

Prime Meridian

Tokyo

Berlin

Jerusalem

London

Boston

Richmond

Miami

Kansas City

Los Angeles

Sun 01:00 11

Sun 00:00 12

Sun 24:00 12

23:00 11

22:00 10

21:30 9

20:00 8

19:00 7

18:00 6

17:00 5

16:00 4

15:00 3

14:00 2

13:00 1

Sun 12:00 0

11:00 1

10:00 2

09:00 3

08:00 4

07:00 5

06:00 6

05:00 7

04:00 8

03:00 9

02:00 10

Sun 01:00 11

UTC–04:00 means the time is 4 hours *behind* the time at the prime meridian (i.e., earlier in the day — it's the UTC time *minus* 4 hours). UTC+04:00 means the time is 4 hours *ahead* of the time at the prime meridian (i.e., later in the day — it's the UTC time *plus* 4 hours).

To clarify, while time zones are 15° wide in theory, in reality, time zone lines do not fall perfectly every 15°. Instead, the zones are jagged, because what city wants to be split into two time zones because it falls on the line? And there are exceptions — China, for example, uses the same time across the whole country, despite spanning more than 15° longitude.

The International Date Line

Starting at the UTC time zone (the zone the prime meridian is in), time zones continue about every 15° longitude until we reach 12 hours in either direction. At that point, we're at what we call the International Date Line. This line is located at approximately 180° longitude. When crossing this line, travelers gain or lose a day, but the time of day stays the same (after all, the sun is still at the same spot overhead).

The idea of an International Date Line might seem odd at first, but think about it for a minute. If it's midnight at the prime meridian, then it would be noon at 180° to the east (+12 hours), and at 180°to the west (–12 hours). Only it would be noon the day before if we went west (–12 hours from midnight is noon on the previous day, as midnight marks a new day).

Unless you're traveling near the International Date Line, you can find the time differences between two locations without taking into account the date line. For example, we can find the difference in time zones between a town in Alaska and Russia by looking at the difference in time traveling the other way around the world (as shown on the map), thereby avoiding the dateline altogether.

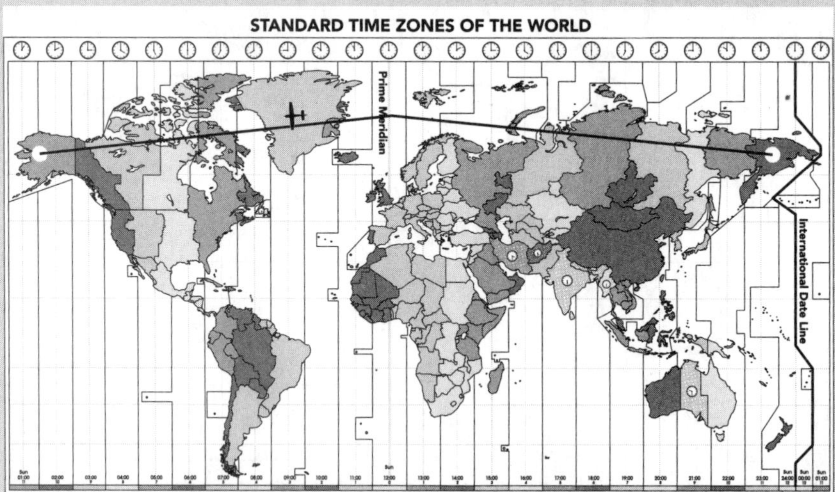

Even though we're avoiding the dateline, the number of hours between two locations might still cause us to be on a different day. For example, if two cities are 8 hours apart, and it's 2 a.m. in the easternmost city, it's going to be 6 p.m. the previous day in the western city — 8 hours before 2 a.m. In other words, we can figure out the date changes without dealing with the International Date Line by simply looking at the difference in times. Again, unless you're traveling near the International Date Line, you don't typically need to think about it.

Since our primary purpose in looking at time zones is to see negative numbers in action and not to spend a long time learning the ins and outs of telling time, we'll not include any problems that require crossing the International Date Line in this course.

Finding the Difference Between Time Zones

The time in Brasília is UTC–03:00 (i.e., 3 hours *before* UTC time). The time in Shanghai, China, on the other hand, is UTC+08:00 (i.e., 8 hours *after* UTC time). What's the difference in time between the two cities?

Notice that we've not been told the current time in either city . . . and we don't need to know it to answer the question. All we're trying to figure out is the difference in time between those two cities.

We can figure out the differences in time the same way we figured out the differences in longitude and latitude: by subtracting one from another and taking the absolute value.

Example: What is the difference in time between Brasília (UTC–03:00) and Shanghai (UTC+08:00)?

Remember, UTC–03:00 means a time 3 hours *before* UTC time, which we could think of as –3 hr. UTC+08:00 means a time 8 hours *after* UTC time, which we could think of as +8 hr. If we find the absolute value of the difference between –3 and +8, then, we'll know the difference in time between these zones.

$-3 - +8 = -11; |-11| = 11$

There's an 11-hour difference between the time in Brasília and the time in Shanghai.

Note: We could also have found the difference starting at +8. Since we're finding the absolute value of the difference, it doesn't matter which number we subtract from which.

$+8 - -3 = 11; |11| = 11$

Some countries (including the USA) follow what's called Daylight Savings Time during a portion of the year. This can affect the number of hours behind or ahead of UTC time a country is. An online search can easily tell you a country's current relationship to UTC time.

Finding the Time in a Different Time Zone[2]

Sometimes, we want to know more than the difference in time. We want to know what the actual time is in another city given the current time in ours.

Once we know the difference in time between two locations, we can use that information to find the actual time in one of the locations if we know the time in the other.

We need to *add* the time difference to the time if we're moving from west to east, and *subtract* it if we're moving from east to west. After all, the sun rises in the east, so it's always later in the day to the east.

Can't I Just Use Electronics to Convert Time Zones?

While you can use a phone, computer, or clock to give you the time in another country, it's helpful to know the basics of how time zones work and how to find a time difference yourself if needed. That way, you'll be able to mentally translate from one time zone to another without having to rely on a device. It also gives you practice with absolute value and negative numbers, both of which are important skills.

Example: If it's 2 p.m. on October 5 in Brasília (UTC–03:00), what time will it be in Shanghai (UTC+08:00)?

In the last example, we found the difference in time between these two locations: 11 hours. Now, we want to find the actual time in Shanghai when it's 2 p.m. on October 5 in Brasília. Shanghai is *east* of Brasília, so we need to *add* the difference in time (11 hours), as it will be that many hours later in Shanghai.

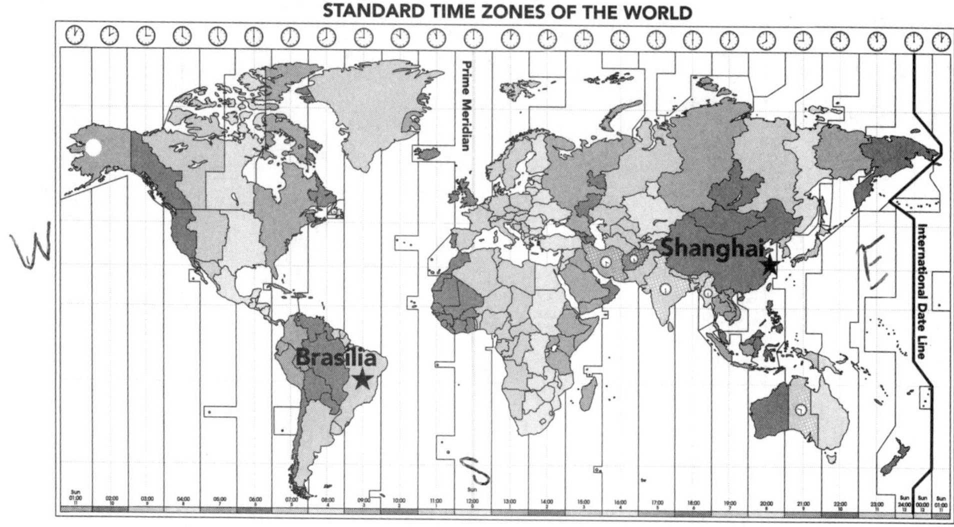

Shanghai is east of Brasília.

2 p.m. + 11 hours = 1 a.m. the *next morning* (October 6)

On the other hand, if we were starting at the more eastern location, we'd have to subtract to find the time at the western location.

Example: If it's 1 a.m. on October 6 in Shanghai (+8 UTC), what time is it in Brasília (–3 UTC)?

Shanghai is *west* of Brasília, so we need to *subtract* the difference in time. Again, we already found that the difference in time is 11 hours.

1 a.m. – 11 hours = 2 p.m. the *previous day* (October 5)

Time Before Time Zones

Prior to the mid-to-late 1800s, each locality operated off its own time based on the sun's movement in their area (or when the local factory or church sounded their whistle or bell). This meant that sundials in towns relatively short distances apart would read noon a minute or two before or after each other. Small differences like this didn't matter for years — but those distances began to matter once railroad travel made more precise timekeeping necessary.

For a fascinating look at the history of timekeeping and some of the challenges that had to be overcome, check out the first two chapters of *Exploring the World of Mathematics* by John Hudson Tiner.[3]

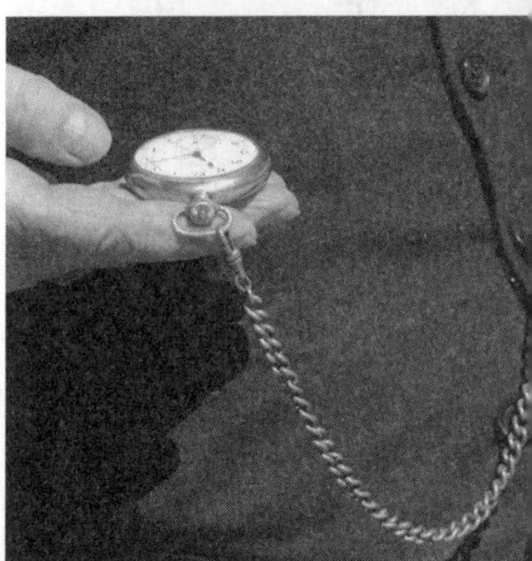

Keeping Perspective

Time zones are one example of men using math to help them with a real-life problem (that of having a consistent way to communicate about time). Remember that math is a tool we can use to help us complete the tasks God has given us here on earth. It's not an isolated subject, but rather a language system that helps us describe God's creation, including the passage of time.

2.7 Chapter Synopsis and the Speed of Light

Both **fractions** and **negative numbers** are extremely helpful "tools" to have in your mathematical "toolbox." Before moving forward, make sure you're comfortable performing the basic operations (adding, subtracting, multiplying, and dividing) with fractions and with negative numbers.

Remember these two key facts:

- **The fraction line can be thought of as a division symbol.**
- **Each negative sign means *the opposite of.***

Before we finish this chapter, let's take a look at one more example of math in action.

The Speed of Light

Have you ever wondered how we know how fast light travels? Facts like these did not just appear in the pages of science books. Men used their God-given abilities to explore God's creation using — you guessed it — math!

Ole Christensen Rømer (1644–1710)

Danish astronomer Ole Christensen Rømer[4] (1644–1710) realized light had a definite speed after examining the time it took for Io (one of Jupiter's moons) to become visible after an eclipse. He noticed that during certain times of the year when the earth is farther away from Jupiter, it takes longer for Io to appear after an eclipse. This is because the light takes longer to reach the earth when the earth is farther away.

Now, you might still be wondering where the math was in all that. Well, even though the word "math" wasn't mentioned in the previous paragraph, math was used to measure and record the time it took for Io to appear and to compare those times. Math is the tool scientists use to explore God's creation.

And as we use math to explore God's creation, we find ourselves pointed to the Creator. In this case, light's consistent speed (which math helped us discover) testifies to God's consistency. Hebrews 1:3 tells us Jesus is "upholding all things by the word of his power." He is the One who holds light together and causes it to operate in the same predictable fashion! The speed of light is constant because God is constant. He does not change based on our moods or the situations in which we find ourselves. God is the same today as He was when He parted the Red Sea and turned water into wine.

> *For I am the LORD, I change not; therefore ye sons of Jacob are not consumed (Malachi 3:6).*

[CHAPTER 3]

Exploring Unknowns and Equations

3.1 Introducing Unknowns

In the first chapter, we reviewed the "big picture" of math. In the last chapter, we looked at a few core notations we use to describe quantities and consistencies.

It's time now to explore solving problems involving what we call unknowns. As we do, we'll apply and build on the principles and notations we've looked at so far.

Understanding Unknowns

The word **unknown** is a short way of writing "an unknown quantity."[1] While you may not have formally looked at unknown quantities, or unknowns, before, you've encountered and worked with them informally for years.

For a simple example of an unknown, say you went to the store to buy a music CD. The store was running a special where you could get 4 CDs for the same price as 1. If you were planning on buying 1 CD anyway, how many additional CDs would you get because of the special? We can think of the number of additional CDs as an unknown. Using a question mark to represent it, we could represent this problem like this:

$$1 + ? = 4$$

You know that to get from 1 to 4, you need 3 more. So the unknown in this case is 3.

$$1 + \mathbf{3} = 4$$

Now, I know you'd typically solve a problem like this one mentally. But whether mentally or on paper, you're really finding an unknown.

For another example of unknowns, consider the relationships between aspects of shapes. When we looked at the principles of geometry back in Book 1, we discovered that the consistent relationship between the area, length, and width of a rectangle is always the same. The size of the rectangle might change, but if a shape is a rectangle, its area will always equal its length times its width.

length

width

Area = length • width

We used a formula to describe this relationship. Notice that we used **letters as placeholders to stand for numbers** — the area, length, and width of a rectangle.

$$A = \ell \bullet w$$

These letters represent unknown quantities, or unknowns. We didn't specify the exact value of the area, length, or width — instead, we used symbols (in this case, letters) to stand for the quantities, whatever they were.

By using letters to represent the area of a rectangle, we represented a mathematical relationship — in this case, the relationship between the area, length, and width in any rectangle. We use the knowledge of this relationship to find the area of various rectangles.

You've also dealt with unknowns when working with word problems. For example, there's a relationship between the number of people in the family attending an event, the cost per person, and the total cost for the family.

While the letter we use to represent an unknown doesn't really matter, you'll notice that math books tend to use *x*, *y*, and *z*, along with *a*, *b*, and c. There's a reason why these letters are used more frequently (it's due to a convention you'll learn about in Lesson 13.3).

total cost for family = number of people in family attending • cost per person

or, more simply,

$$t = n \bullet p$$

The t, n, and p in the above equation are all unknown quantities, or unknowns — we didn't specify how many people there were in the family, how many would be attending, or the cost per person. Instead, we used letters to stand for the total cost, number of people in family attending, and the cost per person.

We will often use letters as placeholders for unknowns. In fact, we could have used a letter back in our CD example instead of a ?. Which letter we use isn't important — the letter is but a placeholder to stand for a quantity.

$$1 + ? = 4 \quad or \quad 1 + c = 4 \quad or \quad 1 + x = 4$$

Multiplication Sign

To avoid confusion with the letter x, we will not use x as a multiplication sign in problems containing unknowns. Instead, we'll use either a dot (•) or parentheses.

While we often use letters as placeholders for unknowns, there's nothing to say we *have* to use letters. In the past, many would refer to an unknown using a word, such as "heap," or "cosa" (which means "thing"). Many Hindu writers used the abbreviation "ya" to refer to an unknown number. Different symbols have also been used. For example, the Greek mathematician Diophantus (c. 275) used Ϛʹ to refer to an unknown, while Stevin (1585) used ①. Letters are merely one way of representing unknowns.[2]

Using Letters

Just as we use numbers to **name** quantities ("1" names a single quantity), to **identify** (the numbers in a telephone number identify a specific telephone line), and to **order** (such as the 5th most popular song of the year), we also use letters to **name** quantities ("*x*" names an unknown quantity), **identify** (license plates use letters as well as numbers to identify a plate), and to **order** (we might list the first item in a list as *a*, the second as *b*, etc.). Like numerals, letters are a helpful naming tool.

Keeping Perspective

As we begin applying the *same principles* we've been using to work with known quantities to unknown quantities (which we call **unknowns**), keep in mind that the letters you'll begin seeing are merely placeholders to stand for a quantity we haven't specified. They are additional symbols we use to help us describe God's creation.

3.2 Understanding Equality

In order to really work with unknowns, we have to grasp the concept of equality. While this is a concept you've been using for years, we're going to dig a little deeper into it.

Working with Equalities

As I'm sure you already know, an **equal sign** indicates that the quantities on both sides of the sign are equal.

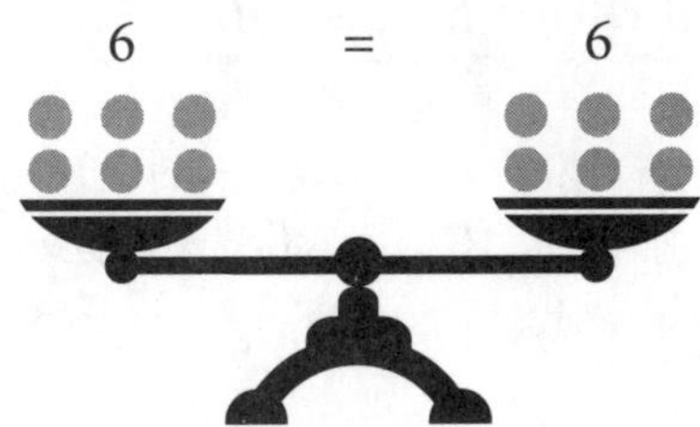

If we add a quantity to one side, then we'd have to add the *same* quantity to the other side in order for the equation to stay equal.

Added 2 to Both Sides

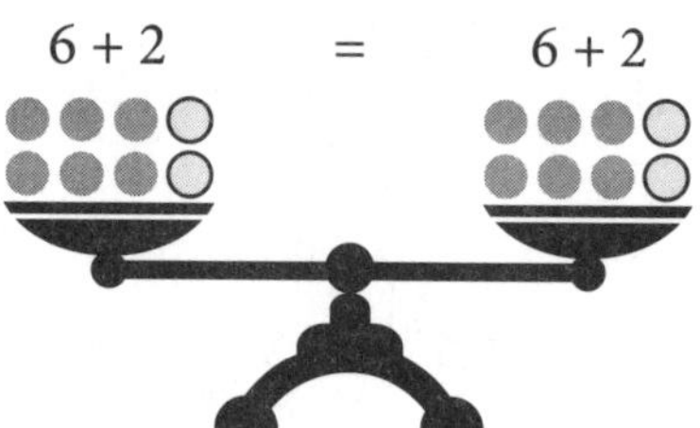

So long as we add the *same quantity* to *both sides*, the sides remain equal.

Likewise, notice that if we subtract the *same quantity* from *both sides* of an equation, the sides stay equal.

Subtracted 2 from Both Sides

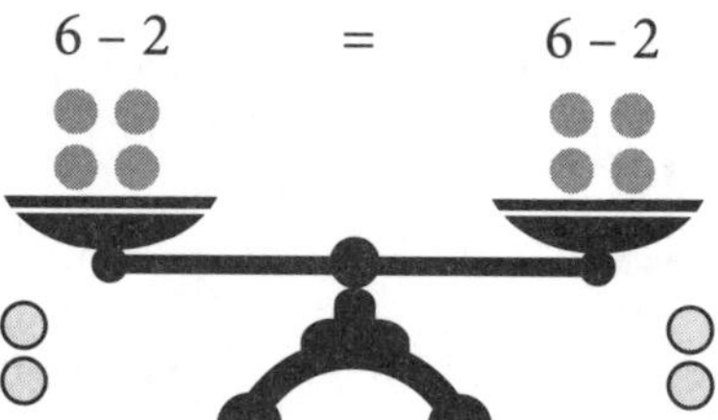

When we multiply or divide *both sides* of an equation by the same quantity, the sides again stay equal.

Multiplied Both Sides by 2

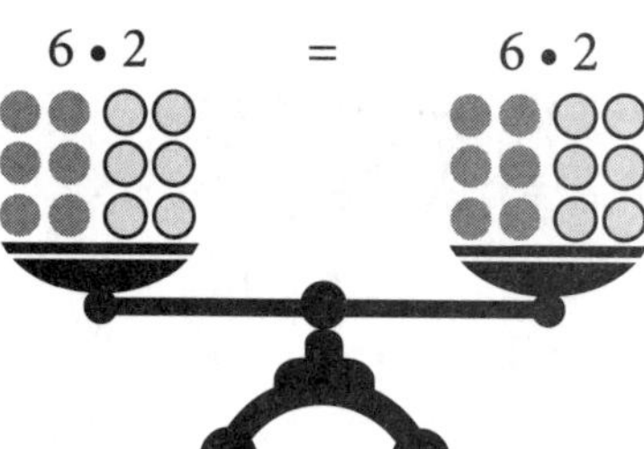

Divided Both Sides by 2

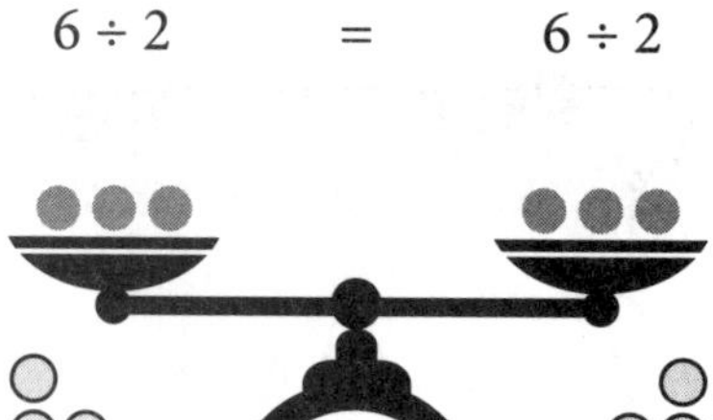

In short, an equal sign means that both sides are equal, or in balance. **So if we perform the *same operation* using the *same quantity* for both sides, the sides will still be equal!**

Swapping Entire Sides of an Equation

Not only can we add, subtract, multiply, or divide *both sides* of an equation by the *same quantity* without affecting the equality of the sides, we can also swap the *entire* left side of an equation with the *entire* right side of that equation.

Why? Because equal means equal — since we swapped the *entire* sides, we didn't affect the equality of them.

$6 + 2 = 8$ *and* $8 = 6 + 2$

$6 - 2 = 4$ *and* $4 = 6 - 2$

$2 \bullet 6 = 12$ *and* $12 = 2 \bullet 6$

$6 \div 3 = 2$ *and* $2 = 6 \div 3$

Important Note — When swapping the sides of an equation, we're moving the *entire* expression from one side to the other. We're *not* changing anything about the expression itself. For example, in $6 \div 3 = 2$, we can switch the $6 \div 3$ to the right side.

$6 \div 3 = 2$ *and* $2 = 6 \div 3$

But we would be changing the value if in the process we changed the order of $6 \div 3$ to $3 \div 6$. We have to move the *entire* expression without changing the order.

$6 \div 3$ does *not* mean the same as $3 \div 6$

$6 \div 3 = 2$ *but* $2 \neq 3 \div 6$

Now, of course, addition and multiplication are commutative and associative, so if all we had was addition or all we had was multiplication on one side of the equation, we *could* switch the order without changing the value of the expression.

$6 + 2 = 8$ *and* $2 + 6 = 8$ *and* $8 = 6 + 2$ *and* $8 = 2 + 6$

$2 \bullet 6 = 12$ *and* $6 \bullet 2 = 12$ *and* $12 = 2 \bullet 6$ *and* $12 = 6 \bullet 2$

However, be careful. Only switch the order if you know you can because of a property. Otherwise, you'll end up changing the value of the expression! It's safest to develop the habit of swapping *entire expressions*, and then only break from that if you know you can without changing the value of the expression.

Representing Relationships

Why do we care that quantities are equal? I'm glad you asked! One of the key things we do in math is look at how quantities relate — that is, at the *relationship* between them. And many of these relationships can be expressed as an **equality** (i.e., "a symbolic expression of the fact that two quantities are equal; an equation"[3]).

For example, $A = \ell \bullet w$ expresses the *relationship* between the area, length, and width of a rectangle. Notice the equal sign; the equal sign lets us know that the area *equals* the length times the width.

When you solve word problems, you use equalities to express relationships. For example, the total money you have left after an event will equal the money you started with, plus any money you were given, minus any money you spent.

ending \$ = beginning \$ + \$ gained – \$ spent

$$e = b + g - s$$

Understanding equalities is going to help us better understand how to work with many real-life relationships. In fact, in the next lesson, we'll begin using the principle of equality to help us solve problems containing unknowns.

Keeping Perspective

God's faithfulness ensures that objects will consistently add, subtract, multiply, and divide. Thus, **when we add, subtract, multiply, or divide *both sides* of an equation by the *same quantity*, the sides of the equation remain equal.** And since equal means equal, **we can swap the *entire* expression on the left of an equal sign with the *entire* expression on the right, or vice versa.**

As you solve the problems on Worksheet 3.2, ponder God's faithfulness. Just as He is faithful to keep His covenant with the "ordinances" of heaven and earth (making it possible for us to rely on addition, subtraction, multiplication, and division to work consistently), He will be faithful to everything else He says in His Word. He will be faithful to save . . . and faithful to punish.

> *But the Lord is faithful, who shall stablish you, and keep you from evil (2 Thessalonians 3:3).*

3.3 Equalities and Unknowns

It's time now to look at equalities that include unknowns. We're going to use the *same principle* of adding, subtracting, multiplying, or dividing *both sides* of an equation by the *same quantity* to find the value of an unknown.

Let's say we are trying to save \$19 for a purchase, and we've saved \$13 so far. How much do we have left to save?

While this is a problem you could solve mentally, let's look at it on a scale for a minute. We know that \$13 plus some quantity (which we'll represent with an x) equals \$19.

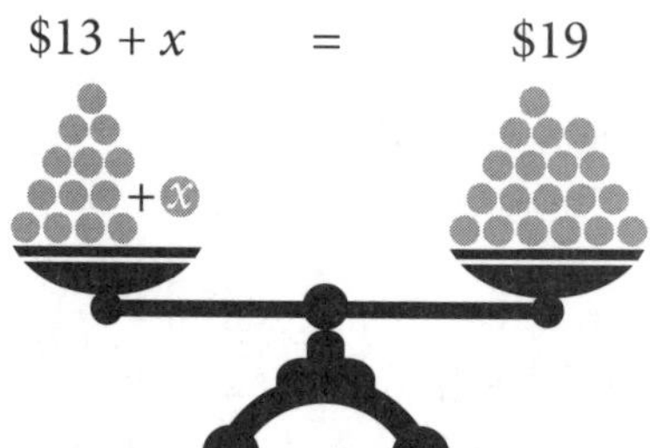

So the question is, how do we find the value of x? Let's take a look.

Finding an Unknown

Remember, if we add, subtract, multiply, or divide *both sides* of an equation by the *same quantity*, both sides will stay equal. So if we subtract \$13 from both sides, we'll be left with x on the left side. Since both sides of our equation will still be equal, the right side will then show us what x equals!

Subtracted \$13 from Both Sides

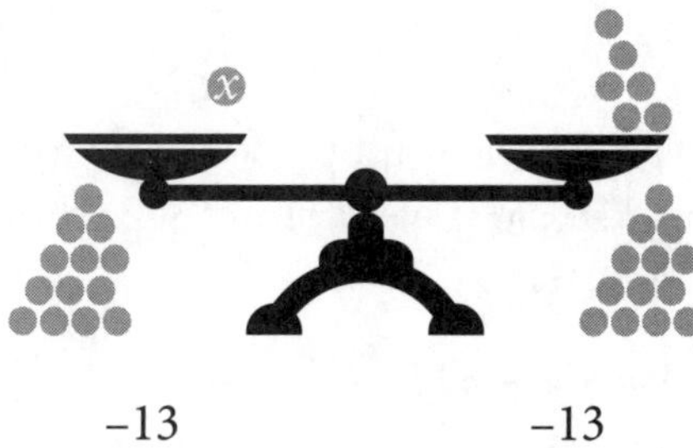

We now know that the value of x is \$6. Note that if we substitute this value back into our original equation, it holds true. \$13 + \$6 does indeed equal \$19.

Value We Found for x Inserted into the Original Equation

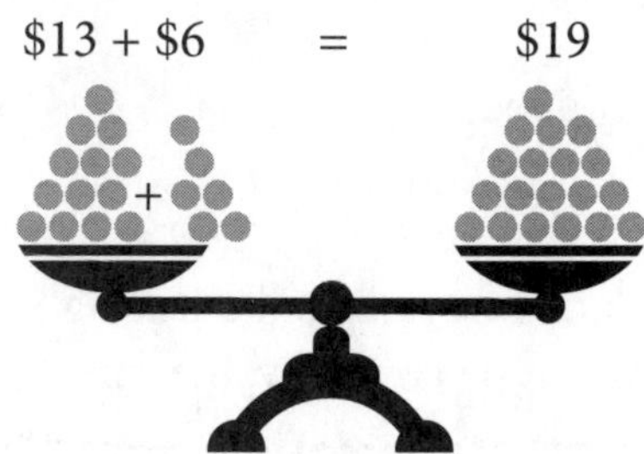

Now, I hope right now you're pausing for a minute and going *wow*. Because of the consistent way God holds this universe together, we can rely on operations to operate (pun intended) so consistently that we can subtract the same quantity from both sides of an equation and be so confident that the answer will still be in balance that we can use that answer to tell us the value of an unknown!

This technique of separating an unknown on one side of an equation in order to find its value is one we're going to be using extensively. While we illustrated it using subtraction, since that was the easiest to show visually on a scale, the same principle applies with other operations.

> To find an unknown in an equation, **get the unknown on a side by itself.** Do this by performing the *same operation* using the *same quantity* to *both sides* of the equation.

While you can find many unknowns mentally, knowing how to find an unknown by isolating it on one side of an equation will help you solve problems that would otherwise be difficult or impossible. It's a technique you will use frequently — and one that ultimately works because of the consistent way God causes objects to add, subtract, multiply, and divide.

Looking at the Details

I'm sure you'll agree that it's not practical to draw a scale every time we want to find the value of an unknown — nor is it necessary. The scale was simply a visual to show the process. Let's now walk through finding a couple of unknowns on paper.

Example: $x + \$13 = \$19$

To find the value for x, we want to isolate x on a side by itself. We know *x plus $13* equals $19. So if we *subtract $13* from both sides, we'll end up finding the value for x.

$$x + \$13 - \mathbf{\$13} = \$19 - \mathbf{\$13}$$

Now let's simplify. $13 – $13 equals 0, leaving us $x + 0$, or more simply, x on the left. And $19 – $13 equals $6, leaving us $6 on the right.

$$\mathbf{x = \$6}$$

Note: We could have used cross outs to show how subtracting $13 canceled out the + $13.

$$x + \cancel{\$13 - \mathbf{\$13}} = \$19 - \mathbf{\$13}$$

$$\mathbf{x = \$6}$$

Now we can check our work by substituting $6 for x in the original equation. If we found the correct value, the equation will hold true.

Original equation:

$$x + \$13 = \$19$$

Substituting $6 for x:

$$\mathbf{\$6} + \$13 = \$19$$

This is true . . . $6 + $13 does equal $19. We did the math correctly.

We just did on paper the same thing we'd shown before on a scale.

Starting Equation

$13 + x = $19

=

Subtracted $13 from Both Sides

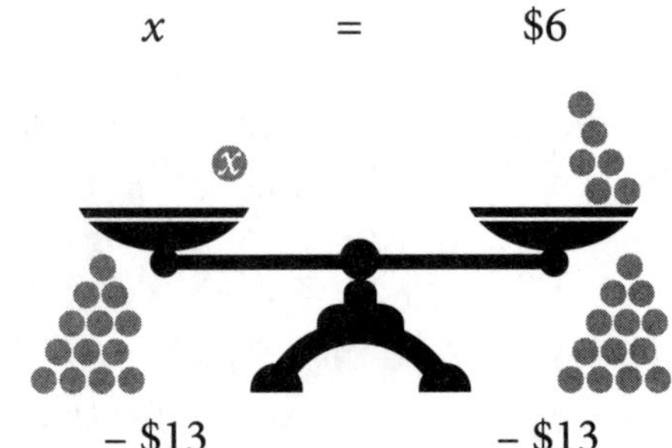

Understanding the Why

While it was easy on the scale to see how subtracting \$13 from both sides found the value for x, some of you might be wisely wondering how that works mathematically. After all, the order of operations says to add and subtract from left to right. So in x + \$13 – \$13 we should add x and \$13 first and *then* subtract \$13, right?

True . . . except remember that we can think of subtraction as an addition of a negative number . . . and that addition is commutative and associative. Even though we didn't write out the plus sign (and many people don't), **we were really viewing the subtraction of \$13 as an addition of –\$13.** Thus we were able to add \$13 and –\$13, which equals 0.

$$x + \mathbf{\$13 + -13}$$

$$x + \mathbf{0}$$

You might also wonder how we knew mathematically what number to subtract. Well, as we saw back in Lesson 2.4, the additive inverse is the name we give to the number that, added to another, equals 0. We know that +\$13 and –\$13 are **additive inverses**. So by subtracting \$13 (which we can think of as adding –\$13) we got 0. And since adding 0 doesn't change the value of a number (there's the **identity property of addition**), we knew adding +\$13 and –\$13 would leave us with x.

$$x + 0 \text{ simplifies to } x$$

The properties and principles we looked at in the first two chapters are ones we'll rely on again and again. And why can we rely on these properties and principles to work? Because God is governing all things in a consistent, predictable way. Once again, our ability to use math ultimately goes back to God's faithfulness.

Example: $x - 2 = 4$

To find the value for x, we want to isolate x on a side by itself. We know *x minus 2* equals 4. So if we *add 2* to both sides, we'll end up finding the value for x.

$$x - 2 + \mathbf{2} = 4 + \mathbf{2}$$

Now, let's simplify. We know that –2 and + 2 are additive inverses, so they will equal 0. And since adding 0 doesn't change the value of a number, our left-hand side will simplify to x. On the right, we'll have 4 + 2, or 6.

$$\mathbf{x = 6}$$

Note: We could have used cross outs to show how adding 2 canceled out the subtraction of 2.

$$x \cancel{- 2 + 2} = 4 + 2$$

$$\mathbf{x = 6}$$

Now we can check our work by substituting 6 for x in the original equation. If we found the correct value, the equation will hold true.

Original equation:

$x - 2 = 4$

Substituting 6 for x:

$\mathbf{6} - 2 = 4$

This is true . . . 6 – 2 does equal 4. We did the math correctly.

Keeping Perspective

If we perform the same operation (using the same quantity) to both sides of an equation, the sides remain equal. Why? Because God holds creation together in a consistent, predictable enough fashion that we can rely on the fact that if we perform the *same operation* using the *same quantity* to both sides of an equation, they'll stay equal.

3.4 More with Equalities and Unknowns

In the last lesson, we saw that we can find an unknown in an equation by getting the unknown on a side by itself. We do this by performing the *same operation* using the *same quantity* to *both sides* of the equation.

While all of our examples in the last lesson were of problems involving addition and subtraction, in real life, we'll encounter problems that require using other operations too. In this lesson, let's take a look at examples involving multiplication and division.

Example: $2 \bullet x = 8$

We'll start by dividing *both sides* by 2 (the *same quantity*). We'll show this using a fraction line.

$$\frac{2 \bullet x}{2} = \frac{8}{2}$$

Now, since we only have multiplication in the numerator, we can simplify $\frac{2 \bullet x}{2}$ the same way we have been simplifying fractions. In this case, we'll divide both the numerator and the denominator by 2, leaving us with x equaling 4.

$\frac{2 \bullet x}{2} = \frac{8}{2}$ is another way of writing $(2 \bullet x) \div 2 = 8 \div 2$. Both the fraction line and the ÷ symbol show division.

$$\frac{\cancel{2} \bullet x}{\cancel{2}} = \frac{\overset{4}{\cancel{8}}}{\cancel{2}}$$

$$\mathbf{x = 4}$$

Now we can check our work by substituting 4 for x in the original equation. If we found the correct value, the equation will hold true.

Original equation:

$$2 \bullet x = 8$$

Substituting 4 for x:

$$2 \bullet \mathbf{4} = 8$$

This is true . . . 2 • 4 does equal 8. We did the math correctly.

While we're focusing on the math side to learn the skill, don't lose sight of the fact that unknowns (such as x) represent quantities. For example, the x in this example could stand for the cost of each item if we buy 2 items for $8.

2 • x = $8,
where x is the cost of each olive oil bottle
and $8 is the total cost of both bottles.

Dividing the *Entire* Sides

It's important to note that the fraction line means to divide the *entire* numerator by the *entire* denominator. In the case of $\frac{2 \bullet x}{2}$, $2 \bullet x$ are factors making up a product. By dividing one of the factors, we are accomplishing the same thing that we would be if we divided the end product. To see this, let's put the actual value into the expression instead of x.

$$\frac{2 \bullet 4}{2}$$

2 • 4 equals 8. $\frac{8}{2}$ equals 4. This is the same answer we would obtain by crossing out the 2s.

$$\frac{2 \bullet 4}{2} = \frac{8}{2} = 4 \qquad \frac{\cancel{2} \bullet 4}{\cancel{2}} = 4$$

But the same does not hold true when there's addition or subtraction involved. For example, $\frac{8+2}{2}$ means to divide the *sum of* 8 and 2 (or 10) by 2. Notice that we would have gotten the wrong answer if we'd simply crossed out the 2s, as we'd be dividing only *part* of the numerator by 2.

$$\frac{8+2}{2} = \frac{10}{2} = 5 \qquad \frac{8+\cancel{2}}{\cancel{2}} \neq 8$$

Correct **Incorrect**

Once again, we're continuing to build on the properties and principles we looked at in the first two chapters. And why can we rely on these principles to work? Because God is governing all things in a consistent, predictable way. Once again, our ability to use math ultimately goes back to His faithfulness.

Example: $x \div 2 = \$4$

To make $x \div 2 = \$4$ easier to work with, let's rewrite it using a fraction.

$$\frac{x}{2} = \$4$$

If we multiply *both sides* by 2 (the *same quantity*), the multiplication will reverse the division by 2 (i.e., the 2s cancel out), and we'll have found the value of x.

$$\mathbf{2} \bullet \frac{x}{2} = \$4 \bullet \mathbf{2}$$

$$\frac{\cancel{2} \bullet x}{\cancel{2}} = \$4 \bullet 2$$

$$\mathbf{x = \$8}$$

Now we can check our work by substituting $8 for x in the original equation. If we found the correct value, the equation will hold true.

Original equation:

$$x \div 2 = \$4$$

Substituting \$8 for x:

$$\$8 \div 2 = \$4$$

This is true . . . \$8 ÷ 2 does equal \$4. We did the math correctly.

Again, to find an unknown in an equation, **get the unknown on a side by itself.** Do this by performing the *same operation* using the *same quantity* on *both sides* of the equation.

Keeping Perspective

Now, you might be wondering *why* you need to learn to find unknowns by isolating them on one side of an equation. All of the problems we've looked at so far have been so simple you could have easily solved them in your head.

While that's true so far, later in this course we'll see how to use this technique to solve problems we couldn't otherwise solve. We're practicing on simple problems to learn the basics, much as you practiced learning how to read by sounding out simple words.

As you practice finding unknowns, keep in mind that our ability to change both sides of an equation the same way without affecting the equality relies on the consistencies God created and sustains. If He were not keeping multiplication and division operating the same way in creation, we'd have no basis to assume that multiplying or dividing by the same quantity would leave both sides of an equation that represented a real-life problem equal . . . nor could we rely on the identity property of multiplication to hold true. All of math depends on God's faithfulness in holding creation together.

3.5 Applying Unknowns

Now that you know a little about unknowns, let's begin using what you've learned to help us describe real-life consistencies.

Distance, Speed, and Time

The distance you can travel depends on how fast you are going (your speed) and the time you travel. We could write a formula expressing the relationship this way:

$$d = s \cdot t$$

$$\textit{distance} = \textit{speed} \cdot \textit{time}$$

We can then use this formula to find missing values by simply plugging in values we know and using what we learned about equality to find the value we don't know.

The relationship between distance, speed, and time is also sometimes written like this: $d = r \bullet t$, where r stands for the *rate* of speed. Remember, the letters are just placeholders; which ones we use can vary. The important thing is to understand what the letters represent.

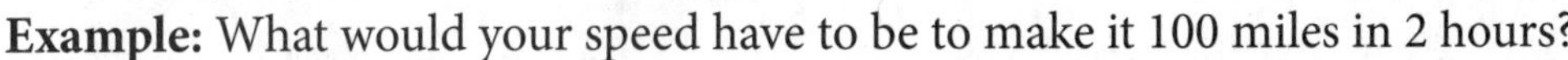

Example: What would your speed have to be to make it 100 miles in 2 hours?

Let's look at the values we know and what we need to find. We've been told the time (t) and distance (d). We need to find the speed (s).

$d = 100$ mi

$s = ?$

$t = 2$ hr

Let's substitute the values we know into the relationship:

$$d = s \bullet t$$

$$\mathbf{100\ mi} = s \bullet \mathbf{2\ hr}$$

Now all we need to do is get the unknown (the speed, which is represented by the letter s) on a side by itself. We can do this by dividing *both sides* by 2 hours. We'll use the fraction sign to represent the division.

Dividing both sides by 2 hr:

$$\frac{100\text{ mi}}{\mathbf{2\ hr}} = \frac{s \bullet 2\text{ hr}}{\mathbf{2\ hr}}$$

$$\frac{\overset{50}{\cancel{100}}\text{ mi}}{\cancel{2}\text{ hr}} = \frac{s \bullet \cancel{2\text{ hr}}}{\cancel{2\text{ hr}}}$$

$$\frac{50\text{ mi}}{\mathbf{hr}} = s$$

The speed equals $\frac{50\text{ mi}}{\text{hr}}$, more commonly written 50 mph, $50\frac{\text{mi}}{\text{hr}}$, or 50 miles per hour.

$50\frac{\text{mi}}{\text{hr}}$ is read "50 miles per hour." For now, speed will always be in miles per hour.

Unit Time — When working with units that are written like a fraction (such as $\frac{\text{mi}}{\text{hr}}$), think of the fraction line as meaning *per*. Thus $\frac{\text{mi}}{\text{hr}}$ means miles *per* hour — that is, the miles we can go per hour. Both $\frac{50\text{ mi}}{\text{hr}}$ and $50\frac{\text{mi}}{\text{hr}}$ mean 50 miles per hour. In fact, we can think of "hr" as "**1** hr." After all, what we're really saying is that we're going 50 miles in 1 hour. All of the expressions below mean the same thing.

$$\frac{50\text{ mi}}{\text{hr}} \quad \textit{or} \quad 50\frac{\text{mi}}{\text{hr}} \quad \textit{or} \quad \frac{50\text{ mi}}{1\text{ hr}}$$

Parties

Let's say you are planning a party. You have 25 guests and want to give them all party favors. If you have $100 to spend, how much can you spend on favors per guest?

Obviously, you'd divide $100 by 25 to get the answer: $4. But again, this could be written out using the principles you've learned this week.

Example: $25 \cdot x = \$100$

We can find the answer by dividing both sides by 25.

Dividing both sides by 25:

$$\frac{25 \cdot x}{25} = \frac{\$100}{25}$$

$$\frac{\cancel{25} \cdot x}{\cancel{25}} = \frac{\cancel{\$100}^{\$4}}{\cancel{25}}$$

$$\mathbf{x = \$4}$$

Keeping Perspective

Again, while you *could* solve the problems we're looking at right now mentally, use them to practice the skill of finding unknowns on paper. Right now, we only have one unknown in problems, but in real life, we often have more than one unknown we need to find . . . or more than one step we have to go through to find the unknown. The principles you are learning will help you solve these more involved problems as we get to them.

3.6 Finding Missing Sides

Let's look at how finding unknowns combines with geometry to help us find missing sides. Say you needed to find the missing side of this irregular hexagon (all measurements are in feet). You know that its perimeter is 65 feet, and you know the lengths of five of the sides, but you need to find the length of the sixth.

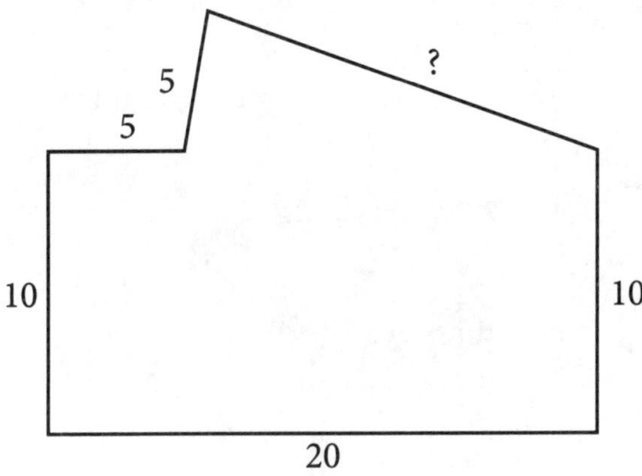

Example: Find the missing side of the irregular hexagon above.

Now, you know that the perimeter equals the sum of all the sides. And you know what the perimeter and all the sides but one equal.

65 ft = 5 ft + 5 ft + 10 ft + 20 ft + 10 ft + ?

Using x to stand for the ?, we can write the equation like this:

65 ft = 5 ft + 5 ft +10 ft + 20 ft + 10 ft **+ x**

So how do you find the unknown side? Start by adding the numbers you know (i.e., simplifying each side of the equation as much as you can), and then subtracting or adding to *both* sides of the equation until you have the unknown (represented by x) on a side of the equation by itself.

Simplifying the right side by adding the known numbers:

65 ft = **50 ft** + x

Subtracting 50 ft from (i.e., adding –50 ft, which is the additive inverse of 50 ft) to **both sides** of the equation:

65 ft + **–50 ft** = 50 ft + x + **–50 ft**

15 ft = x

It's always a good idea to substitute the unknown value you've found back into the original equation to make sure it works. (If it doesn't, you made a mistake somewhere along the line.)

Check:

65 ft = 5 ft +5 ft + 10 ft + 20 ft + 10 ft + **15 ft**

Yes, this is true! 5 ft +5 ft +10 ft +20 ft +10 ft +15 ft does equal 65 ft.

Simplify First

In the above example, notice that we added all the known numbers before we solved for x. Unless you have a reason not to, simplify each side of the equation (that is, express it as simply as possible, such as by adding, subtracting, multiplying, and dividing whatever you can) before you try to solve for an unknown.

Let's take a look now at a volume problem.

Example: Find the width of this fish tank (which is a rectangular prism) if its volume is 60 ft³.

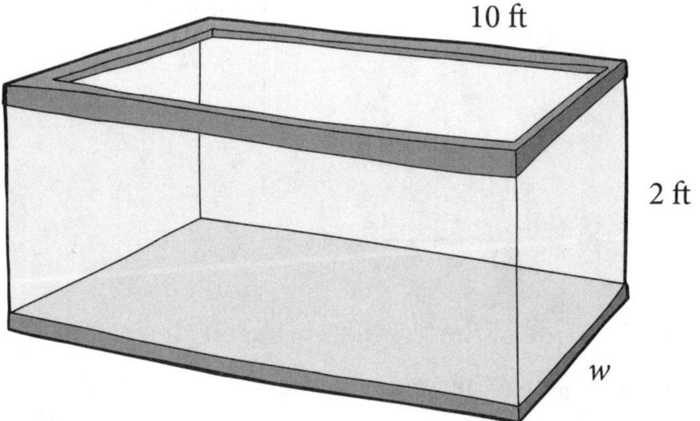

Write the formula:

$V = B \bullet h$

We can further specify this formula for a rectangular prism by specifying that the area of the base (B) is found by multiplying the length by the width.

More specific formula:

$V = \ell \bullet w \bullet h$

Substitute known values into the formula:

$\mathbf{60\ ft^3 = 10\ ft} \bullet w \bullet \mathbf{2\ ft}$

Simplify by multiplying 10 ft by 2 ft:

$60\ ft^3 = \mathbf{20\ ft^2} \bullet w$

Find w by dividing both sides by 20 ft²:

$$\frac{60\ ft^3}{\mathbf{20\ ft^2}} = \frac{20\ ft^2 \bullet w}{\mathbf{20\ ft^2}}$$

$$\frac{\overset{3\,ft}{\cancel{60\ ft^3}}}{\cancel{20\ ft^2}} = \frac{\cancel{20\ ft^2} \bullet w}{\cancel{20\ ft^2}}$$

$\mathbf{3\ ft} = \boldsymbol{w}$

Again, notice that we simplified each side of the equation before we tried to find the unknown.

Check: Let's substitute 3 ft for w.

$60\ ft^3 = 10\ ft \bullet w \bullet 2\ ft$

$60\ ft^3 = 10\ ft \bullet \mathbf{3\ ft} \bullet 2\ ft$

Yes! 2 ft • 3 ft • 10 ft does indeed equal 60 ft³. We solved the problem correctly.

Keeping Perspective

Using letters as placeholders for numbers allows us to use the information we know to find the information we don't know in all sorts of situations, from planning parties to distance calculations to finding the missing side of a prism. Once again, though, the only reason we can work with numbers this way is because we live in a consistent universe held together by a faithful God. His faithfulness ensures that creation remains consistent enough for us to use formulas to describe it.

3.7 Unknowns and Altitude

Now that you've practiced finding the value of unknowns, it's time to apply the skills you've learned to another setting. As we do, we'll see once again that math truly is a useful tool.

Understanding Altitude

Altitude is a concept we use all the time, although we may not often use the word. When we say a building is 300 ft tall, we're really saying that it's altitude, or height, relative to the ground is 300 ft.

Altitude is simply "the height of a thing above a reference level, especially above sea level or above the earth's surface. Also called 'elevation.'"[4] In other words, altitude helps us describe the height of something in relation to a specific reference level.

In the case of a building, we view the ground as our reference level. Mathematically, that means we think of the ground as having an altitude (or height) of 0 feet, meters, or whatever unit we're using to measure. We can then view altitudes (or heights) above ground level as positive, and those below (such as for the basement level or underground parking) as negative.

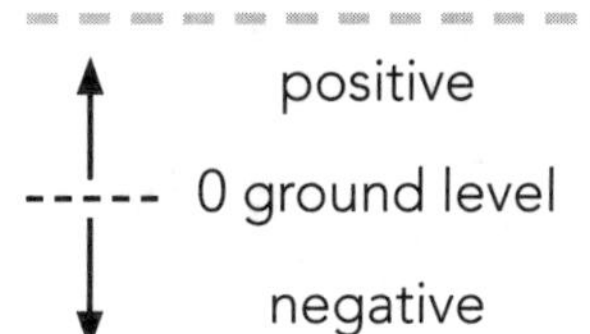

Notice the use of negative numbers to show altitudes *below* the reference level. Negative numbers help us describe creation!

When finding the area of a triangle, for example, you use the *height*, or altitude, of the triangle. Notice that in this case, the height is relative to the base of the triangle. The base is the fixed reference level we've used to find the height, or altitude, of a triangle.

height

base

Sea level is a common reference level for altitude. If you hear that a town has an altitude of 6,000 ft, that means its ground level is 6,000 ft above sea level.

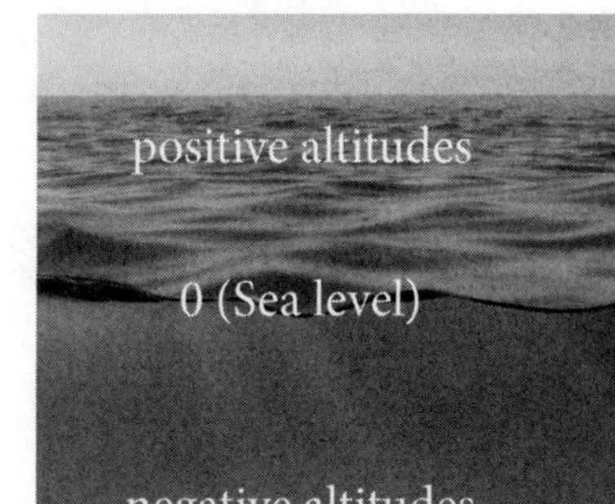

I hope you're seeing that altitude *depends on* or changes based on what we use as our reference level. If measured from sea level, a ski lift station might have an altitude of 9,000 ft. However, if we want to look at the altitude of the top of the mountain relative to that ski lift station, we could look at that same ski lift station as our reference level, viewing it's altitude as 0 ft.

9,000 ft (if measured compared to sea level
0 ft (if our reference level)

To avoid confusion, in problems we'll use the word **altitude** to refer strictly to altitude in relation to sea level, and **height** to refer to altitude in relation to some other fixed reference level. Don't let the term "altitude" confuse you; we're using it simply to refer to height relative to sea level.

Using Unknowns to Explore Altitude

In real life, we often need to look at problems related to altitude (or height). At what rate does a plane change altitude as it takes off? At what rate do dolphins, submarines, and divers descend into the ocean (i.e., change altitude)? At what rate does an elevator change height as it travels between floors?

This formula could be written using different letters. For example, we could have used an *h* instead of an *a* for the altitude (or height).
$h = r \bullet t + h_i$
Again, remember, the letters are just placeholders.

When changing altitude, the altitude (or height) you'll end up at depends on the rate at which you're your changing altitude (or height), the time over which you change altitude (or height), and the altitude (or height) at which you started. We could describe this using a formula.

Altitude (or Height) Formula:

$$a = r \bullet t + a_i$$

altitude (or height) = rate of change in altitude (or height) • time + initial altitude (or height)

The subscript *i* indicates that the *a* stands for the initial altitude (or height). The rate in the formula represents the average rate of change in altitude (or height).

As we have been doing with other formulas, we can use this formula, coupled with what we know about unknowns, to solve real-life problems.

Example: What would be the rate of change in altitude of a helicopter that takes off from sea level and reaches an altitude of 100 ft in 5 seconds?

altitude = 100 ft

initial altitude = 0 ft

Let's look at the values we know and what we need to find. We've been told the time (t) and the altitude (a), as well as the initial altitude (a_i—we know that it is 0 ft since we were told we're starting at sea level). We need to find the rate of change in altitude (r).

$a = 100$ ft

$r = ?$

$t = 5$ sec

$a_i = 0$ ft

Let's substitute the values we know into the relationship:

$$a = r \bullet t + a_i$$

$100 \text{ ft} = r \bullet 5 \text{ sec} + 0 \text{ ft}$

Now, since adding 0 doesn't change the value (the identity property of addition), we can ignore the addition of 0 ft. (In fact, you may see problems with an initial altitude of 0 written this way from the beginning.)

$100 \text{ ft} = r \bullet 5 \text{ sec}$

Now all we need to do is get the unknown (the rate, which is represented by the letter r) on a side by itself. We can do this by dividing both sides by 5 seconds. We'll use the fraction sign to represent the division.

Dividing both sides by 5 seconds:

$$\frac{100 \text{ ft}}{\mathbf{5 \text{ sec}}} = \frac{r \bullet 5 \text{ sec}}{\mathbf{5 \text{ sec}}}$$

$$\frac{{}^{20}\cancel{100} \text{ ft}}{\cancel{5} \text{ sec}} = \frac{r \bullet \cancel{5 \text{ sec}}}{\cancel{5 \text{ sec}}}$$

$\frac{\mathbf{20 \text{ ft}}}{\mathbf{sec}} = \boldsymbol{r}$, which we could also write as $20 \frac{\text{ft}}{\text{sec}} = r$

A rate of $20 \frac{\text{ft}}{\text{sec}}$ would result in going from an altitude of 0 ft to an altitude of 100 ft in 5 seconds.

Real-life problems are often much more complicated than this one. But whether complicated or simple, we can use math formulas (and unknowns!) to help us describe and work with situations.

For now, we'll look only at problems that have an initial altitude (or height) of 0.

Negative Unknowns Applied

Up until now, all of our problems involving unknowns have only had positive numbers. However, as we work with altitude (or height), we end up dealing with negative numbers too.

Let's look at another helicopter example. This time, though, instead of the helicopter *ascending* to 100 ft from sea level, let's look at a helicopter that has to *descend* into a valley 100 ft below sea level.

Example: Suppose a helicopter is flying at an altitude of 0 ft (sea level) across a valley that's 100 ft below sea level. If it descends into the valley, at what rate would the helicopter have to change altitude in order to descend to the bottom (an altitude of –100 ft) in 5 seconds?

Again, let's look at the values we know and what we need to find.

$a = -100$ ft

$r = ?$

$t = 5$ sec

$a_i = 0$ ft (We were told we were starting at sea level.)

Now let's substitute the values we know into the formula.

$$a = r \bullet t + a_i$$

$$-100 \text{ ft} = r \bullet 5 \text{ sec} + 0 \text{ ft}$$

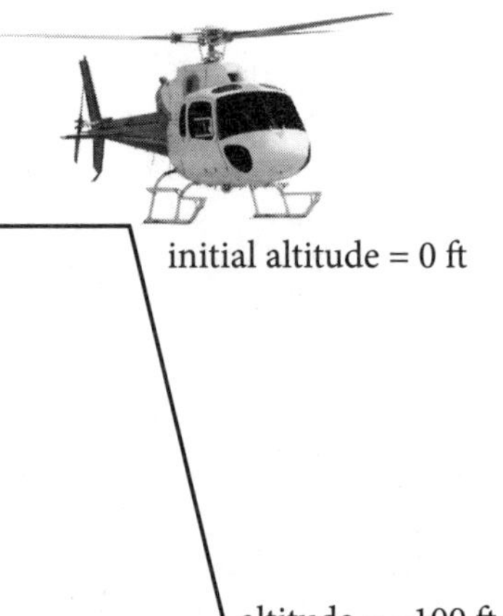

This simplifies to

$$-100 \text{ ft} = r \bullet 5 \text{ sec}$$

Now all we need to do is to get the unknown (represented by the letter *r*) on a side by itself. We can do this by dividing both sides by 5 seconds. Again, since the fraction sign represents division, we'll use it to represent the division.

$$\frac{-100 \text{ ft}}{\mathbf{5\ sec}} = \frac{r \bullet 5 \text{ sec}}{\mathbf{5\ sec}}$$

$$\frac{\overset{20}{-\cancel{100}} \text{ ft}}{\cancel{5} \text{ sec}} = \frac{r \bullet \cancel{5 \text{ sec}}}{\cancel{5 \text{ sec}}}$$

$\frac{\mathbf{-20\ ft}}{\mathbf{sec}} = \boldsymbol{r}$, which we could also write as $-20\frac{\text{ft}}{\text{sec}} = r$

A rate of $-20\frac{\text{ft}}{\text{sec}}$ would result in going from an altitude of 0 ft to an altitude of –100 ft in 5 seconds.

Notice that this time, the rate (*r*) ended up being a negative number. We found its value the same way we have been, though—by separating it on a side by itself.

Don't let negative numbers in problems confuse you. Just as we can add, subtract, multiply, and divide the same positive number to *both sides* of an equation without changing the equality of the expressions, we can do the same thing with negative numbers. We just need to be sure to apply the rules for adding, subtracting, multiplying, and dividing negative numbers we covered back in Chapter 2 when we do.

Keeping Perspective

Well, I hope you had fun exploring altitude. The problems in your workbook will help you continue to use math to understand the world around us so you'll be equipped to use the skills your learning to serve the Lord in different settings.

Since real-life settings often include negative numbers, you'll notice that many problems in your workbook will too. Again, don't let the negatives confuse you. The principles you've learned about how to find the value of an unknown still apply. Simply combine them with what you know about negative numbers.

3.8 Chapter Synopsis and Leonhard Euler

We began this chapter learning that we can use letters and symbols to help us describe God's creation, and how we use the word **unknown** to refer to an "unknown quantity."[5] We saw that we've already been using letters to stand for unknowns for years in formulas and word problems.

Leonhard Euler (1707–1783)

We also explored the concept of equality, seeing that if we performed the *same operation* using the *same quantity* to *both sides* of an equation, both sides remain equal. We used this knowledge to find the value of an unknown by isolating it on one side of the equation.

We'll continue to learn to work with unknowns and equality as we move forward. First, though, let's take a moment to look at the life of Leonhard Euler (pronounced "oiler"; 1707–1783), a godly man God gifted with an amazing mathematical mind.

Leonhard Euler

Euler has been called "the leading mathematician and theoretical physicist of the eighteenth century."[6] He left his mark on nearly every branch of math. He wrote a prodigious amount — one resource I read estimated that "his publications during his working life averaged about 800 pages a year,"[7] and another called him "the most prolific mathematician in history."[8] In addition to numerous other works, Euler wrote math textbooks.

Beyond being a brilliant mathematician, however, Euler's life provides a beautiful illustration of a famous mathematician who truly viewed math as a testimony to God and who served the Lord despite tremendous challenges.

Euler's father had been a preacher, and Euler himself, wanting to please his father, had studied to become a minister as well. Fortunately, his father eventually realized that God had clearly designed his son to be a mathematician instead of a preacher.

After failing to obtain a math position in Basle, Switzerland (his home city), though, Euler eventually ended up moving to Russia for a position at the St. Petersburg Academy that was supposed to be in the medical section. But things did not go as planned. As one book explains,

> *The liberal Empress Catherine I (the widow of Peter the Great) died on the very day that Euler set foot on Russian soil. The heir was a minor, and the ruling faction inaugurated a repressive regime in which the Academy was looked upon as an unnecessary luxury. In the resulting confusion, Euler was able to slip quietly into the mathematical section; the medical post was forgotten.*[9]

God used the confusion following the empress's death not only to move Euler into a math position, but also to help him complete tasks. Euler feared the spies who literally were everywhere. Unable to do much else, Euler applied himself with all the more diligence to his mathematical pursuits.

Euler's life had its fair share of trials. While still fairly young (probably in his early 30s),[10] Euler lost sight in one eye. Later, he lost sight in his other eye too. But Euler didn't waste time in self-pity. God had blessed Euler with an amazing capacity to calculate mentally and remember things, so he kept on solving math problems despite not having good eyesight. As one biographer comments,

> *He was able to do difficult calculations mentally, some of these requiring him to retain in his head up to 50 places of accuracy!*[11]

Euler was definitely a man with a remarkable intellect. Yet unlike many of the French philosophers of his time, Euler recognized that his intellect needed to be submitted to God's authority. One time, a French philosopher named Diderot came to Russia and began spreading his skepticism about God's existence. The ruler asked Euler to combat him.

While none of his biographers question Euler's staunch Christian faith, some do question the validity of the story of Diderot and Euler. I've included it, as it goes back to a very early source[13] and the doubts seem raised more because people can't understand Euler's faith. Whether the interchange with the philosopher happened this way or not, however, the point remains: Euler was a brilliant mathematician who trusted God.

> *Diderot was informed that a learned mathematician was in possession of an algebraical demonstration of the existence of God, and would give it before all the Court, if he [Diderot] desired to hear it. Diderot gladly consented. . . . Euler advanced toward Diderot, and said gravely, and in a tone of perfect conviction: "Sir, $\frac{a + b^n}{n} = x$, hence God exists; reply!"*[12]

Diderot was embarrassed and immediately went back to France. While one could argue that $\frac{a + b^n}{n} = x$ is not proof of God's existence (all of math testifies to God's faithfulness, but we cannot prove God's existence using human reasoning; our faith lies on something ever so much firmer — God's Word), God saw fit to let Euler's simple faith and bold confidence baffle the French philosopher.

May we, like Euler, use math while praising and trusting the Creator of all.

Fractions, Unknowns, and Equations

4.1 Solving Problems with Fractions and Unknowns (Addition and Subtraction)

In this chapter, we're going to take a look at how we can apply the *same principles* we looked at in the last chapter to problems involving fractions. We'll start in this lesson with addition and subtraction problems.

Fractions and Unknowns

Let's say someone purchased an additional $\frac{3}{8}$ of an acre, giving them a total of $4\frac{1}{4}$ acres. You want to know how much land they had before the purchase.

$$x + \frac{3}{8} = 4\frac{1}{4}$$

We can solve this the ***same way*** we would if working with whole numbers — by adding or subtracting the *same quantity* to *both* sides of the equation.

Subtract $\frac{3}{8}$ from (i.e., add the additive inverse, or $-\frac{3}{8}$, to) both sides of the equation:

$$x + \frac{3}{8} + -\mathbf{\frac{3}{8}} = 4\frac{1}{4} + -\mathbf{\frac{3}{8}}$$

Simplify by rewriting $4\frac{1}{4}$ as $\frac{17}{4}$, multiplying it by $\frac{2}{2}$ to rewrite it as $\frac{34}{8}$ so it is an improper fraction with the same denominator as $\frac{3}{8}$, and then completing the subtraction:

$$x = \frac{34}{8} + -\frac{3}{8}$$

$$x = \mathbf{\frac{31}{8}}$$

$$x = \mathbf{3\frac{7}{8}}$$

They started with $3\frac{7}{8}$ acres.

Doing the Same Thing to *Both* Sides of the Equation Doesn't Change the Value

Remember, we can add, subtract, multiply, divide, etc., the *same quantity* to *both sides* of an equation without changing its value. The equal sign means the equation is equal, or in balance. So if one side has an operation performed on it, the other part has to have the *same operation* performed using the *same quantity*, or they will no longer be equal.

Again, picture a scale. When you have a scale that is balanced, both sides of the scale are equal.

$$6 = 6$$

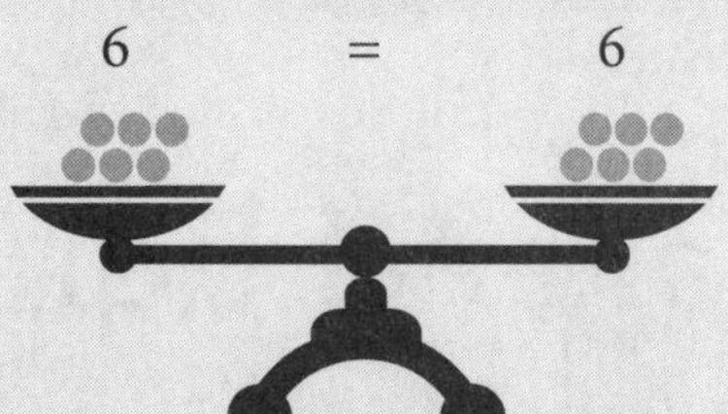

If you add, subtract, multiply, or divide one side of a scale by a quantity, you have to add, subtract, multiply, or divide the other side by the *same quantity*, or the scale will get out of balance.

Added $\frac{1}{2}$ to Both Sides

$$6 + \frac{1}{2} = 6 + \frac{1}{2}$$

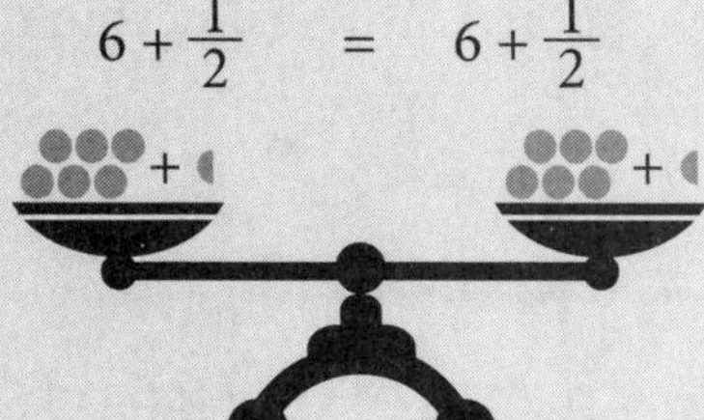

Subtracted $\frac{1}{2}$ from Both Sides, which is the Same as Adding $-\frac{1}{2}$ to Both Sides

$$6 - \frac{1}{2} = 6 - \frac{1}{2}$$

Likewise, in an equation, the value of all the numbers on the left equals the values of all the numbers on the right. For them to remain equal, then, whatever we do to one side, we must also do to the other side.

While you may be wondering why we need to spend so much time understanding equality and the concept that we can add, subtract, multiply, or divide the *same quantity* to *both sides* of an equation, it's a skill used extensively as we seek to use math to explore God's creation. Thus it's vital to make sure we grasp and know how to work with equations involving both unknowns and fractions.

Keeping Perspective

Once again, we're applying the *same principles* we looked at with integers to fractions. Throughout math, you'll find the same principles applied over and over again to new notations and situations. The number of notations we need reminds us that God created a universe more intricate than we could imagine . . . which is why we need so many different mathematical notations and techniques to help us describe it.

While many mathematicians would love to take the glory for math, the glory goes to the One who created and sustains this universe so consistently — and who gave us a mind capable of exploring it. Our ability to observe and think is a gift from God.

I didn't quite grasp that fact until a concussion had me unable to operate for months. No matter how hard I tried, I just could not think at times. God has our bodies do amazing things for us that we take for granted.

As you complete Worksheet 4.1, praise God for giving you the ability to learn and think. If you struggle with a concept, run to God. He understands math perfectly and can help you learn what you need to learn.

> *For who maketh thee to differ from another? and what hast thou that thou didst not receive? now if thou didst receive it, why dost thou glory, as if thou hadst not received it? (1 Corinthians 4:7).*

As an example of men taking the glory for math, consider this quote from Denis Guedj: "Mathematicians are architects of complex systems."[1] To what is he giving the glory for math? Mathematicians.

4.2 Solving Problems with Fractions and Unknowns (Multiplication and Division)

It's time now to take a look at more problems involving fractions and unknowns. This time, rather than addition, we'll look at problems in which our unknown is being multiplied or divided by a fraction.

Fractions and Unknowns

Let's say someone gets a bonus of one twentieth of his monthly salary. If the amount of the bonus was $60, what was the amount of his salary?

If we use x to represent the monthly salary, we could represent the problem this way:

$$\frac{1}{20} \cdot x = \$60$$

In other words, we want to find the number that, if we take $\frac{1}{20}$ of it, gives us $60.

How do we do this? The *same way* we would if we were working with integers: by performing the *same operation* using the *same quantity* to *both sides* of the equation. So to find $\frac{1}{20} \bullet x = \$60$, **we need to divide *both sides* by $\frac{1}{20}$.**

A fraction doesn't change how we solve the problem. To solve a problem with a fraction, we **follow the *same* principles** we've been using with integers. Again, we want to keep our equation in balance. As long as we multiply or divide both sides by the *same amount*, the sides of the equation will remain equal.

Example: $\frac{1}{20} \bullet x = \$60$

Divide both sides by $\frac{1}{20}$:

$$\frac{\frac{1}{20} \bullet x}{\mathbf{\frac{1}{20}}} = \frac{\$60}{\mathbf{\frac{1}{20}}}$$

Remember, the fraction line represents division.

We'll complete the division by inverting and multiplying:

$$\frac{1}{20} \bullet x \bullet \mathbf{\frac{20}{1}} = \$60 \bullet \mathbf{\frac{20}{1}}$$

$$\frac{1}{\cancel{20}} \bullet x \bullet \frac{\cancel{20}}{1} = \$60 \bullet \frac{20}{1}$$

$$\mathbf{x = \$1{,}200}$$

We found our answer!

Notice that if we substitute \$1,200 for x in the original equation, the equation holds true.

Original equation:

$$\frac{1}{20} \bullet x = \$60$$

Substituting \$1,200 for x:

$$\frac{1}{20} \bullet \mathbf{\$1{,}200} = \$60$$

$$\mathbf{\$60 = \$60}$$

Once again, **the same principles you've been using with integers and decimals apply to fractions as well** — you just have to couple them with the things you already know about fractions.

This holds true with multiplication too: **we can multiply both sides by the same fraction without changing the value.** Let's take a look at an example.

Example: $\dfrac{x}{4\frac{4}{5}\text{ lb}} = 5$

Example Meaning: Say we divide apples into $4\frac{4}{5}$ lb packages, and end up with 5 packages. How many apples did we have to start with?

Here, we need to *multiply* both sides by $4\frac{4}{5}$ to find the unknown.

Rewrite the mixed number as an improper fraction to avoid mistakes:

$$\frac{x}{\frac{\mathbf{24}}{\mathbf{5}}\textbf{ lb}} = 5$$

Multiply both sides by $\frac{24}{5}$ to cancel out the division:

$$\frac{x}{\frac{24}{5}\text{ lb}} \bullet \frac{24}{5}\text{ lb} = 5 \bullet \frac{24}{5}\text{ lb}$$

$$\boldsymbol{x = 24\textbf{ lb}}$$

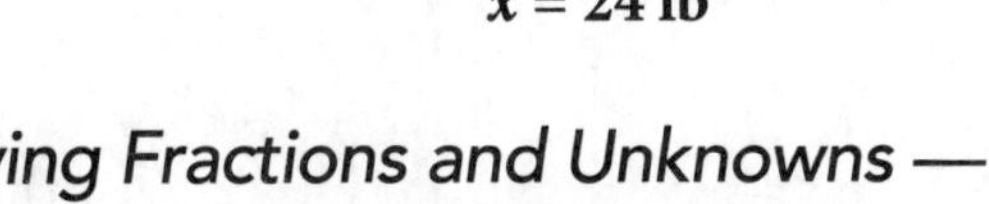

Applying Fractions and Unknowns — Finding the Volume of a Pyramid

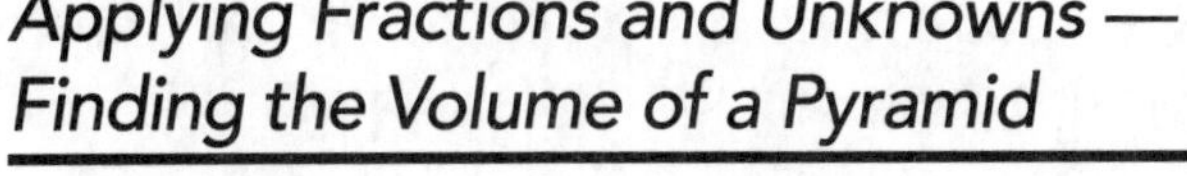

Back in Book 1, you learned how to find the volume of several different three-dimensional (solid) objects, such as the prism and the cylinder.

Prism

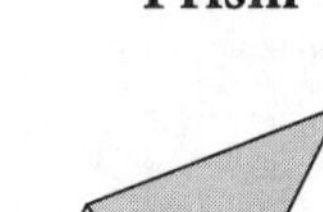

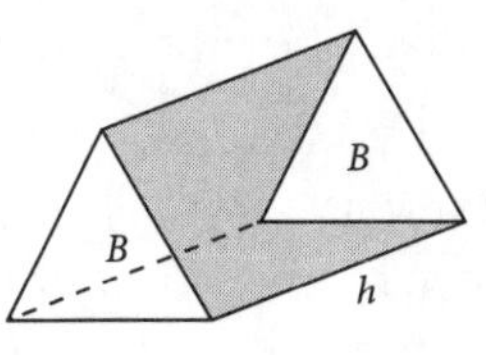

Cylinder

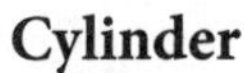

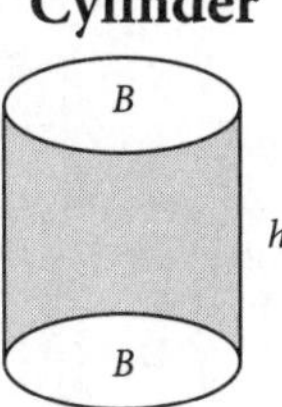

It's time now to learn how to find the volume of another three-dimensional (solid) object: the pyramid. The formula to find the volume of a pyramid includes — you guessed it — a fraction.

First, though, what is a pyramid? A **pyramid** is the name of a three-dimensional solid whose base is a polygon but whose sides are triangles that come to a point. While when we think of pyramids, most of us think of the Egyptian pyramids, which have square bases, pyramids can have any polygon as a base.

Pyramid

(a solid whose base is a polygon and whose sides are triangles that come to a point)

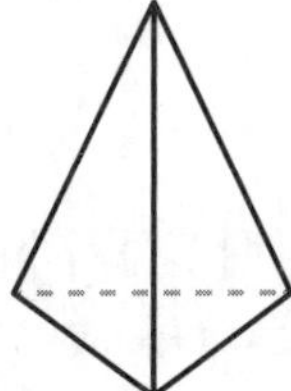

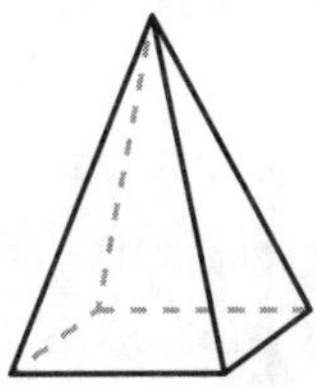

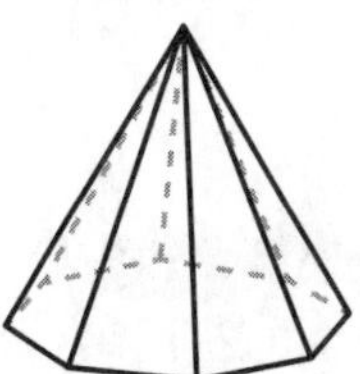

Because of the way the sides of a pyramid come to one central point, a pyramid's volume always equals $\frac{1}{3}$ the volume it would if it were a prism. We can express this relationship as a formula like this:

$$V = \frac{1}{3} \cdot B \cdot h$$

$$\textit{Volume} = \frac{1}{3} \cdot \textit{area of the base} \cdot \textit{height}$$

Notice the fraction, along with the letters used as placeholders!

Now that we know this relationship, we can find the volume of any pyramid.

Example: Find the volume of a pyramid whose base is 40 square feet and whose height is 20 feet.

$V = \frac{1}{3} \cdot \mathbf{40\ ft^2} \cdot \mathbf{20\ ft}$
$V = \mathbf{266.67\ ft^3}$

Why a Mixture of Lowercase and Uppercase Letters?

You might be wondering why we used a lowercase letter *h* for height, but the capital letters *B* and *V* for base and volume. We could have used a lowercase *B* and *V* too — or any letter or symbol, for that matter. But since we typically use a lowercase *b* to mean the *length* of the bottom (i.e., the *base*) of a triangle or parallelogram, we used a capital *B* to differentiate that we're meaning the *entire area* of the polygon that forms the base of a pyramid. Similarly, since scientists typically use a lowercase *v* to stand for velocity (speed in a specific direction), to aid in differentiating between the two, we used an uppercase *V* for volume.

The important thing is to remember that, however it is written, the formula for volume represents the relationship between the volume, the area of the base, and the height of a pyramid.

Keeping Perspective

Once again, we're applying the *same principles* we looked at with whole numbers to fractions. And once again, we can do that because of the underlying consistencies God created and sustains. On Worksheet 4.2, you'll have a chance to practice both the skill and applying the skill to finding the volume of some actual Egyptian pyramids.

4.3 Viewing Division as Multiplication

In the last lesson, we practiced solving problems such as the following.

Example: $\frac{1}{2} \bullet x = 50$

Divide both sides by $\frac{1}{2}$:

$$\frac{\frac{1}{2} \bullet x}{\frac{1}{2}} = \frac{50}{\frac{1}{2}}$$

Invert and multiply to complete the division:

$$\frac{1}{2} \bullet x \bullet \frac{2}{1} = 50 \bullet \frac{2}{1}$$

$$\frac{1}{\cancel{2}} \bullet x \bullet \frac{\cancel{2}}{1} = 50 \bullet \frac{2}{1}$$

$$\mathbf{x = 100}$$

In math we look for the easiest, most concise way to solve a problem. Easier methods save us time and, in the long run, make it possible for us to solve more complicated problems. And there's an easier way to solve problems like these!

Rather than writing out the division and *then* inverting and multiplying, we could have jumped right to multiplying both sides by the inverse of $\frac{1}{2}$.

Example: $\frac{1}{2} \bullet x = 50$

Divide by multiplying both sides of the equation by the inverse:

$$\frac{1}{2} \bullet x \bullet \frac{2}{1} = 50 \bullet \frac{2}{1}$$

$$\frac{1}{\cancel{2}} \bullet x \bullet \frac{\cancel{2}}{1} = 50 \bullet \frac{2}{1}$$

$$\mathbf{x = 100}$$

All we did in the above example was skip the step of writing out the division, jumping right to the completing of it by multiplying by the multiplicative inverse.

Notice that while we completed the multiplication in a separate line, we could have solved the whole problem in one step, as shown in the following example.

Example: $\frac{1}{2} \bullet x = 50$

$$\frac{1}{\cancel{2}} \bullet x \bullet \frac{\cancel{2}}{1} = 50 \bullet \frac{2}{1}$$

$$\mathbf{x = 100}$$

While for clarity we'll continue to show the completion of the multiplication in a separate step, know that you can do them both on the same line when solving problems.

Let's take a look at another example.

Example: $\frac{2}{3} \bullet x = 8$

$$\frac{\mathbf{3}}{\mathbf{2}} \bullet \frac{2}{3} \bullet x = 8 \bullet \frac{\mathbf{3}}{\mathbf{2}}$$

$$\frac{\cancel{3}}{\cancel{2}} \bullet \frac{\cancel{2}}{\cancel{3}} \bullet x = {}^{4}\cancel{8} \bullet \frac{\mathbf{3}}{\cancel{2}}$$

$$\mathbf{x = 12}$$

We can think of division as **multiplying by the multiplicative inverse (i.e., the reciprocal).** Both are different ways to accomplish the same thing.

$$\frac{1}{4} \div \frac{1}{4} = 1 \quad or \quad \frac{1}{4} \bullet \frac{\mathbf{4}}{\mathbf{1}} = 1$$

$$\frac{2}{3} \div \frac{2}{3} = 1 \quad or \quad \frac{2}{3} \bullet \frac{\mathbf{3}}{\mathbf{2}} = 1$$

This holds true with whole numbers too.

$$8 \div 8 = 1 \quad or \quad 8 \bullet \frac{\mathbf{1}}{\mathbf{8}} = 1$$

$$12 \div 12 = 1 \quad or \quad 12 \bullet \frac{\mathbf{1}}{\mathbf{12}} = 1$$

In fact, the "shortcut" we just saw of skipping right to the step of multiply by the inverse applies to whole numbers as well.

Example: $3 \bullet x = \frac{2}{3}$

We need to divide both sides by 3. We can do that by multiplying by the inverse of 3.

$$3 \bullet x \bullet \frac{\mathbf{1}}{\mathbf{3}} = \frac{2}{3} \bullet \frac{\mathbf{1}}{\mathbf{3}}$$

$$\cancel{3} \bullet x \bullet \frac{1}{\cancel{3}} = \frac{2}{3} \bullet \frac{1}{3}$$

$$\mathbf{x = \frac{2}{9}}$$

The more you learn in math, the more you'll apply the same principles you already know to help you solve different problems.

Keeping Perspective

Why is it important to realize we can divide by multiplying by the inverse? Well, for one thing, multiplication is associative and commutative, while division is not. Viewing division as multiplication enables us to apply the associative and commutative properties to problems. Again, we're looking at the consistent way God causes objects to multiply and divide and finding ways to work with those consistencies so that we can solve real-life problems.

4.4 Fractions with an Unknown in the Denominator

Let's continue looking at unknowns and fractions by examining what to do when an unknown is in the denominator of a fraction.

Fractions containing unknowns in the denominator are just another way of representing what you've been doing for years when you've found a missing number in a division problem.

Example: 20 divided by what number equals 4?

Old way of writing:

$20 \div ? = 4$

Same thing represented using a fraction:

$$\frac{20}{?} = 4$$

Same thing represented using an x instead of a *?*:

$$\frac{20}{x} = 4$$

No matter how we write it, the answer is 5, as 20 divided by 5 equals 4.

Let's look at an actual example of what the example above could represent. Say we know someone started with \$20 and divided that money evenly among some friends. Each friend got \$4. How many friends did the money get divided among?

Here we have $\$20 \div x = \$4$, which we could also write as $\frac{\$20}{x} = \$4$

Now, while it's obvious that x equals 5, let's look at how we could solve for x mathematically so we'll be able to apply the skill to problems that aren't so intuitive. How do we isolate x on a side by itself when it's in the denominator of a fraction? Again, by applying the same principles we have been. While isolating x will take one additional step than we've had so far, we can still follow the same general process. Let's take a look.

Example: $\frac{\$20}{x} = \$4$

To begin with, we need to get x out of the denominator. We'll do so by multiplying *both sides* of the equation by x. It doesn't matter that we don't know x's value — we know that whatever it is, we're multiplying both sides by that *same quantity*, so the equation will stay in balance.

$$x \bullet \frac{\$20}{x} = \$4 \bullet x$$

Notice that the two xs on the left side of the equation cancel out.

$$\cancel{x} \bullet \frac{\$20}{\cancel{x}} = \$4 \bullet x$$

$$\$20 = \$4 \bullet x$$

Now it's easy to see how to solve for x. We need to divide both sides by \$4 in order to isolate x on a side by itself. We can do that using a fraction line as we have been, or, as we saw in the last lesson, by multiplying both sides by the inverse of \$4 (which is $\frac{1}{\$4}$).

$$\frac{\$20}{4} = \frac{\$4 \bullet x}{\$4} \quad or \quad \$20 \bullet \frac{1}{\$4} = \$4 \bullet x \bullet \frac{1}{\$4}$$

Either way, the \$4s cancel out, leaving us with a value for x.

$$\frac{\overset{5}{\cancel{\$20}}}{\cancel{4}} = \frac{\cancel{\$4} \bullet x}{\cancel{\$4}} \quad or \quad \overset{5}{\cancel{\$20}} \bullet \frac{1}{\cancel{\$4}} = \cancel{\$4} \bullet x \bullet \frac{1}{\cancel{\$4}}$$

$$\mathbf{\$5 = x} \quad or \quad \mathbf{\$5 = x}$$

It's important to note that, in the example above, we multiplied *both sides* of the equation by x. Even though we didn't know x's value at first, we knew that since we were multiplying *both sides* by that *same value* (x), the sides would stay equal. It doesn't matter if we know the quantity we're adding, subtracting, multiplying, or dividing an equation by or if it's an unknown; so long as we use the same quantity, the sides will remain equal.

Keeping Perspective

When solving problems with fractions and unknowns, remember the basic rules. These rules apply whether you're dealing with *known* or *unknown* quantities.

It doesn't matter that we don't know the value for x — because God governs this world so consistently, we can multiply both sides of an equation by x, knowing that whatever its value, it will follow the "rules" of multiplication, affecting both sides the same way. In other words, God governs creation with such unerring faithfulness that we can manipulate unknowns with the same confidence we could if we knew their value!

As you study math, don't forget to pause and stand in awe of the Creator and sustainer. We serve a faithful, covenant-keeping God we can trust. And He will be just as faithful to everything else He says in His Word.

> *For ever, O LORD, thy word is settled in heaven. Thy faithfulness is unto all generations: thou hast established the earth, and it abideth. They continue this day according to thine ordinances: for all are thy servants. Unless thy law had been my delights, I should then have perished in mine affliction. I will never forget thy precepts: for with them thou hast quickened me (Psalm 119:89–93).*

4.5 A Closer Look at Negative Numbers and Fractions

It's time to take a closer look at negative numbers and fractions and see if we can

1. observe how the consistency of division that God created and sustains works with fractional notation and
2. apply this consistency to problems we couldn't otherwise solve.

Consider this example involving negative numbers and an unknown.

Example: $x - \frac{-50}{2} = 15$

Complete division of $\frac{-50}{2}$:

$x - \mathbf{-25} = 15$

Two negative signs make a positive, as we have the opposite of the opposite:

$x + \mathbf{25} = 15$

Subtract 25 from (i.e., add −25 to) both sides of the equation:

$x + 25 + \mathbf{-25} = 15 + \mathbf{-25}$

$\mathbf{x = -10}$

In the example above, we could simply complete the division (−50 ÷ 2), getting −25, and then solve. But what if we had a different fraction — one that we wouldn't get a whole number if we divided?

Let's say we had $x + \frac{4}{-5} = 15$. How would we solve this *without rounding the answer*?

Let's backtrack for a moment. $\frac{4}{-5}$ means 4 ÷ −5. We've already seen that, since each negative sign means *the opposite of*, if we're dividing with one negative sign, we end up with a negative answer (the opposite of), but if we have two, we end up with a positive answer (the opposite of the opposite is a positive). We keep bouncing back and forth from positive to negative as the number of negative signs increases. **In fact, if we have an odd number of negative signs, we get a negative answer, while an even number of signs gives a positive answer.**

So, even though we don't want to complete the division right now in $\frac{4}{-5}$, we know that since there's only *one negative sign* in $\frac{4}{-5}$, the answer will be *negative*. So we can safely **pull the negative sign out in front of the fraction**, making it $-\frac{4}{5}$, as the negative will apply to the result when we complete the division (remember, $\frac{4}{5}$ means 4 ÷ 5).

Example: $x + \frac{4}{-5} = 15$

Move the negative sign in front of the fraction, as we know the result will be negative:

$$x + -\frac{4}{5} = 15$$

Now we can solve for our unknown by adding the additive inverse (in this case, $\frac{4}{5}$) to both sides and simplifying:

$$x + -\frac{4}{5} + \frac{4}{5} = 15 + \frac{4}{5}$$

$$\mathbf{x = 15\frac{4}{5}}$$

Note that we can move a negative sign in front of a fraction even if there's already a negative sign there.

Example: $x - \frac{-1}{5} = \frac{4}{5}$

Move the negative sign in front of the fraction, as we know the result will be negative:

$$x - -\frac{1}{5} = \frac{4}{5}$$

Simplify (since the opposite of an opposite is a positive, the two negative signs can be replaced by a positive sign):

$$x + \frac{1}{5} = \frac{4}{5}$$

Add the additive inverse (in this case, $-\frac{1}{5}$) to both sides and simplify:

$$x + \frac{1}{5} + -\frac{1}{5} = \frac{4}{5} + -\frac{1}{5}$$

$$\mathbf{x = \frac{3}{5}}$$

Now let's consider another problem, this time one that has two negative signs in the fraction.

Example: $x + \frac{-2}{-3} = 10$

Because we know that a negative divided by a negative equals a positive, we know that –2 divided by –3 will be positive. So we can *remove* both the negative signs, leaving us with this:

$$x + \frac{2}{3}$$

We can now easily solve for x by adding the additive inverse (in this case, $-\frac{2}{3}$) to both sides and simplifying:

$$x + \frac{2}{3} + -\frac{2}{3} = 10 + -\frac{2}{3}$$

$$\mathbf{x = 9\frac{1}{3}}$$

When you encounter problems with negative numbers in a fraction, remember that the fraction represents division. Then use what you know about dividing negative numbers to solve the problem. Each negative sign means *the opposite of*, so one negative sign means the fraction will yield a negative answer, and two negative signs means the fraction will yield a positive answer.

One Negative Sign	One Negative Sign	Two Negative Signs
$\frac{8}{-2} = -\frac{8}{2} = -4$	$\frac{-8}{2} = -\frac{8}{2} = -4$	$\frac{-8}{-2} = \frac{8}{2} = 4$
Negative Answer	*Negative Answer*	*Positive Answer*

Example: Solve $x - \frac{2}{-3} = 5$

Move the negative sign in front of the fraction, as we know the result will be negative:

$$x - -\frac{2}{3} = 5$$

Two negatives make a positive:

$$x + \frac{2}{3} = 5$$

Solve for the unknown by adding the additive inverse (in this case, $-\frac{2}{3}$):

$$x + \frac{2}{3} + -\frac{2}{3} = 5 + -\frac{2}{3}$$

$$\boldsymbol{x = 4\frac{1}{3}}$$

Keeping Perspective

Once again, we're looking at how division works with positive and negative numbers (i.e., how our notational system describes God's creation) and extrapolating on that to solve problems that we couldn't otherwise. You'll see this theme throughout all of upper math. While the problems and rules may get more involved, the basic principles remain the same. And those principles rely on an underlying assumption that the universe is consistent and predictable — an assumption that only makes sense with the God of the Bible.

4.6 Chapter Synopsis

In this chapter, we applied the *same principles* we'd been learning to problems containing fractions and unknowns. You may have noticed that it takes a few more steps to solve problems containing fractions, but hopefully you saw that **the basic process of finding an unknown remained the same.**

Now I know you might be wondering why you have to learn to work with unknowns. A lot of the problems we've covered so far could be solved mentally. But the principles and problem-solving skills you're learning will prove useful, no matter what you end up doing in life. As we move on in the course, we'll begin applying the skills you've been learning to a wide variety of situations.

I also hope you're seeing how we're applying the same principles you've been using for years with whole numbers to unknowns. We can rely on unknowns to follow the same consistencies known numbers do because we live in a universe that operates consistently. This consistency in turn points us to the biblical Creator.

Apart from the God of the Bible, it doesn't make sense why creation would be consistent enough that we can safely know that in real-life situations (and not just in a textbook) adding, subtracting, multiplying, and dividing the same amount to both sides of an equation will always keep the equation in balance. How could chance produce consistency like that? Math's underlying consistency points to the God of the Bible and the truth of God's Word.

> *For the invisible things of him from the creation of the world are clearly seen, being understood by the things that are made, even his eternal power and Godhead; so that they are without excuse (Romans 1:20).*
>
> *I am God, and there is none like me (Isaiah 46:9).*

Application Note — Math and Witnessing

Next time you're in a conversation with someone and you find out they believe they got here by chance, ask the Lord if there's a way to share with them how the very consistencies around us (which math describes) point to a Creator. If you'd like to learn more about how to witness by challenging people's worldview, take a look at *The Ultimate Proof of Creation* by Dr. Lisle. (A free video presentation by the same name is currently available online — see endnote for details.)[2]

You can also view a short video of witnessing using math as a lead-in at www.ChristianPerspective.net/math/POM2

[CHAPTER 5]

Ratios, Proportions, and Unknowns

5.1 Ratios and Proportions Revisited

As you may have noticed, we keep revisiting basic concepts. That's because math builds on itself! We merely keep adding aspects that help us solve additional situations we find in God's creation. It's time now to revisit ratios and proportions, looking at them in light of what we've explored so far with unknowns. As we do, we'll discover that we can combine ratios, proportions, and unknowns to help us explore various aspects of God's creation.

Ratios

As we covered in Book 1, a **ratio** is a fancy name for using division to compare quantities. Ratios can be written different ways. For example, you'll sometimes see them written using a colon (as in 3:1). However, since fractions represent division, ratios are also written as fractions (as in $\frac{3}{1}$). Expressing ratios as fractions makes working with ratios easy, as we already know how to add, subtract, multiply, and divide fractions.

3 cups flour

1 cup sugar

Ratio = relationship found by dividing one quantity by the other

Ratio of flour to sugar: 3:1 or $\frac{3}{1}$ | Ratio of sugar to flour: 1:3 or $\frac{1}{3}$

Sometimes it's helpful to complete the division in a ratio, leaving a whole or decimal answer.

Example: Express the ratio $\frac{90}{4}$ as a decimal number.

Remember, the fraction line represents division, so to convert to a decimal, we've only to complete the division.

$$\frac{90}{4} = 90 \div 4 = 22.5$$

Proportions

Let's now review **proportions**. A proportion is a fancy name for two equal ratios (i.e., two ratios that are equivalent fractions). The ratios below are a proportion, as they are both equal.

$$\frac{1}{2} = \frac{4}{8}$$

You can figure out if two ratios form a proportion by looking to see if they are equivalent fractions.

For example, if we multiply $\frac{1}{2}$ by $\frac{4}{4}$ (a fraction worth 1), we get $\frac{4}{8}$.

$$\frac{1}{2} \bullet \frac{4}{4} = \frac{4}{8}$$

$\frac{1}{2}$ and $\frac{4}{8}$ are equivalent fractions, so they form a proportion.

$$\frac{1}{2} = \frac{4}{8}$$

Remember, multiplying or dividing by a fraction worth 1 (such as $\frac{4}{4}$) doesn't change the amount. Both $\frac{1}{2}$ and $\frac{4}{8}$ represent the same amount. We can see this graphically on a circle.

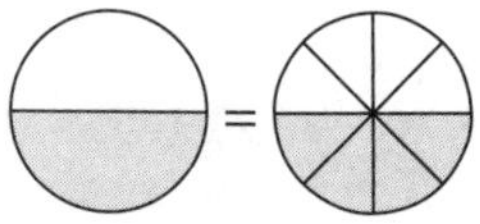

=

On the other hand, $\frac{1}{2}$ and $\frac{3}{8}$ do *not* form a proportion, as they are not equivalent fractions. You cannot multiply or divide one by a fraction worth 1 in order to get the other.

$$\frac{1}{2} \neq \frac{3}{8}$$

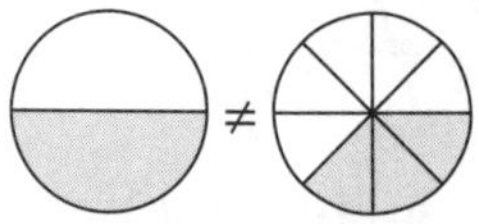

≠

You already know how to find unknowns within proportions. In the past, the missing number (i.e., the unknown) in a proportion was represented with a question mark. Now that you know how to use letters to represent unknowns, we'll use a letter instead. *But the same principles you have been using still apply.*

Example: If it takes 1.5 hours to weed 20 square feet of garden space, how long will it take to weed 60 square feet of garden space, assuming you weed at the same rate?

Since we're weeding at the same rate, the ratio between the time it takes and the garden space we weed will stay the same. Thus we can solve this by setting up a proportion. Notice we've used an *x* rather than a *?* to represent the missing number.

$$\frac{1.5 \text{ hr}}{20 \text{ ft}^2} = \frac{x}{60 \text{ ft}^2}$$

Now we need to see what the denominator in the first ratio was multiplied or divided by to reach the denominator in the second ratio. In order for the ratios to be the same, the numerator will have been multiplied or divided by the same amount.

In this case, $60 \text{ ft}^2 \div 20 \text{ ft}^2 = 3$; the denominator in the first ratio was multiplied by 3.

$$\frac{1.5 \text{ hr}}{20 \text{ ft}^2} = \frac{x}{60 \text{ ft}^2}$$

multiplied by 3

So the entire first ratio would need to be multiplied by $\frac{3}{3}$ (a fraction worth 1) to result in an equivalent ratio.

$$\frac{1.5 \text{ hr}}{20 \text{ ft}^2} \bullet \frac{3}{3} = \frac{\mathbf{4.5 \text{ hr}}}{60 \text{ ft}^2}$$

It will take 4.5 hr to weed 60 ft^2 at the same rate as 1.5 hr per 20 ft^2.

Term Reminder

We have names to help us refer to different parts of a proportion. In the proportion shown, "2" and "6" are called the **extremes**, while "3" and "4" are called the **means**.

Extremes Means

$$\frac{2}{3} = \frac{4}{6}$$

Proportions and Similar Shapes

Similar shapes are an example of proportions in action. We call shapes similar if they're the *same except for their size* — that is, if one is just a scaled up or down version of the other. In a similar shape, all of the corresponding angles (angles representing the same part of the shapes) are congruent (that is, "identical in form"[1]) and all of the corresponding sides (sides representing the same part of the shapes) are **proportional** — that is, the ratios between their corresponding parts form a proportion.

The rectangles shown below are similar. Thus all of their corresponding angles are congruent, and all of their corresponding sides are proportional — that is, whatever ratios we set up comparing corresponding sides, we'll find that they form a proportion.

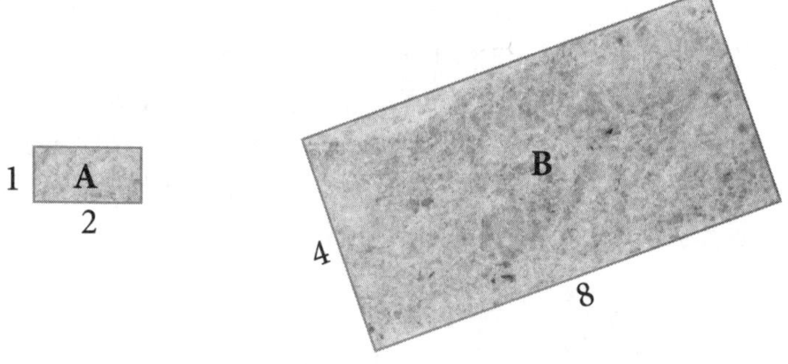

$$\frac{\textit{width of rectangle A}}{\textit{length of rectangle A}} = \frac{\textit{width of rectangle B}}{\textit{length of rectangle B}}$$

$$\frac{1}{2} = \frac{4}{8}$$

If we know two shapes are similar, then, we can set up a proportion to find the length of missing sides.

Example: If the following two triangles are similar, find the length of the missing side.

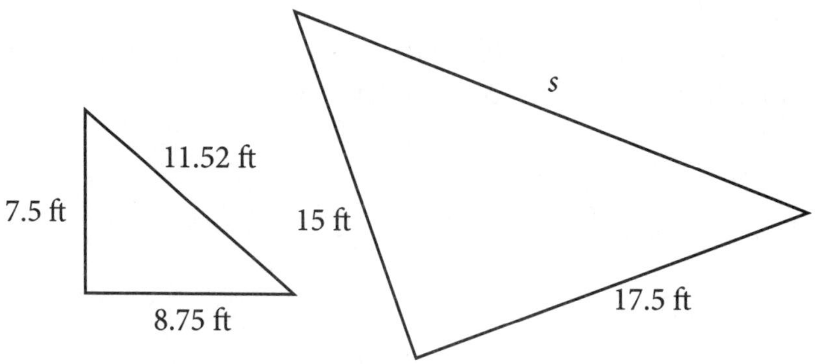

$$\frac{7.5 \text{ ft}}{11.52 \text{ ft}} = \frac{15 \text{ ft}}{s}$$

We need to see what the numerator in the first ratio was multiplied or divided by to reach the numerator in the second. In order for the ratios to be the same, the denominator will have been multiplied or divided by the same amount.

In this case, 15 ft ÷ 7.5 ft = 2; the numerator in the first ratio was multiplied by 2.

multiplied by 2

$$\frac{7.5 \text{ ft}}{11.52 \text{ ft}} = \frac{15 \text{ ft}}{s}$$

So the entire first ratio would need to be multiplied by $\frac{2}{2}$ (a fraction worth 1) to result in an equivalent ratio.

$$\frac{7.5 \text{ ft}}{11.52 \text{ ft}} \bullet \frac{2}{2} = \frac{15 \text{ ft}}{\mathbf{23.04 \text{ ft}}}$$

The missing side is 23.04 feet.

Different Ratios

In the previous example, since we knew the triangles were similar, there were a number of different proportions we could have set up to find the length of the missing side(s). While we looked at the proportion between the height and the diagonal of each triangle (the first proportion shown below), we could have looked at the proportion between the base and diagonal of each triangle, at the proportion between the diagonals of both triangles and the bases of both triangles, or at a number of other proportions.

$$\frac{\textit{height of triangle A}}{\textit{diagonal of triangle A}} = \frac{\textit{height of triangle B}}{\textit{diagonal of triangle B}} \qquad \frac{7.5 \text{ ft}}{11.52 \text{ ft}} = \frac{15 \text{ ft}}{s}$$

$$\frac{\textit{base of triangle A}}{\textit{diagonal of triangle A}} = \frac{\textit{base of triangle B}}{\textit{diagonal of triangle B}} \qquad \frac{8.75 \text{ ft}}{11.52 \text{ ft}} = \frac{17.5 \text{ ft}}{s}$$

$$\frac{\textit{diagonal of triangle A}}{\textit{diagonal of triangle B}} = \frac{\textit{base of triangle A}}{\textit{base of triangle B}} \qquad \frac{11.52 \text{ ft}}{s} = \frac{8.75 \text{ ft}}{17.5 \text{ ft}}$$

The point is to remember that the ratio between the sides of each triangle is the same, and then to form a proportion that accurately compares corresponding sides. We could not, for instance, use the proportion below, as it's comparing the ratio between the ***height*** and the diagonal of one triangle with the ratio between the ***base*** and diagonal of the other. The height and base are not corresponding sides!

$$\frac{\textit{height of triangle A}}{\textit{diagonal of triangle A}} = \frac{\textit{base of triangle B}}{\textit{diagonal of triangle B}}$$

Incorrect

Ratios, Proportions, and Unit Conversion

As you use math to explore God's creation or help in real-life situations, you will likely encounter different units of measure. But good news! While the *words* may change, the *principles* remain the same. All you need to know is the *ratio* by which two units relate, and you can convert from one unit into another.

Remember, dividing a number by itself equals 1. So since 12 inches and 1 foot both represent the *same* distance, $\frac{12 \text{ in}}{1 \text{ ft}}$ *and* $\frac{1 \text{ ft}}{12 \text{ in}}$ are both ratios worth 1 — they're the same quantity divided by the same quantity. In this course, we'll refer to a ratio between two units that is worth 1 as a **conversion ratio**. A conversion ratio shows us how two units compare.

We looked in Book 1 at three different ways to convert between units. They all use the conversion ratio.

In the "Conversion via the Ratio Shortcut" method, we simplified as we multiplied. You'll find that this method works best on multi-step conversions. Multiplying by the conversion ratio works because multiplying by 1 doesn't change the value of a number (there's that identity property of multiplication) and a conversion ratio is always a ratio worth 1, as both the numerator and the denominator represent the *same* distance, capacity, etc., just in different units.

Example: Convert 72 inches to feet.

Conversion via a Proportion	Conversion via the Ratio Shortcut	Conversion via Mental Math
$\frac{12\text{ in}}{1\text{ ft}} = \frac{72\text{ in}}{?\text{ ft}}$	$\overset{6}{\cancel{72}}\ \cancel{\text{in}} \cdot \frac{1\text{ ft}}{\underset{1}{\cancel{12}}\ \cancel{\text{in}}} = 6\text{ ft}$	We know 1 foot equals 12 inches, so 72 inches divided by 12 will give us our feet $72 \div 12 = 6$
Answer: 6 ft	Answer: 6 ft	Answer: 6 ft

Converting Square and Cubed Units Reminder

The "Conversion via the Ratio Shortcut" method makes it easy to convert square and cubed distance units.

$$12\ \cancel{\text{in}^2} \bullet \frac{1\text{ ft}}{12\ \cancel{\text{in}}} \bullet \frac{1\text{ ft}}{12\ \cancel{\text{in}}} = \frac{12\text{ ft}^2}{144} = 0.08\text{ ft}^2$$

$$12\ \cancel{\text{in}^3} \bullet \frac{1\text{ ft}}{12\ \cancel{\text{in}}} \bullet \frac{1\text{ ft}}{12\ \cancel{\text{in}}} \bullet \frac{1\text{ ft}}{12\ \cancel{\text{in}}} = \frac{12\text{ ft}^3}{1{,}728} = 0.01\text{ ft}^3$$

We multiplied by $\frac{1\text{ ft}}{12\text{ in}}$ more than once in order to cancel out all of the inches. Remember, 12 in^2 is a shorthand way of representing 12 in • in (the superscript ^{2} is an exponent — it tells us how many times to multiply inches by itself), so we have to multiply 12 in^2 by $\frac{1\text{ ft}}{12\text{ in}}$ two times in order to cancel out both the inches. Likewise, 12 in^3 is a shorthand way of representing 12 in • in • in, so we have to multiply 12 in^3 by $\frac{1\text{ ft}}{12\text{ in}}$ three times in order to cancel all of the inches. To demonstrate, we've rewritten each conversion writing out in^2 and in^3.

$$12\ \cancel{\text{in}} \bullet \cancel{\text{in}} \bullet \frac{1\text{ ft}}{12\ \cancel{\text{in}}} \bullet \frac{1\text{ ft}}{12\ \cancel{\text{in}}} = \frac{12\text{ ft} \bullet \text{ft}}{144} = \frac{12\text{ ft}^2}{144} = 0.08\text{ ft}^2$$

$$12\ \cancel{\text{in}} \bullet \cancel{\text{in}} \bullet \cancel{\text{in}} \bullet \frac{1\text{ ft}}{12\ \cancel{\text{in}}} \bullet \frac{1\text{ ft}}{12\ \cancel{\text{in}}} \bullet \frac{1\text{ ft}}{12\ \cancel{\text{in}}} = \frac{12\text{ ft} \bullet \text{ft} \bullet \text{ft}}{1{,}728} = \frac{12\text{ ft}^3}{1{,}728} = 0.01\text{ ft}^3$$

Example: 2,000 pounds (abbreviated lb) equals 1 ton. How many tons is 500 pounds?

Conversion via a Proportion	Conversion via the Ratio Shortcut	Conversion via Mental Math
$\frac{500\text{ lb}}{x} = \frac{2{,}000\text{ lb}}{1\text{ ton}}$	$500\ \cancel{\text{lb}} \cdot \frac{1\text{ ton}}{2{,}000\ \cancel{\text{lb}}} = \frac{500\text{ ton}}{2{,}000}$	$500 \div 2{,}000 = 0.25$
Answer: 0.25 tons	Answer: 0.25 tons	Answer: 0.25 tons

Important Note

You'll find common conversion ratios on the reference sheets you were given from the *Teacher Guide*, as well as in the appendix of this book. Unless instructed otherwise, you can consult these sheets when completing your worksheets.

Keeping Perspective

Looking at the ratios around us helps us learn a lot about God's creation. For example, in Book 1 we saw that the ratio between the number of spirals going each direction in a sunflower is always approximately the same and that this ratio enables the most number of seeds to fit in a sunflower head. Ratios are also incredibly helpful in solving real-life problems, as we'll see as we move forward.

5.2 Cross Multiplication

So far, we've followed the process in the following example to find the unknown (i.e., the missing number) in a proportion.

Example: If we use 1 yd of ribbon for every 4 bows, how many yards do we need to make 12 bows? 3 yards! Duh!

We're dealing with this proportion:

$$\frac{1 \text{ yd}}{4 \text{ bows}} = \frac{x}{12 \text{ bows}}$$

We can find x by figuring out what the denominator on the left was multiplied or divided by to get the denominator on the right.

$$\frac{1 \text{ yd}}{4 \text{ bows}} = \frac{x}{12 \text{ bows}}$$

multiplied by 3

Now we can multiply or divide the numerator on the left by the same amount as the denominator (so the whole ratio would be multiplied or divided by a fraction worth 1, keeping it equivalent).

$$\frac{1 \text{ yd}}{4 \text{ bows}} \bullet \frac{3}{3} = \frac{3 \text{ yd}}{12 \text{ bows}}$$

The missing number (i.e., the unknown) in the proportion — shown here by x — is 3 yd.

Basically, we've been finding x by figuring out what fraction worth 1 (in the example, $\frac{3}{3}$) we needed to multiply or divide by and then using that to find x. Multiplying or dividing by 1 doesn't change the value (the identity property of multiplication) — which is why we end up with an equivalent ratio.

There's another way to go about finding the unknown in a proportion. It's called cross multiplication. While you may already know the bottom-line technique, let's walk through why the technique works so you can understand it better. To understand the technique, though, we need to first look at two principles.

Principle 1: Multiplying by the Multiplicative Inverse of an Equivalent Fraction Equals 1

When we multiply a fraction by its multiplicative inverse (i.e., the reciprocal), we reverse the division and end up with a fraction worth 1.

For example, $\frac{4}{1}$ is the multiplicative inverse of $\frac{1}{4}$. When we multiply $\frac{1}{4}$ by $\frac{4}{1}$, we end up with a fraction worth 1.

$$\frac{1}{4} \bullet \frac{4}{1} = \frac{4}{4} = 1$$

Logically, then, if we multiplied a fraction by the multiplicative inverse of any *equivalent* fraction, we could also reverse the division and end up with a fraction worth 1.

For example, $\frac{1}{4}$ and $\frac{3}{12}$ are equivalent fractions — they both represent the same quantity.

$$\frac{1}{4} = \frac{3}{12}$$

If we multiply $\frac{1}{4}$ by $\frac{12}{3}$ (the multiplicative inverse of $\frac{3}{12}$), we get a fraction worth 1.

$$\frac{1}{4} \bullet \frac{12}{3} = \frac{12}{12} = 1$$

This brings us to the first principle: just as multiplying by the multiplicative inverse equals 1, **multiplying by the multiplicative inverse of an *equivalent fraction* equals 1.**

Principle 2: The Product of the Extremes and the Product of the Means are Equal to Each Other

Now, notice that a shortcut for multiplying the first ratio in a proportion by the multiplicative inverse of the second would be to multiply the extremes and to multiply the means.

$$\mathbf{\frac{1}{4} = \frac{3}{12}}$$

Multiplying One Ratio by the Reciprocal of the Other	**Multiplying the Extremes and the Means**
$\frac{12}{3}$ is the reciprocal of $\frac{3}{12}$.	
$\frac{1}{4} \bullet \frac{12}{3}$	$\frac{1}{4} = \frac{3}{12}$ 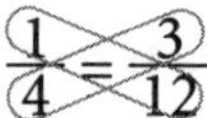
product of numerators: 1 • 12 = 12	product of extremes: 1 • 12 = 12
product of denominators: 4 • 3 = 12	product of means: 4 • 3 = 12

The product of the extremes and the product of the means were *both* 12. Finding the product of the extremes and the product of the means is a shorthand way of finding what the numerator and the denominator would be if we multiplied one ratio in the proportion by the reciprocal of the other. Thus the product of the extremes and the product of the means will always be equal to each other.

Cross Multiplication

If the product of the extremes and the product of the means are always equivalent, we can represent their products using an equation, and then use that equation to find the value of an unknown. For example, let's replace 3 in the proportion we've been looking at with an *x*.

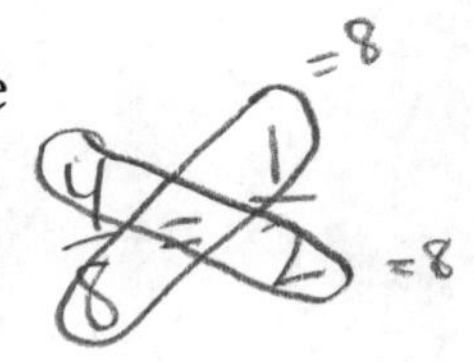

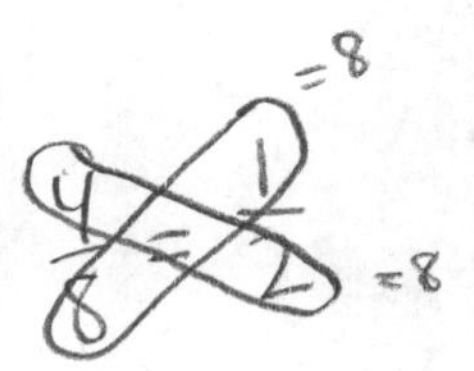

$$\frac{1}{4} = \frac{x}{12}$$

Now let's multiply the extremes and multiply the means.

$$\frac{1}{4} = \frac{x}{12} \qquad 4 \bullet x \qquad 1 \bullet 12$$

Since we know these products are equal, we can put an equal sign between them, writing an equation.

$$1 \bullet 12 = 4 \bullet x$$

> We call the technique of multiplying the extremes, multiplying the means, and setting their products as equal **cross multiplication**.

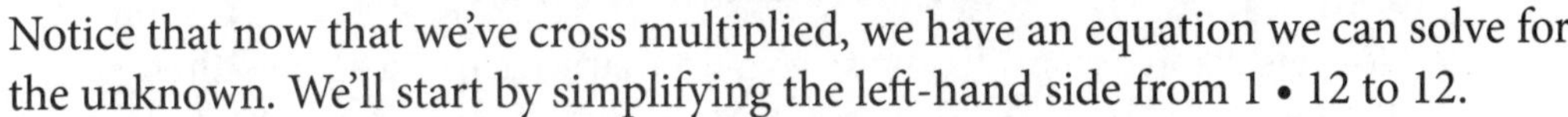

Notice that now that we've cross multiplied, we have an equation we can solve for the unknown. We'll start by simplifying the left-hand side from 1 • 12 to 12.

$$12 = 4 \bullet x$$

And now we can isolate *x* on one side of an equality by dividing *both sides* by 4 (or multiplying both sides by the multiplicative inverse — $\frac{1}{4}$):

Dividing Both Sides	**Multiplying Both Sides by the Multiplicative Inverse**
$\frac{12}{4} = \frac{4 \bullet x}{4}$	$12 \bullet \frac{1}{4} = 4 \bullet x \bullet \frac{1}{4}$
$\frac{12}{4} = \frac{\cancel{4} \bullet x}{\cancel{4}}$	${}^{3}\cancel{12} \bullet \frac{1}{\cancel{4}} = \cancel{4} \bullet x \bullet \frac{1}{\cancel{4}}$
$3 = x$	$3 = x$

> The product of the extremes and the product of the means in a proportion will always be equal because it is a shortcut for multiplying one ratio by the multiplicative inverse of an equivalent ratio. We can use this knowledge to find the unknown in a proportion by cross multiplying — multiplying the means and the extremes and setting their products as equal.

Applying the Technique

Let's use cross multiplication to find the unknown in a few proportions.

Example: If a recipe calls for 1.5 teaspoons of vanilla per 6 muffins, and we want to use the recipe in a commercial bakery to make 240 muffins, how many teaspoons of vanilla should we use?

We have this proportion:

$$\frac{1.5 \text{ tsp}}{6 \text{ muf}} = \frac{x}{240 \text{ muf}}$$

Let's start by cross multiplying:

$$\frac{1.5 \text{ tsp}}{6 \text{ muf}} = \frac{x}{240 \text{ muf}}$$

$$1.5 \text{ tsp} \bullet 240 \text{ muf} = 6 \text{ muf} \bullet x$$

Now we'll simplify the left side of the equation by multiplying 1.5 tsp by 240 muf:

$$\mathbf{360 \text{ tsp}} \bullet \text{muf} = 6 \text{ muf} \bullet x$$

Notice that we kept the units. The muffin unit will cancel out later, leaving us with the appropriate unit (teaspoons).

Now we'll solve to find x. Notice again that we can do so by either dividing both sides, or by multiplying both sides by the multiplicative inverse.

Dividing Both Sides	Multiplying Both Sides by the Multiplicative Inverse
$\frac{360 \text{ tsp} \bullet \text{muf}}{6 \text{ muf}} = \frac{6 \text{ muf} \bullet x}{6 \text{ muf}}$	$360 \text{ tsp} \bullet \text{muf} \bullet \frac{\mathbf{1}}{\mathbf{6 \text{ muf}}} = 6 \text{ muf} \bullet x \bullet \frac{\mathbf{1}}{\mathbf{6 \text{ muf}}}$
$\frac{{}^{60}\cancel{360} \text{ tsp} \bullet \cancel{\text{muf}}}{\cancel{6} \cancel{\text{muf}}} = \frac{\cancel{6} \cancel{\text{muf}} \bullet x}{\cancel{6} \cancel{\text{muf}}}$	${}^{60}\cancel{360} \text{ tsp} \bullet \cancel{\text{muf}} \bullet \frac{1}{\cancel{6} \cancel{\text{muf}}} = \cancel{6} \cancel{\text{muf}} \bullet x \bullet \frac{1}{\cancel{6} \cancel{\text{muf}}}$
60 tsp = *x*	**60 tsp = *x***

Once again, get in the habit of simplifying each side of the equation (performing whatever operations you can) before solving for x — it will prove especially helpful on more complicated equations. In the previous example, we simplified the left side by multiplying 1.5 tsp by 240 muf before solving for x.

Example: If these two rectangles are similar (i.e., their angles are the same and their sides are proportional), find the dimension of the missing side.

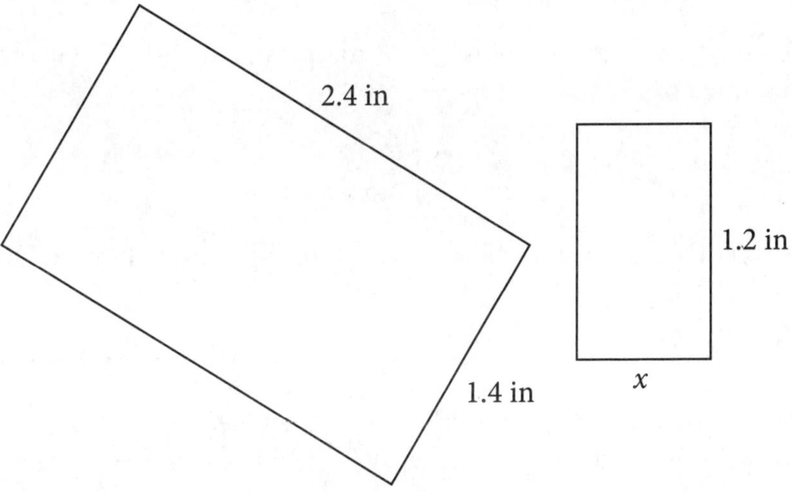

Since we know the two rectangles are similar, we can set up a proportion and use cross multiplication to quickly find the missing side. It doesn't matter that we have decimal numbers in the proportion — the same principles apply.

$$\frac{2.4 \text{ in}}{1.4 \text{ in}} = \frac{1.2 \text{ in}}{x}$$

Cross multiply:

$$2.4 \text{ in} \bullet x = 1.4 \text{ in} \bullet 1.2 \text{ in}$$

Simplify:

$$2.4 \text{ in} \bullet x = \mathbf{1.68 \text{ in}^2}$$

Solve for the unknown:

Dividing Both Sides

$$\frac{2.4 \text{ in} \bullet x}{\mathbf{2.4 \text{ in}}} = \frac{1.68 \text{ in}^2}{\mathbf{2.4 \text{ in}}}$$

$$\frac{\cancel{2.4} \cancel{\text{in}} \bullet x}{\cancel{2.4} \cancel{\text{in}}} = \frac{1.68 \cancel{\text{in}^2}^{\text{ in}}}{2.4 \cancel{\text{in}}}$$

$$\mathbf{x = 0.7 \text{ in}}$$

Multiplying Both Sides by the Multiplicative Inverse

$$2.4 \text{ in} \bullet x \bullet \frac{\mathbf{1}}{\mathbf{2.4 \text{ in}}} = 1.68 \text{ in}^2 \bullet \frac{\mathbf{1}}{\mathbf{2.4 \text{ in}}}$$

$$\cancel{2.4} \cancel{\text{in}} \bullet x \bullet \frac{1}{\cancel{2.4} \cancel{\text{in}}} = 1.68 \cancel{\text{in}^2}^{\text{ in}} \bullet \frac{1}{2.4 \cancel{\text{in}}}$$

$$\mathbf{x = 0.7 \text{ in}}$$

Notice the answer in the example is in the correct unit (inches). If you do the math correctly, you will have the correct unit at the end of a problem.

Keeping Perspective

Each new problem-solving tool builds on prior knowledge. Cross multiplication builds on various concepts, such as division, multiplication, and fractions . . . along with the identity property of multiplication! At its core, it rests on the consistency with which God holds all things together — a consistency that makes math possible.

5.3 More with Time

For some time now, you've been using the relationship that the distance equals the speed multiplied by the time.

$$d = s \bullet t$$
$$distance = speed \bullet time$$

In this lesson, we're going to explore this relationship a little more deeply.

Finding the Time

Up until now, you've only solved to find either the speed or the distance using the $d = s \bullet t$ relationship, but sometimes it may be helpful to figure out the time.

Example: How long will it take to travel 80 miles at 40 miles per hour?

Let's start by substituting the values we know into the formula.

$$d = s \bullet t$$

$$\textbf{80 mi} = \frac{\textbf{40 mi}}{\textbf{1 hr}} \bullet t$$

We know the speed and the distance, but not the time. So how do we find time? Well, if we multiply both sides by the multiplicative inverse of $\frac{40 \text{ mi}}{1 \text{ hr}}$ (i.e., divide both sides by $\frac{40 \text{ mi}}{1 \text{ hr}}$), we'll have separated t by itself and found its value. Notice that when we do, the miles cross out and we're left with an answer in hours.

Notice that we wrote the speed as a ratio of miles per hour. Remember the word *per* clues you into knowing you're dealing with a ratio. We're looking not just at miles, but at the miles traveled *per* hour.

$$80 \text{ mi} \bullet \frac{\textbf{1 hr}}{\textbf{40 mi}} = \frac{40 \text{ mi}}{1 \text{ hr}} \bullet t \bullet \frac{\textbf{1 hr}}{\textbf{40 mi}}$$

$$^{2}\cancel{80 \text{ mi}} \bullet \frac{1 \text{ hr}}{\cancel{40 \text{ mi}}} = \frac{\cancel{40 \text{ mi}}}{1 \cancel{\text{hr}}} \bullet t \bullet \frac{1 \cancel{\text{hr}}}{\cancel{40 \text{ mi}}}$$

$$\textbf{2 hr} = \boldsymbol{t}$$

Notice that in the example we isolated t by multiplying both sides of the equation by the multiplicative inverse. While we could have isolated t by dividing both sides by $\frac{40 \text{ mi}}{1 \text{ hr}}$ and completing the division by inverting and multiplying, multiplying both sides by the multiplicative inverse saved us a step.

Now that you are familiar with how multiplying by the multiplicative inverse does the same thing as dividing, we're going to stop showing both methods and only show the one that is simpler for the current problem.

Minutes and Hours

Sometimes when working with time, we have to convert between minutes and hours.

Example: Suppose I'm going somewhere 5 miles away, and I want to know how long it will take if I travel at 15 miles per hour.

Substitute known values into the formula:

$$d = s \bullet t$$

$$\mathbf{5\ mi} = \frac{\mathbf{15\ mi}}{\mathbf{1\ hr}} \bullet t$$

Multiply both sides by the multiplicative inverse of $\frac{15\text{ mi}}{1\text{ hr}}$ (i.e., divide both sides by $\frac{15\text{ mi}}{1\text{ hr}}$):

$$5\text{ mi} \bullet \frac{\mathbf{1\ hr}}{\mathbf{15\ mi}} = \frac{15\text{ mi}}{1\text{ hr}} \bullet t \bullet \frac{\mathbf{1\ hr}}{\mathbf{15\ mi}}$$

$$5\cancel{\text{ mi}} \bullet \frac{1\text{ hr}}{15\cancel{\text{ mi}}} = \frac{\cancel{15\text{ mi}}}{\cancel{1\text{ hr}}} \bullet t \bullet \frac{\cancel{1\text{ hr}}}{\cancel{15\text{ mi}}}$$

$$\frac{5\text{ hr}}{15} = t\text{, which simplifies to } \frac{1\text{ hr}}{3} = t$$

In the example above, we ended up with a partial number of hours. Since we typically refer to portions of an hour in minutes, let's convert this answer into minutes. **Remember, you can convert units of time the same way you convert other units.** Since there are 60 minutes in an hour, the conversion ratio between minutes and hours is $\frac{60\text{ min}}{1\text{ hr}}$ or $\frac{1\text{ hr}}{60\text{ min}}$.

We'll use $\frac{60\text{ min}}{1\text{ hr}}$ to convert $\frac{1\text{ hr}}{3}$, or $\frac{1}{3}$ hr, to minutes, as that will cause the hours to cancel out.

$$\frac{1\cancel{\text{ hr}}}{\cancel{3}} \bullet \frac{\cancel{60}\text{ min}}{1\cancel{\text{ hr}}} = 20\text{ min}$$

When converting between units, **use the conversion ratio that will cause the units to cancel out,** leaving your answer in the units you need.

Let's look at another example. This time, we'll have to convert in order to solve the problem.

Example: How far can you go in 10 minutes at a speed of 40 mph?

Substitute known values:

$$d = s \bullet t$$

$$d = \frac{\mathbf{40\ mi}}{\mathbf{1\ hr}} \bullet \mathbf{10\ min}$$

Oops! Do you see a problem with this equation? The units won't cancel out — one number is in minutes and the other is in hours. We have to first express them both in the same unit.

In this case, it's simplest to change the 1 hour to 60 minutes.

$$d = \frac{40 \text{ mi}}{\textbf{60 min}} \bullet 10 \text{ min}$$

Now the units will cross out and we can simplify to find the value of *d*.

$$d = \frac{\overset{2}{\cancel{40}} \text{ mi}}{_{3}\cancel{60} \cancel{\text{min}}} \bullet 10 \cancel{\text{min}}$$

$$d = \frac{\textbf{20 mi}}{\textbf{3}}$$

$$\boldsymbol{d = 6.67 \text{ mi}}$$

Note: We could have converted the minutes to hours instead — it just would have been a longer process.

Convert the minutes:

$$\cancel{10} \cancel{\text{min}} \bullet \frac{1 \text{ hr}}{\cancel{60} \cancel{\text{min}}} = \frac{1}{6} \text{ hr}$$

Solve, using $\frac{1}{6}$ hr instead of 10 min for *t*:

$$d = s \bullet t$$

$$d = \frac{\textbf{40 mi}}{\textbf{1 hr}} \bullet \frac{\textbf{1}}{\textbf{6}} \textbf{ hr}$$

$$d = \frac{\cancel{40} \text{ mi}}{1 \cancel{\text{hr}}} \bullet \frac{1}{\cancel{6}} \cancel{\text{hr}}$$

$$d = \textbf{6.67 mi}$$

Important Note

If we hadn't written the units out when solving the example problem, we might not have realized the need to convert, leaving us with a terribly wrong answer! Including units is very important — especially in more complicated problems where mistakes are harder to spot.

Keeping Perspective

We all deal with time all the "time" . . . and math can help us find the answers we need in a "timely" way! As you explore time today, remember that math's very existence reminds you that you serve a God you can trust all the time. (And with that, it's "time" to stop making time puns.)

5.4 Proportions and the Pressure and Volume of a Gas

Let's take a quick look at another application of proportions found in God's creation. When a gas is forced into a smaller volume, it exerts more pressure. The smaller the volume, the greater the pressure the gas exerts. The greater the volume, the less pressure the gas exerts (after all, the gas molecules have a larger volume in which to float around).

Since this relationship is so constant, we can set up a proportion comparing the pressure and volume of the *same gas* at two different times. Assuming the gas's temperature doesn't change, the pressure and volume at the first measurement will relate to the final pressure and volume of the next measurement like this:

$$\frac{P_1}{P_2} = \frac{V_2}{V_1}$$

Subscript Numbers

In the formula $\frac{P_1}{P_2} = \frac{V_2}{V_1}$, P_1 and V_1 stand for the pressure and volume of the gas at the first measurement, while P_2 and V_2 stand for the pressure and volume of the same gas at the second measurement. **The subscripts $_1$ and $_2$ differentiate which pressure and volume we mean.** Using subscripts to differentiate between different pressures, volumes, distances, velocities, etc., is a common convention that you'll encounter.

We can use this proportion — which is a mathematical expression of a consistency God holds in place — to help us solve problems. As we do, we'll also employ cross multiplication.

Example: If a toy balloon contains 2.5 quarts of gas (V_1) and exerts a pressure of 1 atmosphere (P_1), to what size will it shrink if its pressure changes to 5 atmospheres (P_2), assuming the temperature stays the same?

This example is based on one given in *Secondary Arithmetic*, an early 1900s math book.[2]

What do we know? We've been told our initial volume (V_1) is 2.5 quarts, and our initial pressure (P_1) is 1 atmosphere. We want to know the final volume (V_2) if the pressure changes to 5 atmospheres.

Now we can substitute these values into the proportion. We'll use the abbreviation atm for atmosphere and qt for quarts.

$$\frac{\textbf{1 atm}}{\textbf{5 atm}} = \frac{V_2}{\textbf{2.5 qt}}$$

Cross multiply:

$$\frac{1\text{ atm}}{5\text{ atm}} = \frac{V_2}{2.5\text{ qt}}$$

$$1\text{ atm} \bullet 2.5\text{ qt} = 5\text{ atm} \bullet V_2$$

Simplify:

$$\textbf{2.5 atm} \bullet \textbf{qt} = 5\text{ atm} \bullet V_2$$

Solve for the unknown by dividing both sides by 5 atm:

$$\frac{2.5\text{ atm} \bullet \text{qt}}{5\text{ atm}} = \frac{5\text{ atm} \bullet V_2}{5\text{ atm}}$$

$$\frac{\textbf{2.5 qt}}{\textbf{5}} = \boldsymbol{V_2}$$

$$\textbf{0.5 qt} = V_2$$

Tada! We have our answer.

Since our purpose is to show math's usefulness rather than to explore pressure and volume, we only touched on the relationship between pressure and volume of gases. It's a relationship you'll probably explore more in science . . . only now you have a taste for how math aids us in exploring it! While science books don't always explain the math behind the concepts they teach, math applies throughout science.

Keeping Perspective

The beginning of a physics book from 1910 points out the reliance of science upon the unfailing regularity of creation.

> *The sun set last night and rose again this morning, and we are sure that it will set again to-night and rise again to-morrow morning. In fact, from all our experiences with Nature we have learned that she always acts in such a perfectly regular way that we can predict what will happen under a given set of circumstances.*[3]

This physics book is making the case that science depends on the regularity all around us — a regularity that is as constant as the sun's rising and setting. It's this regularity that lets us record the relationship between the pressure and volume of a gas and expect it to hold true, no matter the actual values.

Now, we could argue with the book in that some aspects of creation are so incredibly complex that we can't predict them (for example, we can't predict an electron's exact location in an atom). We could also point out that there are often more details involved than a formula takes into account (for instance, more than pressure and volume may affect a gas). Nevertheless, the principle that we live in an amazingly consistent, predictable universe holds true. All of modern science is based upon the fact that creation is consistent.

The Bible tells us it's God who holds this amazing regularity together. From the rising of the sun to the way the volume of a gas affects its pressure to the way speed and time relate, He governs things reliably. The fact that we can reduce things such as pressure and volume to a math equation emphasizes once again just how reliable creation is . . . and in turn how reliable the One holding creation together is. You can rely on God absolutely.

> *The heavens declare the glory of God; and the firmament sheweth his handywork. Day unto day uttereth speech, and night unto night sheweth knowledge. There is no speech nor language, where their voice is not heard (Psalm 19:1–3).*

5.5 Proportions and Levers

Before we move on, let's explore another application of proportions: levers. As we do, you'll discover that math helps us design these useful machines.

So what is a lever? A lever is a machine that helps us lift heavy objects. More specifically, a lever is "a rigid bar resting on a pivot, used to help move a heavy or firmly fixed load with one end when pressure is applied to the other."[4] A lever has two competing forces acting on it. (A force can be thought of as "a push or pull."[5])

In the picture, the man is applying force to one side, and the weight of the rock is applying force on the other side.

A lever also has a pivot point — the rod the man is using to lift the rock is resting on a pivot point. Each force is separated from the pivot point by some distance.

A lever's pivot point is technically called the "fulcrum."

Let's label the picture to clarify.

F_1 and F_2 = The two forces (pushes/pulls/weights) at work on the lever. In the picture with the man and the rock, the forces are the weight of the rock and the effort/weight the man's applying.

d_1 and d_2 = The distances between the forces and the pivot point.

Important Note: The subscripts $_1$ and $_2$ simply differentiate between the two forces and distances. In this case, both the letters with a subscript $_1$ refer to the force/distance of the man, while both the letters with a subscript $_2$ refer to the force/distance of the rock.

While we labeled the picture with the subscripts $_1$ referring to the man and the subscripts $_2$ referring to the rock, we could use the subscripts $_1$ to represent either the man or the rock, and the subscripts $_2$ to represent the other. The point of the subscripts is to differentiate between the force/distance of the man and the force/distance of the rock.

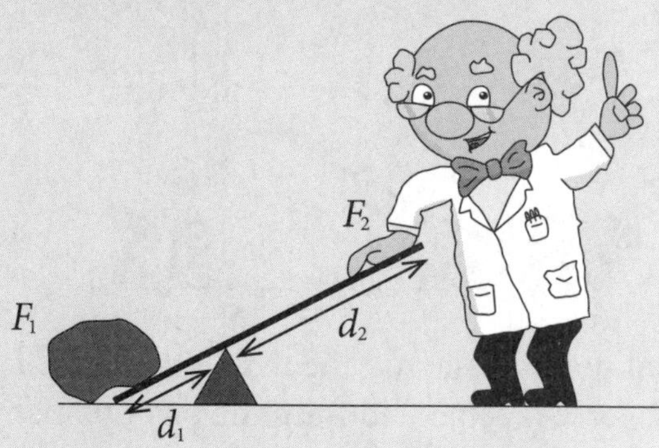

So how much force does the man need to apply to move the rock?

Math can help us find out! There's a mathematical relationship between the forces applied and the distances between each force and the pivot point.

$$\frac{F_1}{F_2} = \frac{d_2}{d_1}$$

Relationship Between Forces and Distances in a Lever

Note: This relationship describes an ideal lever. In real life, no lever is perfectly ideal — some of the force applied gets lost in operation. However, this formula gets us close.

Notice that we expressed the relationship using a proportion . . . which means you can use cross multiplication to find an unknown value when you know all of the others. Let's take a look at two examples. As we do, we'll learn a little more about how levers work.

Applying Levers

Example: Suppose a man is applying a force 2 feet (d_1) from the pivot point of a lever, and the 60-pound (F_2) rock he is trying to move is resting 1 foot (d_2) away from the pivot point. How much force must the man exert to lift the rock?

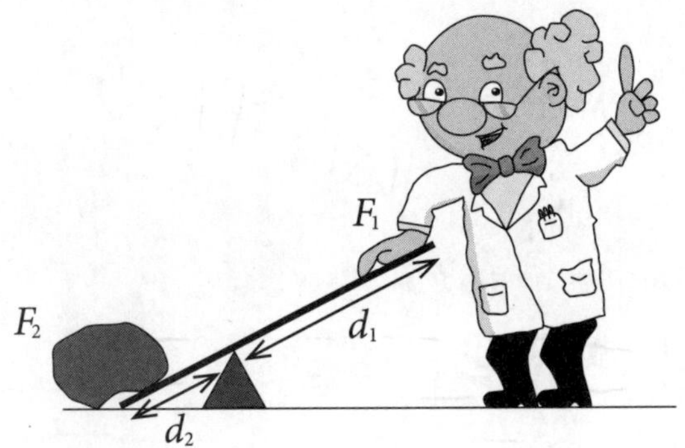

Original formula:

$$\frac{F_1}{F_2} = \frac{d_2}{d_1}$$

Substitute known numbers:

$$\frac{F_1}{\mathbf{60\ lb}} = \frac{\mathbf{1\ ft}}{\mathbf{2\ ft}}$$

Cross multiply:

$$F_1 \bullet 2\text{ ft} = 60\text{ lb} \bullet 1\text{ ft}$$

Simplify:

$$F_1 \bullet 2\text{ ft} = \mathbf{60}\text{ lb} \bullet \text{ft}$$

Divide both sides by 2 ft:

$$\frac{F_1 \bullet 2\text{ ft}}{\mathbf{2\ ft}} = \frac{60\text{ lb} \bullet \text{ft}}{\mathbf{2\ ft}}$$

$$\frac{F_1 \bullet \cancel{2\text{ ft}}}{\cancel{2\text{ ft}}} = \frac{\overset{30}{\cancel{60}}\text{ lb} \bullet \cancel{\text{ft}}}{\cancel{2}\cancel{\text{ft}}}$$

$$\mathbf{F_1 = 30\ lb}$$

Notice how the units cross out, leaving us pounds, which is a measure of force.

The man must exert 30 lb of force to lift the 60-lb rock.

Example: Suppose the man is now trying to lift an even heavier rock that weighs 100 pounds (F_2). Once again, the rock is 1 foot (d_2) away from the pivot point. But let's say he decides to apply his force farther away from the pivot point, pressing down 4 feet (d_1) from the pivot point instead of 2 ft as he did before. How much force must he exert to move the rock?

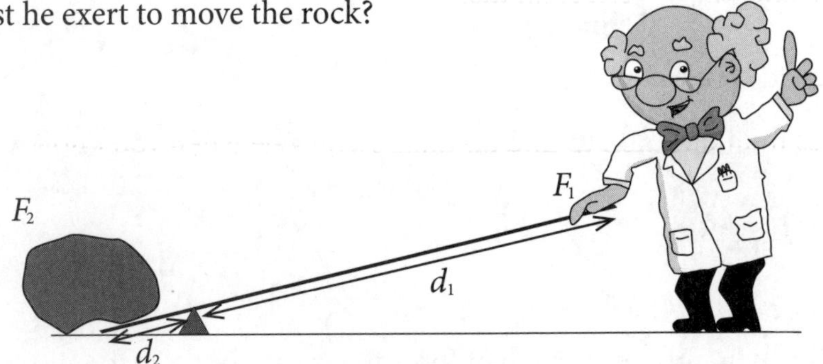

Original formula:

$$\frac{F_1}{F_2} = \frac{d_2}{d_1}$$

Substitute known numbers:

$$\frac{F_1}{\mathbf{100\ lb}} = \frac{\mathbf{1\ ft}}{\mathbf{4\ ft}}$$

Cross multiply:

$$F_1 \bullet 4\ \text{ft} = 100\ \text{lb} \bullet 1\ \text{ft}$$

Divide both sides by 4 ft:

$$\frac{F_1 \bullet 4\ \text{ft}}{\mathbf{4\ ft}} = \frac{100\ \text{lb} \bullet \text{ft}}{\mathbf{4\ ft}}$$

$$\frac{F_1 \bullet \cancel{4\ \text{ft}}}{\cancel{4\ \text{ft}}} = \frac{^{25}\cancel{100}\ \text{lb} \bullet \cancel{\text{ft}}}{\cancel{4}\ \cancel{\text{ft}}}$$

$$F_1 = \mathbf{25\ lb}$$

The man must exert 25 lb of force to lift the 100-lb rock.

Example: Suppose the man is now trying to lift that same 100-pound rock (F_2), only this time he positions the rock so that it is 2 feet (d_2) from the pivot point. He again applies his force 4 feet (d_1) from the pivot point, as he did in the last example. How much force must he exert to move the rock?

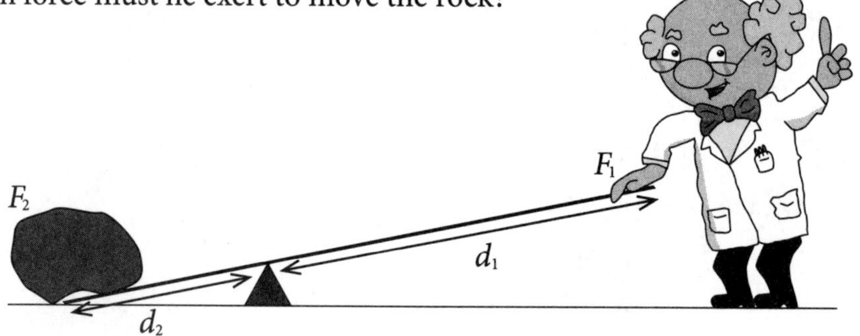

Original formula:

$$\frac{F_1}{F_2} = \frac{d_2}{d_1}$$

Substitute known numbers:

$$\frac{F_1}{\mathbf{100\ lb}} = \frac{\mathbf{2\ ft}}{\mathbf{4\ ft}}$$

Cross multiply:

$$F_1 \bullet 4\ \text{ft} = 100\ \text{lb} \bullet 2\ \text{ft}$$

Divide both sides by 4 ft:

$$\frac{F_1 \bullet 4\ \text{ft}}{\mathbf{4\ ft}} = \frac{100\ \text{lb} \bullet 2\ \text{ft}}{\mathbf{4\ ft}}$$

$$\frac{F_1 \bullet \cancel{4\ \text{ft}}}{\cancel{4\ \text{ft}}} = \frac{^{25}\cancel{100}\ \text{lb} \bullet 2\ \cancel{\text{ft}}}{\cancel{4}\ \cancel{\text{ft}}}$$

$$F_1 = \mathbf{50\ lb}$$

The man must exert 50 lb of force to lift the 100-lb rock.

Thinking It Through

Even though the rock in the second example was heavier than the rock in the first example (100 lb instead of 60 lb), the man had to apply less force to move it because he stood farther away from the pivot point. The increased distance caused his force to lift a larger force. In the third example, though, the rock was farther away from the pivot point too. This caused the man to need more force to move it than he did when the rock was close to the pivot point.

In the type of lever we looked at, by increasing the distance between the pivot point and where we apply the force or by decreasing the distance between the pivot point and the object we want to move, we can move heavier objects. Again, there's a mathematical relationship between the forces and distances. By understanding this relationship, we can better design levers.

Keeping Perspective

You'll hopefully learn more about levers and how they work in science (or if you're curious, there are lots of resources online or at the library). Our purpose here wasn't to fully understand levers, but rather to see yet another example of how math helps us explore God's creation. By recording the relationship between the forces and distances involved in lifting an object, we can figure out on paper what kind of a lever we need to lift objects. We can rely on our computations to work because we know the universe is held together by an unchanging, faithful God who governs all things consistently.

5.6 Chapter Synopsis and Archimedes

In this chapter, we've reviewed **ratios** and **proportions**, building on our previous knowledge. Along the way, we learned a shortcut (**cross multiplication**) for finding an unknown in a proportion, and we applied our knowledge to various real-life settings.

I hope by now you're catching a glimpse of how much math builds on itself. If you ever encounter a math concept that seems complicated, break it down into concepts you understand and then build from there.

Archimedes

Just how powerful can a lever be? Well, Archimedes, a brilliant mathematician and inventor from the town of Syracuse who lived a couple of hundred years before the birth of Christ, is credited for saying something to the effect of "give me a fulcrum [pivot point] on which to rest, and I will move the earth."[6]

Archimedes (c. 287–212 B.C.)

As you might guess from that boast, Archimedes was incredibly gifted mechanically. Yet sadly, he only developed the contrivances he did for extraordinary causes, such as to save his city, appease a king, or prove a point. He "declared that 'every kind of art which was connected with daily needs was ignoble and vulgar.'"[7] Archimedes would never have used math simply to aid the everyday life of his fellow man. Like most of the other Greek mathematicians, Archimedes viewed math as an intellectual pursuit — something above common labor.

As one of his biographers quoted,

> *In the words of Plutarch, "he possessed so lofty a spirit, so profound a soul, and such a wealth of scientific knowledge that, although these inventions had won for him the renown of more than human sagacity, yet he would not consent to leave behind him any written work on such subjects, but, regarding as ignoble and sordid the business of mechanics and every sort of art which is directed to practical utility, he places his whole ambition in those speculations in the beauty and subtlety of which there is no admixture of the common needs of life."*[8]

While in the quote above, Plutarch painted Archimedes' attitude toward daily things as admirable, Archimedes' attitude prevented him from helping mankind with their daily tasks as much as he could have. God gifted Archimedes with an incredible gift for mechanical inventions and innovation, yet Archimedes' beliefs kept him from using that gift to its full extent. Our beliefs matter — and as was the case with Archimedes, our lives show what we believe.

The Bible exhorts us with this: "And whatsoever ye do, do it heartily, as to the Lord, and not unto men;" (Colossians 3:23). In a Christian worldview, the daily things in life are as important as the "royal" things. Right back in the Garden of Eden, God gave Adam work to do in tending the garden of Eden. Whatever task we're working on is the one which we have the privilege of working on with all our heart, depending and worshiping God as we do.

> *And the LORD God took the man, and put him into the garden of Eden to dress it and to keep it (Genesis 2:15).*
>
> *And whatsoever ye do in word or deed, do all in the name of the Lord Jesus, giving thanks to God and the Father by him (Colossians 3:17).*

Archimedes' Death

In his *A Short Account of the History of Mathematics*, Walter Ball tells the story of how Archimedes was killed when the Romans invaded Syracuse in 212 B.C. Although the Roman commander specifically told his men not to kill Archimedes, as he admired Archimedes for all the incredible devices he had used to keep the Romans at bay, his orders were disregarded. Accounts differ as to the details of why the commander's command wasn't obeyed. It is said Archimedes was found deep in thought working a geometry problem in the sand (the typical way of writing problems back then). He told the soldier not to ruin his work, and the offended soldier killed the great mathematician. Whether that was the case or whether the soldiers killed him to pilfer from him, we don't know. But we do know that Archimedes often lost himself entirely in math problems.[9]

[CHAPTER 6]

Percents, Unknowns, and Rearranging Equations

6.1 Revisiting Percents

Let's take this lesson to look at one important application of math that comes up regularly in daily life: percent problems. Whether it's with tips, discount coupons, sales tax, interest rates, nutritional facts, or survey results, we all encounter percents on a regular basis.

Remembering the Meaning

As we saw in Book 1, **percents** are a shorthand way to express ratios as fractions of 100. Rather than writing $\frac{6}{100}$, we can write 6%. The % sign stands for *percent*, or *per hundred*. It tells us that the number represents that amount *per* hundred.

Keeping in mind the meaning of the percent sign will help you work with percents. Since all percents represent portions of 100, we can add and subtract them, just as we would fractions with the same denominator.

$$45\% + 23\% = 68\%$$
$$68\% - 23\% = 45\%$$

To multiply and divide percents, however, you'll guard against errors if you convert to a fraction or a decimal and then multiply or divide. Converting percents to fractions or decimals is simple.

Converting to Fractions and Decimals

To convert a percent to a *fraction*, simply remove the percent sign and add a denominator of 100 (after all, the percent sign is another way of writing a denominator of 100, and the fraction line means division), and then simplify or rewrite as needed.

Example: Convert 45% to a fraction.

$\frac{45}{100}$, which simplifies to $\frac{9}{20}$

Example: Convert 68.5% to a fraction.

$\frac{68.5}{100}$, which we could rewrite as $\frac{137}{200}$

(We multiplied both the numerator and the denominator by $\frac{2}{2}$ to get rid of the decimal. $\frac{68.5}{100} \bullet \frac{2}{2} = \frac{137}{200}$)

To convert a percent to a *decimal*, simply divide the percent by 100 (remember, the percent sign is another way of writing a denominator of 100) and remove the percent sign.

Example: Convert 45% to a decimal.

$\frac{45}{100}$ or $45 \div 100 = 0.45$

Example: Convert 68.5% to a decimal.

$\frac{68.5}{100}$ or $68.5 \div 100 = 0.685$

Converting from Fractions and Decimals

It's simple to convert *fractions of 100* to a percent — after all, the % sign means *per hundred*, so we can simply replace a denominator of 100 with a percent sign.

Example: Convert $\frac{5}{100}$ to a percent.

$\frac{5}{100} = 5\%$

What about converting integers, decimals, and fractions with denominators other than 100? Let's consider *integers* and *decimals* first. Before we jump to the "rule," let's think this task through for a minute. If we could rewrite an integer or a decimal as a fraction of 100, then it would be easy to convert to a percent. We can do that by multiplying the integer or decimal by $\frac{100}{100}$ (since $\frac{100}{100}$ equals 1, multiplying by $\frac{100}{100}$ will not change the value of the integer or decimal, as any number times 1 equals itself).

Example: Convert 3 to a percent.

$3 \bullet \frac{100}{100} = \frac{300}{100} = 300\%$

Example: Convert 0.45 to a percent.

$0.45 \bullet \frac{100}{100} = \frac{45}{100} = 45\%$

Example: Convert 0.685 to a percent.

$0.685 \bullet \frac{100}{100} = \frac{68.5}{100} = 68.5\%$

Now, you probably already knew that you could convert integer and decimal numbers to percents by **simply multiplying the number by 100 and then adding the percent sign.** Know, though, that this "rule" is a shortcut for writing the quantity over a denominator of 100 (that's what we're doing when we multiply by 100) and then replacing the denominator with a % sign (after all, the sign means *per hundred*).

As for converting *fractions with denominators other than 100* to percents, you could either

1. rewrite the fraction so its denominator is 100, and then replace the denominator with a % sign or
2. complete the division in the fraction, and then convert from the decimal to a percent.

Both of these methods ensure we keep the same meaning in the new notation.

Example: Convert $\frac{4}{5}$ to a percent.

Method 1: Rewrite as a fraction of 100.

$$\frac{4}{5} \bullet \frac{20}{20} = \frac{80}{100}$$

Now, since the % sign means per hundred, we can rewrite $\frac{80}{100}$ as 80%.

Method 2: Convert to a decimal and then to a percent.

$$\frac{4}{5} = 4 \div 5 = 0.8 \bullet \frac{100}{100} = \frac{80}{100} = 80\%$$

Revisiting Percentages

A 25%-off sale, a 6% tax rate, a 20% tip — we encounter percents all the time in real life. And we often need to calculate the *dollar amount* that percent represents (i.e., the actual dollars we'll save from the sale, spend in tax, or leave for a tip). How do we figure this out?

Well, as you hopefully remember from Book 1, one way to find the actual quantity would be to **set up a proportion**. After all, a percent represents a rate *per hundred*. It tells us the ratio, or relationship, but doesn't specifically tell us the actual quantity. We can find the actual quantity using a proportion.

For example, if we want to find 5% of $50, we want to find the amount that represents the same portion of $50 as 5 does out of 100. We can find this using a proportion.

Example: Find 5% of $50

$$\frac{5}{100} = \frac{x}{\$50}$$

Cross multiply:

$$5 \bullet \$50 = 100 \bullet x$$

Simplify:

$$\mathbf{\$250} = 100 \bullet x$$

In Book 1, we would have found 5% of $50 with this proportion: $\frac{5}{100} = \frac{?}{\$50}$. Notice that we did the same thing, except we used *x* instead of *?* as a placeholder.

Divide by 100:

$$\frac{\$250}{\mathbf{100}} = \frac{100 \bullet x}{\mathbf{100}}$$

$$\frac{\$250}{100} = \frac{\cancel{100} \bullet x}{\cancel{100}}$$

$$\mathbf{\$2.50 = x}$$

Percentage is often used synonymously with percent. However, to keep it easy to tell what we're referring to, we'll use the term "rate" or "percent" if we mean the rate or ratio per hundred, and "percentage" if we mean the **result we'd get if we found the portion of a base the rate represents.**

We'll call the number we just found — the actual amount the percent represents — the **percentage**.

$50 was what we'll call the **base**. The base is the number *of which* we're taking a percent. If you're leaving a tip, your bill before the tip would be the base. If you're making a purchase, the cost before tax or a discount would be the base.

We'll call 5% the percent or the **rate**. We'll use the term "rate" in this course, as technically we could have a rate per thousand, million, or any other denominator . . . although the rate will usually be a percent (an amount *per hundred*).

To clarify, here's the proportion with the parts of it labeled.

Rate → $\frac{5}{100} = \frac{\$2.50}{50}$ ← **Percentage** (\$2.50), **Base** (50)

Now that we have terms to describe the different components of a percent problem, let's express their relationship as a formula. The rate always equals the percentage divided by the base. After all, the ratio *per hundred* will be the same ratio as that between the percentage and the base — that is, they form a proportion.

$$R = \frac{P}{B}$$

$$Rate = \frac{Percentage}{Base}$$

When using this formula, keep in mind that the rate will typically be a percent — a portion of a hundred. The rate will be one ratio in the proportion, and the $\frac{Percentage}{Base}$ will be the other. You may be familiar with a different formula and method for finding a percentage — we'll get to that in the next lesson. For now, re-familiarize yourself with the terms we use when working with percent problems and with finding them via a proportion.

Keeping Perspective

Fractions, decimals, and **percents** are all different ways of recording quantities. Each notation proves useful. Remember, we can use different notations to describe God's creation.

6.2 Rearranging Formulas

In the last lesson, we revisited **percents** and used proportions to help us find a percentage of a number.

$$Rate = \frac{Percentage}{Base} \quad or \quad R = \frac{P}{B}$$

You may recall from the last book that another way to find a percentage is by multiplying the rate times the base.

$$Rate \bullet Base = Percentage \quad or \quad R \bullet B = P$$

We mentioned then that we'd take a look in this book at why both formulas yield the same answer. Well, that time has come.

Two Formulas; Same Meaning

As you know, we can add, subtract, multiply, and divide *both sides* of an equation by the *same quantity* without changing the meaning. For example, to find x in the equation $12 = \frac{x}{4}$, we'd multiply *both sides* of the equation by 4.

$$12 = \frac{x}{4}$$

$$12 \bullet \mathbf{4} = \frac{x}{\cancel{4}} \bullet \cancel{\mathbf{4}}$$

$$\mathbf{48 = x}$$

Let's take this concept one step further. Just as we can add, subtract, multiply, and divide *both sides* of an equation by the *same value* without changing the meaning, we can add, subtract, multiply, and divide *both sides* of an equation by the *same unknown* without changing the meaning . . . even if the entire equation has only unknowns. Because we know God governs this universe consistently, we know that as long as we add, subtract, multiply, and divide *both sides* of the equation by the *same quantity* — whether its value is a known or an unknown, and whether the rest of the equation has known or unknown quantities — we won't have changed the equation's meaning.

Let's apply this to our percentage formula. We can multiply both sides by B (the base) to rewrite the equation with P (the percentage) on a side by itself.

$$Rate = \frac{Percentage}{Base} \quad or \quad R = \frac{P}{B}$$

Multiply both sides by *Base* or *B*:

$$Rate \bullet \mathbf{Base} = \frac{Percentage}{Base} \bullet \mathbf{Base} \quad or \quad R \bullet \mathbf{B} = \frac{P}{B} \bullet \mathbf{B}$$

$$Rate \bullet Base = \frac{Percentage}{\cancel{Base}} \bullet \cancel{Base} \quad or \quad R \bullet B = \frac{P}{\cancel{B}} \bullet \cancel{B}$$

$$Rate \bullet Base = \mathbf{Percentage} \quad or \quad R \bullet B = \mathbf{P}$$

Both $R \bullet B = P$ and $R = \frac{P}{B}$ express the *same* relationship.

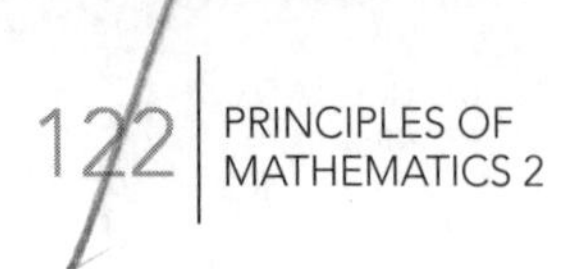

Two Different Ways to Represent the Same Relationship

$Rate = \frac{Percentage}{Base}$	$Rate \bullet Base = Percentage$
$R = \frac{P}{B}$	$R \bullet B = P$

As we saw in Book 1, it's easier to find the percentage using $R \bullet B = P$, since the equation already has the percentage (P) on a side by itself.

Example: What is 5% of $100?

All we need to do is substitute the values we know for R and B. Since it's easier to multiply by a decimal than a fraction, we'll express our rate as a decimal.

$$R \bullet B = P$$

$$\mathbf{0.05 \bullet \$100} = P$$

$$\mathbf{\$5} = P$$

While those are the only two ways we looked at in Book 1 to write the relationship between the rate, base, and percentage, we could also rearrange the equation so that B (the base) is on a side by itself. We'll start with this formula:

$$R \bullet B = P$$

Now let's divide both sides by R to separate B on a side of its own:

$$\frac{R \bullet B}{\mathbf{R}} = \frac{P}{\mathbf{R}}$$

$$\frac{\cancel{R} \bullet B}{\cancel{R}} = \frac{P}{R}$$

$$B = \frac{P}{R}$$

Three Different Ways to Represent the Same Relationship

$Rate = \frac{Percentage}{Base}$	$Rate \bullet Base = Percentage$	$Base = \frac{Percentage}{Rate}$
$R = \frac{P}{B}$	$R \bullet B = P$	$B = \frac{P}{R}$

It's helpful to pick one of these ways of expressing the relationship and memorize it. You can then rearrange it as needed to solve a particular problem.

Rearranging Other Formulas

In the last chapter, we looked at these proportions:

$\frac{P_1}{P_2} = \frac{V_2}{V_1}$	$\frac{F_1}{F_2} = \frac{d_2}{d_1}$
Relationship between pressure and volume of a gas when the temperature is constant	Relationship between forces and distances in a lever

We solved problems with both formulas by substituting known numbers and then cross multiplying. However, we *could* cross multiply the unknowns themselves, thus rearranging the formula.

$\frac{P_1}{P_2} = \frac{V_2}{V_1}$	$\frac{F_1}{F_2} = \frac{d_2}{d_1}$
$\frac{P_1}{P_2} = \frac{V_2}{V_1}$	$\frac{F_1}{F_2} = \frac{d_2}{d_1}$
$\mathbf{P_1 \bullet V_1 = P_2 \bullet V_2}$	$\mathbf{F_1 \bullet d_1 = F_2 \bullet d_2}$

We could then use the bolded equations as our formulas instead to solve problems.

The point is that it's often helpful to rearrange formulas. Rearranged formulas can make the math simpler and can help us better understand the relationship.

Swapping Entire Sides of an Equation

Not only can we rearrange formulas to solve for different unknowns, but just as we did with known numbers back in Lesson 3.2, we can also swap the left side of the equation with the right side, and vice versa, when dealing with unknowns.

Shown with Known Numbers			***Shown with an Unknown***		
$6 + 2 = 8$	*and*	$8 = 6 + 2$	$x + 2 = 8$	*and*	$8 = x + 2$
$6 - 2 = 4$	*and*	$4 = 6 - 2$	$x - 2 = 4$	*and*	$4 = x - 2$
$2 \bullet 6 = 12$	*and*	$12 = 2 \bullet 6$	$2 \bullet x = 12$	*and*	$12 = 2 \bullet x$
$6 \div 3 = 2$	*and*	$2 = 6 \div 3$	$x \div 3 = 2$	*and*	$2 = x \div 3$

This holds true when we have all unknowns as well, such as in a formula.

$$R \bullet B = P \quad \textit{and} \quad P = R \bullet B$$

In fact, because formulas can be rearranged following the same principles we use with known numbers, **you'll often see the same formula expressed many different ways.** However it is written, the relationship remains the same.

Important Reminder

When switching the sides of an equation, we're moving the *entire expression* from one side to the other. We're *not* changing anything about the expression itself. For example, in $x - 6 = 8$, we can switch the $x - 6$ to the right side.

$$x - 6 = 8 \quad \textit{and} \quad 8 = x - 6$$

But we would be changing the meaning if in the process we changed the order of $x - 6$ to $6 - x$. We have to move the whole expression without changing it in order for the equation to mean the same thing.

$x - 6 = 8$ does *not* equal $8 = 6 - x$

In $x - 6$, we're subtracting 6 from x; in $6 - x$, we're subtracting x from 6. Those are two different meanings.

Note: Technically, if all we have is addition or multiplication on one side of an equation, then the order within that side doesn't matter, as addition and multiplication are both associative and commutative. However, it's best to get used to moving the entire sides without changing anything else.

The bottom-line principle is that we can work with unknowns the same way we do with known numbers. Because of the consistent way God holds all things together, it doesn't matter if we know the value of a quantity or not. We can count on that quantity to operate according to the consistent ordinances God created and sustains.

Important! Stop and reread the above until you're sure you understand the concept. This idea of working with unknowns the same way we do with known quantities is key. You'll keep building on the idea over and over again.

Keeping Perspective

Because creation is so consistent, we can rely on addition, subtraction, multiplication, and division to operate the same way no matter what value an unknown represents. Thus, we can apply the principles and rules we use with known numbers to unknowns with confidence, knowing that whatever the unknown's value, it will "follow the rules," so to speak.

This sort of confidence in a consistent universe points us upward to the biblical God. Only a faithful, powerful God could keep this universe operating with the kind of unerring consistency required to work with unknowns, knowing that, whatever the actual values are, they'll operate in a predictable, recordable fashion.

6.3 Finding Rates and Bases

Up until now, you've been given the rate and the base and asked to find the percentage. Sometimes, though, we know the percentage and want to find either the rate or the base. It doesn't matter what number in a percent problem you need to find — all you need to remember is the basic relationship (that is, the formula), and you can rearrange and solve to find whatever information you need. Let's take a look at some examples.

While we'll be using *Rate • Base = Percentage* as our starting point to solve each problem since it's often easiest to remember the relationship this way, as we saw in the last lesson, you could use this relationship arranged any way (i.e., you could use $Rate = \frac{Percentage}{Base}$ or $Base = \frac{Percentage}{Rate}$ instead, as they represent the same relationship). **The important thing is to remember the relationship between rate, percentage, and base in one arrangement or another, and to identify and use the correct numbers for rate, percentage, and base.**

Example: Find the rate if your base is \$14.30 and your percentage is \$1.55.

Substitute the values given into the formula:

$$R \bullet B = P$$

$$R \bullet \mathbf{\$14.30} = \mathbf{\$1.55}$$

Divide both sides by \$14.30 to find R:

$$\frac{R \bullet \$14.30}{\mathbf{\$14.30}} = \frac{\$1.55}{\mathbf{\$14.30}}$$

$$\frac{R \bullet \cancel{\$14.30}}{\cancel{\$14.30}} = \frac{\$1.55}{\$14.30}$$

$$\boldsymbol{R} = \mathbf{0.1084}, \text{ or } \mathbf{10.84\%}$$

We can check our answer by substituting the value we found for the rate back into the initial equation.

$$R \bullet \$14.30 = \$1.55$$

$$\mathbf{0.1084} \bullet \$14.30 = \$1.55$$

This is true — our answer checks out.

Technically, we get \$1.55012 when we use a value of 10.84% for *R*. The difference is because 10.84% is a rounded value.

Now, unfortunately, real-life problems don't come labeled with rate, base, and percentage. Instead, we'll typically have to think through which number is which. This can be challenging at times, especially at first. But the more you practice, the easier it should get. Let's look at the *same problem* we just examined, only this time, we'll have to identify the rate, base, and percentage ourselves.

Example: Suppose you have a bill of \$14.30 at a restaurant. You've got \$1.55 of coins in your wallet. Figure out if this is a high enough percent of your bill to leave as the tip.

Let's think this through for a minute. What are we trying to find? It can be helpful to think through the situation in general. When you're leaving a tip, you usually leave a percent (such as 20%) of your bill. In this problem, we know the amount of the bill, and we know the potential tip value, but we don't know the percent that tip value represents. So we're trying to find the percent, or the rate. Of what number do we want to find that rate? Of the bill. So \$14.30 is the base, which would make \$1.55 the percentage. Now we can find the answer, just as we did in the last example.

Substitute the values given into the formula:

$$R \cdot B = P$$

$$R \cdot \mathbf{\$14.30} = \mathbf{\$1.55}$$

Divide both sides by $14.30 to find R:

$$\frac{R \cdot \$14.30}{\mathbf{\$14.30}} = \frac{\$1.55}{\mathbf{\$14.30}}$$

$$\frac{R \cdot \cancel{\$14.30}}{\cancel{\$14.30}} = \frac{\$1.55}{\$14.30}$$

$$R = \mathbf{0.1084}\text{, or } \mathbf{10.84\%}$$

We can check our answer by substituting the value we found for the rate back into the initial equation.

$$R \cdot \$14.30 = \$1.55$$

$$\mathbf{0.1084} \cdot \$14.30 = \$1.55$$

This is true — our answer checks out.

Since 10.84% is a pretty low tip, we now know the change in our wallet isn't enough.

Identifying the Rate, Base, and Percentage

The most challenging part of solving percentage problems is correctly identifying the rate, base, and percentage. Here is some basic guidance to help you.

The **rate** is the portion we're trying to find. It's typically a percent — that is, the portion of 100 we're trying to find. You can typically identify it by the % sign.

The **base** is the number of which we want to find a certain rate — that is, the number we're multiplying the rate by. As we saw in Book 1, multiplication can be thought of in terms of *of*. When we multiply 6 • 5, we're taking 6 sets *of* 5. When we multiply $3 \cdot \frac{1}{2}$, we're taking 3 sets *of* $\frac{1}{2}$. Since the rate is multiplied by the base, the word *of* can help you identify the base. While the word *of* might not always be used in the problem (and real-life problems don't come labeled with words at all), you can think in terms of "the rate *of* the base equals the percentage" and see which number fits as the base. That is, what's the number *of which* you want to find the rate?

For example, in the previous example, even though the word *of* was not used in the problem, we could think through what number we were trying to find the rate *of*. We wanted to know what rate *of* $14.30 equals $1.55.

The **percentage** is the result of multiplying the rate and the base. If you identify your rate (which is easy, since it's typically a percent) and your base (look for the number *of* which you want to find the rate), the percentage will be the remaining number. The word *equals* can also help you identify it. Again, think in terms of "the rate of the base *equals* the percentage" —

while the problem may not use the word *equals*, you can often see which number would fit when you read the relationship aloud.

Another way to identify the rate, base, and percentage is to remember the proportion we looked at in the last lesson. You know the rate is one of the ratios, and then all you need to figure out is which number represents a portion *of* the other number — that is, which is the numerator and which is the denominator in the other ratio.

$$Rate = \frac{Percentage}{Base}$$

Whatever method works for you is fine, so long as you identify the correct values. Our examples, though, will use *Rate • Base = Percentage.*

The bottom-line key to solving percent problems is to understand what you're trying to find so you're not blindly inserting numbers into an equation. This comes with practice. **The more you practice identifying the parts of a percent problem, the easier it should get . . . and the more prepared you'll be to apply the skill in real life.**

Keeping in mind the guidance from the box above, let's consider two additional examples. Notice how in each one, thinking about the number *of* which we want to find the rate helps us identify the base.

Example: Suppose a 5% tax is charged on a $90 item. How much will we pay in tax?

Let's start by finding the rate, which in this case is 5%. Now let's ask ourselves *of what number* do we want to find 5%? After all, the rate *of* the base equals the percentage. We want to find 5% *of* $90. So $90 is our base. We must be looking for the percentage — the amount we'll pay in tax.

Substitute the values given in the formula and solve:

$$R \bullet B = P$$

$$\mathbf{0.05 \bullet \$90} = P$$

$$\mathbf{\$4.50} = P$$

We will have to pay $4.50 in tax.

Again, we can check our answer by substituting the value for P and seeing if the equation holds true.

$$0.05 \bullet \$90 = P$$

$$0.05 \bullet \$90 = \mathbf{\$4.50}$$

We could also have thought of this in terms of a proportion. The 5% tax is a rate of $\frac{5}{100}$. We want to set up an equivalent ratio to this. We'd have this: $\frac{5}{100} = \frac{P}{\$90}$

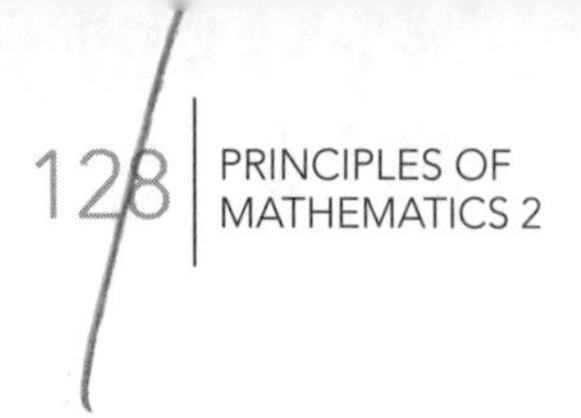

Example: Suppose you receive a 5% commission on every sale you make. If you receive $50 in commission, how many dollars of sales did you make?

Here we know 5% is the rate. Now let's ask ourselves of what number do we want to find 5%? We get 5% of the total sales. The total sales is the base. Remember, the rate of the base equals the percentage. So what's the percentage? Well, we know 5% of the total sales equals $50. $50 is the percentage.

We could also have thought of this in terms of a proportion. The 5% tax is a rate of $\frac{5}{100}$. We want to set up an equivalent ratio to this. We'd have this: $\frac{5}{100} = \frac{\$50}{B}$

Substitute the values given into the formula:

$$R \bullet B = P$$

$$\mathbf{0.05} \bullet B = \mathbf{\$50}$$

Divide both sides by 0.05 to find B:

$$\frac{0.05 \bullet B}{\mathbf{0.05}} = \frac{\$50}{\mathbf{0.05}}$$

$$\frac{\cancel{0.05} \bullet B}{\cancel{0.05}} = \frac{\$50}{0.05}$$

$$\mathbf{B = \$1{,}000}$$

Check:

$$0.05 \bullet B = \$50$$

$$0.05 \bullet \mathbf{\$1{,}000} = \$50$$

As with any other skill, identifying rate, base, and percentage gets easier with practice. Your worksheets will help you master the skill.

Keeping Perspective

Just as you've been using math to find missing numbers in other relationships (perimeter, area, volume, levers, time, etc.), you can apply those same principles to finding rates, bases, and percentages. Since these types of relationships are common in real life, you'll find that familiarizing yourself with solving percent problems of double value will help your math skills *and* help you quickly deal with the real-life percent problems you encounter.

6.4 Force and Motion

It's time now to explore a famous and important consistency. Before we jump into it, let's review a science term called **force**. As we mentioned when we looked at levers, force is the "push or pull"[1] on objects.

Back in the late 1600s, a man named Isaac Newton discovered what are known as the *laws of motion* that describe mathematically the consistent way God causes objects to respond to pushes and pulls (i.e., how they respond to force). Because

God causes everything — from a tiny pin to a massive airplane — to respond to those pushes and pulls consistently, we can express this relationship as a mathematical "law."

Here's Newton's Second Law of Motion expressed as a formula:

$$F = m \bullet a$$

$$\textit{Force} = \textit{mass} \bullet \textit{acceleration}$$

(While you'll learn more about these terms if you study physics, for now you can think of mass as weight, and acceleration as change of speed in a certain direction.)

Using this "law," we can figure out how fast objects will accelerate (i.e., change speed in a certain direction) due to forces applied to them.

And just as we did with the percent formula ($R \bullet B = P$), we can rearrange the equation to find the values we don't know.

Example: Find the mass if the force is 5 and the acceleration is 10.

Substitute values we know into the formula:

$F = m \bullet a$

$\mathbf{5} = m \bullet \mathbf{10}$

Divide both sides by 10:

$\frac{5}{\mathbf{10}} = \frac{m \bullet 10}{\mathbf{10}}$

$\frac{5}{10} = \frac{m \bullet \cancel{10}}{\cancel{10}}$

$\mathbf{0.5} = \boldsymbol{m}$

Check:

$5 = m \bullet 10$

$5 = \mathbf{0.5} \bullet 10$

$5 = \mathbf{5}$

We've purposefully left off units of measure in this example, as our goal was to show the math rather than get into the science of measuring force, mass, and acceleration.

In the problem above, we substituted the known values and then rearranged to find the unknown (the mass). Sometimes, though, we want to rewrite a formula in order to see in general how one unknown relates to the others. For example, how does the mass always relate to the force and the acceleration? We can find this by rearranging the formula so that mass (m) is on a side by itself.

Example: Solve $F = m \bullet a$ for m.

We can solve for m (i.e., find the mass) by dividing both sides by the acceleration.

$$\frac{F}{\boldsymbol{a}} = \frac{m \bullet a}{\boldsymbol{a}}$$

$$\frac{F}{a} = \frac{m \bullet \cancel{a}}{\cancel{a}}$$

$$\frac{F}{a} = \boldsymbol{m}$$

We now have rearranged the formula so it's easy to see how the mass relates to the force and the acceleration. What if we wanted to know how the acceleration relates to the force and mass? We could rearrange the formula so that a was on a side of the equation by itself. In fact, you'll get a chance to do just that when you complete Worksheet 6.4.

Keeping Perspective

Stop and ponder the miracle of $F = m \bullet a$ for a moment. God governs this universe so consistently that we can mathematically record and predict how much force will be needed to move an object based on its mass. We can reduce movement to a formula and apply it to thousands of situations, knowing it will work because *God is a faithful God.*

Just as God is faithful to hold the universe together, He is faithful to His promises to you too. Reflect today on how God has kept His Word to you and to those around you.

6.5 Chapter Synopsis and Sir Isaac Newton

We sure covered a lot of ground in this chapter, didn't we? We started with revisiting **percents** (a shorthand way to express ratios as fractions of 100). We then reviewed how to find a **percentage**, and then eventually learned how to find other missing numbers in a percent problem (such as the **base** or the **rate**). We practiced the same skill while exploring force and motion.

One key point to take away from this chapter is that, because of God's faithfulness in holding all things together, **we can rearrange formulas as needed to find missing information.** It doesn't matter if we know the amount we're adding, subtracting, multiplying, or dividing both sides of the equation by, or whether we're dealing with all unknowns — as long as we change both sides of the equation the same way, we know our equation will be in balance. After all, whatever number it is, God is keeping this universe together in a consistent way, and it will add, subtract, multiply, or divide the same way on both sides of the equation.

Original Equation

$x = x$

Added *y* to Both Sides

$x + y = x + y$

Our equation is still in balance, as y — whatever its value — is being added to ***both sides.***

Sir Isaac Newton

Sir Isaac Newton (1642–1727)[3]

Since we looked at force and motion a little in the last lesson, let's take a look at the man who discovered the laws of motion. Gifted with an incredible ability to apply math practically, Sir Isaac Newton, commonly referred to as Newton, clearly saw this universe as a complex machine created and held together by God.

Newton concludes his work the *Principia* (in which he explained the law of gravity) with several pages of reflections on God. He stated,

> *This most beautiful system of the sun, planets, and comets, could only proceed from the counsel and dominion of an intelligent and powerful Being.*[2]

Newton's life serves as a good rebuttal to the belief so prevalent in our culture that a biblical worldview is incompatible with science and progress. Although Newton's theology was not perfect, he clung steadfastly to the Lord and what He believed the Scriptures to say. He recognized that the incomprehensible God of the Bible, not "fate" or "nature" or even a God we could fully understand, had created all things.

Here is another quote from the third book of the *Principia*,

> *And from his true dominion it follows that the true God is a living, intelligent, and powerful Being; and, from his other perfections, that he is supreme, or most perfect. He is eternal and infinite, omnipotent and omniscient; that is, his duration reaches from eternity to eternity; his presence from infinity to infinity; he governs all things and knows all things that are or can be done.*[4]

Newton's childhood was not easy. He was born premature, and people were surprised he survived. His father died before his birth, and his mother remarried when Newton was three, leaving Newton to live with his grandmother for several years. Later, Newton entered the university as "a poor scholar," probably performing many menial tasks to work his way through school.[5] After graduating with his BA, a plague interrupted his further career at the college, forcing the university to close and sending Newton home.

But Newton used this forced time back home to explore God's universe. Those years he spent at home ended up becoming Newton's most productive years — years that laid the groundwork for much of his life's accomplishments. He later said of those years, "All this was in the two plague years of 1665–1666. For in those days I was in the prime of my age for invention and minded Mathematics and Philosophy more than at any time since."[6] After the plague, Newton returned to the university and became a Fellow and later a Lucasian Professor of Mathematics (at the young age of 27, no less!) — but his diligence *through* the forced time back home during the plague is a wonderful reminder to us to rejoice in whatever God allows into our lives and to seek to honor Him in it.

Fascinating Fact

Newton taught himself many math concepts by studying books on his own.

[CHAPTER 7]

Simplifying Expressions

7.1 Simplifying Multiplication

A large portion of math is about learning conventions, notations, and techniques that help us simplify expressions.

What do we mean by simplifying expressions? Well, remember that an **expression** is "a collection of symbols that jointly express a quantity."[1] For example, $4 \bullet 5$ is an expression — 4, 5, and • are a collection of symbols that together express the quantity 20. Thus when we refer to **simplifying an expression**, we mean to express it so it's as easy to understand and work with as possible.

Now, you've already been simplifying expressions for years. $4 \bullet 5$ simplifies to 20. Both $4 \bullet 5$ and 20 represent the same quantity, only 20 is a simpler way of expressing that quantity.

$$4 \bullet 5 = 20$$

$\frac{4}{6}$ simplifies to $\frac{2}{3}$; both $\frac{4}{6}$ and $\frac{2}{3}$ represent the same quantity, only $\frac{2}{3}$ is a simpler way of expressing that quantity.

$$\frac{4}{6} = \frac{2}{3}$$

In this chapter, we're going to look at some ways to simplify expressions involving unknowns. That way, you'll be even better equipped to handle the real-life problems you encounter.

Let's start by taking a look at a convention that we can often use to simplify how we express multiplication.

Expressing Multiplication Simply

When we're multiplying all numerals, we have to use a multiplication sign; when working with letters or non-numerical symbols, we don't need to write the multiplication sign. The convention is that **"*the absence of a sign* between letters or between a figure [numeral] and a letter indicates *multiplication*."**[2]

Below are a few examples.

$3 \bullet x$ (3 sets of x, or $x + x + x$) can be written as $3x$

$5 \bullet \pi$ (5 sets of π, or $\pi + \pi + \pi + \pi + \pi$) can be written as 5π

$y \bullet x$ (y sets of x) can be written as yx

This convention should not be totally unfamiliar to you. You've already been omitting multiplication signs in front of parentheses, knowing that whatever is outside of the parentheses gets multiplied by whatever is inside.

$$2(5) = 2 \bullet 5 = 10$$

We've also shown geometry formulas using this convention at times. For example, the figure below shows the three ways used in Book 1 to represent the perimeter of an equilateral (all sides equal) triangle using s to represent the length of each side. Notice that in the last way, we omitted the multiplication sign.

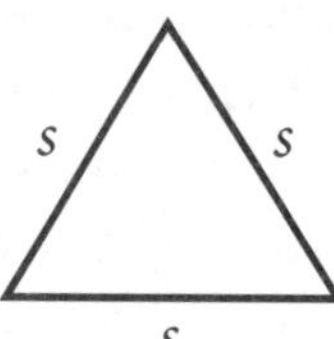

Perimeter of a Triangle $= s + s + s$ *or* $3 \bullet s$ *or* $3s$

As always, make sure you understand the principle. The principle is to omit multiplication signs when you can without leading to ambiguity.

If we have units of measure, we'll often need a multiplication sign even with an unknown in order to avoid confusion. For example, we wouldn't write 10 ft • x as 10 ft$x$, because that would be confusing. Instead, we'd continue to use the • or parentheses.

10 ft • x *or* (10 ft)x

Obviously, if we replace an unknown with its value, we'll have to include a multiplication sign. For instance, if we knew that the value of s in $3s$ was 5, then we'd write 3(5) or $3 \bullet 5$. We couldn't write 35, as that would not be the same meaning as $3 \bullet 5$.

Expressing Multiplication Simply in Formulas

Let's take a look at an example of working with a formula where unnecessary multiplication signs have been omitted.

We saw in the last chapter that we can rearrange formulas to solve for different unknowns. For example, we can rearrange the percent formula to solve for the base.

Example: Rearrange $R \bullet B = P$ to solve for the base (B).

Divide both sides by R:

$$\frac{R \bullet B}{\mathbf{R}} = \frac{P}{\mathbf{R}}$$

$$\frac{\cancel{R} \bullet B}{\cancel{R}} = \frac{P}{R}$$

$$B = \frac{P}{R}$$

The following example shows the *same thing* written without a multiplication sign. Even though we've not written the sign, RB means R *times* B. Thus, we can still rearrange the formula the same way we did before.

Example: Rearrange $RB = P$ to solve for the base (B).

Divide both sides by R:

$$\frac{RB}{\mathbf{R}} = \frac{P}{\mathbf{R}}$$

$$\frac{\cancel{R}B}{\cancel{R}} = \frac{P}{R}$$

$$B = \frac{P}{R}$$

A Convention Is a Convention

It's important to differentiate between the adopted conventions in math and the underlying consistencies. God created the underlying consistencies, and they remain the same throughout time. Multiplication consistently works the same way. The way we describe consistencies, though, can and does vary. For example, you now know quite a few ways to describe multiplication.

God's creation is so amazingly complex and intricate, though, that we frequently need to modify conventions in different branches of math in order to describe it. When you get to calculus, you'll learn that in calculus the letter *d* is considered a special symbol rather than an unknown. So in calculus, *dx* does not mean *d* times *x*, but rather something completely different.

Again, remember to view conventions as helpful tools to describe God's creation . . . tools that can be modified if needed to serve the end: exploring and solving real-life problems. Above all, remember that we need so many different tools in math because God created an incredible universe. He is much greater than we could ever conceive!

More Related Conventions

There's also a convention about whether to write $3 \bullet x$ or $x \bullet 3$ as $3x$ or as $x3$. Since multiplication is commutative (order doesn't matter — see Lesson 1.3), both $3 \bullet x$ and $x \bullet 3$ yield the same product. So rather than writing them both ways, the convention is to always put the numeral first. We would write both $3 \bullet x$ and $x \bullet 3$ (x sets of 3) as $3x$ rather than as $x3$, and both $2 \bullet \pi$ and $\pi \bullet 2$ as 2π.

This convention applies when we insert values into formulas too. For example, you know the rate times the base equals the percentage ($R \bullet B = P$, or $RB = P$). Let's say you know the base is \$100 and the percentage is \$5. Rather than writing $R\$100 = \$5$, put the numerical value before the unknown, like this: $\$100R = \$5$.

We also follow a consistent convention in reading multiplications by unknowns. Rather than saying "three times x," **we read $3x$ as "three x."**

Following consistent conventions makes it easier to instantly take in and work with equations.

Keeping Perspective

It's joked that mathematicians are lazy.

> *Mathematics is being lazy. Mathematics is letting the principles do the work for you so that you do not have to do the work for yourself. — George Pólya*[3]

While we don't want to be lazy, we do look for simple ways to complete a task. Not writing multiplication signs when we don't have to is definitely one of those extremely useful time-and-trouble-saving conventions. It makes expressions easier to read and work with, as we'll see in the next lesson.

As you complete the worksheet in the *Student Textbook*, remember that the only reason we're able to develop useful conventions is because God created us with this ability. He gave man the capacity for naming and developing useful (and hopefully simpler) ways of describing the quantities and consistencies He created and sustains. He wired us with the ability to solve problems and express His world mathematically.

7.2 Combining Like Terms

Okay, now that you know about the convention of omitting multiplication signs when we can, let's return to the main focus of this chapter: simplifying expressions.

We're going to take a look at an equation that has multiple multiplications of an unknown and look at how it can be solved quite simply.

Multiple Multiplications

Let's say we are starting a knitting business. We buy 2 skeins of yarn the first time we go to the store, and then go back for another 5 skeins. If we spent \$56 altogether and we know each skein cost the same amount, how much did it cost per skein?

Let's use x to represent the cost for one skein. The first time, we bought 2 skeins, or $2x$ (two times the cost of one skein would be the cost of two skeins). At another store, we bought 5 skeins, or $5x$ (five times the cost of one skein would be the cost of five skeins). We know these costs added together equal \$56, so we have this equation: $2 \bullet x + 5 \bullet x = \$56$, which we can express more simply as $2x + 5x = \$56$.

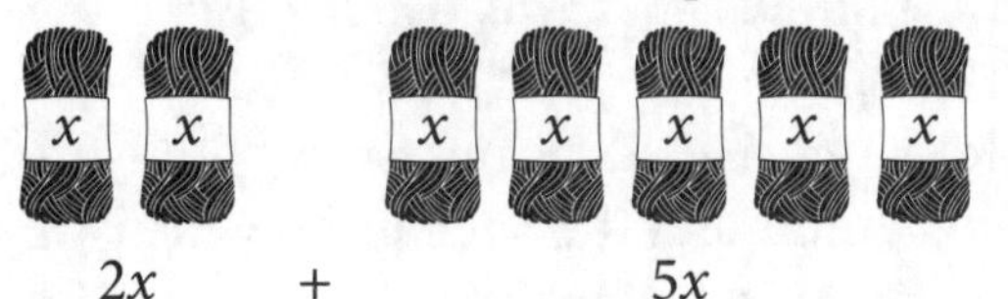

$2x \quad + \quad 5x \quad = \$56$

> Notice how omitting the multiplication signs made the equation easier to read. $2x + 5x = \$56$ is much less cumbersome to write and read than $2 \bullet x + 5 \bullet x = \$56$. Yet both equations mean the *same thing.*

Now, to solve $2x + 5x = \$56$, we need to first simplify $2x + 5x$. How do we do that? Let's take a look.

Example: $2x + 5x = \$56$

Remember that x is a placeholder for the cost of one skein of yarn. Two skeins will cost 2 times the cost of one skein ($2x$), and five skeins will cost 5 times the cost of one skein ($5x$), making the total 7 times the cost of one skein ($7x$).

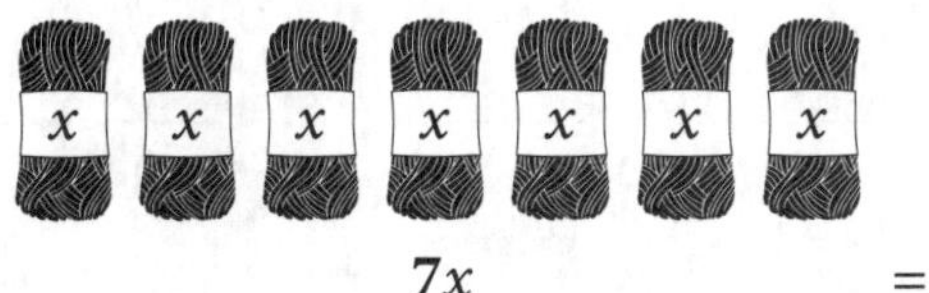

$7x \quad = \$56$

Now we can solve to find the cost of one skein of yarn (x) the same way we have in other problems: by isolating the unknown on one side of the equation. In this case, we can do this by dividing both sides by 7:

$$\frac{7x}{7} = \frac{\$56}{7}$$

$$\frac{\cancel{7}x}{\cancel{7}} = \frac{\cancel{\$56}^{8}}{\cancel{7}}$$

$$\mathbf{x = \$8}$$

Each skein of yarn cost us \$8.

Notice that if we substitute \$8 for x in the original equation, we find that it holds true.

$$2(\mathbf{\$8}) + 5(\mathbf{\$8}) = \$56$$

$$\mathbf{\$16} + \mathbf{\$40} = \$56$$

$$\mathbf{\$56} = \$56$$

Term Time

When we're referring to the multiplier of one or more unknowns, we'll call the multiplier the **coefficient** of the unknown(s). Thus, we would call the 2 and the 5 in $2x$ and $5x$ coefficients, as the 2 and 5 are multipliers of an unknown (x).

Note: You'll learn a more comprehensive definition for coefficients in algebra (they have a broader use than the one explained here).

Notice that in the example, we simplified $2x$ and $5x$ by adding the coefficients of x together ($2 + 5 = 7$). After all, the 2 and the 5 tell us how many times to multiply x. By adding them together, we're counting the total number of times we need to multiply x.

When we added the coefficients together, we were **combining like terms.** Combining like terms is an extremely important simplification technique, so it warrants further examination.

Understanding the Principle

As you've probably noticed, words can have different meanings in math than they do in everyday English. "Terms" is one of those words that can be used different ways.

In normal speech, we use the word *term* to refer to "a word or phrase used to describe a thing or to express a concept."[4] In a mathematical sense, though, we'll use the word **term** to describe an "expression or quantity, the parts of which are not separated by + and – signs."[5] Each circle below represents a single term.

$$2x + 5x = \$56$$

The idea behind the term "term" is that it represents a complete quantity that we can then add or subtract to other quantities. We could look at the entire fraction below as a single term (the complete fraction is representing a single quantity that we could then add or subtract to other quantities), or at the individual quantities that are not separated by + or – signs as terms.

$$\frac{5 + 6 \cdot 5}{20} + 7$$

Now, $2x$ and $5x$ are what we call **like terms** or **similar terms**. Like or similar terms are both multiplications of the same unknown. Since both $2x$ and $5x$ are multiplications by the same unknown, we could **combine them by adding the coefficients together** (the 2 and the 5), giving us $7x$.

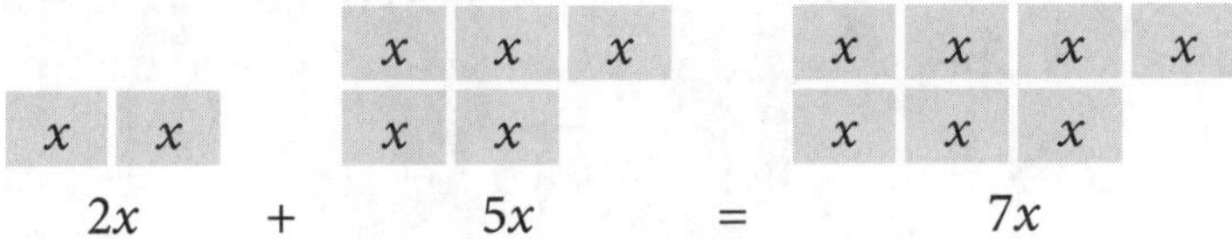

On the other hand, say we bought 2 skeins of yarn at one price and then 5 skeins at another store for a different price, spending a total of \$56 altogether. Using y to represent the price of the first 2 skeins and x to represent the price of the remaining 5 skeins, we'd have this:

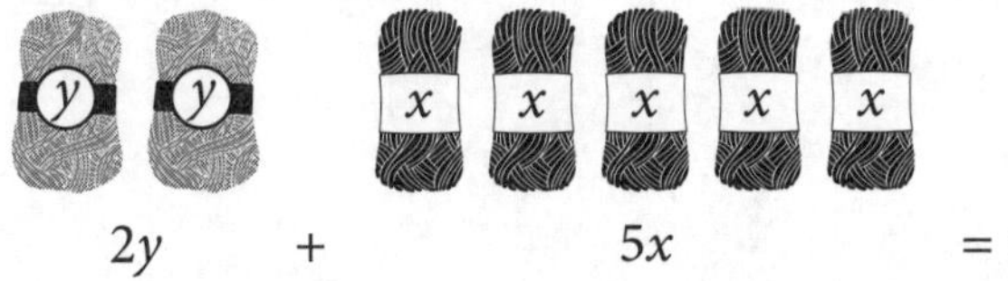

Here, $2y$ and $5x$ are *not* like terms. The y and the x represent *different* costs. They're different placeholders. Thus we *couldn't* add the coefficients for $2y + 5x$, since the unknowns (y and x) are different, meaning their values could be different.

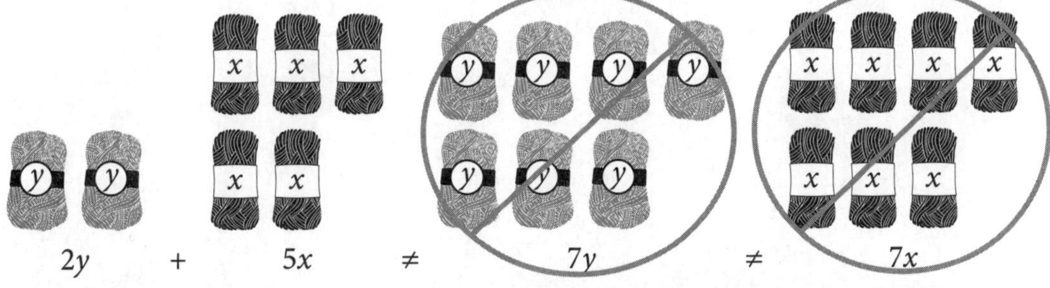

We can only combine like terms — that is, terms that have the same unknown. **We combine like terms by adding their coefficients.** After all, the coefficients tell us how many times to multiply the unknown. Adding the coefficients merely adds up the total number of times the unknown needs to be multiplied.

Keeping Perspective

In order to solve equations, we frequently need to first simplify expressions. One way to do that is to **combine like terms.** We do this by adding the **coefficients** (a term often used in describing the multiplier of an unknown). Once we've combined the like terms, we can then often solve for the unknown the same way we have been: by isolating it on one side of the equation.

7.3 Combining Like Terms with Coefficients of 1

Let's continue exploring how to combine like terms by considering a slightly different scenario. Suppose we purchase only 1 skein of yarn, and then later buy an additional 5 at the same price. Our new total is $48. We would have this equation:

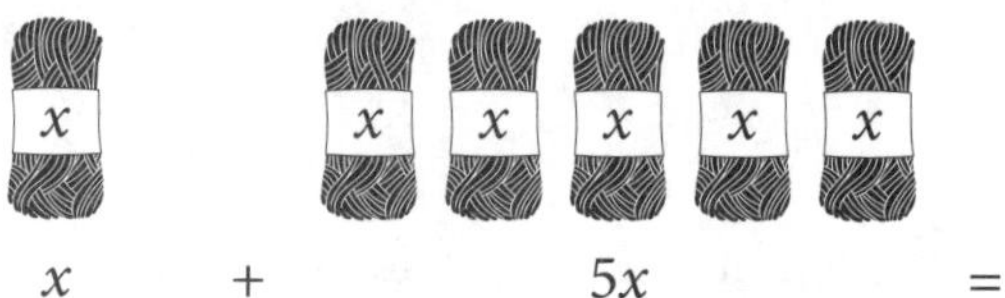

$x \quad + \quad 5x \quad = \$48$

How do we add x and $5x$? Well, think about what x represents for a minute. Although we haven't written a 1, x really means 1 set of x. We want to take it 1 time. Thus, we can *think of x as having a coefficient of 1*, combine the like terms by adding the coefficients, and solve to find x.

Example: $x + 5x = \$48$

Think of x as $1x$:

$\mathbf{1}x + 5x = \$48$

Add the coefficients:

$\mathbf{6x} = \$48$

Divide both sides by 6:

$\frac{6x}{\mathbf{6}} = \frac{\$48}{\mathbf{6}}$

$\frac{\cancel{6}x}{\cancel{6}} = \frac{\cancel{\$48}^{8}}{\cancel{6}}$

$\mathbf{x = \$8}$

Each skein of yarn costs $8.

If we substitute $8 for x in the original equation, we'll find that $8 is indeed the value for x that makes the equation hold true.

$x + 5x = \$48$

$\mathbf{\$8} + 5(\mathbf{\$8}) = \$48$

$\$8 + \mathbf{\$40} = \$48$

$\mathbf{\$48} = \$48$

We can think of any unknown as having a coefficient of 1. After all, x means 1 set of x, s means 1 set of s, and y means 1 set of y.

Another way to think about it is to remember the identity property of multiplication — that multiplying by 1 doesn't change the value of a quantity. Thus, just as 5 equals the same as 1 • 5, so x equals the same as 1 • x.

Keeping Perspective

That identity property of multiplication sure has a way of popping up all over the place, doesn't it? It's useful to remember that multiplying by 1 doesn't change the value — that, in fact, we can think of any value as 1 *set of* that value. So if you encounter an unknown without a written coefficient, you can think of it as having a coefficient of 1.

7.4 Combining Like Terms with Fractional Coefficients

As we use math to explore God's creation and help with real-life tasks, we encounter problems with fractional as well as whole-number coefficients. For example, if someone makes $\frac{1}{2}$ an unknown amount, we could represent that as $\frac{1}{2} \cdot x$, which can be shortened to $\frac{1}{2}x$. Here, $\frac{1}{2}$ is the coefficient of x.

The good news is that the *same principles* we've been using with whole-number coefficients apply to fractional coefficients too. In this lesson, we'll take a look at a couple of examples of simplifying expressions that include fractional coefficients.

Remember, in the case of fractional multiplication, it's helpful to think of the multiplication as finding a portion of another number. $\frac{1}{2} \cdot x$, or $\frac{1}{2}x$, means $\frac{1}{2}$ of x.

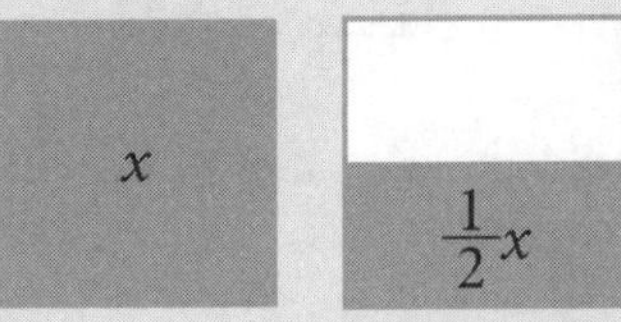

It doesn't matter what value x ends up being — when we find $\frac{1}{2}x$, we're finding $\frac{1}{2}$ of that value.

Adding Like Terms with Fractional Coefficients

Let's say someone gets a bonus of $\frac{1}{20}$ of his weekly salary, and then another bonus of $\frac{3}{5}$ his normal weekly salary (he must be doing a great job!). If the bonuses total \$300, how much is his normal salary?

If we use x to represent the normal salary, we would have this equation:

$$\frac{1}{20}x + \frac{3}{5}x = \$300$$

How do we solve this equation? We combine like terms with fractional coefficients the *same way we do like terms with whole-number coefficients*, remembering to rewrite the fractions so they have the same denominator in order to add them.

Example: $\frac{1}{20}x + \frac{3}{5}x = \$300$

Rewrite so the fractions have the same denominator:

$$\frac{1}{20}x + \mathbf{\frac{12}{20}}x = \$300$$

Combine the like terms by adding the coefficients together:

$$\mathbf{\frac{13}{20}}x = \$300$$

Divide both sides by $\frac{13}{20}$ to find x (which we do by inverting and multiplying):

$$\frac{13}{20}x \cdot \mathbf{\frac{20}{13}} = \$300 \cdot \mathbf{\frac{20}{13}}$$

$$\frac{\cancel{13}}{\cancel{20}}x \cdot \frac{\cancel{20}}{\cancel{13}} = \$300 \cdot \frac{20}{13}$$

$$\mathbf{x = \frac{\$6{,}000}{13}}\text{, or } \mathbf{\$461.54}$$

\$461.54 is the normal salary.

When the Coefficient Is One

Let's change the problem up a little. Say someone gets a bonus of $\frac{1}{20}$ of his weekly salary. If the amount of his normal salary plus the bonus is \$420, how much is his normal salary?

If we use x to represent the normal salary, we would have this equation:

$$x + \frac{1}{20}x = \$420$$

We can find the unknown (the normal salary) easily if we remember that we can think of x as having a coefficient of 1.

Example: $x + \frac{1}{20}x = \$420$

View x as $1x$:

$$\mathbf{1}x + \frac{1}{20}x = \$420$$

Rewrite so the coefficients have the same denominator:

$$\mathbf{\frac{20}{20}}x + \frac{1}{20}x = \$420$$

Combine the terms by adding the coefficients together:

$$\mathbf{\frac{21}{20}}x = \$420$$

Divide both sides by $\frac{21}{20}$ to find x (which we do by inverting and multiplying):

$$\frac{21}{20}x \cdot \mathbf{\frac{20}{21}} = \$420 \cdot \mathbf{\frac{20}{21}}$$

$$\mathbf{x = \$400}$$

The normal salary is \$400.

Important Note

Notice that we rewrote $1x$ as $\frac{20}{20}x$ in order to add it to $\frac{1}{20}x$, giving us $\frac{21}{20}x$. Use improper fractions as coeffiecients rather than mixed numbers, as they are simpler to read and work with.

Keeping Perspective

Notice that we keep applying the *same principles* over and over again. We're looking at the consistent way God causes objects to add and multiply, and applying that consistency to help us work with unknowns as well as with known numbers, and with fractional coefficients as well as with whole-number ones.

7.5 Chapter Synopsis and Eureka!

This chapter, we explored

- representing multiplication by simply **omitting the multiplication sign** when we can without changing the meaning. $3x$ is a shorthand way of writing $3 \cdot x$. We also learned to always write the numerical value first (we write $3x$ rather than $x3$).
- referring to the multiplier of one or more unknowns as the **coefficient** of the unknown(s). *Example*: In $3x$, we call 3 the *coefficient* of x.
- **combining like terms** by adding together the coefficients, remembering that we can think of an unknown that doesn't have a coefficient written as having a coefficient of 1. *Example*: $x + 2x = 3x$

If representing multiplication without a symbol and combining like terms still feels a bit foreign, don't be discouraged. In many ways, parts of math are similar to learning any other skill. At first, you have to think and pay attention to what you're doing, but after awhile, it becomes second nature, much like riding a bike, speaking a language, or playing an instrument.

Math in Action: Eureka![6]

Since we touched on problem-solving skills this chapter, let's take a look at a famous math problem of antiquity. Have you ever heard the expression "Eureka!" used to indicate figuring something out? That expression was popularized by a problem solved by the Greek mathematician Archimedes (the same Archimedes whom we looked at in Lesson 5.6).

The king of Syracuse, King Hieron, had ordered and received a gold crown. The crown weighed the correct weight, but the king wasn't convinced that the crown was made of pure gold. How could he tell if the makers had slipped some silver into the gold when making the crown?

The king posed that question to Archimedes. According to the story passed down, Archimedes figured out how to find the answer while watching how his body displaced water when he took a bath. He was so excited about hitting upon a method to test whether the crown was truly gold that he went racing home shouting "Eureka!" ("I have found it!"[7]) through the streets.

So how did Archimedes figure out if the crown was pure gold? While history is vague on the details, let's look at the way most accounts assume Archimedes followed to determine the gold content.

If we fill a bucket to the top with water, and then add an object (like a crown) to it, what happens?

Some water will overflow from the bucket to make room for the object. The amount of water that overflows depends on the volume of the object. The larger the volume, the more water overflows. So two objects that have the same volume should cause the same amount of water to overflow.

So how does this help us see if a crown is pure gold? Well, we could take a bar of pure gold that weighs the same as the crown. We know that if the crown is made of pure gold too, then its volume should be the same as the volume of the bar of pure gold. After all, they'd both be the *same weight* of the *same substance* . . . so their volume should be the same.

And how can we see if their volumes are the same? By putting the bar and the crown each in full buckets and measuring how much water overflows!

If water that overflows is the same, then the crown is made of pure gold; if it is different, then it is not pure gold.

Archimedes' experiment confirmed the king's suspicion: the crown was not pure gold.

The story of Archimedes and the crown is a good example of an important aspect of problem solving: thinking through how to get from what we know to what we want to know.

Archimedes had a problem to solve — and there weren't any hints as to how to solve it. He had to come up with a way to prove the crown's composition. And he did it by using weights (measure), volume (geometry), and other math concepts.

When you encounter word problems that seem unusual, know that the solution is usually a simple one, but sometimes it takes thought and time to get to it. Break it apart and think about what you know and what you need to know. Don't hesitate to pray and ask for wisdom — after all, God is the One holding math together and the source of all wisdom.

The fear of the LORD is the beginning of wisdom: and the knowledge of the holy is understanding (Proverbs 9:10).

The problems in this curriculum that seem challenging are designed to give you opportunities to apply what you're learning in a new setting so that you'll be able to solve problems in real life.

[CHAPTER 8]

Negative Numbers and Unknowns

8.1 Negative Signs and Unknowns

Since negative signs have a way of showing up in all sorts of situations, we're going to take the chapter to look more closely at how to work with equations that include negative signs and unknowns. Basically, we'll learn to apply what we *already know* about negative numbers with what we *already know* about unknowns and simplifying expressions to problems involving both.

Let's start by reviewing once again what the negative sign means and look at how that applies when we're dealing with an unknown.

Negative Signs Before Unknowns

As you know, a negative sign means *the opposite of.*

-5 means *the opposite of* 5

This applies to unknowns too.

$-x$ means *the opposite of* x

> A negative sign in front of an unknown means the same as it would if it were in front of a known number: to find the opposite of the value.
>
> -5 means *the opposite of* 5
> $-x$ means *the opposite of* x

Now, x could still be a positive or a negative number. Either way, though, the negative sign tells us to take *the opposite of* x's value.

Evaluate is a word you'll often see used in math books. It means to find the value of the expression, equation, etc.; that is, to "express numerically."[1]

Example: Evaluate $-x$ if x equals 8.

Let's substitute 8 for x to find the answer.

$-x$

–8

Example: Evaluate $-x$ if x equals –8.

Let's substitute –8 for x to find the answer.

$-x$

– –8

The opposite of the opposite of 8 is positive 8.

8

Example: Evaluate $5 - x$ if x is –2

Let's substitute –2 for x.

$5 - x$

5 – **–2**

Since the opposite of the opposite of 2 is positive 2, this simplifies to 7:

5 + **2**

7

Now, you might be wondering when we'd ever need to evaluate an expression like this. Subtracting unknowns (which could be negative) turns up all the time as we explore the consistencies God created and sustains around us. Let's take a look at an example.

Remember, a subscript number (such as the $_0$ in p_0) doesn't mean to perform any sort of operation — the subscript number is part of the symbol we're using to specify the unknown. In this case, the subscript $_0$ is differentiating the initial position from the current position.

Example: If our current position relative to home (p) is +30 mi and our initial postition relative to home (p_0) was –60 mi (i.e., 60 mi in *the opposite* direction), what was the change in our position?

Here, we want to find the *change in* position. To find this, we need to take the current position (p) and subtract the initial position (p_0) from it. This will tell us how the position has changed.

$p - p_0$

Let's substitute the values we were given. Notice the negative signs!

30 mi – –60 mi

Now let's simplify, remembering that two negative signs make a positive (the opposite of the opposite is a positive):

30 mi + 60 mi

Now we can complete the addition to find the answer.

90 mi

Think about what the answer we just found means. We started at –60 mi from home and now we're at 30 mi from home. So now we're at 90 mi more in the positive direction than we were at the beginning — our *change* was +90 mi.

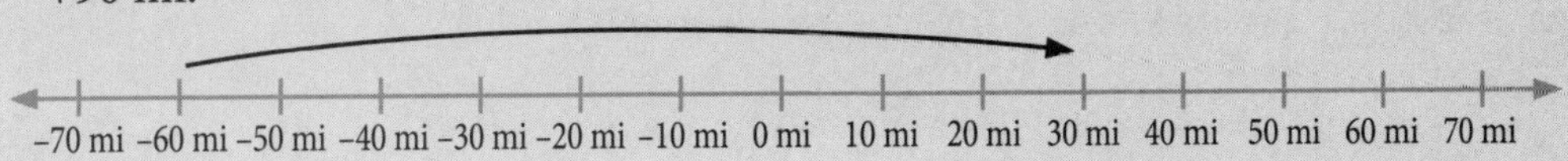

Don't let negative signs in problems fool you. You have all the tools you need to solve them. Just remember that each negative sign means *the opposite of*.

Keeping Perspective

Hopefully nothing in this lesson was new or a surprise to you. Once again, we were applying what we *already knew* to some additional situations we'd not yet explored. Train yourself not to panic when you encounter a problem that seems unfamiliar. Just because you have not seen a problem like the one you're trying to solve does not mean you can't solve it.

8.2 Revisiting the Additive Inverse

You've already been using negative numbers combined with unknowns to solve equations. For example, you've isolated x in $x + 10 = 50$ by adding –10 (the additive inverse of +10) to both sides of the equation.

Example: $x + 10 = 50$

Add –10 (the additive inverse of +10) to both sides:

$$x + 10 + \mathbf{-10} = 50 + \mathbf{-10}$$

$$\mathbf{x = 40}$$

It's time now to apply this *same principle* to rearranging formulas.

Remember, the additive inverse is the number that, added to a number, equals 0. The additive inverse is always the opposite of the number. For example, 5 is the additive inverse of –5, and –5 is the additive inverse of +5. –5 and +5 are opposites. When we add them together, we get 0. If you walk 5 miles in one direction and then turn around and walk 5 miles in the opposite direction, you'll end up back where you started.

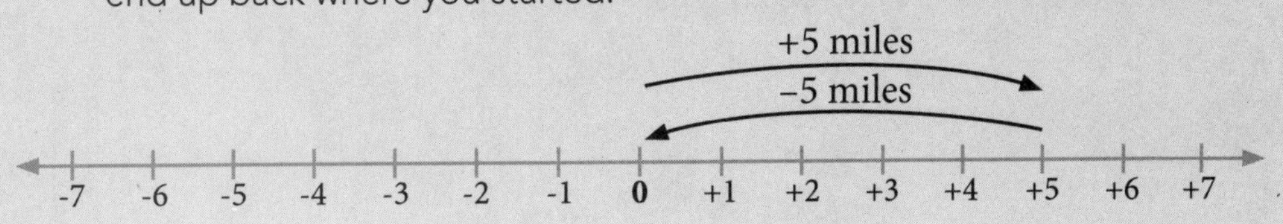

Rearranging Formulas with the Additive Inverse

While we don't know an unknown's value (it's unknown!), we know that whatever it is, if it's added to its additive inverse, it will equal 0.

$$w + -w = 0 \quad \text{and} \quad -w + w = 0$$

We can use this knowledge to help us rearrange letters within equations or formulas in order to find the desired unknown. Let's say our take-home salary (commonly called the net salary) equals the amount we make (our gross salary) minus whatever is held back for taxes (called withholdings) or other purposes (such as health insurance, donations, etc.). Assuming we only have withholdings taken out of our salary, we'd have this relationship:

$$\textit{net salary} = \textit{gross salary} - \textit{withholdings}$$

Which can be reduced to a formula:

$$n = g - w$$

Now let's say that rather than finding n, we're interested in finding g. Can we rearrange the equation to solve for g?

Absolutely! We can rearrange $n = g - w$ so as to find the value for g by *adding w to both sides* of the equation.

$$n + \mathbf{w} = g - w + \mathbf{w}$$

Now, the $-w$ and $+w$ on the right side are additive inverses . . . they'll equal 0. Thus, we've just solved for g!

$$n + w = \mathbf{g}$$

If we wanted to, we could rewrite this so that g is on the left, making it even easier to tell that we've solved the equation for it. (Remember, swapping the *entire sides* of an equality doesn't change the meaning — see Lesson 6.2.)

$$g = n + w$$

All we did was apply the *same tools* we've been using with actual numbers to help us work with unknowns.

Keeping Perspective

Once again, we're continuing to apply the same tools to new settings. You'll continue this process throughout math.

8.3 Combining Like Terms with Negative Coefficients

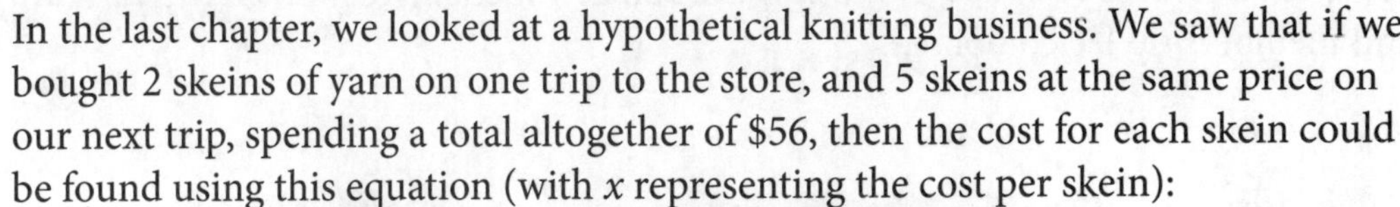

In the last chapter, we looked at a hypothetical knitting business. We saw that if we bought 2 skeins of yarn on one trip to the store, and 5 skeins at the same price on our next trip, spending a total altogether of \$56, then the cost for each skein could be found using this equation (with x representing the cost per skein):

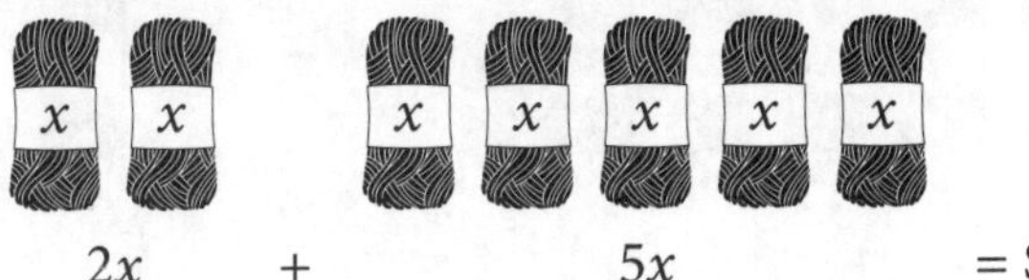

$2x \quad + \quad 5x \quad = \$56$

What if, after purchasing the 2 and the 5 skeins, we *returned* 3 skeins, receiving \$24 for the returned yarn? Instead of spending \$56, we would have spent \$56 – \$24, or \$32. Now we could set up the following equation, using x to represent the cost per skein of yarn:

$2x \quad + \quad 5x \quad + \quad -3x \quad = \$32$

Notice that we represented the costs we returned as *negative* costs — they're the *opposite of costs* we incurred. Let's take a look at how to combine like terms when negative coefficients are involved.

Whether negative or positive, we can still combine like terms. Just as $2 + 5 + -3$ equals 4, $2x + 5x + -3x$ equals $4x$. **When combining like terms, we add the coefficients.** This applies whether the coefficients are positive or negative.

Example: $2x + 5x + -3x = \$32$

Combine like terms:

$\mathbf{4x} = \$32$

Divide both sides by 4:

$$\frac{4x}{\mathbf{4}} = \frac{\$32}{\mathbf{4}}$$

$$\frac{\cancel{4}x}{\cancel{4}} = \frac{\cancel{\$32}^{\,8}}{\cancel{4}}$$

$$\mathbf{x = \$8}$$

If we substitute \$8 for x in the original equation, we'll find that \$8 is indeed the value for x that makes the equation hold true.

$2(\mathbf{\$8}) + 5(\mathbf{\$8}) + -3(\mathbf{\$8}) = \$32$

$\mathbf{\$16 + \$40 + -\$24} = \$32$

$\mathbf{\$32} = \$32$

Let's make the situation a tad more complicated. Let's say that in addition to buying the 2 skeins of yarn, then the 5 skeins, and then returning 3 of those skeins, in the middle of our shopping (before we made the return but after we made all the purchases) we also had a flat yearly membership fee of $20 to a knitting club. We spent a total of $52 ($52 is $32 plus the $20 membership fee) on all the yarn and membership fee combined.

We'd now have this problem:

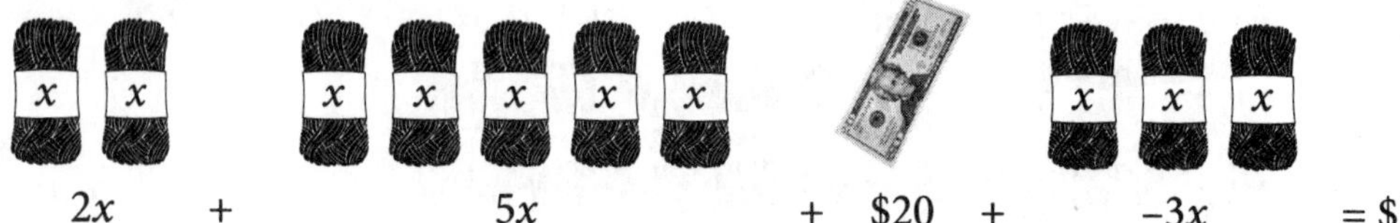

$2x$ + $5x$ + \$20 + $-3x$ = \$52

This is the same problem as before, except we have one more step involved.

Example: $2x + 5x + \$20 - 3x = \$52$

Combine like terms:

$\mathbf{4x} + \$20 = \$52$

Add –\$20 to both sides:

$4x + \$20 + \mathbf{-\$20} = \$52 + \mathbf{-\$20}$

$4x = \mathbf{\$32}$

Divide both sides by 4:

$\frac{4x}{\mathbf{4}} = \frac{\$32}{\mathbf{4}}$

$\frac{\cancel{4}x}{\cancel{4}} = \frac{\$\cancel{32}^{8}}{\cancel{4}}$

$\mathbf{x = \$8}$

Let's look at another problem involving different yarn. Suppose this time we purchase 5 skeins of yarn, and then later return 1 of those skeins. In the end, we spent $24. How much did each skein cost?

$5x$ − x = \$24

How do we simplify $5x - x$ so we can solve for x? Well, remember that subtracting x can be thought of as *adding* $-x$ . . . and $-x$ can be thought of as $-1x$. So we can still combine the like terms and solve just as we have been.

> Remember, we can multiply any number by 1 without changing the value. Thus, $-x$ equals $-1x$. In fact, many find it useful to think of $-x$ as -1 times x, or $(-1)x$.

Example: $5x - x = \$24$

View $-x$ as $+ -1x$:

$5x + \mathbf{-1}x = \$24$

Combine like terms:

$\mathbf{4x} = \$24$

Divide both sides by 4:

$$\frac{4x}{\mathbf{4}} = \frac{\$24}{\mathbf{4}}$$

$$\frac{\cancel{4}x}{\cancel{4}} = \frac{\cancel{\$24}^{6}}{\cancel{4}}$$

$\boldsymbol{x = \$6}$

Keeping Perspective

Whether representing a return, miles traveled in a different direction, money owed, acceleration in a negative direction, or something else altogether, negative signs help us describe and solve real-life situations. The purpose of becoming familiar with them is so that they don't trip us up when we encounter them.

Remember that the whole reason we're even able to use math outside a textbook is because God gave us that ability. He created us able to think, reason, and in a very limited way, "think His thoughts after Him" (Johannes Kepler). Negative numbers are part of the arsenal of tools we use to help us describe His creation. They allow us to express the pull of gravity on earth (we describe it as a *negative* force to differentiate it from forces pushing upward toward space), the flow of electricity in one direction (to differentiate it from electricity flowing in the opposite direction), money that is owed (to differentiate it from money we have earned), and so much more.

8.4 Surprised by Negatives

As you advance into problems with more steps, you'll often encounter negative signs in problems that don't appear to have anything to do with negative numbers. For example, let's say we have \$10 when we head to the store and \$8 when we come home. How much did we spend?

We could express this using an unknown to stand for what we spent:

$$10 - x = 8$$

Now, it's obvious that x must equal 2 (10 minus 2 equals 8), but what if this problem had been more involved? How would we have solved it? Let's take a look at how to solve problems like this mathematically so we'll be able to solve more complicated problems when we encounter them.

Example: $10 - x = 8$

We'll start by adding –10 to both sides.

$$10 - x = 8$$

$$10 + \mathbf{-10} - x = 8 + \mathbf{-10}$$

$$\mathbf{-x = -2}$$

Yikes! What do we do? We now know what *the opposite of* x equals, but what does x equal?

We can find the value for x a couple of different ways. We could add x to both sides of the equation, and then add 2 to both sides of the equation.

Add x to both sides:

$$-x + \mathbf{x} = -2 + \mathbf{x}$$

$$\mathbf{0} = -2 + x$$

Add 2 to both sides:

$$0 + \mathbf{2} = -2 + x + \mathbf{2}$$

$$\mathbf{2 = x}$$

We added parentheses around –x and –2 to make it clear that we're multiplying the *entire side* by –1. Parentheses are often helpful when dealing with negative numbers to avoid any confusion regarding the negative signs.

There's a faster way, though. Look again at the equation we had after adding –10 to both sides:

$$-x = -2$$

We could have multiplied both sides of this equation by –1. (Remember, we can multiply *both sides* of an equation by the same quantity and the sides will remain equal.)

$$(\mathbf{-1})(-x) = (-2)(\mathbf{-1})$$

Now, let's simplify this. We know that (–2)(–1) equals 2. But what about (–1)(–x)? Well, remember that when there are two negative signs in a multiplication, the negative signs cancel out, as we're taking the opposite of the opposite, which is a positive. So even though we don't know x's value, we know that the opposite of it times the opposite of 1 will equal $1x$, as the negative signs will cancel out in the multiplication.

$\mathbf{1x} = 2$, which simplifies to $\mathbf{x} = 2$

Notice that if we substitute 2 for x in the original equation, the equation holds true.

$$10 - x = 8$$

$$10 - \mathbf{2} = 8$$

This is true. We did the math correctly.

Let's look at another example.

Example: $10 - x = 20$

Let's start by adding –10 to both sides.

$10 + \mathbf{-10} - x = 20 + \mathbf{-10}$

$-x = 10$

Now let's multiply both sides by –1.

$(\mathbf{-1})(-x) = 10(\mathbf{-1})$

In $(-1)(-x)$, we again have two negative signs, so the negative signs cancel each other out, as the opposite of the opposite is a positive. $(-1)(-x)$ equals $1x$.

$\mathbf{1x = -10}$, which simplifies to $\mathbf{x = -10}$

Multiplying by –1

Another way to look at multiplying $(-1)(-x)$ is to think of the $-x$ as $(-1)(x)$.

$(-1)(-x)$ *becomes* $(-1)(-1)(x)$

We then complete the multiplication of the –1s, leaving us with $(1)(x)$.

$(-1)(\mathbf{-1})(x)$ becomes $(\mathbf{1})(x)$, or more simply, x

Keeping Perspective

In the problem we looked at today, we had negative numbers ($-x$, –2, and –1) temporarily. While the original problem didn't appear to have anything to do with negative numbers, we had to know how to deal with negative numbers in order to find the value of x.

Since negative numbers have a way of showing up when trying to solve a problem, it's important to be comfortable with them. Again, they're tools to help us describe God's creation . . . sometimes in ways you'd least expect!

Once again, we're combining tools to help us solve more and more complicated situations. You'll see over and over again throughout math that we keep revisiting the same principles over and over again, applying them to additional situations.

8.5 When the Unknown Is on Both Sides of the Equation

Up until now, the unknown we've been trying to find has been on one side of the equation, but sometimes we will have the same unknown on *both* sides of the equation.

For example, let's say that you want to find the amount of money someone made before a \$200 a week raise they received. You also know that after the raise, they make 3 times what they made before (it was a good raise!). Using x to represent the amount they made before the raise, you'd have this relationship:

$$x + \$200 = 3x$$

How do you solve this? Well, it's not as hard as you might think. If we add $-x$ to *both sides* of this equation, we'll have rearranged it so the unknown is only on one side.

$$x + \mathbf{-x} + \$200 = 3x + \mathbf{-x}$$
$$\mathbf{\$200 = 2x}$$

Important! Even though we don't know the value of x, when we add $-x$ to *both* sides of the equation, we know we're adding the *same quantity* to both sides of the equation. Thus the equation will stay in balance.

Now we can divide to solve for x.

$$\frac{\$200}{2} = \frac{2x}{2}$$

$$\frac{\overset{\$100}{\cancel{\$200}}}{\cancel{2}} = \frac{\cancel{2}x}{\cancel{2}}$$

$$\mathbf{\$100 = x}$$

The employee made \$100 a week before the raise.

Let's check our math by substituting \$100 for x in the original equation.

$$x + \$200 = 3x$$
$$\mathbf{\$100} + \$200 = 3(\mathbf{\$100})$$
$$\mathbf{\$300 = \$300}$$

The math checks out.

Keeping Perspective

Don't let a problem that looks slightly different than what you've seen before confuse you. Break the problem down into steps, simplifying each side as you go and applying the tools you've learned in combination.

Learning to solve problems is a lot like learning to read. Just as in reading you first had to learn the different letter combinations used to describe sounds, so in math you first have to learn the symbols and conventions used to describe mathematical relationships. Just as reading becomes easier and easier as you practice sounding out words, so reading the language of mathematics becomes easier and easier as you practice solving problems.

8.6 Chapter Synopsis

While we didn't cover anything new in this chapter, we applied what we already knew to negative numbers, making sure we were equipped to simplify expressions involving negative unknowns as well as expressions with positive unknowns. We saw that the *same principles* apply to negative unknowns as positive unknowns. The key principle to remember when working with negative numbers is that a negative sign means *the opposite of.*

As you continue to study math, you'll find yourself continuing to expand on and build on the basics you already know. If you find yourself wondering why we need so many different techniques, know that it's because we live in an amazing, complex universe. Each technique helps us describe an aspect of God's incredible creation.

Yet all of math rests on the same basic principles — which all ultimately rest on God's faithfulness in holding all things together.

[CHAPTER 9]

Parentheses, the Distributive Property, and Unknowns

9.1 Parentheses and Nested Parentheses

Back in Lesson 1.2, we reviewed the order of operations, an agreed-upon convention that tells us the order in which the operations in an expression should be completed when simplifying the expression. This order tells us to solve parentheses, or grouped numbers, first, then exponents and roots, then multiplication and division, and then addition and subtraction. By having an agreed-upon order, it's clear what an expression means.

Example: Simplify $\frac{5}{9}(20 - 32)$

Solve within the parentheses first:

$\frac{5}{9}(-12)$

Multiply $\frac{5}{9}$ by -12 and simplify:

$-\frac{60}{9}$

$-\frac{20}{3}$

$-6\frac{2}{3}$

We're going to take this chapter to take a closer look at problems containing parentheses. Along the way, we'll review the distributive property and apply it to help us solve problems containing both parentheses and an unknown.

Let's start our explorations by looking at how parentheses can help us describe converting temperature from Fahrenheit to Celsius.

Parentheses and Temperature Conversions

The conversion between Fahrenheit and Celsius isn't as straightforward as other conversions. To convert Fahrenheit to Celsius, we have to subtract 32 degrees and then multiply that result by $\frac{5}{9}$.

Example: Convert 70 degrees Fahrenheit to degrees Celsius.

Subtract 32°:

$70° - 32° = 38°$

Multiply the result by $\frac{5}{9}$:

$$38° \bullet \frac{5}{9} = \frac{190°}{9} = 21.11°$$

70 degrees Fahrenheit is 21.11 degrees Celsius.

Now, we could have used parentheses to express this problem more concisely.

We can represent that we need to subtract 32° from 70° and *then* multiply the difference by $\frac{5}{9}$ like this:

$$\frac{5}{9}(70° - 32°)$$

Notice that we used the parentheses to group together the operation that needed to be completed first, thereby writing the entire process in one expression rather than as two separate expressions.

Example: Convert 70 degrees Fahrenheit to degrees Celsius.

$\frac{5}{9}(70° - 32°)$

Solve within the parentheses:

$\frac{5}{9}(\mathbf{38°})$

Complete the multiplication:

$\mathbf{\frac{190}{9}}$

Convert to a decimal:

21.11°

In fact, we could go one step further and use parentheses to help us write a formula for converting between Fahrenheit and Celsius.

Formula for Converting Between Fahrenheit and Celsius:

$$C = \frac{5}{9}(F - 32°)$$

where C = degrees in Celsius and F = degrees in Fahrenheit

Nested Parentheses

So far, we've limited our use of parentheses to a single pair of parentheses. But as you continue to study God's creation in greater detail, you'll find yourself needing additional groupings at times. For example, suppose that, per person, it costs $2 (shoe rental) plus $4 (bowling cost) to bowl. If there are 5 people in a family and the family wants to budget enough money for all 5 people to bowl 7 times a year, how much should they budget?

Here, we need to add the $2 and $4 to find the cost per person, *then* multiply that by 5 people to find the cost for the entire family each time they bowl, and *then* multiply that by the number of times they want to budget for per year (7).

Rather than writing one expression for the addition, another for the first multiplication, and another for the final multiplication, we can show the entire problem as one expression by using **nested parentheses** — that is, parentheses within parentheses.

7(5($2 + $4))

Because it gets hard to read nested parentheses, brackets [ ] are often used instead of parentheses for the outer grouping when there's an inner pair of parentheses. Below is another way of writing 7(5($2 + $4)).

7[5($2 + $4)]

Whether written with brackets or two sets of parentheses, we can simplify nested groupings the same way. We need to **start with the innermost grouping and work our way out.**

Example: 7[5($2 + $4)]

Step 1: Solve the innermost grouping.

7[5(**$2 + $4**)]

7[5(**$6**)]

We've now found the cost per person to bowl: $6.

Step 2: Solve the next grouping.

7[**$30**]

We've now found the cost for the entire family to bowl each time they go: $30.

Step 3: Complete the final multiplication.

$210

We've now found the cost for the entire family to bowl 7 times a year: $210.

The family should budget $210.

Think carefully about the example we just solved. Calculating how much it would cost for the entire family to bowl is the type of problem you've been solving since elementary school. Only in elementary school, you would have solved this type of problem as three separate problems, like this:

cost per person to bowl = \$2 + \$4 = \$6

cost for the entire family of 5 to bowl each time they go = 5 • \$6 = \$30

cost for the entire family to bowl 7 times = 7 • \$30 = \$210

Using nested parentheses, we expressed all of these steps as one problem:

cost for the entire family to bowl 7 times = 7[5(\$2 + \$4)]

Keeping Perspective

Parentheses are part of the language side of mathematics. We use them to group operations that need to be performed before others.

As we mentioned back in Lesson 1.2, other methods have also been used to indicate groupings instead of parentheses. Two different historical ways of writing (4 + 5)3 are shown here.[1]

$$\overline{4+5} \bullet 3 \qquad 4+5,\, 3$$

While the quantities and consistencies God created and sustains remain constant, the symbols we use to describe them can and do vary. God gave man the ability to think creatively and adopt different methods for describing His creation.

As you study the language side of mathematics, remember that you are trying to learn a language to help you clearly describe the quantities and consistencies God created and sustains.

9.2 Parentheses, the Distributive Property, and Unknowns

We saw in the last lesson that parentheses help us group numbers on which operations need to be completed first.

We looked at the formula for converting between Fahrenheit and Celsius:

$$C = \frac{5}{9}(F - 32°)$$

In the last lesson, we only used the formula to convert from Fahrenheit to Celsius. Thus, we always knew what F in the formula represented. But what if we want to convert a temperature in Celsius to Fahrenheit? Could we use the formula to find F if we know C?

For example, if we know it's 20 degrees Celsius, can we find the degrees Fahrenheit?

$$20° = \frac{5}{9}(F - 32°)$$

Yes, we can find the value of F the same way we would the value of other unknowns — by isolating it on a side of the equation by itself. But how do we do that? After all, we have to subtract 32° from F . . . but we don't know F's value!

It's time to review the distributive property and look at how it can help us solve problems like this one.

Applying the Distributive Property

Distributive Property Review

The distributive property is a name to describe the fact that if you distribute multiplication among addends and then add those results together, you'll get the same result as if you first did the addition and then multiplied the sum.

Example: Find 2(3 + 4)

With distribution:	Adding first:
2(3 + 4)	2(3 + 4)
2(**3**) + 2(**4**)	2(7) = 14
6 + **8** = 14	

No matter whether we distribute the multiplication among addends or add the addends together first, the answer is the same.

Why? Because of the consistent way addition and multiplication work. The distributive property expresses a reality about the consistency of addition and multiplication God holds in place. The distributive property ultimately works because of God's faithfulness in holding all things together consistently.

Okay . . . so how does the distributive property help us find unknowns? Let's take a closer look. We'll do so with a simple percent example, and then return to temperature.

Example: Suppose your purchase totaled \$50. You know you bought two items, one of which cost \$30 before tax. You don't remember the cost of the other item, but you know you were charged 6% tax on both items. How much was the other item?

> Multiplying by 1.06 is the same as finding 100% plus the 6% tax, as 100% + 6% = 106%, or 1.06. See Lesson 9.4 of Book 1 for details.

Let's write this problem out, using x to stand for the item of which we want to find the price.

$$1.06(\$30) + 1.06(x) = \$50 \quad or \quad 1.06(\$30 + x) = \$50$$

In the equation on the left, we're multiplying each item by 1.06 to find its total with tax, and *then* adding them together to find the total.

In the equation on the right, we're adding the items we purchase and then multiplying their total to find the total with tax.

Both equations are two different ways of thinking about the problem. Let's take a closer look, though, at how to solve $1.06(\$30 + x) = \$50$, as you need to know how to handle problems written this way. While there's an unknown inside the parentheses, we can use the distributive property to help us solve this.

Distribute the multiplication:

$$1.06(\$30 + x) = \$50$$

$$1.06(\mathbf{\$30}) + 1.06(\boldsymbol{x}) = \$50$$

Notice that now we are multiplying each of the items by 1.06 to find its total with tax rather than adding them together first. In other words, we arrived at the other approach to the problem we mentioned up front!

Simplify:

$$\mathbf{\$31.80} + \mathbf{1.06}\boldsymbol{x} = \$50$$

Now we can solve to find x by isolating it on one side of the equation.

Add –\$31.80 to both sides:

$$\$31.80 + \mathbf{-\$31.80} + 1.06x = \$50 + \mathbf{-\$31.80}$$

$$\mathbf{1.06}\boldsymbol{x} = \mathbf{\$18.20}$$

Divide both sides by 1.06:

$$\frac{1.06x}{\mathbf{1.06}} = \frac{\$18.20}{\mathbf{1.06}}$$

$$\frac{\cancel{1.06}x}{\cancel{1.06}} = \frac{\$18.20}{1.06}$$

$$\boldsymbol{x} = \mathbf{\$17.17}$$

Notice that if we substitute \$17.17 into the original equation, we find that the math checks out.

Technically, we get \$50.0002 when we use a value of \$17.17 for x. The difference is due to rounding (\$17.17 is a rounded answer).

$$1.06(\$30 + x) = \$50$$

$$1.06(\$30 + \mathbf{\$17.17}) = \$50$$

$$1.06(\mathbf{\$47.17}) = \$50$$

$$\mathbf{\$50} = \$50$$

Distributing the multiplication enabled us to solve a problem we otherwise couldn't have.

Let's take a look at applying this property when we have *subtraction* inside the parentheses, such as in $4(2 - x) = 10$.

The distributive property only works on *addends* that make up a sum. Remember, though, that we can **view subtraction as an addition of a negative number.** For example, we can view $4(2 - x) = 10$ as $4(2 + -x) = 10$. We can now use the distributive property to find the unknown!

Distribute the multiplication and simplify:

$$4(2 + -x) = 10$$

$$4(\mathbf{2}) + 4(\mathbf{-x}) = 10$$

$$\mathbf{8 + -4x} = 10$$

Notice that we simplified 4(−x) to −4x. Remember, we can think of −x as (−1)x. So we can think of 4(−x) as 4(−1)(x), which we can simplify to −4x.

Add −8 to both sides:

$$8 + -4x + \mathbf{-8} = 10 + \mathbf{-8}$$

$$-4x = 2$$

Divide both sides by −4:

$$\frac{-4x}{\mathbf{-4}} = \frac{2}{\mathbf{-4}}$$

$$\frac{\not{-}4x}{\not{-}4} = \frac{2}{-4}$$

$$x = -\frac{2}{4}\text{, which simplifies to } -\frac{1}{2}$$

We often view subtraction as an addition of a negative number without writing out the + sign. The key is to view the negative sign as part of the number that follows it.

Example: Suppose that you know you left the store having spent a total of \$20. You purchased a \$33 item and returned an item, but you can't remember the price of the returned item. You also know you were charged 6% tax on the purchase, and credited 6% on the return.

Using x to stand for the returned item, we could represent this mathematically like this:

$$1.06(\$33 - x) = \$20$$

Think of the parentheses as (\$33 + $-x$) and distribute the multiplication:

$$1.06(\$33 + \mathbf{-x}) = \$20$$

$$1.06(\$33 + -x) = \$20$$

$$1.06(\mathbf{\$33}) + 1.06(\mathbf{-x}) = \$20$$

Simplify:

$$\mathbf{\$34.98 + -1.06x} = \$20$$

Add −\$34.98 to both sides:

$$\$34.98 + \mathbf{-\$34.98} + -1.06x = \$20 + \mathbf{-\$34.98}$$

$$\mathbf{-1.06x = -\$14.98}$$

Again, we could also have written this problem as 1.06(\$33) + 1.06(−x) = \$20. After all, we could find the cost with tax of each item and then add them together instead of adding them together and then finding the tax. Notice that when we distribute the multiplication, we end up with this equation.

Divide both sides by –1.06:

$$\frac{-1.06x}{\mathbf{-1.06}} = \frac{-\$14.98}{\mathbf{-1.06}}$$

$$\frac{\cancel{-1.06}x}{\cancel{-1.06}} = \frac{-\$14.98}{-1.06}$$

$$\mathbf{x = \$14.13}$$

Again, if we substituted \$14.13 into the original equation for *x*, we can verify that we've successfully found the value for *x*.

Technically, we get \$20.0022 when we use a value of \$14.13 for x. The difference is due to the rounding we did when solving the problem.

$$1.06(\$33 - x) = \$20$$

$$1.06(\$33 - \mathbf{\$14.13}) = \$20$$

$$1.06(\mathbf{\$18.87}) = \$20$$

$$\mathbf{\$20} = \$20$$

\$20 dollars does equal \$20. We found the correct value for *x*.

Distributive Property and the Temperature Formula

Now that we have reviewed the distributive property and used it to find the unknown in a couple of everyday examples, it's time to return to the temperature problem we began the chapter with: converting 20 degrees Celsius to Fahrenheit. Now we can easily solve this using the distributive property.

Example: Convert 20 °*C* to °*F*.

Formula for converting between Celcius and Fahrenheit:

$$C = \frac{5}{9}(F - 32°)$$

Substitute known values:

$$\mathbf{20°} = \frac{5}{9}(F - 32°)$$

Distribute the multiplication, being careful to view –32° as a negative number:

$$20° = \frac{5}{9}(F + -32°)$$

$$20° = \frac{5}{9}(F + -32°)$$

$$20° = \frac{5}{9}\mathbf{(F)} + \frac{5}{9}\mathbf{(-32°)}$$

Simplify:

$$20° = \frac{5}{9}\mathbf{F} + -\frac{\mathbf{160°}}{\mathbf{9}}$$

Add $\frac{160°}{9}$ to both sides of the equation:

$$20° + \frac{\mathbf{160°}}{\mathbf{9}} = \frac{5}{9}F + -\frac{160°}{9} + \frac{\mathbf{160°}}{\mathbf{9}}$$

$$\frac{\mathbf{340°}}{\mathbf{9}} = \frac{5}{9}F$$

Divide both sides by $\frac{5}{9}$, which we do by multiplying by $\frac{9}{5}$:

$$\frac{340°}{9} \bullet \frac{\mathbf{9}}{\mathbf{5}} = \frac{5}{9}F \bullet \frac{\mathbf{9}}{\mathbf{5}}$$

$$\frac{\overset{68}{\cancel{340}}°}{\cancel{9}} \bullet \frac{\cancel{9}}{\cancel{5}} = \frac{\cancel{5}}{\cancel{9}}F \bullet \frac{\cancel{9}}{\cancel{5}}$$

$$\mathbf{68° = F}$$

20° Celsius equals 68° Fahrenheit.

We could check the answer by substituting 68° for F in the original equation:

$$20° = \frac{5}{9}(\mathbf{68°} - 32°)$$

$$20° = \frac{5}{9}(\mathbf{36°})$$

$$20° = \mathbf{20°}$$

Now I know this example may look hard, but each step is not hard. Complicated-looking problems are simple when you take them step by step.

Keeping Perspective

Notice that once again, we're just applying the *same principles* we learned in basic math to help us work with unknown as well as known numbers. We didn't cover anything *new* today — rather, we explored how to apply what we had already been doing with known numbers to unknowns.

As you use the distributive property with unknowns, remember that the distributive property merely describes a consistency that holds true with multiplication. And why does it hold true? Because of the consistent way God governs this universe!

9.3 Positive Signs, Parentheses, and the Distributive Property

As we've seen, parentheses are a useful grouping tool. In the last lesson, we used the distributive property to help us remove parentheses when an unknown was inside of them. In this lesson, we're going to continue looking at parentheses, the distributive property, and unknowns, focusing on problems in which a parenthesis is directly preceded by a positive sign.

For example, let's suppose that you want to find the total you spent over two days. Your total will equal the sum of the total you spent each day.

total spent day 1 + total spent day 2 = total for both days

Let's say your total the first day was \$5, and the second day you spent \$4 and \$36. You'd have this equation:

$$\$5 + (\$4 + \$36) = \textit{total for both days}$$

Notice that we put the \$4 and \$36 inside of parentheses, as the relationship said to add the *total* for each day together. Now, while in this case we could simply complete all the addition and solve the problem, what would we do if the parentheses contained an unknown — if we didn't remember the amount of the \$36 purchase, for instance, but knew the total purchases for both days was \$45?

$$\$5 + (\$4 + x) = \$45$$

Notice that we now have an unknown *inside* the parentheses. How can we solve this? There doesn't appear to be anything to distribute.

Well, we know from the identity property of multiplication that multiplying by 1 doesn't change the value of a quantity. **So we could multiply the parentheses by 1 and distribute the 1 without changing the value.**

Multiply the parentheses by 1:

$$\$5 + 1(\$4 + x) = \$45$$

We can now distribute the 1 the same way we distributed other quantities in the last lesson!

Distribute the multiplication by 1 and simplify:

$$\$5 + 1(\$4 + x) = \$45$$
$$\$5 + 1(\mathbf{\$4}) + 1(\boldsymbol{x}) = \$45$$
$$\$5 + \mathbf{\$4} + \boldsymbol{x} = \$45$$

We were able to remove the parentheses by multiplying the parentheses by 1. However, we didn't need to write out the distribution. Notice that we would have arrive at $\$5 + \$4 + x = \$45$ by simply removing the parentheses.

Removing the parentheses from

$$\$5 + (\$4 + x) = \$45$$

gives us

$$\$5 + \$4 + x = \$45$$

When a set of parentheses is preceded by a + sign, multiply the values inside the parentheses by 1 and distribute the 1. You can do this by simply removing the parentheses. After all, multiplying by positive 1 doesn't change the value, so distributing a positive 1 isn't going to change the value.

Once the parentheses have been removed, we can easily solve to find x.

Simplify:

$$\$5 + \$4 + x = \$45$$

$$\mathbf{\$9} + x = \$45$$

Add –$9 to both sides of the equation:

$$\$9 + x + \mathbf{-\$9} = \$45 + \mathbf{-\$9}$$

$$x = \mathbf{\$36}$$

Keeping Perspective

While today's lesson may have felt a little obvious, sometimes it's worth stating the obvious. It's important to understand that parentheses are a grouping symbol that tells us to solve whatever is inside the parentheses first. We can only remove parentheses after we've performed the operations inside them *or* if we know that removing the parentheses will preserve the same meaning (such as if we're able to distribute the multiplication).

9.4 Parentheses in Action

We've been spending a lot of time lately looking at the mechanics of simplifying expressions involving unknowns. It's time to take a break from the mechanics to remind ourselves why we're learning these simplification techniques: so we can solve real-life problems.

In fact, we're going to take the entire lesson to walk through one problem. While this problem is more in-depth than any of the ones we've looked at so far, it's a good illustration of the type of real-life problems you'll be able to solve once you get familiar with the mechanics we've been exploring.

Example: At a local election there were only 2 candidates, and 1,280 votes were cast. The winning candidate won by only 40 votes. How many votes were cast for each candidate?

It might initially look as if we don't have enough information to answer the question. After all, we don't know the total votes cast for *either* candidate. We have *two unknowns* right now — the votes cast for the loser and the votes cast for the winner.

All we know is that the sum of the votes equals 1,280, and that the votes for the winner equal 40 more than the votes for the loser.

1,280 = *votes for the loser* + *votes for the winner*

votes for the winner = *votes for the loser* + 40

If we use x to stand for the votes for the loser, we could describe the votes for the winner as $x + 40$. This would give us the following:

This problem is adapted from a math book[2] from the early 1900s.

votes for the loser = x

votes for the winner = $x + 40$

We know the total votes cast here were 1,280. Since there were only 2 candidates, the votes for the loser plus the votes for the winner must equal 1,280.

1,280 = *votes for the loser* + *votes for the winner*

$1{,}280 = \mathbf{x + (x + 40)}$

Do you see what we just did? **We found a way to express the problem using only one unknown.**

Notice we put parentheses around $(x + 40)$. Why? Because we know that *the sum of* $x + 40$ represents the votes for the winner. So when we substitute $x + 40$ for the votes for the winner, we used parentheses to show that we were replacing the votes for the winner with the *sum of* $x + 40$.

Let's solve $1{,}280 = x + (x + 40)$ to find x.

Remove the parentheses:

$1{,}280 = x + (x + 40)$

$1{,}280 = x + \mathbf{x + 40}$

Note: We removed the parentheses because we knew that we could multiply the parentheses by 1, distribute that 1, and the values would be the same, as multiplying by 1 doesn't affect the values of anything inside the parentheses. We didn't bother to write out the steps, since multiplying by 1 doesn't affect the values.

Combine like terms:

$1{,}280 = \mathbf{2x} + 40$

Subtract 40 from both sides:

$1{,}280 - \mathbf{40} = 2x + 40 - \mathbf{40}$

$1{,}240 = 2x$

Divide both sides by 2 to find x:

$\frac{1{,}240}{\mathbf{2}} = \frac{2x}{\mathbf{2}}$

$\frac{{}^{620}\cancel{1{,}240}}{\cancel{2}} = \frac{\cancel{2}x}{\cancel{2}}$

$\mathbf{620 = x}$

Now remember, x represented the votes for the loser. So now we can find the vote for the winner by simply substituting the value we found!

votes for the winner = $x + 40$

Now that we know $x = 620$, this would mean:

votes for the winner = $\mathbf{620} + 40$

votes for the winner = $\mathbf{660}$

We'll check our math by substituting values back into the original relationships:

votes for winner = *votes for the loser* + 40

660 = **620** + 40

660 = **660**

total votes = *votes for the loser* + *votes for the winner*

1,280 = **620 + 660**

1,280 = **1,280**

We just solved a problem that had *two* missing pieces of information. By looking at how those pieces *related to each other*, we were able to find one missing piece and then use it to find the other.

There's More Than One Way to Peel an Onion (or Solve a Problem)

In the example we just explored we could have used x to represent votes for the winner rather than the votes for the loser.

If so, we would show the relationship this way:

votes for the winner = x
votes for the loser = x – 40
Total = *votes for loser* + *votes for winner*
1,280 = (x – 40) + x

If we complete this problem, we'll come out with the same values for the winner and loser we did before. Only this time, x will represent the winner.

1,280 = **2x** – 40

Add 40 to both sides:

1,280 **+ 40** = 2x – 40 **+ 40**

1,320 = 2x

Divide both sides by 2 to find x:

$$\frac{1{,}320}{\mathbf{2}} = \frac{2x}{\mathbf{2}}$$

$$\frac{{}^{660}\cancel{1{,}320}}{\cancel{2}} = \frac{\cancel{2}x}{\cancel{2}}$$

660 = x

Since we used x to represent the votes for the *winner*, we need to substitute to find the votes for the *loser*.

votes for loser = x – 40
votes for loser = **660** – 40
votes for loser = **620**

We arrived at the same answers as before: 660 votes for the winner and 620 votes for the loser. It doesn't matter which unknown you solve for, so long as you keep the relationships accurate and are consistent in your use of the unknown.

Keeping Perspective

While you won't be required to solve problems with two unknowns without lots of hints right now, I hope the example we looked at gave you a glimpse of how the skills you're learning can be used. Remember, math isn't a bunch of meaningless rules or numbers. It's a way of describing real-life consistencies God created and sustains. As such, it applies outside of a textbook! You can use the skills you're learning in math to help you in whatever occupation or sphere of influence to which God calls you.

9.5 Parentheses, the Distributive Property, Unknowns, and Negative Numbers

Because grouping numbers is so very helpful, especially as equations get more and more in-depth, we need to take one more lesson to look at applying the distributive property to help us deal with parentheses containing unknowns. Specifically, we're going to take a look at situations involving negative numbers. Once again, we'll be applying what we already know to help us in new situations.

Parentheses Preceded by a Negative Number

Distributive Property and Negative Numbers

In order to properly distribute the multiplication when the multiplier is preceded by a negative sign, **view the multiplier as a negative number.**

Example: Find 5 – 2(3+4)

With distribution:	Adding first:
$5 + -2(3 + 4)$	$5 - 2(3 + 4)$
$5 + -2(\mathbf{3}) + -2(\mathbf{4})$	$5 - 2(\mathbf{7})$
$5 + \mathbf{-6} + \mathbf{-8} = \mathbf{-9}$	$5 - \mathbf{14} = \mathbf{-9}$

Viewing a multiplier preceded by a negative sign as a negative number preserves the intended meaning. For example, the expression 5 – 2(3 + 4) means to subtract 2 times the total inside the parentheses from 5. If we don't distribute the negative sign,[3] we'll end up only subtracting *part* of the total, which gives us an *incorrect* answer.

Notice how in the example below, instead of subtracting 6 and 8, we end up subtracting 6 and *adding* 8, thus getting an incorrect answer.

Incorrect:

$5 - 2(3 + 4)$

$5 - 2(3) + 2(4)$

$5 - \mathbf{6} + \mathbf{8} = 6$

I can't say it enough times: **train yourself to look at subtraction as the addition of negative numbers.**

Let's apply the distributive property to unknowns. Say someone earned \$200, and then bought 2 DVDs at \$14 each plus 2 shirts, the price of which he can't remember. He now has \$100 left of the money he earned. How much did he spend on each shirt?

Let's write this out, using x to stand for the price of each shirt:

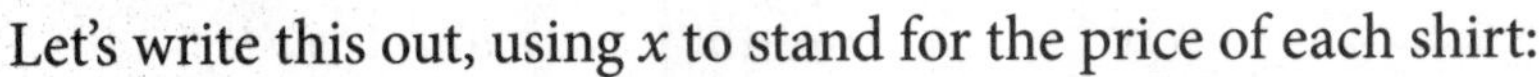

$$\$200 - 2(\$14) - 2x = \$100 \quad \textit{or} \quad \$200 - 2(\$14 + x) = \$100$$

In the equation on the left, we're subtracting the costs of the 2 DVDs and the 2 shirts separately. In the equation on the right, we're adding the cost of each DVD and shirt together, multiplying it by 2, and then subtracting that product from \$200. Both are different ways of approaching the same problem.

Let's take a closer look at how to solve $\$200 - 2(\$14 + x) = \$100$, as you need to know how to handle problems written this way. Notice there's an unknown inside the parentheses, so we *can't* simply complete the addition and then multiply. We can, however, distribute the multiplication.

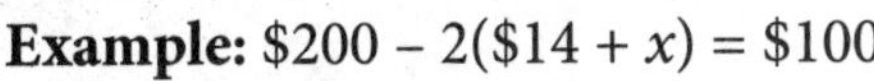

Example: $\$200 - 2(\$14 + x) = \$100$

Distribute –2:

$$\$200 - 2(\$14 + x) = \$100$$

$$\$200 + \mathbf{-2(\$14)} + \mathbf{-2(x)} = \$100$$

Notice that we are now subtracting the costs of the DVDs and the shirts separately, rather than adding them together first. In other words, we arrived at the other approach to the problem we mentioned up front.

Simplify:

$$\$200 + \mathbf{-\$28} + \mathbf{-2x} = \$100$$

$$\mathbf{\$172} + -2x = \$100$$

Add –\$172 to both sides of the equation:

$$\$172 + \mathbf{-\$172} + -2x = \$100 + \mathbf{-\$172}$$

$$\mathbf{-2x = -\$72}$$

Divide both sides of the equation by –2:

$$\frac{-2x}{\mathbf{-2}} = \frac{-\$72}{\mathbf{-2}}$$

$$\frac{\cancel{-2}x}{\cancel{-2}} = \frac{\cancel{-\$72}^{\$36}}{\cancel{-2}}$$

$$\mathbf{x = \$36}$$

Each shirt cost \$36.

We can check the answer by substituting \$36 for x in the original equation:

$$\$200 - 2(\$14 + \mathbf{\$36}) = \$100$$

$$\$200 - 2(\mathbf{\$50}) = \$100$$

$$\$200 - \mathbf{\$100} = \$100$$

$$\mathbf{\$100} = \$100$$

Parentheses Preceded by a Negative Sign

Sometimes, all we may have in front of a set of parentheses is a negative sign.

For example, suppose we knew that a game of bowling cost \$2 in shoe rental, but we couldn't remember the cost per game. We knew we'd started with \$8 in our wallet, and ended with \$3 after renting shoes and playing one game of bowling. We'd have this problem:

$$\$8 - (\$2 + x) = \$3$$

Notice that we've used parentheses to group the total costs of the shoe rental and the cost per game (x). We want to subtract the total cost from \$8, as \$8 minus the total we spent will equal the \$3 left in our wallet.

But how can we solve this since we don't know the cost per game (x)?

Let's take a look.

Example: $\$8 - (\$2 + x) = \$3$

As we've seen, multiplying by 1 doesn't change the value of a number (the identity property of multiplication). So let's multiply the values inside the parentheses by 1.

$$\$8 - 1(\$2 + x) = \$3$$

Now we have an equation we know how to solve! We can distribute the -1, just as we did the -2 in the previous section.

To clarify, we'll add a plus sign before the -1, as we have to be sure to view the -1 as a negative number in order to properly distribute the multiplication.

$$8 + \mathbf{-1}(2 + x) = 3$$

Distribute -1 and simplify:

$$8 + (-1)(2 + x) = 3$$

$$\$8 + \mathbf{-1(\$2)} + \mathbf{-1(x)} = \$3$$

$$\$8 + \mathbf{-\$2} + \mathbf{-x} = \$3$$

$$\mathbf{\$6} + -x = \$3$$

Add –6 to both sides:

$\$6 + \mathbf{-\$6} + -x = \$3 + \mathbf{-\$6}$

$\mathbf{-x = -\$3}$

Multiply both sides by –1:

$(-x)\mathbf{(-1)} = (-\$3)\mathbf{(-1)}$

$\mathbf{x = \$3}$

Check the answer by substituting \$3 for x in the original equation:

$\$8 - (\$2 + \mathbf{\$3}) = \$3$

$\$8 - \mathbf{(\$5)} = \$3$

$\mathbf{\$3} = \$3$

This is true. We found the correct value for x.

Distributing multiplication between addends — including distributing a negative sign — preserves the intended meaning. Both \$8 – (\$2 + \$3) and \$8 + –\$2 + –\$3 mean to subtract a total of \$5 from \$8. When we have an unknown inside the parentheses, distributing the multiplication can help us solve what we otherwise wouldn't be able to.

When a set of parentheses is preceded by a – sign, distribute the – sign by multiplying the values inside the parentheses by 1 and distributing –1.

Example: Simplify $-(2 + x)$

$\mathbf{-1}(2 + x)$

$(-1)\mathbf{(2)} + (-1)\mathbf{(x)}$

$\mathbf{-2 + -1x}$, or $-2 + -x$

Understanding that you can multiply any quantity by 1 without changing its value (the identity property of multiplication) is crucial. In fact, it can be helpful to think of there being an understood 1 next to every unknown or parentheses.

$a = \mathbf{1}a$ $\qquad$ $-a = \mathbf{-1}a$

$x = \mathbf{1}x$ $\qquad$ $-x = \mathbf{-1}x$

$(x + 5) = \mathbf{1}(\mathbf{1}x + 5)$ $\qquad$ $-(2 + x) = \mathbf{-1}(2 + \mathbf{1}x)$

However you think of it, know that **you can multiply by 1 without changing the value.**

Keeping Perspective

Each new rule in math builds on previous principles or rules, ultimately going back to the underlying consistency God created and sustains. The rules and conventions, like a language system, help us represent and work with that consistency.

9.6 Chapter Synopsis and the Beauty of Mathematics

We've been looking a lot at unknowns in this course and at how to find them. In this chapter, we focused on applying the **distributive property** to find an unknown inside **parentheses** (a grouping).

Once again, we've been applying what we *already know* about known numbers to help us work with unknowns. We can apply the same principles to unknowns that we do to known quantities because of the unerringly consistent way God holds all things together.

While we haven't used the word, as we've been exploring unknowns and how to work with them, we've really been learning the core principles of the branch of math called algebra. While the word "algebra" sounds intimidating, **algebra** is simply "the part of mathematics in which letters and other general symbols are used to represent numbers and quantities in formulae and equations"[4] or "the science which teaches how to determine unknown quantities by means of those that are known."[5]

Don't let algebra intimidate you. It's simply the branch of math where we learn to apply the *same principles* we've been using with known quantities to unknowns, thereby being equipped to explore the quantities and consistencies God created and sustains around us to an even deeper level.

The Beauty of Mathematics

Have you ever thought about the beauty God placed around us? He could have made everything all one color — but instead, He wove together a vast variety of hues. He put interest everywhere we look.

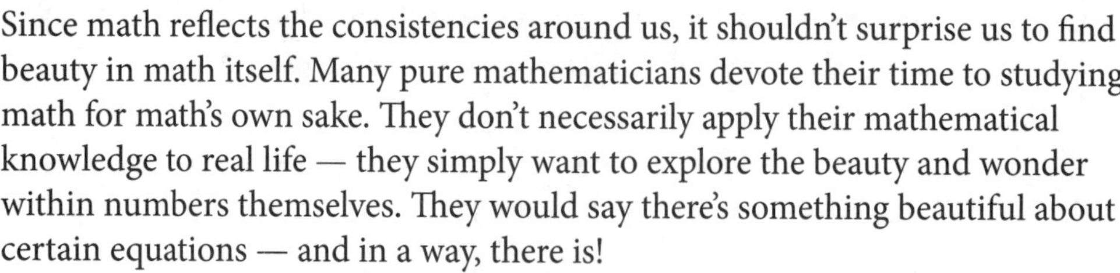

Since math reflects the consistencies around us, it shouldn't surprise us to find beauty in math itself. Many pure mathematicians devote their time to studying math for math's own sake. They don't necessarily apply their mathematical knowledge to real life — they simply want to explore the beauty and wonder within numbers themselves. They would say there's something beautiful about certain equations — and in a way, there is!

As creatures made in God's image, we can recognize the beauty of math itself. It's good to recognize the beauty in math at every level, much as we would recognize the beauty of a painting. We should always remember, though, that God is the master artist — if men are able to paint a beautiful picture, it is only because God made us in His image (and our picture is but a copy of the picture God has painted). Math's beauty ultimately points us to God's creativity and care.

[CHAPTER 10]

Inequalities

10.1 Understanding Inequalities

So far, we've focused our study on equations — that is, statements "that the values of two mathematical expressions are equal (indicated by the sign =)."[1] When we see an equal sign, we know that the expression on the left *equals* the expression on the right.

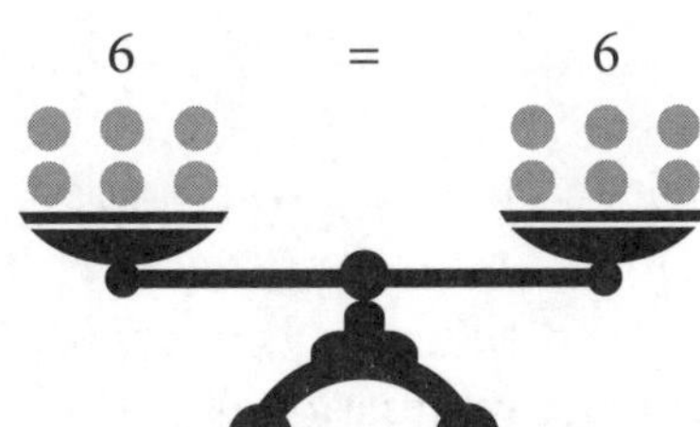

In real life, though, we also sometimes encounter what we call **inequalities**, or expressions that are *not* equal.[2]

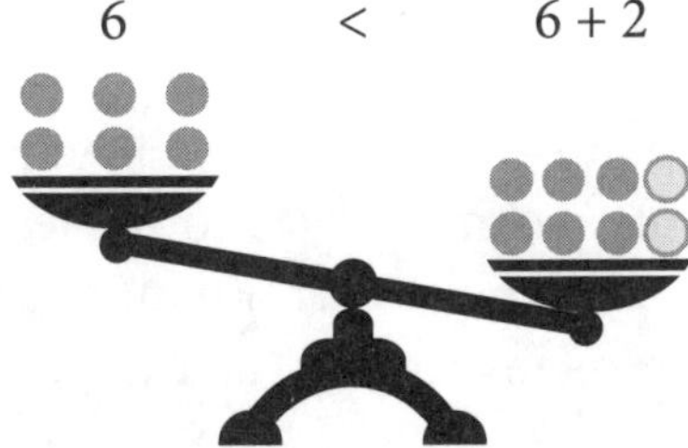

You should already be familiar with the symbols we use to represent unequal relationships. However, let's review these symbols and their meanings.

Reviewing the Symbols

The chart shows the inequality symbols we mentioned in Book 1. These symbols give us a concise language to compare expressions.

Symbol	Name
>	greater than
≥	greater than or equal to
=	equal to

Symbol	Name
<	less than
≤	less than or equal to
≠	does not equal

Notice that the *greater than or equal to* symbol is the same as the *greater than* symbol, except for a line underneath it. It looks like a mix between the *greater than* sign and the *equal to* sign. That's because it is! *Greater than or equal to* means that the expression on the one side could be either greater than *or* equal to the expression on the other side.

> greater than
= equal to
≥ greater than *or* equal to

The same is true regarding the *less than or equal to* sign. It is a combination of the *less than* and *equal to* signs, as it means either less than *or* equal to.

< less than
= equal to
≤ less than *or* equal to

We think in terms of inequality all the time without recognizing it. We may need to arrive at a meeting in *less than* 3 hours or get *greater than* 8 hours of sleep a night. Inequality symbols are formalized ways of expressing what our brain is already doing automatically in many situations.

Sometimes we simply know two quantities aren't equal, but we don't know exactly how they're not equal. For instance, we know that we can't divide by 0, so if we know we need to divide the distance we've traveled by the speed, we know we can only do so if the speed *does not equal* 0.

We also sometimes need to express situations where expressions could be either unequal *or* equal. For example, we might need to spend *less than or equal to* \$20 on a gift, exercise *more than (greater than)* a certain number of minutes each day, or get *greater than or equal to* a certain score on an exam.

Keeping Perspective

Inequalities, like equalities, give us a helpful way to describe how quantities relate. Only instead of showing us that two expressions are equal, they show us that one expression is greater than, greater than or equal to, less than, less than or equal to, or not equal to another expression.

As you review the symbols we use to represent inequality, know that our modern symbols are not the only way inequalities have been expressed! Many different symbols have been used, a few of which are shown here.[2]

Greater than	Greater than or Equal to	Less than	Less than or Equal to
[illegible]	[illegible]	[illegible]	[illegible]
[illegible]	≧	[illegible]	≦

10.2 Inequalities and Unknowns

Many real-life problems involving unknowns can best be described by an inequality. For example, let's say you need your total cumulative points in a contest to be *greater than* 400 to win a prize. If you have already earned 150 points, you would still need to earn greater than 250 points in order to end up with greater than 400 points. We could express this with an inequality, using x to represent the number of points you still need to earn:

$$x > 250$$

Let's take a look at what this inequality means.

Multiple Possible Values

When we see $x = 250$, we know that x has a single value: 250. If we were to think of all the values x could be as a set, or collection, that set would only contain one value: 250.

When x is on one side of an inequality, though, the unknown could equal many different values. That is, the set, or collection, of possible values for x would contain multiple values. In the case of $x > 250$, x needs to be *greater than* 250. It doesn't matter how much greater than 250 — you just need *greater than* 250 points to win the prize. The value for x could be 251, 254.3, 270.8, etc. — any value *greater than* 250 points works.

For another example, suppose you need at least a 70 on an exam in order to get a B in a course. We would say your score has to be *greater than or equal to* 70, as it won't matter if it's above 70, but it must be at least 70. Using x to represent your score, you'd have this:

$$x \geq 70$$

Again, in an inequality, we're not specifying one specific value for x; instead, we're *specifying a set of multiple possible values.*

Multiple values for an unknown is perhaps easiest to see on a number line. On a number line, we use an **open point** (one that's not shaded in) to show that a point is not included, and a **closed point** (one that is shaded in) to show that it is. We can use arrows to show multiple values.

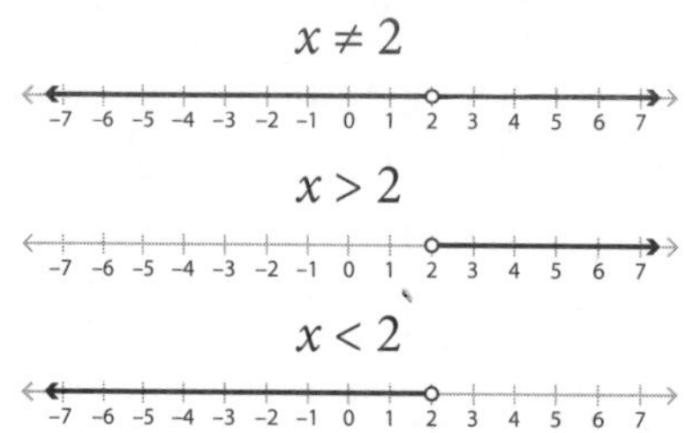

Notice that the points at 2 in this column are open; this shows that 2 *is not* included in the possible values for x.

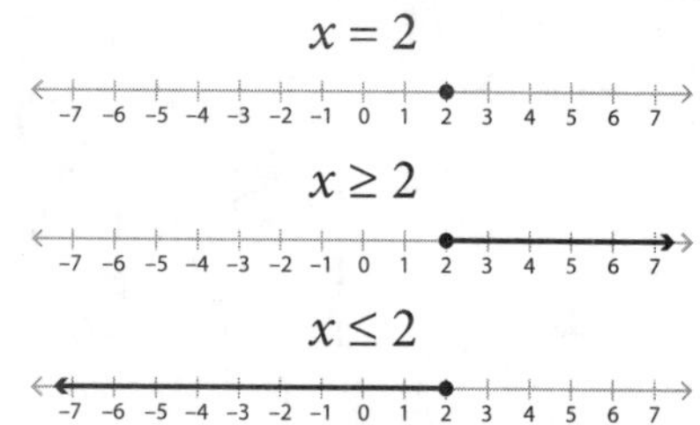

Notice that the points at 2 in this column are closed; this shows that 2 *is* included in the possible values for x.

Keeping Perspective

I hope you're catching the usefulness of inequality symbols. They give us a way of specifying multiple possible values rather than one specific value, giving us a handy way of describing *more than* a certain income, *less than* a certain amount, etc.

10.3 Swapping Sides of an Inequality

As you already know, when working with equalities, it doesn't matter which side of the equal sign each expression is on, as long as both sides are equal. For example, $2 \bullet 5 = 10$ and $10 = 2 \bullet 5$.

Swapping expressions separated by an = sign doesn't change the meaning.

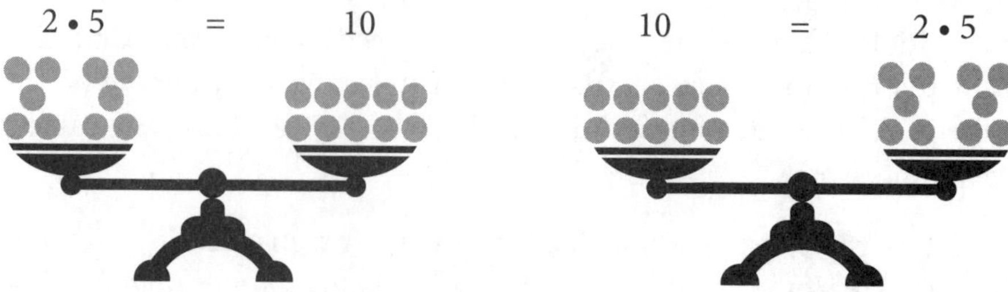

While the same would hold true for $\neq$, the same does *not* hold true for the other inequalities, as they're comparing which side is greater than the other. For example, $3 < 4$, but we can't simply switch the 3 and the 4 and say that $4 < 3$, as 4 is *not* less than 3.

Swapping expressions separated by a $<$, $>$, $\leq$, or $\geq$ without changing the direction of the inequality symbol *does* change the meaning.

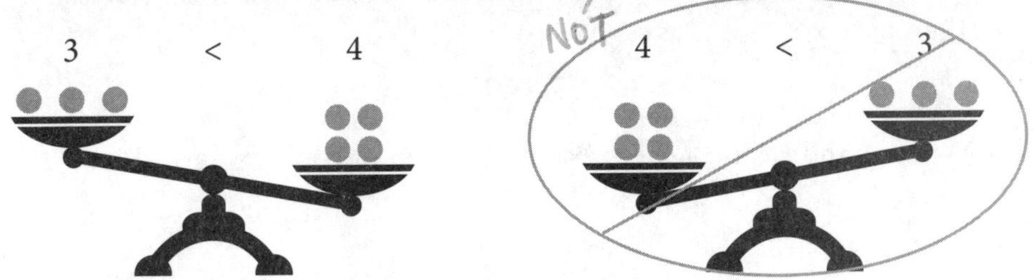

If we want to list the 4 on the left side of the inequality, we can, however, keep the same meaning (that 3 is less than 4) by flipping the inequality sign when we switch the sides.

When we swap expressions separated by a $<$, $>$, $\leq$, or $\geq$, we have to switch the direction of the inequality symbol.

$3 < 4$ and $4 > 3$ both show the same relationship. Saying that 3 is less than 4 is describing the same inequality as saying that 4 is greater than 3.

In fact, we can read inequalities in either direction. For example, we could read the inequality $9 > x$ as "9 is greater than x" or as "x is less than 9." Both are two different ways of describing the same inequality. A great way to see this is on a number line.

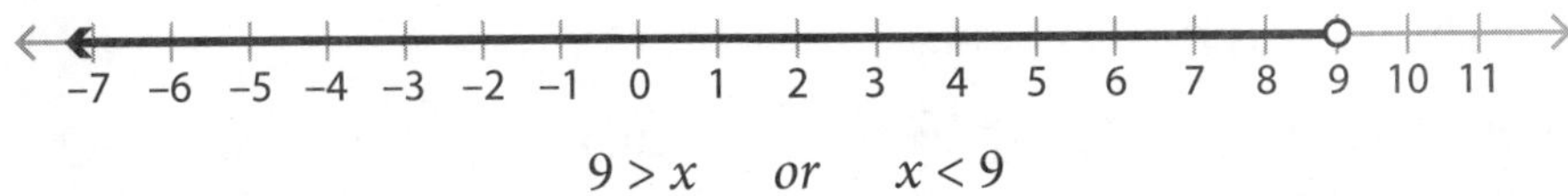

$$9 > x \quad or \quad x < 9$$

It's easy to know which way to face the sign if you remember that, no matter how we rearrange the inequality, the larger side of the sign goes with the greater number. Notice that in both cases below, we've put the larger side of the sign next to the greater number.

$$7 < 8 \quad or \quad 8 > 7$$

This is true for unknown numbers as well as known. For example, if we want to show that x is greater than 7, we've only to make sure x is on the larger side of the sign.

$$7 < x \quad or \quad x > 7$$

Hungry Alligators
Some people find it useful to think of the sign as an alligator's mouth, remembering that the alligator is always going to "eat" the greater number.

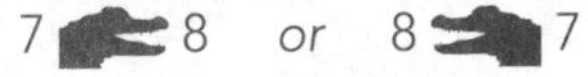

While the ins and outs of inequalities are most likely review for you, it's important to understand these underlying principles as we begin using them with unknowns. For example, you're going to begin to encounter relationships such as this one:

$$60 \div x < 5$$

Here, we don't know what x equals . . . but we know that 60 divided by it will be less than 5. It's important to understand that you can also think of this as 5 is greater than $60 \div x$.

$$5 > 60 \div x$$

Both $60 \div x < 5$ and $5 > 60 \div x$ represent the same unequal relationship.

Keeping Perspective

In order to keep the relationship the same, when we swap expressions separated by a $<$, $>$, $\leq$, or $\geq$ symbol, we have to switch the direction of the inequality symbol. Because of the consistent way God governs all things, it doesn't matter if we know the quantities we're dealing with or not. We can rely on them to operate in a predictable fashion.

10.4 Finding the Value of an Unknown in an Inequality

Now that we have looked at inequality symbols and what they mean with unknowns, it is time to learn how to find the value of an unknown in an inequality. For example, how much can we spend if we know we need \$4 to pay for parking and we have \$10 total?

While the answer is obvious (if we have \$10 and need to save \$4, we have \$6 to spend), let's represent this mathematically in order to use it to get a better understanding of inequalities.

Up until now, we would have written this problem as an equation, using it to find the *max* we could spend. Here, x represents the max we could spend.

Original problem:

$$x + \$4 = \$10$$

Add –\$4 to both sides:

$$x + \$4 + \mathbf{-\$4} = \$10 + \mathbf{-\$4}$$

$$\boldsymbol{x = \$6}$$

In reality, though, we don't *have* to spend all \$6. After all, who wouldn't want to spend less if they could? We could spend any amount *less than or equal to* \$6. We could better convey what we mean by using x to represent the amount we *could* spend, and using an inequality to find the entire *set of numbers* that, added to \$4, are less than or equal to \$10.

$x + \$4 \leq \$10$

While our brains can automatically figure out that it can spend less than the max without the aid of an inequality, inequalities can help us better express what we're meaning.

Let's take a closer look at solving for an unknown in an inequality. We'll start by looking at what happens when we add, subtract, multiply, or divide *both sides* of inequalities using known numbers, and then apply the same principle when unknowns are involved.

What You Do to One Side . . .

What would happen if we added an amount to just one side of an inequality? After all, the sides are already unequal, right? Look at what happens when we add 3 to only the left side of $6 > 4$.

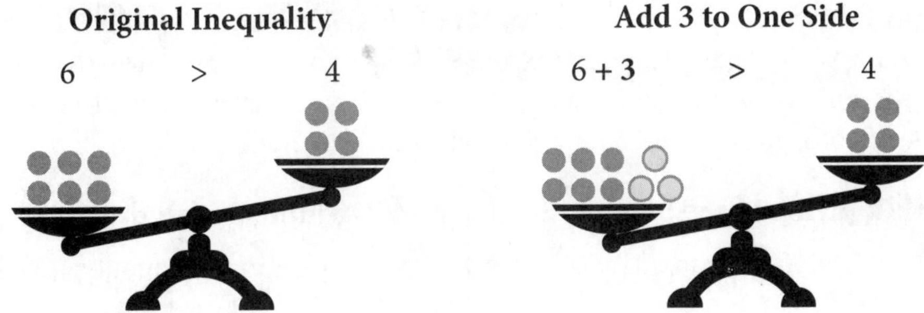

While the inequality in this case is still true (9 is still greater than 4), we've *changed the relationship*. The left side is now 5 greater than the right side, rather than 2 greater. In order to keep the relationship the same, we have to **add, subtract, multiply, or divide the *same amount* to *both sides* of the inequality, just as we have been with equalities.**

We can add, subtract, multiply, or divide *both sides* of an inequality by the same *positive* number without changing the meaning of the inequality.

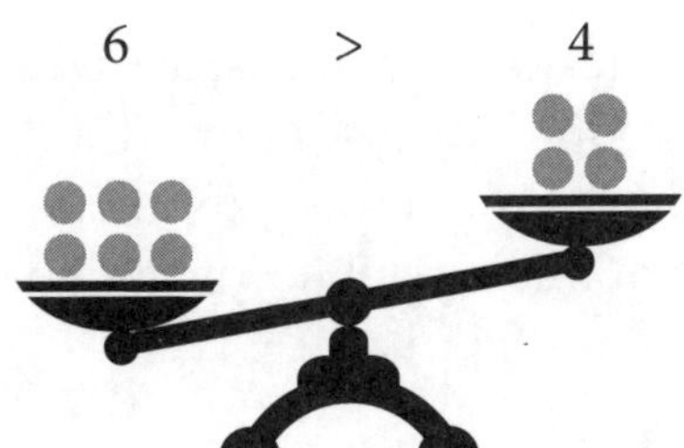

Adding 2 to Both Sides

$6 + 2 \quad > \quad 4 + 2$

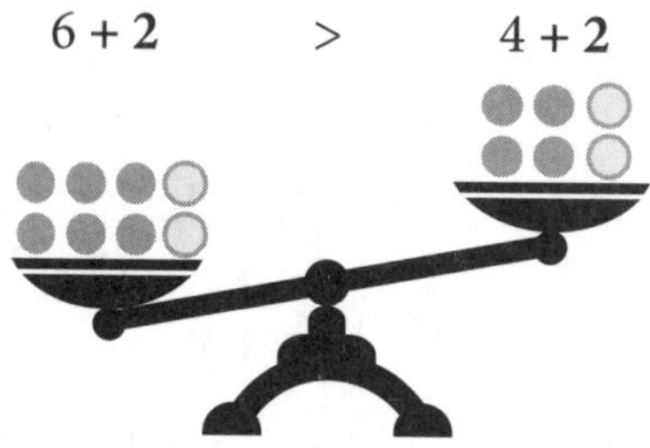

Subtracting 2 from Both Sides

$6 - 2 \quad > \quad 4 - 2$

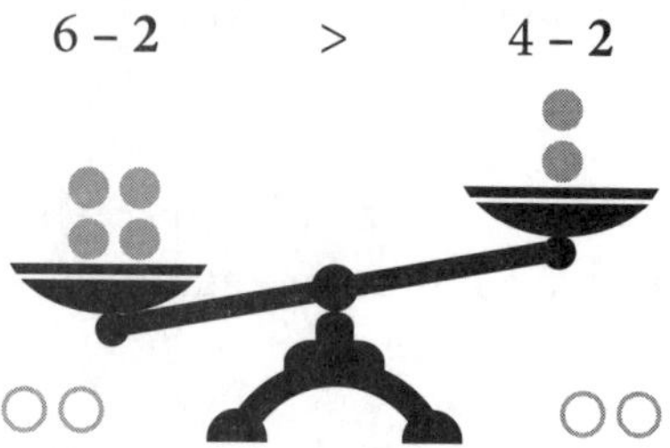

Multiplying Both Sides by 2

$6 \cdot 2 \quad > \quad 4 \cdot 2$

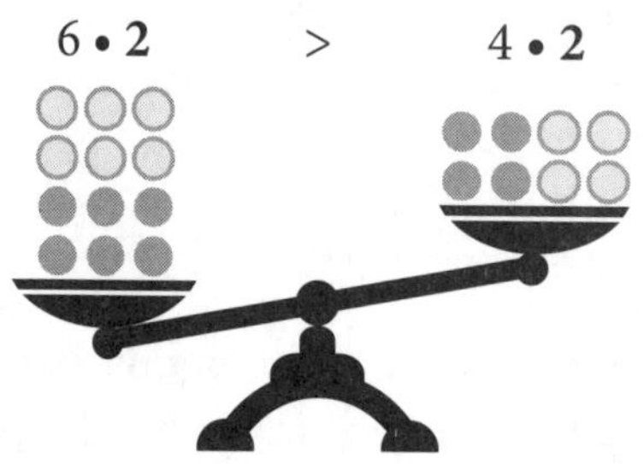

Dividing Both Sides by 2

$6 \div 2 \quad > \quad 4 \div 2$

However, with the inequalities $<$, $>$, $\leq$, and $\geq$, when we multiply or divide both sides of the inequality by a *negative number*, the inequality symbol must be switched to keep the meaning of the inequality. Remember, the negative sign means *the opposite of*. So multiplying or dividing by a negative number takes *the opposite of* both sides, which changes which side is greater.

If we had not changed the direction of the signs, we would have ended up with untrue statements.

Multiplying Both Sides by –2

Original inequality:

$6 > 4$

Multiplying both sides by –2 *and* switching the direction of the symbol:

$$6 \cdot -2 < 4 \cdot -2$$

$$-12 < -8$$

Notice that we end up with a true statement: –12 is less than –8.

Dividing Both Sides by –2

Original inequality:

$6 > 4$

Dividing both sides by –2 *and* switching the direction of the symbol:

$$\frac{6}{-2} < \frac{4}{-2}$$

$$-3 < -2$$

Notice that we end up with a true statement: –3 is less than –2.

Finding Unknowns in an Inequality

Whether dealing with equalities or inequalities, we live in a consistent universe held together by a consistent God. Because of this, we can confidently build on the knowledge we know (such as the consistent way objects add and subtract) to find unknowns. Let's take a look at finding unknowns inside inequalities.

Example: How much can we spend if we've already spent \$5 and need to spend a total of less than or equal to \$20?

Original problem:

$x + \$5 \leq \$20$

Add –\$5 to both sides:

$x + \$5 + \mathbf{-\$5} \leq \$20 + \mathbf{-\$5}$

$x \leq \$15$

Now it's clear that we can spend *less than or equal to* \$15.

A good habit to form is to look closely at your ending inequality to make sure that it makes sense. While this is sometimes hard to see with unknowns, it's nevertheless a helpful habit that will reduce careless errors.

Example: If we're planning a wedding and plan for 100 servings, how much per serving can we afford if we have a budget of \$500 to spend on the cake?

Using x to represent the price per serving, we'd have this inequality:

$100x \leq \$500$

In other words, the price per serving times 100 servings must be less than or equal to \$500.

How do we solve this? Well, we can divide both sides by 100, just as you would if there were an equal sign.

$$\frac{100x}{\mathbf{100}} \leq \frac{\$500}{\mathbf{100}}$$

$$\frac{\cancel{100}x}{\cancel{100}} \leq \frac{\$\cancel{500}^{5}}{\cancel{100}}$$

$\mathbf{x \leq \$5}$

We can afford ≤ \$5 per serving.

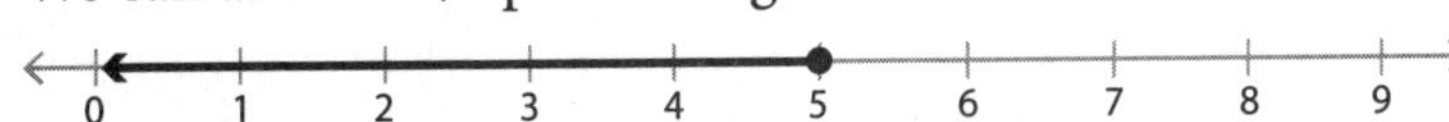

Negative Numbers and Inequalities

It's worth noting that while an inequality may technically include negative numbers, negative numbers don't always make sense for a particular situation. In both of the examples we looked at, for example, it wouldn't make sense for x to be a negative value. Even though the inequalities $x \leq \$15$ and $x \leq \$5$ include all values less than or equal to \$15 and \$5, *including negative values*, we know from the situations given that we are only interested in positive values for x. It would not make sense to spend negative costs for the gift or the wedding cake.

Keeping Perspective

As I was discussing inequalities with someone, it came up how there's no equal to God. We simply can't equate Him to anyone or anything else. God is greater and holier than we could ever think or imagine.

> *To whom will ye liken me, and make me equal, and compare me, that we may be like? (Isaiah 46:5)*

Yet it is easy to fall into making God out to be like us or like what we think He should be. Most of us can smile at the Israelites and at how often they made idols for themselves instead of worshiping God, yet we can easily fail to see that we are doing the same thing. Whenever we think of God as something other than what He's revealed Himself to be, we're fashioning our own god in our mind.

For example, many people think that since they wouldn't send people to hell, that God won't either. Yet God makes it very clear in His Word that He will judge sin, and that if we have not placed our trust in Jesus, hell is exactly what we deserve and will receive (Romans 6:23; Galatians 6:7; Acts 4:12; John 14:6; Revelation 21:8). We need to heed what the Bible says about God and not make the mistake of fashioning Him into what we want Him to be — His thoughts are much, much greater than our own.

> *For my thoughts are not your thoughts, neither are your ways my ways, saith the LORD. For as the heavens are higher than the earth, so are my ways higher than your ways, and my thoughts than your thoughts (Isaiah 55:8–9).*

10.5 Chapter Synopsis and the Human Brain

In this chapter, you got a chance to explore inequalities. We saw how, because of the consistent way God governs all things, we're able to find unknowns in inequalities as well as in equations.

Here are a few key things we covered:

- **How to represent everyday comparisons** between non-equal quantities using mathematical symbols. After all, not everything is equal!
- **How to show inequalities** on a number line.
- **How to preserve the meaning when swapping expressions separated by a $<$, $>$, $\leq$, or $\geq$ sign** by switching the direction of the inequality symbol.
- **How to solve problems dealing with inequalities** the same way we would solve an equality unless you need to multiply or divide an inequality with a $<$, $>$, $\leq$, or $\geq$ by a negative number. In that case, we have to reverse the direction

of the inequality sign (*less than* becomes *greater than*, etc.) in order to keep it accurate.

Basically, we saw that, with a little modification, we could expand tools we already had in our mathematical tool belt (such as number lines and solving for unknowns) to solve problems involving unequal expressions. You'll find as you continue in math that many of the more advanced concepts are simply a modification of something you already know.

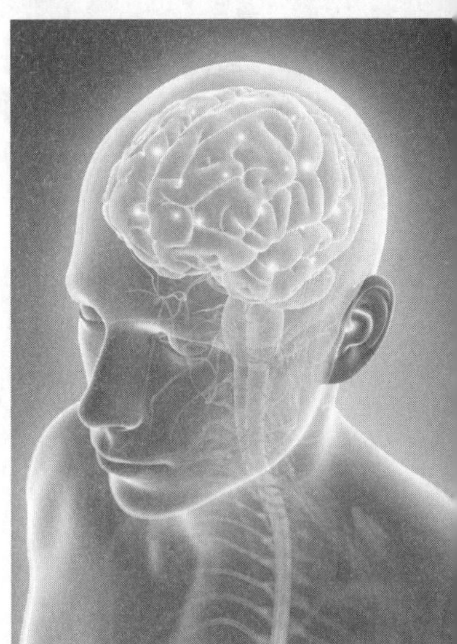

The Human Brain: A Miracle

Stop and ponder for a moment the miracle occurring right now in your brain. You're able to read these words! Your eyes are taking in an image. Your brain is processing that image, connecting it with what you've learned about language, and giving you an interpretation — all that within a split second.

We don't often think of the miracle going on inside our brain . . . until it doesn't work. A concussion once left my brain not working normally for many months. As a result, I have been realizing how truly reliant we are on the Lord for even the brainpower to be able to learn and use math. As you continue adding tools to your mathematical tool belt and expanding others, ponder the miracle that's allowing your brain to process the information and learn — and praise God for the abilities He's given you.

[CHAPTER 11]

Statistics

11.1 Statistics Review

In this chapter, we're going to take a break from mechanics and look at a branch of mathematics called statistics. **Statistics** is "the mathematics of the collection, organization, and interpretation of numerical data; especially, the analysis of population characteristics by inference from sampling."[1] The word statistics can also mean "a collection of numerical data,"[2] but to keep the meaning clear, we'll use the abbreviation **stat** when we mean the data itself, and statistics when we mean the mathematics of collecting, organizing, and interpreting that data. While you may never have to personally collect, organize, or interpret much numerical data yourself, understanding statistics will aid you in understanding the stats you'll encounter throughout your life.

Let's begin the chapter with a quick review of the process of *collecting, organizing,* and *interpreting* data. We covered this process in Book 1, so it should be review for you (look back at Chapter 12 in Book 1 if you have any questions).

Collecting Data

When collecting **data** (i.e., "Facts that can be analyzed or used in an effort to gain knowledge or make decisions; information"[3]), it's important to collect the *right* data — the data needed in order to come to accurate conclusions.

Sometimes, collecting data involves measuring and recording results. For example, the high temperature for a specific location each day during the week could be measured and recorded, and we'd then have comprehensive data on that week's high temperatures (provided, of course, that our thermometer was accurate . . . and that we wrote down the correct numbers . . . and that we measured the highest temperature).

Often, though, it's not possible to collect comprehensive data. In that case, it's common to collect data from a *sample*, or "portion," of the whole group.

Term Reminder

A **sample** is "the portion of a population selected for analysis."[4] The whole group we're considering is called the **population**. If we were collecting opinions of all the students attending a college, for instance, all students attending the college would be the population, and those whose opinion we actually collected would be the sample.

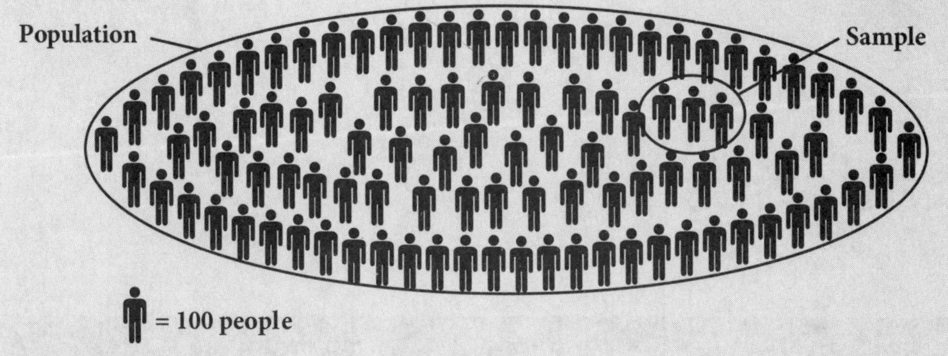

In order to collect useful data, a sample needs to be a *random* selection of the population that is *large enough* that we can accurately use it as a basis for conclusions about the entire population. For example, if we want to figure out the opinion of all the students attending a specific college on an issue, interviewing all students attending one particular class, students from another college, or only a handful of random students attending the college would all be invalid samples. We would need to interview enough randomly chosen students attending the specific college in question to have an idea of the opinions of all the students attending that college.

Organizing Data

After data is collected, it's helpful to organize the data in order to draw conclusions from it. We'll look at multiple different ways to organize data throughout this chapter, but for now, let's review the basic concept of making a **frequency distribution** — that is, of making a table that makes it easier to see how frequently (i.e., "how often") each "outcome"[5] or **data point** (a fancy name for a specific piece of data within the group of data) appears.

In the example, we've tallied up the number of times each outcome/data point appeared (the tally column), recorded that number in the frequency column, and also found the **relative frequency** (the percent of the total each frequency represents). The actual columns in a frequency distribution table can vary, as long as we somehow show how frequently the different outcomes appear.

Example: Make a frequency distribution table for these high temperatures a hypothetical city had during the first week in August: 99, 80, 82, 83, 85, 86, 82.

FREQUENCY DISTRIBUTION TABLE

Temperature	Tally	Frequency	Relative Frequency
	Draw a mark each time the temperature is in the data.	*Use your Tally column to write the frequency of each temperature.*	*Divide the frequency by the total number of data points (in this case, 7), expressing the quotient as a percent.*
99°	/	1	14.29%
86°	/	1	14.29%
85°	/	1	14.29%
83°	/	1	14.29%
82°	//	2	28.57%
80°	/	1	14.29%

Often, it's more meaningful to summarize the data into groups and then look at the frequency appearing in each group. The table below shows the *same data* summarized into 5° groupings.

Temperature	Tally	Frequency	Relative Frequency
≥ 91°	/	1	14.29%
86°–90°	/	1	14.29%
81°–85°	////	4	57.14%
76°–80°	/	1	14.29%

The groups make it easier to draw conclusions from the data. We can now tell that 57.14% of the temperatures were between 80°–85°.

Notice the greater than or equal to sign (≥) before 91° in the table above — inequalities are used in statistics too! Notice, though, that the remaining groups don't use an inequality sign; instead, we've simply listed the lowest number and the highest number in the group. After all, in this case, 86°–90° is easier to read than ≥ 86° and ≤ 90°.

Graphs are another tool that help us organize data. The chart below reviews the main graphs we covered in Book 1.

Graph Review

Different types of graphs are useful in different settings. Here's a brief refresher of a few graphs. (See the resources in the endnote[6] for more details on when to use what graph.)

Pie Graphs — Pie graphs make it easy to see what portion of a whole is represented. The pie graph below shows the same data we made a frequency distribution table of — notice how the graph visually shows what portion of all the high temperatures (i.e., the whole) fell in each grouping.

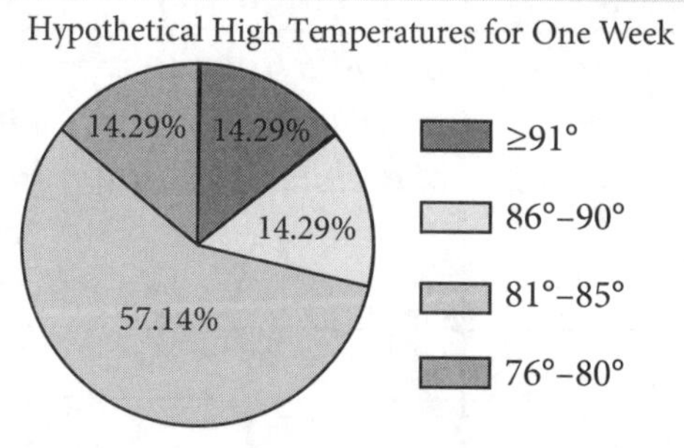

Bar Graphs/Column Graphs/Histograms — Bar graphs (which are also called column graphs if the bars are vertical) help show how data compares with other data. Histograms are bar graphs with grouped data (i.e., with ranges). The examples below are examples from Book 1.

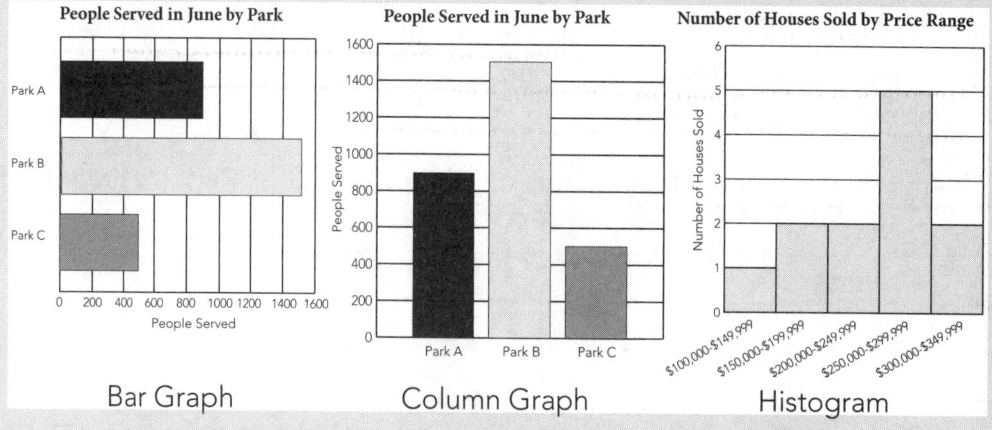

Bar Graph | Column Graph | Histogram

Line Graphs — Line graphs help show how data compares with other data, only they make it easier to see small differences and patterns. Notice how the line graph of the high temperatures we made a frequency distribution table of makes it easy to see the small fluctuations and the general pattern in the high temperatures.

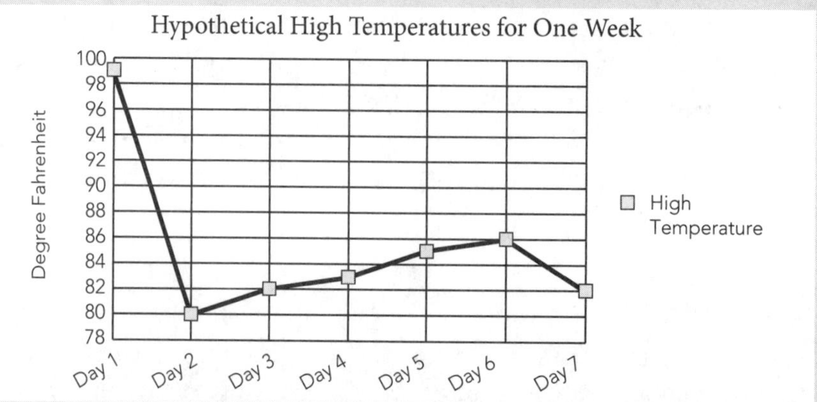

Notice how all of the graphs organize data so we can take it in at a glance. **As the saying goes, a picture is truly worth a thousand words!**

Interpreting Data

Now for the third aspect of statistics: interpreting data. Based on the hypothetical high temperatures we collected and organized, what conclusions can we reach?

We have to be careful when interpreting data . . . and when reading conclusions others have made. For example, if when collecting high temperatures the typical high was between 81°–85°, saying that the city has a typical high in the 80s would not be an accurate conclusion. While *this* particular week's data fell mainly in the 80s, one week's worth of data is hardly enough to base a conclusion on! The city could be having an incredible heat wave . . . or cooler-than-usual temperatures.

Whether purposefully or accidentally, stats can easily get presented in a misleading way. We'd be wise to look critically at conclusions drawn, asking questions. One of the main reasons we'll be looking at statistics together is so that you'll be better able to think through stats you encounter.

Interpreting Survey Results

When looking at survey results and trying to decide if the results confirm the interpretation presented, it's helpful to look at two numbers called the margin of error and the confidence level. We explored both of these numbers in Book 1, but they're important enough to warrant a quick review. The **margin of error** tells us the expected range of error between the number quoted and what we would expect if we sampled the entire population under consideration. The **confidence level** tells us how confident we are that our results are accurate within the listed margin of error.

For example, suppose an election survey sent to a sample of random voters in a district showed that 51% of those surveyed favored Candidate B.

Those in Favor of Candidate B = 51%

Notice that this means 51% of the voters surveyed favor Candidate B. How reflective is this number of the opinion of *all* the voters in the district? Well, look at the fine print at the bottom of the survey. Let's say it says this:

Survey has a 90% Confidence Level and a MOE of ±5%.

The margin of error (MOE) of ±5% means that we should expect the result listed — the 51% — to vary from the opinion of the total population by 5 percent in either direction. In other words, we expect the percent of the whole population in favor of Candidate B to be somewhere between 46%–56%. Statistically, since only a sample was surveyed, we can only expect the results to reflect the whole within a certain percentage — calculated here to be within 5%.

The confidence level of 90% means that the survey has a 90% chance of being accurate within the 5% margin of error listed, and a 10% chance of being off by greater than the 5% margin of error listed. In other words, we're 90% sure that 46%–56% of the population is in favor of Candidate B, but there's a chance that, if we'd surveyed the whole population instead of a sample, we'd find different results.

Next time an election approaches and you read an article claiming that one candidate is "clearly" in the lead, look at the margin of error and confidence level. If one candidate is in the lead by 51% over another candidate at 49% and there's a ±5% margin of error, we don't really know which candidate is in the lead! The ±5% margin of error tells us that the percent in favor of each candidate could be 5% in either direction of the percent listed.

Keeping Perspective

While that was a pretty fast-paced review, I hope it gave a broad picture of the process of statistics: collecting, organizing, and interpreting data. We'll explore the statistical process in more depth throughout the rest of the chapter. One thing we'll see again and again is that it's very, very, very (did I say that enough times?) easy to misrepresent a stat, leading the viewer to a conclusion other than what the data really shows. By understanding more about the statistical process, however, you'll be better equipped to sift through misrepresentations and cut to the truth.

And should you ever need to present stats (in a meeting, in a debate tournament, in a 4-H presentation, to a congressman you're lobbying, etc.), hopefully our studies will equip you to present the data in a truthful way. As God's children, we want to live and present truth in all we do.

> *God is not a man, that he should lie; neither the son of man, that he should repent: hath he said, and shall he not do it? or hath he spoken, and shall he not make it good? (Numbers 23:19)*
>
> *Wherefore putting away lying, speak every man truth with his neighbour: for we are members one of another (Ephesians 4:25).*

11.2 Line Graphs and Trends

In the last lesson, we reviewed the core components of statistics: *collecting*, *organizing*, and *interpreting* data. In this lesson, we're going to take a more detailed look at a tool that helps us organize data: line graphs. We'll also touch on trends, a term you're likely to hear in everyday life.

Since line graphs are a type of coordinate graph, let's first briefly review the basics of coordinates.

Reviewing Coordinates

Coordinates are numbers that we use to indicate a position. More technically, they're "each of a group of numbers used to indicate the position of a point, line, or plane."[7] We measure coordinates using an **axis** (**axes** if plural): a "fixed reference line for the measurement of coordinates."[8] Notice the axes shown on the map. The axes are basically number lines, one going horizontally, and the other vertically.

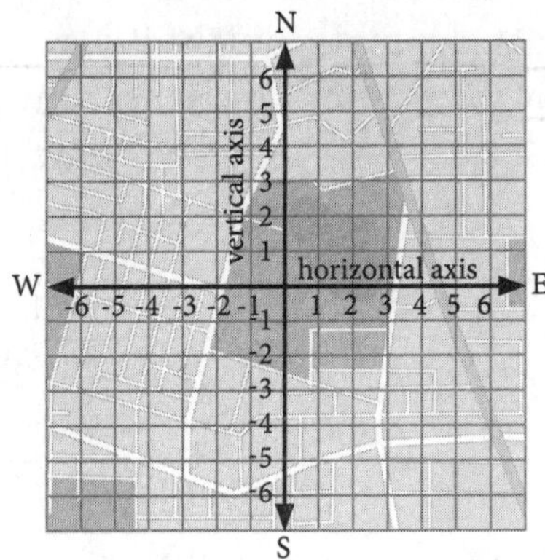

The arrows on each axis are simply reminders that we could continue the graph further.

Let's look at an example of coordinates. The coordinates (4, 5) refer to a position 4 points over horizontally and 5 points up vertically from the point marked 0. How did we know the 4 meant the horizontal distance? Well, the standard convention is to **always list the horizontal coordinate first, followed by the vertical coordinate.** This standard format enables everyone to know which number means what.

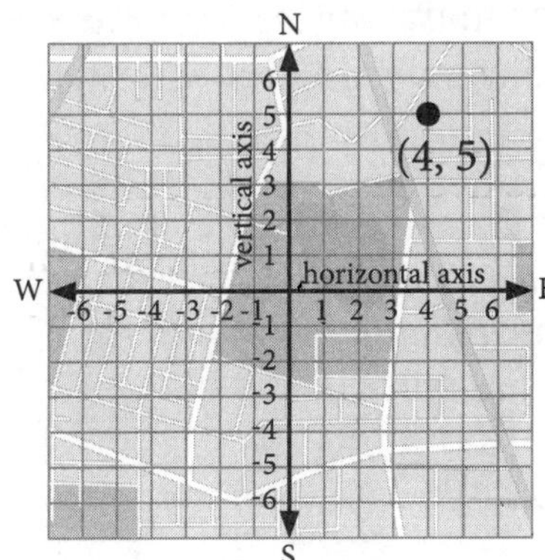

Did You Know . . . ?

When you set the resolution of your computer monitor, you're choosing how many little boxes the computer uses in its coordinate system. A resolution of 1,600 by 900 means there are 1,600 pixels (boxes) horizontally and 900 vertically. The more pixels used, the more precise the image.

Note: An actual screen has many more pixels than the boxes shown.

You'll hear the term resolution in connection with other technology as well. For example, you might hear the term "1080p" or "1080i" connected with high definition. The 1080 is a way of counting how many little boxes (pixels) make up the height of the coordinate system that's capturing or displaying the video.

Line Graphs

Now that we've reviewed coordinates, let's take a closer look at line graphs. **Line graphs** are a type of coordinate graph that make it easy to see small changes and to compare two different sets of data.[9] For example, let's say a state wants to compare the number of books that have been borrowed at 2 libraries over 5 years in order to determine where to spend their funding. They have the following 2 sets of data.

Library 1:

Year	Books Borrowed *(rounded to the nearest thousand)*
2011	101,000
2012	86,000
2013	86,000
2014	82,000
2015	79,000

Library 2:

Year	Books Borrowed *(rounded to the nearest thousand)*
2011	12,000
2012	16,000
2013	21,000
2014	25,000
2015	36,000

A line graph could make this data easier to compare. We'll use one axis to represent the years, and another the books borrowed. Since it's easiest to see the change in whatever we graph on the vertical axis and since we're interested in the change in the number of books, we'll put that data on the vertical axis, and the year on the horizontal axis.

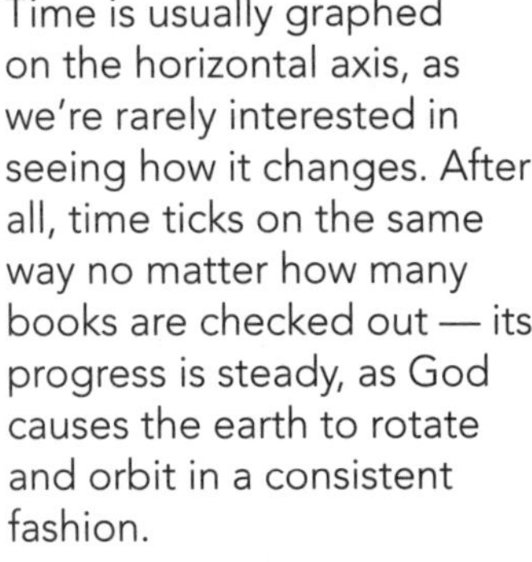

Time is usually graphed on the horizontal axis, as we're rarely interested in seeing how it changes. After all, time ticks on the same way no matter how many books are checked out — its progress is steady, as God causes the earth to rotate and orbit in a consistent fashion.

We next need a scale for our axes — that is, we need to determine how much each box will represent. In this case, we'll make each vertical box represent 10,000 books, and each horizontal box a year.

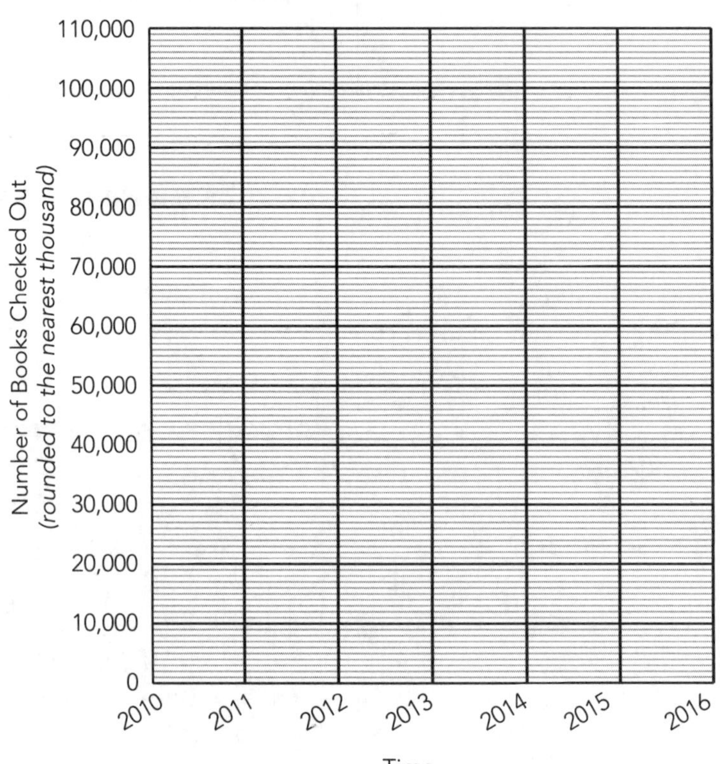

Now we can draw a point on the coordinate system for each year of Library 1. The first point will go at 2011 and 101,000, since in 2011, Library 1 had 101,000 books checked out. The next point will go at 2012 and 86,000, and so forth.

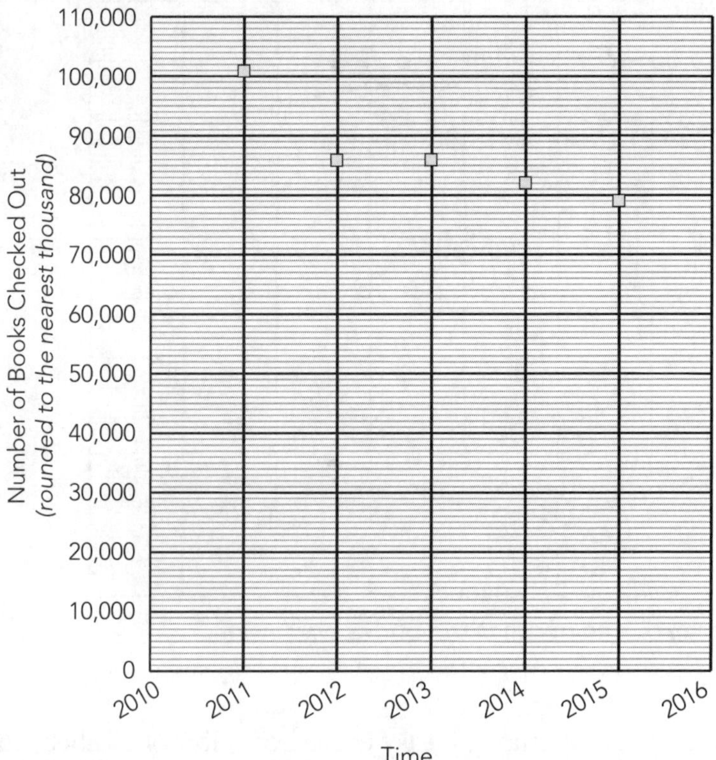

We'll now connect the points. Notice how easy it is to see how in general, the total books checked out for this library has declined.

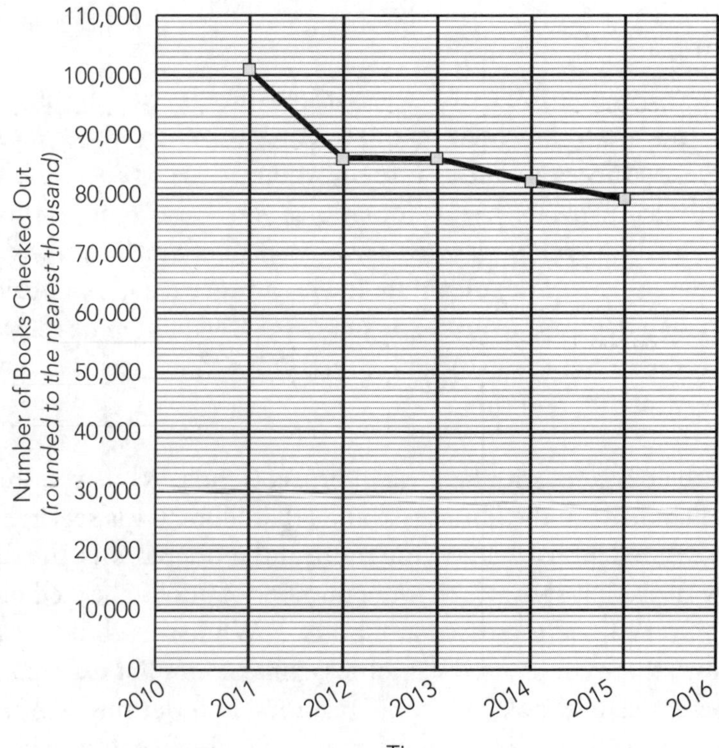

If we do the same thing for Library 2, we can easily compare the two results.

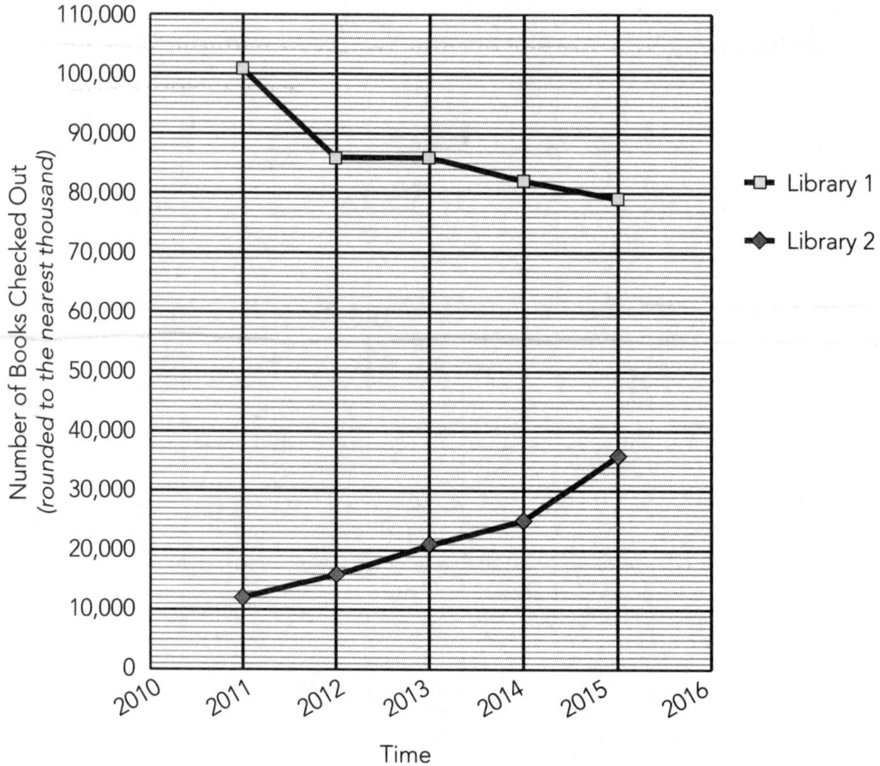

Notice how the line graph makes it easy to see how Library 1's checkouts have declined, while Library 2's have steadily risen. We would say that there's a **downward trend** in checkouts for Library 1, and an **upward trend** in checkouts for Library 2.

Term Time

The word **trend** is one you'll hear a lot in statistics. It is a fancy term for describing the "general inclination or tendency."[10] When we see a general increase, we say there's an upward trend; when we see a general decrease, we say there's a downward trend. Sometimes you'll also hear *positive trend* instead of *upward trend*, or *negative trend* instead of *downward trend*, but be sure you understand the meaning. If a downward trend is a positive thing (such as a decrease in crime or sickness), it will often be referred to as a positive trend rather than a negative one. Once again, terms can be used different ways at different times.

Now, we have to be careful with how we interpret trends. While you might be tempted to conclude from the libraries' trends that Library 1 is serving fewer and fewer patrons, while Library 2 is serving more and more patrons, the data alone does not show this. All it shows is that the number of books checked out has decreased at Library 1 and increased at Library 2. While this could mean Library 1 is losing patrons, there could also be another explanation. For example, Library 1 could have increased its ebook collection, resulting in fewer physical checkouts but serving more patrons. We need more information before we draw a conclusion.

Keeping Perspective

As you practice using **line graphs** to show **trends** or patterns, over time, remember that we're using graphs to help us picture data. Notice how much easier it is to see a trend on a graph! Graphs give us a visual way of organizing data.

11.3 Scatter Graphs and Correlation

It's time to continue organizing data with graphs by looking at a **scatter graph**. A scatter graph is similar to a line graph, only in a scatter graph, we don't draw a line connecting the data points. Scatter graphs help us compare two or more sets of data to see if there's any sort of "mutual relationship or connection,"[11] or what we call **correlation**, between them.

To illustrate, consider this problem given in a math book from the early 1900s:

> *"Hastings measured (in kilograms) the strength of the right fore-arms of 5,476 children, of ages from 5 years to 16 years. He found the average strength as follows:"*[12]

Hastings' results are given below.

Age	Average Forearm Strength *(in kilograms)*	Age	Average Forearm Strength *(in kilograms)*	Age	Average Forearm Strength *(in kilograms)*
5	4.9	9	13.1	13	22.6
6	7.0	10	14.7	14	25.4
7	9.2	11	18.0	15	28.9
8	10.6	12	19.7	16	33.3

Let's graph this on a scatter graph (basically, a line graph without the lines) to see if there's a correlation (i.e., relationship) between a child's age and their forearm strength.

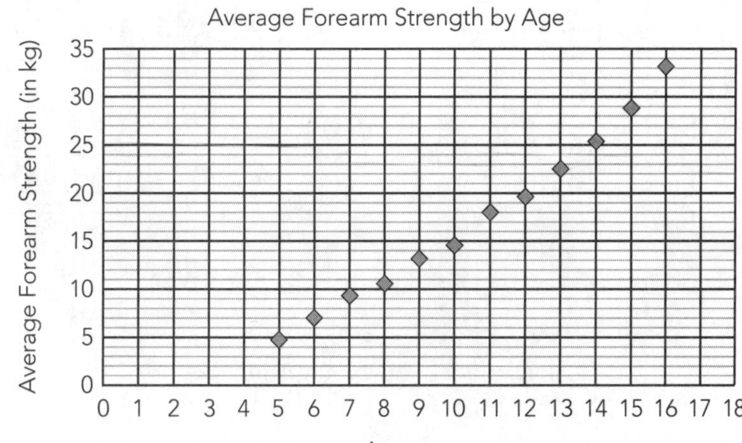

Now it's easy to see the correlation, or relationship, between a child's age and forearm strength. In general, there appears to be a general increase in forearm strength with a child's age — at least for the ages we've looked at here. We would call this a **positive correlation**.

Let's look at another example. Say a company wanted to see if there was a relationship between price and sales of a product (which we'll call "Product A"). The company experimented by raising the price and tracking the sales. Notice that the graph makes it easy to see that in this case there is a correlation, or relationship, between the number sold and the price. This time, we would say there's a **negative correlation**, since, when looked at from left to right, the values incline downward, showing that, in general, sales declined when the price increased.

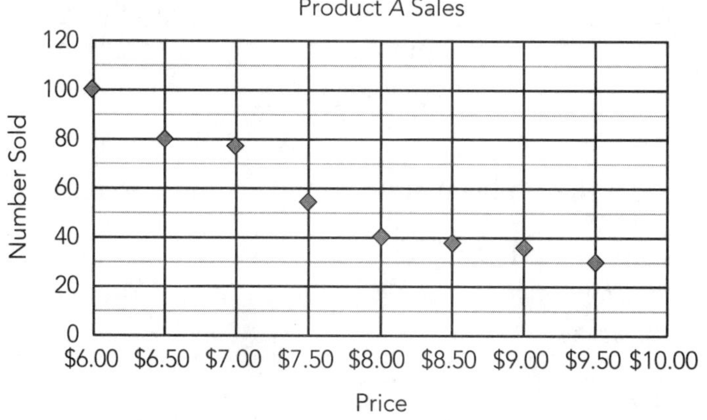

In contrast, there's probably not a correlation, or relationship, between the inches of precipitation and the number of houses in a neighborhood. The graph below is an example of a graph that shows **little correlation**.

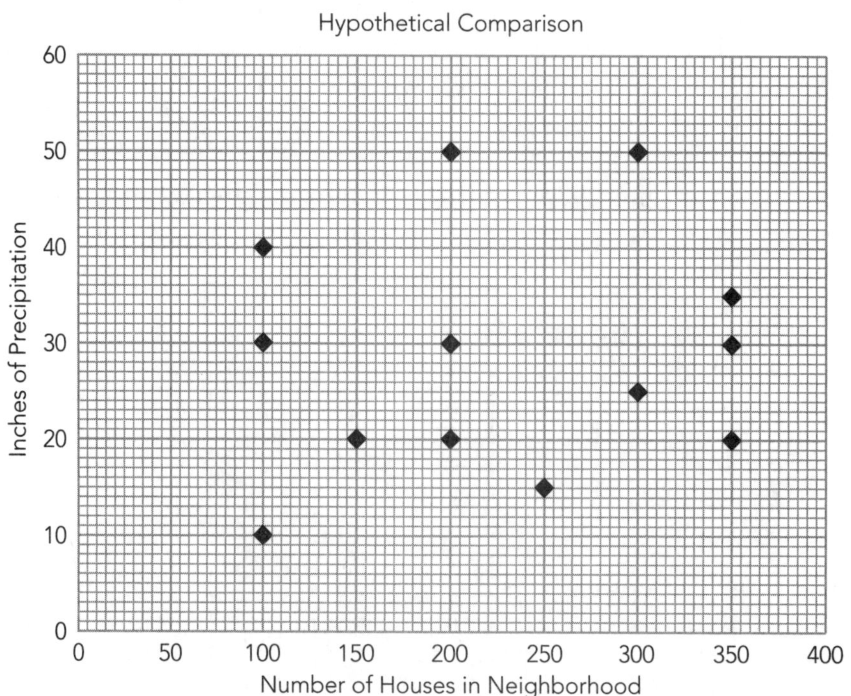

Keeping Perspective

Correlation is a fancy term for a connection or relationship between two separate groups of data. Knowing whether or not data is correlated helps us draw conclusions (such as that arms get stronger as kids grow . . . or that an increased sales price caused a decrease in sales . . . or that the precipitation isn't affected by the number of houses in a neighborhood). **Scatter graphs** make it easy to see these correlations.

It's worth noting that we need to be careful about the conclusions we draw from correlations. For example, a claim based on the "Average Forearm Strength by Age" graph that the older someone gets, the stronger they become would be deceptive. While we could conclude that the average forearm strength increases for the ages 5–16, at some point, we would expect the average forearm strength to level out as children become adults and reach their full stature and strength. Then at some age we'd expect the average forearm strength to start decreasing. We should also ask about the margin of error and confidence level of the data itself. *Always be careful to look twice at conclusions drawn off stats.*

11.4 Stem-and-Leaf Plots

There are many ways to organize data. While up until now we've only looked at frequency distributions and graphs, let's take a look at a non-graphical approach to organizing data: the stem-and-leaf plot.

In a stem-and-leaf plot, rather than *drawing* a graph, we simply *separate the numbers* themselves in order to organize them.

For example, consider the following data of a class's test scores:

90 95 80 80 87 76 74 73 72 70 69 65 50

Suppose we want to see how many scores fall in the 90s, 80s, 70s, etc. We can do this by listing all of the tens place digits in one column, which we'll call "Stems."

Stems
9
8
7
6
5

Now, let's make a second column called "Leaves." In this column, we'll write down the ones digit of every score next to the appropriate "stem" (i.e., tens digit). That way, we'll be able to see how many scores go with each "stem" — that is, how many are in the 90s, 80s, 70s, etc. Let's start with 90. Since 90 has a tens digit of 9 and a ones digit of 0, we'll put a 0 in the "Leaves"' column on the same row as the 9.

Test Scores

90	95	80	80	87
76	74	73	72	70
69	65	50		

Stems	Leaves
9	0
8	
7	
6	
5	

We'll now do the same thing for 95, writing the "leaf" of 5 in the same row as the 9.

Stems	Leaves
9	0 5
8	
7	
6	
5	

We'll continue in this manner, writing each ones digit (i.e., each "leaf") next to the appropriate "stem."

Stems	Leaves
9	0 5
8	0 0 7
7	6 4 3 2 0
6	9 5
5	0

Notice how there are more "leaves" in the 7 row than in any of the other rows. That tells us that more of the scores fall in the 70s than in the 50s, 60s, 80s, or 90s.

Suppose the next year we again collected the class test scores, getting these scores instead:

91 92 90 85 82 81 81 80 77 75 70 65 59

We could add another leaf column to the other side, thereby making it easy to compare how the scores increased or decreased.

When writing the "leaves" for Year 2, we worked from right to left. That way, the column would align on the right no matter how many leaves went with each stem.

Leaves (Year 2)	Stems	Leaves (Year 1)
0 2 1	9	0 5
0 1 1 2 5	8	0 0 7
0 5 7	7	6 4 3 2 0
5	6	9 5
9	5	0

Notice how it's easy to see that in the second year, the number of "leaves" for 9 and 8 increased, while the number of leaves for 7, 6, and 5 decreased or stayed the same. This tells us that the class had more students score in the 90s and 80s than it did the year before, and fewer or the same in the 50s–70s.

Often people will claim the data proves some point they want to make. For example, someone could claim based on the test score improvement we just looked at that the teaching in this class clearly improved the second year, causing there to be more grades in the 80s and 90s. While that initially sounds viable (and it could be the case), there could be other explanations for the improvement. The teacher could have been more generous with his grading, the test could have been easier, the students could have been unusually bright, etc. We can't draw a conclusion about the capabilities of a teacher based on one class's test scores.

Before you believe a conclusion based on stats, always dig around to see if it's a reasonable one and if there might be other explanations.

When organizing data using a stem-and-leaf plot, the data determines what the stems and leaves are. With the test scores, we made the tens digit the stems, since we wanted to see how many scores fell in the 90s, 80s, 70s, etc. If we had data containing numbers in the millions, though, we might make the millions place the "stem" instead of the tens place. In that case, we could round the number to the nearest hundred thousands place so that we'd still only have one "leaf" to record. The point is to use whatever "stem" and "leaves" would best help us organize the data without having to draw an official chart.

Example: Draw a stem-and-leaf plot of the following hypothetical data regarding the number of people dwelling in each city within a county. Round each number to the nearest thousand; make the "stems" the ten thousands and the "leaves" the thousands.

45,679 42,432 41,897 30,456 27,567 25,235

Rounded numbers:

46,000 42,000 42,000 30,000 28,000 25,000

Stem and Leaf Plot:

Stems	Leaves
4	6 2 2
3	0
2	8 5

This plot shows that more of the hypothetical cities have populations in the 40,000s than in the 20,000s or 30,000s.

Keeping Perspective

While you won't often encounter a stem-and-leaf plot in the news since they're not as visually easy to process as a graph, they're another tool we can use to organize data.

11.5 Average and Distribution

In Book 1, we looked at another non-graphical way of organizing data: an average. It's time to review averages, as well as to further explore the concept of distribution.

Reviewing Average

The **average** (also called the **mean**) is a way of describing the center of the data. It's found by dividing the sum of all the data points (remember, a data point is a specific piece of data within the group of data) by the number of data points.

$$\textbf{\textit{average}} = \frac{\textbf{\textit{total of data points}}}{\textbf{\textit{number of data points}}}$$

Example: Find the average of 4, 5, 6, 10, 2, and 7.

$$average = \frac{total\ of\ data\ points}{number\ of\ data\ points} = \frac{4 + 5 + 6 + 10 + 2 + 7}{6} = \frac{34}{6} = 5.67$$

The average is 5.67.

An average summarizes the data into a single number representing the middle of the data. While we found an average of 5.67 for 4, 5, 6, 10, 2, and 7, there are data points above and below 5.67. The average is simply a way of summarizing the data.

Let's look at another example.

Example: Suppose we conducted an experiment about how plants responded to a new fertilizer (which we'll call Fertilizer A). We had a control group of 59 plants that were not given any fertilizer, and a group of 59 plants that were fertilized with Fertilizer A. After a week, we measured the growth in inches (rounded to the nearest half inch) for the 59 plants that were fertilized, getting these results: 0, 0.5, 0.5, 1, 1, 1, 1.5, 1.5, 1.5, 1.5, 1.5, 2, 2, 2, 2, 2, 2, 2.5, 2.5, 2.5, 2.5, 2.5, 2.5, 2.5, 2.5, 3, 3, 3, 3, 3, 3, 3, 3, 3, 3.5, 3.5, 3.5, 3.5, 3.5, 3.5, 3.5, 3.5, 4, 4, 4, 4, 4, 4, 4.5, 4.5, 4.5, 4.5, 4.5, 5, 5, 5, 5.5, 5.5, 6

What was the average growth of the fertilized plants?

$$average = \frac{total\ of\ data\ points}{number\ of\ data\ points}$$

$total\ of\ data\ points = 0 + 0.5 + 0.5 + 1 + 1 + 1 + 1.5 + 1.5 + 1.5 + 1.5 + 1.5 + 2 + 2 + 2 + 2 + 2 + 2 + 2.5 + 2.5 + 2.5 + 2.5 + 2.5 + 2.5 + 2.5 + 2.5 + 3 + 3 + 3 + 3 + 3 + 3 + 3 + 3 + 3 + 3.5 + 3.5 + 3.5 + 3.5 + 3.5 + 3.5 + 3.5 + 3.5 + 4 + 4 + 4 + 4 + 4 + 4 + 4.5 + 4.5 + 4.5 + 4.5 + 4.5 + 5 + 5 + 5 + 5.5 + 5.5 + 6 = 177$

$number\ of\ data\ points = 59$

$$average = \frac{177}{59} = 3$$

The average growth of the fertilized plants was 3 in.

In the previous example, notice that some plants grew much more than 3 in and others grew much less than 3 in. The average summarizes the middle of the data.

Averages and Distribution

While the average is sometimes a helpful summarizing number, it doesn't always tell us the full picture. It can also help to look at the distribution of the data, seeing if most of the results are near the average, or if the results vary greatly. For instance, if half the plants hadn't grown at all and the other half had grown 6 in, the average would have still been 3 in . . . only 3 in would not be a realistic result to expect (we should expect either no growth or 6 in of growth).

Notice that if we look at a frequency distribution of the data from the hypothetical fertilizer experiment, we see that in this case, the results are distributed between 0 in and 6 in, with about 80% falling between 1.5 in and 4.5 in.

Frequency Distribution

Growth	Tally	Frequency	Relative Frequency
0 in	I	1	1.69%
0.5 in	II	2	3.39%
1 in	III	3	5.08%
1.5 in	卌	5	8.47%
2 in	卌 I	6	10.17%
2.5 in	卌 III	8	13.56%
3 in	卌 IIII	9	15.25%
3.5 in	卌 III	8	13.56%
4 in	卌 I	6	10.17%
4.5 in	卌	5	8.47%
5 in	III	3	5.08%
5.5 in	II	2	3.39%
6 in	I	1	1.69%
			Total = 99.97%

Total would be 100% without rounding.

The **distribution** is even easier to see on a column graph.

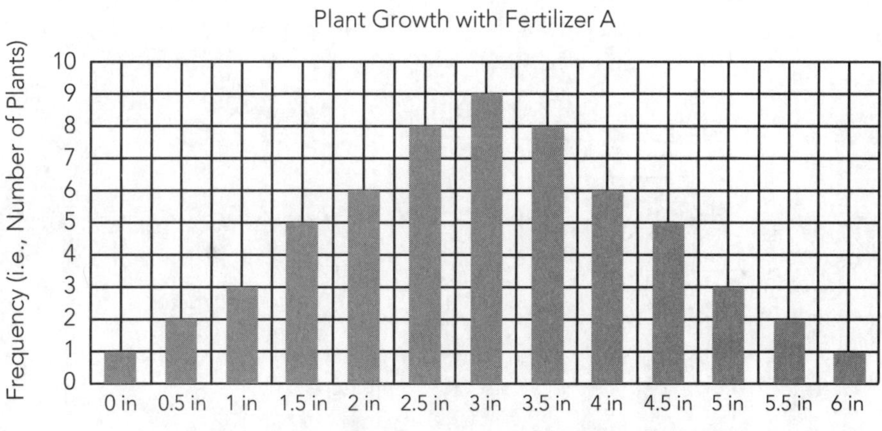

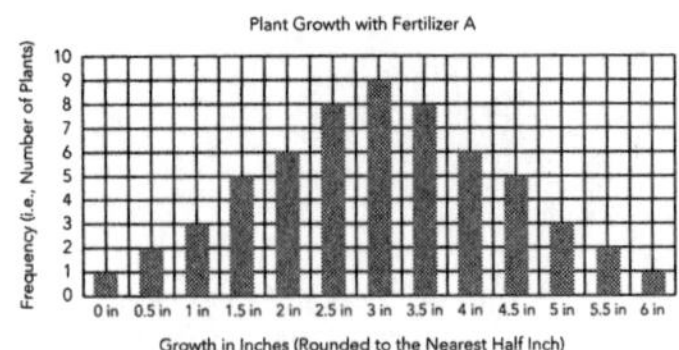

On the graph, we can tell instantly that the average is also the most frequent result — that is, the **mode**. The height of the columns is determined by the number of plants at each height — that is, by the number of results for 0 in, 0.5 in, 1 in, etc. Since 3 in — the average — is the tallest column, this means that 3 in was the result that appeared the most.

The results are evenly distributed (i.e., spread out) on both sides of that average (the columns get smaller on both sides of the average in the same manner). This tells us that the average is also the **median**. 3 in is in the center of the data — there are an equal number of results on both sides of it.

Median and Mode

We covered median and mode in Book 1, but here's a quick review. The **median** is the absolute middle number of a set of data — i.e., the number that would be found if we arrange all the data in order and find the one in the middle.

Example: Find the median of 0, 0.5, 0.5, 1, 1, 1, 1.5, 1.5, 1.5, 1.5, 1.5, 2, 2, 2, 2, 2, 2, 2.5, 2.5, 2.5, 2.5, 2.5, 2.5, 2.5, 2.5, 3, 3, 3, 3, 3, 3, 3, 3, 3.5, 3.5, 3.5, 3.5, 3.5, 3.5, 3.5, 3.5, 4, 4, 4, 4, 4, 4, 4.5, 4.5, 4.5, 4.5, 4.5, 5, 5, 5, 5.5, 5.5, 6

The data points are already arranged in order, so we just need to find the number in the middle.

29 data points

0, 0.5, 0.5, 1, 1, 1, 1.5, 1.5, 1.5, 1.5, 1.5, 2, 2, 2, 2, 2, 2, 2.5, 2.5, 2.5, 2.5, 2.5, 2.5, 2.5, 2.5, 3, 3, 3, (3), 3, 3, 3, 3, 3, 3.5, 3.5, 3.5, 3.5, 3.5, 3.5, 3.5, 3.5, 4, 4, 4, 4, 4, 4, 4.5, 4.5, 4.5, 4.5, 4.5, 5, 5, 5, 5.5, 5.5, 6

29 data points

The median is 3.

Note: When there are an even number of data points, there is not just one number in the middle. We find the median by taking the average (i.e., mean) of the two numbers closest to the middle.

Example: *Find the median of 4, 5, 6, 10, 2, and 7.*

Arrange all the data points in order: 2, 4, 5, 6, 7, 10

Number in the middle:

2 data points 2 data points

2, 4, (5, 6), 7, 10

median

$$\frac{(5 + 6)}{2} = 5.5$$

The median is 5.5.

The **mode** is the most frequent data point.

Example: Find the mode of 0, 0.5, 0.5, 1, 1, 1, 1.5, 1.5, 1.5, 1.5, 1.5, 2, 2, 2, 2, 2, 2, 2.5, 2.5, 2.5, 2.5, 2.5, 2.5, 2.5, 2.5, 3, 3, 3, 3, 3, 3, 3, 3, 3, 3.5, 3.5, 3.5, 3.5, 3.5, 3.5, 3.5, 3.5, 4, 4, 4, 4, 4, 4, 4.5, 4.5, 4.5, 4.5, 4.5, 5, 5, 5, 5.5, 5.5, 6

The most frequent data point is 3 (it appears 9 times), so it is the mode.

Note: Not all sets of data have a mode or a single mode. When no data point occurs more frequently than any other, there is no mode.

Example: *Find the mode of 4, 5, 6, 10, 2, and 7.*

There is no mode, as no number appears more frequently than any other.

When there's a tie for which data point appears the most, there is more than one mode.

Example: *Find the mode of 69, 69, 70, 70, 72, 72, 80, 82*

In this case, 69, 70, and 72 are the modes, as they all appear more than any other number.

The average, median, and mode are all useful ways of expressing the *measure of central tendency*, i.e., the middle of the data.

Now, let's say we tested a different fertilizer mix (Fertilizer B) the next week on 59 plants, and got different results from our experiment, in which the average was still approximately 3 in (2.99, which rounds to 3), but the graph looked like this:

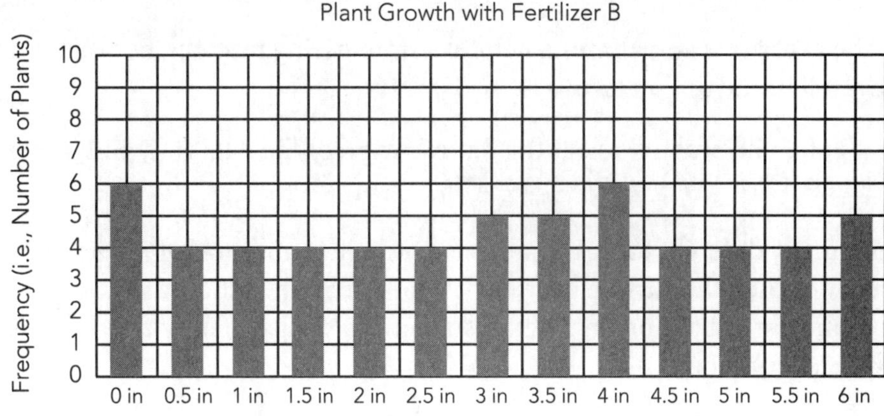

Notice the distribution is now *not* even on both sides of the average (3 in), nor is the average the most frequent result (i.e., the tallest column/mode).

If you go on to explore statistics in more depth, you'll learn that looking at the distribution of data proves incredibly useful in interpreting the data and figuring out what conclusions you can draw. We're only touching on it here, but hopefully the glimpse gives you a taste for how many different aspects to data there are to look at when drawing a conclusion.

Keeping Perspective

While **averages**, **modes**, and **medians** can be helpful summarizing numbers, it can also be helpful to look at the data's **distribution** — that is, at how spread out the results are. All of these are tools in a statistician's toolbox to help him interpret data . . . and another tool in your toolbox to help you question the data you're quoted to see if it matches the claims made.

11.6 Chapter Synopsis and Carl Friedrich Gauss

Well, we've reached the end of a quick tour of **statistics** — the branch of math in which we *collect*, *organize*, and *interpret* data.[13] After reviewing the basics of gathering data, we spent most of our time looking at organizing and interpreting data. We saw

- that tables, graphs, and plots (including **frequency distribution tables, line graphs, stem-and-leaf plots,** and **scatter graphs**) can help us organize data so it's easier to interpret
- that we can look to see the general **trend**, or pattern
- that we can look at whether two different sets of data are **correlated** (i.e., whether there's any relationship between them)
- that the **average** is sometimes a helpful summarizing number, but that it doesn't always tell us the full picture
- that it's often helpful to look at the **distribution** of the data (i.e., how spread out the data is)

There are many different tools we can use to organize and interpret data. While we've only touched the surface of statistics, hopefully the little we've covered will help you understand the process better so you can see past faulty conclusions and ask informed questions.

Carl Friedrich Gauss

Let's take a minute to look at a man who contributed so much to math that he earned the title "Prince of Mathematics." While his contributions were not limited to any one field of math, he certainly contributed to statistics. In fact, a specific distribution is sometimes called Gaussian distribution after him.

Carl Friedrich Gauss entered the world as the son of a bricklayer on April 30, 1777 (almost a year after America declared independence from Britain). He later joked that he could reckon before he could talk,[14] as he was incredibly gifted in math from a young age.

Although gifted in math, Gauss debated about pursuing philology (the study of languages) instead of mathematics. In the end, math won out, and Gauss left his mark on the discipline. One source went as far as to say that "most of the whole science of mathematics has undergone a complete change of form by virtue of Gauss's work."[15]

Carl Friedrich Gauss (1777–1855)

Sadly, though, Gauss missed out on getting credit for many of the discoveries he made because he didn't want to publish anything until he had perfectly polished it. (Sometimes we have to be willing for others to see our mistakes!) One by one, others discovered and published his discoveries instead. For example, he realized there were multiple geometries before others, but he never published his thoughts on the topic, so someone else got the credit.

Gauss didn't inherit the title the "Prince of Mathematics"; he worked hard to contribute what he did to math. He served as professor of mathematics and director of the observatory at Göttingen, remaining inside the city (one account said he even slept in his observatory[16]) for more than 40 years with one exception: to go to a work-related conference.

As you solve math problems, remember that the many rules and notations we use today didn't just appear in the textbook — it took a lot of time and hard work from many people. While their efforts would have been in vain if God were not holding all things together consistently and if He had not given men the ability to explore creation, we can learn from the diligence of men like Gauss.

> *If others would but reflect on mathematical truths as deeply and as continuously as I have, they would make my discoveries.*[17] *— Gauss*

[CHAPTER 12]

Probability

12.1 Introduction to Probability

From predicting weather to understanding how likely it is you'll get the roll you need to win a board game to setting insurance prices to understanding genetics, probability is a useful and exciting branch of mathematics.

And just what is probability? Well, probable means "likely to happen or to be true,"[1] so **probability** is the study of the likelihood of something. Probability is often taught alongside statistics, as in probability we often use data about the past to help us figure out how likely something is to happen in the future.

In this lesson, let's take a look at the overall concept of probability using simple examples. Throughout the rest of this chapter, we'll explore the mathematics of probability in more depth and touch on some of its many applications.

Calculating Probability

Have you ever wondered what the probability is of rolling a ⚄ on a regular die? Well, one way to calculate the probability of a specific **event** (an event is a fancy name for "the actual outcome or final result"[2] or "something that happens"[3]) taking place is to divide the number of outcomes that give us the event (i.e., the result) with the total number of possible outcomes.

$$\textit{probability of an event} = \frac{\textit{outcomes that produce event}}{\textit{total possible outcomes}}$$

In the case of the die, there are 6 sides to a die, 1 of which is a ⚄. Every time you roll a die, then, one of those 6 sides is going to end up on top. So there are 6 total possible outcomes, 1 of which is a ⚄.

Six Sides of a Die

The probability formula we're using assumes that each of the total possible outcomes is equally likely of occurring. In this course, all of our outcomes will be equally likely.

$$\textit{probability of rolling a} ⚄ = \frac{\textit{outcomes that produce} ⚄}{\textit{total possible outcomes}} = \frac{1}{6} = 0.1667 = 16.67\%$$

There's a 16.67% probability of rolling a ⚄ on a standard die.

Notice that we expressed the probability as a percent by dividing the outcomes that produce the result we're interested in by the total possible outcomes. While probability can be expressed using other notations (such as a ratio or decimal), unless specified otherwise, **in this course, express probability as a percent, rounded to two decimal places.** For example, express a probability of $\frac{1}{6}$ as 16.67%.

Let's look at a couple more probability examples.

Example: All 26 of the letters of the alphabet are in a hat, and Henry pulls a letter out of the hat. What is the probability that he'll pick a B?

Here, the total possible outcomes are 26 — the person pulling a letter out could pick any one of the 26 letters in the alphabet. Out of the letters in the alphabet, 1 is a letter B, so only 1 outcome produces the result we're interested in.

$$\textit{probability of an event} = \frac{\textit{outcomes that produce event}}{\textit{total possible outcomes}}$$

$$\textit{probability of picking a B} = \frac{1}{26} = 0.03846 = 3.85\%$$

There's a 3.85% probability Henry will pick a B.

Example: There are 2 pink shirts, 2 yellow shirts, and 3 green shirts in a drawer. If you randomly pull out a shirt, what's the probability of picking a yellow shirt?

Here, the total possible outcomes is 2 + 2 + 3, or 7. Out of the possible shirts we could pick, 2 are yellow. So 2 of the possible outcomes will give us a yellow shirt.

$$\textit{probability of an event} = \frac{\textit{outcomes that produce event}}{\textit{total possible outcomes}}$$

$$\textit{probability of picking a yellow shirt} = \frac{2}{7} = 0.2857 = 28.57\%$$

There's a 28.57% probability of picking a yellow shirt.

Understanding the Big Picture

We've been looking at what is known as **theoretical probability** — that is, probability determined by dividing the outcomes that produce the event by the total possible outcomes.

Experimental probability, on the other hand, would be the result of experimenting (no surprise there). For example, you could find the experimental probability of getting a ⚄ by rolling a die over and over again and tracking your results.

The more times you experiment, the more the experimental probability will match the theoretical probability. For example, because there's one of each of ⚀⚁⚂⚃⚄⚅ on a 6-sided die and because God created a consistent universe in which gravity and other physics operate consistently on the die, if we roll a die enough times, on average we'll get a ⚄ one out of every six times. Yet along the way, we might get two ⚄s . . . and then not get a ⚄ for a long time. However, the more times we roll the die, the more closely we'll average getting one ⚄ for every six rolls.

The fact that the more times we do something, the more our actual experience will equal the theoretical probability we find mathematically is called the **law of large numbers**. This "law" reminds us that probability helps predict on a large scale, but doesn't necessarily help us know an individual outcome. God is the One governing each individual outcome — the only reason we can use probability to predict outcomes on a large scale is because He has chosen to govern this universe in a predictable fashion. *Probability expresses how likely an outcome seems; it doesn't tell us what an individual outcome will be.*

Keeping Perspective

While we used a die as an example of probability since most people have tossed a die before, you'll see in the remaining lessons in this chapter that the concept of probability applies in numerous fields and situations. While you may never need to actually compute the probability of an event occurring yourself, understanding the concept will help you understand probabilities you encounter in your life . . . and perhaps make you a tougher opponent to beat the next time you play a board game.

As you use probability, keep in mind that God is the One governing every detail, and He already knows the exact future. In fact, probability itself is only possible because there's consistency in the universe. If the world were operating without God's hand, we shouldn't expect to find the consistent patterns we do (or even to be able to trust our brains in discerning those patterns). Even in something random such as throwing a die, there's consistency. Gravity is operating consistently on that die, ensuring each side has an equal chance of landing face up. We can only use probability to help us make educated guesses because the universe is ordered by a consistent God.

12.2 Expressing and Applying Probability

In the last lesson, we learned how to calculate probability using simple examples. Now, let's take a bigger look at probability in action. Before we do, though, we have to first take a closer look at what it means for an event to be 100% probable — and at how we can sometimes find probability by addition and subtraction.

100% Probable

Probabilities can *always* be expressed as a percent ranging from 0% to 100%. After all, you can't get any surer than 100% . . . or any less certain than 0%!

Also, we think of it as being 100% probable that one of the possible outcomes will take place. After all, if the event occurs, one of the possible outcomes has to happen. **Thus the sum of all the possible outcomes will always total 100%.** For example, when we roll a die, it's 100% probable that we'll get a result (barring, of course, a dog doesn't swallow the die while it's in midair ☺). One of the sides is going to turn up on top. Since there are 6 sides and each of them is equally likely to turn up on top, the probability of rolling any 1 of those sides is $\frac{1}{6}$. If we were to add up the probability of rolling each of the different possible outcomes, we'd end up at 100%.

Six Possible Outcomes When You Roll a Die

probability of an event $= \frac{\textit{outcomes that produce event}}{\textit{total possible outcomes}}$

probability of rolling a ⚀ $= \frac{1}{6}$

probability of rolling a ⚁ $= \frac{1}{6}$

probability of rolling a ⚂ $= \frac{1}{6}$

probability of rolling a ⚃ $= \frac{1}{6}$

probability of rolling a ⚄ $= \frac{1}{6}$

probability of rolling a ⚅ $= \frac{1}{6}$

---

sum of probabilities $= \frac{6}{6} = 100\%$

Knowing this can help us compare and work with probabilities. For example, let's say we want to know the probability of *not* getting a ⚃ when we roll a die. Since we know the probability of getting a ⚃ is $\frac{1}{6}$, or 16.67%, the probability of *not* getting a ⚃ is 100% – 16.67%, or 83.33%. Notice that this is the *same answer* we would have obtained had we counted up the possible outcomes that do not yield a ⚃ (5, as 5 out of the 6 sides of a die do *not* yield a ⚃) and divided them by the total possible outcomes.

$$\textit{probability of an event} = \frac{\textit{outcomes that produce event}}{\textit{total possible outcomes}}$$

$$\textit{probability of } \text{not } \textit{rolling a } ⚃ = \frac{5}{6} = 83.33\%$$

Keep this in mind as we take a look at a couple of everyday probability applications.

Applying Probability to Baseball Statistics

Probability and statistics are often lumped together, both in curriculum and practice. One reason is because statistics helps us collect, organize, and interpret[4] data, and then probability helps us look at that past data and use it to figure out a probability of a future event.

For example, you learned back in Book 1 how to find a batting average using this relationship:

$$\textit{batting average} = \frac{\textit{hits}}{\textit{at-bats}}$$

As we mentioned in Book 1, batting averages are typically expressed rounded to the third decimal place (the thousandths place), so we will round them to the thousandths place as well.

Example: Find the batting average if a player has 9 hits in 46 at-bats

$$\textit{batting average} = \frac{\textit{hits}}{\textit{at-bats}}$$

$$\textit{batting average} = \frac{9}{46}$$

$$\textit{batting average} = 0.196$$

Now, let's add probability to the mix. The batting average we just found means that the player hit the ball 0.196 or 19.6% of the time. We could say that the probability, or likelihood, that this player will hit a ball is 19.6%.

Do you see what we just did? *We used the stats collected about past results to predict the probability of a future event occurring.* In a way, a batter's hits are his outcomes that produce the event and his total at-bats are his total possible outcomes. When we divide the two to find the average, we're also finding the probability that the player will hit a ball based on his past record. Does this mean that in the future he'll hit the ball 9 out of 46 times? Absolutely not! After all, he could improve his swing . . . or get injured.

What's the probability that this player will *miss* the ball? Well, if he hits it 19.6% of the time, then he misses it 100% – 19.6%, or 80.4% of the time. It's 80.4% probable that he'll miss the ball.

Note: We could have also found the probability of the player missing the ball by taking his misses divided by his at-bats. If he hits the ball 9 out of 46 times, then he misses 37 out of 46 times. So the probability of missing is $\frac{37}{46}$, *or 80.4%.*

Applying Probability to Life Insurance

Finding the probability based on stats is done in all sorts of industries. Have you ever wondered how life insurance companies set their rates to make sure they make a profit? They use probability! They look at compiled data (stats!) and use it to predict the likelihood, or probability, of death. They then use this information to help set their rates so that they'll make a profit.

Applying Probability to Weather

Every time you check the weather you're using — you guessed it — probability! While we don't often think about it as probability, when we say there's an 80% chance of rain, what we're really saying is that there's an 80% probability that it will rain (so bring that umbrella!).

The actual math behind determining the probability of rain is a little more complicated than the simple probabilities we've learned to calculate. However, it's an example of the principles of probability in action.

By the way, if there's an 80% probability it will rain, what's the probability it won't rain? 20%, as 100% – 80% = 20%.

Beyond the probability of rain, probability also helps answer questions such as whether a town should evacuate for a hurricane . . . or whether a forest fire is likely (and thus whether a fire ban needs to go into effect). While the actual math is beyond the scope of this course, know that the principles you're learning have a lot of more advanced real-life applications too.

Keeping Perspective

Not to sound too cheesy, but the probability is pretty high that you'll encounter probability in one form or another in your life. Even if you personally don't find the probability of an event, you're going to encounter probabilities, if only in a weather forecast. Make sure you understand what a probability means so you'll be able to correctly interpret those you encounter.

12.3 Independent Events

Up until now, we've only looked at finding the probability of a single result, that is, of a single event. But many times we need to find the probability of getting more than one result — that is, the probability of multiple events, or results, taking place.

How we find the probability depends on whether the events (i.e., results) are independent *from* each other or dependent *on* each other. Events are **independent** when the result of one doesn't affect the results of the other. For example, when we roll a die, the probability of rolling a ⚃ doesn't change based on what was rolled previously. So we would say that each roll is an **independent event**. On the other hand, events are **dependent** when one affects the other. For example, if a game has a pile of cards that people draw from, the probability of drawing a specific type of card changes based on how many cards (and how many of that type of card) have already been drawn out of the pile. Each event (in this case, each draw of a card) is an example of a **dependent event**, as it affects the next event.

In this lesson, we're going to look at the probability of independent events taking place. In the next lesson, we'll look at dependent events.

Finding the Probability of Independent Events

Say we're playing Yahtzee and need to roll two ⚃s on our last roll in order to win. The probability of rolling a ⚃ on the first die is $\frac{1}{6}$, since there are 6 possible numbers that could land on top, one of which is a ⚃.

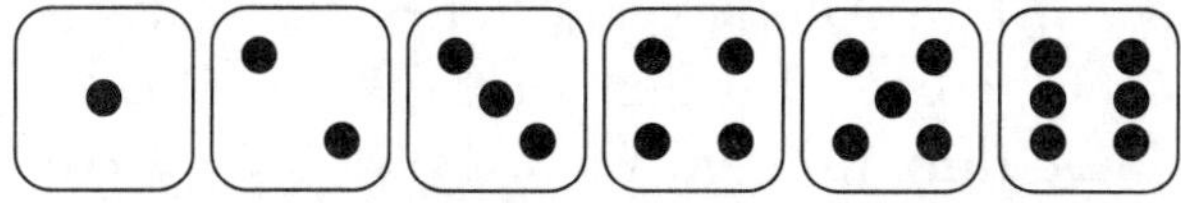

6 possible outcomes, 1 of which is a ⚃

Likewise, the probability of rolling a ⚃ on the second die is also 1 out of 6.

What's the probability of rolling a ⚃ on *both* dice?

When each event is independent from the other like this, the probability of them both occurring can be found by multiplying the individual probabilities together. In other words, we **multiply the probability of each event occurring to find the probability of both events occurring.**

$$\frac{1}{6} \bullet \frac{1}{6} = \frac{1}{36} = 0.0278 = 2.78\%$$

Now, you might be wondering why we multiply to find the event of more than one event occurring. Well, from a probability perspective, we will only roll a ⚃ on the first die 1 out of every 6 times. So $\frac{5}{6}$ of the time we won't roll a ⚃. During the $\frac{1}{6}$ of a time we do, we'll only roll a ⚃ on the second die $\frac{1}{6}$ of the time. So that leads $\frac{1}{6} \bullet \frac{1}{6}$, or $\frac{1}{36}$, probability of rolling a ⚃ on both dice.

> The probability of independent events occurring is found by multiplying the probability of each of the events occurring.

In the case of rolling two ⚃s, we only had two events (i.e., results). However, this same principle holds true for any number of independent events.

Example: What is the probability of rolling 5 ⚀s in a row on a die?

Since the likelihood of rolling a ⚀ on each roll of a die is $\frac{1}{6}$, the likelihood of rolling 5 ⚀s in a row is this:

$$\frac{1}{6} \bullet \frac{1}{6} \bullet \frac{1}{6} \bullet \frac{1}{6} \bullet \frac{1}{6} = \frac{1}{7{,}776} = 0.00013 = 0.013\%$$

Note: Although rolling 5 ⚀s in a row might seem impossible, it theoretically could happen. Remember, probability cannot tell us what will happen; it can only help us make a more logical guess about whether an event is reasonable to expect. It seems quite unlikely we'll roll 5 ⚀s in a row.

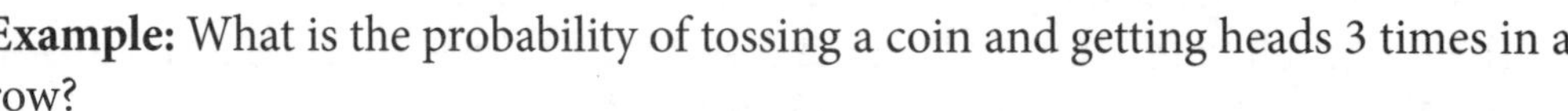

Example: What is the probability of tossing a coin and getting heads 3 times in a row?

Each time, we have 2 possible outcomes, 1 of which is heads. So the probability of rolling a head on each toss is $\frac{1}{2}$. Thus the probability of rolling a head three times in a row is $\frac{1}{2} \bullet \frac{1}{2} \bullet \frac{1}{2} = \frac{1}{8} = 0.125 = 12.5\%$.

Keeping Perspective

As you continue to develop your probability skills, remember that probability is a useful real-life tool. One example of probability's applications is in helping us describe electrons in an atom. One model of the atom views the electrons as a "cloud" around the nucleus of an atom. In this model, while the electrons don't have a precise orbit, we can use probability to help predict the general regions within the "cloud" in which electrons will be. While many of the cool applications of probability require more math than we've covered, know that the principles you're learning apply in all sorts of places — including the microscopic.

12.4 Dependent Events

In the last lesson, we saw how to find the probability of independent events — that is, of events in which the result of one doesn't affect the results of the other. Each roll of a die or toss of a coin is an independent event — that is, the probability of rolling a ⚀ or getting heads doesn't change based on a previous roll or toss. Every time you roll a die, there's a $\frac{1}{6}$, or 16.67%, probability of rolling a ⚀; every time you toss a coin, there's a $\frac{1}{2}$, or 50%, probability of getting heads.

Other events, though, are what we call **dependent events** — that is, one event affects the other event. If you're randomly picking teammates by drawing a number out of a hat, every time someone draws a number, there's one less number left in the hat. Each draw affects the probability of the next draw by reducing the numbers left in the hat.

In this lesson, we're going to take a look at how to find the probability of dependent events.

Dependent Events

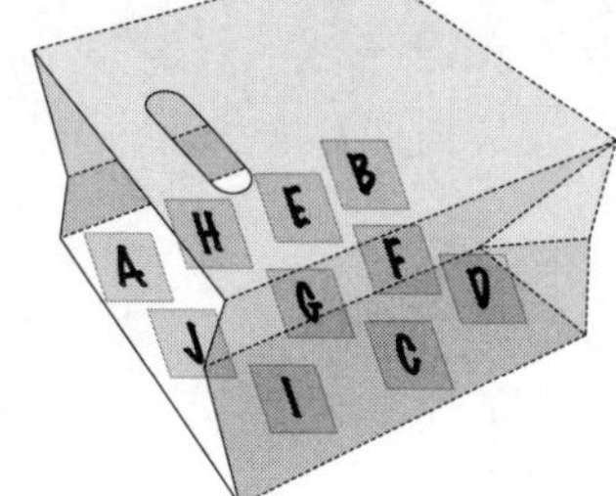

Suppose you put pieces of paper with the ten letters A–J in a bag. What would the probability be of the first person drawing an A and the second person drawing a B if each person kept the number they drew and didn't put it back in the bag?

Well, you know the probability of drawing an A on the first draw would be $\frac{1}{10}$, or 10%, as there are 10 possible letters the person could draw, 1 of which is an A.

10 possible outcomes, 1 of which is an A

$$\textit{probability of drawing an A} = \frac{1}{10}$$

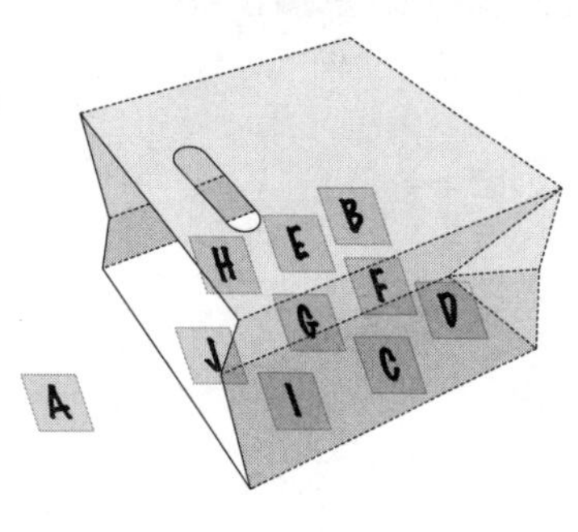

However, the second person would only have 9 possible letters he could draw, as *the first person already removed the letter A!* Thus, the probability of drawing a B on the second draw when the first person drew an A would be $\frac{1}{9}$.

9 possible outcomes, 1 of which is a B

$$\textit{probability of drawing a B} = \frac{1}{9}$$

The probability of *both* of these events taking place would be $\frac{1}{10} \bullet \frac{1}{9} = \frac{1}{90}$, or 1.11%. After all, $\frac{1}{10}$ of the time the first person will draw an A, and then $\frac{1}{9}$ of those times the second person will draw a B. So there's a $\frac{1}{90}$ probability of the first person drawing an A *and* the second person drawing a B.

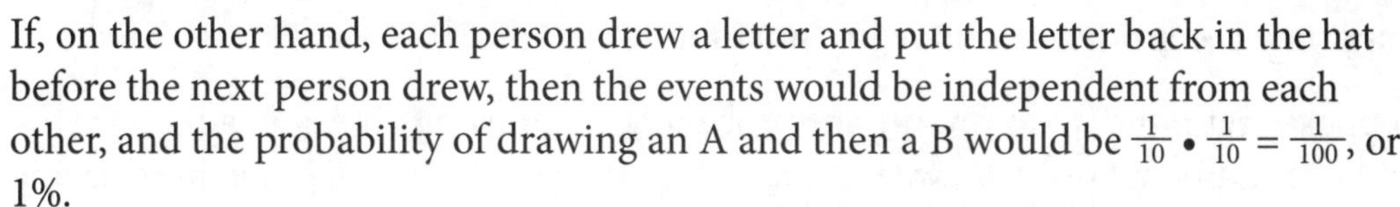

If, on the other hand, each person drew a letter and put the letter back in the hat before the next person drew, then the events would be independent from each other, and the probability of drawing an A and then a B would be $\frac{1}{10} \bullet \frac{1}{10} = \frac{1}{100}$, or 1%.

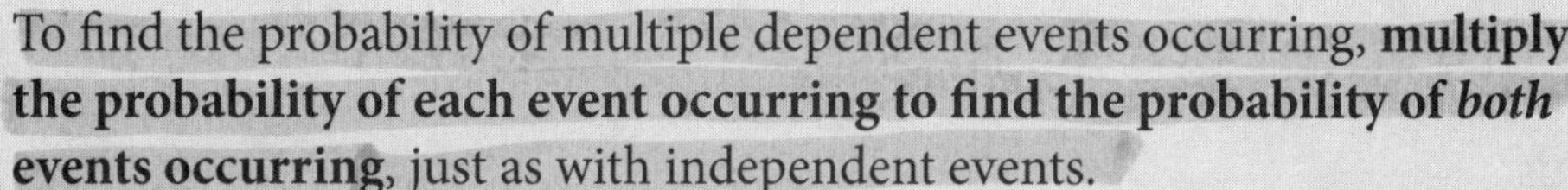

To find the probability of multiple dependent events occurring, **multiply the probability of each event occurring to find the probability of *both* events occurring**, just as with independent events.

Only when dealing with dependent events, **account for any changes caused by the previous event when you find the probability of the next event.**

Example: If there are 12 marbles in a bag, 4 of which are spotted, what is the probability of drawing a spotted marble on your first two draws if each marble is not put back inside the bag after its drawn?

Probability of drawing a spotted marble on the first draw:

12 marbles; 4 of which are spotted

$$\textit{probability of drawing a spotted marble} = \frac{4}{12}$$

Probability of drawing a spotted marble on the second draw, after 1 spotted marble has been removed:

11 marbles; 3 of which are spotted

probability of drawing a spotted marble $= \frac{3}{11}$

Probability of *both* events occurring:

$$\frac{4}{12} \bullet \frac{3}{11} = \frac{12}{132} = 0.0909 = 9.09\%$$

There's a 9.09% chance the first two marbles drawn will be spotted in this scenario.

Notice that in the above example, the first event (i.e., the first draw) not only resulted in decreasing the total possible outcomes, but also caused the outcomes that result in a spotted marble to decrease from 4 to 3, as we removed a spotted marble. **Always be careful to think through what the previous events affect.**

Factorials — Learning the Notation

As you may have noticed by this point, math is filled with different terms and notations. These terms and notations help us easily communicate — that is, once you learn their meaning.

One term you'll hear in probability is **factorial**. To understand factorials and their importance, consider the following situation.

Suppose that rather than finding the probability of drawing an A and a B on the first two draws out of a bag, we wanted to find the probability of 26 people drawing the 26 letters of the alphabet out of a bag in order.

The first person would have a $\frac{1}{26}$ of drawing an A, the second a $\frac{1}{25}$ of drawing a B, and so forth. So to find the probability of each letter being chosen in order, we'd have this:

$$\frac{1}{26} \bullet \frac{1}{25} \bullet \frac{1}{24} \bullet \frac{1}{23} \bullet \frac{1}{22} \bullet \frac{1}{21} \bullet \frac{1}{20} \bullet \frac{1}{19} \bullet \frac{1}{18} \bullet \frac{1}{17} \bullet \frac{1}{16} \bullet \frac{1}{15} \bullet$$
$$\frac{1}{14} \bullet \frac{1}{13} \bullet \frac{1}{12} \bullet \frac{1}{11} \bullet \frac{1}{10} \bullet \frac{1}{9} \bullet \frac{1}{8} \bullet \frac{1}{7} \bullet \frac{1}{6} \bullet \frac{1}{5} \bullet \frac{1}{4} \bullet \frac{1}{3} \bullet \frac{1}{2} \bullet \frac{1}{1}$$

Now, that's a long list of multiplications to write and calculate! Let's see if we can find a simpler way to both express and complete the multiplication. Notice in this case that the numerators are all 1, as there's only 1 of each letter in the bag. So we know that since 1 times itself equals 1, our ending numerator will be 1.

But how do we easily express and calculate the denominator? How do we find the product of multiplying an integer (in this case, 26), by one less than itself, and then one less than that, etc., all the way down to 1? That's even a mouthful to say! Thankfully, there's a term that can help us describe this type of multiplication, a notation that makes it easy to write, and a button on the calculator that makes it easy to calculate.

Term — We call "the product of an integer and all the [positive] integers below it"[5] a **factorial**. In trying to find the probability of drawing all of the letters in order out of a bag, the final denominator would be 26 factorial — that is, the product of 26 and all the integers below it.

Notation — Rather than writing "26 factorial," mathematicians use an exclamation mark next to an integer to mean the factorial of that integer. Using this notation, we could represent the lengthy multiplication we've been looking at like this:

$$\frac{1}{26!}$$

Whew! That was a whole lot less writing, wasn't it?

Calculation — We can easily find the factorial of any number using the **factorial button** (look for an x!) on a calculator. When we do, we find that 26! equals approximately 403,291,460,000,000,000,000,000,000, so $\frac{1}{26!}$ equals approximately $\frac{1}{403,291,460,000,000,000,000,000,000}$. Aren't you glad we didn't have to do all the multiplication manually?

While we won't be doing a lot with factorials in this course, it's important that you understand how helpful mathematical notations can be. Using the symbol ! can save us from a *lot* of writing. Don't ever let a foreign-looking symbol intimidate you — the symbol is likely an agreed-upon notation that, once you understand the meaning, will make solving problems simpler.

Some calculators don't have a factorial button. If that's the case, you can use an online calculator. Just type in the integer to the left of the exclamation mark, and then type an exclamation mark.

Also note that if you enter 26! into a calculator, you will probably get an answer that looks like 4.0329146^{26}. This is the same value as 403,291,460,000,000,000,000,000,000, only written in scientific notation. We'll look at scientific notation in Chapter 16. In the meantime, you won't be asked to find factorials that a calculator displays in scientific notation.

Keeping Perspective — Probability and Origins

Here's a brief summary of finding the probability of multiple events:

- To find the probability of multiple events occurring, **multiply the probability of the individual events.**
- If an event changes the probability of the next event (i.e., if the events are **dependent events**), you have to take that into account when computing the probability of the next event.

Before we conclude the lesson, let's take a look at an application of probability you might not expect.

While we already know that the universe did not get here by accident because of the record we have in the Bible, we can use probability to help illustrate just how illogical it is to believe that the universe arose by chance. Take a look at the probability given in this exert from *Creation* magazine.

> *The probability of the chance formation of a hypothetical functional 'simple' cell, given all the ingredients, is acknowledged*[6] *to be worse than 1 in $10^{57,800}$. This is a chance of 1 in a number with 57,800 zeros. It would take 11 full pages*

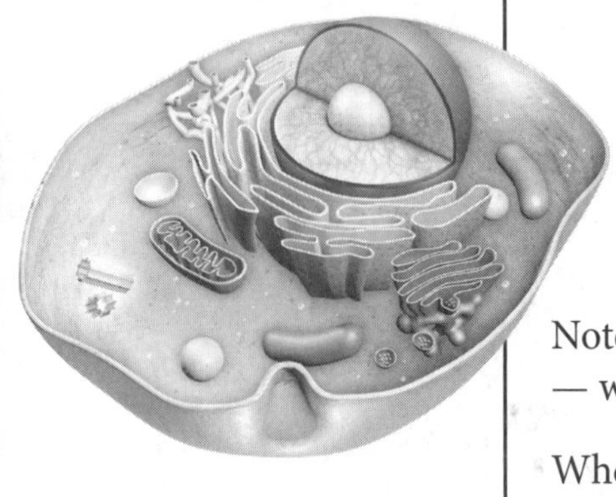

of magazine type to print this number. To try to put this in perspective, there are about 10^{80} (a number with 80 zeros) electrons in the universe. Even if every electron in our universe were another universe the same size as ours that would 'only' amount to 10^{160} electrons. — Don Batten, *Creation Magazine*[7]

Note that $10^{57,800}$ — a number that would take 11 full magazine pages to print — was the probability of *one single cell* arising by chance.

When you look at the probability, it takes a lot of faith to believe a single cell arose by chance, let alone the entire universe! Now, of course, believing in God takes faith too. Both evolution and creation are faith-based, as they *both* deal with the past (and the past can't be proven or observed). Scientists weren't there . . . but God was, and He's told us what happened in His Word. We get to decide if we'll believe what He says or if we'll put our confidence in the ever-changing theories of man.

See www.answersingenesis.org/home/area/faq/probabilities.asp for more information on probability and origins.

The question, as Ken Ham puts it so well in *The Answers Book for Kids*, is, "Do you trust God, who knows everything, who has always been there, who never changes, and who doesn't tell a lie OR a human being who doesn't know everything, changes his mind, changes his story, and wasn't always there?"[8]

12.5 The Fundamental Counting Principle

Up until now, when you've been asked to find the probability of an event or multiple events, you've always been told the number of possible outcomes. Sometimes, though, it's not quite so obvious how many possible outcomes there are. For example, what's the probability of getting a specific phone number if they're randomly assigned? Or leaving probability out of it for a moment, how many unique phone numbers can there be in a single area code?

Let's take a closer look at how we can find the number of possible outcomes, both when working with a probability problem and when simply trying to figure out the number of real-life possible combinations, such as the number of unique telephone numbers.

The Fundamental Counting Principle

Let's start with a simple example. When rolling two dice at the same time, you know you'll end up with a sum somewhere between 2 and 12. After all, you could roll ⚀⚀ (which would result in a sum of 2), ⚅⚅ (which would result in a sum of 12), or some combination in between.

Let's see how likely it is to roll a specific sum. We'll do so by figuring out all the possible combinations we could get from two dice and organizing them by their sum.

All Possible Combinations of Two Dice Arranged by Sum

Sum of Two Dice	Combinations that Produce Sum	
2	⚀⚀	1 combination
3	⚀⚁ ⚁⚀	2 combinations
4	⚀⚂ ⚁⚁ ⚂⚀	3 combinations
5	⚀⚃ ⚁⚂ ⚂⚁ ⚃⚀	4 combinations
6	⚀⚄ ⚁⚃ ⚂⚂ ⚃⚁ ⚄⚀	5 combinations
7	⚀⚅ ⚁⚄ ⚂⚃ ⚃⚂ ⚄⚁ ⚅⚀	6 combinations
8	⚁⚅ ⚂⚄ ⚃⚃ ⚄⚂ ⚅⚁	5 combinations
9	⚂⚅ ⚃⚄ ⚄⚃ ⚅⚂	4 combinations
10	⚃⚅ ⚄⚄ ⚅⚃	3 combinations
11	⚄⚅ ⚅⚄	2 combinations
12	⚅⚅	1 combination

total possible combinations = 1 + 2 + 3 + 4 + 5 + 6 + 5 + 4 + 3 + 2 + 1 = 36

There are 36 total combinations possible on two dice, 6 of which give us a combined sum of a 7. So the probability of rolling a combined sum of a 7 is $\frac{6}{36}$, or 16.67%.

Now, that was a lot of work! Remember, in math we try to find simpler ways to get the job done — that is, we use the intellect God gave us, coupled with the consistencies He created and sustains, to find mathematical "tools" that simplify tasks. Let's take a closer look at a simpler way to find the probability of rolling a combined sum of a 7.

While we eventually need to look at both dice as a single event since we're interested in their combined sum, let's temporarily look at them as separate events. When we do, it's easy to see that each die could yield 6 possible outcomes.

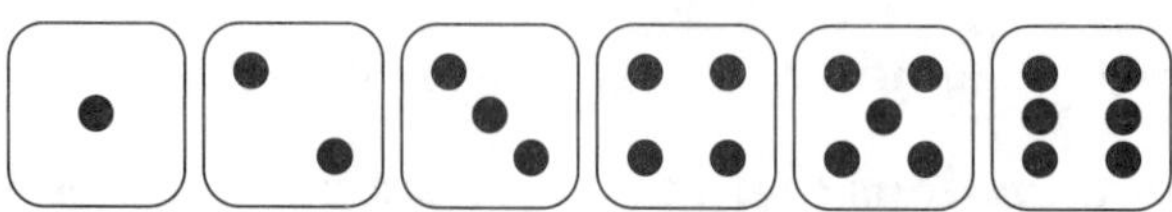

6 Possible Outcomes from Each Die

So if the first die could yield 6 possible outcomes and the second die could yield 6 possible outcomes, and any one of the outcomes from one die could be paired with any one of the outcomes from the other die, it follows that there are **6 • 6, or 36**, different ways the two dice could combine. We can use simple multiplication to show us the number of possible outcomes we could obtain from two dice. There's no need to laborously think through each possibility and make a chart.

We just arrived at what's called the **fundamental counting principle**. This principle basically states that we can find the total possible outcomes of two or more events (i.e., results) by multiplying the possible outcomes of each.

We can use the fundamental counting principle to help us find the total possible outcomes in order to then find the probability of an event (i.e., result).

Example: If you have 10 ties and 5 shirts, any of which can be worn with any other, how many total different possible outfits could you put together? If you randomly select a tie and shirt, what's the probability of picking a specific combination?

$\textit{total possible outcomes} = 10 \bullet 5 = 50$

We could put together 50 outfits out of 10 ties and 5 shirts, as any shirt can be paired with any tie.

$\textit{probability of picking 1 specific combination} = \frac{1}{50} = 0.02 = 2\%$

Possible Outcomes and Telephone Numbers

How many different telephone numbers can we assign to *a single area code*? Well, in the countries using the North American Numbering Plan (the USA is one), we never start a telephone number with a 0 or 1, so the first digit will be a number between 2–9. The remaining digits will be a number from 0–9. So there are 8 different possible outcomes for the first digit (2–9), and 10 different possible outcomes (0–9) for each of the other digits.

See http://www.nanpa.com/about_us/abt_nanp.html for more details about the numbering plan for telephone numbers in North America. The chart shown here is based on the one they have listed on their site.[9]

Telephone Numbers in One Area Code

$NXX - XXXX$

$N = \textit{any number from } 2\text{–}9$

$X = \textit{any number from } 0\text{–}9$

Now, it would take a long time to manually add up all the different possible combinations. After all, only *one* digit would have to change in order for the number to be different.

Thankfully, we can use math (specifically, the fundamental counting principle) to do the calculating for us. All we have to do is multiply the possible options for *each* digit, and we'll find the total possible combinations.

$$\textit{total possible outcomes} = 8 \bullet 10 \bullet 10 \bullet 10 \bullet 10 \bullet 10 \bullet 10 = 8{,}000{,}000$$

Each area code can theoretically contain up to 8 million different numbers (I say theoretically because, in reality, some numbers don't get used). Now aren't you glad we didn't have to manually count each of those possible outcomes?

Note: Approximately 8 million phone numbers (some numbers aren't used) might sound like a lot, but when you think about the fact that companies can reserve blocks of numbers and that families may have a home, work, and multiple cell numbers, phone numbers get assigned more quickly than you might think.

Keeping Perspective — More Applications

The more math you learn, the more you'll discover that concepts continue to build on each other . . . and that there's always more you could learn! While we've touched on the basics of probability, whole courses are devoted to it.

There's so much more to math and how it applies and explores God's creation than any human can ever fully know. God, however, knows and understands it all. In fact, He created and sustains the world math seeks to describe.

> *O LORD, our Lord, how excellent is thy name in all the earth! who hast set thy glory above the heavens. . . . When I consider thy heavens, the work of thy fingers, the moon and the stars, which thou hast ordained; What is man, that thou art mindful of him? and the son of man, that thou visitest him? (Psalm 8:1–4).*

12.6 Understanding the Odds / The Dangers of Gambling

You may have heard the expression "what are the odds of that." The "odds" of something happening are very similar to the "probability of" something happening. Only with **odds**, we compare the outcomes that produce the event with the outcomes that do not produce the event rather than with the total outcomes.

For example, if 6 out of the 36 possible combinations of two dice produce a combined sum of a 7, then the remaining 30 do *not* produce a combined sum of a 7. So the *odds* for rolling a combined sum of a 7 are 6 to 30 (often written 6:30), while the *odds against* rolling a combined sum of a 7 are 30 to 6 (often written 30:6).

Notice that with odds we're comparing 6 (the outcomes that produce a specific event) with 30 (the outcomes that do not produce that event), whereas when we find the *probability*, we compare 6 (the outcomes that produce a specific event) with 36 (the *total possible outcomes*).

$$\textbf{\textit{probability}} = \frac{\textbf{\textit{outcomes that produce event}}}{\textbf{\textit{total possible outcomes}}}$$

$$\textbf{\textit{odds for}} = \frac{\textbf{\textit{outcomes that produce event}}}{\textbf{\textit{outcomes that do not produce event}}}$$

$$\textbf{\textit{odds against}} = \frac{\textbf{\textit{outcomes that do not produce event}}}{\textbf{\textit{outcomes that produce event}}}$$

Also, while we typically express probability as a percent, it's more common to **express the odds with a colon**, as in 6:30 (read "6 to 30"). The colon format makes sense for odds, since it emphasizes the comparison between the two values. **In this course, use a colon to express odds.**

Example: If a player bats at a $\frac{9}{50}$ batting average, what are the odds he will hit the ball when he steps up to the plate? How about the odds that he won't hit the ball?

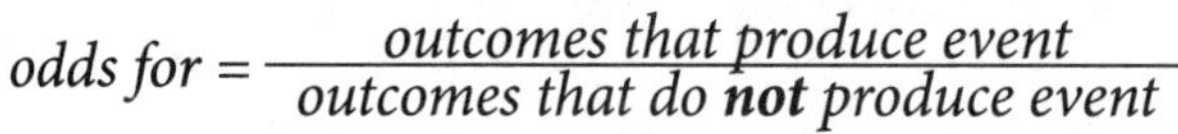

$$\textit{odds for} = \frac{\textit{outcomes that produce event}}{\textit{outcomes that do } \textbf{not} \textit{ produce event}}$$

$$\textit{odds for} = \frac{9}{41}\text{, or 9:41}$$

$$\textit{odds against} = \frac{\textit{outcomes that do } \textbf{not} \textit{ produce event}}{\textit{outcomes that produce event}}$$

$$\textit{odds against} = \frac{41}{9}\text{, or 41:9}$$

Note: The outcomes that do not produce event (41) was found by subtracting 9 (the outcomes that produce event) from the total outcomes (50).

$$50 - 9 = 41$$

The Probability of Losing

Both odds and probability are commonly used in context of games and gambling. The lottery, horse races, casinos, and other establishments all thrive on enticing people to spend money on the chance that they might win a much larger sum of money.

What many people don't stop to consider, though, is the probability of *losing*. Casinos exist because way more people lose than make money, making the casino rich. Some even lose everything they own and shipwreck their futures and families in pursuit of money.

We're going to use math to explore the probability of losing a lottery. Our purpose in doing this is to help cut through some of the pull we're bombarded with in this culture toward various forms of gambling and to show from a mathematical sense how gambling can be quite dangerous.

According to the Virginia Mega Millions website[10] as I'm writing this, the odds of winning the next jackpot are "1 in 258,890,850." Notice that it says 1 *in* 258,890,850 rather than 1 *to* 258,890,850 — even though the word "odds" is used here, we're going to assume[11] that the site is meaning that the probability of winning is $\frac{1}{258,890,850}$. Think about that number for a minute. If we convert it to a percent, we'll see that's a 0.000000386% chance of winning. If we were to round the number to the nearest *millionth*, we'd get a 0% probability of winning.

Let's look at the probability of *losing*. If we subtract 0.000000386% from 100%, we'll find the probability of losing.

$$100\% - 0.000000386\% = 99.999999614\%$$

That's basically a 100% chance of losing!

To put it in terms of the odds, the odds are only 1 to 258,890,849 of winning.

Now granted, there are smaller prizes with their own probabilities and odds. Yet the probability of winning *any* prize (including even the smallest prize of $1) is 6.8%, so we have 93.2% probability of not winning *any prize* at all (not even $1!).

Despite the probability of losing, multitudes of people purchase lottery tickets. A 2008 study found that households earning less than $13,000 a year spend an average of about $645 a year on lottery tickets.[12] That's a lot of money every year! After only 10 years, that would come to $6,450. After 50 years, that would add up to $32,250 dollars. Even if those numbers have changed or are exaggerated, the point remains: the price of tickets adds up. People freely buy lottery tickets with an almost 0% chance of winning.

Again, while no one talks about the probability or odds of losing, they're very real. "According to the 2006 Gross Annual Wager Report, Americans lost nearly $91 billion on all forms of gambling combined."[13]

Keeping Perspective

Well, hopefully our quick look at gambling and the odds will help you be more aware of the truth behind gambling — that the odds are tremendously in favor of *losing*, not gaining. It's easy to become enamored by the thought of "getting lucky" or "getting rich quick" and end up enslaved in what can be a dangerous addiction. Please be careful to guard your heart from the love of money.

> *For the love of money is a root of all sorts of evil, and some by longing for it have wandered away from the faith and pierced themselves with many griefs (1 Timothy 6:10; NASB).*

12.7 Probability and Genetics

God built living things with an incredible code that passes on from one generation to the next. You have thousands of genes (and I don't mean blue jeans!) in your DNA that affect the thousands of different characteristics that make up you. Before we end our brief foray into probability, let's take a lesson to look at how probability helps us explore how traits get passed down from one generation to the next.

A Glance at History

Gregor Mendel (1822–1884)

Back in the 1800s, a monk named Gregor Mendel began experimenting with how traits were passed on from one generation to the next. Specifically, he conducted experiments with pea plants. He discovered some fascinating things about how God built amazing variety into this world. While we'll just take a look at the end conclusions based on his research, know that this information came about through looking at God's creation and exploring it.

> *The power of Mendel's work is that he linked **mathematical analysis** to the study of inheritance. — Michael Windelspecht*[14]

Understanding Genes

Without going into all the details, you have two versions of every gene in your DNA code: one from your mother, and one from your father. The combination you receive determines the traits (eye color, hair color, etc.) you have. That's part of the amazing variety God placed within the DNA code.

You see, some traits are what we call **recessive** — that is, they'll only show up if an offspring receives genes for it from *both* parents. Others are what we call **dominant** — that is, if an offspring receives just *one* gene from one of his parents for that trait, he'll have that trait.

Let's look at a simple example involving Mendel's peas. Mendel discovered that shortness in pea plants is a recessive trait — a pea plant will only be short if both of its "parents" give it a short gene, which we'll represent with an h. If a pea plant gets just one tall gene, which we'll represent with an H, it will be tall.

Now remember, an offspring receives two versions of every gene: one from each "parent." Let's think through the different combinations of what we'll nickname the "height" gene a pea plant could have. It could receive a short gene (h) from both parents, giving it two short genes, or hh. Or it could receive a short gene from one parent and a tall gene from the other, giving it hH or Hh. Or it could receive a tall gene from both parents, giving it HH. If the plant receives hh, it will be short, but with all three of the other possible combinations, the plant will be tall.

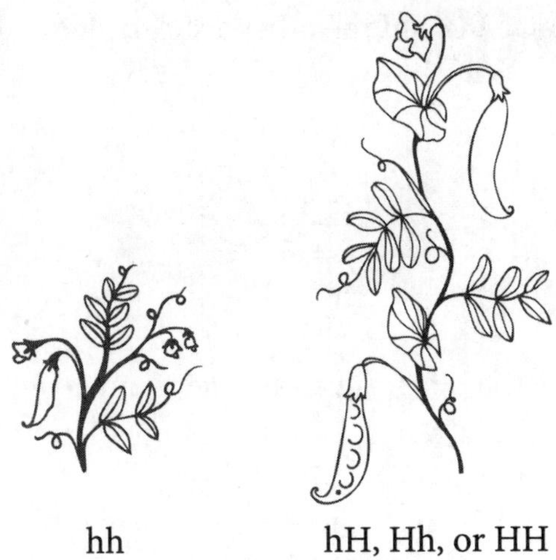

hh hH, Hh, or HH

While you might think we chose the small h for short because it looks smaller than a capital H, we actually chose a capital letter for the tall gene (H) to show that it's the *dominant* trait, and a small letter for the short gene (h) to show that it's the *recessive* trait.

Notice, then, that a tall pea plant could still have the short gene — that is, it could still have the genetic information for shortness.

Let's say that two tall pea plants that both also have a short gene (Hh) get bred together. What different gene combinations could they pass on to their offspring? Well, we know from the fundamental counting principle that we can find the total possible combinations of two or more events by multiplying the possible outcomes of each. In this case, we can view the gene each plant passes on to its offspring as one event. Since each plant has 2 versions of every gene, each plant has 2 possible versions it could pass along to its offspring. Thus, the total possible combinations of genes the offspring could receive is 2 • 2, or 4.

This is easy to see on what we call a Punnett Square. We'll start by drawing a square (well, actually, several squares within a square) and putting the "parent" genes along the sides.

Genes of one tall pea plant

Genes of one tall pea plant	H	h
H		
h		

Let's now fill in the boxes with the different possible combinations of genes the offspring could receive. Each parent could give a tall gene (H), giving the offspring two tall genes (HH).

	H	h
H	HH	
h		

One parent could give a tall gene and the other a short, giving the offspring a tall and a short gene (Hh).

	H	h
H	HH	(Hh)
h	(hH)	

Or both parents could give the offspring a short gene, giving the offspring two short genes (hh).

	H	h
H	HH	Hh
h	hH	(hh)

Whether the offspring was tall or short would depend on which set of genes it receives. If the offspring receives even one tall gene, it will be tall since the tall gene is dominant; if the offspring receives *only* short genes (hh), it will be short.

	H	h
H	HH *tall*	Hh *tall*
h	hH *tall*	hh *short*

Again, note that this is a simple example. Some traits are not simply dominant and recessive. In *Building Blocks in Life Science*, Dr. Gary Parker illustrates this using flowers, explaining that "crosses of pink-flowered four o'clocks with genes Pp produce three variations of flower color: red (PP), pink (Pp), and white (pp)."[15] Some traits are also determined by more than one gene. The genetic code is truly amazing!

Probability Time

Okay, let's bring probability into the mix here. What's the probability of getting a short pea plant with the two tall plants we've been looking at? There are 4 possible gene combinations that could get passed along. Out of those, only 1 will result in a short pea plant. So there's a $\frac{1}{4}$, or 25%, probability of getting a short pea plant whenever these 2 pea plants are bred together.

	H	h	
H	HH	Hh	4 possible combinations; 1 of which (hh) will result in a short plant.
h	hH	hh	

What's the probability of getting 2 short pea plants in a row from these 2 tall plants? Well, there's a $\frac{1}{4}$ probability each time, and each event (i.e., result) is independent from the other, so there'd be a $\frac{1}{4} \cdot \frac{1}{4} = \frac{1}{16}$, or 6.25%, probability of getting two short pea plants in a row.

We can use probability to see how likely (or unlikely) certain traits are to pass along.

The Bigger Picture

Now, you might be wondering why we care what the probability is of two pea plants with genes Hh producing a short pea plant. On a practical level, understanding genetics can help us breed plants and animals with more desirable traits. On a deeper level, understanding genetics gives us a glimpse into God's amazing creative design. The Bible tells us that God created plants and animals according to their kinds.

> *And God said, Let the earth bring forth grass, the herb yielding seed, and the fruit tree yielding fruit after his kind, whose seed is in itself, upon the earth: and it was so. . . . And God created great whales, and every living creature that moveth, which the waters brought forth abundantly, after their kind, and every winged fowl after his kind: and God saw that it was good. . . . And God said, Let the earth bring forth the living creature after his kind, cattle, and creeping thing, and beast of the earth after his kind: and it was so (Genesis 1:11–24).*

Notice the repeated use of the word "kind." God created "kinds" of animals and plants, including within that kind the genetic code that could produce all the different variations within that kind we have today.

By ingraining incredible variety within kinds, God not only created an interesting world, but He also made it possible for living things to survive in the various climates that make up our now-fallen world. For example, some genes might result in traits that help an animal or plant survive in hot climates. Those offspring without that gene would die off in a hot area or move on to a cooler part of the world, leaving behind only those with the hot-climate-friendly gene . . . who would then pass that gene on to their offspring.

This process is often referred to as *natural selection*, and evolutionists like to point to it as evidence for plants and animals changing from one kind to another. But that is not the case. For one kind to evolve into another kind, there would need to be a *gain* of information from one generation to another. But what we observe is the opposite of that: a *loss* of information. When two tall pea plants have a short offspring, that offspring has lost the tall gene. After all, the original plants had genes of Hh; the short offspring now has a gene of hh. It has *lost* the gene for tall (H) and now *only* has short genes. The small pea plant may look different from its parents, but it hasn't *gained* any information — the small gene was present in both parents, just not shown because of their tall gene (H). The offspring has *lost* information — it no longer has the genetic information for being tall (H).

Natural selection is the exact opposite of changing from one kind into another; it results in a *loss* of information, not a gain.

Also, while we observe variations *within a kind* (such as different heights in pea plants), we don't observe changes from one kind to another (a pea plant doesn't become a celery stalk).

For more information on genetics and a biblical worldview, see the free resources referenced in the endnotes.[16]

Understanding genes also helps us understand how Noah fit all the animals on the ark (he only had to take two of every *kind*) and how all the people of the world go back to one man and woman (Adam and Eve), just as the Bible says.

Keeping Perspective

There is so much variety within our genetic code it's staggering.

> *The number of atoms estimated in the entire universe is in the order of a 1 followed by 80 zeros. But the number of combinations of unique children that a male and female human could potentially procreate is even more than this. There's phenomenal variability in our genes. DNA is the most complex phenomenal storage system in the universe. When one considers the amount of information that God put in our DNA — one just has to stand back in awe of our Creator. It is mind-boggling.*
> — *Ken Ham and A. Charles Ware*[17]

Needless to say, there's much more to genetics and our DNA code that we could explore in a lesson. Hopefully, the little we looked at, though, gives you a glimpse at the incredible way God built variety into His creation and at how probability helps us explore yet another aspect of His handiwork.

Keep in mind, though, that while we can figure out the probability of certain traits passing along, it's God who determines the intricate details of each new living creature. You are created exactly how God wove you together. While genes give us a glimpse into the mechanisms He uses to accomplish His purposes and probability gives us a way of looking at the big picture and the results over large numbers (i.e., if we combine enough pea plants with Hs, how often should we expect to get hh), it does *not* tell us an individual outcome. You are uniquely designed by a caring Creator.

> *For You formed my inward parts; You wove me in my mother's womb (Psalm 139:13; NASB).*

12.8 Chapter Synopsis

We've covered a lot of territory in this chapter as we've looked at how to understand, express, and apply probability. Here are a couple of key points to remember:

- **Probability** is a way of expressing the likelihood of an **event** (i.e., a result) occurring. It doesn't tell us what *will* happen — only how *likely* it is to happen. The **law of large numbers** expresses the idea that the more times we do something, the more our actual experience will equal the theoretical probability found mathematically. Probability can always be expressed as a percent between 0–100% — you can't get any more probable than 100%, or less probable than 0%.

- **We can find the probability** for a single event by taking the total number of outcomes that produce that event and dividing that by the total possible outcomes; we find the probability of **independent events** occurring by multiplying the probability of each event occurring, and of **dependent events** the same way, only being careful to adjust the probability of each event to account for changes caused by the previous event.

- A **factorial** is "the product of an integer and all the [positive] integers below it."[18] It's expressed using an exclamation mark. For example, 3! means 3 • 2 • 1. Factorials are a useful notation used in probability, as well as elsewhere in math.

- The **fundamental counting principle** helps us find the total possible outcomes. This principle basically states that we can find the total possible outcomes of two or more events (i.e., results) by multiplying the possible outcomes of each.

- **Odds** are very similar to probability, only we're comparing the outcomes that produce an event with those that do not produce that event rather than with the total possible outcomes. We commonly express odds as a ratio like this: 3:1.

  - $\textit{probability of a result occurring} = \dfrac{\textit{outcomes that do produce event}}{\textit{total possible outcomes}}$

  - $\textit{odds for a result occurring} = \dfrac{\textit{outcomes that produce event}}{\textit{outcomes that do } \textbf{not} \textit{ produce event}}$

  - $\textit{odds against a event occurring} = \dfrac{\textit{outcomes that do } \textbf{not} \textit{ produce event}}{\textit{outcomes that produce event}}$

Above all, remember that while we can look at the probability of different events, God is the One who knows and controls the future.

The Bible tells us of several times when people cast lots to determine an outcome. Casting lots is similar to drawing a number, throwing a die, or flipping a coin and letting the outcome determine your actions. While this might seem like a random way to decide, God makes it clear that nothing — not even the casting of a lot — is independent from His control.

And they said every one to his fellow, Come, and let us cast lots, that we may know for whose cause this evil is upon us. So they cast lots, and the lot fell upon Jonah (Jonah 1:7).

The lot is cast into the lap; but the whole disposing thereof is of the LORD (Proverbs 16:33).

We can rest knowing that our wise Heavenly Father watches over every detail of His creation, noticing every tiny sparrow that falls. *Nothing* happens to us by chance.

Are not two sparrows sold for a farthing? and one of them shall not fall on the ground without your Father (Matthew 10:29).

Exploring Mathematical Relationships

13.1 Constants, Variables, and Relationships Between Variables

Now that we've had a chance to get a taste for statistics and probability, it's time to return to looking at equations and inequalities. Only this time, rather than focusing on the mechanics of finding unknowns, we're going to look at how equations and inequalities help us describe real-life relationships.

The concept of using math to describe real-life relationships is not a new one. In fact, when solving geometry problems, you've worked with the *relationships* between the perimeter, area, and volume and the sides of shapes.

Example: Find the length of a rectangular deck that's 6 ft wide and has an area of 72 ft².

You know the *relationship* between the area, length, and width is $A = \ell w$, so to find the length, you substitute the values you know and then solve for ℓ.

$$A = \ell w$$

$$\mathbf{72\ ft^2} = \ell(\mathbf{6\ ft})$$

$$\frac{\mathbf{72\ ft^2}}{\mathbf{6\ ft}} = \frac{\ell(\mathbf{6\ ft})}{\mathbf{6\ ft}}$$

$$\frac{\cancel{72}^{12}\ \cancel{ft^2}^{ft}}{\cancel{6}\ \cancel{ft}} = \frac{\ell(\cancel{6\ ft})}{\cancel{6\ ft}}$$

$$\mathbf{12\ ft} = \ell$$

When solving word problems, you've looked at the *relationship* between the different elements of a word problem in order to find the requested piece of information.

Example: How many total slices of pizza do you need if you plan 2 slices for each guest and you expect 30 guests?

Relationship between slices of pizza and guests:

Total pizza slices = number of slices per guest • number of expected guests

Relationship expressed using letters:

$T = sg$

Inserting known values and solving:

$T = 2(30)$

$T = \mathbf{60}$

You would need 60 slices of pizza.

It's time now, though, to explore mathematical relationships in more depth by looking not just for a single value (such as the area or the total slices of pizza) but at how the unknowns in a relationship relate *to each other* — that is, at the **relation**, or relationship, between them. For example, if we need 2 slices of pizza per guest, how does the total slices of pizza relate to the number of guests?

The term ***relation*** is one you'll hear in math. We're using it to mean "the way in which two or more concepts, objects, or people are connected; a thing's effect on or relevance to another."[1] While there's a more technical definition, this definition encapsulates the core idea.

Obviously, the greater the number of guests, the more slices of pizza you need. The fewer the guests, the less pizza you need.

While that may seem obvious, looking at how different values relate *to each other* proves valuable. To begin exploring these relations, we first need to understand a couple of important terms.

Understanding Constants and Variables

We use the term **constant** to refer to a quantity whose value we know is constant (i.e., fixed or unchanging) and **variable** to describe a quantity whose value can vary.

Every numeral is a constant. For example, 5, $\frac{1}{2}$, –8, and 1.2563 all represent a fixed value. Some letters are also constant. For example, even though we use a π (which is a Greek letter p) to describe pi, its value is fixed, making it a constant. It is always the irrational number that begins 3.14 and continues on and on.

Other letters, though, are variables — that is, their value can vary. For example, the value of x can vary depending on what we're using it to represent. It is a variable. In the formula $A = \ell w$ that we use to find the area of a rectangle (*Area = length • width*), A, ℓ, and w are all variables, as they all represent values that can vary.

Looking at the Relationship Between Variables

It's often helpful to look at the relationship, or relation, *between* variables. How does one vary as the other varies?

For example, let's say we were in charge of designing a rectangular sign. We know the customer wants the length of the sign to be 10 ft, but we can make the width any value from 1 ft to 10 ft.

In this situation, the length (ℓ) is a *constant* 10 ft. The width and the area (w and A), though, are variables . . . we could insert different values for them. Let's look at how changing the width affects the area.

Area = ?

width = ?

length = 10 ft

Take a look at what happens to the area if we pick a few different widths.

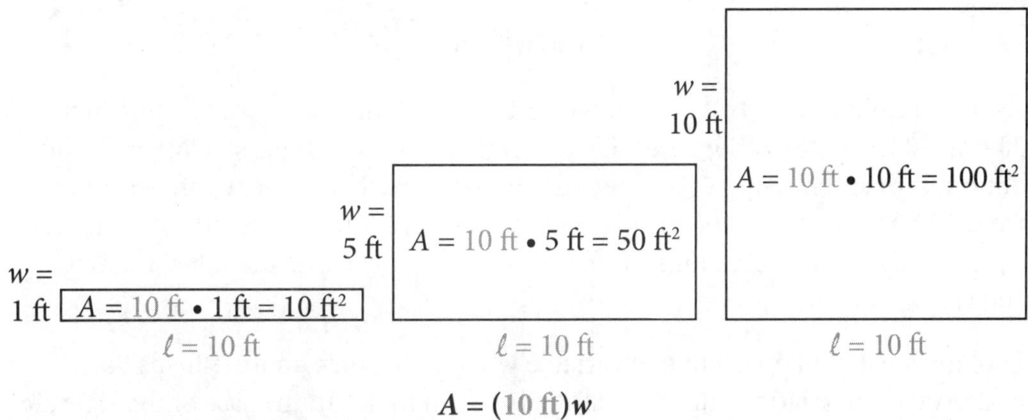

Notice that as the width *increases* from 1 ft to 5 ft to 10 ft, the area *increases* from 10 ft^2 to 50 ft^2 to 100 ft^2. On the other hand, if we were to look at the signs shown from right to left, we'd see that as the width *decreases* from 10 ft to 5 ft to 1 ft, the area *decreases* too. After all, in this example, the area always equals 10 times the width . . . thus, as the width increases or decreases, the area has to as well by the same factor.

Let's look at a different scenario. Say we charge for the sign by the square foot and the customer was only willing to pay for 100 ft^2. The customer didn't have any restrictions on the measurement of the length or width.

In this case, the area (A) is now a *constant* 100 ft^2, while the length and width (ℓ and w) have values that could vary. Let's take a look at how changing the width affects the length.

Area = 100 ft^2

width = ?

length = ?

As the width changes, the area doesn't change (it is constant). Instead, the length decreases as the width increases, and increases as the width decreases (after all, the product of the length and the width has to equal the same amount: 100 ft²).

$w =$ 1 ft $\quad A = 100 \text{ ft}^2 \quad \ell = 100$ ft

$w =$ 5 ft $\quad A = 100 \text{ ft}^2 \quad \ell = 20$ ft

$w =$ 10 ft $\quad A = 100 \text{ ft}^2 \quad \ell = 10$ ft

$$\mathbf{100\ ft^2} = \ell w$$

As the width *increases* from 1 ft to 5 ft to 10 ft, the length *decreases* from 100 ft to 20 ft to 10 ft. On the other hand, if we were to look at the signs starting with the bottom sign and moving up to the top sign, we'd see that as the width *decreases* from 10 ft to 5 ft to 1 ft, the length *increases* from 10 ft to 20 ft to 100 ft. After all, the two values multiplied together have to continually equal the same amount: 100 ft².

Looking at what happens to one variable when we change another helps us understand the relationship, or relation, between them. In the case of the signs, it could help us decide on a width, length, or area, depending on our need.

Keeping Perspective

Well, that's a brief introduction to **constants**, **variables**, and the relationship (or **relation**) between variables. Throughout this chapter, we're going to have fun looking in more depth at variables and at the relationship, or relation, between them. Doing so will help equip you to understand and work with real-life problems you encounter in your own life.

13.2 Independent and Dependent Variables

In real life, many variables *depend on* the value of other variables. The total you spend at a store *depends on* the products you put in your cart, the time it takes you to travel down the highway at 60 miles an hour *depends on* how far you travel, and the amount of flour you need in a recipe *depends on* how many batches of the recipe you're making.

Let's explore the dependency of one variable on another in more depth.

Independent and Dependent

Picture a vending machine. When you press a button (and insert the payment, of course), a specific item in the machine falls to the bottom. Which item you receive is *dependent on* which button you press. There's a relationship between the *input* (what button you press) and the *output* (what comes out).

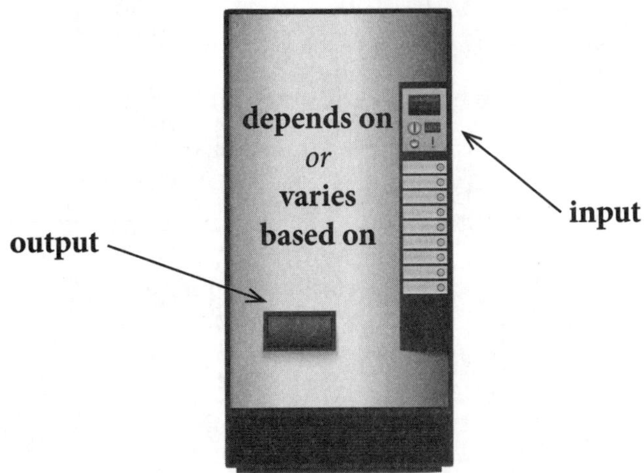

In a similar way, we can think of the relationship between variables as having an *input* and an *output*. For example, let's look back at a relationship we mentioned in the last lesson:

$$\textit{Total pizza slices} = \textit{slices per guest} \bullet \textit{number of expected guests}$$

or

$$T = sg$$

If we view *s* (the slices per guest) as a constant 2 slices, then we'd have this:

$$T = 2g$$

In $T = 2g$, the *output* we get for the total pizza slices (T) *depends on* the value we *input* for the number of guests (g). If we expect 5 guests, then the input is 5, and we need 10 total pizza slices (that is, we'll get an output of 10 pizza slices). If we expect 10 guests, then the input is 10, and we need 20 pizza slices total (that is, the output is 20 pizza slices). This is easily seen on a table.

g (input)	***T* = 2*g***	***T*** (output)
5	$T = 2(\mathbf{5})$	10
10	$T = 2(\mathbf{10})$	20

When we designed a sign in the last lesson with a fixed length, we thought of the area as *depending on* what value we chose for the width. We could have shown this in a chart too.

In the examples, while we didn't write out the units for every input and output, notice that if we had, we would have ended with an appropriate unit.

$A = (10\text{ ft})(1\text{ ft}) = 10\text{ ft}^2$

$\ell = \frac{100\text{ ft}^2}{1\text{ ft}} = 100\text{ ft}$

If we're substituting numbers into an equation correctly, the units should always cancel out, leaving us in a logical unit. If they don't, you know you made a mistake somewhere. So even though you don't have to write out the units for every input and output, you should make sure you solve with the units once to verify that the units work out.

w (input, in ft)	$A = (10\text{ ft})w$	A (output, in ft²)
1	$A = (10)(\mathbf{1}) = 10$	10
5	$A = (10)(\mathbf{5}) = 50$	50
10	$A = (10)(\mathbf{10}) = 100$	100

On the other hand, when we designed a sign with a fixed area, we thought of the *length* as *depending on* what value we chose for the width. Again, we could show this in a chart.

w (input, in ft)	$100\text{ ft}^2 = \ell w$, which we could rewrite as $\ell = \frac{100\text{ ft}^2}{w}$ in order to easily find the value of ℓ	ℓ (output, in ft)
1	$\ell = \frac{100}{1} = 100$	100
5	$\ell = \frac{100}{5} = 20$	20
10	$\ell = \frac{100}{10} = 100$	10

Since the output depends on the input, it's common to refer to whatever variable we use to represent the input as the **independent variable** (its value is *independent* and can be whatever we choose to make it). The variable representing the output is referred to as the **dependent variable** (its value *depends* on the value of the input).

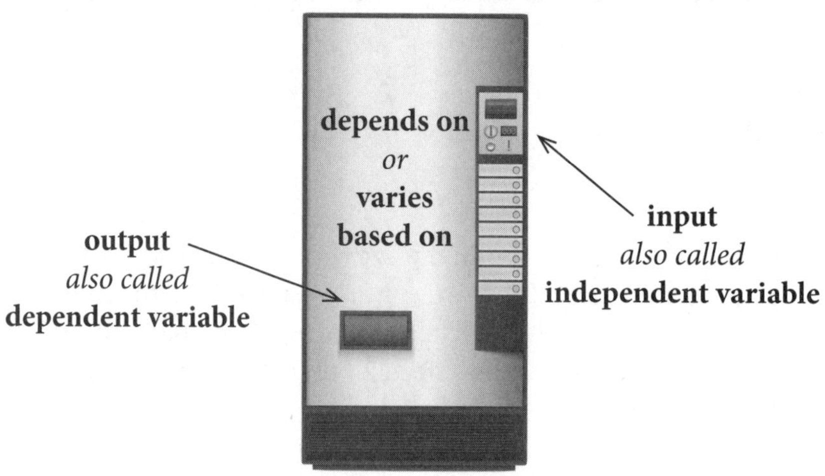

Here are the more official definitions:

> "An **independent variable** is a variable whose values don't depend on changes in other variables."[2]

> "A **dependent variable** is a variable whose value depends on the values of one or more other independent variables."[3]

Which variable we view as dependent can often change based on the situation. We have to look at which variable's value *depends on* or *varies based on* the value of the other.

In the case of ordering pizza for a party, the total we need to order *depends on* or *varies based on* the number of guests. So in the relationship $T = 2g$, we'd say that T is the dependent variable, and g is the independent variable. (It wouldn't make sense to say that the number of guests depends on the pizza ordered.)

In the case of area, width, and length, though, which variable we view as the independent one is different in different situations. When we had a constant length of 10 ft, we could view the area as dependent on the width, and see how it varies as the width changed. In this case, we'd call A the dependent variable and w the independent variable. However, we could also look at how the width would have to change based on different areas we choose (which would make sense to do if the customer was paying for the sign by the area). In this case, then, we'd think of w as the dependent variable and A as the independent variable.

Keeping Perspective

It's important to know that a variable can be dependent on another variable. If we need 2 slices of pizza per guest expected at a party, then the number of slices we need is *dependent on* the number of guests. If we need \$5 for every ticket we buy for a show, then the total amount of money we need to purchase tickets is *dependent on* the number of tickets we buy.

We're surrounded by real-life relationships in which one variable is dependent on another. The terms **dependent variable** and **independent variable** give us mathematical terminology to describe this dependency.

Remember, though, that the only reason it makes sense to explore relationships between variables is because there are consistent, real-life relationships. It's creation's underlying consistency — which God created and sustains — that makes it possible for us to describe real-life relationships mathematically.

A chart you can use to help keep track of input, output, independent variables, and dependent variables, along with other related terms we'll be covering, is included in Appendix A.

13.3 Using x and y for Independent and Dependent Variables

Back in Lesson 3.1, we mentioned that math books tend to use the letters x, y, and z, along with a, b, and c, more than other letters. Well, the time has finally come to learn why.

x, y, and z

A common convention is to use x **to represent the independent variable** in a mathematical relationship, and y **to represent the dependent variable**. In this

While math books typically use x and y as variables, science books usually use more descriptive letters, such as t for time, d for distance, ρ (a Greek letter) for density, etc. After all, in math, we're often working on learning the skills and techniques abstractly, while in science we are applying the math to a specific situation.

course, you can assume we've followed this convention whenever you see both x and y in an equation. By knowing the convention, you'll instantly know which variable to view as dependent and which to view as independent.

When working with the letters x and y all day, it's easy to forget that we're not merely completing a paper exercise. There's a reason to learn how to work with mathematical relationships — they help us describe the real-life relationships all around us.

For example, $y = x + 100$ could be representing the relationship between the perimeter and a side of a polygon, where all of the sides except one total 100 ft.

$$y = x + 100$$
$$P = s + 100 \text{ ft}$$

Or it could be representing the relationship between someone's total weekly earnings and what they earn from tips, if they also receive a \$100 set salary.

$$y = x + 100$$
$$w = t + \$100$$

Don't let the y and x fool you into thinking the skills you're learning are meaningless.

Why a, b, and c?

You'll also see a lot of the letters a, b, and c in math books. Why? Because there's a convention to use them to represent *constants*. In other words, we use the end of the alphabet to represent variables, and the beginning to represent constants. Again, though, this is just a convention. If we know what the constant is representing, we might use a letter that is more descriptive.

Keeping Perspective

For an example of mathematical relationships in action, consider a spring. When you pull on a spring or try to compress it, it exerts resistance, or force, against you. The more you stretch that spring out or try to compress it, the more force it exerts, trying to return to its natural state.

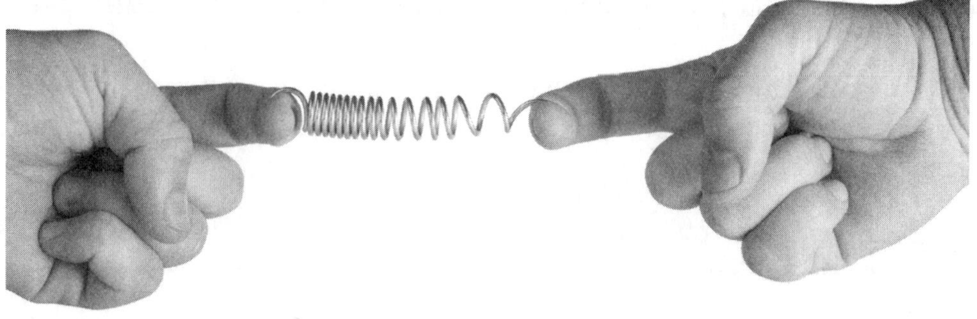

There's a relationship, or relation, between the force and the amount the spring is stretched or compressed. The force is dependent on the amount the spring is stretched or compressed. The greater the distance the string is stretched or compressed, the greater the force the spring exerts in trying to return to its natural state. Using F to represent the force the spring exerts, k to represent a constant known as the spring constant, and d to represent the amount the spring is stretched or compressed, we can show the relationship like this:

$$F = -kd$$

Notice that this relationship could also be expressed as $y = -ax$ . . . only since it's a science example, we've used the letters typically used for force, the spring constant, and displacement (a fancy name for "the amount by which a thing is moved from its normal position"[4]).

On Worksheet 13.3, you'll get a chance to explore this relationship in more depth. Springs are just one example of a real-life mathematical relationship. We're surrounded by a consistent universe held together by a consistent God, and math gives us a way to explore those consistencies. Every time you get into a car, you benefit from the knowledge car makers gained from understanding the relationship between the force and distance in springs, as there are springs over each tire that help absorb the bumps on the road (quite literally). Math truly is a useful tool.

The k in the formula equals a constant known as the spring constant. The value of the spring constant is different for different springs (some springs are tougher to stretch than others).

13.4 Functions

It's time now to learn a fancy term that helps us describe many mathematical relationships (including all the ones we've looked at in this chapter). It's a pretty important term — and one you'll hear frequently in future math classes.

Understanding Functions

While you'll learn a more technical definition in upper math, the concept of a function isn't hard. Simply put, a **function** is a relationship, or relation, between an input and an output where for every input there's only one output.

Let's return to the vending machine example we looked at back in Lesson 13.2. A vending machine is a great example of a function. For every button you press (i.e., every input), you get one, and only one, output. While sometimes some of the buttons produce the same output (some vending machines have more than one button you can press for water, for example), for every button you press, you get one and only one output.

While both these imputs will result in the same output (water), each button produces only one output.

The key distinguishing feature of a function is that there's only one output for each input. When wouldn't there be? Well, suppose we had this relationship:

$$y = \pm x$$

Notice the ± sign before the x. Watch what happens if we input a value of 3 to this relationship.

$$y = \pm 3$$

Notice that y has two possible values — y could be either +3 or –3. For every input of x in $y = \pm x$, there are two possible values for y: a positive value and a negative one. This relationship is not a function.

Likewise $y > x$ is not a function, as for every value of x, there are many values y could be.

With the exception of $y = \pm x$ and $y > x$, though, all of the relationships between variables in this chapter have been functions.

A Function of

As you begin exploring mathematical relationships between variables, you'll often hear the phrase **a function of**. In $A = (10 \text{ ft})w$, for example, we could say that *A is a function of w*. All we mean by this is that A's value is dependent on w's value in such a way that for every input of w, there's one, and only one, value for A.

Likewise, if we wanted to play around with different values for the area and see how they affected the width, then we'd say that *w is a function of* A. All we mean by this is that w's value is dependent on A's in such a way that for every input of A, there's one, and only one, value for w.

Functions Aren't Just Equations

It's important to mention that not all relations or functions can be described by an equation.

For example, consider this table showing hypothetical precipitation data for a city:

2015 Monthly Precipitation in a City (hypothetical data)

Month	1	2	3	4	5	6	7	8	9	10	11	12
Monthly Precipitation (in inches)	3	2	4	4	4	7	1	6	8	4	5	4

While there's not a mathematical *equation* that can describe the relationship between the month and precipitation, there's still a *relationship* between the month and the precipitation. Picture each of the months for this year as buttons on a vending machine — for every value you pick for month, you'd get one, and only one, value for precipitation. So even though we can't describe the relationship with a single equation, we could still view the precipitation as a *function* of the month.

Important! Notice that in the table we looked at above, some months had the same inches of precipitation. We can still think of the precipitation as a function of the month, though, as for each input (month) there's only one output (precipitation measurement). However, we could *not* look at the month as a function of the monthly precipitation. After all, picture the different monthly precipitation values as buttons on a vending machine — when you pick the value of 4 for monthly precipitation, you'd get a month of 3, 4, 5, 10, *or* 12. There's not only *one* output for every input.

Keeping Perspective

Wondering why we need another term? Well, there are certain techniques (which are beyond the scope of this course) that we can use in exploring mathematical relationships between variables that only work if we're dealing with a relationship in which every input yields one, and only one, output. Thus, we need a word to describe relationships with this property . . . and thus the need for the term **function**.

13.5 Domains

Some relationships only hold true for certain values. In the pizza function we've been exploring all chapter, for instance, having a negative number of guests wouldn't make sense. The function between the total pizza slices and number of guests only makes sense when g is greater than or equal to 0.

We could specify this using an inequality.

$T = 2g$, when $g \geq 0$

Total pizza slices = 2 • *number of expected guests,* when the number of guests is greater than or equal to 0

We call the set of values that the independent variable can possibly be the **domain**. In $T = 2g$, when $g \geq 0$, all numbers greater than or equal to 0 are the *domain*.

Important! The domain is not always written out. When dealing with real-life problems, always stop to think through what inputs make sense. For example, whether or not the domain is specified, you know that having a negative number of guests wouldn't really make sense. Thus when comparing the total pizza slices needed and the number of guests at a party, you only care about positive number of guests.

Sometimes, we need to specify a domain that includes both a starting and ending value. For example, suppose you're ordering CDs in bulk to resell. You've been told it will cost $7 a CD if you order more than 10 but less than or equal to 20 CDs.

Let's put this in math terms:

total cost = 7 • *number of CDs*
holds true only when the number of CDs
is more than 10 but less than or equal to 20

And now let's reduce this to symbols:

$$t = 7c, \text{ when } c > 10 \text{ and } \leq 20$$

Now, mathematicians love to find ways to write more concisely. Concise writing, once you're familiar with the convention, makes math problems easier to write and quicker to understand. By putting c in the middle of both inequality symbols, we can represent this domain more concisely.

$$t = 7c, \text{ when } \mathbf{10 < c \leq 20}$$

Putting c in the middle of the two inequality signs is simply a more compact way of showing the domain, $10 < c \leq 20$ means that c must be greater than 10 *and* less than or equal to 20.

As we saw back in Lesson 10.2, we can show the possible values for an unknown on a number line by using a closed point if that number is an included value, and an open point if it is not.

$x > 2$	$x \geq 2$
Open point shows that 2 is *not* included in values for x.	Closed point shows that 2 *is* included in the values for 2.

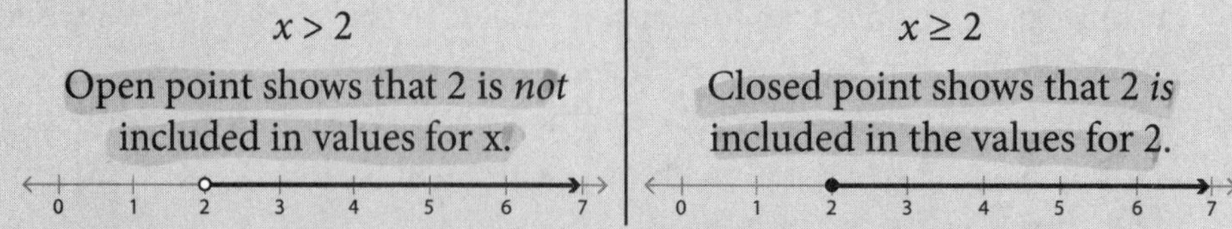

Domains with starts and ends can also be shown on a number line by using a point at the start and a point at the end. In the example below, the open point at –5 shows that –5 is *not* an included value, while the closed point at 2 shows that 2 *is* an included value.

$$-5 < x \leq 2$$

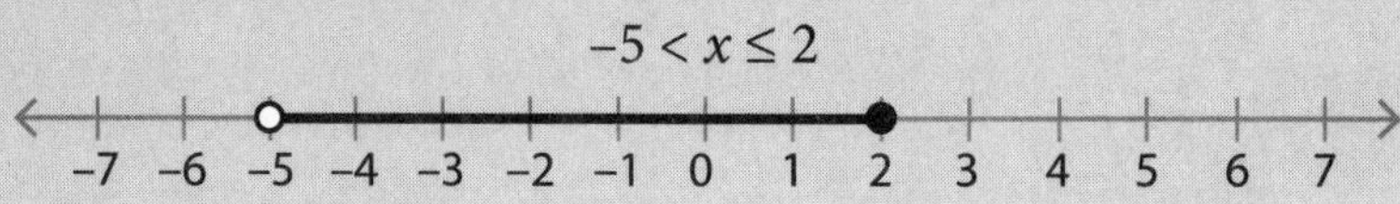

Keeping Perspective

Since many relationships only hold true for certain values, we'll sometimes need to specify a **domain** — a set of possible values for the "input." Inequality symbols give us a concise way to do this. Once again, we're learning how to use symbols (inequalities this time) to help us communicate about the real-life quantities and consistencies God created and sustains.

13.6 Chapter Synopsis

In this chapter, we've begun using math to help us understand the relationship *between variables*. Along the way, we learned a few key terms:

- **Constants** refer to quantities whose value is fixed or unchanging.
- **Variables** refer to quantities whose value can vary.
- **Independent variable** is a name for "a variable whose values don't depend on changes in other variables"[5]; an x is commonly used to show the independent variable. It's helpful to think of the independent variable as an *input* to a relationship.
- **Dependent variable** is a name for "a variable whose value depends on the values of one or more other independent variables"[6]; y is commonly used to show the dependent variable. It's helpful to think of the dependent variable as the *output* of a relationship.
- **Function** is a relationship, or relation, between an input and an output where for every input there's only one output.
- **Domain** is the set of all the values the independent variable can be.

The main thing to remember from this chapter is that we can explore the relationship between variables. This in turn helps us understand how changing one variable (speed, price per person, width, etc.) will affect another (distance, total cost, area, etc.).

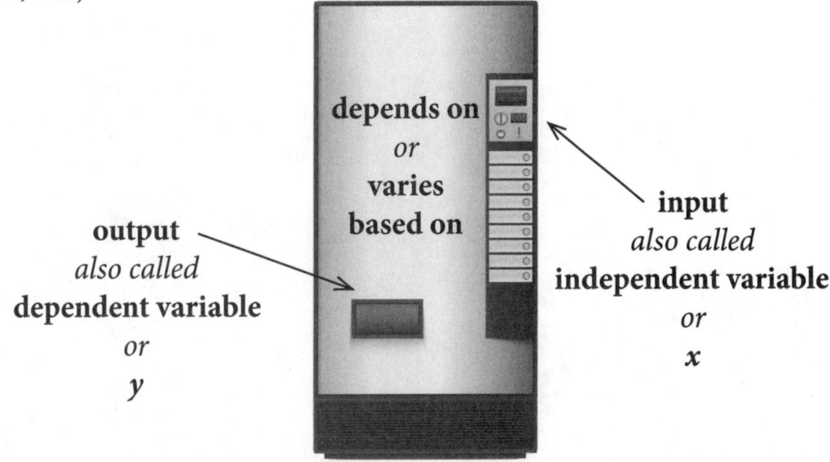

[CHAPTER 14]

Graphing Mathematical Relationships

14.1 Picturing Relationships

In this chapter, we're going to continue our explorations of relationships between variables. Rather than just looking at more equations, though, we're going to use graphs to help us.

Back when we looked at statistics, we reviewed several different types of coordinate graphs. Coordinate graphs not only help us picture *data*, but they also help us picture *relationships between variables.*

Viewing Relationships Graphically

To illustrate how graphs picture relationships, we'll walk through graphing a simple relationship: $y = 10x$.

Remember, even though we're using y and x to make it easy to identify the dependent and independent variables, $y = 10x$ could represent any number of real-life relationships. For example, it could represent the relationship between the area and width of a rectangle when the length is a constant 10 ft.

$$y = 10x$$
$$A = (10 \text{ ft})w$$

Or it could represent the relationship between the distance and time when the speed is a constant 10 $\frac{\text{mi}}{\text{hr}}$.

$$y = 10x$$
$$d = (10 \tfrac{\text{mi}}{\text{hr}})t$$

Or it could represent the relationship between the percentage and the rate when the base is a constant \$10.

$$y = 10x$$
$$P = \$10R$$

To see $y = 10x$ graphically, we need to have coordinates to graph. We can find coordinates by picking a couple of values for x (the independent variable/input) and finding the corresponding y values (the dependent variable/output). We could pick any values for x within the domain — we'll pick 1, 5, and 10.

x (independent variable/ input)	$y = 10x$	y (dependent variable/ output)
1	$y = 10(\mathbf{1}) = 10$	10
5	$y = 10(\mathbf{5}) = 50$	50
10	$y = 10(\mathbf{10}) = 100$	100

Remember, the convention is to list the horizontal coordinate first, and then the vertical coordinate. So in (1, 10), 1 is the horizontal coordinate, and 10 is the vertical coordinate.

We can use the x and y values we just found as coordinates. The x value will be the horizontal coordinate, and the corresponding y value will be the vertical coordinate. So we have these three sets of coordinates: (1, 10), (5, 50), and (10, 100).

Why did we use the x values as the horizontal coordinates and the y values as the vertical coordinates? Well, we typically want to see the change in the dependent variable (we want to see how the output varies based on the input), and this is easier to see if **the dependent variable (in this case, y) is graphed on the vertical axis.**

Since we commonly use y to represent the dependent variable (the output) and x to represent the independent variable (the input) and since we typically graph the dependent variable on the vertical axis and the independent variable on the horizontal axis, **the vertical axis is referred to as the y-axis and the horizontal axis as the x-axis.**

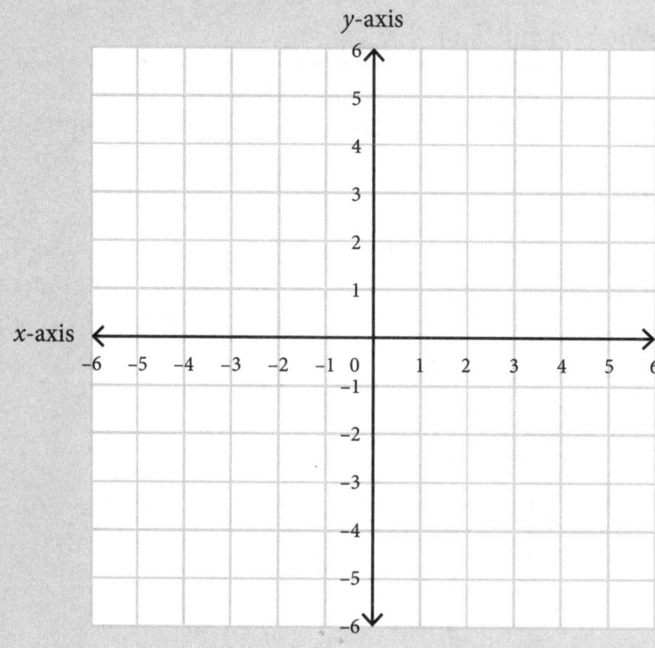

Now let's graph the coordinates.

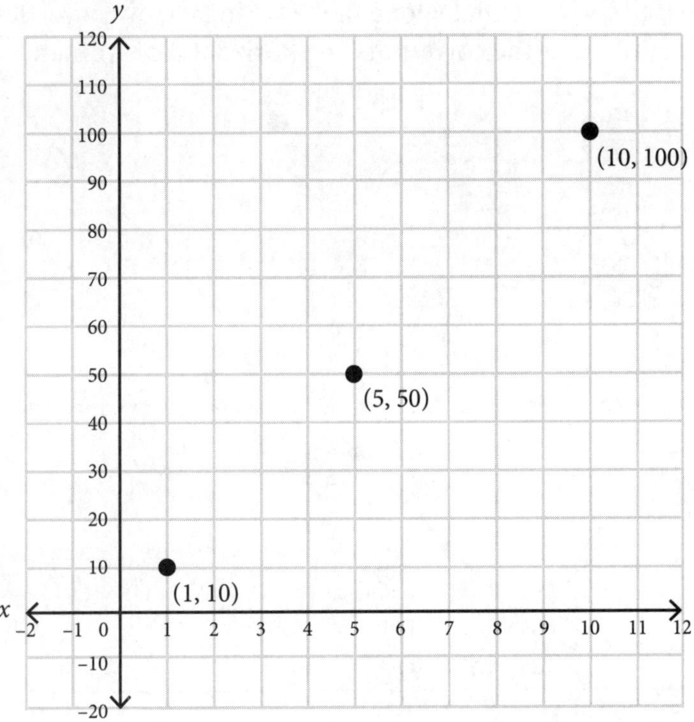

$y = 10x$

Now, we could keep graphing more values by choosing additional values for x. But, whatever values we choose for x, the value for y (the vertical coordinate) will always be 10 times the value of x (the horizontal coordinate).

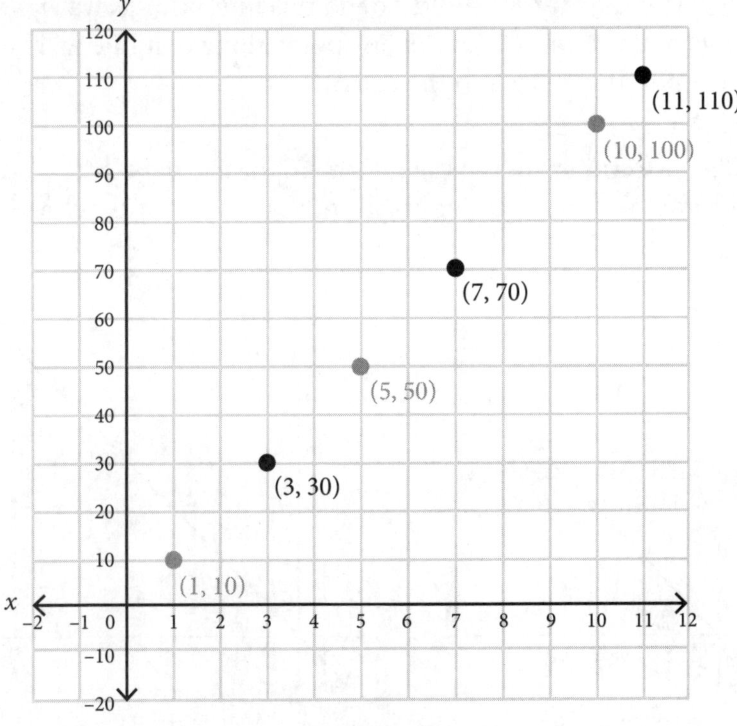

$y = 10x$

Notice that if we connect any two points, forming a straight line that extends in both directions, all the points fall along that line. In fact, every vertical coordinate along that line is 10 times the corresponding horizontal coordinate.

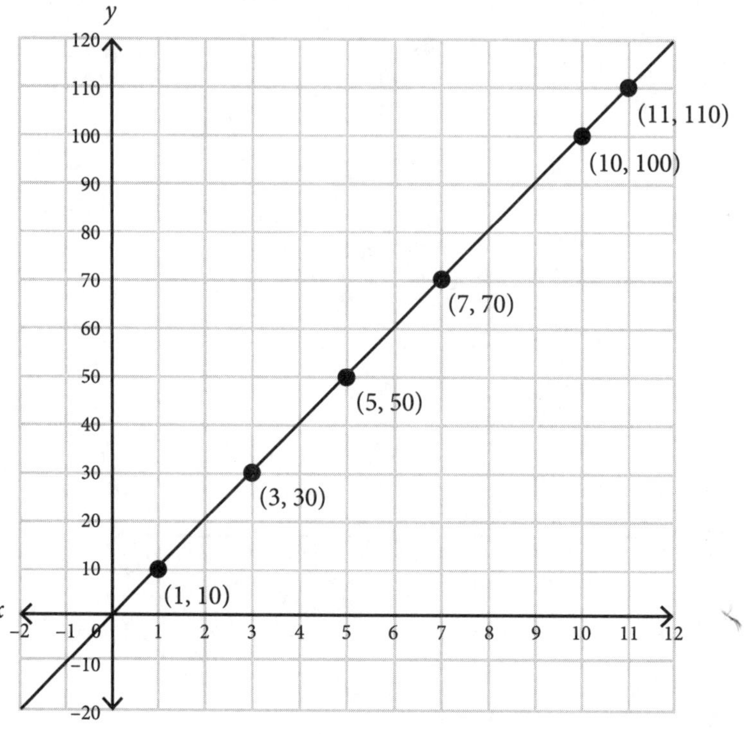

$y = 10x$

The line pictorially shows the relationship in which every vertical coordinate is 10 times the horizontal one. We could extend this line as far as we wanted to in either direction, and the coordinates of any point along that line will be a valid input and corresponding output in the equation.

Sometimes we'll add arrows to the line to emphasize the fact that we can extend the line. You'll encounter graphs both with and without arrows.

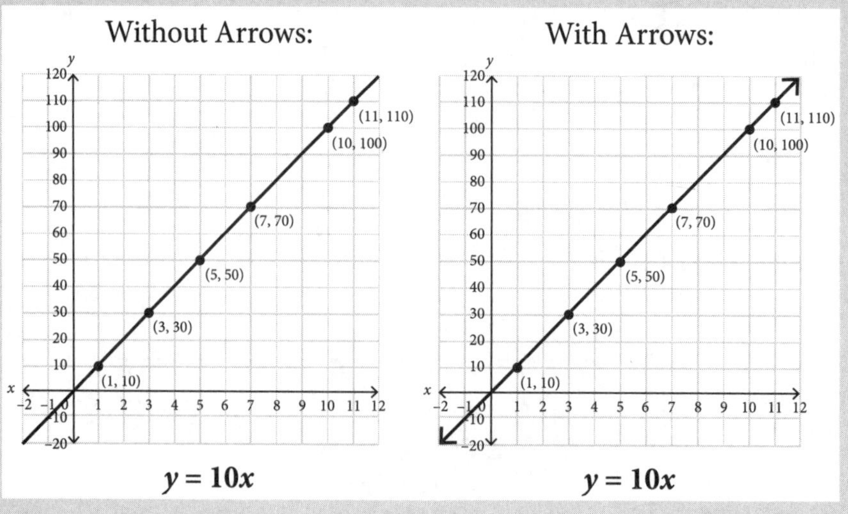

Sometimes, it may not make sense to extend a line in both directions. For example, if you're only interested in positive values, you wouldn't want to extend the line in the negative direction. Always use your common sense when interpreting graphs.

Linear Equations

In this chapter, we're going to focus on graphing equations that produce a straight line when graphed. Not surprisingly, we have a term to help us describe all equations that produce a straight line when graphed. We call them **linear equations**. Since *linear* means "having the form of or resembling a line,"[1] the name makes sense.

One of the reasons math may sometimes seem confusing is that each branch of math often modifies a term's meaning or adds a new term that's similar, although slightly different. Don't let these terms confuse you — we have so many of them because *each term is a way of categorizing relationships based on a different attribute.* Having a variety of terms gives us a more precise language with which to communicate.

See Appendix B for an explanation of how to tell from a graph if the relationship is a function.

For example, if we want to emphasize that an equation produces a straight line when graphed, we'll use the term *linear equation*. When we're talking about how each input in a relationship has only one output, we'll refer to the relationship as a *function*. Each term categorizes the relationship based on a different attribute.

Different Relationships; Different Graphs

While we're focusing on linear equations in this chapter, not all relationships are linear!

For example, if we were to graph $y = \frac{100}{x}$, we'd end up with this graph:

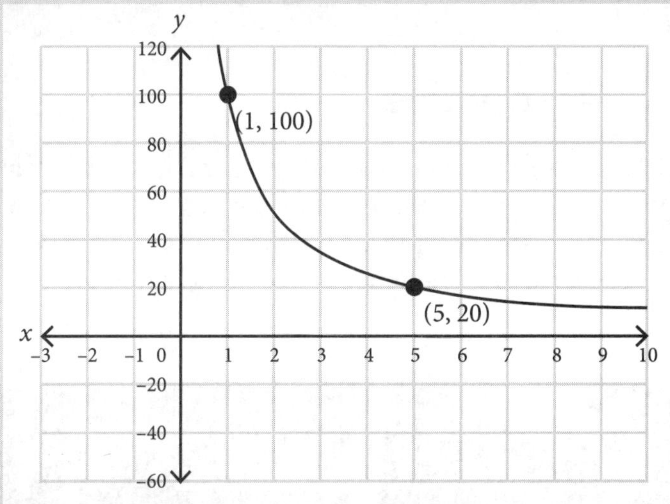

$$100 = yx \quad or \quad y = \frac{100}{x}$$
when $x > 0$

Whether linear or not, graphs give us a visual way of seeing the relationship between variables.

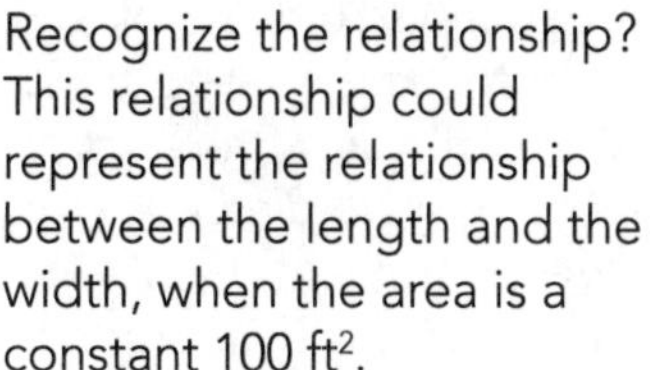

Recognize the relationship? This relationship could represent the relationship between the length and the width, when the area is a constant 100 ft².

$100 \text{ ft}^2 = \ell \bullet w$ or $\ell = \frac{100 \text{ ft}^2}{w}$
when w is > 0

Or it could represent the relationship between time and speed when the distance is 100 km.

$100 \text{ km} = s(t)$ or $s = \frac{100 \text{ km}}{t}$
when $t > 0$

Or it could represent a number of other relationships. Don't ever let the y and x fool you into thinking an equation is meaningless.

Different Variables

As we mentioned in the last chapter, while math books are filled with the letters x and y, science books and other fields that apply math are often filled with letters that are more meaningful to what a specific equation is representing. Whether the equation is written using x and y or other variables, the principle remains the same: **put the independent variable on the horizontal axis, or *x*-axis, and the dependent variable on the vertical axis, or *y*-axis.** The graph below is the *same graph* labeled differently depending on the variables used in the equation.

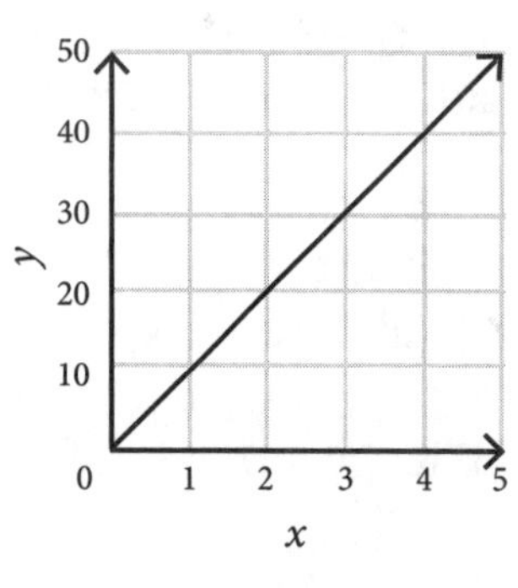

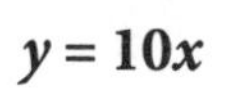

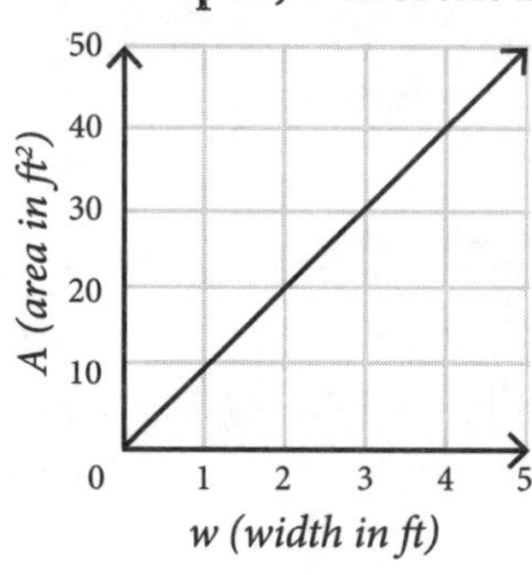

$A = (10 \text{ ft})w$

(the change in the area of a rectangle as the width changes when the length is a constant 10 ft)

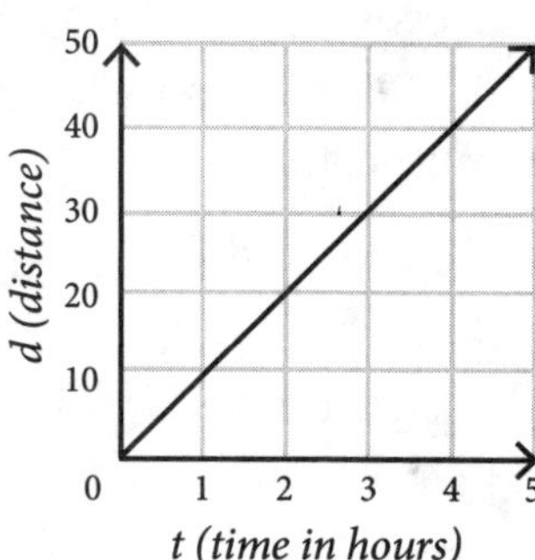

$d = (10 \frac{\text{mi}}{\text{hr}})t$

(the change in the distance as the time changes when the speed is a constant 10 miles per hour)

Notice that the graphs here show only the final line with no points labeled; you'll often see computer-generated graphs that look like this.

Notice also the arrow pointing in the positive direction on the lines. While we didn't specify the domains for the equations, the area and distance equations wouldn't make sense for values less than 0. So we only drew the arrow in the positive direction. We'll further explore how to show domains on a graph in Lesson 14.3.

Keeping Perspective

Coordinate graphs help us picture the relationship between variables. As we learn to use graphs to explore **linear equations** in more depth, remember that we can do so because we serve a consistent, faithful God who is governing this universe in a predictable, able-to-be-explored way.

14.2 The Mechanics of Graphing Linear Equations

Ready to practice graphing relationships yourself? I hope so, because it's time to begin. Again, we're going to limit ourselves to linear equations — equations that produce a straight line when graphed. As you practice graphing equations in this chapter, you're going to get to "picture" some familiar relationships.

Learning the Mechanics

So how do you graph a linear equation? Well, the idea is to accurately draw the line that represents the solutions to the equation. One way to do this is to find 2 sets of coordinates that are solutions to the equation and graph those coordinates, using a ruler to connect the resulting points into a line. The coordinates of every point along that straight line will be a valid input and output to the same linear equation.

The steps below summarize the graphing process:

- **Step 1: Find coordinates to graph.** Choose values for the independent variable (i.e., inputs) and substitute each one into the equation to find the corresponding value for the dependent variable (i.e., the corresponding output).

  Unless you know you're only interested in certain values, **you can pick any values for the independent variable** (i.e., any inputs).

- Again, you only need 2 sets of coordinates to graph; however, to make it easier to draw a straight line, it's often helpful to find 3 sets of coordinates. We'll use 3 in our examples. As mentioned in the last lesson, we **graph the independent variable on the horizontal axis and the dependent variable on the vertical axis.** So use the values for the independent variable (i.e., the inputs) as the horizontal coordinates and the corresponding values for the dependent variable (i.e., the outputs) as the vertical coordinates.

- **Step 2: Graph the coordinates.** Once you've found sets of coordinates to graph, graph those coordinates and connect the points with a straight line (use a ruler) to see the relationship visually. Be sure to also label your graph so it's clear what you're graphing.

And that's all there is to it! Let's walk through a couple of examples.

Example: Graph the linear equation $y = -20x$.

Step 1: Find coordinates to graph. We can find coordinates to graph by picking 3 values for x (i.e., 3 inputs), substituting them into the equation, and finding the corresponding y values (i.e., the corresponding outputs).

The chart below shows this process. We've put the column showing the calculations to the right, as it's easier to see the coordinates we obtain for x and y if those columns are next to each other. On worksheets, you can perform these calculations mentally or on a calculator.

x (independent variable/input/ horizontal coordinate)	y (dependent variable/output/ vertical coordinate)	$y = -20x$
–1	20	$y = -20(\mathbf{-1}) = 20$
0	0	$y = -20(\mathbf{0}) = 0$
1	–20	$y = -20(\mathbf{1}) = -20$

We've now found 3 sets of coordinates to graph: (–1, 20), (0, 0), and (1, –20).

Step 2: Graph the coordinates. We'll now graph the coordinates we found, draw a straight line connecting them, and label the graph.

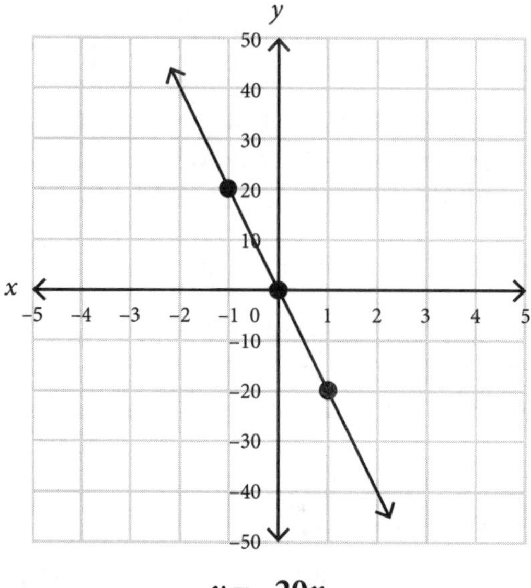

$y = -20x$

You might wonder when we'd want to multiply x by –20. Remember, the negative sign means the opposite of. So –20 could mean *losing* (the opposite of gaining) at a rate of $20 a day, 20 hours in the opposite direction (that is, 20 hours in the past), etc. It could also mean that whatever x is representing, we want to take the opposite of it. After all, $-20x$ means the same thing as $20(-x)$.

Negative Time

Remember, a negative sign means *the opposite of*. So a time of –40 seconds means *the opposite of* 40 seconds, or 40 seconds in the past. So the graph helps us see that 40 seconds in the past, an elevator changing height at a rate of $5\frac{\text{ft}}{\text{sec}}$ that is at a height of 0 feet right now was at a height of –200 feet, or –200 feet below the ground level.

Example: Graph how the elevator's height changes over time if the height is changing at a consistent rate of 5 feet per second (we're not stopping anywhere) and we're starting at a height of 0 ft. The linear equation to graph is $h = (5\frac{\text{ft}}{\text{sec}})t + 0$, which simplifies to $h = (5\frac{\text{ft}}{\text{sec}})t$.

Step 1: Find coordinates to graph.

Let's substitute a couple of values for time into the equation $h = (5\frac{\text{ft}}{\text{sec}})t$ to find the corresponding output.

t (independent variable/input/ horizontal coordinate, in sec)	h (dependent variable/output/ vertical coordinate, in feet)	$h = (5\frac{\text{ft}}{\text{sec}})t$
–40	–200	$h = (5)(\mathbf{-40}) = -200$
0	0	$h = (5)\mathbf{0} = 0$
40	200	$h = (5)\mathbf{40} = 200$

We now have 3 sets of coordinates to graph: (–40, –200), (0, 0), and (40, 200).

Step 2: Graph the coordinates.

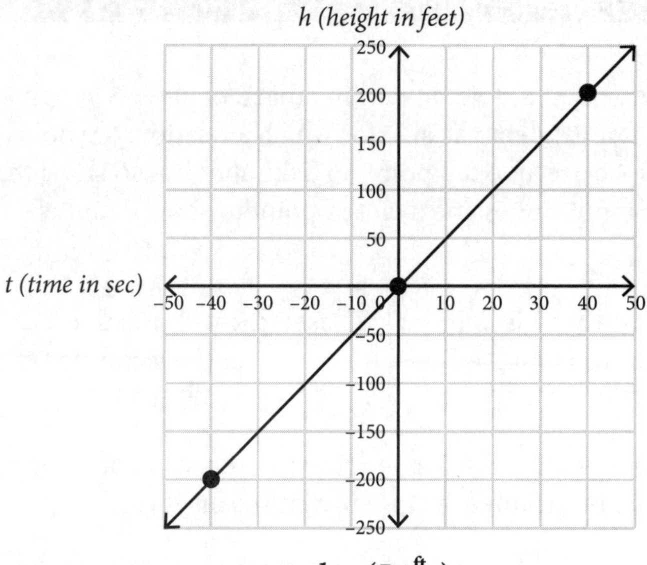

$$h = (5\frac{\text{ft}}{\text{sec}})t$$

(the height over time at a constant rate of change in height of $5\frac{\text{ft}}{\text{sec}}$)

Note that we could have used an *a* to stand for the height instead of an *h*, making the equation $a = (5\frac{\text{ft}}{\text{sec}})t$. As we mentioned in Lesson 3.7, the actual letters used can vary. However, since we're using the word *height* instead of *altitude*, we chose an *h*.

Keeping Perspective

As you practice graphing linear equations, keep in mind what you're really doing: visually showing the relationship between variables.

Graphs make it easy to instantly see the output of a relationship for a wide variety of inputs. For instance, notice how easy the graph makes it to see how much total will be spent based on how many times a $15 commuter train is ridden.

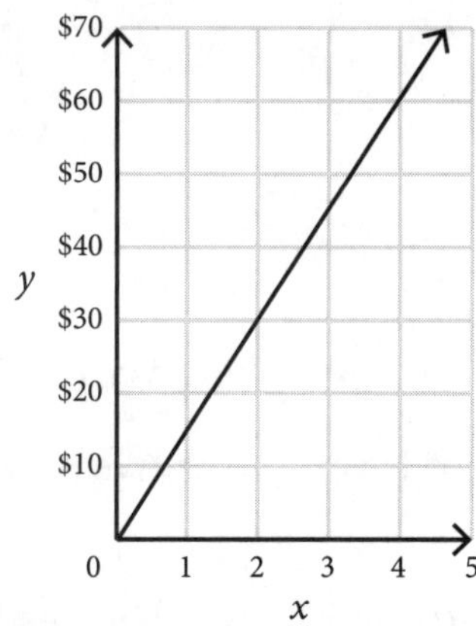

$$y = \$15x$$

total spent = $15(*number of times train is ridden*)

Now, you might be wondering why you need to learn to graph. Granted, many people don't take the time to graph an equation in order to make a decision. Yet by learning to graph equations, you are training yourself to recognize the relationships between variables. This in turn can help you assess real-life problems and decisions that come your way, regardless of what field or sphere of influence the Lord leads you to pursue.

14.3 Showing the Domain on a Graph

In the last chapter, we explored domains, seeing that a *domain* is simply the set of all the values for the independent variable for which a relationship holds true. We reviewed the fact that we use an open point on a number line to show that a value is *not* included in the input values and a closed point to show that it is.

$x > 2$

Open point shows that 2 is *not* included in values for x.

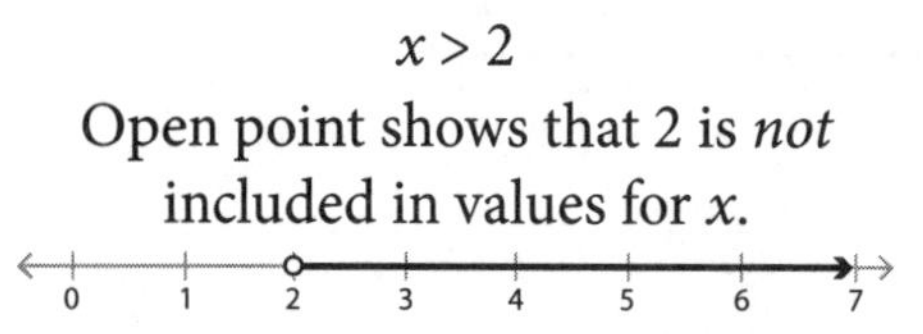

$x \geq 2$

Closed point shows that 2 *is* included in the values for x.

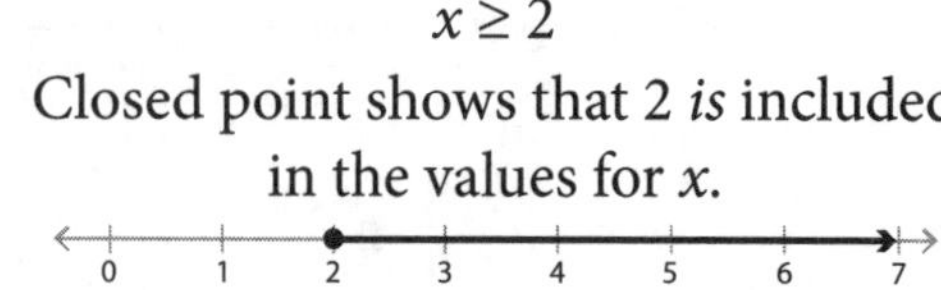

Well, the same convention applies when graphing on a coordinate graph: an open point means a value is not included; a closed point means it is.

For example, on the graph below of the equation $y = 8x$, where $x > 1$, we've drawn an open point where x is 1 to show that 1 is *not* included in the values for x; we've then extended the line only in the positive direction, as x has to be *greater than 1*.

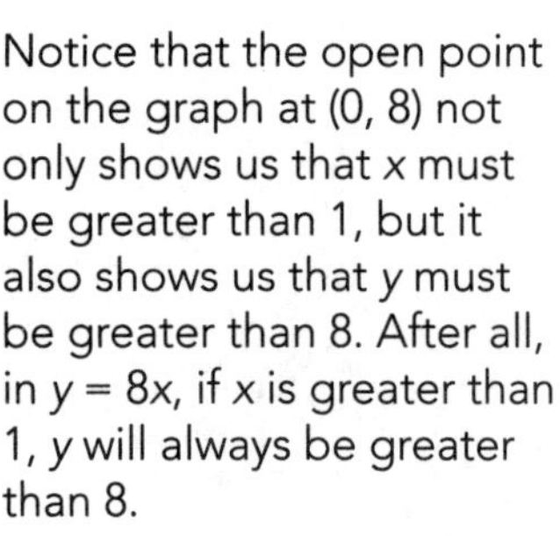

Notice that the open point on the graph at (0, 8) not only shows us that x must be greater than 1, but it also shows us that y must be greater than 8. After all, in $y = 8x$, if x is greater than 1, y will always be greater than 8.

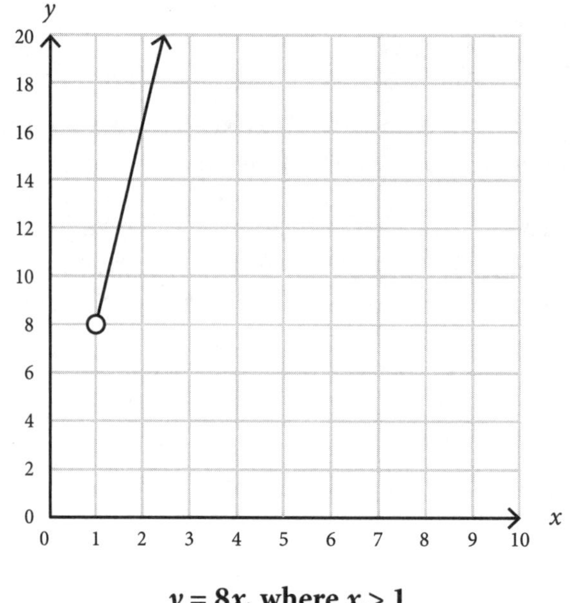

$y = 8x$, where $x > 1$

Let's take a look at a couple of other examples. We'll use a relationship we looked at in the last chapter.

Example: Graph the linear equation $T = 2g$, where $g \geq 0$.
View T as the dependent variable. (This equation represents this relationship: *Total slices of pizza* = 2 • *number of expected guests*, where the number of guests is greater than or equal to 0.)

Notice the domain specified for g. This tells us that g has to be greater than or equal to 0. (After all, it wouldn't make sense to have a negative number of guests!) So when graphing this, we'll draw a closed point at 0, only extending the line in the positive direction.

g (independent variable/input/ horizontal coordinate)	t (dependent variable/output/ vertical coordinate)	**$T = 2g$, where $g \geq 0$**
0	0	$T = 2(\mathbf{0}) = 0$
20	40	$T = 2(\mathbf{20}) = 40$
30	60	$T = 2(\mathbf{30}) = 60$

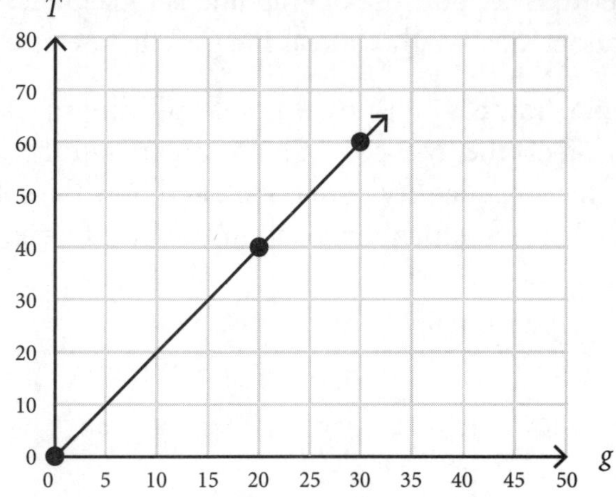

$T = 2g$, where $g \geq 0$
(*Total slices of pizza* = 2 • *number of expected guests*, where the number of guests is ≥ 0)

Example: Graph the linear equation $T = 2g$, where $g > 0$. View T as the dependent variable. (This equation represents this relationship: *Total slices of pizza* = 2 • *number of expected guests*, where the number of guests is greater than 0.)

Notice that we've been asked to graph the same equation as in the previous example, only this time we want to graph it when the domain is $g > 0$ rather than $g \geq 0$. So our graph will look the same, except that we'll use an open point at 0 rather than a closed point to show that 0 is not included in the domain.

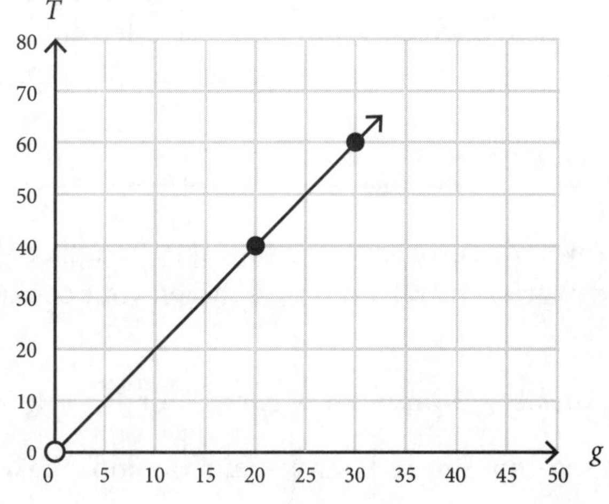

$T = 2g$, where $g > 0$

(*Total slices of pizza* = 2 • *number of expected guests*, where the number of guests is > 0)

Keeping Perspective

Closed and open points allow us to visually show the values for which a relationship holds true. That way, anyone looking at the graph can instantly and accurately see the relationship between the variables.

Always remember that the purpose of graphing is to help picture and work with real-life relationships. Math is a real-life tool that helps us with tasks.

Notice, for example, how easy it is to see graphically how a change in the quantity ordered affects the total cost of buying team t-shirts (assuming it costs \$5 per shirt for any quantity under \$50), and how the solid and open points show the values for which this relationship holds true.

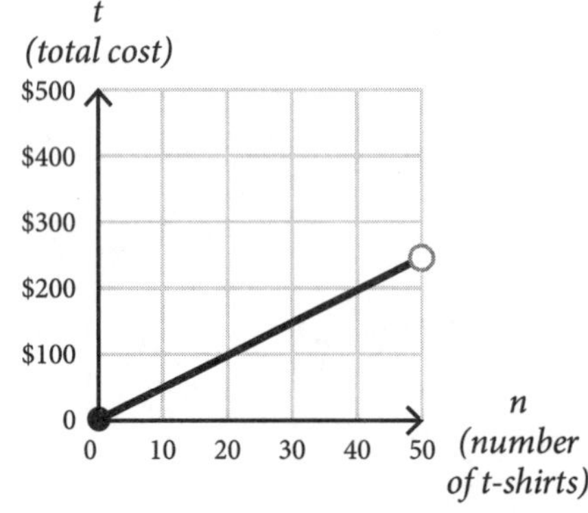

$t = \$5n$**, where** $0 \leq n < 50$
(*total cost* = \$5 • *number of t-shirts*)

14.4 Y-Intercept

It's time now to dig a little deeper into the graphs of linear equations and take a look at what we call the y-intercept. Now I know y-intercept sounds a little intimidating, but it's not. In fact, let's use a cookie example to make it sweeter.

Understanding Y-Intercept

Suppose you are throwing a party and need to make enough cookies for each guest to have 3. You could express the relationship between your cookies and guests like this:

cookies = 3 • *number of guests* or $c = 3g$

Let's graph this relationship. Since negative guests wouldn't make sense, we'll graph this for where $g \geq 0$.

g (independent variable/input/ horizontal coordinate)	c (dependent variable/output/ vertical coordinate)	**$c = 3g$, where $g \geq 0$**
0	0	$c = 3(\mathbf{0}) = 0$
10	30	$c = 3(\mathbf{10}) = 30$
20	60	$c = 3(\mathbf{20}) = 60$

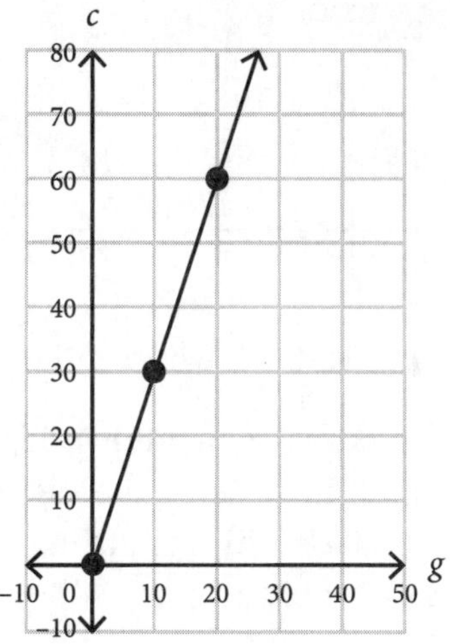

$c = 3g$, where $g \geq 0$

cookies = 3 • *number of guests,* where the *number of guests* ≥ *0*

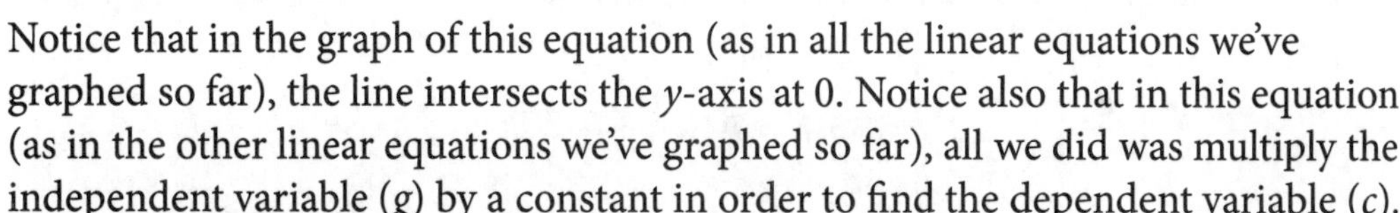

Notice that in the graph of this equation (as in all the linear equations we've graphed so far), the line intersects the *y*-axis at 0. Notice also that in this equation (as in the other linear equations we've graphed so far), all we did was multiply the independent variable (*g*) by a constant in order to find the dependent variable (*c*).

But now suppose again that you're throwing a party and need to make enough cookies for each guest to have 3. This time, you want to also make 10 additional cookies to give to a neighbor. You would have this equation:

$$c = 3g + \mathbf{10}, \text{ where } g \geq 0$$

Notice that this is the same equation we graphed before, except that now we're adding 10 cookies. When we graph this equation, we find that it still forms a straight line . . . only that line doesn't pass through (0, 0). Instead, when *g* equals 0, *c* equals 10. This results in the line crossing the *y*-axis at 10 rather than at 0.

g (independent variable/input/ horizontal coordinate)	c (dependent variable/output/ vertical coordinate)	**$c = 3g + 10$, where $g \geq 0$**
0	10	$c = 3(\mathbf{0}) + 10 = 10$
10	40	$c = 3(\mathbf{10}) + 10 = 40$
20	70	$c = 3(\mathbf{20}) + 10 = 70$

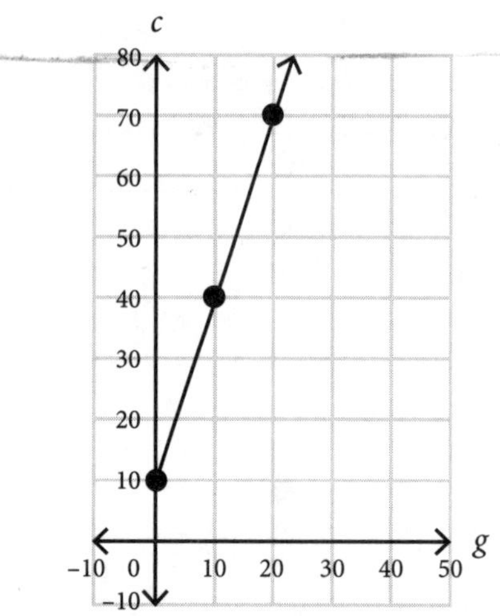

$c = 3g + 10$, where $g \geq 0$

Because we *added a value other than 0*, when the independent variable is 0, the dependent variable is no longer 0. Instead, it's the value of the constant added. In this case, c equals 10 when g equals 0. This results in the line intersecting the y-axis at 10. Basically, the line shifts up by 10.

Let's change it up a bit. What if we want to make enough cookies for each guest to have 3, but we want to subtract 10 from that amount, as we already have 10 cookies on hand from a batch we made the other day. Now we'd have this equation and graph:

$c = 3g + \mathbf{-10}$, where $g \geq 0$

g (independent variable/input/ horizontal coordinate)	**c** (dependent variable/output/ vertical coordinate)	**$c = 3g - 10$, where $g \geq 0$**
0	−10	$c = 3(\mathbf{0}) - 10 = -10$
10	20	$c = 3(\mathbf{10}) - 10 = 20$
20	50	$c = 3(\mathbf{20}) - 10 = 50$

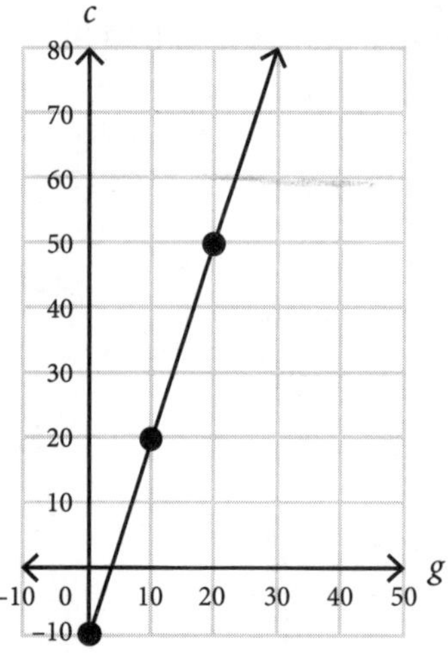

$c = 3g - 10$, where $g \geq 0$

Notice that we ended up with the same basic graph, except this time, the *line shifted down by 10*, intersecting the y-axis at −10.

We call the vertical coordinate where a line intersects, or intercepts, the y-axis its ***y*-intercept**. Assuming we're using the dependent variable values as the vertical coordinates and the independent variable values as the horizontal coordinates, **the *y*-intercept will be the dependent variable's value when the independent variable is 0.**

To illustrate, we've re-shown the cookie graphs below, circling the y-intercepts and showing what the dependent variable equals when the independent variable (g) is 0.

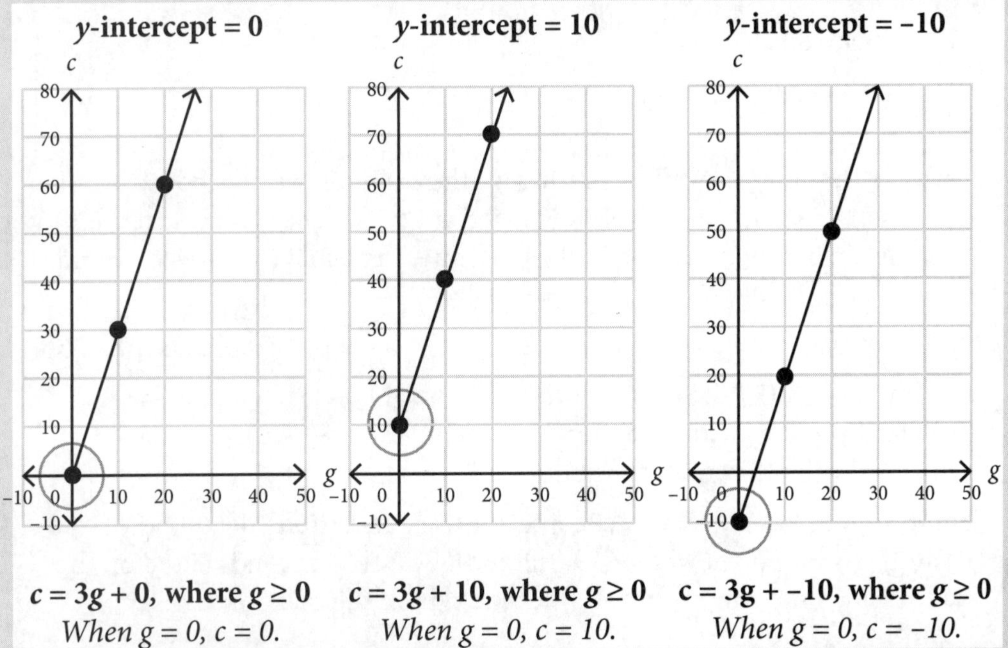

Note: When the y-intercept is 0, we typically don't bother to write it out, so you'll commonly see $c = 3g + 0$ written as $c = 3g$. After all, adding 0 doesn't change the value of the equation.

While we're focusing on lines, the definition of a y-intercept isn't limited to linear (i.e., straight-line) equations. The y value of where any curve (whether straight or not) intersects the y-axis is known as the y-intercept.

If you keep in mind what the y-intercept means, it's easy to identify it.

Example: What is the y-intercept of $y = 5x + 80$?

We can find the y-intercept a couple of different ways.

1. Graph the equation and look at where the line intersects the y-axis.

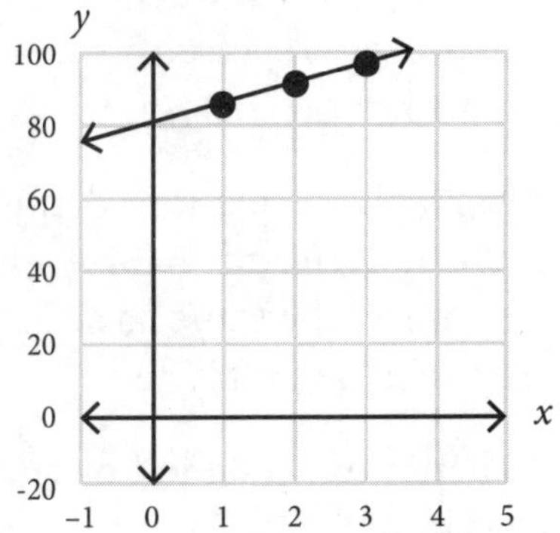

80 is the y-intercept, as that's where the line intersects the y-axis.

2. Solve for when the independent variable equals 0. That will tell us when the line will intersect the *y*-axis.

Original equation:

$y = 5x + 80$

Substitute 0 for x:

$y = 5(\mathbf{0}) + 80$

$y = \mathbf{0} + 80$

$y = \mathbf{80}$

80 is the *y*-intercept.

Let's talk about one possible meaning for the equation we just looked at ($y = 5x + 80$). Back in Lesson 3.7, we looked at how we could represent the relationship between altitude (or height), rate, and time using this equation:

$$a = r \bullet t + a_i$$

altitude (or height) = rate of change in altitude (or height) • time + initial altitude (or height)

Up until now, all of the initial altitudes (or heights) we've graphed have been 0. Now that we know about *y*-intercept, however, we can graph problems with other initial altitudes (or heights).

For example, let's say that a helicopter starts at an altitude of 80 ft (i.e., +80 ft) and we want to see what its altitude will be after 5 seconds based on the rate at which it changes altitude. We would have this relationship:

$$a = (5 \text{ sec})r + 80 \text{ ft}$$

Notice how this is the same basic relationship we looked in the previous example ($y = 5x + 80$), only instead of *y* and *x*, we used *a* and *r*. Again, always remember that the skills you're learning in apparently meaningless problems apply outside of a textbook!

Keeping Perspective

The ***y*-intercept** is a fancy name for the vertical coordinate where the line (or curve in some relationships) intersects the *y*-axis. It will be the value of the dependent variable (which we often use *y* to represent) when the independent variable (which we often use *x* to represent) is 0.

In the process of exploring *y*-intercept, we graphed equations that initially look a little more complicated. Yet while $c = 3g + 10$ and $c = 3g + -10$ might appear more complicated than $c = 3g$, they are all the same basic equation, only in the first two cases, an extra 10 are added or subtracted.

So why are we exploring *y*-intercepts? To better understand how graphs record real-life relationships, and the relationships themselves. Knowing the *y*-intercept helps us know what the output will be when the input is 0 (which can tell us the cookies needed when there are no guests, the starting distance, the initial height of plants before the experiment began, etc.).

As we explore relationships, remember that we ultimately can only use math outside of a textbook because God truly is the everlasting God who never grows weary. If multiplication and addition weren't consistent day in and day out, we wouldn't have any basis for saying that, in real life, 3 times 0 consistently equals 0 (and thus no way of predicting what the output of $c = 3g$ would be when g equals 0). It's ultimately God's faithfulness that makes it possible to apply math to real-life situations.

> *Hast thou not known? hast thou not heard, that the everlasting God, the LORD, the Creator of the ends of the earth, fainteth not, neither is weary? there is no searching of his understanding (Isaiah 40:28).*

14.5 Slope

It's time to look at another term that will help us better understand the graphs of linear equations: slope.

The term *slope* is not an entirely foreign one. After all, we're all familiar with using the term in connection to the steepness of a hill, trail, or mountain. But what exactly do we mean by a "steep slope" or a "downward slope"? Let's take a closer look at slopes of hills, and then apply what we learn to slopes of lines.

Slopes of Hills

We describe the steepness of a slope based on how much vertical change there is in comparison to horizontal change. The chart below illustrates this. Notice that we've called a slope positive if, when viewed from left to right, we're heading uphill; we've called a slope negative if, when viewed from left to right, we're heading downhill.

	Positive Slopes	**Negative Slopes**
gradual slopes	vertical change; horizontal change	vertical change; horizontal change
steeper slopes	vertical change; horizontal change	vertical change; horizontal change
very steep slopes	vertical change; horizontal change	vertical change; horizontal change

So how do we describe a slope mathematically? After all "gradual," "steep," and "very steep" could have different meanings to different people. Mathematically, we **describe slope as the ratio between the vertical change and the horizontal change.**

In other words, if we gain 1 mile in altitude while at the same time traveling 5 miles east of where we started, then we'd say the slope is $\frac{1 \text{ mi}}{5 \text{ mi}}$, or $\frac{1}{5}$.

Slope can be expressed as a decimal or percent too. If we complete the division in $\frac{1}{5}$, we get 0.2, or 20%.

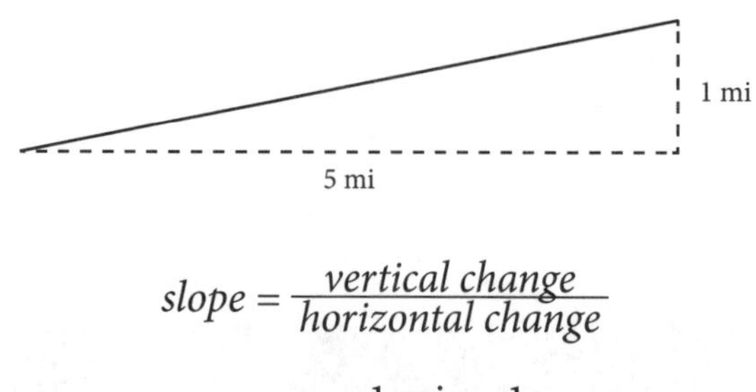

$$slope = \frac{vertical\ change}{horizontal\ change}$$

$$slope = \frac{1 \text{ mi}}{5 \text{ mi}} = \frac{1}{5}$$

At every point along a hill with a slope of $\frac{1}{5}$, we'll have climbed $\frac{1}{5}$ the distance vertically as we've traveled horizontally. The steepness of the slope is determined by how quickly we're changing altitude as we travel, which is the same as the ratio between the *vertical change* and the *horizontal change.*

Slopes of Lines

The slope of a line, like the slope of a mountain, is the ratio between the *vertical change* and the *horizontal change.* When finding the slope of a line, we're not typically given the change in the vertical position and the change in the horizontal position. Instead, we have to find that change ourselves. We can do this by picking two points along the line and looking at the *difference* between their vertical coordinates and their horizontal coordinates.

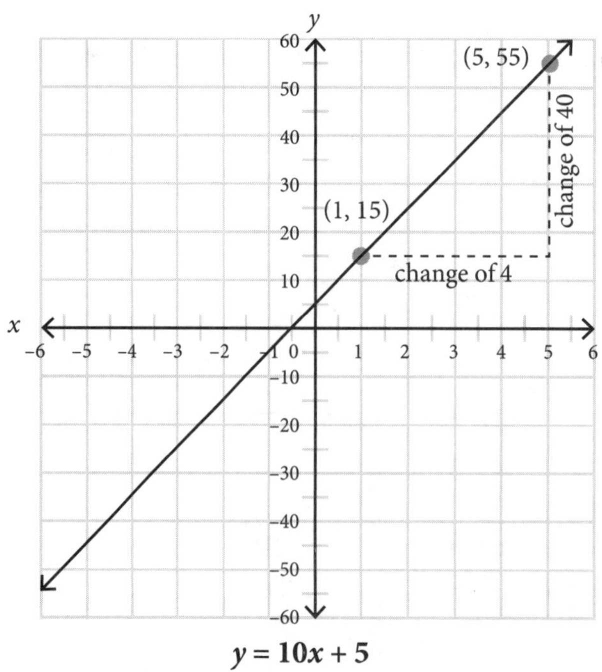

$y = 10x + 5$

Change in the vertical coordinates:
The y coordinates for the two points we chose are 55 and 15, so the vertical change equals 55 – 15, or 40.

Change in the horizontal coordinates:
The x coordinates for those same two points are 5 and 1, so the horizontal change equals 5 – 1, or 4.

$$\mathbf{slope = \frac{vertical\ change}{horizontal\ change}}$$

$$\mathbf{slope = \frac{40}{4} = 10}$$

On a straight line, no matter what two points we pick to find the change in y and the change in x, we'll get the same slope. After all, the line is straight, so its slope, or inclination, is consistent.

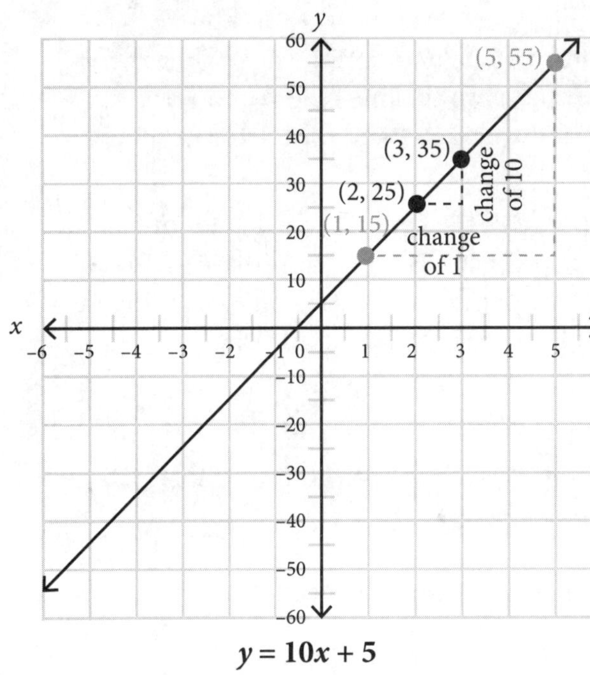

$y = 10x + 5$

Change in the vertical coordinates:
The y coordinates for the two points we chose are 35 and 25, so the vertical change equals 35 – 25, or 10.

Change in the horizontal coordinates:
The x coordinates for those same two points are 3 and 2, so the horizontal change equals 3 – 2, or 1.

$$slope = \frac{vertical\ change}{horizontal\ change}$$

$$slope = \frac{10}{1} = 10$$

No matter what points we choose, since the line is straight, the slope will be the same. The ratio between the vertical change and the horizontal change for any 2 points along the line is 10. The slope of $y = 10x + 5$ is 10.

Rise over Run

There's a saying to help remember how to find the slope. It's called **rise over run**. In other words, find the slope by dividing the *rise* (the vertical change) by the *run* (the horizontal change).

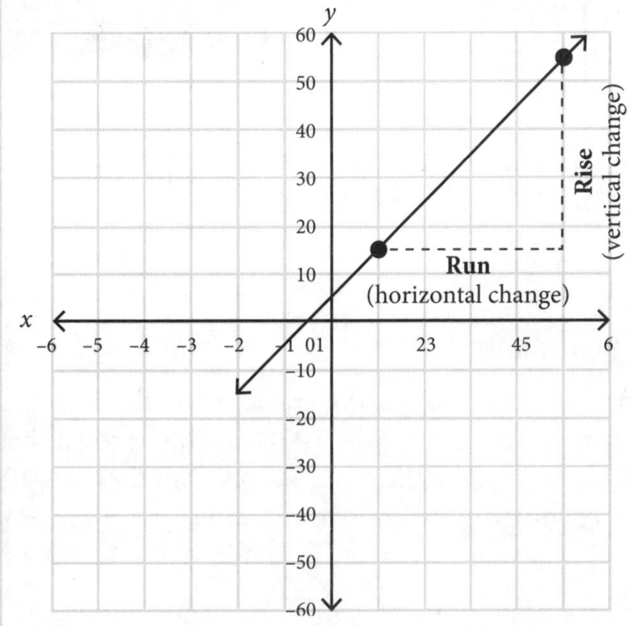

$$slope = \frac{vertical\ change}{horizontal\ change} \quad \text{or} \quad slope = \frac{rise}{run}$$

Morris Kline[2] explains slope like this: "In our everyday experience we use the notion of the slope of a hill. What we mean by the slope is the number of feet we travel up, which is called the rise, divided by the number of feet of horizontal travel, which is called the run. Thus if we . . . rise 2 feet while moving horizontally 6 feet, we say that the slope is $\frac{2}{6}$ or $\frac{1}{3}$."

We could also show that we need to take the change in the vertical coordinates divided by the change in the horizontal coordinates like this:

$$\frac{y_2 - y_1}{x_2 - x_1}$$

The x_2 and y_2 stand for coordinates for one point on the line, while the x_1 and y_1 are coordinates of another point on the line. The y_2 and y_1 stand for the vertical coordinates, and the x_2 and x_1 stand for the horizontal coordinates.

Another way to represent the change in the vertical coordinates divided by the change in the horizontal coordinates is to use a Δ —the Δ symbol means "change in" . . . yes, we have a symbol for just about everything in math! Using this symbol, we could represent slope like this:

$$\frac{\Delta y}{\Delta x}$$

No matter how we write it, though, the idea is to **find the vertical change and divide that by the horizontal change.**

The examples below walk through finding the slope of a couple of lines.

Example: Find the slope of the line shown.

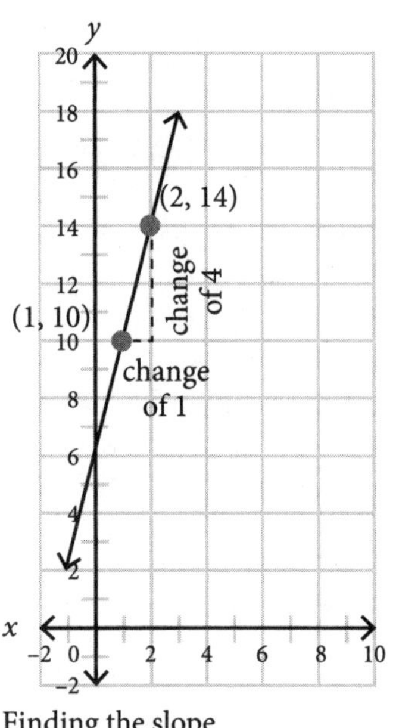

Finding the slope

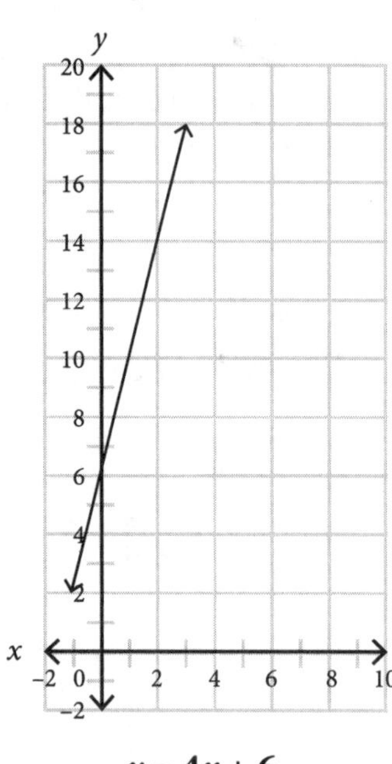

$y = 4x + 6$

The sidebar shows how we picked two points along the line and found the vertical change (4) and the horizontal change (1). We could have chosen any two points; we picked (2, 14) and (1, 10). Now we can find the slope by looking at the ratio between the vertical and horizontal change.

$$slope = \frac{vertical\ change}{horizontal\ change}$$

$$slope = \frac{14 - 10}{2 - 1} = \frac{4}{1} = 4$$

The slope is 4.

Key Point to Remember

We can pick any two points along the line to use in finding the slope of the line. Since the line is straight, the ratio between the vertical change and the horizontal change will be the same between any 2 points. It's easier, however, to pick whole numbers when you can.

Example: Find the slope of the line shown.

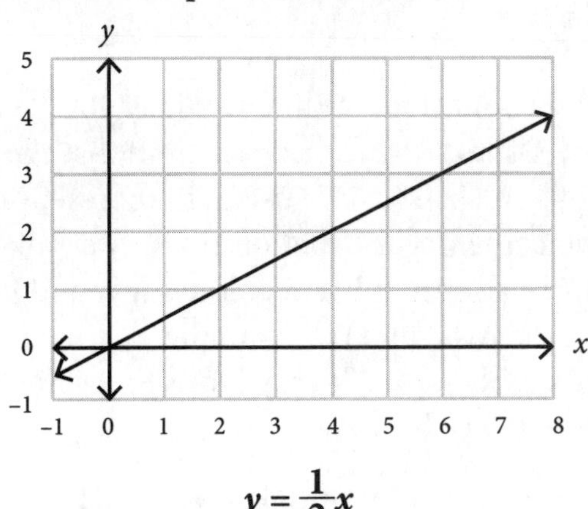

$y = \frac{1}{2}x$

Again, we can pick any two points along the line to use; we'll use (2, 1) and (6, 3).

$$slope = \frac{vertical\ change}{horizontal\ change}$$

$$slope = \frac{3 - 1}{6 - 2} = \frac{2}{4} = \frac{1}{2}$$

The slope is $\frac{1}{2}$.

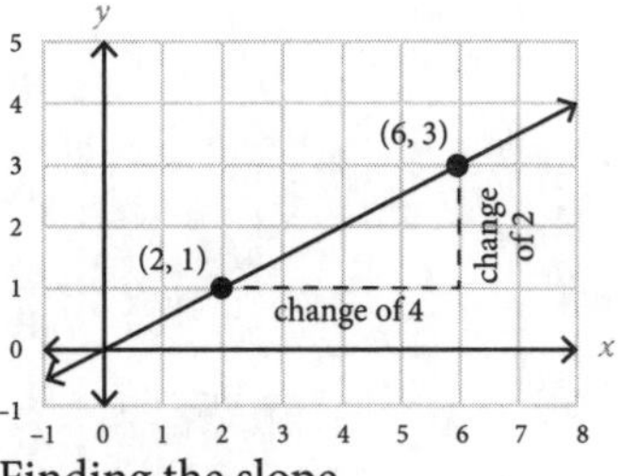

Finding the slope

Example: Find the slope of the line shown.

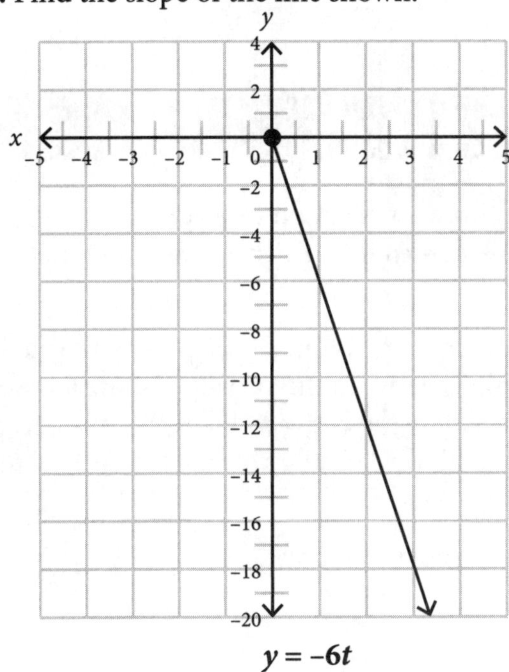

$y = -6t$

$$slope = \frac{vertical\ change}{horizontal\ change}$$

$$slope = \frac{-12 - -6}{2 - 1} = \frac{-6}{1} = -6$$

The slope is –6.

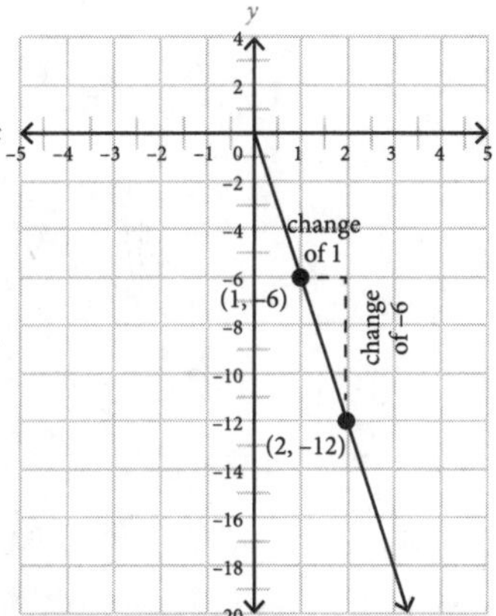

Finding the slope

In this example, we have a negative slope (–6). Notice that the line, when looked at from left to right, slopes downward — it truly does have a negative slope! And what could this negative slope represent?

A skier's change in height relative to the top of the mountain as he skis down the slope, the total dollars owed if a fee is charged every day, etc.

Example: Find the slope of the line shown.

Notice that this time, the coordinates have units. The horizontal coordinates represent hours, while the vertical coordinates represent miles. We'll want to keep track of the units as we find the slope.

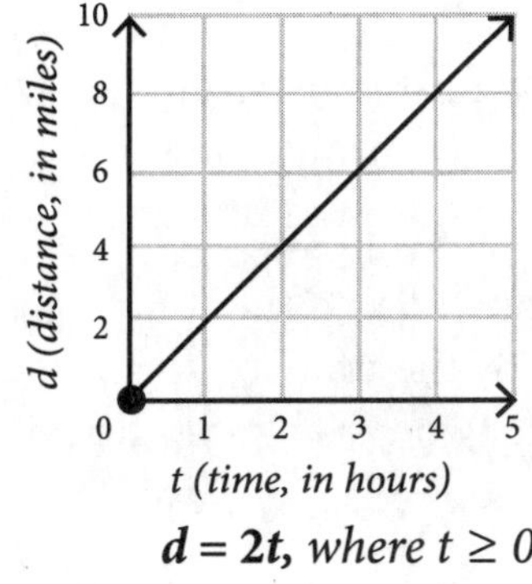

$d = 2t$, where $t \geq 0$

$$slope = \frac{vertical\ change}{horizontal\ change}$$

$$slope = \frac{4\ mi - 2\ mi}{2\ hr - 1\ hr} = \frac{2\ mi}{1\ hr} = 2\frac{mi}{hr}$$

The slope is $2\frac{mi}{hr}$.

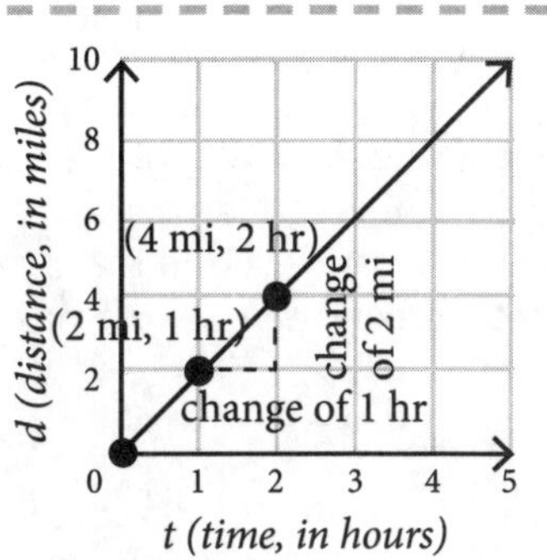

Finding the slope

Keeping Perspective

Well, I hope you had fun learning about slope. While you may at times wonder why you need to find the slope of a line, keep in mind that the graphs we're exploring, while they may seem abstract, are useful in representing real-life relationships. For example, the linear equation $y = \frac{1}{2}x$ we looked at in this lesson could represent the relationship between the sugar and flour needed in a recipe (half as much sugar as flour) or a number of other real-life relationships. The use of y and x simply makes it easy for us to instantly see the dependent and the independent variables.

By familiarizing yourself with mathematical relationships, you'll be better equipped to handle the real-life relationships you encounter.

14.6 Finding the Equation

Up until now, you've always been given an equation to graph. In real life, though, we sometimes need to graph data and *then* find the linear equation that best describes the data.

For example, say we collected data for an experiment that had two variables. We may not *know* what the relationship is between the variables is. In fact, we might be trying to discover if there is a relationship between them and, if so, what it is. By graphing the values we obtained, we'll be able to visually see if there is a relationship between them.

Let's do this with these hypothetical experiment results:

x	y
1	20
5	100
15	300
20	400

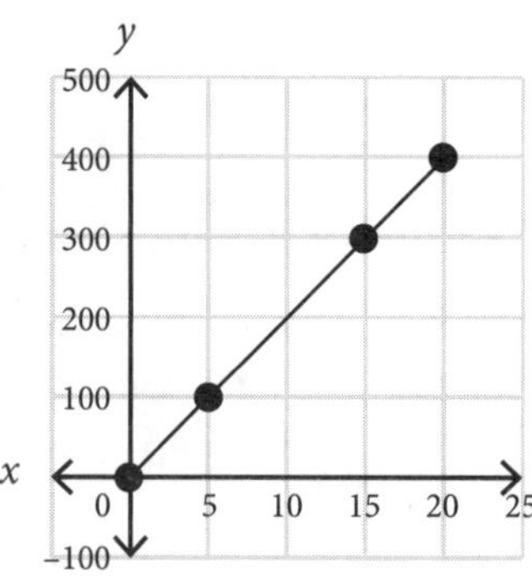

Not all experiments will show a relationship between variables. For example, there's probably not a relationship between the number of times you check on a pot of water and how quickly it boils. (And we all know that a watched pot never boils!) Plus, in real life, experiment results will not typically fall *perfectly* along a straight line like this. However, if the results are all close to falling along a line, we might conclude the difference is due to measurement error or other factors.

The graph helps us see that there is a relationship between the two variables in the experiment. But what exactly is that relationship? How can we describe the relationship using an equation?

To answer these questions, let's explore how to find the equation a linear graph (i.e., graph of a straight line) represents. By the time we finish, you'll be equipped to figure out the relationship between the two variables in the experiment. In fact, you'll get to do just that on Worksheet 14.6.

Slope-Intercept Form

We know how to find the slope and y-intercept by looking at a graph. Now it's time to go one step further and see how we can use the values we find for the slope and the y-intercept to write an equation that describes the line.

To illustrate, let's revisit an equation we looked at last lesson: $y = 10x + 5$. Notice that 10 is the slope of this line while 5 is the y-intercept. Notice that in the equation, 10 (the slope) is the multiplier of the independent variable, while 5 (the y-intercept) is a constant added to that product.

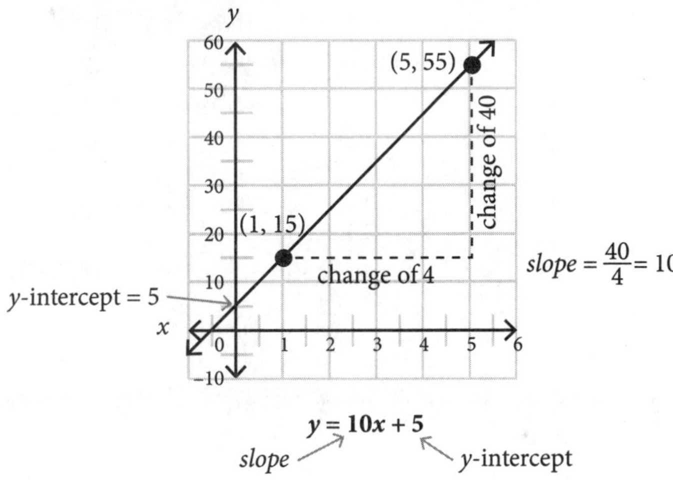

The equation $y = 10x + 5$, as well as all of the other linear equations we've graphed so far, follow the same general format:

dependent variable = ***slope***(*independent variable*) + ***y-intercept***

When an equation is written in this format, we say it's in **slope-intercept form**. After all, on the right side of the equation, the slope (which is multiplied by the independent variable) comes first, and then the y-intercept.

Now, there's a simpler way to describe slope-intercept form. We can use letters to stand for the dependent variable, slope, independent variable, and y-intercept. The typical way of expressing slope-intercept form is $y = mx + b$.

Slope-Intercept Form

dependent variable = slope(independent variable) + y-intercept

$$y = mx + b$$

While slope-intercept form is technically a way of describing a format for writing linear equations, we can also use it like a formula.

To express most lines mathematically, simply find the slope and the y-intercept, and arrange the values in slope-intercept form.

The letters m and b chosen are merely a convention — we really could use other letters. In fact, other countries do![3] Remember, a letter is a placeholder to represent a quantity.

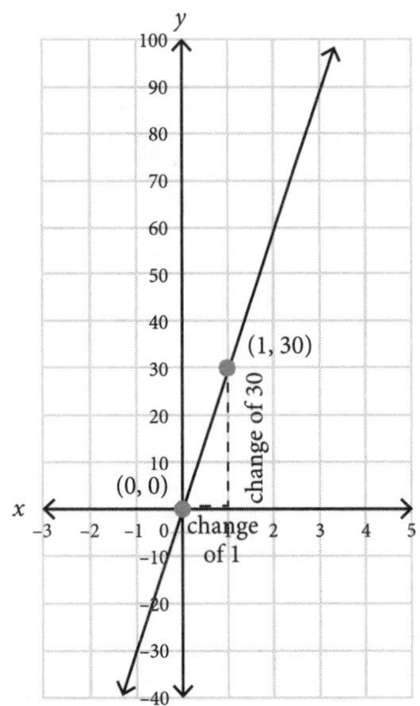

Finding the slope

Remember, we could pick any two points off which to find the slope. Smaller values make for easier math, though, so we chose (0, 0) and (1, 30).

Example: Find the equation of this line.

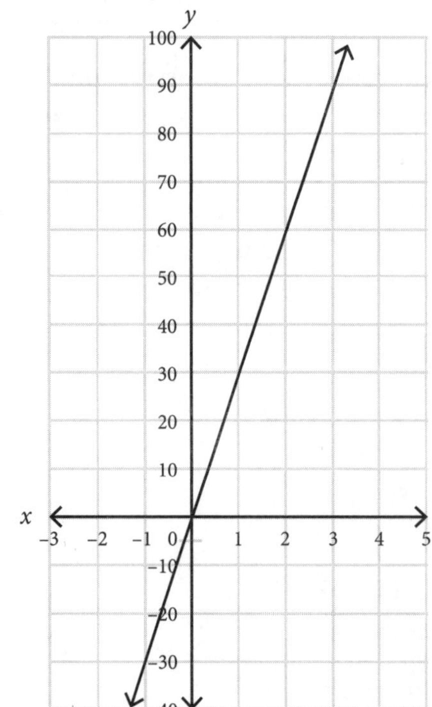

Finding the slope:

$$slope = \frac{vertical\ change}{horizontal\ change}$$

$$slope = \frac{30}{1} = 30$$

Finding the y-intercept:

The line intersects the y-axis when y equals 0, so the y-intercept is 0.

Substitute the slope and y-intercept we found into the slope-intercept form to find the equation of the line:

$y = mx + b$

$y = \mathbf{30x + 0}$, which simplifies to

$\mathbf{y = 30x}$

Note: Since adding 0 doesn't change the value, we don't typically write out y-intercepts of 0.

Check: If we substitute values for x into $y = 30x$, we see that no matter what value we choose for x, the resulting value for y would give us coordinates that are indeed points along the line. This line does indeed represent the equation $y = 30x$.

x (independent variable/input)	y (dependent variable/output)	$y = 30x$
−1	−30	$y = 30(\mathbf{-1}) = \mathbf{-30}$
3	90	$y = 30(\mathbf{3}) = \mathbf{90}$

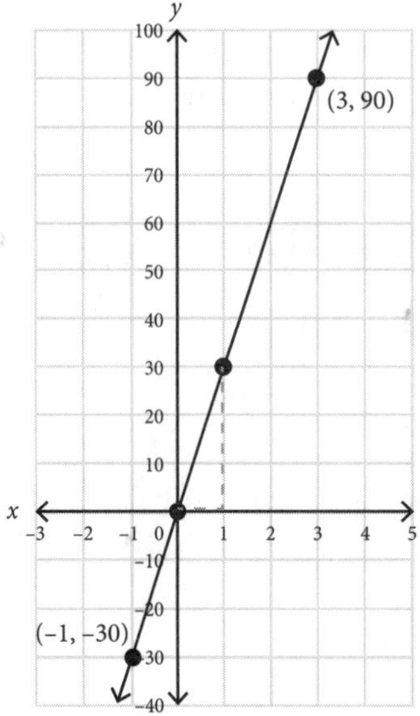

Example: Find the equation of this line.

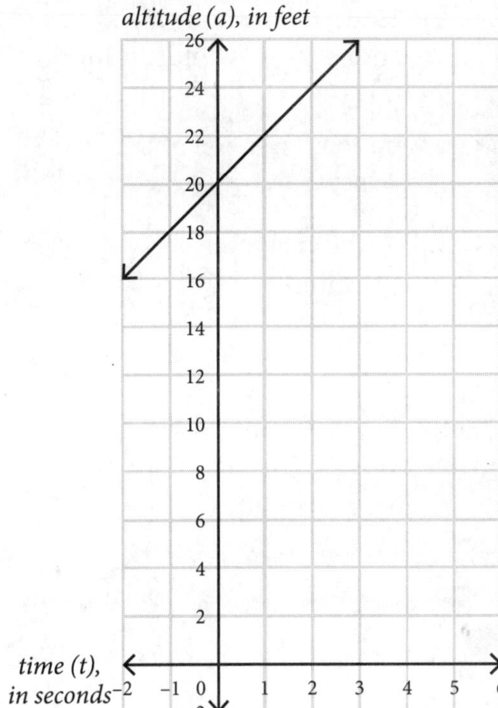

Finding the slope:

$$slope = \frac{vertical\ change}{horizontal\ change}$$

$$slope = \frac{2 \text{ ft}}{1 \text{ sec}} = 2\,\frac{\text{ft}}{\text{sec}}$$

Finding the y-intercept:

The line intersects the y-axis when y equals +20 ft, so the y-intercept is +20 ft.

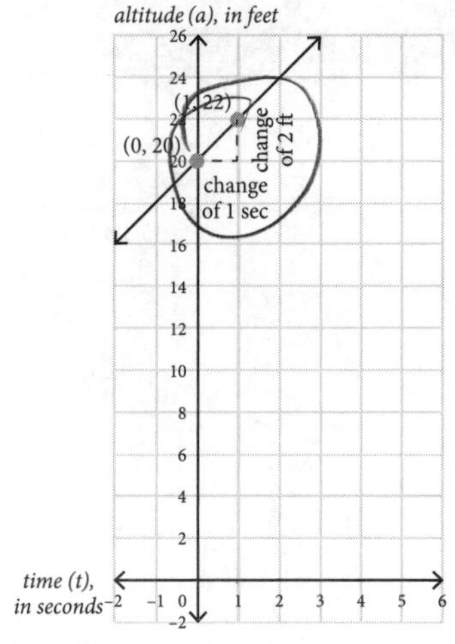

Finding the slope

Now that we have found the slope ($2\,\frac{\text{ft}}{\text{sec}}$) and the y-intercept (20 ft), it's time to substitute these values into the slope-intercept form:

$$y = mx + b$$

$$a = (2\,\frac{\text{ft}}{\text{sec}})t + 20 \text{ ft}$$

Notice that we used the letters a and t instead of y and x and that we included $\frac{\text{ft}}{\text{sec}}$ and ft since the problem and graph used those variables and units.

Check: If we substitute values for t into $a = (2\,\frac{\text{ft}}{\text{sec}})t + 20$ ft, we see that for any value for t we could choose, the resulting value for a would give us coordinates that are indeed points along the line. This line does indeed represent the equation $a = (2\,\frac{\text{ft}}{\text{sec}})t + 20$ ft.

t (independent variable/ input, in secc)	***a*** (dependent variable/ output, in ft)	$a = (2\frac{\text{ft}}{\text{sec}})t + 20 \text{ ft}$
−1	18	$a = 2(-1) + 20 = 18$
2	24	$a = 2(2) + 20 = 24$

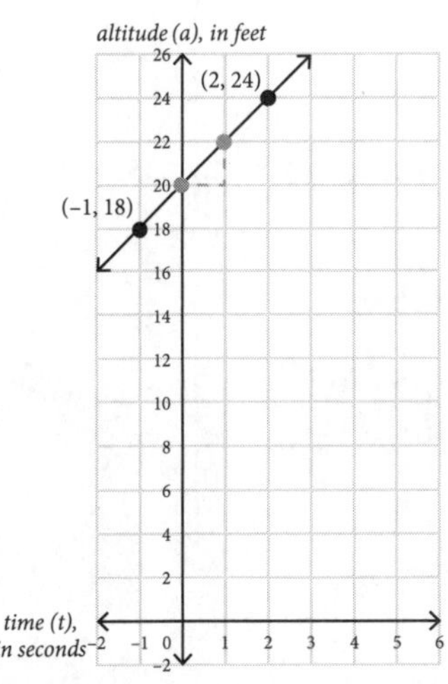

Understanding Slope-Intercept Form

While we've been giving you all equations in slope-intercept form, it's important to note that we could express a relationship in a different form. For instance, we could rewrite $y = 10x + 5$ as $y - 10x = 5$.

Example: Rewrite y = $10x + 5$ so x and y are on the same side of the equation.

Add $-10x$ to both sides:

$$y + \mathbf{-10x} = 10x + 5 + \mathbf{-10x}$$

$$y - 10x = 5$$

While $y = 10x + 5$ and $y - 10x = 5$ both represent the same relationship, $y - 10x = 5$ is not arranged in slope–intercept form. Thus, the slope and the y-intercept are not in the positions they are in $y = mx + b$.

Slope-intercept form ($y = mx + b$) is a way of writing an equation. Using it makes it super easy to represent a line mathematically — but know that equations can be written other ways too.

Other Linear Graphs

Towards the beginning of the lesson, we said that you can use the slope-intercept form to express *most* linear (i.e., straight-line) graphs. **In fact, if an equation can be written in slope-intercept form, it will produce a straight line when graphed** and it can be thought of as both a linear equation and a function.

However, not all linear graphs can be described in slope-intercept form, nor can all linear graphs be thought of as representing functions. The exceptions are completely vertical lines.[4] Notice that in a completely vertical line, x has a fixed value, and y's value doesn't depend on x's, nor is there one y value for each x value (y could be a number of values).

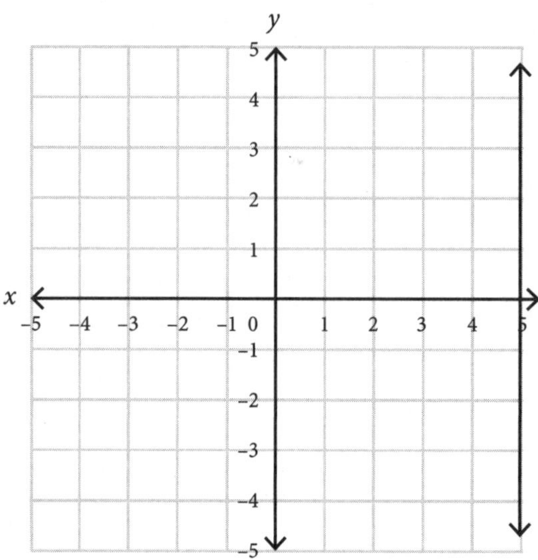

$x = 5$

Keeping Perspective

Graphs give a pictorial representation of a relationship. Now you not only know how to graph a linear equation, but you also know how to find the linear equation that describes a line.

One of the beauties of coordinate graphing is that it combines tools from geometry with tools from algebra. For example, we could look at an angle on a graph and use a formula to describe the line that forms the angle.

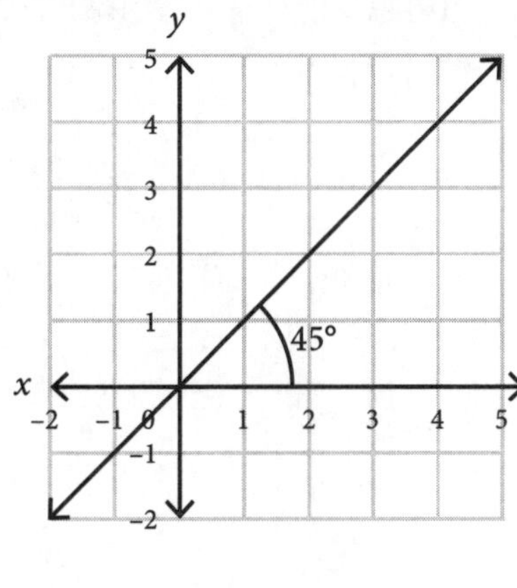

$$y = x$$

(formula that describes a line that forms a 45° angle)

As you continue exploring mathematical relationships with graphing, pause and praise the Creator of all. Remember that we're only able to represent and work with equations because God gave us this ability. He created us capable of thinking, exploring the world around us, and solving problems. He is the faithful, consistent God governing the universe.

14.7 The Line of Best Fit

Throughout this chapter we've been exploring linear equations — equations that result in a straight line when graphed. In the last lesson, we learned how we could even graph data from an experiment and, if the data fell along a straight line, find the equation that describes the relationship between variables.

It's worth noting, though, that in real life, many times actual data will not *perfectly* fall along a straight line. However, we can still often find the line that *best describes* the relationship.

Line of Best Fit

The following graph shows the body temperature of a typhoid patient measured in 3-hour intervals.[5]

Why is the temperature decreasing? Well, the data doesn't tell us. It would make sense for the temperature to decrease, though, if the patient is recovering.

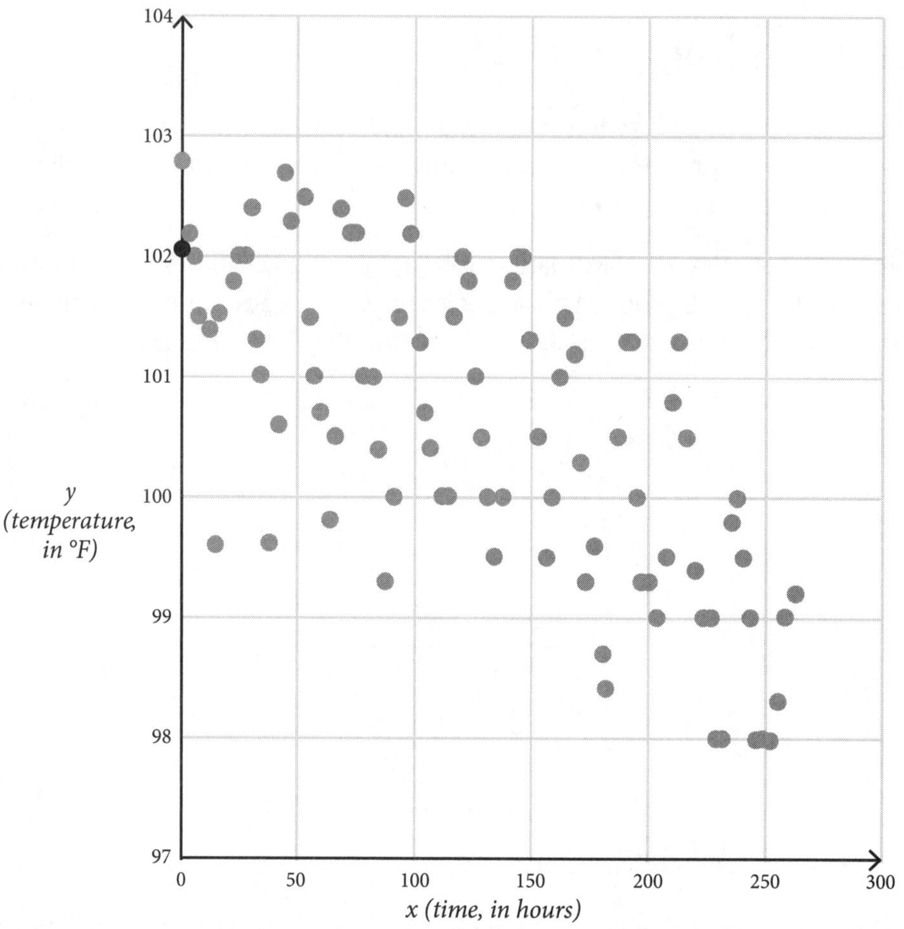

Temperature over Time of a Typhoid Patient

Notice how the graph helps us quickly see the general trend of the data. We can instantly see that the temperature decreased over time. However, there may be times where we will want to dig a little deeper.

Even though there's not a perfect relationship between the temperature and time in this scenario, it's possible to mathematically calculate what we call the **line of best fit** (which will also sometimes be called the **trend line**) — the straight line that would *best represent* the relationship between two variables.

While we won't go into the math of finding the line of best fit, here's a picture of the fever temperatures over time with the line of best fit drawn.

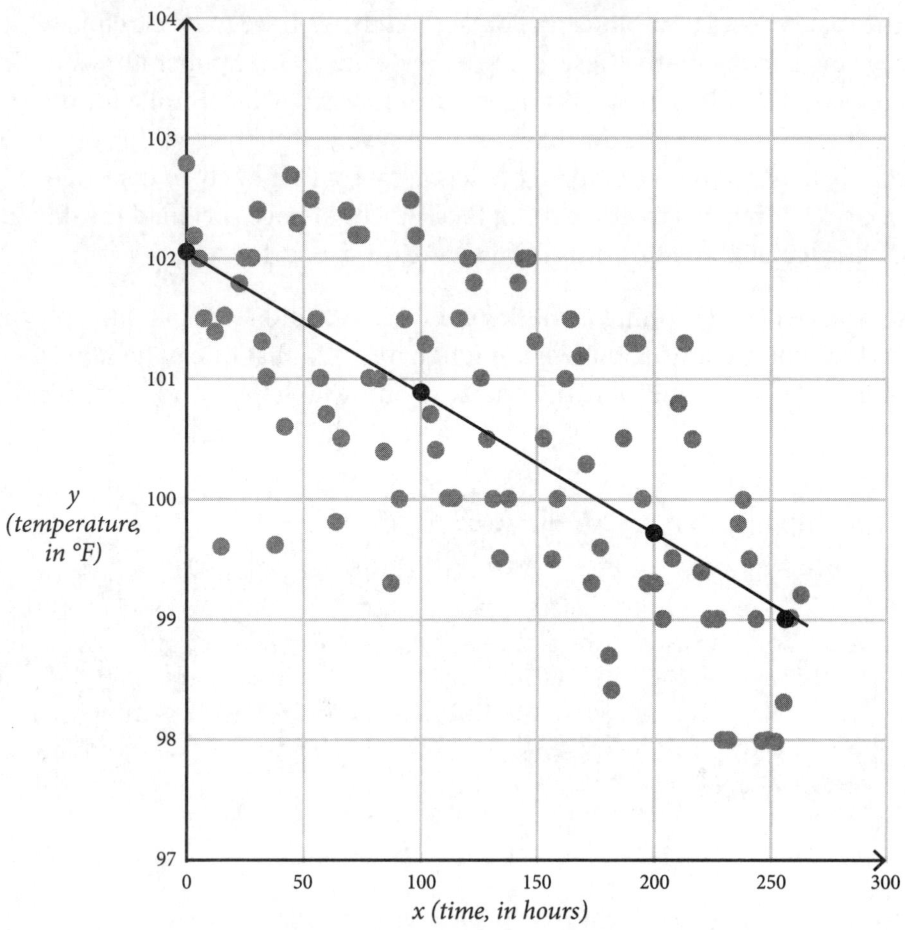

Fever Temperature over Time of a Typhoid Patient

Now, let's figure out what equation this line represents. In this case, the line intercepts the y-axis at 102.06 °F, so 102.06 °F is the y-intercept. The slope can be found by dividing the vertical change by the horizontal change for any two points along the line. If we were to zoom in on the line and find the slope by looking at the vertical change and the horizontal change for any two points, we would get a slope of −0.0116. So we have this linear equation:

$$y = -0.0116x + 102.06$$

We can use this equation to help us make predictions about what will happen at other values. For example, if we use a value of 270 hours for x in the equation, we'll see that y will be 98.93 °F.

$$y = -0.0116(\mathbf{270}) + 102.06$$

$$y = \mathbf{-3.132} + 102.06$$

$$y = \mathbf{98.93}$$

Now, let's talk about what that value means. So far, the patient's actual temperatures have fallen both above and below the line of best fit. So we shouldn't expect the patient's temperature to fall at exactly 98.93 °F after 270 hours. However, this number gives us an *idea* of what to expect if the trend continues.

As is the case whenever we interpret data, though, we have to be careful about drawing conclusions. In this case, since we're dealing with temperature and time, we have to be careful about assuming this relationship will continue for other values. After all, we don't know that it will, and we definitely wouldn't expect it to once a patient recovers (the patient's temperature isn't likely to continue to decrease once it returns to normal). In fact, we could have specified the domain for which we calculated the line of best fit: where $0 \leq x \leq 261$.

The data we've been graphing is the result of one typhoid fever patient. So while we can draw conclusions about what might happen to that one patient, we'd need a lot more data before we could generalize about what happens to other typhoid patients.

Is the Line of Best Fit Really a Fit?

In the example we walked through, the line of best fit was a fairly good representation of the data, as most of the data was somewhat near the line. This is not always the case. If most of the data is nowhere near the line of best fit, the line of best fit is obviously not a very good representation of the data. The *line of best fit* only proves helpful if there's a general linear relationship between the two variables.

Keeping Perspective

As we use math to explore the world around us, we will encounter data that doesn't relate together precisely. Finding the **line of best fit** (which will also sometimes be called the **trend line**) can prove helpful. In this lesson, we used it to help describe the approximate relationship between one particular typhoid patient's temperature and the time that has passed.

In the process of exploring this relationship, we used inequalities, statistics, graphing, and equations. Math builds on itself, combining tools and skills to handle more complicated situations. As you continue learning new ways to apply mathematical tools, keep praising the Creator and seeking to learn to use each new tool and skill for His glory.

> *And whatsoever ye do, do it heartily, as to the Lord, and not unto men; Knowing that of the Lord ye shall receive the reward of the inheritance: for ye serve the Lord Christ (Colossians 3:23–24).*

14.8 Chapter Synopsis and René Descartes

Well, we've reached the end of our short look at picturing relationships using coordinate graphing. We saw

- that we can picture the relationship between variables using a coordinate graph. To make it easier to see how the dependent variable changes, we'll typically **put the dependent variable (i.e., the output) on the vertical axis, and the independent variable (i.e., the input) on the horizontal axis.**
- that we graph **linear equations** by finding at least two sets of coordinates, graphing those coordinates, and connecting them with a line.
- that we can show the values for which an equation holds true by using closed or open points.

We also explored ***y*-intercept** and **slope**, and then applied what we had learned to find the equation a line describes using **slope-intercept form**. We ended with a brief look at the **line of best fit** (which will also sometimes be called the **trend line**).

I hope you've gotten a glimpse for the usefulness of picturing relationships graphically. On a graph, we can easily see different inputs and outputs to an equation without manually calculating each one. It's been said that "a picture is worth a thousand words" . . . and coordinate graphs prove no exception.

Again, the purpose of picturing mathematical relationships is to better understand and work with the real-life mathematical relationships around us. It's a tool to help us describe God's creation and serve the Lord in various fields and settings.

Let's finish by taking a look at the life of a man closely connected with the history of coordinate graphing: René Descartes.

René Descartes

While we haven't used this term, the coordinates we've been using to graph equations are sometimes called **Cartesian coordinates** after the French mathematician René Descartes (pronounced "dā'kärt"[6] — note the "cartes" in both Des*cartes* and *Carte*sian). Descartes published "the first treatise"[7] on what's known as analytic geometry, some aspects of which we've been exploring this chapter.

René Descartes (1596–1650)

Despite his contributions to math, Descartes was actually more of a philosopher than a mathematician. He recognized that the Greek teaching and mysticism nearly universally embraced in the culture of his day could not explain truth, but rather than returning to biblical truths, he turned instead to his own reasoning and tried to find a foundation for truth there.

> *To Descartes the principal source of knowledge is in our intelligence. . . . It is intelligence that distinguishes truth from error . . .*

> *we must study our intelligence, which itself alone can know, though imagination, senses, and memory may aid it.*[8]
>
> *. . . he seeks for proofs, not from without but from within, and this he does by showing what is involved in any simple fact, such as that I know.*[9]

Descartes based his philosophy on the idea that "I think, hence I am."[10] His thinking, not God's Word, was his starting point.

Not only is our own thinking an unbiblical starting point, but it's logically unsound as well. After all, why should we even trust our own reasoning if we don't start with the assumption that God created us in His image and gave us the ability to reason?

Astrophysicist and creation researcher Dr. Jason Lisle points out the unsoundness of starting with our own reasoning in depth in his book *The Ultimate Proof of Creation*. Here's one quote:

> *If evolution were true, science would not make sense because there would be no reason to accept the uniformity of nature upon which all science and technology depend.*
>
> *Nor would there be any reason to think that rational analysis would be possible since the thoughts of our mind would be nothing more than the inevitable result of mindless chemical reactions.*[11]

While Descartes argued for God's existence, he did so starting with his own reasoning as the source for truth rather than on God's Word. Sadly, his thinking has become more and more prevalent in our culture. Yet the Bible warns us that it's foolish to trust our own hearts. Our faith rests, not on the basis of human reasoning, but on an unchanging God.

> *He that trusteth in his own heart is a fool: but whoso walketh wisely, he shall be delivered (Proverbs 28:26).*
>
> *The fool hath said in his heart, There is no God. They are corrupt, they have done abominable works, there is none that doeth good (Psalm 14:1).*
>
> *Trust in the LORD with all thine heart; and lean not unto thine own understanding. In all thy ways acknowledge him, and he shall direct thy paths (Proverbs 3:5–6).*

[CHAPTER 15]

Exponents and Unknowns

15.1 Reviewing Exponents

It's time now to continue exploring relationships between variables by looking at relationships that involve exponents, including volume, exponential growth, and earthquakes. Before we do that, though, let's do a quick review of exponents.

Reviewing Exponents

As we saw in Book 1, we can represent repeated multiplication more concisely using exponents. For example, we can represent 2 • 2 • 2 as 2^3. The superscript 3 tells us to multiply 2 by itself 3 times. Likewise, we can represent ft • ft • ft as ft^3. The superscript 3 tells us to multiply ft by itself 3 times.

Notice in the chart on the next page that we wrote the number that needs to be multiplied (which we call the **base**), and then we wrote a superscript number (which we call the **exponent**) indicating the number of times the base should be multiplied.

Also notice in the chart that we've used the word *power* to read the different quantities. For example, we read 2^4 as "two to the fourth *power*." While the word *power* is sometimes omitted (people will sometimes refer to 2^4 as "two to the fourth"), it's a good term to know. A **power** is "the product which we obtain by multiplying a number once or several times by itself."[1] So when we say "two to the fourth power," we're referring to the *product* of multiplying 2 by itself 4 times—that is 16, as 2 • 2 • 2 • 2 = 16.

While a *power* technically refers to the *product* of multiplying a base by itself a certain number of times and an *exponent* is the number written down to show us how many times to multiply the base, you'll also often hear the terms *power* and *exponent* used synonymously.[2]

Notation	Meaning	Read
2^0	1	Two to the zeroth power
2^1	2	Two to the first power
2^2	2 • 2	Two to the second power / two squared *called "squaring" a number*
2^3	2 • 2 • 2	Two to the third power / two cubed *called "cubing" a number*
2^4	2 • 2 • 2 • 2	Two to the fourth power
2^5	2 • 2 • 2 • 2 • 2	Two to the fifth power
2^6	2 • 2 • 2 • 2 • 2 • 2	Two to the sixth power
2^7	2 • 2 • 2 • 2 • 2 • 2 • 2	Two to the seventh power
2^8	2 • 2 • 2 • 2 • 2 • 2 • 2 • 2	Two to the eighth power
2^9	2 • 2 • 2 • 2 • 2 • 2 • 2 • 2 • 2	Two to the ninth power
2^{10}	2 • 2 • 2 • 2 • 2 • 2 • 2 • 2 • 2 • 2	Two to the tenth power

We could continue the chart with other powers (2^{11}, 2^{12}, 2^{13}, etc.).

A Number Raised to the Zeroth Power

Wondering why a base raised to the zeroth power equals 1? Let's take a quick look.

Since we can multiply any number by 1 without changing its value (there's that identity property of multiplication again), we can think of the exponent as telling us to take 1 *times* the base multiplied by itself a certain number of times.

$2^3 = 1 \bullet 2 \bullet 2 \bullet 2$

$4^2 = 1 \bullet 4 \bullet 4$

If we think of all exponents as telling us to take 1 *times* the base multiplied by itself a certain number of times, then any base raised to the zeroth power would mean to multiply 1 by the base 0 times . . . in other words, to not multiply 1 by anything, leaving us with 1.

$2^0 = 1$

$4^0 = 1$

Multiplying 1 by the base zero times leaves us with 1.

While we typically don't bother to think of multiplying by 1 when we simplify an exponent, know that we could, and that when we do, powers of 0 make sense.

Exponents and Negative Numbers

Consider the following:

$$(-2)^3$$

Just as 2^3 means $2 \bullet 2 \bullet 2$, so $(-2)^3$ means $-2 \bullet -2 \bullet -2$. And what does that equal? Well, since each negative sign means the opposite of, it would equal –8.

$$-2 \bullet -2 \bullet -2 = -8$$

odd number is negative
even number is positive

The opposite of the opposite of the opposite equals a negative.

On the other hand, $(-2)^4$ will yield a positive answer.

$$-2 \bullet -2 \bullet -2 \bullet -2 = 16$$

The opposite of the opposite of the opposite of the opposite equals a positive.

Important Note

Notice that we put parentheses around –2 in $(-2)^3$ and $(-2)^4$. If we had not, it would have meant to multiply +2 the requested number of times, and then take the opposite of the result. In the case of 2^4, one way gives us a negative answer, and the other a positive.

$$-2^4 = -(2 \bullet 2 \bullet 2 \bullet 2) = -16 \quad (-2)^4 = -2 \bullet -2 \bullet -2 \bullet -2 = 16$$

Revisiting the Order of Operations

Remember to follow the order of operations when solving problems involving exponents.

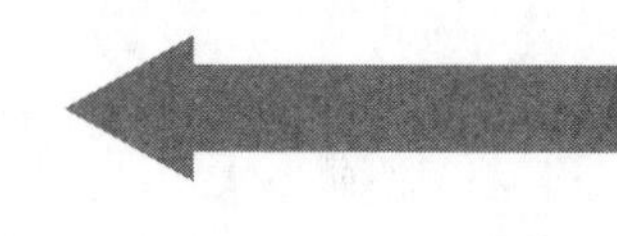

Order of Operations

1. Solve anything within parentheses first, using the following order (which is the same order we'll follow outside of parentheses too):
   a. Simplify exponents and roots, from left to right.*
   b. Multiply or divide, from left to right.
   c. Add or subtract, from left to right.
2. Next simplify exponents and roots, from left to right.*
3. Now multiply or divide, from left to right.
4. Last, add or subtract, from left to right.

**There will not be any roots until they are reviewed in Lesson 17.1.*

Reminder: The order of operations is an agreed-upon convention so we all know what is meant by a mathematical expression.

Example: $2(1 + 5)^2$

Solve within the parentheses:

$2(\mathbf{6})^2$

Simplify the exponents:

$2(\mathbf{36})$

Complete the multiplication:

72

Order of Operations Note: The order of operations determines how we complete calculations. As you've seen, when working with unknowns, we're not always able to complete the calculations without first rearranging the equation. The rules we follow when working with unknowns take into account the order of operations and preserve the meaning. The rules we follow work because of the consistent way God causes addition, subtraction, multiplication, and division to operate.

Example: $8x + 2x + 5^2 = 20$

There are no parentheses, so the first step is to simplify the exponents and roots.

$8x + 2x + \mathbf{25} = 20$

Now, let's combine like terms.

$\mathbf{10x} + 25 = 20$

And now let's find x by isolating it on a side of the equation by itself.

$10x + 25 + \mathbf{-25} = 20 + \mathbf{-25}$

$10x = \mathbf{-5}$

$\frac{10x}{\mathbf{10}} = -\frac{5}{\mathbf{10}}$

$\frac{\cancel{10}x}{\cancel{10}} = -\frac{5}{10}$

$\mathbf{x = -\frac{1}{2}}$

Example: $x \bullet 2 + 5 = 26$

Here, we have to first complete the multiplication of $x \bullet 2$. While we can't fully complete the multiplication since we don't know x's value, let's rewrite $x \bullet 2$ as $2x$ for clarity.

$\mathbf{2x} + 5 = 26$

We can find x by isolating it on a side of the equation by itself.

$2x + 5 - \mathbf{5} = 26 - \mathbf{5}$

$2x = \mathbf{21}$

$\frac{2x}{\mathbf{2}} = \frac{21}{\mathbf{2}}$

$\frac{\cancel{2}x}{\cancel{2}} = \frac{21}{2}$

$\mathbf{x = 10.5}$

Notice that we would have gotten a different answer had we not followed the order of operations but instead added 2 and 5 at the beginning.

$x \bullet 2 + 5 = 26$

$x \bullet 7 = 26$

$\frac{7x}{7} = \frac{26}{7}$

$\frac{7x}{7} = \frac{26}{7}$

$\mathbf{x = 3.71}$

Incorrect

Keeping Perspective

Exponents are useful notations to help us express quantities concisely. It's much simpler to write 2^8 than $2 \bullet 2 \bullet 2 \bullet 2 \bullet 2 \bullet 2 \bullet 2 \bullet 2$.

While we're focusing on the mechanics of exponents right now, don't lose sight of the purpose of the mechanics. We're learning these notations *so that* we can describe real-life relationships that involve repeated multiplication, such as population growth, earthquakes, and gravity, to name a few.

15.2 Exponents and Unknowns

Many real-life relationships involve repeated multiplication. Take the relationship between the area and sides of a square, for instance.

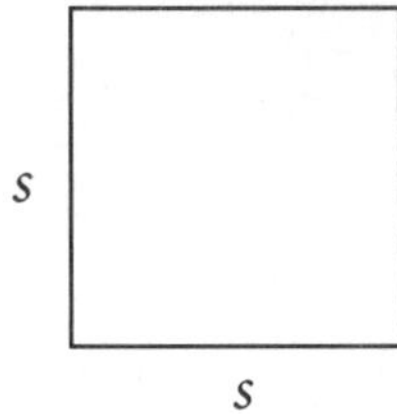

$$Area = side \bullet side$$

$$A = s \bullet s$$

As we saw in Book 1, we can represent the repeated multiplication more concisely using an exponent.

$$A = s \bullet s$$

$$A = s^2$$

Exponents are a shorthand way of representing repeated multiplication, whether we're dealing with known numbers or unknowns.

Example: Represent $x \bullet x \bullet x \bullet x$ using an exponent.

Answer: x^4

Example: Represent y^3 using a multiplication sign.

Answer: $y \bullet y \bullet y$

Working with Exponents and Unknowns

It's simple to work with formulas involving exponents. Simply substitute known values as you have been, remembering that the exponent tells us how many times to multiply the base.

Example: Find the area of a square that has sides of 2 ft.

All we have to do is substitute 2 ft for s in the formula and complete the multiplication to find the area.

Original formula:

$$A = s^2$$

Substitute 2 ft for s:

$$A = (\mathbf{2\ ft})^2$$

Complete the multiplication:

$$A = \mathbf{2\ ft \bullet 2\ ft}\text{, which equals } 4\text{ ft} \bullet \text{ft, or } \mathbf{4\ ft^2}$$

The area is 4 ft^2 (i.e., 4 square feet).

Example: Find y if $y = x^3$ and $x = 5$.

All we have to do is substitute 5 for x in $y = x^3$, and complete the multiplication.

$$y = x^3$$

$$y = \mathbf{5^3}$$

$$y = \mathbf{5 \bullet 5 \bullet 5}$$

$$y = \mathbf{125}$$

Notice that in the first example, we enclosed 2 ft in parentheses when we substituted it for s, giving us $A = (2\text{ ft})^2$. That's because without the parentheses, we would have had $A = 2\text{ ft}^2$, which would mean that A equaled 2 square feet, or 2 ft • ft, rather than 2 ft • 2 ft, or 4 ft^2. In the second example, we didn't bother to put parentheses around the 5 in $y = 5^3$, as there was no unit of measure. However, we could have still enclosed the 5 inside of parentheses if we wanted to. Both $y = 5^3$ and $y = (5)^3$ mean the same thing.

Keeping Perspective

Exponents are shorthand for repeated multiplication, whether we're dealing with a known number or an unknown. Throughout the rest of this chapter, we'll explore relationships involving exponents in more depth. For now, familiarize yourself with using this handy notation to represent repeated multiplications, whether of known or of unknown quantities.

As always, keep in mind that the equations you work with, while they don't always come labeled with a meaning, can represent all sorts of real-life relationships. For example, $y = x^3$ might represent the volume of a cube. The volume of a cube equals the length of one of its sides times itself three times ($V = s^3$) . . . which could also be written $y = x^3$. Although you'll see a lot of *xs* and *ys* in math books, those letters are simply placeholders.

s *s* *s*

$V = s^3$

Volume = $(side)^3$

15.3 Graphs of Functions with Exponents

Let's use graphing to get a better picture for the relationship between variables in which the independent variable (x) is raised to a power. While you won't be asked to graph any of these relationships yourself and while we'll only look at a couple of examples, it's important to begin to understand that different relationships look different on a graph.

All of the relationships we'll be looking at in this lesson will still be functions; however, they will not be linear functions (i.e., they won't result in a straight line when graphed).

Graphing Functions with Exponents

Let's consider two simple equations: $y = x^2$ and $y = x^3$. Let's start by looking at only positive values for x and see what these relationships look like on a graph.

x	y	$y = x^2$
0	0	$y = 0^2 = 0$
2	4	$y = 2^2 = 4$
4	16	$y = 4^2 = 16$

x	y	$y = x^3$
0	0	$y = 0^3 = 0$
2	8	$y = 2^3 = 8$
4	64	$y = 4^3 = 64$

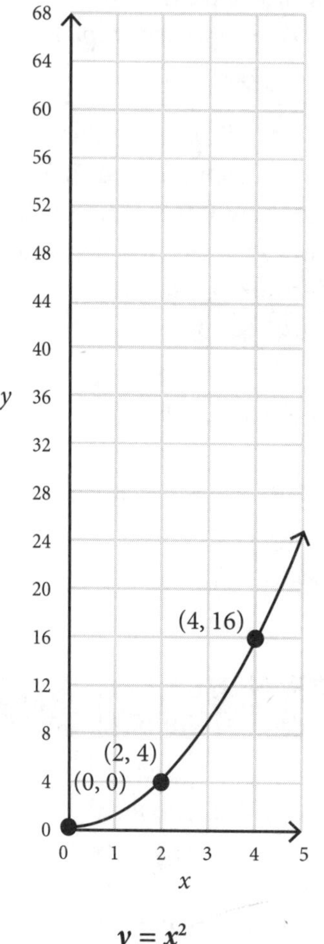

$y = x^2$

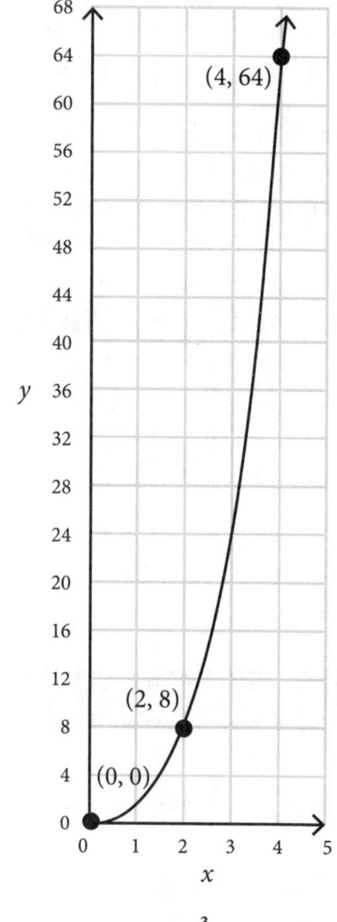

$y = x^3$

Notice that when graphed, these relationships result in a curve that gets steeper and steeper rather than a straight line. After all, the greater the number we insert for x, the greater the product will be when we raise that number to a power. In $y = x^3$, when x is 2, y is 8. But when x is 4, y is 64.

Making it Practical

While we used y and x to keep the equations generic above, the $y = x^2$ and $y = x^3$ are essentially the same equations (only using different letters) as those for the area of a square and the volume of a cube: $A = s^2$ and $V = s^3$.

Now, let's look at what $y = x^2$ and $y = x^3$ look like when we include negative values for the independent variable. Below are the same two graphs, only this time, we've included negative values.

x	y	$y = x^2$
−2	4	$y = (-2)^2 = 4$
−4	16	$y = (-4)^2 = 16$

x	y	$y = x^3$
−2	−8	$y = (-2)^3 = -8$
−4	−64	$y = (-4)^3 = -64$

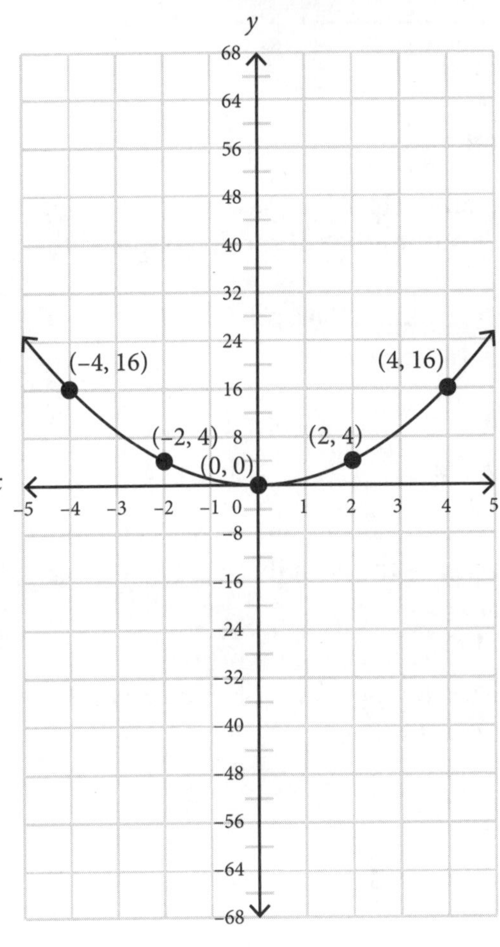

$y = x^2$

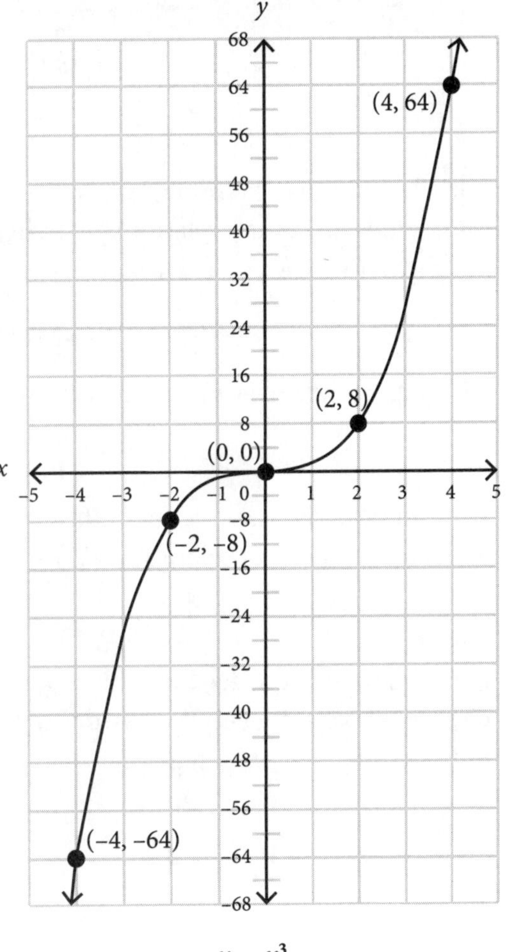

$y = x^3$

Notice that in x^2, when we insert a negative value for x, we still end up with a positive value for y. After all, a negative times a negative equals a positive. In x^3, though, when we insert a negative value for x, the value for y is also negative, since a negative times a negative times a negative equals a negative. This results in a different curve when graphed.

> The main point is that graphs show us how variables relate to each other. A graph helps us see how changing the independent variable will affect the dependent variable.

Before we conclude, let's graph a couple of real-life relationships that include a exponent and see how graphs can make it easier to see relationships. For example, the following graph makes it easy to see that the volume of a cube with 50 in sides is 125,000 in^3.

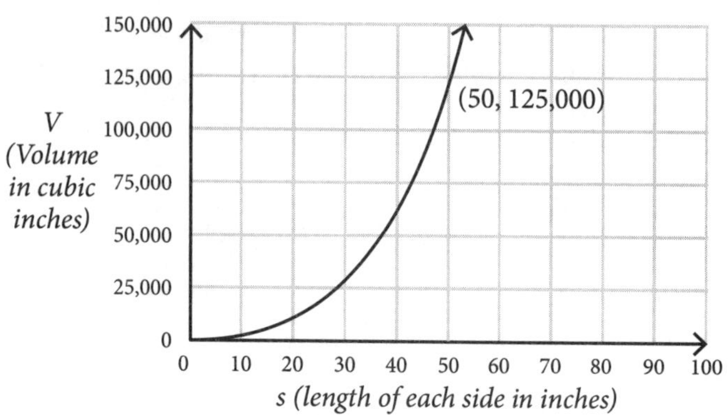

$$V = s^3\text{, when } s > 0$$

For a less familiar example, let's look at an example from physics. Without going into details, here's the relationship between a certain type of acceleration and the velocity and radius of a circle:

$$\textit{centripetal acceleration} = \frac{\textit{velocity} \bullet \textit{velocity}}{\textit{radius of the circle}}$$

Let's express the relationship using letters:

$$a = \frac{v \bullet v}{r} \quad \text{or} \quad a = \frac{v^2}{r}$$

Let's suppose the value of the radius (r) of a circle is a constant 10. We could now look at centripetal acceleration (a) as a function of the velocity (v).

$$a = \frac{v^2}{10}$$

Suppose we want to see how the centripetal acceleration (a) will change as we change the velocity (v). We can do this easily on a graph!

Since the units of measure in this example are unfamiliar, we've purposefully left them off.

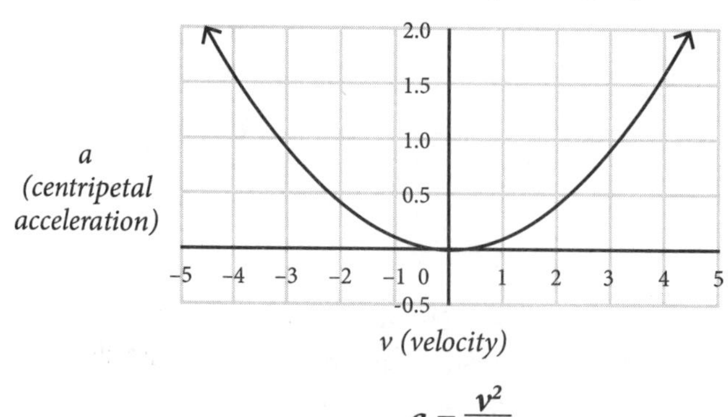

$$a = \frac{v^2}{10}$$

(the change in acceleration as the velocity changes when the radius is 10)

Notice how easy the graph makes it to see the relationship between the centripetal acceleration and the velocity. We can now see at a glance how increasing or decreasing the velocity will change the centripetal acceleration.

Keeping Perspective

Again, in this course, you won't be asked to graph equations where the independent variable is raised to a power. We included them in this lesson to illustrate the point that graphs help us picture relationships, that relationships are not all linear, and that graphs prove a useful tool in helping us understand the amazingly complex world God created and sustains.

15.4 Using a Calculator with Exponents

Since you will sometimes be allowed to use your calculator when solving a problem with an exponent, let's take a quick look at the mechanics of simplifying exponents on a calculator.

Simplifying Exponents on a Calculator

On exponent problems where it indicates you can use a calculator, look for your **exponent button**. Your calculator's exponent button might look like either of the following buttons:

or

To simplify a number raised to a power on a calculator, input the base (the number you're multiplying), press the exponent button (y^x or ^), and then input the exponent (the number of times to multiply the base). Press the equal button (=) if needed to see the product.

Example: Find 44^5

Enter 44 (the base) into the calculator.

Press y^x or ^.

Enter 5 (the exponent) into the calculator.

Press =. *(This step may not be necessary on your calculator.)*

Finding Squares on a Calculator

Many calculators also have a **square button.**

This button assumes an exponent of 2. If you need to square a number (multiply it by itself), this button can save you time. Just enter the number, and then press this button.

Your calculator's buttons may look slightly different. If these instructions don't seem to work, look at your calculator's instruction manual.

Example: Find 24^2

Enter 24 (the base) into the calculator.

Press x^2.

Press =. *(This step may not be necessary on your calculator.)*

Keeping Perspective

While it's important to know how to use calculators, it's also important that you *not* rely on them to the point that you don't understand what they're doing. It's all too easy to input numbers into a calculator and forget what those numbers mean. Above all, remember that calculators are only possible because math is so consistent (and thus we can pre-program a machine to solve problems) . . . and math is only so consistent because God is consistently holding all things together.

15.5 Exponential Growth

It's time to learn about a really cool application of exponents and unknowns: **exponential growth**. We'll start by exploring the concept, and then we'll see how exponents help us describe this type of growth quite simply.

Linear Versus Exponential Growth

Some things grow at a steady rate. For example, suppose a specific tree grows an average of 18 in each year. Notice that if we were to graph this average growth over time, we'd end up with a straight line.

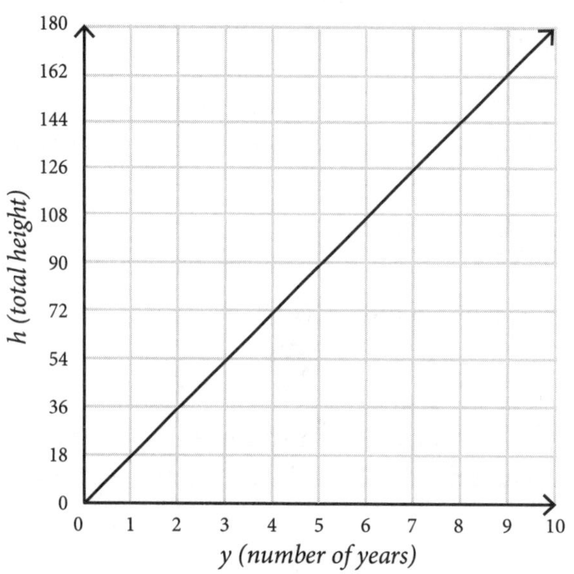

$y = 18 \text{ in} \cdot x$

(total height = 18 in • the number of years)

We call growth that results in a straight line when graphed **linear growth** (notice the *line* in *linear*).

Another kind of growth, though, is what we call **exponential growth**. For example, suppose a man makes $10,000 a year. If every year, he gets a raise of 10% of his salary (yes, I know that's a very high raise . . . we're using 10% because 10% is a super easy number to work with, since the decimal system is based on 10), at the end of one year, he'd get a raise for 0.10 • $10,000, or $1,000. At the end of two years, he'd get a raise of 10% of his salary again, only this time, his salary is already $11,000, so his raise would be 0.10 • $11,000, or $1,100. At then end of three years, he'd get a 10% raise again, only now his salary is already $12,100, so his raise would be 0.10 • $12,100, or $1,210.

If we were to keep going and then graph the growth of this man's salary over time, we'd end up with the curve shown.

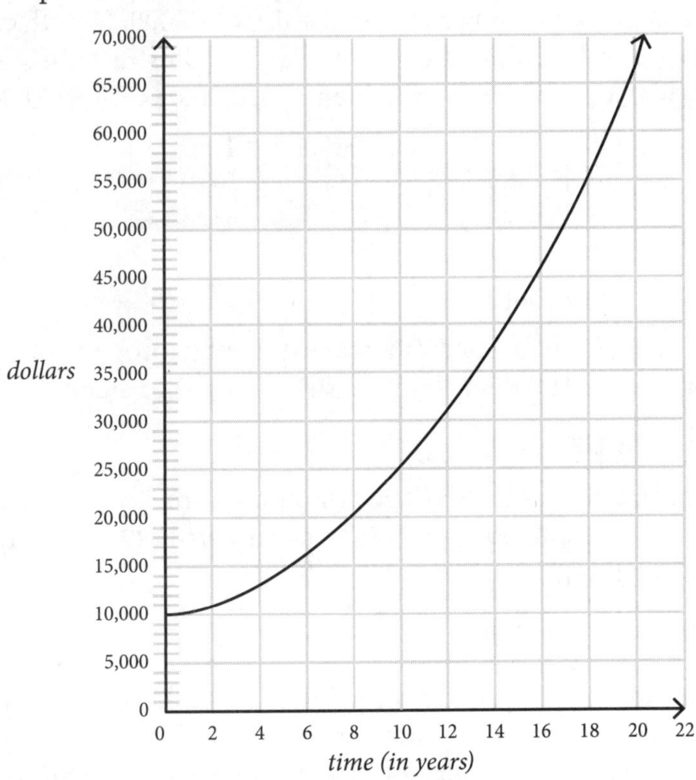

Notice that the growth of the salary is relatively small at first, but then the growth each year gets more and more as the salary from which the 10% raise is computed is greater and greater.

Simplifying Exponential Growth

Now, the graph showed us that the salary after 20 years would be about $67,000, but what if we needed to calculate this man's salary after 20 years without a graph . . . or to find a more precise value that we can see on the graph? It would be rather tedious to find all the salary and raises for 20 years.

Remember, in math, we look for simpler ways to calculate numbers. Thankfully, there's a much simpler way to describe exponential growth. Rather than jumping right to the formula, though, let's walk through the process using the example we have been of a \$10,000 salary, with a yearly raise of 10%.

At the end of the first year, the salary is \$10,000 *plus* 0.1 • \$10,000.

\$10,000 + 0.1 • \$10,000 =

\$10,000 + \$1,000 = \$11,000

Notice that we're taking the previous salary (\$10,000) *plus* 10% of the previous salary (0.1 • \$10,000). That will tell us the new salary after a 10% raise. Another way to write this would be using parentheses.

\$10,000(1 + 0.1)

\$10,000(1 + 0.1) means the same thing as \$10,000 + 0.1 • \$10,000. In both cases, we're finding the previous salary plus 10% of that salary. To illustrate, the steps below show how \$10,000(1 + 0.1) can be rewritten as \$10,000 + 0.1 • \$10,000.

Distribute the multiplication in \$10,000(1 + 0.1):

\$10,000(1 + 0.1)

\$10,000(**1**) + \$10,000(**0.1**)

Simplify \$10,000(1) to \$10,000 (there's that identity property of multiplication — multiplying by 1 doesn't change the value):

\$10,000 + \$10,000(0.1)

Rewrite \$10,000(0.1) as 0.1 • \$10,000 (multiplication is commutative, so the order doesn't matter, and parentheses and • are both valid ways to show multiplication):

\$10,000 + **0.1 • \$10,000**

Now, why do we want to write the problem as \$10,000(1 + 0.1)? Well, each year, we have to take the previous year's salary and add to it 10% of the previous year's salary. Now that we know that multiplying by (1 + 0.1) does the same thing as adding the previous year's salary *plus* 10% of that salary, an easy way to calculate this for each year is to multiply the previous year's salary by (1 + 0.1). So since we know the salary after one year is \$10,000(1 + 0.1), we can multiply that by another (1 + 0.1) to find the salary after 2 years.

\$10,000(1 + 0.1)**(1 + 0.1)**

And if we wanted to find the ending salary after 3 years, we'd multiply by an additional (1 + 0.1).

\$10,000(1 + 0.1)(1 + 0.1)**(1 + 0.1)**

Since each (1 + 0.1) finds the ending salary after another year, we can find the ending salary for *any* number of years by simply multiplying by (1 + 0.1) by itself once for each year. Notice the repeated multiplication involved. We could represent this so much simpler with exponents!

$$\$10{,}000(1 + 0.1)(1 + 0.1)(1 + 0.1) =$$

$$\mathbf{\$10{,}000(1 + 0.1)^3}$$

In fact, we could express the whole process of calculating exponential growth using a formula.

Exponential Growth

$\boldsymbol{P = P_0(1 + r)^t}$, where

P = *final amount after growth* (in the example, the final salary)

P_0 = *initial amount before growth* (in the example, the initial salary)

r = *rate of growth over a specified period of time* (in the example, the percent of the raise)

t = *the number of specified periods of time that have passed* (the periods of time *must* be the same period of time used for the rate — in the example, years)

Why does the formula use P and P_0? We'll see in the next lesson that, since this formula is often used in describing population growth, the P stands for the final *population*, and the P_0 for the initial *population*. Remember, a subscript $_0$, such as the one used in P_0, is a common way of indicating a starting value. Unlike exponents, subscript letters or numbers are part of the symbol representing an unknown.

We can now use this relationship to easily calculate the final amount after growth.

Example: Find the salary after 20 years if the starting salary is \$10,000 and each year the salary grows at a rate of 10%.

Formula:

$P = P_0(1 + r)^t$

Substitute known numbers:

$P = \mathbf{\$10{,}000}(1 + \mathbf{0.1})^{\mathbf{20}}$

Solve inside the parentheses:

$P = \$10{,}000(\mathbf{1.1})^{20}$

Simplify 1.1^{20} using the calculator's exponent button:

$P = \$10{,}000(\mathbf{6.727499949})$

Complete the multiplication:

\$67,275

Order Matters

As we start working with problems containing exponents, remember to follow the order of operations. Notice that we added 1 + 0.1 first, getting 1.1, and then found the value of 1.1 raised to the 20th power.

Keeping Perspective

Notice how exponents are quite useful in describing exponential growth. They truly are a handy way of representing repeated multiplications.

15.6 Population Growth

In the last lesson, we explored the concept of exponential growth. While we limited our explorations in the lesson and corresponding worksheet to problems dealing with money, let's now look at the exponential growth of plant, animal, and people populations.

Unlike money, populations don't grow in a tidy, completely describable manner. All babies aren't conveniently born on December 31 each year to make for a consistent time at which a population increases. Instead, there's continual birth and death.

However, the growth is still exponential. Consider a population of viruses. When a virus cell multiplies, it increases the number of virus cells that can then multiply themselves, which will then increase the number of virus cells that can then multiply themselves. In other words, there will be growth upon the growth. The bigger the virus cell population gets, the more the growth will occur, as there will be more and more virus cells multiplying themselves.

While the formula we have been using for exponential growth doesn't take into account the continual rate at which real populations change, it can be used to give a general approximation of population growth, especially for small periods of time and small populations. We can sometimes predict population growth with greater accuracy using a different formula, but that is beyond the scope of this course.

Whatever formula we use, predicting population growth isn't an exact science. After all, we're *assuming* that the population will grow at a specific rate . . . which may not happen. Nevertheless, estimating population growth often still proves quite helpful.

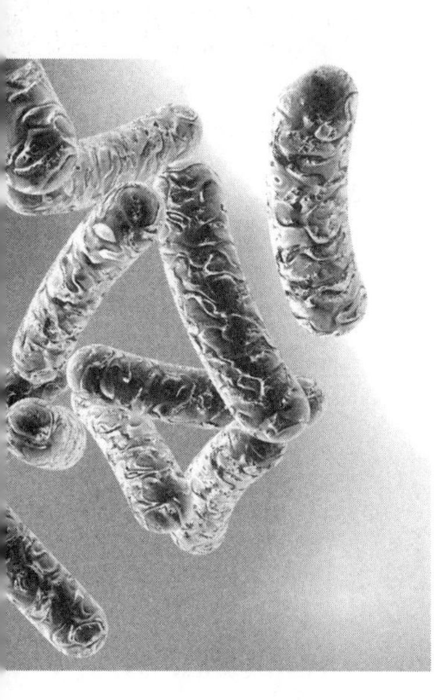

It is easy to see now why we use P and P_0 in $P = P_0(1 + r)^t$, isn't it? The P stands for the final population, and the P_0 for the initial population.

Example: If the initial population of bacteria was 300 and the bacteria is growing at an approximate rate of 4% each hour, what would the approximate ending population be after 60 hours? Round to the nearest whole number.

The initial population is 300, the time is 60 hours, and the rate is 4%, or 0.04, an hour. Notice that we're assuming that the growth occurs every hour, while in reality it's constantly occurring. Nevertheless, we can still find an approximation.

Formula:

$$P = P_0(1 + r)^t$$

Substitute known numbers:

$$P = \mathbf{300}(1 + \mathbf{0.04})^{\mathbf{60}}$$

Solve inside the parentheses:

$$P = 300(\mathbf{1.04})^{60}$$

Simplify 1.04^{60} using the calculator's exponent button:

$$P = 300(\mathbf{10.51962741})$$

Complete the multiplication:

$P = \mathbf{3{,}156}$ (rounding to the nearest whole number)

Notice that we could also graph the relationship between the ending population and the time that has passed, thereby seeing the growth for multiple hours visually. While you won't be asked to graph any non-linear equations in this course, the graph is included here to give you a visual picture of the relationship.

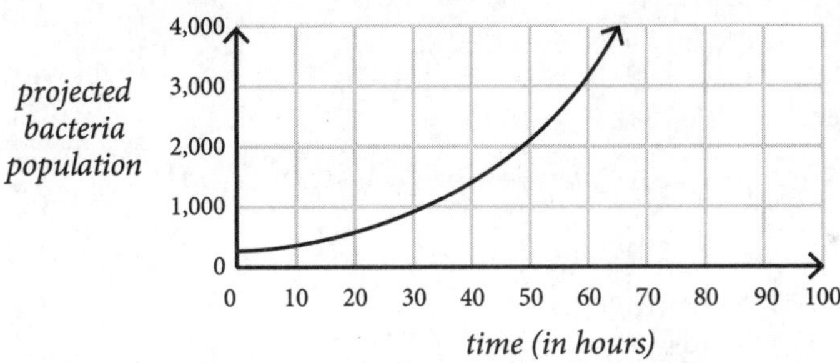

Approximate Growth of 300 Bacteria at a 4% Growth Rate per Hour

Example: Based on census data, the city's population grew an average of 6% a year over the last 10 years. If this growth continues (6% a year) and if the current population is 5,000 people, approximately how many people will the city have in 20 years?

In this case, the initial population is 5,000, the time is 20 years, and the rate is 6%, or 0.06, a year. Again, notice that we're assuming the growth is a yearly growth, when in reality populations are constantly changing. Nevertheless, we can still find an approximation.

Formula:

$P = P_0(1 + r)^t$

Substitute known numbers:

$P = \mathbf{5{,}000}(1 + \mathbf{0.06})^{\mathbf{20}}$

Solve inside the parentheses:

$P = 5{,}000(\mathbf{1.06})^{20}$

Simplify the 1.06^{20} using the calculator's exponent button:

$P = 5{,}000(\mathbf{3.207135472})$

Complete the multiplication:

$P = \mathbf{16{,}035.68}$

Again, a graph of the relationship can give us a visual picture of the overall relationship between the ending population and the years that have passed.

Notice that in both of the example graphs, we viewed P (the ending population) as the dependent variable and t (the time in hours) as the independent variable. In these relationships, our independent variable was the exponent.

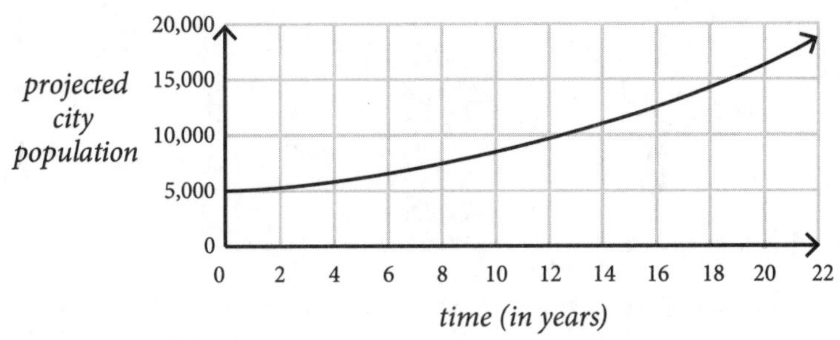

Population Growth and the Biblical Timeline

The Bible teaches that we are all descendents of Noah and his sons, who got off the ark nearly 4,400 years ago. Many people wonder how the earth could have as many people as it does in such a short timeframe. Wouldn't we need many more years to get the present population?

Actually, when we do the math, we find that the earth's current population could have easily grown from 8 to what it is today in around 4,400 years. In fact, the math raises questions as to how the earth's population could be what it is if the biblical timeframe were *not* true. If humans have been on earth for tens of thousands of years, we'd expect a much greater population. See the articles referenced in the endnote for further information.[3]

Keeping Perspective

Predicting a population growth often proves quite helpful in real life. It allows us to plan for and better understand the growth of various populations.

Population growth often brings up various ethical challenges, such as how to deal with various population growths. Always remember to let biblical principles guide how you use mathematics.

15.7 Exponential Decay

In exponential growth, a population keeps growing exponentially, resulting in an ever-*increasing* population. Sometimes, though, the opposite happens: there's an ever-*decreasing* population. For example, if we found an antibacterial medicine that would cause a 2% *decrease* each hour in a bacteria population, we would have a negative rate of growth (a 2% decrease is a rate of –0.02).

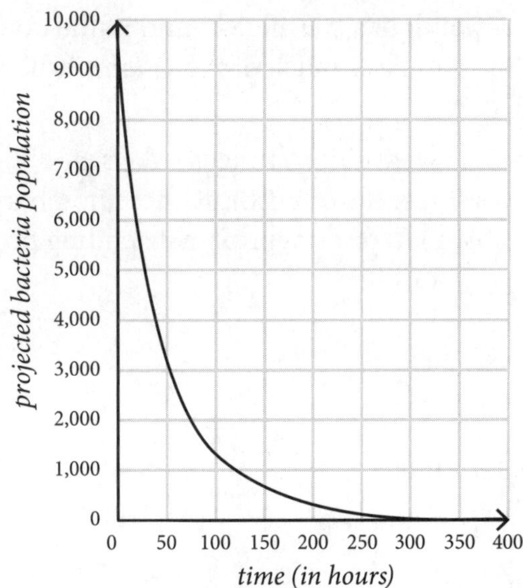

Change in 10,000 Bacteria at a *Negative* 2% Growth Rate per Hour

Notice that the graph of the decreasing bacteria population looks backward to an exponential growth curve. Rather than increasing gradually at first and then rapidly, the total viruses decreased rapidly at first (the 2% decrease gets taken off a larger population) and then more gradually as the population dwindles (making the 2% decrease less and less significant). We call this kind of decay **exponential decay**.

The formula for both exponential growth and decay is the same, with the only difference being the value of the rate. If the rate of growth is positive, we're dealing with exponential growth; if the rate of growth is less than 0 but greater than −1, then we're dealing with exponential decay.

Exponential Growth: $P = P_0(1 + r)^t$

when $r > 0$

Exponential Decay: $P = P_0(1 + r)^t$

when $0 > r > -1$

We can solve problems dealing with exponential decay the same way we did with exponential growth.

Important Note: The growth and decay of real-life populations does not occur on the minute, hour, day, etc. It's a continuous growth or decay. The formula we're using, however, is approximating the decay as if it all occurred at a specific time. We can sometimes use a different formula to find a closer approximation, but doing so is beyond the scope of this course.

Example: Suppose that the amount of a specific vitamin in the body decays exponentially at a rate of 5% a day. How much of the vitamin will be left after 6 days if there was 400 mg to start?

Here, the rate is –5%, or –0.05, the time is 6 days, and the starting population (P_0) is 400 mg. If we substitute these numbers into the formula, we'll be able to find the approximate ending population (P).

Formula:

$$P = P_0(1 + r)^t$$

Substitute known numbers:

$$P = (\mathbf{400\ mg})(1 + \mathbf{-0.05})^{\mathbf{6}}$$

Simplify inside the parentheses:

$$P = (400\text{ mg})(\mathbf{0.95})^6$$

Simplify 0.95^6 using the calculator's exponent button:

$$P = (400\text{ mg})(\mathbf{0.735091891})$$

Complete the multiplication:

$$P = \mathbf{294.04\ mg}$$

The vitamin would have decreased to 294.04 mg.

As with exponential growth, we could look at the relationship between the vitamin left in the body and the time on a graph to get a picture of the decay over time.

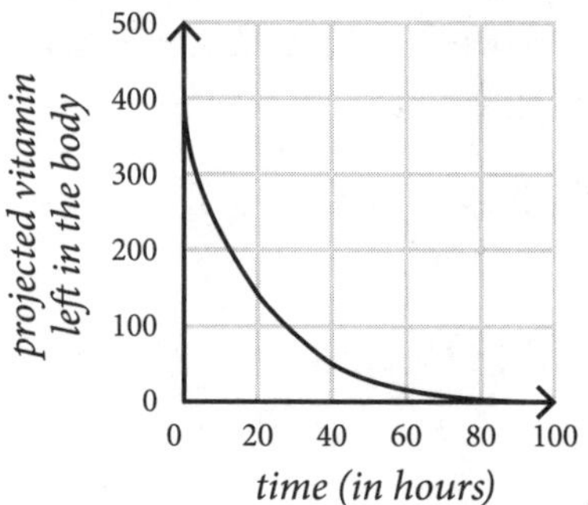

Applying Exponential Decay: Radiometric Dating

The formula we'd use to find the exponential decay of elements in rocks is slightly different than the one we've been using (we'd use $P = P_0e^{rt}$). We won't be learning the math behind radiometric dating in this course. Instead, we'll be focusing on the general principle.

You may have heard of radiometric dating. The basic theory behind radiometric dating is that certain "parent" elements in rocks decay into other "daughter" elements at a specific rate. If we know the amount of the original "parent" elements (the P_0), the amount of the current "parent" elements (the P), and the rate of the decay (the r), then we can use math to find the time that has passed (the t).

All that sounds pretty good in theory, doesn't it? There are some major problems, though. It's all based on a lot of assumptions! As *The Revised and Expanded Answers Book*[4] points out, scientists weren't there when the rocks they're dating were formed, so they're basing the numbers they're using for the original number of elements (the P_0) and the rate at which the decay occurred (the r) on what they see occurring in the present. They're also assuming that none of the original or "daughter" elements escaped from or got added to the rock — that everything in the past occurred as it is in the present. These are *huge* assumptions!

In the bacteria example we began the lesson with, we could observe the decline of the bacteria population. We were not basing our conclusion on assumptions about the original population of bacteria. The bacteria example is an illustration of observational science — observing God's creation in the present and using the abilities He gave us to describe and understand it. Finding the age of a rock, though, moves out of the realm of observational science and into the realm of history and belief. It's filled with starting assumptions.

There's much that could be said about the contradictions and problems with radiometric dating. For example, the same rock will often be dated differently based on which element is used to date it. As another example, the fairly recent (1980) eruption of Mount St. Helens points to issues with radiometric dating. After the eruption, Dr. Steven Austin (Institute for Creation Research) was able to gather rocks that we know formed during the eruption and had them radiometrically dated. The rocks were dated between 340,000 to 2.8 million years. Since we know the rocks had just been formed, these dates testified to an error with the starting assumptions of the dating method.[5] However, the point here is that radiometric dating is a good example of how we need to question the *starting assumptions* used. Don't just assume that because math has been used, the answer supports a claim made.

If the numbers we use in an equation are based on faulty assumptions, it doesn't matter how sound the math is — the answer will be mistaken.

> *Scientists do not measure the age of rocks, they measure isotope concentrations, and these can be measured extremely accurately. However, the "age" is calculated using assumptions about the past that cannot be proven.*
>
> *We should remember God's admonition to Job, "Where were you when I laid the foundations of the earth?" (Job 38:4). — The Revised and Expanded Answers Book[6] [Scripture quote from the NKJV]*

To learn more about radiometric dating and its flaws, check out the resources on www.AnswersinGenesis.org.

Keeping Perspective

Whether recording growth or decay, exponents help us describe God's creation. But, as we saw with radiometric dating, we need to be careful *how* we apply math — faulty assumptions lead to faulty conclusions. Always remember to hold everything up to the truth of God's Word. God, unlike scientists, *was* there in the past. His Word can be trusted absolutely.

15.8 Chapter Synopsis and Earthquakes

In this chapter, we reviewed exponents: a handy notation for representing repeated multiplication more concisely. Using exponents, we can simplify $2 \bullet 2$ to 2^2, $s \bullet s \bullet s$ to s^3, and $(1 + 0.1)(1 + 0.1)$ to $(1 + 0.1)^2$. Since many real-life relationships (such as the area of a square, the volume of a cube, and exponential growth and decay) include repeated multiplication, exponents come in quite handy in describing God's creation.

Before we end, let's take a look at yet another example of exponents in action.

Earthquakes

The relationship between the magnitude and the energy of an earthquake can be expressed using — you guessed it — exponents! While scientists are always trying to find more accurate ways of measuring earthquakes and their magnitude and energy (they're not exactly easy to measure!), the general relationship that's used to estimate energy is given below.[7] In the formula, E stands for energy, and the M stands for the magnitude of the earthquake. Notice the exponent![8]

$$10^{11.8+1.5M} = E$$

Always remember that the techniques you study in math apply outside of a textbook. Also remember that God's Word gives us answers to explain what we find as we do.

Earthquakes, the Fall, and the Gospel

As we use math, we encounter incredible evidence of God's design. But we also encounter heartbreak, suffering, and death, as is the case with earthquakes. The Bible, though, gives us answers to why suffering and death exist — and gives us good news nothing (not even earthquakes) can shake or take away.

The Bible tells us that death came into this world as a result of man's sin. Earthquakes were not part of God's original creation. Instead of getting angry at God for the bad things that happen, we should remember that sin is serious. It's sin that brought death and suffering into the world.

> *And God saw every thing that he had made, and, behold, it was very good. And the evening and the morning were the sixth day (Genesis 1:31).*
>
> *Wherefore, as by one man sin entered into the world, and death by sin; and so death passed upon all men, for that all have sinned (Romans 5:12).*
>
> *For we know that the whole creation groaneth and travaileth in pain together until now (Romans 8:22).*

The Bible also gives us very, very good news. One day, there will be a new heavens and earth where there will be no more suffering or death — all will again be very good.

> *And I saw a new heaven and a new earth: for the first heaven and the first earth were passed away; and there was no more sea. . . . And God shall wipe away all tears from their eyes; and there shall be no more death, neither sorrow, nor crying, neither shall there be any more pain: for the former things are passed away (Revelation 21:1–4).*

God's new kingdom will be an amazing place. Yet not everyone will enter it. The Bible also tells of eternal punishment — a punishment that makes the suffering we see here on earth look light.

> *And I saw the dead, small and great, stand before God, . . . And whosoever was not found written in the book of life was cast into the lake of fire (Revelation 20:12, 15).*

> *But the fearful, and unbelieving, and the abominable, and murderers, and whoremongers, and sorcerers, and idolaters, and all liars, shall have their part in the lake which burneth with fire and brimstone: which is the second death (Revelation 21:8).*

God is going to punish sin — and we have all sinned. Revelation 21:8 tells us liars shall have their part in the lake of fire — and who hasn't told a lie? If God judges us on our own merit, we're all worthy of death.

Yet God made a way for us to be redeemed, escaping the punishment we deserve and entering into His glorious coming kingdom. That way is Jesus.

> *For the wages of sin is death; but the gift of God is eternal life through Jesus Christ our Lord (Romans 6:23).*

> *Be it known unto you all, and to all the people of Israel, that by the name of Jesus Christ of Nazareth, whom ye crucified, whom God raised from the dead, even by him doth this man stand here before you whole. This is the stone which was set at nought of you builders, which is become the head of the corner. Neither is there salvation in any other: for there is none other name under heaven given among men, whereby we must be saved (Acts 4:10–12).*

> *For God so loved the world, that he gave his only begotten Son, that whosoever believeth in him should not perish, but have everlasting life (John 3:16).*

So you see, the Bible gives us answers for the suffering and death we find around us — and an offer of eternal life in heaven, where there will be no more suffering or death. Next time you're talking with a friend, look for a way to lead the conversation to the gospel. Eternity is real — and right around the corner.

[CHAPTER 16]

More with Exponents

16.1 Exponents in Denominators

As we use math to explore God's creation, we find ourselves needing to *divide by* quantities raised to a power. Notice the exponent in the *denominator* of the fraction in the formula below (which is a formula for calculating the gravitational force being exerted on an object . . . something we can only calculate because of the amazingly consistent way God governs all things).

$$F = G(\frac{m_1 m_2}{r^2})$$

Note: Remember, the subscripts (the tiny 1 and 2 on m_1 and m_2) are not exponents. They are part of the symbol we're using to stand for unknowns. In this case, m_1 stands for the mass of one object, and m_2 the mass of another object. The r stands for the distance between the two masses.

We're not going to explore this formula, as it requires the use of numbers that are quite unwieldy (G equals 0.0000000000667408). However, we are going to take a look at a few simple examples of exponents in the denominator of fractions to make sure we're equipped to handle them when we encounter them.

Finding Exponents in the Denominator

Example: Find $\frac{81}{3^2}$

$\frac{81}{3^2}$ equals $\frac{81}{3 \bullet 3} = \frac{81}{9} = 9$

Notice that in the example above we ended up dividing by 3^2, or 9. Remember, the fraction line means division.

Example: Find $\frac{80}{10^2}$

$$\frac{80}{10^2} = \frac{80}{10 \bullet 10} = \frac{80}{100} = \frac{4}{5}$$

Keeping Perspective

Once again, we're continuing to build on principles we already know to help us handle more and more situations. Exponents give us a concise way of describing aspects of God's creation and solving real-life problems. In fact, on Worksheet 16.1 you'll get a chance to use them in conjunction with probability problems. For instance, what's the probability of rolling five ⚁s in a row? Since there's a $\frac{1}{6}$ probability of rolling a ⚁ each time, there's a $\frac{1}{6} \bullet \frac{1}{6} \bullet \frac{1}{6} \bullet \frac{1}{6} \bullet \frac{1}{6}$ probability of rolling five ⚁s in a row. We could represent the probability more concisely as $\frac{1}{6^5}$.

16.2 Negative Exponents

We saw in the last lesson how exponents sometimes turn up in the denominators of fractions — that is, that we sometimes need to *divide* by a quantity raised to a power.

In this lesson, it's time to learn about a handy way of expressing dividing by numbers that are raised to a power (that is, exponents in denominators): negative exponents. Using this notation, we could rewrite $F = G(\frac{m_1 m_2}{r^2})$ as $F = Gm_1m_2r^{-2}$. Notice the r^{-2}. What's the negative sign in front of the exponent all about? Let's take a look.

Understanding Negative Exponents

We saw back in Lesson 2.3 that the multiplicative inverse of a number is the number that, when multiplied by another number, equals 1. The multiplicative inverse of 2 is $\frac{1}{2}$, as $2 \bullet \frac{1}{2} = \frac{2}{2}$, or 1.

Let's apply this concept to exponents for a moment. The multiplicative inverse of 2^2 is $\frac{1}{2^2}$, as $2^2 \bullet \frac{1}{2^2}$ equals 1.

$$2^2 \bullet \frac{1}{2^2} = \frac{2^2}{2^2} = \frac{4}{4} = 1$$

Now, another way to write the multiplicative inverse of a number raised to a power is to put a negative sign in front of the exponent. For example, 2^{-2} is another way of writing the multiplicative inverse of 2^2.

$$2^{-2} = \frac{1}{2^2}$$

A *negative sign* in front of an exponent is another way of writing the *multiplicative inverse of* the base raised to that power.

Below is a chart illustrating negative exponents. Notice that in each case, the negative sign in front of the exponent means the *multiplicative inverse* of the normal meaning.

Notation	Meaning	Read
2^{-1}	$\frac{1}{2^1}$ *or* $\frac{1}{2}$	Two to the negative first power
2^{-2}	$\frac{1}{2^2}$ *or* $\frac{1}{2 \cdot 2}$	Two to the negative second power
2^{-3}	$\frac{1}{2^3}$ *or* $\frac{1}{2 \cdot 2 \cdot 2}$	Two to the negative third power
2^{-4}	$\frac{1}{2^4}$ *or* $\frac{1}{2 \cdot 2 \cdot 2 \cdot 2}$	Two to the negative fourth power
2^{-5}	$\frac{1}{2^5}$ *or* $\frac{1}{2 \cdot 2 \cdot 2 \cdot 2 \cdot 2}$	Two to the negative fifth power
2^{-6}	$\frac{1}{2^6}$ *or* $\frac{1}{2 \cdot 2 \cdot 2 \cdot 2 \cdot 2 \cdot 2}$	Two to the negative sixth power
2^{-7}	$\frac{1}{2^7}$ *or* $\frac{1}{2 \cdot 2 \cdot 2 \cdot 2 \cdot 2 \cdot 2 \cdot 2}$	Two to the negative seventh power
2^{-8}	$\frac{1}{2^8}$ *or* $\frac{1}{2 \cdot 2 \cdot 2 \cdot 2 \cdot 2 \cdot 2 \cdot 2 \cdot 2}$	Two to the negative eighth power
2^{-9}	$\frac{1}{2^9}$ *or* $\frac{1}{2 \cdot 2 \cdot 2 \cdot 2 \cdot 2 \cdot 2 \cdot 2 \cdot 2 \cdot 2}$	Two to the negative ninth power
2^{-10}	$\frac{1}{2^{10}}$ *or* $\frac{1}{2 \cdot 2 \cdot 2 \cdot 2 \cdot 2 \cdot 2 \cdot 2 \cdot 2 \cdot 2 \cdot 2}$	Two to the negative tenth power

Since we can't divide by 0 (it is considered an invalid operation), we also can't have 0 raised to a negative power. For example, 0^{-2} would mean $\frac{1}{0^2}$, which would mean $1 \div 0 \cdot 0$, which simplifies to $1 \div 0$ (an invalid operation).

Again, remember that a negative sign means *the opposite of.* While a negative sign normally means the *additive inverse* of a number, when it's before an exponent, the negative sign means the *multiplicative inverse* of the base raised to that power.

Finding Negative Exponents on a Calculator

You can simplify negative exponents on a calculator the same way you do positive exponents, only on some calculators you'll need to enclose the exponent inside parentheses so the calculator knows the negative sign applies to the exponent.

Example: Find 44^{-2}

Enter 44 (the base) into the calculator.

Press y^x or ^.

Enter –2 (the exponent) into the calculator. *(You'll need to enter the 2 first and then the – sign on some calculators, and the – sign first and then the 2 on others. Play around with your calculator on this example until you get the correct answer. Also, be sure to use the negative button and not the minus sign.)*

The calculator should show an answer of 0.000516529.

From r^2 to r^{-2}

For those of you wondering how we rewrote $F = G(\frac{m_1m_1}{r^2})$ as $F = Gm_1m_2r^{-2}$, here's a quick explanation. Since we can view division as multiplying by the multiplicative inverse (see Lesson 4.3), we can think of the division by r^2 as a multiplication by $\frac{1}{r^2}$. Thus, we could rewrite $F = G(\frac{m_1m_1}{r^2})$ like this:

$$F = G(m_1m_2) \bullet \frac{1}{r^2}$$

And then we can rewrite $\frac{1}{r^2}$ using a negative exponent as r^{-2}, giving us $F = (Gm_1m_2) \bullet r^{-2}$ or $F = Gm_1m_2r^{-2}$.

Don't worry if you didn't follow every detail of writing $F = G(\frac{m_1m_1}{r^2})$ as $F = Gm_1m_2r^{-2}$. We won't be looking at unknowns and negative exponents in depth in this course. This example is included here to give you a glimpse into how what you're learning applies in helping us describe God's creation. The important thing is to understand that a negative exponent is another way of writing the multiplicative inverse of a base raised to a power. So 2^{-2} is another way of writing $\frac{1}{2^2}$ and r^{-2} is another way of writing $\frac{1}{r^2}$.

Keeping Perspective

Negative exponents, like so many other aspects of math, are *conventions*, or agreed-upon ways of writing, that help us clearly describe and work with real-life consistencies. Negative exponents are simply a shorthand way of representing *the multiplicative inverse* of the base raised to that power. For example, 5^{-9} means $\frac{1}{5^9}$.

16.3 Scientific Notation

As we explore God's creation using math, we come across extremely unwieldy numbers. For example, the mass of the earth has been calculated at approximately 5,972,200,000,000,000,000,000,000 kg — that's a really lengthy number! Can you imagine trying to write this number often, let alone multiplying or dividing it with other lengthy numbers?

We also encounter lengthy microscopic numbers, such as the rest mass of an electron (approximately 0.000000000000000000000000000000911 kg). Again, imagine trying to keep track of all those zeros!

In Book 1, we looked at how to express unwieldy numbers 1 and greater in a notation called scientific notation. We saw that using **scientific notation**, we can represent 5,972,200,000,000,000,000,000,000 kg as 5.9722 x 10^{24} kg.

Scientific notation is based on using powers of 10 to describe the different places in the decimal place-value system. *Each place* in the decimal system can be described by 10 raised to a power. Notice the negative exponents used to represent decimal places!

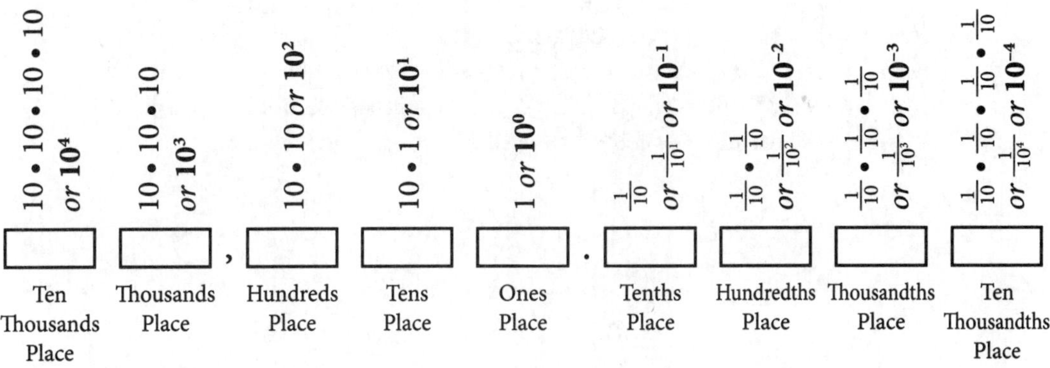

In scientific notation, a number is written with just one non-zero digit to the left of the decimal point multiplied by 10 raised to whatever power would be necessary to move the digits to the appropriate place. For example, 0.8 in scientific notation would be 8 x 10^{-1}. Notice that if you multiply 8 by 10^{-1} (i.e., $8 \bullet \frac{1}{10}$), you'll get 0.8. Both 0.8 and 8 x 10^{-1} represent the same quantity.

So how exactly do we work with scientific notation? I'm glad you asked! Let's take a look.

Converting from Scientific Notation

It's super easy to convert from scientific notation to decimal notation. All we have to do is complete the multiplication.

Example: Express 4.9 x 10^2 in decimal notation.

Complete the multiplication:

4.9 x 10^2

4.9 x **10** x **10**

4.9 x **100 = 490**

Example: Express 4.9×10^{-2} in decimal notation.

Complete the multiplication:

$$4.9 \times 10^{-2}$$

$$4.9 \times \frac{1}{10^2}$$

$$4.9 \times \frac{1}{10 \cdot 10}$$

$$4.9 \times \frac{1}{100} = 0.049$$

Multiplying and Dividing by 10 Reminder

Since our place-value system is based on 10, multiplying and dividing by 10 is simple. When we multiply by 10, we move the decimal one place to the right, as that increases the value of each digit by 10; when we divide by 10, we move the decimal one place to the left, as that decreases the value of each digit by 10.

$$4.9 \cdot 10 = 49.$$

Decimal point moved to the right one place.

$4.9 \div 10$ *or* $4.9 \cdot \frac{1}{10} = 0.49$

Decimal point moved to the left one place.

What about when we multiply or divide by other powers of 10 — such as 10^2? Well, 10^2 means $10 \cdot 10$, so we would need to move the decimal point *two* places to the right or left to increase the value of each digit by $10 \cdot 10$.

$$4.9 \cdot 10^2 = 490.$$

Decimal point moved to the right two places.

$4.9 \div 10^{-2}$ *or* $4.9 \cdot \frac{1}{10^2} = 0.049$

Decimal point moved to the left two places.

Converting to Scientific Notation

To convert a number to scientific notation, we simply

1. Move the decimal point so there's only one digit to its left.
2. Multiply by 10 raised to whatever power is needed to put the digits in the appropriate places.

Example: Express 490 in scientific notation.

Move the decimal point so there's only one digit to its left.

4.90

We can drop the zero, as 4.90 and 4.9 prepresent the same value.

4.9

Multiply by 10 raised to whatever power is needed to put the digits back in the appropriate places. When we rewrote 490 as 4.9, we moved the decimal point two places to the *left*.

4.90

By moving the decimal point two places to the *left*, we essentially *divided* by 10^2, or 100.

$490 \div 10^2 = 490 \div 100 = 4.90 = 4.9$

We now need to multiply *by the same power of 10* we divided by in order to keep the value the same.

$4.9 \times \mathbf{10^2}$

Notice that if we were to complete the multiplication of 4.9 and 10^2, we'd end up with 490. Both 4.9×10^2 and 490 represent the same quantity.

When we rewrite a number in scientific notation, we're not changing the value, but rather are expressing the place value by multiplying by a power of 10.

Let's look at an example that involves a negative power of 10.

Example: Express 0.049 in scientific notation.

Move the decimal point so there's only one non-zero digit to its left.

4.9

Multiply by 10 raised to whatever power is needed to put the digits back in the appropriate places. When we rewrote 0.049 as 4.9, we moved the decimal point two digits to the *right*.

0.049

By moving the decimal point two places to the *right*, we essentially *multiplied* by 10^2.

$0.049 \times 10^2 = 0.049 \times 10 \times 10 = 4.9$

Now, to express the original value, we need to reverse the multiplication we just did. We can do that by multiplying by the *inverse* of 10^2, or 10^{-2}. Remember, 10^{-2} means $\frac{1}{10^2}$, or 1 *divided by* 10^2.

4.9×10^{-2}

Go ahead and do the math. You'll find that 4.9×10^{-2} does indeed equal 0.049. By multiplying by the *inverse* of 10^2 (i.e., 10^{-2}), we put the decimal back into the correct location. We're essentially undoing the multiplication we did when we multiplied by 10^2 to move the decimal point to the right.

$$4.9 \times 10^{-2} = 4.9 \times \frac{1}{10^2} = \frac{4.9}{10^2} = 4.9 \div 10^2 = 0.049$$

Because multiplying and dividing by 10 in the decimal system is simply a matter of moving the decimal point to the right or left, you can easily find what power 10 should be raised to by counting the number of digits the decimal point moved. If the decimal point moved to the *left*, then you'll need to multiply by 10 raised to the same number of digits the decimal point moved. If you moved the decimal point to the *right*, then you'll need to multiply by *the inverse of* 10 raised to the same number of digits the decimal point moved.

Example: 4,000

Move the decimal point to the *left* 3 digits.

4,000

Multiply by 10 raised to the 3rd power.

4×10^3

Example: 0.0004

Move the decimal point to the right 4 digits.

0.0004

Multiply by *the inverse of* 10 raised to the 4th power.

4×10^{-4}

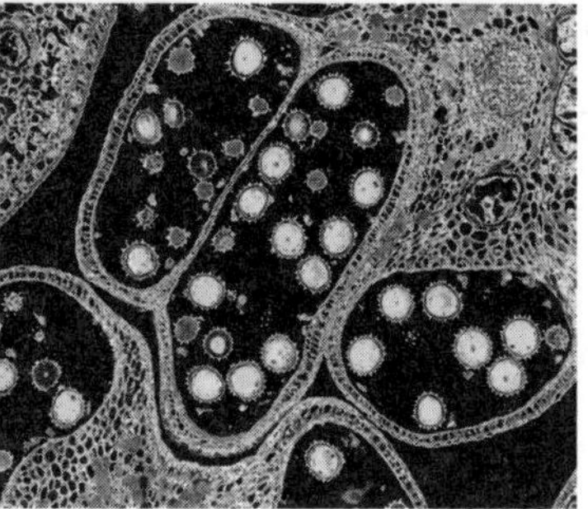

Keeping Perspective

5,972,200,000,000,000,000,000,000 kg = 5.9722×10^{24} kg
0.000000000000000000000000000000911 kg = 9.11×10^{-31} kg

Scientific notation sure makes unwieldy numbers easier to work with! Always remember that each notation you learn in math is a useful tool that helps us describe the world in which we live.

Our need for scientific notation reminds us of the enormity and complexity of God's creation. Just think: God created and sustains both the tiny electron and the largest galaxy!

For the LORD is a great God, and a great King above all gods. In his hand are the deep places of the earth: the strength of the hills is his also. The sea is his, and he made it: and his hands formed the dry land. O come, let us worship and bow down: let us kneel before the LORD our maker (Psalm 95:3–6).

16.4 Performing Operations in Scientific Notation on a Calculator

Sometimes, you'll want to add, subtract, multiply, or divide numbers written in scientific notation. If your calculator supports scientific notation, it's not hard to input numbers and then perform operations on them. Let's take a quick look.

Inputting in Scientific Notation

The instructions that came with your calculator can help you in inputting scientific notation, but here are some general guidelines. You'll want to

1. input the decimal portion of the number,
2. press the EE button,
3. input the power of 10, and then
4. press the = button.

Example: Enter 4.256 x 10^5 on a calculator.

Enter 4.256 into the calculator.

Press EE.

Enter 5 (the power of 10) into the calculator.

Press = to see the answer: 425,600.

Example: Enter 4.256 x 10^{-5} on a calculator.

Enter 4.256 into the calculator.

Press EE.

Enter –5 (the power of 10) into the calculator. (Be sure to use the negative button and not the minus sign.)

Press = to see the answer: 0.00004256.

If you do not have an EE button, look to see if EE is written *above* one of the other buttons. On some calculators, some buttons have two functions — the one on it ***and*** the one above it. To input a number in scientific notation if the EE is written above a button, follow the same steps explained above and shown in the examples, except press the 2nd button before pressing the button that has EE above it. This will cause the calculator to use the button's second meaning (in this case, EE).

Numbers Displayed on a Calculator Reminder

Not only can you input scientific notation into a calculator, but many calculators will display results in scientific notation if they run out of room to show an answer.

For example, if I type 800,000,000 x 90,000 into my calculator, I get 7.2^{13}. The "13" off to the right represents the exponent of 10 in scientific notation. In other words, this is the calculator's way of displaying 7.2 x 10^{13}.

Some calculators or computer programs will include an "E" or "e" (makes sense, since "e" is the first letter in "exponent"). On these calculators, 7.2 x 10^{13} would be displayed as 7.2e13 or 7.2E13. Some may even put a positive sign before the exponent (7.2e+13

Even though 7.2^{13} is how we typically write 7.2 raised to the 13th power (that is, 7.2 multiplied by itself 13 times), it is some calculators' way of displaying 7.2×10^{13}.

or 7.2E+13) to show that the exponent is positive (or a negative sign to show that it is negative).

Different Ways Calculators/Computer Programs Display 7.2×10^{13}

7.2^{13}

7.2e13

7.2E13

7.2e+13

7.2E+13

Performing Operations in Scientific Notation

Once you have a number inputted, you can then press the appropriate button to add, subtract, multiply, divide, etc.

Example: Multiply 4.256×10^5 by 4.256×10^{-5}. Give your answer rounded to the third decimal place when written in scientific notation.

Input 4.256×10^5 into the calculator.

Press **x** (the times button).

Input 4.256×10^{-5} into the calculator.

Press **=** to see the answer: 18.113536, which equals 1.8113536×10^1.

Keeping Perspective

So why would you want to perform operations with scientific notation on a calculator? Because as we use math as a real-life tool, we encounter numbers that are cumbersome otherwise.

16.5 More with Combining Like Terms

Now that you're familiar with exponents and with using them to help us describe different aspects of God's creation, let's explore a few additional tools we can use to help us work with exponents when we encounter them.

Sometimes we encounter situations where we need to add or subtract unknowns raised to powers. For example, let's say we've tiled a floor with the same-size square tiles. We know the area of each tile is s^2 (the length of one side times itself). So the area of 4 tiles would be $s^2 + s^2 + s^2 + s^2$, or $4s^2$ — that is 4 times s^2.

s^2	s^2
s^2	s^2

area of 4 tiles $= 4 \bullet s^2 = 4s^2$

And if we wanted to add that to the area of an additional 3 tiles, we'd have $4s^2 + 3s^2$.

area of 4 tiles + *area of 3 tiles*

$4s^2 + 3s^2$

Obviously, the area of 4 + 3, or 7, tiles would be 7 times the area of one tile, or $7s^2$.

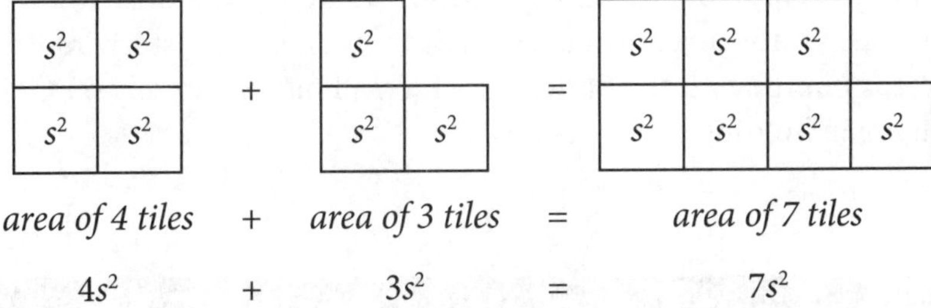

While the answer was obvious in this scenario, let's take a minute to explore the concept.

Combining Like Terms

Back in Lesson 7.2, we discovered that we could combine like terms. We know that 2 of an unknown ($2x$) plus 5 of the same unknown ($5x$) will equal 7 of that unknown ($7x$).

$2x + 5x = 7x$

This same principle applies when the unknown is raised to a power. 2 of an unknown squared ($2x^2$) plus 5 of the same unknown squared ($5x^2$) will equal 7 of that unknown squared ($7x^2$).

$2x^2 + 5x^2 = 7x^2$

Obviously, though, 2 of an unknown ($2x$) plus 5 of the same unknown squared ($5x^2$) could not be combined together. They're not like terms. In $2x$, we're multiplying by an unknown, while in $5x^2$ we're multiplying by the unknown times itself.

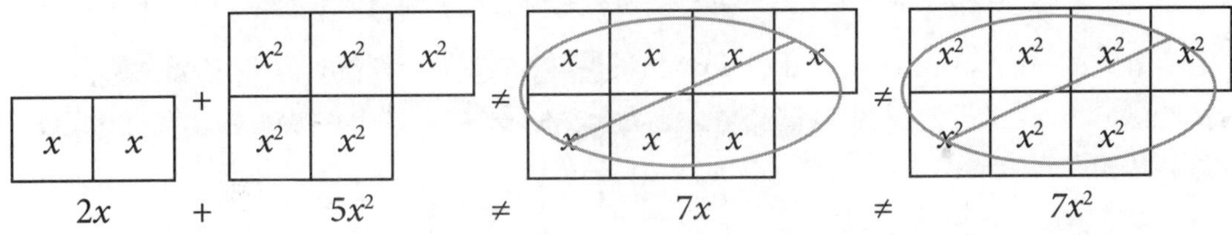

We can only combine like terms. Like terms are terms that have the same unknowns raised to the *same powers.*

To return to our tile example, when we saw that $4s^2 + 3s^2$ equals $7s^2$, we were combining like terms!

Keeping Perspective

Again, we keep applying the *same principles* to new situations. You'll find this pattern repeated over and over again as you continue studying math. Math keeps building on the basics . . . which all ultimately rely on God's faithfulness in holding all things together.

16.6 More with Multiplication and Division

There's so much more we could explore regarding working with exponents! Yet if you remember that an exponent tells us how many times to multiply the base by itself and the basic rules you *already know* about working with quantities, you'll be able to work with exponents with ease.

As an illustration, let's take a look at a couple of scenarios involving multiplying and dividing with exponents.

Multiplying Unknowns with Exponents

As we use math to explore God's creation and complete real-life tasks, we encounter a need to multiply unknown quantities that are raised to a power. Sometimes, we can't complete the multiplication unless we know the value of the unknown. But when the *base is the same*, we *can* simplify the expression. To see how, let's first look at a multiplication example with known quantities that have the *same base*: $2^3 \bullet 2^2$.

Think about what each of the exponents mean. Since 2^3 represents $2 \bullet 2 \bullet 2$ and 2^2 represents $2 \bullet 2$, $2^3 \bullet 2^2$ represents $(2 \bullet 2 \bullet 2) \bullet (2 \bullet 2)$, or 2^5.

Notice that we could have obtained 2^5 by adding the exponents (2 and 3) together. ***If the base is the same,* we can multiply the quantities by *adding* the exponents together.**

$$2^3 \bullet 2^2 = 2^{3+2} = 2^5$$

$$2 \bullet 2 \bullet 2 \bullet 2 \bullet 2 = (2 \bullet 2 \bullet 2)(2 \bullet 2) = 2 \bullet 2 \bullet 2 \bullet 2 \bullet 2$$

This same "rule" applies to unknowns too! It doesn't matter that we don't know the value for the unknown — we can still keep track of how many times it is being multiplied by itself.

$$x^3 \bullet x^2 = x^{3+2} = x^5$$
$$x \bullet x \bullet x \bullet x \bullet x = (x \bullet x \bullet x)(x \bullet x) = x \bullet x \bullet x \bullet x \bullet x$$

Adding the exponents to complete the multiplication only works if the base is the same. We cannot add the exponents if they have different bases. It is easy to see why, if we think through an example.

Example: Simplify $4^3 \bullet 2^2$

$$4^3 \bullet 2^2 = (4 \bullet 4 \bullet 4)(2 \bullet 2) = 256$$

Notice that while we were able to simplify above by calculating the actual values for each factor, we would not have found the correct answer if we had added the exponents together, as the bases are different.

$$4^3 \bullet 2^2 \neq 4^5 \neq 2^5$$
$$4 \bullet 4 \bullet 4 \bullet 2 \bullet 2 \neq 4 \bullet 4 \bullet 4 \bullet 4 \bullet 4 \neq 2 \bullet 2 \bullet 2 \bullet 2 \bullet 2$$
$$256 \neq 1{,}024 \neq 32$$

While this seems pretty obvious with known numbers, it's important to point out, as it applies to unknowns as well.

$$x^3 \bullet y^2 \neq x^5 \neq y^5$$
$$x \bullet x \bullet x \bullet y \bullet y = (x \bullet x \bullet x)(y \bullet y) \neq x \bullet x \bullet x \bullet x \bullet x \neq y \bullet y \bullet y \bullet y \bullet y$$

Example: Simplify y^3y^5

Remember, two unknowns written next to each other mean to multiply. The expression y^3y^5 means the same thing as $y^3 \bullet y^5$.

If we remember what the exponents means, we can easily simplify.

$$(y \bullet y \bullet y) \bullet (y \bullet y \bullet y \bullet y \bullet y) = y \bullet y \bullet y \bullet y \bullet y \bullet y \bullet y \bullet y = y^8$$

We could also take a shortcut and add up all the repeated multiplication by simply adding the exponents together.

$$y^3y^5 = y^{3+5} = y^8$$

The same principles we're looking at with positive exponents apply with negative exponents too, only we won't be exploring multiplying and dividing unknowns with negative exponents in this course.

Dividing Unknowns with Exponents

As we use math to explore God's creation and complete real-life tasks, we also encounter a need to divide quantities raised to a power.

If you remember what an exponent means and use a fraction line to represent the division, it's easy to divide quantities raised to a power *if the base is the same.* Notice how the division simply cancels out the multiplication.

$$2^3 \div 2^2 = (2 \bullet 2 \bullet 2) \div (2 \bullet 2) = \frac{2 \bullet \cancel{2} \bullet \cancel{2}}{\cancel{2} \bullet \cancel{2}} = 2$$

This same principle applies to unknowns as well.

$$x^3 \div x^2 = (x \bullet x \bullet x) \div (x \bullet x) = \frac{x \bullet \cancel{x} \bullet \cancel{x}}{\cancel{x} \bullet \cancel{x}} = x$$

Now, there's a faster way to keep track of how many of the repeated multiplications cancel out. If the base is the same, we can divide quantities with exponents by subtracting the exponents. Thus we could divide $x^3 \div x^2$ by subtracting 2 from 3, like this:

Remember, any quantity raised to the first power equals itself. Thus x^1 equals x.

$$x^3 \div x^2 = x^{3-2} = x^1 = x$$

If the bases are the same, we can multiply quantities with exponents by adding the exponents, and divide them by subtracting the exponents. Adding or subtracting the exponents keeps track of the multiplication or division for us.

Example: Simplify $\frac{y^7}{y^5}$

Remember, the fraction line means to divide, and exponents tell us to multiply the base repeatedly.

$$\frac{y^7}{y^5} = \frac{y \bullet y \bullet \cancel{y} \bullet \cancel{y} \bullet \cancel{y} \bullet \cancel{y} \bullet \cancel{y}}{\cancel{y} \bullet \cancel{y} \bullet \cancel{y} \bullet \cancel{y} \bullet \cancel{y}} = y \bullet y = y^2$$

We could also take a shortcut and figure out how many repeated multiplications are left after the division by simply subtracting the 5 from the 7.

$$\frac{y^7}{y^5} = y^{7-5} = y^2$$

Subtracting the exponents to complete the division only works *if the base is the same*. We *cannot* subtract exponents with different bases. After all, we wouldn't be dividing by the same quantity, so the division wouldn't cancel out the multiplication.

Geometry Time

Would it surprise you to learn that you've already been applying what we've been looking at this lesson? Well, you have! Let's take a quick look at how.

Example: Multiply 6 ft^2 by 5 ft to find the volume of a rectangular prism with a base that has an area of 6 ft^2 and that has a height of 5 ft.

$$6 \text{ ft}^2 \bullet 5 \text{ ft} = 30 \text{ ft}^3$$

Notice that we multiplied ft^2 by ft, getting ft^3. It's easy to see why we end up with ft^3 if we rewrite ft^2 as ft • ft.

$$6 \textbf{ ft} \bullet \textbf{ft} \bullet 5 \text{ ft} = 30 \text{ ft}^3$$

We could also have found the correct unit of measure for the answer by adding the exponents, remembering that ft can be thought of as ft^1, as an exponent of 1 means the same thing as the base by itself.

$$6 \text{ ft}^2 \bullet 5 \text{ ft}^1 = 30 \text{ ft}^{2+1} = 30 \text{ ft}^3$$

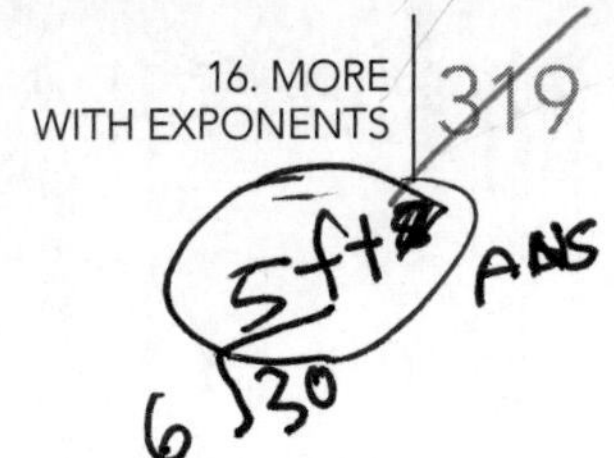

Example: Divide 30 ft³ by 6 ft² to find the height of a rectangular prism that has a volume of 30 ft³ and a base with an area of 6 ft².

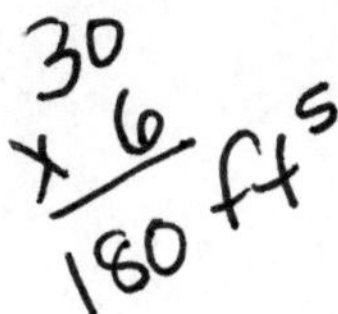

$$\frac{\overset{5}{\cancel{30}}\ \cancel{ft^3}^{\,ft}}{\cancel{6}\ \cancel{ft^2}} = 5\text{ ft}$$

Notice that we just divided ft³ by ft²! We knew the answer would be in ft, as we know that ft³ represents ft • ft • ft and ft² represents ft • ft. Thus ft³ divided by ft² leaves us with ft.

$$\frac{30\text{ ft} \bullet \text{ft} \bullet \text{ft}}{6\text{ ft} \bullet \text{ft}} = \frac{30\text{ ft} \bullet \cancel{\text{ft}} \bullet \cancel{\text{ft}}}{6\,\cancel{\text{ft}} \bullet \cancel{\text{ft}}} = 5\text{ ft}$$

We could also have found the answer by subtracting the exponents, remembering again that an exponent of 1 means the same thing as the base by itself.

$$5\text{ ft}^{3-2} = 5\text{ ft}^1 = 5\text{ ft}$$

The point is not to change how you work with units of measure, but rather to illustrate that you've already been working with exponents a lot more than you might have thought.

Keeping Perspective

Again, there's a lot more we could look at with exponents, but hopefully the little we've covered has illustrated that they're a useful notation for representing repeated multiplication — and that if you remember that, you'll be equipped to work with them, even if you forget the "rule."

Exponents, along with the rest of math, are notations to help us describe and work with real-life quantities. We can only multiply and divide quantities raised to powers using rules because we can rely on multiplication and division to work consistently . . . which we can do because of the consistency with which God is holding all things together.

16.7 Chapter Synopsis and a Glance at History

In this chapter, we had a chance to explore exponents in more depth and to apply them to scientific notation. In the process, we looked at a lot of the "language" side of math — how to use negative exponents, how to work with scientific notation, how to combine like terms with exponents, how to multiply exponents together when the base is the same, etc. Each rule or method we explored helped us learn how to express quantities and consistencies God created and sustains using a specific notation.

Let's end with a glance at history that illustrates the usefulness of using letters and exponents when working with unknowns.

A Glance at History

Math hasn't always involved letters or symbols. In fact, working with unknowns often used to be expressed in words or abbreviations rather than in letters and symbols. In her book *A Survey of Mathematics,*[1] Vivian Shaw Groza gives the following example of how the same problem could be expressed in words (known as rhetorical algebra), abbreviations (known as syncopated algebra), and symbols (known as symbolic algebra — what we use today):

Rhetorical Algebra

Three multiplied by the cube of the unknown number from which six multiplied by the square of the unknown number is subtracted is equal to the sum of five and the product of four and the unknown number.

Syncopated Algebra

3 Cu $\overline{m}$ 6 Sq ae 4 no p 5

Symbolic Algebra[2]

$3x^3 - 6x^2 = 4x + 5$

Can you imagine trying to solve pages of equations written in rhetorical or syncopated algebra? Symbols (including exponents) make it much easier to write, read, and work with unknowns! As you study more of the "language" of math, know that the different notations and conventions do indeed make it easier to communicate about and explore quantities and consistencies.

[CHAPTER 17]

Square Roots and Unknowns

17.1 Square Roots

Now that we've explored exponents, we're going to spend this chapter looking at a related concept: roots. We'll find that they, like exponents, help us describe and work with the real-life relationships God has placed around us.

Let's start today by making sure we understand what's meant by a square root. In the next lesson, we will begin to apply square roots to unknowns.

Understanding Square Roots

Exponents allow us to represent repeated multiplication. When we *square* a number, we mean to multiply it by itself. A *square root* reverses a squared number. It asks for a number that, times itself, equals the given number.

4 *squared* (written 4^2) = $4 \bullet 4$, or 16.

the *square root* of 16 (written $\sqrt{16}$) = 4, since $4 \bullet 4 = 16$

Just as 4^2 (4 *squared*) represents the repeated multiplication of $4 \bullet 4$, $\sqrt{16}$ (the *square root* of 16) represents the division necessary to reverse that repeated multiplication. A **square root** (often shown with a $\sqrt{\ }$ symbol) is a way of concisely asking for the number that, times itself, will equal the number given.

Two Square Roots

Since a negative number times itself yields a *positive* number, the square root of a positive number could be either positive *or* negative.

$$\sqrt{16} = 4 \text{ or } -4$$

$$4 \bullet 4 = 16 \quad \textit{and} \quad -4 \bullet -4 = 16$$

$$\sqrt{4} = 2 \text{ or } -2$$

$$2 \bullet 2 = 4 \quad \textit{and} \quad -2 \bullet -2 = 4$$

$$\sqrt{64} = 8 \text{ or } -8$$

$$8 \bullet 8 = 64 \quad \textit{and} \quad -8 \bullet -8 = 64$$

In Book 1, you learned to express that a square root could be either positive or negative by writing a ± in front of your answer. We emphasized this point because it's important to realize that there is both a positive and a negative square root for every positive real number.

In algebra and much of upper math, though, it's common to assume that a positive root is meant when you see a root sign ($\sqrt{\ }$) unless told otherwise. This avoids a lot of ambiguity and confusion, especially as we begin exploring more complex relationships.

From now on, unless you're asked to give both the negative and the positive square root, **you can assume the positive square root is meant**. In real life, don't assume a positive square root when a negative answer could make sense.

Finding a Square Root

Think about what we're trying to find when we are finding a square root. We want to find a number that, times itself, equals the given number. In other words, we need to find the *factor* that, times itself, equals the number of which we're finding the square root. Any thoughts as to a technique that can help us find the factors of a number?

Factoring! If we find the prime factors of a number, we can more easily spot the square root.

Example: Find $\sqrt{4}$

Let's start by factoring 4.

4
∧
2 • 2

Factoring makes it easy to see that the square root of 4 — the number that, times itself, equals 4 — is 2.

Example: Find $\sqrt{36}$

Let's start by factoring 36.

36
∧
3 • 12
∧
3 • 4
∧
2 • 2

36 expressed as the product of its prime factors: 3 • 3 • 2 • 2

The square root isn't instantly obvious this time. But notice that it takes two 3s and two 2s multiplied together to make 36. We're looking for a number that, times itself, equals 36. We can clump prime factors together to find a factor that, times itself, will equal 36. Our answer would be 2 • 3, or 6.

$(2 \cdot 3) \cdot (2 \cdot 3) = 36$

$6 \cdot 6 = 36$

$\sqrt{36} = 6$

It's not always necessary to find all the prime factors. Sometimes you'll know the square root just by thinking through your multiplication facts. In fact, with 36, you knew 6 • 6 = 36. However, knowing how to find the square root by factoring is both helpful in understanding square roots and useful for finding square roots you don't know.

Keeping Perspective

While square roots should be review for you, we'll begin exploring in the next lesson how square roots aid us in finding unknowns. Like exponents, we'll find square roots quite useful in working with real-life mathematical relationships.

17.2 Square Roots and Unknowns (and Squaring Both Sides of an Equation)

Now that we've reviewed square roots, it's time to look at how to use them with unknowns. Once again, we'll find that the *same principle* that applies to known quantities applies to unknowns as well.

Square Roots of Squares

Consider this expression:

$$\sqrt{4^2}$$

Any idea what it means? Well, it's asking for the square root of 4^2. Since 4^2 equals 16, $\sqrt{4^2}$ is another way of writing $\sqrt{16}$.

$$\sqrt{4^2} = \sqrt{16}$$

The answer to both of these expressions is 4, as 4 • 4 equals 16.

Notice that we could have easily seen the answer just by looking at $\sqrt{4^2}$. If the square root of a number is the number that, times itself, equals the number, then the square root of 4^2 is going to be 4. The answer is obvious if we remember the meaning of square roots and exponents: we know that the square root of a squared number will be the base that's being squared.

$$\sqrt{8^2} = 8$$

$$\sqrt{10^2} = 10$$

$$\sqrt{115^2} = 115$$

This holds true for unknowns too. In the following expressions, it doesn't matter that we don't know the value for the unknown. We know the square root of the unknown squared will be the unknown itself.

$$\sqrt{v^2} = v$$

$$\sqrt{x^2} = x$$

$$\sqrt{a^2} = a$$

Starting in the next lesson, we'll use this concept to help us solve many problems. Taking the square root of numbers that are squared proves quite useful.

Squaring Both Sides of an Equation

Now let's say that we know that $\sqrt{x} = 4$. How do we find x?

Well, think about what the square root sign means. It indicates the number that, times itself, equals a given number. If we know the square root of x is 4, we know that x must be 4 • 4, or 16. After all, $\sqrt{16} = 4$.

Now, let's think about how we could have found that mathematically. Just as we can multiply both sides of an equation by the same quantity without changing the equality, we can square both sides of an equation without changing the equality.

Example: $\sqrt{x} = 4$. Find x.

Square *both sides* of the equation:

$(\sqrt{x})^2 = (4)^2$

What does $(\sqrt{x})^2$ mean? Well, we know $\sqrt{x} \bullet \sqrt{x}$ has to equal x, as a square root means a number that, times itself, equals the quantity under the $\sqrt{\ }$ sign.

$x = 16$

Keeping Perspective

The more you learn in math, the more you'll keep building on the same basic principles. In this lesson, we built on the concept of square roots, exponents, and equality to help us find the value of an unknown under a square root symbol. All of math rests on the fundamental principles you've been learning since elementary school, which in turn rest on God's faithfulness in holding all things together.

17.3 Taking the Square Root of Both Sides

You've learned quite a bit so far about finding unknowns. For instance, you've learned that adding, subtracting, multiplying, or dividing the *same amount* from *both sides* of an equation doesn't alter the equality. The equation stays in balance.

It's time now to dig a little deeper and build on the principles you know to work with relationships involving square roots.

Taking the Square Root of Both Sides of an Equation

Just as we can divide both sides of an equation by the same quantity without changing the equality, we can also take the square root of both sides of an equation without changing the equality.

Example: $64 = 64$

$\sqrt{64} = \sqrt{64}$

$\mathbf{8 = 8}$

Taking the square root of *both sides* of an equation proves most useful in solving for unknowns.

Example: $64 = x^2$

How do we find x? Well, if we take the square root of both sides, we'll find the value of x. After all, we saw in the last lesson that the square root of a squared number is the number itself, so the square root of x^2 is x.

$$\sqrt{64} = \sqrt{x^2}$$

$$\mathbf{8 = x}$$

Let's apply this concept to a practical example. We know that the area of a square equals the length of one of its sides squared.

$$Area = side^2 \quad \text{or} \quad A = s^2$$

So let's say we want to figure out how long to make the sides of a square if we want it to take up an area of 25 ft^2.

Example: Find the sides of a square with an area of 25 ft^2.

Substitute known values:

$$A = s^2$$

$$25 \text{ ft}^2 = s^2$$

Now, how do we find the value of s? By taking the square root of both sides of the equation! That will tell us the number that, times itself, equals 25 ft^2.

$$\sqrt{25 \text{ ft}^2} = \sqrt{s^2}$$

$$\mathbf{5 \text{ ft} = s}$$

Notice that when we found $\sqrt{25 \text{ ft}^2}$, we ended up with 5 ft. Don't let the units confuse you. Just as the square root of s^2 is s, so the square root of ft^2 is ft. After all, if we multiply 5 ft by 5 ft, we do indeed end up with 25 ft^2.

Back in Book 1, you learned this formula for finding the length of each side of a square when you knew the area:

$$\sqrt{Area} = side \quad \text{or} \quad \sqrt{A} = s$$

We mentioned then that you'd learn in Book 2 how we came up with this formula. Well, that time has come.

We came up with this formula by taking the square root of both sides of the formula for finding the area of a square.

Formula for finding the area of a square:

$$A = s^2$$

Take the square root of *both sides:*

$$\sqrt{A} = \sqrt{s^2}$$

Simplify (we know the square root of s^2 will be s):

$$\sqrt{A} = \mathbf{s}$$

It doesn't matter if we're dealing with known numbers or unknowns — we can take the square root of *both sides* of an equation.

Keeping Perspective

In this lesson, we saw that we can **take the square root of both sides of an equation**. As you begin working with more involved mathematical relationships, you'll use the principle of performing the *same operation* of the *same amount* to both sides of an equation over and over again to find unknowns. As you do, remember that the whole reason we can work with mathematical relationships and unknowns to begin with is because of the consistent way God holds all things in place.

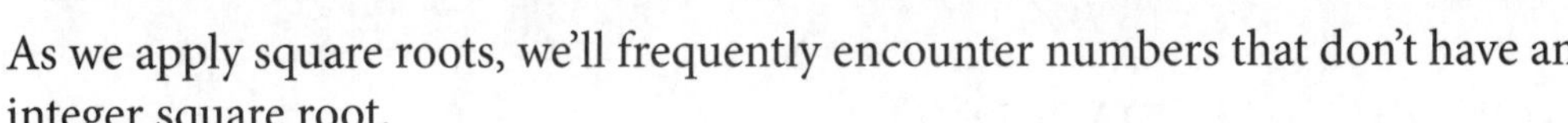

17.4 Approximating Square Roots and Finding Square Roots on a Calculator

As we apply square roots, we'll frequently encounter numbers that don't have an integer square root.

For example, what is $\sqrt{65.5}$? We know that it's more than 8, as $8 \bullet 8$ equals 64. But it's less than 9, as $9 \bullet 9$ equals 81.

So the $\sqrt{65.5}$ is between 8 and 9.

If we needed a more exact answer, we could estimate some different values until we narrowed down the square root more precisely. For example, we might see if $\sqrt{65.5}$ is 8.10.

$$8.10 \bullet 8.10 = 65.61$$

Hmm . . . we're very close, but $\sqrt{65.5}$ is less than 8.10, as we want the number that, when squared, equals 65.5, not 65.61. So let's try a number slightly less than 8.10, such as 8.09.

$$8.09 \bullet 8.09 = 65.45$$

Well, 8.09 was too low. $\sqrt{65.5}$ is somewhere between 8.09 and 8.10.

We could keep trying numbers to pin $\sqrt{65.5}$ down, or we could use a calculator to do the calculations for us.

To find a square root on a calculator, look for the square root button, which should look something like this:

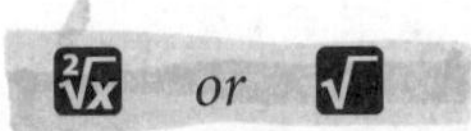

Square Root Button

(The x in the button on the left is just a placeholder to represent whatever quantity is under the square root sign.)

Example: Find $\sqrt{65.5}$

Enter 65.5 into the calculator.

Press  or √.

$\sqrt{65.5} = 8.0932070281\ldots$

On some calculators, you'll have to press the square root button *first*, and then enter the number of which you want to find the square root. Take some time to be sure you know how to find the square root on your calculator.

Note that the calculator will automatically give the positive square root.

We focused this lesson on learning the skill of approximating square roots and finding them on a calculator. The purpose of familiarizing ourselves with square roots is to be equipped to apply them. For instance, say we wanted the area of a square garden to be 65.5 ft^2. What length should we make each side? We could answer the question by finding the square root of 65.5 ft^2 . . . which we learned how to do both through approximating or using a calculator.

Keeping Perspective

Worksheet 17.4 will help you practice both approximating square roots and finding them on a calculator. While the calculator will obviously be easier, approximating square roots will help you become familiar with square roots. The goal is to be equipped to use square roots as a tool, no matter what type of number you encounter.

17.5 Pythagorean Theorem

It's time now to apply square roots to help us explore a handy relationship related to right triangles. To understand this relationship, though, we have to first learn about right triangles.

Right Triangles

A **right triangle** is a triangle with a right angle (a 90° angle, which we mark with a ⅂, as shown in the picture). In a right triangle, we call the two sides forming the right angle **legs**, and the side opposite the right angle the **hypotenuse**.

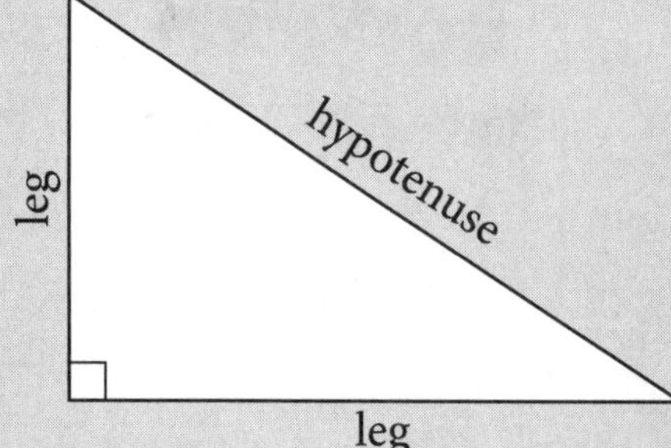

Right triangles prove incredibly useful in describing all sorts of distances — some of which you wouldn't at first suppose they could. For example, we can look at a rectangle (such as a soccer field, bookcase, door, etc.) as two right triangles put together.

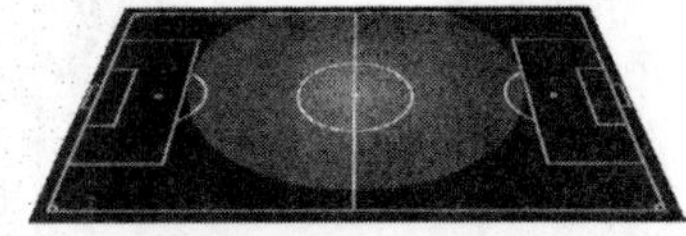

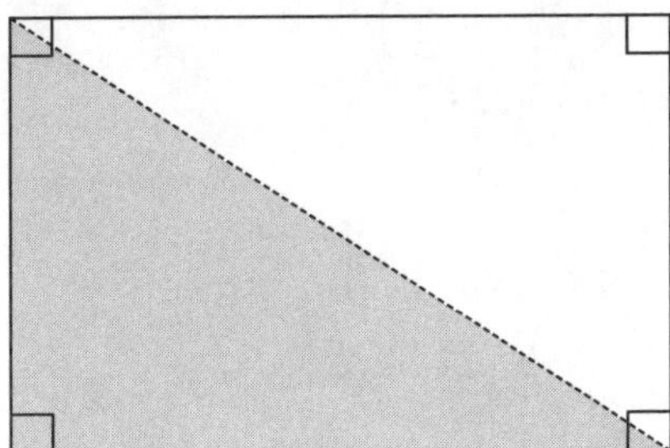

Understanding the Relationship

In a right triangle, if we square all the sides, the square of the hypotenuse will equal the sum of the squares of the other two sides. This relationship is known as the **Pythagorean theorem**. It is typically expressed like this:

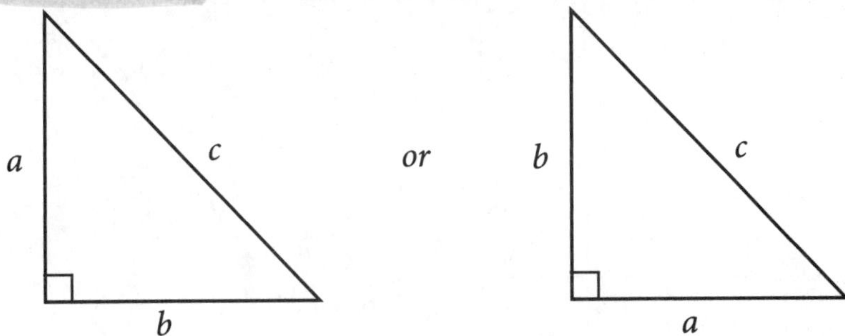

Pythagorean Theorem:

$$a^2 + b^2 = c^2$$

where c stands for the length of the hypotenuse of a right triangle, and a and b stand for the length of the two legs of the same right triangle

> Don't let the letters a, b, and c confuse you. It doesn't matter which leg we view as a and which we view b — the Pythagorean theorem is simply stating that if we square both legs and add them together, it equals the square of the hypotenuse. This relationship has to hold true in order to form a triangle with a right angle.

Let's take a look at a triangle and see the theorem in action. The sides of the right triangle below are 3, 4, and 5 centimeters (you can measure them if you like).

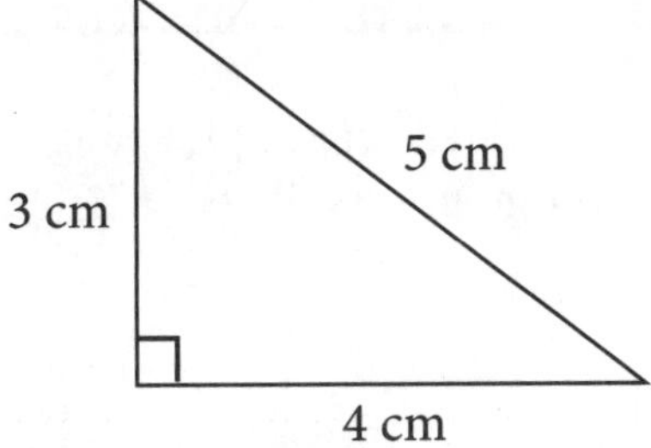

If we were to substitute these measurements into $a^2 + b^2 = c^2$ and simplify, notice that the Pythagorean theorem holds true.

Substitute known values:

$$a^2 + b^2 = c^2$$

$$\mathbf{(3\ cm)^2 + (4\ cm)^2 = (5\ cm)^2}$$

Simplify:

$$\mathbf{9\ cm^2 + 16\ cm^2 = 25\ cm^2}$$

$$\mathbf{25\ cm^2} = 25\ \text{cm}^2$$

The following picture shows this visually. In it, we've built actual squares off each side. The sum of the area of the squares built off the two legs equals the sum of the area of the square built off the hypotenuse. The square of both legs equals the square of the hypotenuse.

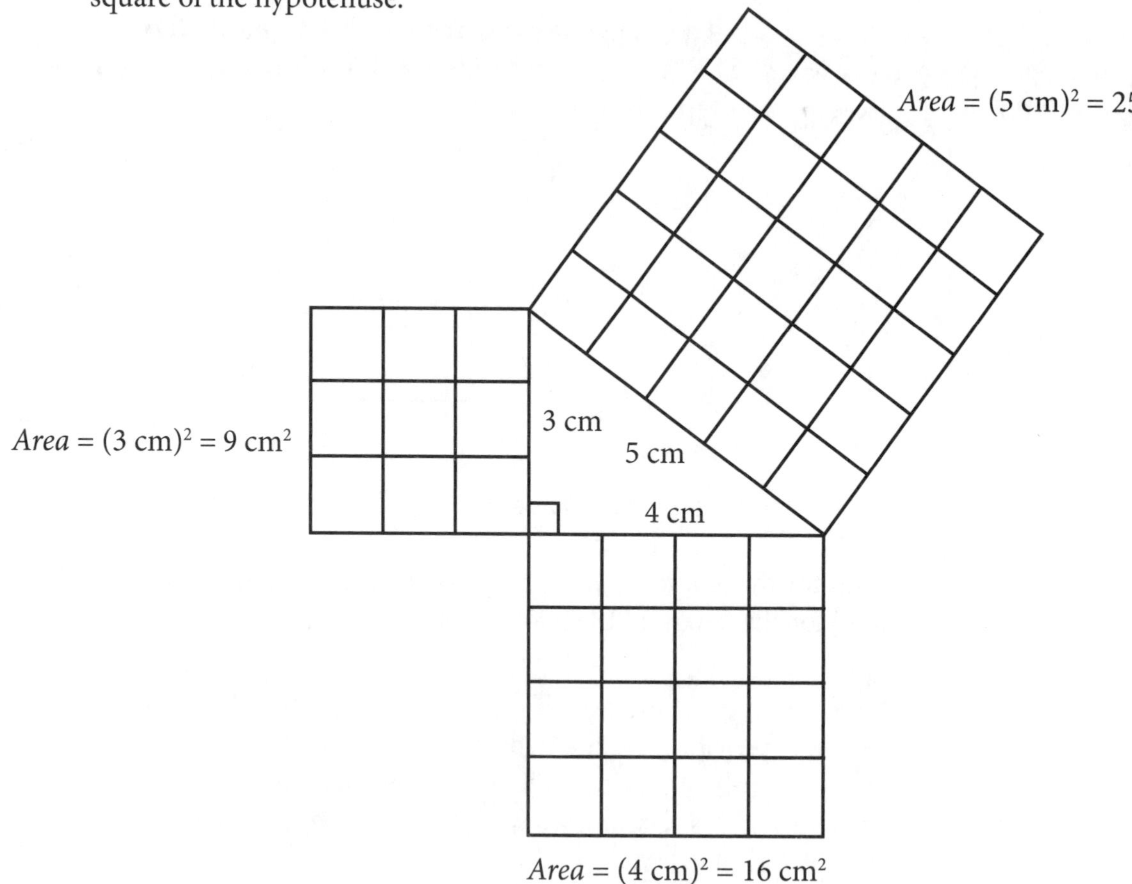

$$\mathbf{9\ cm^2 + 16\ cm^2 = 25\ cm^2}$$

Using the Relationship

You may be wondering why we care that, in a right triangle, the square of the sides equals the square of the hypotenuse. Well, it can help us find the length of a missing side.

Say we know the lengths of the legs of a right triangle, but don't know its hypotenuse. We can use the knowledge of the relationship between the legs and the hypotenuse (i.e., the Pythagorean theorem) to figure out the missing dimension.

Example: Use the Pythagorean theorem to find the missing side of this triangle.

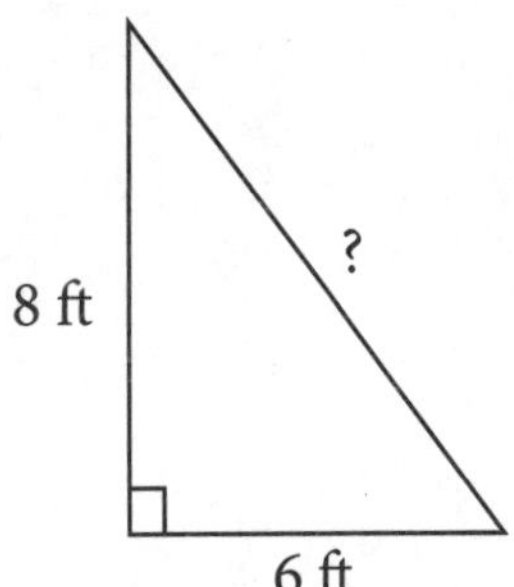

How do we know the 8 ft and 6 ft sides are the two legs and the side marked with a question mark is the hypotenuse (represented by *c* in the formula)? Because the hypotenuse is the side opposite the right angle, while the legs are the sides that form the right angle. Since the side marked with a ? is opposite the right angle, we know it is the hypotenuse, while the other two sides are the legs.

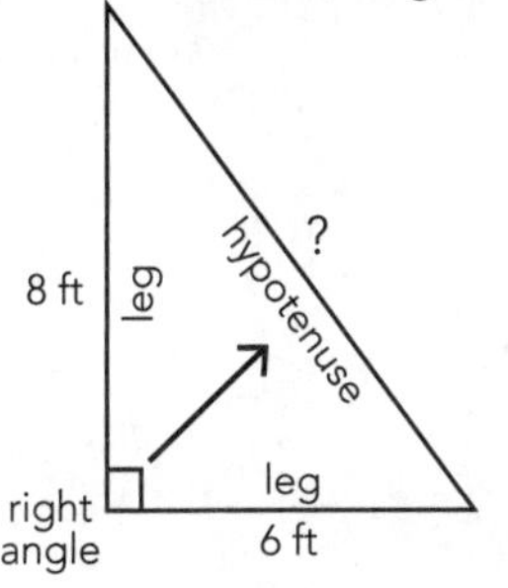

Pythagorean theorem:

$a^2 + b^2 = c^2$

Substitute known lengths — we know the lengths of the two legs (a and b — again, it doesn't matter which leg we view as a and which one we view as b . . . the point is simply to add their squares together):

$\mathbf{(6\text{ ft})^2 + (8\text{ ft})^2} = c^2$

Simplify:

$\mathbf{36\text{ ft}^2 + 64\text{ ft}^2} = c^2$

$\mathbf{100\text{ ft}^2} = c^2$

Now we've found c^2, but we still need to find c. We can easily do this by taking the square root of both sides of the equation.

$\sqrt{100\text{ ft}^2} = \sqrt{c^2}$

$\mathbf{10\text{ ft} = c}$

Let's take a look at a real-life example of how the Pythagorean theorem can help us find a missing distance.

Example: Suppose you know that a certain soccer field[1] has a length of 105 m and a width of 68 m. If we're standing at one corner, how far would we walk if we walked diagonally across the field?

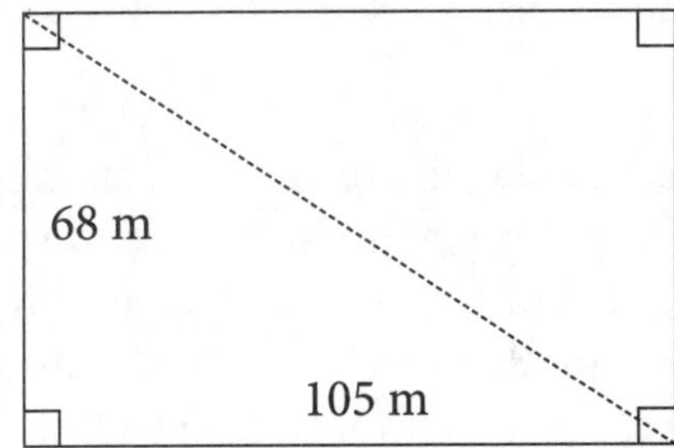

Notice that since a soccer field is a rectangle (and a rectangle has all right angles), we can think of the diagonal as dividing the field into two identical right triangles. We know the legs of the right triangles, but we need to find the hypotenuse (the diagonal). We can use the Pythagorean theorem to find this!

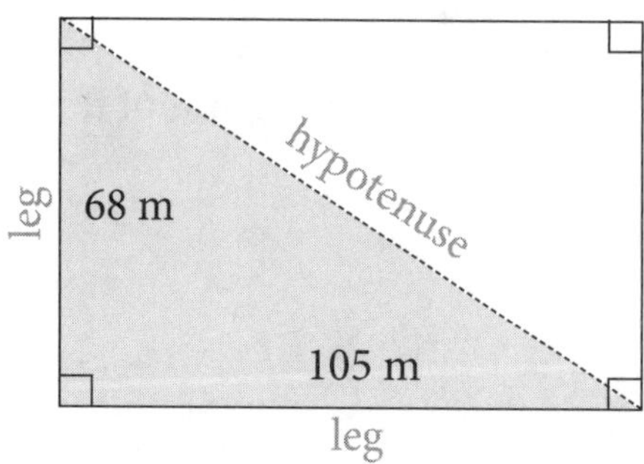

Pythagorean theorem:

$a^2 + b^2 = c^2$

Substitute known lengths — we know the lengths of the two legs (a and b — it doesn't matter which leg we view as a and which one we view as b):

$\mathbf{(68\text{ m})^2 + (105\text{ m})^2} = c^2$

Simplify:

$\mathbf{4{,}624\text{ m}^2 + 11{,}025\text{ m}^2} = c^2$

$\mathbf{15{,}649\text{ m}^2} = c^2$

Now we've found c^2, but we still need to find c. We can easily do this by taking the square root of both sides of the equation.

$\sqrt{15{,}649\text{ m}^2} = \sqrt{c^2}$

While finding the square root of 15,649 m^2 would be rather tedious manually, we can find it easily on a calculator, giving us the answer: a number that rounds to 125.1 m.

$\mathbf{125.1\text{ m}} = c$

Keeping Perspective

Just as we can take the square root of the area to find the length of each side of a square, we can use square roots to help us find missing sides in a right triangle. In both cases, we're using the information we know to find the information we don't know.

As you learn more about exploring the complexities of God's creation, you'll find that the relationships will gradually become more involved and require more concepts to solve. Don't let the complexities overwhelm you — just remember to break each problem into steps. Above all, remember that the very complexities point us to God's greatness — He created and sustains each relationship! Truly His wisdom and might know no bounds.

17.6 More with the Pythagorean Theorem

In working with exponents and unknowns, sometimes we'll encounter equations that require more than one step to solve. Don't let multi-step problems intimidate you: break them down into steps.

For example, consider this problem:

$$x^2 + 16 = 80$$

Here, x^2 isn't on a side by itself to start with, but there's no need to panic. We know that we can add the *same* amount to *both* sides of the equation. If we add –16 to both sides, then, we'll be left with x^2 on a side by itself and can then find x by taking the square root.

Example: $x^2 + 16 = 80$

Add –16 to both sides of the equation:

$x^2 + 16 + \mathbf{-16} + = 80 + \mathbf{-16}$

$x^2 = \mathbf{64}$

Take the square root of both sides:

$\sqrt{x^2} = \sqrt{64}$

$\mathbf{x = 8}$

In the last lesson, we only used the Pythagorean theorem to find the hypotenuse — the side we've been representing with c. But with a few more steps, we can use the Pythagorean theorem to find *any* missing side in a right triangle.

Example: Find the missing side in this right triangle.

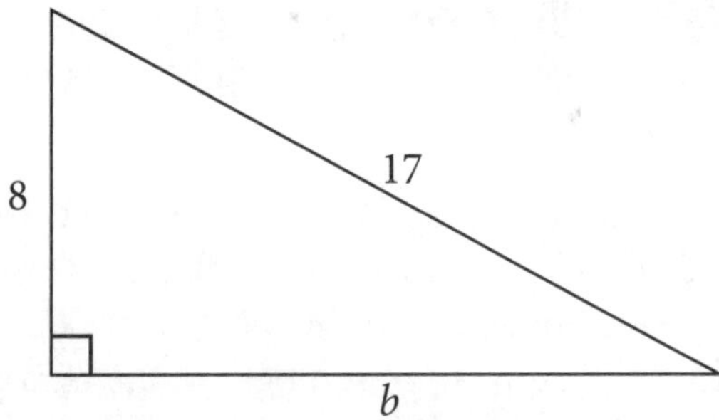

Pythagorean theorem:

$a^2 + b^2 = c^2$

Substitute known values:

$\mathbf{8^2} + b^2 = \mathbf{17^2}$

Simplify exponents:

$\mathbf{64} + b^2 = \mathbf{289}$

Add –64 to *both sides* of the equation:

$64 + \mathbf{-64} + b^2 = 289 + \mathbf{-64}$

Simplify:

$b^2 = \mathbf{225}$

Find the square root of *both sides* of the equation:

$\sqrt{b^2} = \sqrt{225}$

$\boldsymbol{b} = \mathbf{15}$

Keeping Perspective

Much as some works of art require only a couple of techniques, while others require many (combining colors, special brush strokes, painting in layers, etc.), so some math problems require only a couple of techniques to solve, while others require many. As you practice combining different techniques, remember that God's the artist of the complex picture math attempts to describe. While men have developed techniques, God is the One who gives those techniques meaning by holding all things together consistently. He's the One who makes working with unknowns possible.

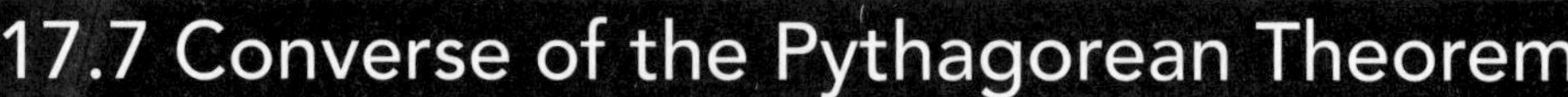

17.7 Converse of the Pythagorean Theorem

Not only can the Pythagorean theorem help us find missing dimensions in a right triangle, but it can also help us tell if a triangle is indeed a right triangle. The Pythagorean theorem describes the fact that *if a triangle is a right triangle, then the sum of the squares of the lengths of the legs will equal the square of the length of the hypotenuse*; the opposite argument, or **converse**, of that is that *if the sum of the squares of the lengths of the legs in a triangle equal the square of the length of the hypotenuse, the triangle is a right triangle.*

While not all converse, or opposite, arguments hold true (just because every toddler cries does not mean that everyone who cries is a toddler), in the case of the Pythagorean theorem, the converse holds true. If the sum of the squares of the lengths of the legs in a triangle equal the square of the length of the hypotenuse, the triangle has to be a right triangle. We call this the **converse of the Pythagorean theorem**.

Converse of the Pythagorean Theorem

If the sum of the squares of the lengths of the legs in a triangle equal the square of the length of the hypotenuse, the triangle is a right triangle.

In other words, if in a triangle, $a^2 + b^2 = c^2$, then the triangle is a right triangle.

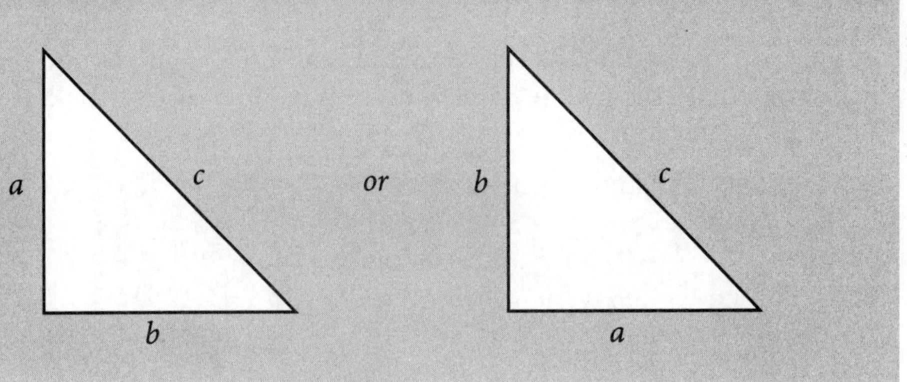

Why do we care that the converse of the Pythagorean theorem is true? Well, let's say we want to make sure we've assembled a sturdy bookcase. The sides of the bookcase should be nailed to the base at right (90°) angles — they can't intersect at a different angle, or the bookcase would totter (not a good thing!). How can we tell if we've got the shelves nailed at the correct angle?

One way is to use the converse of the Pythagorean theorem. A properly built bookshelf would be a rectangle, with all right angles. If the bookcase is truly a rectangle, then a diagonal line from corner to corner would divide the bookcase into two right triangles.

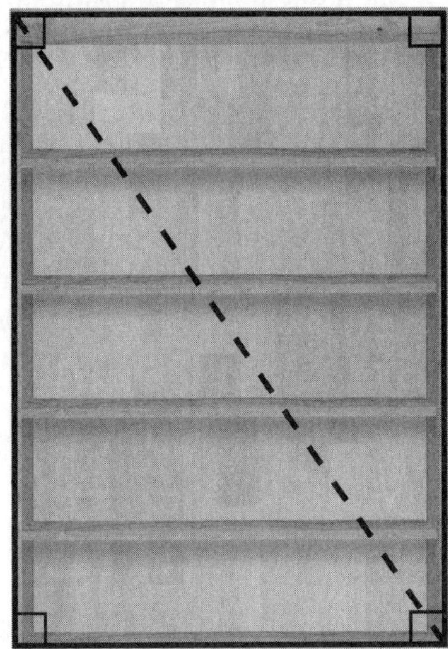

A Properly Built Bookcase

(All right angles; a diagonal line from corner to corner would divide the bookcase into two right triangles.)

Now we can measure the dimensions of a bookcase we're building. We could then use the Pythagorean theorem to figure out what the length of the diagonal from corner to corner would be if the diagonal does indeed form two right triangles. If the actual measurement of the diagonal equals the measurement calculated using the Pythagorean theorem, then we know that the bookcase forms two right triangles, thus telling us that its angles are indeed right angles. If it's different, though, we'd know that we need to adjust the bookcase some more.

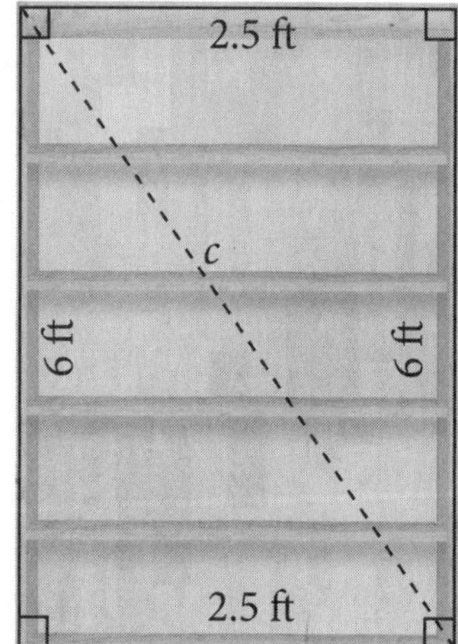

Example: If a rectangular bookcase is 6 ft tall and 2.5 ft wide, what would the length marked *c* in the picture have to measure in order for the bookcase to be built with right angles?

Substitute known values:

$a^2 + b^2 = c^2$

$(\mathbf{6\ ft})^2 + (\mathbf{2.5\ ft})^2 = c^2$

Simplify exponents:

$\mathbf{36\ ft^2} + \mathbf{6.25\ ft^2} = c^2$

Simplify:

$\mathbf{42.25\ ft^2} = c^2$

Take the square root of *both sides*:

$\sqrt{42.25\ \text{ft}^2} = \sqrt{c^2}$

$\mathbf{6.5\ ft} = c$

So *if* the diagonal (c) measures 6.5 ft, then the triangles must be right triangles, meaning the bookcase is built with right angles. If it does not, then we'd better keep tweaking the bookcase until it does.

Keeping Perspective

Since many shapes can be thought of as several triangles, triangles can help us find measurements we might not expect! As we saw in Book 1, shapes help us describe all sorts of aspects of God's creation. By combining what we know about shapes with the techniques we've learned for finding unknowns, we're able to solve even more real-life problems. No matter how many techniques we combine, though, we're ultimately relying on the underlying consistencies God created and sustains and on the fact that God created us capable of appreciating and recording those consistencies.

17.8 Other Roots

Up until now, the only roots we've looked at have been square roots. As we've seen, a square root is a way of asking for the number that, times itself, equals a given number. But let's say that we wanted to find a number that, times itself *three* times (rather than two), equaled a given number. For example, say we knew the volume of a cube was 27 in³, but wanted to find out the measure of each side of the cube. We want to find a number that, times itself three times, equals 27 in³. Is there a way to do that?

$$Volume = s^3$$

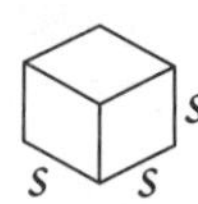

Yes! All we'd need to do is put a superscript 3 in front of the root symbol. This would tell us to find the *cubed* root — the number that, times itself *three* times, equals a given number.

$\sqrt[3]{27}$ asks for the number that, times itself three times, equals 27.

Answer is 3, as 3 • 3 • 3 equals 27.

Whatever superscript number we put to the left of the root sign tells us what root were looking for — that is, the number of times the root would be multiplied by itself to equal the number under the root sign (called the **radicand**).

Root	Meaning	Result
$\sqrt{4}$ *or* $\sqrt[2]{4}$	*the number that, times itself, equals 4*	2, as 2 • 2 = 4
$\sqrt[3]{8}$	*the number that, times itself three times, equals 8*	2, as 2 • 2 • 2 = 8
$\sqrt[4]{16}$	*the number that, times itself four times, equals 16*	2, as 2 • 2 • 2 • 2 = 16
$\sqrt[5]{32}$	*the number that, times itself five times, equals 32*	2, as 2 • 2 • 2 • 2 • 2 = 32
$\sqrt[6]{64}$	*the number that, times itself six times, equals 64*	2, as 2 • 2 • 2 • 2 • 2 • 2 = 64

Notice from the chart that we *could* put a 2 next to the root sign to show the squared root, only it's customary not to bother.

...etc.

In other words, just as exponents can be used to show repeated multiplication, **roots help us express repeated division**. Just as we can use different exponents to show how many times we want to multiply a number, we can use different roots to reverse that repeated multiplication.

Term Time

Radical is another name for a root, **index** is the name for the superscript number that indicates which root we're taking, **radical sign** is another name for the root sign, and **radicand** is a term used to refer to "the quantity under a radical sign."[2]

index → $\sqrt[3]{512} = 8$ ← root *or* radical; radicand; root sign *or* radical sign

It's important to note that the index is not normally written when we're finding the square root. If there's no index, the radical sign by itself means the square root. For example, $\sqrt{16}$ means the same thing as $\sqrt[2]{16}$.

To avoid confusion with an index (the superscript number that indicates which root we're taking), when writing a multiplication next to a square root sign, use parentheses. For example, even though $3\sqrt{64}$ technically means $3 \bullet \sqrt{64}$, if handwritten, it could be easy to mistake the 3 for an index (as in $\sqrt[3]{64}$). So it's safer to develop the habit of including parentheses. For example, write $3(\sqrt{64})$ or $(3)\sqrt{64}$ rather than $3\sqrt{64}$.

Finding Various Roots

It was easy to find the cubed root of 27, since it was a relatively small number. Often, we'll need to factor to find various roots. In this course, **we'll focus on square roots and cubed roots, but the same process applies for finding other roots.**

Example: Find the cubed root of 125 (also written $\sqrt[3]{125}$).

Here we want to find the number that, times itself three times, equals 125. We can figure this out by factoring 125.

```
125
 ^
5 • 25
    ^
  5 • 5
```

Since 5 • 5 • 5 equals 125, 5 is the cubed root of 125.

Example: Find the cubed root of 216 (also written $\sqrt[3]{216}$).

Here we want to find the number that, times itself three times, equals 216. We can figure this out by factoring 216.

```
    216
     ^
   3 • 72
        ^
     8 • 9
     ^   ^
  4 • 2 3 • 3
  ^
2 • 2
```

Notice that none of the prime factors multiplied together three times equal 216. Thus, we have to look at how we could *combine* the prime factors to find a cubed root. Let's arrange all the prime factors in order and look at them: 2 • 2 • 2 • 3 • 3 • 3

Notice that we have three 2s and three 3s. We can combine these to find the factor that, when multiplied by itself 3 times, equals 216.

$$2 \bullet 2 \bullet 2 \bullet 3 \bullet 3 \bullet 3 = 216$$

$$6 \bullet 6 \bullet 6 = 216$$

The cubed root of 216 is 6, as 6 • 6 • 6 equals 216.

There's also a way to find various roots on a calculator using a button that typically has this symbol on it: $\sqrt[x]{y}$. However, for now, you'll need to do your own calculating of cubed roots. While the process may seem tedious, finding a root via factoring will help you familiarize yourself with roots and with the factors that make up numbers, which will help you in understanding many different aspects of math.

Keeping Perspective

Roots, or **radicals**, are another helpful notation to aid us in describing God's creation. As with all the other notations we've looked at, they're part of the "language" of mathematics that we use to concisely describe and work with real-life quantities and consistencies. While much of math focuses on the notations, we need to remember the purpose of learning those notations: to better understand God's creation and to be equipped to use math to His glory in whatever situations He brings into our lives.

17.9 Chapter Synopsis and the Pythagorean Worldview

Well, we've reached the end of our short look at square roots and unknowns. We started by looking at **square roots** and how they undo squaring a number. We then applied that knowledge to help us find various unknowns.

We also explored in depth the relationship between the legs and hypotenuse in a right triangle: the **Pythagorean theorem** ($a^2 + b^2 = c^2$). We used this theorem to find the length of any side of a right triangle when we knew the other two sides, and we used the **converse of the Pythagorean theorem** to tell if a triangle was really a right triangle. Last, we touched on other roots besides square roots.

In ending our explorations, it's fitting that we take a look at the mathematician for which the Pythagorean theorem is named . . . and at how his very theorem contradicted his worldview.

Pythagoras and the Pythagorean Worldview[3]

The Pythagorean theorem is named after a Greek mathematician named Pythagoras. Pythagoras was one of the earlier Greek mathematicians, born somewhere around 570 B.C. He didn't always live in Greece — he spent some time in Egypt, where he may have learned some of their mathematical and religious teachings.

Pythagoras is known, however, for the combination school/religious brotherhood that he founded in Greece. Pythagoras and those in his "brotherhood" are collectively referred to as Pythagoreans.[4] While the Pythagoreans contributed a lot to math, they also worshiped numbers.

> *In fact, he and his followers worshiped numbers as the full intelligibility and the generating source of all things. This veneration is revealed in one of the Pythagorean creedal confessions, "Bless us divine number, thou who generatest gods and men."*
> *— James Nickel,* Mathematics: Is God Silent?[5]

Pythagoras
(c. 570 B.C.–490 B.C.)

The Pythagoreans were very secretive. Those members on the "inside," so to speak, were "bound by oath not to reveal the teaching or secrets of the school."[6] Thus, history is not always totally clear about some of the school's discoveries. We don't even know which discoveries Pythagoras made versus others at the school, since it was common to give Pythagoras credit for everything.

The Pythagorean . . . having been brought up in the study of mathematics, thought that things are numbers . . . and that the whole cosmos is a scale and a number. — Aristotle

All throughout history, men have tried to explain math and the order in creation apart from acknowledging God. Their theories were believed for a time and disproven later. This proved true for the Pythagorean belief too. In fact, as James Nickel points out in *Mathematics: Is God Silent?* the Pythagorean theorem *itself* disproves the Pythagorean worldview![7]

You see, one of the strange teachings of the Pythagorean school was that they believed everything (including fractions) could be reduced one way or another to whole numbers (1, 2, 3, . . .). Even numbers we wouldn't think of as whole (such as $\frac{8}{9}$) can be thought of as a whole number divided by a whole number. In other words, they thought of everything in terms of positive rational numbers.

Yet when we apply the Pythagorean theorem, we encounter numbers that *can't* be described using whole numbers alone.

Consider a right triangle whose legs are both 1.

Pythagorean theorem:

$$a^2 + b^2 = c^2$$

Substitute known values:

$$\mathbf{1}^2 + \mathbf{1}^2 = c^2$$

Simplify:

$$\mathbf{1} + \mathbf{1} = c^2$$

$$\mathbf{2} = c^2$$

Find the Square Root of Both Sides:

$$\sqrt{2} = \sqrt{c^2}$$

$$\sqrt{2} = \mathbf{c}$$

The hypotenuse of a triangle whose legs are both 1 cannot be expressed using rational numbers. It is the $\sqrt{2}$, an irrational number that begins 1.414213562 . . . and continues on and on. There's no fraction or ratio made up of whole numbers that can express this quantity precisely. Not everything can be reduced to a positive rational number! God's creation is much more complicated than that.

As we look at the Pythagorean school and their thinking, and then see how their very theorem contradicted their worldview, we're reminded of the foolishness of man's sinful thinking. God's truth is written in His Word for any who will listen, yet all throughout history, men have tried to ascribe God's glory elsewhere. While most modern mathematicians don't boldly worship numbers the same way the Pythagoreans did, that same spirit of enthroning math and the creation rather than the Creator is still something we need to guard against, both in what we read and in our own lives.

For the wisdom of this world is foolishness with God. For it is written, He taketh the wise in their own craftiness (1 Corinthians 3:19).

Thy word is true from the beginning: and every one of thy righteous judgments endureth for ever (Psalm 119:160).

Because that which may be known of God is manifest in them; for God hath shewed it unto them. For the invisible things of him from the creation of the world are clearly seen, being understood by the things that are made, even his eternal power and Godhead; so that they are without excuse: Because that, when they knew God, they glorified him not as God, neither were thankful; but became vain in their imaginations, and their foolish heart was darkened. Professing themselves to be wise, they became fools, And changed the glory of the uncorruptible God into an image made like to corruptible man, and to birds, and fourfooted beasts, and creeping things. Wherefore God also gave them up to uncleanness through the lusts of their own hearts, to dishonour their own bodies between themselves: Who changed the truth of God into a lie, and worshipped and served the creature more than the Creator, who is blessed for ever. Amen (Romans 1:19–25).

[CHAPTER 18]

Glimpses of Trigonometry

18.1 Introduction and Review

If you've finished Book 1 and the previous chapters in Book 2 of this course, you've had a chance to explore (and hopefully master) the core principles of arithmetic, geometry, algebra, statistics, and probability. It's now time to take a glimpse at the branch of math known as **trigonometry**. Trigonometry means "triangle measure"; not surprisingly, it deals with triangles — right triangles to be exact.

Since we've been exploring right triangles with the Pythagorean theorem, you already know a lot about them. But believe it or not, there's more to learn!

Before we jump into right triangles again, though, let's look at some important geometry definitions and concepts.

> We'll be quickly reviewing a lot of information covered in Book 1. If anything in this lesson doesn't make sense, see Chapter 20 of Book 1 for clarification.

Reviewing Terms

Corresponding sides and angles are sides and angles that represent the same part of the shapes. In the triangles shown, the sides marked with the same letter are all corresponding sides — they represent the same part of the triangles. Likewise, the angles marked with the same letter are all corresponding angles — they also represent the same part of the triangles.

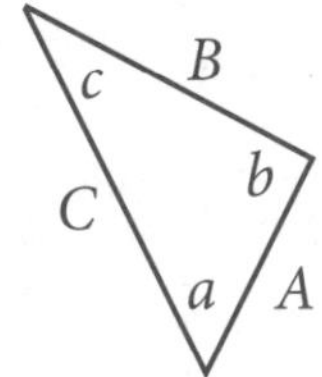

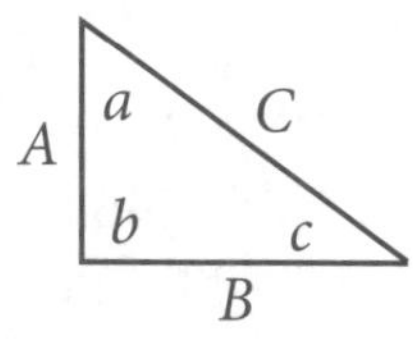

Congruent — Congruent means "identical in form."[1] Since congruent shapes are "identical in form," all of their corresponding sides and angles are also congruent, or "identical in form." Below, the corresponding sides are shown with tick marks, and the congruent angles are shown with arcs (except for right angles, which are all marked with a half-box). Sides with one tick mark are congruent to all other sides with one tick mark; those with two tick marks are congruent to all other sides with two tick marks, etc. Likewise, angles with one arc are congruent; those with two arcs are congruent, etc.

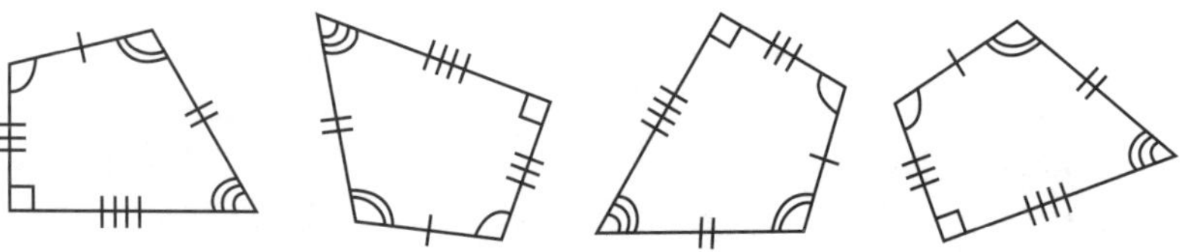

Congruent Shapes
(All corresponding angles and sides are congruent.)

Similar — We call shapes similar if they're the *same except for their size* — that is, if one is just a scaled-up or down version of the other. In a similar shape, corresponding angles are congruent and corresponding sides are **proportional** — that is, the ratios between corresponding sides form a proportion.

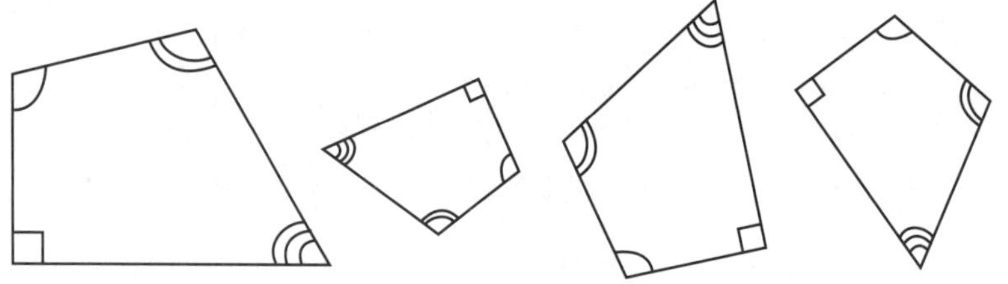

Similar Shapes
(All corresponding angles are the same; corresponding sides are proportional.)

AAA Similarity Theorem

How do we know if shapes are similar? Well, in the case of triangles, if all the corresponding angles in two triangles are congruent, the sides will be proportional too, meaning the triangles will be similar. There's just no way to form triangles with all the same angles and not have the sides proportional too. This fact is referred to as the AAA (angle, angle, angle) similarity theorem.

Example: Are the corresponding sides in these triangles proportional? Why or why not?

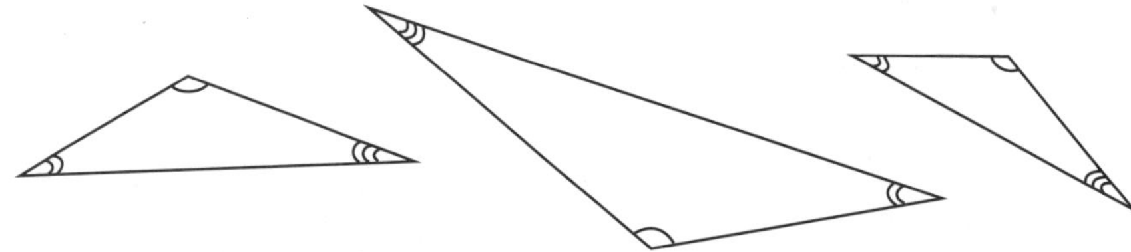

Yes, the sides are proportional. All of their angles are congruent, which means the triangles must be similar, and similar shapes have proportional corresponding sides.

Attributes of a Triangle

The **sum of all the angles in a triangle equals 180°**. The angles simply have to equal 180° in order to form a closed, two-dimensional figure with three straight sides.

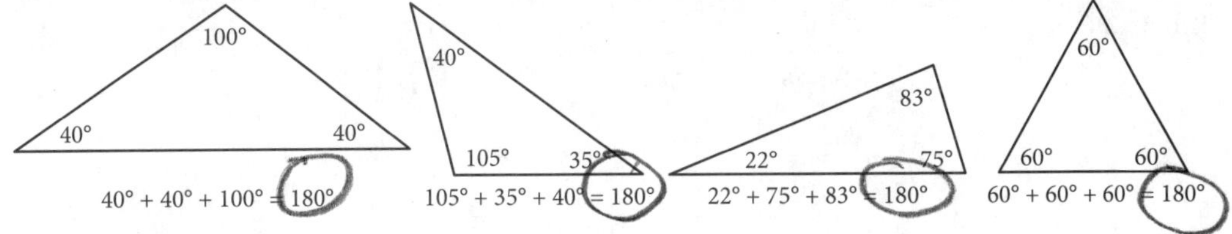

Other Geometries Exist

It's worth pointing out that a triangle can have different definitions and thus different attributes. While in this course (as with most math courses) we're using the common definitions (those from Euclidean geometry), there are other geometry systems that help us describe other aspects of God's creation. In those geometries, definitions (and the attributes and conclusions drawn from those definitions) are different than those in Euclidean geometry.

For example, in spherical geometry (a geometry that helps us work with spheres — such as the earth), the definition of a triangle is different, so the conclusion that the sum of the angles of a triangle always equals 180° does not hold true in spherical geometry.

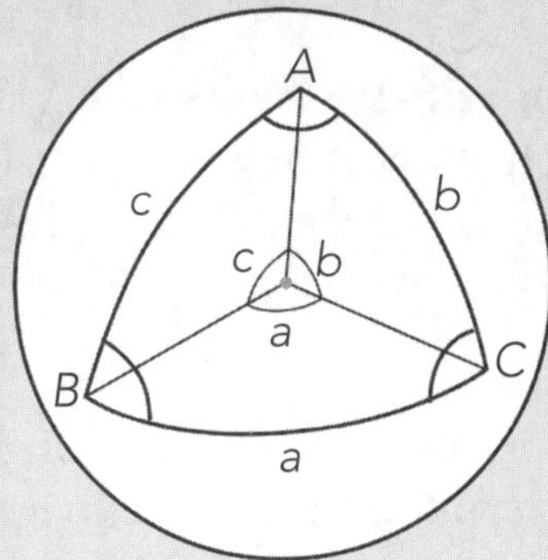

Non-Euclidean geometry is not something you'll be expected to learn in this course. However, it's important to know that other definitions and geometry systems exist. The existence of other systems reminds us that each one is a tool — a way of describing God's universe, which is so complex we need multiple geometries to explore it!

AA Similarity Theorem

Let's say that two triangles have a 40 degree and a 60 degree angle. We don't know the third angle, but we know that the sum of all the angles in each triangle equals 180 degrees. If we set up an equation and solve to find the missing angles, we'll find that they are both equal.

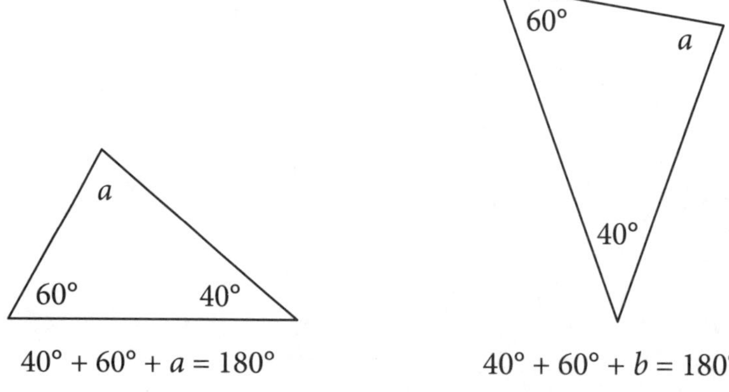

$40° + 60° + a = 180°$ $\qquad$ $40° + 60° + b = 180°$

Simplify:

$\mathbf{100°} + a = 180°$ $\qquad$ $\mathbf{100°} + b = 180°$

Add –100° to both sides:

$100° + \mathbf{-100°} + a = 180° + \mathbf{-100°}$ $\qquad$ $100° + \mathbf{-100°} + b = 180° + \mathbf{-100°}$

$a = \mathbf{80°}$ $\qquad$ $b = \mathbf{80°}$

This brings us to the **AA similarity theorem** (the AA stands for angle-angle), which is a way of describing that two triangles have to be similar if *two sets* of their corresponding angles are congruent. After all, if two sets of corresponding angles are the same, the third will be too, since the total of the angles in a triangle is always 180°.

By knowing this ahead of time, we can tell if two triangles are similar, even if all we know is that two sets of corresponding angles are congruent.

Example: Are these two triangles similar? How do you know?

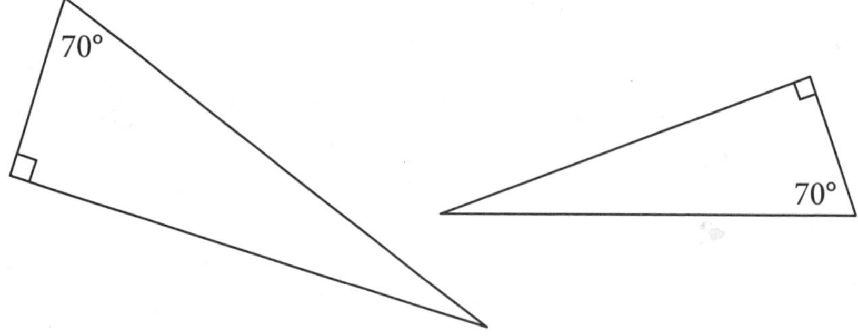

Yes, these triangles are similar, as we know from the AA similarity theorem that if two sets of corresponding angles are congruent, the triangles have to be similar. (The right angles and the 70° angles are congruent.)

Keeping Perspective

As we move into exploring the ratios in right triangles, we'll find ourselves building on the AA similarity theorem. Keep in mind as we do that the AA similarity theorem is simply a logical conclusion based on the definitions we use in Euclidean geometry to describe triangles, congruency, and similarity. Also note that we're only able to come up with definitions to describe shapes and come to conclusions based on those definitions because God gave us the ability to name and explore His creation, to think, and to reason.

For the Christian, our ultimate starting assumption is the truth of God's Word. And when we start with it, it makes sense out of the world around us. In fact, it explains why we can make logical deductions at all: because God created us in His image, gifting us with the ability to think.[2]

18.2 Tangent: A Ratio in Right Triangles

It's time now to begin exploring trigonometry by looking at a specific ratio in right triangles called a tangent.

Exploring the Ratios in Right Triangles

Take a look at the triangles below. Notice that they are all right triangles, since they are all triangles with one right angle. Notice also that they all have a 40° angle. This means they all have two congruent angles — a right, or 90° angle, and a 40° angle. As we reviewed in the last lesson, then, we can conclude by the AA similarity theorem that these triangles are similar.

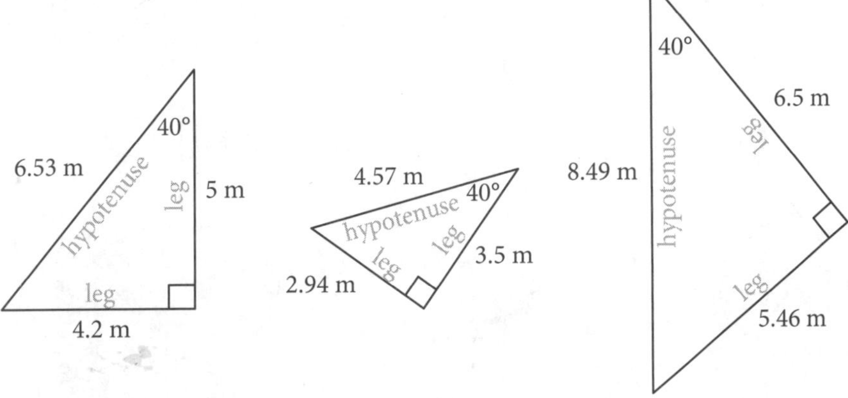

Since the triangles are all similar, the ratios between the corresponding sides will be too (having proportional sides is part of the definition of similar). So if we form a ratio between the leg opposite the 40° angle and the leg next to, or adjacent, to it, we know the ratio will be the same for all the triangles shown.

$$\frac{\textit{leg opposite the } 40° \textit{ angle}}{\textit{leg adjacent to the } 40° \textit{ angle}}$$

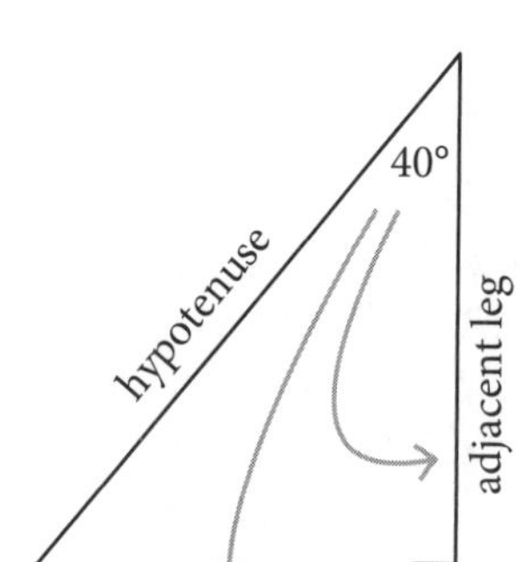

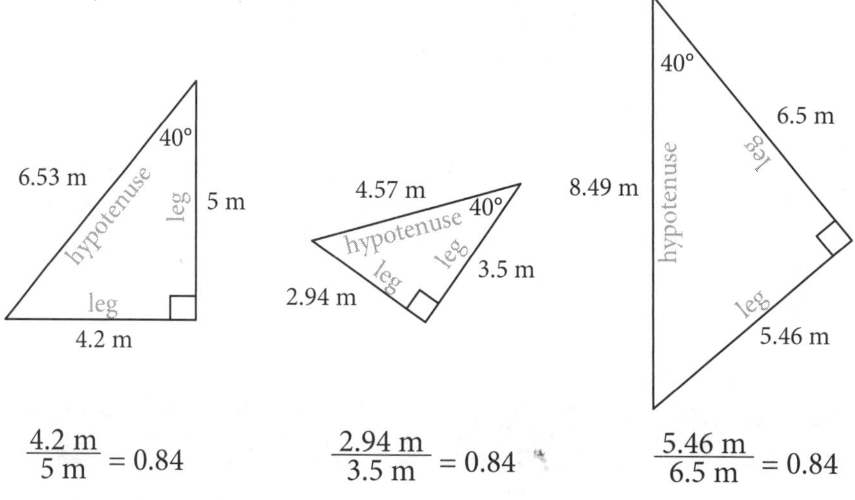

$\frac{4.2 \text{ m}}{5 \text{ m}} = 0.84$ $\frac{2.94 \text{ m}}{3.5 \text{ m}} = 0.84$ $\frac{5.46 \text{ m}}{6.5 \text{ m}} = 0.84$

The more precise ratio between the opposite and adjacent legs of a 40° angle in a right triangle is 0.83909963117. We rounded the ratio to 0.84. The lengths of the sides of the triangles listed are also rounded measurements; if we had used unrounded measurements, we would be able to find the precise ratio.

No matter the size of the right triangle, the ratio between the leg opposite a 40° angle and the adjacent leg is the same. After all, all right triangles with a 40° angle are similar . . . and by definition, similar triangles have proportional sides.

As another example of this, let's look at the ratio of the leg opposite the *unmarked* angle with the leg adjacent to it. We know that the unmarked angle is 50°, since 40° + 90° + **50°** = 180°. Look at what happens when we form a ratio of the leg opposite to each 50° angle with the leg adjacent to the 50° angle.

$$\frac{\textit{leg opposite the } 50° \textit{ angle}}{\textit{leg adjacent to the } 50° \textit{ angle}}$$

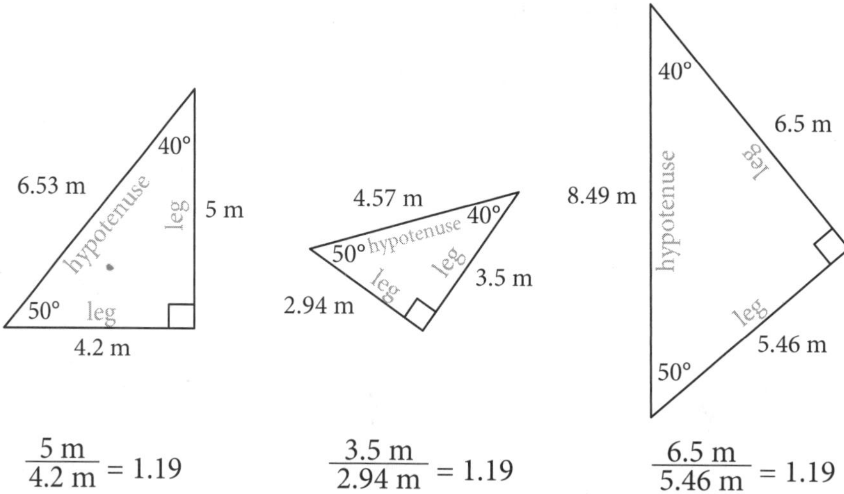

$\frac{5 \text{ m}}{4.2 \text{ m}} = 1.19$ $\frac{3.5 \text{ m}}{2.94 \text{ m}} = 1.19$ $\frac{6.5 \text{ m}}{5.46 \text{ m}} = 1.19$

Notice that once again the ratios are all the same. After all, all right triangles with a 50° angle are similar, as two angles (the right angle and the 50° angle) are congruent (which we know from the AA similarity theorem means the triangles have to be similar). Thus, the ratio between their sides will be proportional.

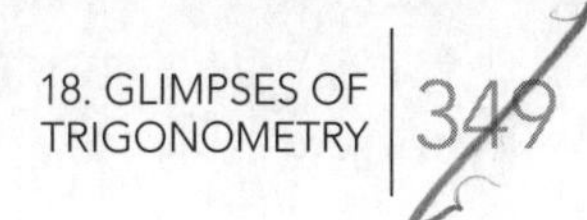

We refer to the ratio between the opposite and adjacent leg of either of the non-right angles in a right triangle as the **tangent** of that angle.

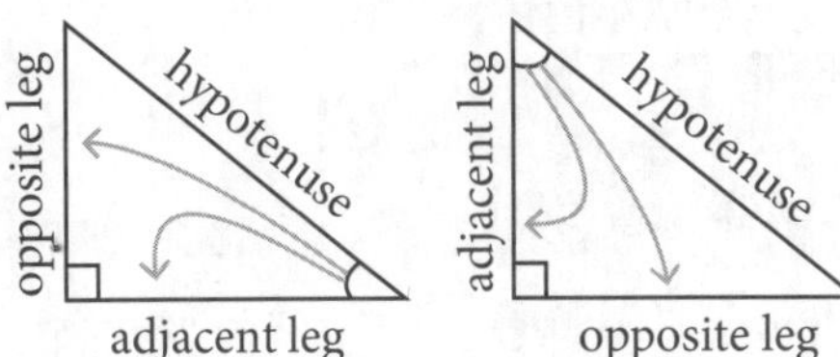

$$\textit{tangent of an angle} = \frac{\textit{opposite leg}}{\textit{adjacent leg}}$$

Computing Tangents

As we saw, the tangent of a specific angle measurement is always the same. After all, all right triangles with another angle measuring the same are similar, so their sides will be proportional (that's part of the definition of similar).

Because the tangent of a specific angle measurement is always the same, **you can find tangents using a calculator**. Simply type the angle size into the calculator and press the TAN button. The calculator will show you the tangent of the angle you input.

TAN is an abbreviation for "tangent."

Example: Find the tangent of a 30° angle.

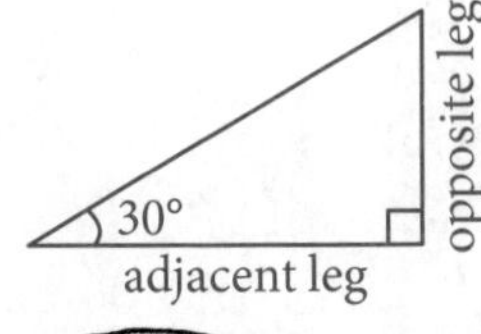

Enter 30 into the calculator.

Press TAN.

Press = (if necessary).

The calculator will display the tangent of a 30° angle: 0.577350269, which rounds to 0.58.

On some calculators, you will need to press TAN and *then* enter the angle size.

The tangent of a particular angle size will always be the same. After all, *all* right triangles with another angle the same measurement will be similar . . . making all of their corresponding sides proportional . . . making the ratio between the leg opposite an angle and the one adjacent to it the same!

Applying Tangents

We can use tangents to find missing information. Say we want to know the height of a building. We can find this using tangents. First, we would walk a short distance from the building, measuring how far we walk as we go.

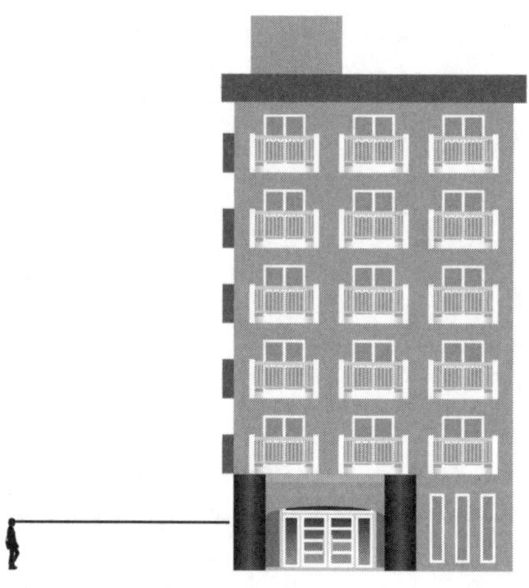

Notice that we can think of the distance between us and the building (i.e., the distance we just walked) as forming one leg of a right triangle, with the building forming the other leg.

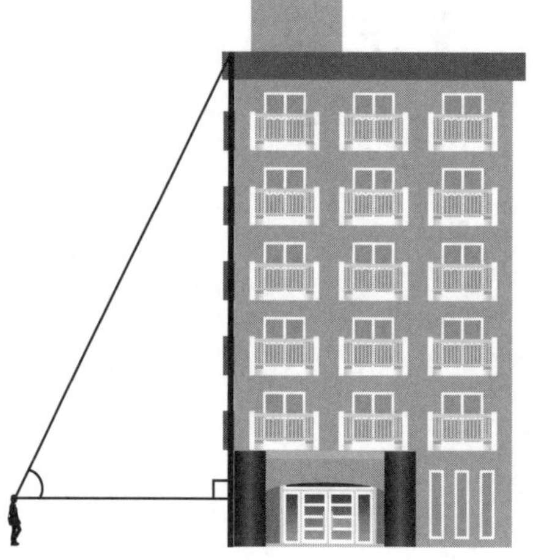

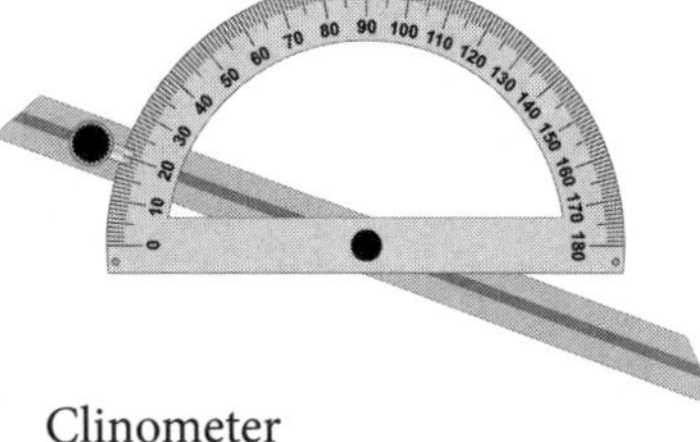

Clinometer

We can measure the angle from where we're standing to the top of the building using a clinometer (a specialized protractor). The height of the building would then be the length of the leg opposite the angle we measured plus the distance from where we measured the angle to the ground (a distance we can easily measure).

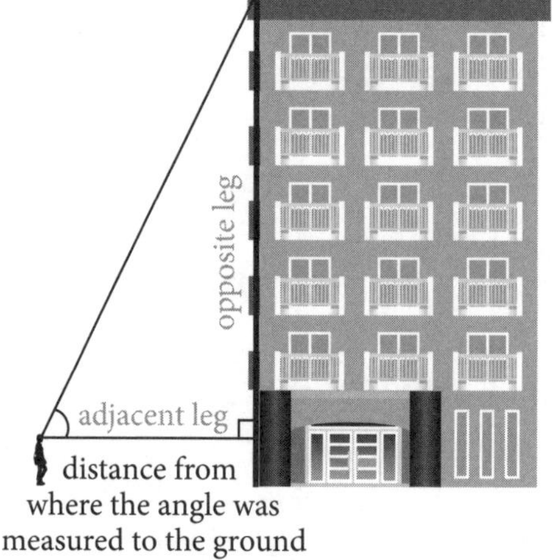

height of building = opposite leg + distance from where the angle was measured to the ground

We can now use what we know about tangents to find the length of the opposite leg, add it to the distance from where the angle was measured to the ground, and thus find the approximate height of the building.

Example: If the angle between a man's eyelevel and the top of the building is 65°, the distance between him and the building is 20 ft, and the distance from his eyelevel to the ground is 5 ft, approximately how tall is the building?

Let's start by looking at the information we know. We'll write the dimensions we've been given on top of the picture.

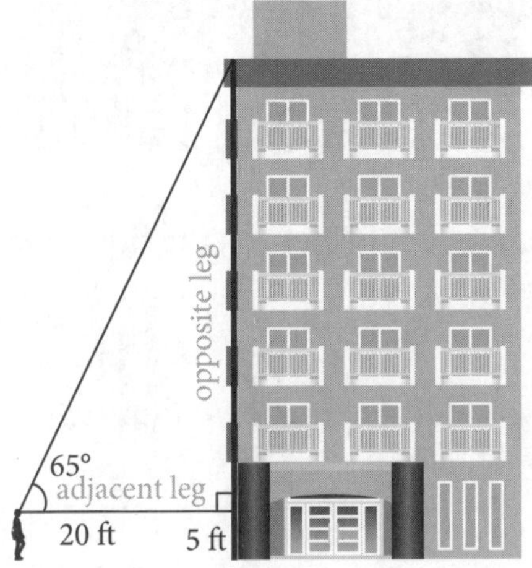

What else do we know? Well, we know that the tangent equals the opposite leg over the adjacent leg.

$$\textit{tangent of an angle} = \frac{\textit{opposite leg}}{\textit{adjacent leg}}$$

Now since we know the length of the adjacent leg and the angle measurement, let's substitute those values into the equation.

$$\textit{tangent of } \mathbf{65°} = \frac{\textit{opposite leg}}{\mathbf{20\ ft}}$$

We also know that we can find the tangent of 65° on a calculator.

$$\textit{tangent of } 65° = 2.144506921$$

So we could substitute 2.144506921 for the tangent of 65°.

$$\mathbf{2.144506921} = \frac{\textit{opposite leg}}{20\text{ ft}}$$

Now we can find the length of the opposite leg by isolating it on one side of the equation. We'll do this by multiplying *both sides* by 20 ft.

$$\mathbf{20\ ft} \bullet 2.144506921 = \frac{\textit{opposite leg}}{20\text{ ft}} \bullet \mathbf{20\ ft}$$

$$\mathbf{42.89\ ft} = \textit{opposite leg}$$

The opposite leg of the triangle rounds to 42.89 ft. Now we need only to add this height to 5 ft (the man's eyelevel to the ground) to find the approximate height of the building.

$$\textit{height of building} = \mathbf{42.89\ ft + 5\ ft}$$

$$\textit{height of building} = \mathbf{47.89\ ft}$$

The building is approximately 48 ft high.

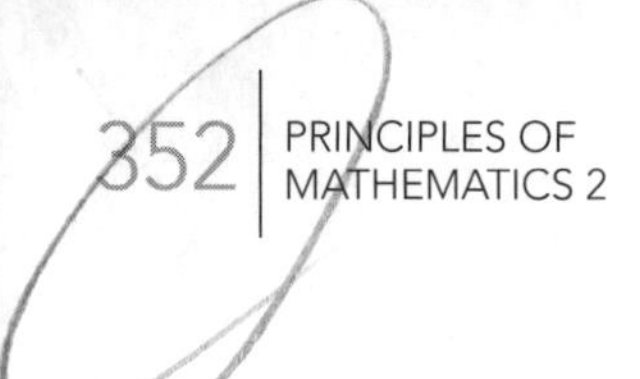

Keeping Perspective

From helping us find the height of a building to many other applications you'll encounter as you learn more math and physics, understanding tangents proves useful. As you familiarize yourself with finding the ratio between the opposite and adjacent leg in right triangles and apply this knowledge to solve problems, remember to praise God for the very ability to do so.

18.3 Sines and Cosines: More Ratios in Right Triangles

In the last lesson, we learned that we call the ratio between the side opposite either of the non-right angles in a right triangle and the side next to it the *tangent* of that angle.

In this lesson, it's time to learn about two additional ratios within right triangles: *sines* and *cosines.*

Understanding Sines

In a right triangle, we call the ratio between the leg opposite an angle and the hypotenuse the **sine** of that angle.

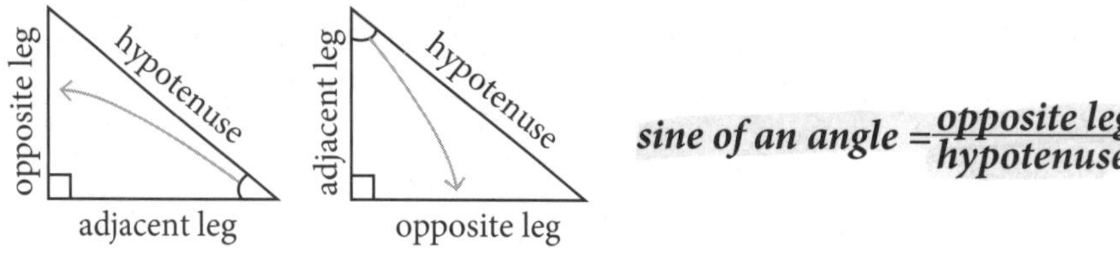

As was the case with tangents, the sine will always be the same for a specific angle measurement. Notice in the following example that for each 40° angle, the sine is the same.

$$\textit{sine of } 40° = \frac{\textit{leg opposite the } 40° \textit{ angle}}{\textit{hypotenuse}}$$

Note that the triangles shown here are the same triangles we found the tangents of in the last lesson. We could have just as easily found the sine for a different set of similar triangles, but we chose the same triangles for illustration purposes.

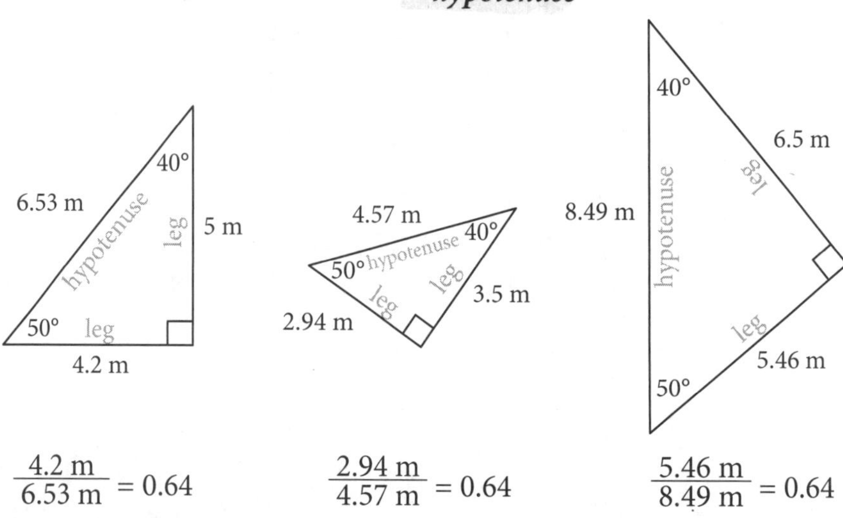

$$\frac{4.2 \text{ m}}{6.53 \text{ m}} = 0.64 \qquad \frac{2.94 \text{ m}}{4.57 \text{ m}} = 0.64 \qquad \frac{5.46 \text{ m}}{8.49 \text{ m}} = 0.64$$

As with tangents, we can let a calculator calculate sines for us. For example, rather than manually computing it, we could have used a calculator to find the sine of 40°. After all, every 40° angle in a right triangle will have the same ratio between the opposite side and the hypotenuse, as every right triangle with a 40° angle is similar, and similar triangles have proportional sides.

Example: Find the sine of a 40° angle.

Enter 40 into the calculator.

Press SIN.

Press = (if necessary).

The calculator will display the sine of a 40° angle: 0.64278761, which rounds to 0.64.

Notice that the calculator abbreviates "sine" as "SIN." "SIN" is a common abbreviation for sine; it only takes three letters to write instead of four. "SIN" is still read as "sine" (with a long i). Also notice that we got a more precise value for sine on the calculator — we could have obtained this more precise value without a calculator too if the measurements for the triangles hadn't been rounded. *Note: On some calculators, you will need to press* SIN *and then enter the angle size.*

Understanding Cosines

In a right triangle, we call the ratio between the leg adjacent to an angle in a right triangle and the hypotenuse the **cosine** of that angle.

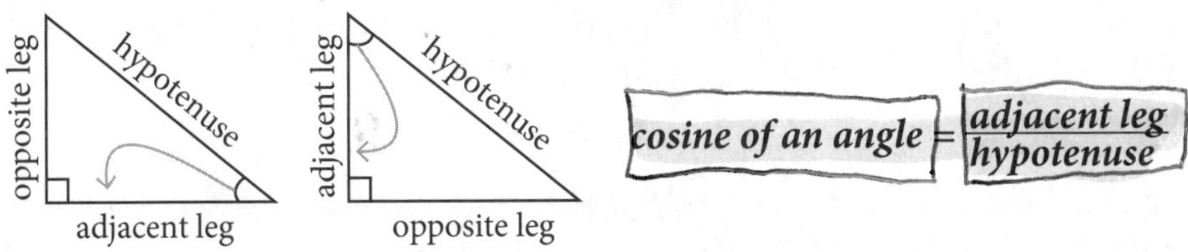

As with tangents and sines, the cosine will always be the same for a specific angle measurement, as all right triangles with an angle that specific angle measurement are similar, meaning their sides are proportional.

$$\textit{cosine of } 40° = \frac{\textit{leg adjacent the } 40° \textit{ angle}}{\textit{hypotenuse}}$$

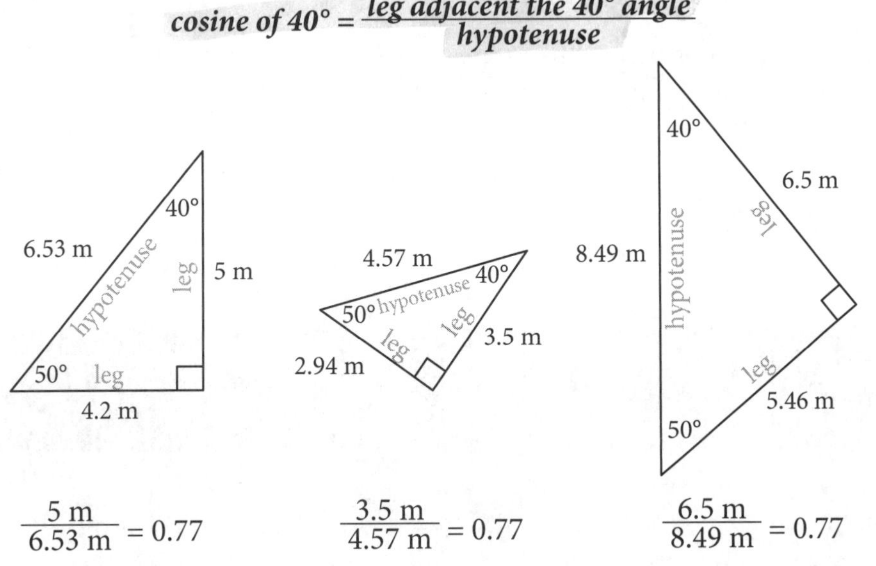

$\frac{5 \text{ m}}{6.53 \text{ m}} = 0.77$ $\frac{3.5 \text{ m}}{4.57 \text{ m}} = 0.77$ $\frac{6.5 \text{ m}}{8.49 \text{ m}} = 0.77$

Again, these triangles have rounded dimensions and thus the sines and cosines would vary a little if we were to calculate them to beyond the hundredths place. If the triangle's measurements had not been rounded, the ratios would be precisely the same no matter how many places we calculated them to.

As with tangents and sines, we can let a calculator calculate cosines for us. For example, rather than computing the cosines of the 40° angle manually like we did above, we could have used a calculator.

COS is an abbreviation for cosine. *Note: On some calculators, you will need to press* COS *and then enter the angle size.*

Example: Find the cosine of a 40° angle.

Enter 40 into the calculator.

Press COS.

Press = (if necessary).

The calculator will display the sine of a 40° angle: 0.766044443, which rounds to 0.77.

Ratios in Right Triangles

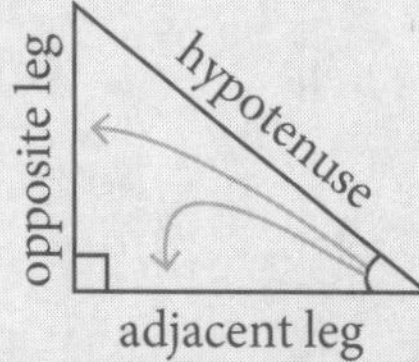

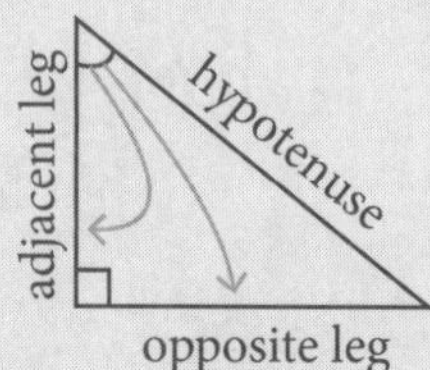

Tangent of an angle — The ratio between the opposite and adjacent leg of either non-right angle in a right triangle.

$$\textit{tangent of an angle} = \frac{\textit{opposite leg}}{\textit{adjacent leg}}$$

Sine of an angle — The ratio between the opposite leg of either non-right angle in a right triangle and the hypotenuse.

$$\textit{sine of an angle} = \frac{\textit{opposite leg}}{\textit{hypotenuse}}$$

Cosine of an angle — The ratio between the adjacent leg of either non-right angle in a right triangle and the hypotenuse.

$$\textit{cosine of an angle} = \frac{\textit{adjacent leg}}{\textit{hypotenuse}}$$

Keeping Perspective

While sine and cosine may not appear that important initially, their applications when coupled with more advanced math concepts are incredible. While you'll have to wait for some of their usefulness until more advanced math courses, know that they help us record sounds, aim a cannon, describe the position of stars, develop GPS navigation, and much more.

18.4 Representing Trigonometric Functions (Function Notation)

As you have hopefully noticed, in math we try to cut down on writing. The more concisely we can represent quantities and relationships, the easier they are to work with (once we master the "language," so to speak). Not surprisingly, then, there's a notation for representing tangents, sines, and cosines more concisely.

Understanding Function Notation

We've seen that the tangent of a 40° angle will be the same (0.84) for any size right triangle. Likewise, we've seen that the sine of a 40° angle will be the same (0.64) for any size right triangle, and the cosine of a 40° angle will be the same (0.77) for any size right triangle. No matter what angle measurement we pick as the "input," we get one "output" for each of the three ratios (tangent, sine, and cosine).

Thus we can view tangent, sine, and cosine as a *function of* the angle measurement. In fact, tangent, sine, and cosine are often referred to as **trigonometric functions**.

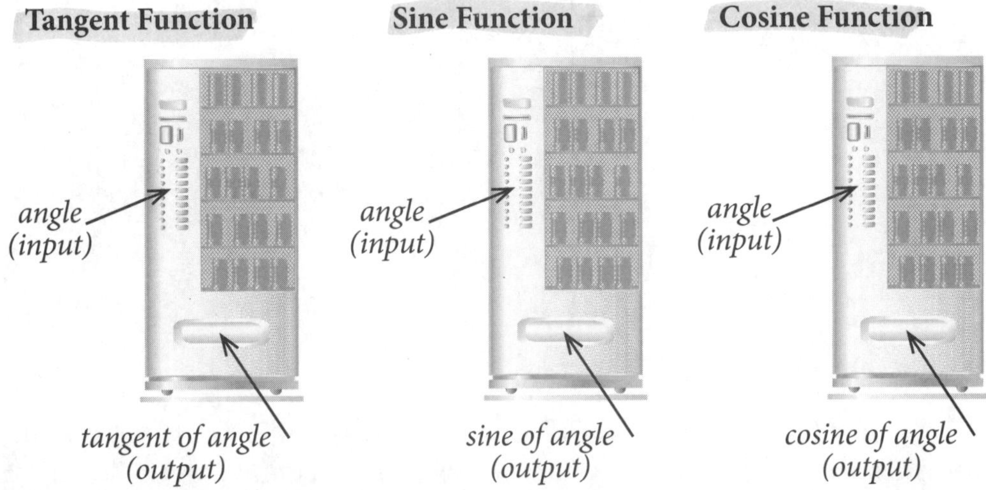

Thus, rather than writing "the sine of 40°" it's common to use a notation that's commonly used with functions. In this notation — called **function notation** — we shorten "sine of 40°" to "sin(40°)".

Notice that in this notation, **the parentheses do *not* mean multiplication**. Instead, they enclose the input to the function — in this case, the angle size. Writing "sin(40°)" is a compact way of indicating the output of the sine function for an input of 40°.

It's common to follow the same notation with tangents and cosines as well, using three-letter abbreviations and parentheses to enclose the angle measurement for which we want to find the sine, cosine, or tangent.

the sine of 40° = sin(40°)

the cosine of 40° = cos(40°)

the tangent of 40° = tan(40°)

Function Notation

name of function(input to function)

What's the Use?

For another glimpse into trigonometry's applications, here's a quick example of how trigonometry helps us describe relationships on coordinate graphs.

Take a look at the coordinate graph below.

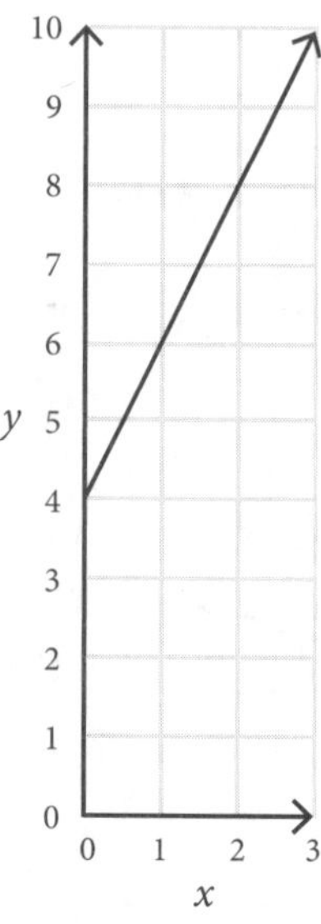

As you know, the slope of a line can be found by dividing the vertical change by the horizontal change. Notice, though, that we can think of the vertical change and the horizontal change as two sides of a right triangle. When we divide the vertical change by the horizontal change, we're really finding the tangent of an angle!

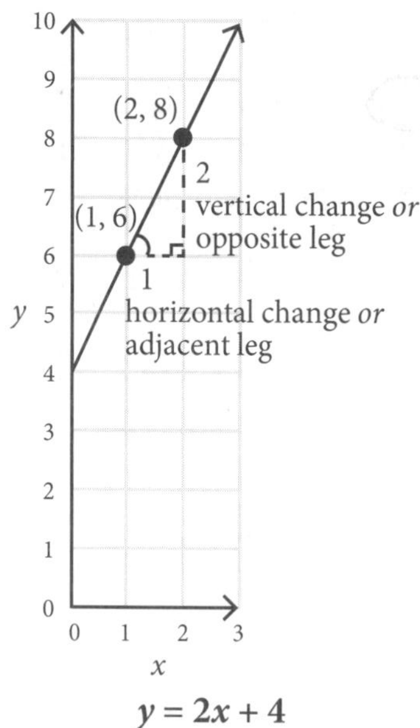

$y = 2x + 4$

$$slope = \frac{\text{change in vertical coordinates}}{\text{change in horizontal coordinates}}$$

$$slope = \frac{8 - 6}{2 - 1} = \frac{2}{1} = 2$$

$$tangent = \frac{\text{opposite leg}}{\text{adjacent leg}}$$

$$\tan = \frac{2}{1} = 2$$

$$\tan(63.43°) = 2$$

Any guesses what the graph above could represent? How about the distance over time at a speed of 2 $\frac{\text{mi}}{\text{hr}}$ and a starting distance of 4 miles…or the number of pages you read a day if you start reading 4 pages a day and then increase by 2 pages each day. Always remember that the skills you're learning apply!

Different branches of math overlap, and as you continue learning math, you'll find yourself using trigonometry coupled with other branches to help you explore a variety of real-life mathematical relationships.

Keeping Perspective

Think of function notation as you would think of a language. A language may initially seem confusing to learn, as you're representing concepts differently. But don't forget that you're representing the same concepts! Ultimately, whether we write "the sine of 40°" or sin(40°), we're representing the same relationship. And, because of God's faithfulness in holding all things together, those relationships — however we write them — help describe God's creation and serve as a real-life tool we can use to serve Him.

18.5 Chapter Synopsis and Sound Waves

Here are few key details to remember from our brief glimpse at trigonometry:

- If two sets of corresponding angles in two triangles are congruent, the triangles have to be similar. This is expressed in the **AA similarity theorem**.
- We have names for the different ratios within right triangles.

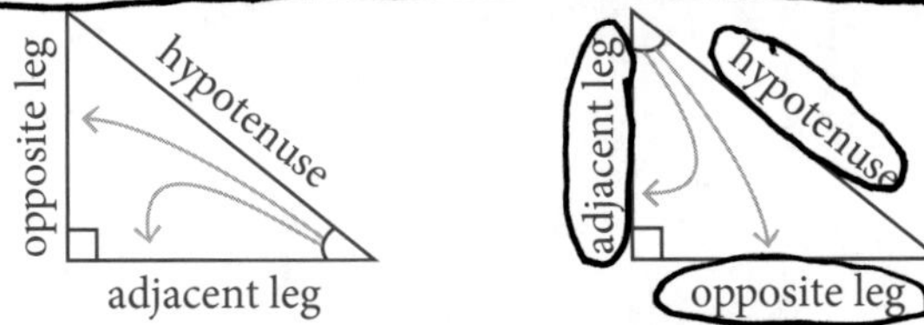

Tangent of an angle — The ratio between the opposite and adjacent leg of either non-right angle in a right triangle.

$$\textit{tangent of an angle} = \frac{\textbf{opposite leg}}{\textbf{adjacent leg}}$$

Sine of an angle — The ratio between the opposite leg of either non-right angle in a right triangle and the hypotenuse.

$$\textit{sine of an angle} = \frac{\textbf{opposite leg}}{\textbf{hypotenuse}}$$

Cosine of an angle— The ratio between the adjacent leg of either non-right angle in a right triangle and the hypotenuse.

$$\textit{cosine of an angle} = \frac{\textbf{adjacent leg}}{\textbf{hypotenuse}}$$

- **The tangent, sine, and cosine are all functions of the angle measurement.** Because there is only one value for each angle measurement (i.e., one output for every input), we can use a calculator to compute the answer for us.
- It's helpful to write trigonometric functions using **function notation**. Function notation is a helpful shorthand way of representing functions. In it, we put the function name next to parentheses containing the input to the function.

  sine of 50° = sin(50°)

  cosine of 50° = cos(50°)

  tangent of 50° = tan(50°)

Let's end our quick look at trigonometry taking a tiny peek at how trigonometry helps us describe sounds.

Sound Waves

Just as we graph other functions, we can graph sines, cosines, and tangents too! When we graph $y = 2x$, we're looking at how y (the output) changes based on the values we use for x (the input). We're looking to see the general relationship, rather than to find one particular answer.

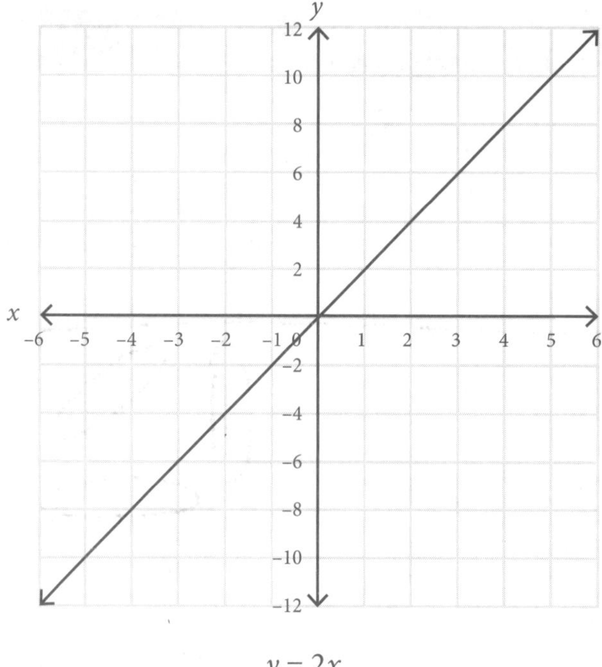

$y = 2x$

Likewise, a graph of a sine shows how the sine value (the output) changes based on the angle measurement (the input) — that is, it gives us a picture of the general relationship between the sine value and the measurement of the angle.

Let's think about what happens to the sine as the measurement of the angle changes. When the angle's measurement is close to 0°, the opposite leg is much smaller than the hypotenuse.

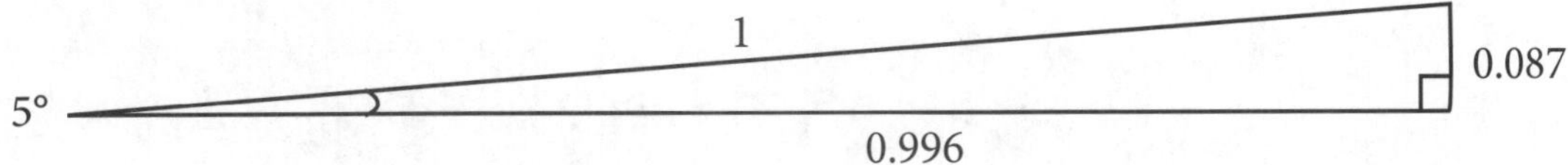

Thus, the sine will be very small, since the sine is found by dividing the opposite side over the hypotenuse. The closer the angle measurement gets to 0°, the closer the sine will get to 0 too, as we'll end up with a very small value when we divide the opposite leg by the hypotenuse.

We've rounded the dimensions in the triangles shown (and thus the resulting sines) to the nearest thousandths.

$$\textit{sine of an angle} = \frac{\textit{opposite leg}}{\textit{hypotenuse}}$$

$$\sin(5°) = \frac{0.087}{1} = 0.087$$

On the other hand, as the angle measurement gets closer to 90°, the opposite leg will get closer and closer to the same length as the hypotenuse. So the closer to 90° the angle we're finding the sine of gets, the closer the sine of the angle will be to 1.

85°
1
0.087
0.996

$$\textit{sine of an angle} = \frac{\textit{opposite leg}}{\textit{hypotenuse}}$$

$$\sin(85°) = \frac{0.996}{1} = 0.996$$

If we were to graph the values of the sine for every angle measurement from 0° to 90°, we'd end up with a graph that looks like this:

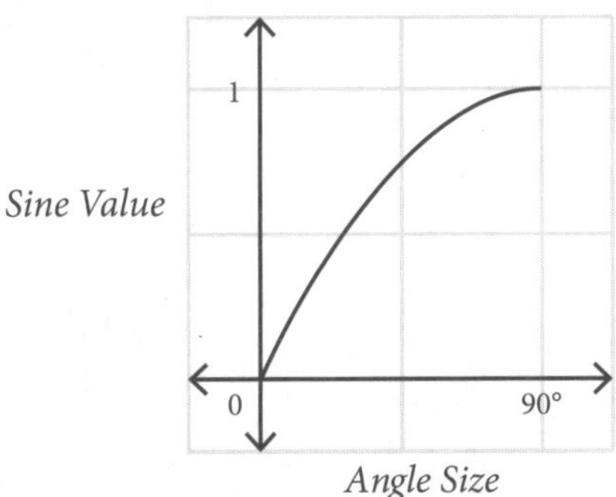

Notice how the graph makes it easy to see the changes in the sine (i.e., the ratio between the opposite and hypotenuse sides) as the angle measurement changes. The graph, though, stops at 90°. This is because in an actual right triangle, our angles have to be less than 90°, as we already have a 90° angle (it's a right triangle), and the sum of all the angles equals 180°. However, in order to graph sounds and use sines to explore other aspects of God's creation, we need to be able to define the value of sine for other angle sizes too. And we can. How? By looking at a triangle on a unit circle.

A unit circle is a circle with a radius one unit long. To make it easy to measure distances, we'll draw the unit circle on top of a horizontal and vertical axis. We'll also label degrees going around the circle.

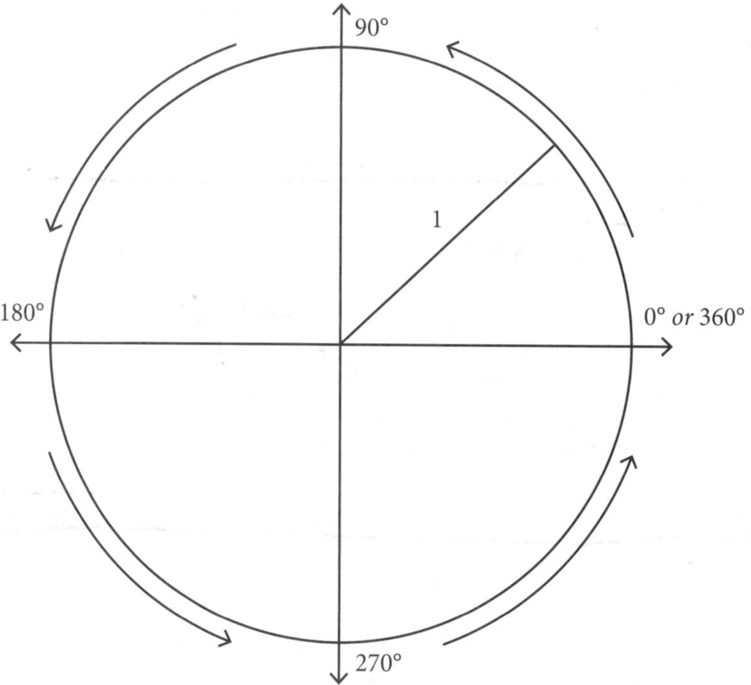

We can form a right triangle with the radius as the hypotenuse at any point along the circle (four examples are shown in the following circle). In each case, the triangle will have a hypotenuse of 1 (the radius), but the ratio between the opposite leg and the hypotenuse will change in order to form a right triangle.

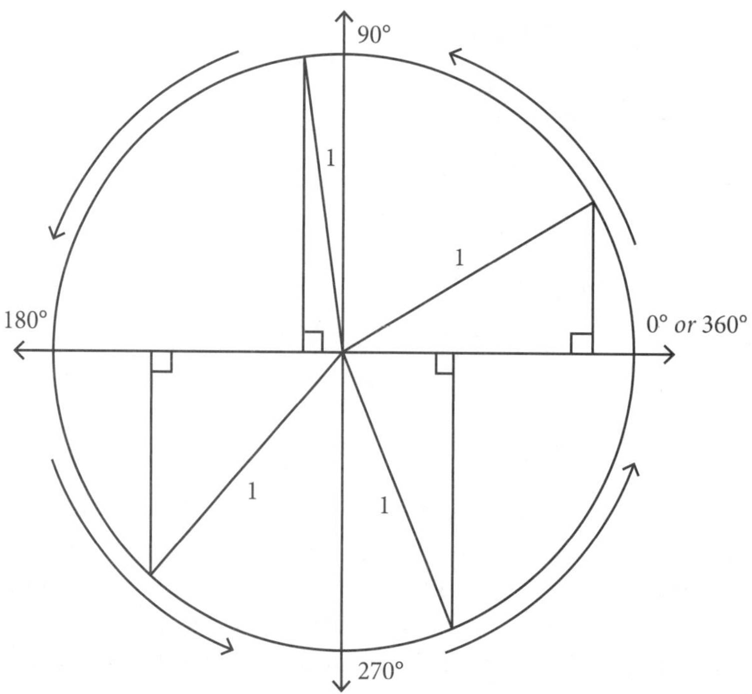

So how does this help us find the sine value for additional angle sizes? Well, notice that while the marked angle in the following triangle is only 45°, on the circle its hypotenuse is located 135° from 0°. So we'll define the sine of 135° as being the ratio between the opposite leg and the hypotenuse of this triangle.

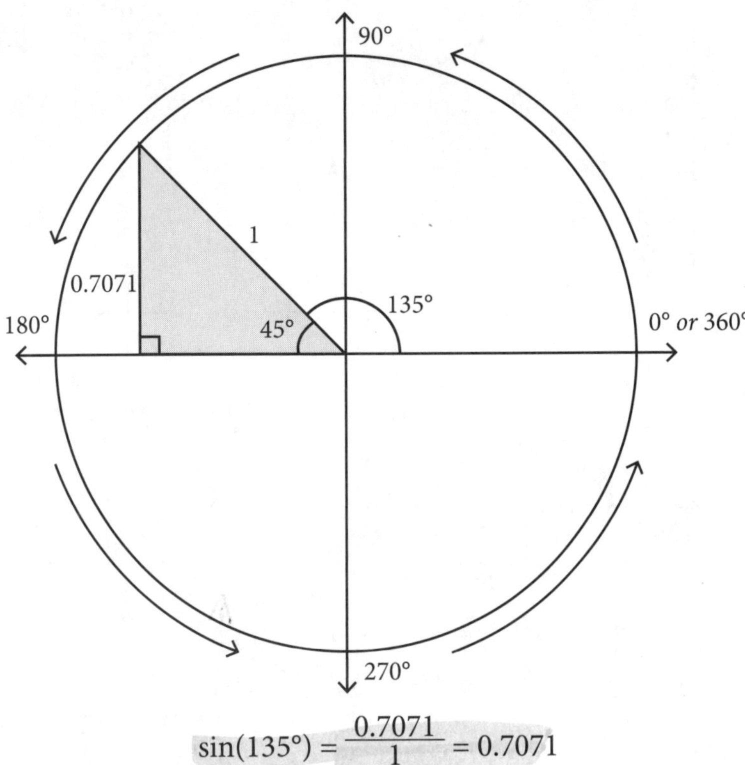

$$\sin(135°) = \frac{0.7071}{1} = 0.7071$$

We'll also view leg lengths under the horizontal axis as negative, resulting in negative signs for certain angle sizes.

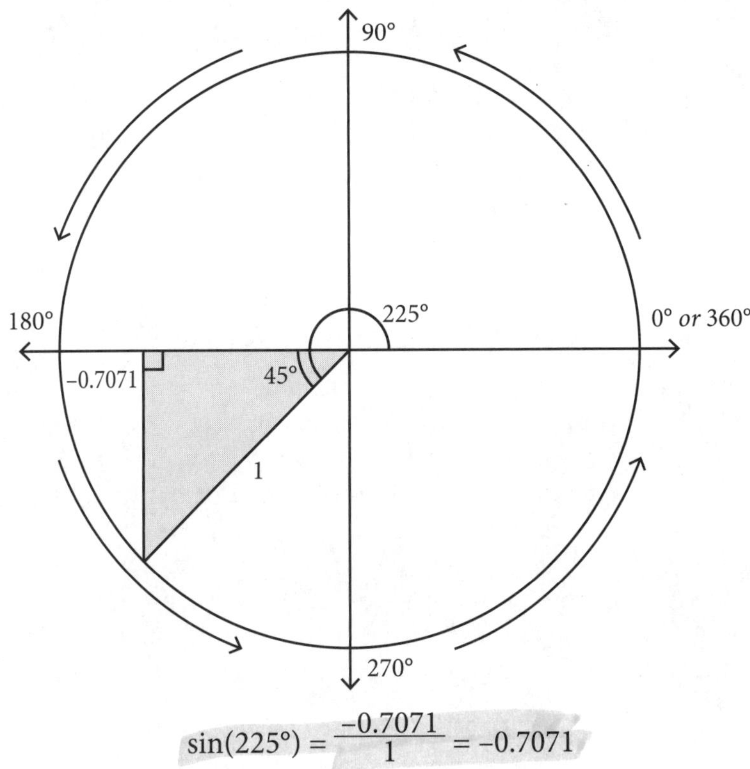

$$\sin(225°) = \frac{-0.7071}{1} = -0.7071$$

Understanding triangles on unit circles is not something you need to understand the mechanics of until more advanced math courses (in fact, there are some other math concepts you need to learn first to fully grasp it).[3] This very general overview is included here simply to give you a taste of how trigonometry helps us describe God's creation.

If we were to graph how the value of sine changes as the angle size changes for additional angle sizes pictured on a unit circle, we'd end up with this graph:

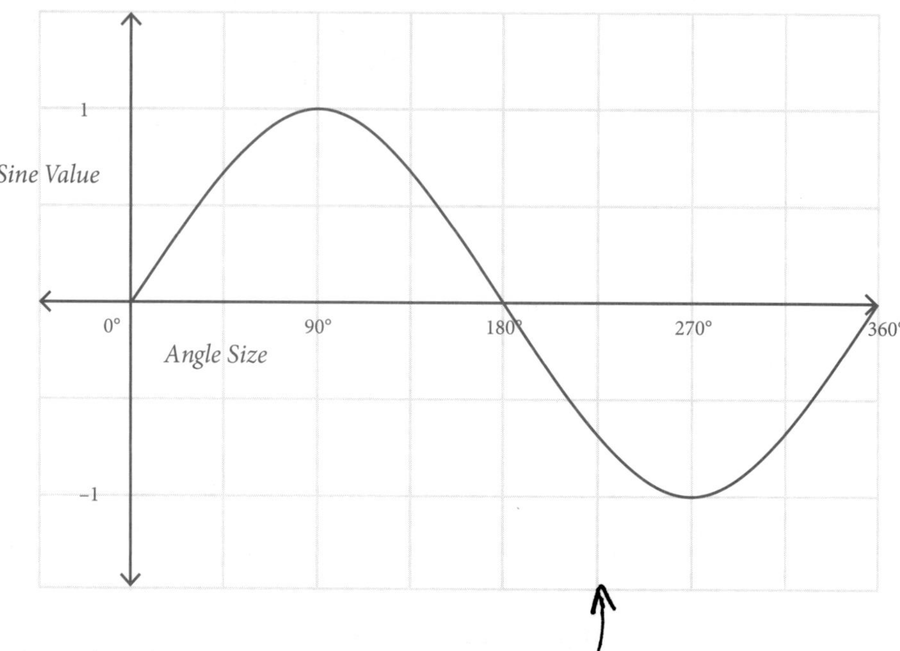

It turns out that this wave-like movement, called a sine wave, proves incredibly useful, as sounds, light, and other aspects of creation travel in this repetitive wave-like pattern. Even though we wouldn't think of these aspects of creation as triangles, we *can* think of them as sine waves . . . and then indirectly use sines to describe them mathematically!

Why would we want to describe sounds mathematically? Well, one reason is that describing sounds mathematically allows us to reproduce sounds digitally.

While the math behind recording sounds is beyond the scope of this course, know that every time you watch a movie or listen to recorded music you're benefiting from the exploration of God's creation using math (including sines) . . . an exploration made possible because of the incredible order, design, and consistency God created and sustains.

Your Ears — Marvels of Engineering

While a sine wave represents a simple sound, most sounds are quite complicated and are represented as the addition of multiple sine waves. While it takes advanced computations to break down these complex sounds into their components in order to record them mathematically, scientists theorize that your ears do something similar using hairs in your inner ear.[4] The more we learn about math and use it to explore the world around us, the more we discover just how much God has given us that we take for granted, down to hairs in our ears that make hearing possible.

Now, I imagine you never anticipated triangles helping us describe sound, did you? I keep stressing this, but I'm not sure I can say it enough times: more advanced math concepts build on the basic tools, letting us describe at a deeper level the intricacies of God's creation. And the more we learn about God's creation, the more we're able to use that knowledge to develop useful tools.

> *O sing unto the LORD a new song: sing unto the LORD, all the earth. Sing unto the LORD, bless his name; shew forth his salvation from day to day. Declare his glory among the heathen, his wonders among all people. For the LORD is great, and greatly to be praised: he is to be feared above all gods (Psalm 96:1–4).*

Abigail
Huld -anne

Sets, Sequences, Symbols, and Unknowns

19.1 Sets and Symbols

While you're likely pretty familiar with sets and sequences already, it's time to take a closer look at these concepts.

Reviewing Sets

Let's start with a quick review of the basics. As we discussed in Book 1, a **set** is any collection — be that a collection of clothes, recipes, tools, books, numbers, or anything else. Sets can be random or based on one or more specific characteristics. For example, we could randomly choose a handful of numbers and call them a set, or we could view all numbers divisible by 5 as a set. A set can be thought of as a grouping.

If we have a set within a set, we have what we call a **subset**. Every member of a subset is also a member of the main set, but not every member of the main set is necessarily a member of the subset. For example, we could think of the set of all red shirts as a subset underneath the set of all shirts — all red shirts are also shirts, but all shirts are not necessarily red.

We often use Venn diagrams to show how different sets, or collections, relate together. The Venn diagram below shows how the set "Red Shirts" is a subset of the set "Shirts."

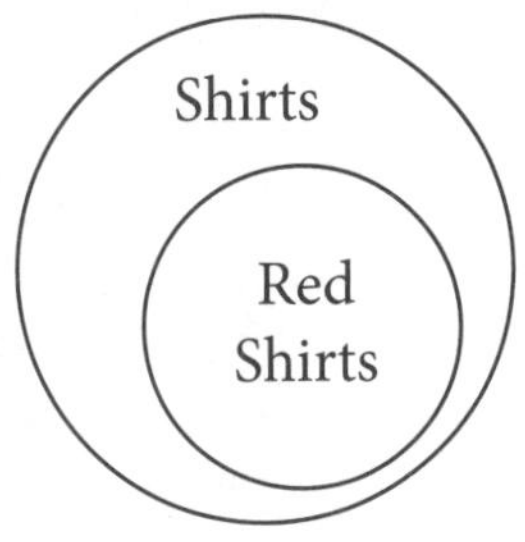

New Term and Symbol

We would call every shirt an element of the set of "Shirts," and every red shirt is also an element of the set of "Red Shirts." An **element** is "an entity that is a single member of a set."[1]

We also have a symbol to show that something is an *element of* a set: ∈. "my favorite shirt ∈ Shirts" means that the shirt we're referring to as "my favorite shirt" is an *element of* the set "Shirts."

Because sets are used extensively in math, there are whole notational conventions regarding how to express them mathematically.

One way to express a set is to use curly braces { }. For example, we could represent a set containing all shirts like this:

{shirts}

And we could represent the set of all shirts and pants like this:

{shirts, pants}

And a set of integers greater than 10 like this:

{11, 12, 13, . . .}

Keeping this in mind, it's time to combine the concept of sets with what we've learned about using letters as placeholders.

Letters for Sets

As we've seen, much of math is a naming process. Adam used names to name the animals back in the Garden of Eden; in math, we use symbols (numerals, letters, etc.) to name the quantities and consistencies around us.

This naming process includes sets. In Book 1, we used words to describe sets of quantities. For instance, we might call the set of all shirts "Shirts."

But rather than naming sets with words, we can name sets with *letters*. Just as we use letters to represent unknowns, we could also use letters to represent *sets*. For example, we could call the set of all shirts *S* and the set of red shirts *R*.

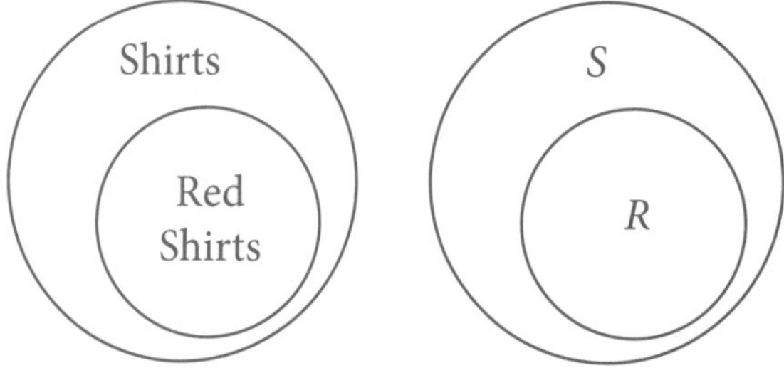

The letter *S* is much shorter to write than "Shirts," and the letter *R* is more concise than "Red Shirts." Using letters to name sets makes it easier to work with problems involving sets, just as using letters as placeholders for unknowns makes it easier to work with problems involving unknowns.

Convention Time

You might wonder why we used S and R instead of s and r. We could have used either; however, in general, mathematicians use a capital letter to stand for an entire set, and a lowercase letter to stand for any member of that set. In this convention, we'd use S to refer to the set of all shirts, and s to refer to a specific shirt. This convention, though, is not followed universally. Always keep in mind that math is a tool — while the underlying consistencies are absolute, the way we describe them can be modified as needed.

Keeping Perspective

The main thing to take away is that we can use letters to stand for sets. We're once again combining mathematical tools in order to describe and explore God's creation.

19.2 Sets and Possible Values

We can think of every variable as having a *set* of possible values.

In $x = 2$, if we were to think of all the values x could be as a set, or collection, that set would only contain one value: 2.

In $x > 2$, if we were to think of all the values x could be as a set, or collection, that set would contain multiple values: every number greater than 2.

In $d = (40\ \frac{\text{mi}}{\text{hr}})t$, where $0\text{ hr} \leq t \leq 5\text{ hr}$, the set of values t can be contains all the values greater than or equal to 0 hr but less than or equal to 5 hr.

In the last lesson, we learned about using the symbol $\in$ to indicate an *element of* a set. Now let's look at how we can use it to help us specify the set of values a variable can be.

Specifying a Set

Let's say that we were laying out a garden, and we need the width to be 8 ft, 10 ft, or 12 ft. We've also decided that the length needed to be 8 ft. We want to see what the area would be at different sizes. We'd have this equation:

$$A = (8\text{ ft})w, \text{ where } w \in \{8\text{ ft}, 10\text{ ft}, 12\text{ ft}\}$$

Notice how we used the $\in$ sign to show that w must be 8 ft, 10 ft, or 12 ft. That is, w must be an *element of* the set {8 ft, 10 ft, 12 ft}.

Specifying a Number Set

It's sometimes helpful to specify the *type of number* a variable can be. For example, suppose we wanted to graph the relationship between the number of ounces of luncheon meat and the number of people attending an event if we need 5 ounces per attendee. We'd have this relationship:

$$y = 5x$$

Now, it wouldn't really make sense for x (the number of attendees) to be less than 0 or to be a fractional amount. After all, a fractional amount of people doesn't make sense. While we could write "where x is any non-fractional value greater than 0," that's pretty cumbersome to write. In math, we try to think of ways to simplify as much as possible. As we saw in Lesson 2.4, we can use a term to refer to the set of all "non-fractional value greater than 0." We refer to that set, or collection, of numbers as "Whole Numbers" or "Natural Numbers."

When working with sets, it's common to use the term *natural numbers* instead of *whole numbers*.

$$y = 5x, \text{ where } x \text{ is any natural number}$$

However, there's a way to communicate natural numbers even more simply. Rather than using a term, we could simply use a symbol! It's common to use an ℕ to refer to the *set* of all natural numbers.

$$y = 5x, \text{ where } x \in \mathbb{N}$$

Notice that using just two symbols — $\in \mathbb{N}$ — we've managed to communicate the idea that for this equation, x must be a non-fractional value greater than 0. That is, x must be an "element of" the set of all natural numbers.

Remember, **the symbol ∈ means "is an element of"** — it's a way of signifying that something is a member of a set. When we write $x \in \mathbb{N}$, we're saying that x must be an *element of* or a *member of* the set of all natural numbers.

Here are some common symbols used to represent different types of numbers:

ℚ = Rational Numbers

ℤ = Integers

ℕ = Natural Numbers

The symbols ℚ, ℤ, and ℕ, along with other symbols for types of numbers we're not covering here, help us quickly communicate the type of number a variable must be (i.e., they tell us of what set of numbers the variable must be a part of). Once you get used to them, the symbols save a lot of writing!

Keeping Perspective

As you study sets, don't get lost in the terms or symbols. You've been using the concept of sets for years. Sets are simply collections. Whenever you organize, you unconsciously sort things into sets. Perhaps you organize your books by fiction or nonfiction. In that case, you could think of all your books as being divided into the sets of "Fiction" and "Nonfiction." If instead you divided your books into books that you've read versus books to be read, you'd have the sets "Read" and "Not Read." If you randomly put your books on the shelves, then your sets might be random collections of "Shelf 1" and "Shelf 2."

Just as we can think of collections of books as sets, we can think of possible solutions to problems as sets. We can also use symbols and terms to help us express those possible solutions more concisely.

Number sets, such as real numbers, whole numbers, etc., are ways of organizing numbers based on their properties, making it easy to refer to all numbers with specific properties. The symbols $\mathbb{Q}$, $\mathbb{Z}$, and $\mathbb{N}$ are agreed-upon shorthand for describing specific number sets, saving our fingers extra writing. These sets prove useful in describing the type of numbers we can handle in an equation. They're part of the language we use to describe God's creation.

19.3 Sequences and Unknowns

As we saw back in Book 1, **sequences** are simply "an ordered set of quantities."[2] In other words, they're a set in which the order matters.

Every time we skip count (i.e., count by 2s, 3s, 4s, etc.), we're really reciting a sequence. Some sequences, such as {2, 4, 6, . . .} have a pattern (each number is 2 greater than the one before it). Others, though, don't. For example, we could think of all of the digits of π as a sequence. The order matters, but there's no discernable pattern.

$$3.14159265358979323 84\ldots$$

While we're thinking of sequences as "an ordered set of *quantities*,"[3] in English, we use the term in a broader way too. For example, the sequence of events in a book is the order in which they happen.

We can use letters to help express the patterns in many sequences. For example, let's use f to stand for some unknown number. We'll make it the first number in a sequence.

$$f$$

Now let's say we want a sequence in which the next value is twice that first value, the third is three times it, the fourth is four times it, the fifth is five times it, and so forth. We could represent this easily.

$$f, 2 \bullet f, 3 \bullet f, 4 \bullet f, 5 \bullet f, \ldots$$

If we omit the multiplication signs, since we don't really need them to show the multiplication, the sequence looks like this:

$$f, 2f, 3f, 4f, 5f, \ldots$$

We've now described all sequences that start with one value, then have an element 2 times that value, then an element 3 times that value, etc.

Example: Find the first five values of the sequence $\{f, 2f, 3f, 4f, 5f, \ldots\}$ when f is 10.

All we have to do is substitute 10 for f and then complete the multiplications.

Substitute 10 for f:

$\{f, 2f, 3f, 4f, 5f, \ldots\}$

$\{\mathbf{10}, 2(\mathbf{10}), 3(\mathbf{10}), 4(\mathbf{10}), 5(\mathbf{10}), \ldots\}$

Complete the multiplication:

$\{10, \mathbf{20}, \mathbf{30}, \mathbf{40}, \mathbf{50}, \ldots\}$

We've now found the values for this sequence when f is 10.

Example: Find the first five values of the sequence $\{f, 2f, 3f, 4f, 5f, \ldots\}$ when f is 2.

All we have to do is substitute 2 for f and then complete the multiplications.

Substitute 2 for f:

$\{f, 2f, 3f, 4f, 5f, \ldots\}$

$\{\mathbf{2}, 2(\mathbf{2}), 3(\mathbf{2}), 4(\mathbf{2}), 5(\mathbf{2}), \ldots\}$

Complete the multiplication:

$\{2, \mathbf{4}, \mathbf{6}, \mathbf{8}, \mathbf{10}, \ldots\}$

We've now found the values for this sequence when f is 2.

Notice that the sequence $\{f, 2f, 3f, 4f, 5f, \ldots\}$ can be used to describe skip counting. In the first example, when f was 10, the sequence became 10, 20, 30, 40, 50, etc. — i.e., counting by 10s. In the second example, when f was 2, the sequence became 2, 4, 6, 8, 10, etc. — i.e., counting by 2s.

Not only does the sequence $\{f, 2f, 3f, 4f, 5f, \ldots\}$ describe skip counting, but it also describes an amazing order God has placed within many sounds. Without going into lots of detail, one of the attributes of sound that we can measure is its frequency. (The frequency of a sound determines how high or low of a pitch we hear.) We measure the frequency of sounds in a unit called Hertz, which is abbreviated Hz.

Now, each note played on an instrument (or sung) has a main sound you hear, as well as subtler sounds, called partials or overtones. The main sound and each of the overtones are all at different frequencies.

If we use the frequency of the main sound as f in the sequence $\{f, 2f, 3f, 4f, 5f, \ldots\}$, we can find the approximate measurements of the frequency of the overtones on all instruments that produce what we call harmonics. While the volume (or more properly, amplitude) of the overtones will vary based on the instrument, the frequency of the overtones will correspond to the next elements in the sequence!

Example: The main sound of the second lowest E on the piano is at 82.41 Hz (when rounded to the tenths place). Find the approximate frequency of the first 4 overtones.

Substitute 82.41Hz for f:

$\{f, 2f, 3f, 4f, 5f, \ldots\}$

{**82.41 Hz**, 2(**82.41 Hz**), 3(**82.41 Hz**), 4(**82.41 Hz**), 5(**82.41 Hz**), . . .}

Complete the multiplication:

{82.41 Hz, **164.82 Hz, 247.23 Hz, 329.64 Hz, 412.05 Hz, . . .**}

The first four overtones are at frequencies of approximately 164.82 Hz, 247.23 Hz, 329.64 Hz, and 412.05 Hz.

Pretty cool, huh? Well, it gets even cooler. The frequencies of the overtones in notes correspond with the frequencies of the main sounds of other notes. By examining the frequencies, we can see mathematically what notes tend to sound pleasing together! Math helps us understand the order God has placed within sound.[4]

Keeping Perspective

As you review sequences and learn to express them with letters, remember that sequences are a way of describing a set in which the order matters. Once again, we're combining math tools in order to dig deeper into the order and design our amazing God has placed all around us — including the very sounds that reach our ears.

19.4 Arithmetic and Geometric Sequences

The terms *arithmetic sequences* and *geometric sequences* help us easily refer to sequences with different properties. Much as it's easier to say "bowl" than it is to describe the characteristics of a bowl every time we refer to one, it's easier to say "arithmetic sequence" or "geometric sequence" than it is to describe the characteristics of these sequences.

In this lesson, we're going to take a look at both arithmetic sequences and geometric sequences. While the terms may be new, you've encountered both of these types of sequences many times. Let's take a look.

Arithmetic Sequences

Arithmetic sequences have what we call a **common difference**. For example, in {2, 4, 6, 8, 10, . . .} each number is 2 plus the previous number. We would say the common difference is 2.

Think about the name common difference for a moment. "Difference" is the term we used in subtraction to refer to the result of subtracting one number from another.

If you subtract any number in {2, 4, 6, 8, 10, . . .} from the one after it, you get . . . another drum roll please . . . 2! Truly, 2 is the common difference of this sequence.

$$10 - 8 = 2 \qquad 8 - 6 = 2 \qquad 6 - 4 = 2 \qquad 4 - 2 = 2$$

As another example, the sequence {*f*, 2*f*, 3*f*, 4*f*, 5*f*, . . .} has a common difference: *f*. If we were to subtract any number in {*f*, 2*f*, 3*f*, 4*f*, 5*f*, . . .} from the one after it, you get . . . another drum roll please . . . *f*!

$$5f - 4f = f \qquad 4f - 3f = f \qquad 3f - 2f = f \qquad 2f - f = f$$

Geometric Sequences

Geometric sequences have what we call a **common ratio**. For example, in {3, 9, 27, 81, 243, . . .} each number is 3 times the previous number. We would say the common ratio is 3, and that {3, 9, 27, 81, 243, . . .} is a geometric sequence.

Think about the name common *ratio* for a moment. We know a ratio is a comparison via division.

If you take the ratio between any element in the sequence shown and the element before it, you get . . . drum roll please . . . 3! Truly, 3 is the common ratio of this sequence.

$$\frac{243}{81} = 3 \qquad \frac{81}{27} = 3 \qquad \frac{27}{9} = 3 \qquad \frac{9}{3} = 3$$

As another example, the sequence {*f*, 5*f*, 25*f*, 125*f*, 625*f*, . . .} has a common ratio of 5. Even though we've used an *f* to stand for an unknown in the sequence, if we take the ratio between each element of the sequence by the element before it, we end up with 5. It doesn't matter what *f*'s value is — the ratio between each element of the sequence and the one before it will be 5.

$$\frac{{}^{5}\cancel{625}\cancel{f}}{\cancel{125}\cancel{f}} = 5 \qquad \frac{{}^{5}\cancel{125}\cancel{f}}{\cancel{25}\cancel{f}} = 5 \qquad \frac{5\cancel{f}}{\cancel{f}} = 5$$

Let's take a look at a geometric sequence in action. In the last lesson, we saw how {*f*, 2*f*, 3*f*, 4*f*, 5*f*,...} helps us describe the frequency of the main sound and overtones of instruments that produce harmonics. Well, there's a geometric sequence that helps us compare the frequency of main sounds with the frequency of *other main sounds that have the same letter names.*

If you're familiar with music, you know that we use letters to describe notes. All of the marked notes on this keyboard are Ds.

What you may not know, though, is that the frequencies of the main sounds in the notes with the same letter names (such as the main sounds of all the Ds) basically follow this geometric sequence: {*f*, 2*f*, 4*f*, 8*f*, 16*f*, . . .}, where *f* is the frequency of the main sound in the lowest note of the letter name.

Example: The lowest D on the piano has a frequency of 36.7 Hz (rounded to the nearest tenth). Find the approximate frequency of the next four Ds on the piano.

Substitute 36.7 for *f*:

{*f*, 2*f*, 4*f*, 8*f*, 16*f*, . . .}

{**36.7 Hz**, 2(**36.7 Hz**), 4(**36.7 Hz**), 8(**36.7 Hz**), 16(**36.7 Hz**), . . .}

Complete the multiplication:

{36.7 Hz, **73.4 Hz**, **146.8 Hz**, **293.6 Hz**, **587.2 Hz**, . . .}

The main sounds in the next four Ds will have frequencies of approximately 73.4 Hz, 146.8 Hz, 293.6 Hz, and 587.2 Hz.

The actual frequencies differ slightly from what is shown here due to rounding differences; keep in mind too that actual pianos won't always be in tune, so their frequencies will likely not be precise.

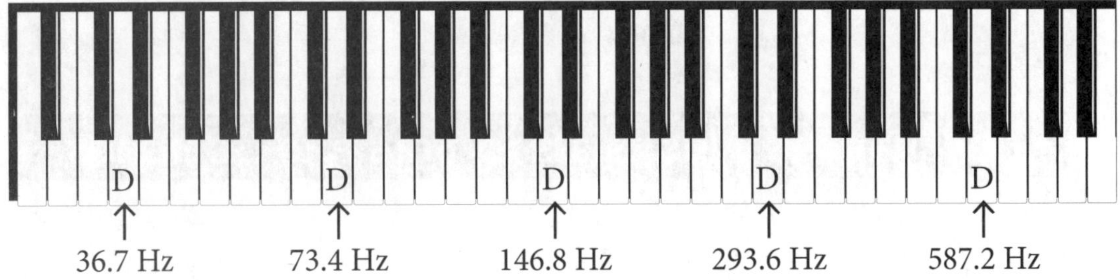

Whole books have been written about the mathematics of music. We use math to look at how notes relate together, the amplitude of overtones in different instruments, the acoustics of the room, how to record sounds, and ever so much more. God created sounds with a mind-boggling depth of richness to them.

Keeping Perspective

Sequences come in all sorts of different patterns. While we focused on **arithmetic** and **geometric sequences** in this lesson, since they're important terms to know, not all sequences are arithmetic or geometric. Sequences can also be **random** . . . or have different patterns!

For example, in {1, 3, 15, 17, 85}, the second element is 2 greater than the previous one (3 – 1 = 2), while the third is 5 times the previous element (3 • 5 = 15). Then the fourth is 2 greater than the previous element again (17 – 15 = 2), and the fifth is 5 times the previous (17 • 5 = 85). So this sequence appears to have a pattern . . . but it's not a completely arithmetic or geometric pattern.

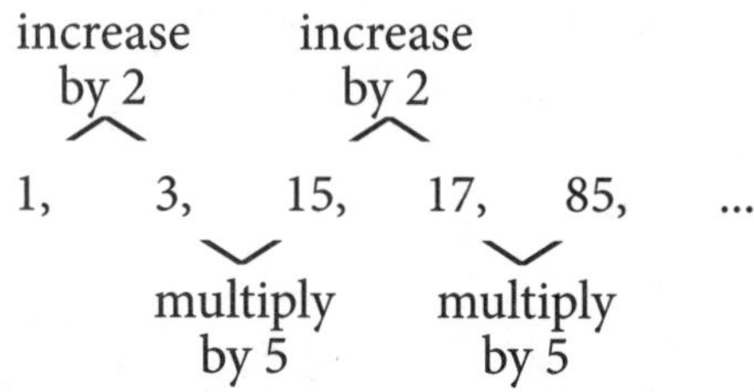

The point? Remember that sequences are simply sets in which the order matters. Sometimes they have a pattern we can describe with a term . . . and sometimes they don't. Understanding sequences and looking at their patterns helps us describe real-life patterns we find — such as the patterns in the frequencies of notes, or the pattern we follow when we count a stack of nickels {5, 10, 15, 20, . . .}.

19.5 Chapter Synopsis and Sets and Searches

Here's a quick recap of some important takeaways:

- A **set** is simply a collection, and a **subset** is a further grouping within a set.
- We often **name sets with letters.**
- **The possible values for any unknown can be thought of as a set.**
- **We use sets to organize numbers based on their properties.** We can also use symbols to specify a specific type of number. For example, $x \in \mathbb{N}$ means that x must be "an element of" the set of natural numbers.
- **Sequences are ordered sets**. We call sequences with a common difference between each element **arithmetic sequences**, and sequences with a common ratio **geometric sequences**. We can use unknowns to help us express sequences.

Now, many of the applications of sets and sequences require more math than we've covered or have time to cover in this course. However, just to give you a taste of some of the cool applications of sets, let's take a birds-eye view of how we benefit from sets whenever we search the Internet.

Sets and Searches

When you search a database (such as when you use an online search engine or a library catalog), the search engine is looking for elements in the "set" of terms you specified. If you searched a library catalog for "jewels" in the title of a book, it's looking for every book with "jewels" in its title. If you add an "OR kings," then, provided it's programmed to recognize the OR, it's looking for every book that has either "jewels" *or* "kings" in its title.

George Boole (1815–1864)

OR is what's known as a Boolean operator. It's part of a branch of math known as Boolean algebra. This algebra is named after George Boole (1815–1864), who came up with the idea of using letters to describe logical arguments. Boolean algebra is "indispensable in the design of computer chips and integrated circuits"[5] because it can reduce logic to simple rules, which in turn can translate into true or false statements, which in turn can translate into on and off flows of electricity (computers run using on and off flows of electricity).

It's important to note that Boolean algebra follows different rules than regular algebra, as it's describing logical statements rather than quantities. Each algebra system is a way of describing God's creation.

[CHAPTER 20]

Glimpses of Consumer Math

20.1 Compound Interest

In this chapter, we're going to take a look at some practical applications of math that affect everyone. Rather than learning new math skills, you'll have a chance to apply the skills you already know to new situations.

The applications we're going to look at are from an area of math known as consumer math. The word *consumer* means "a person who purchases goods and services for personal use."[1] So **consumer math** technically means math that you need to purchase goods and services, although it's usually broadened to include other skills needed in daily life too. While we've already covered a lot of consumer math throughout the course, it's time to touch on a couple of concepts we haven't been able to explore yet.

Interest

To start with, let's take a look at the concept of interest. "**Interest** is a fee (or payment) made for the borrowing (or lending) of money."[2] When you put money in a bank, it typically earns interest — that is, the bank pays you for the temporary use of the money while it's in their bank. They can combine your money with thousands of other peoples' money and invest it. As they make money off the invested money, they share a portion of their earnings with you in the form of interest. Because they have so many customers, unless something goes massively wrong, they still have enough cash on hand to give you whatever you withdraw.

Calculating Interest

Most interest is what we call **compound interest** — money is invested, and the investor earns interest on the initial investment *plus all the previous interest earned.* Since the word **compound** means "to put together into a whole; combine:,"[3] it makes sense that *compound* interest means interest that's added to, or combined with, the investment each time.

Let's say you invest \$10,000 in a bank that earns 4% interest compounded yearly. This means that every year, an interest of 4% is *compounded*, or *combined with*, the money you've invested in the bank. After the first year, you'll earn 4% of \$10,000, or \$400, in interest. After the second year, you'll earn 0.04 of *\$10,400*, or \$416, in interest. Every year that passes you'll earn more interest, as the interest is calculated on the initial investment *plus* all the previous interest earned.

This formula assumes we don't put any money into or take any money out of the investment (i.e., deposit or withdrawal money), but rather let the initial investment grow untouched.

Because money earning compound interest grows exponentially (there's growth on the growth), we can use the *same exponential growth formula* we looked at back in Lessons 15.5 to calculate how money will grow when earning compound interest.

Exponential Growth Formula

$P = P_0(1 + r)^t$, where

P = *final amount after growth* (in the case of interest, the ending amount of money, including all the interest)

P_0 = *initial amount before growth* (in the case of interest, the initial investment)

r = *rate of growth over a specified period of time* (in the case of interest, the rate of growth per compound period)

t = *the number of specified periods of time that have passed* (in the case of interest, the number of compound periods)

In order to accurately apply the exponential growth formula to interest rates, it's important to understand what we mean by a **compound period.** A compound period is "the period of time between the compounding of interest."[4] In other words, a compound period of a year means that every year, the interest is added to the account, increasing the amount off which the interest is calculated the next year.

Example: Suppose you invest \$10,000 at a 4% interest rate. If the interest is compounded yearly, what will your ending balance be in 10 years, assuming you don't withdraw or deposit any money?

Formula:

$P = P_0(1 + r)^t$

Substitute known numbers:

$P = \mathbf{\$10{,}000}(1 + \mathbf{0.04})^{\mathbf{10}}$

Solving inside the parentheses:

$P = \$10{,}000(\mathbf{1.04})^{10}$

Simplify 1.04^{10} using the calculator's exponent button:

$P = \$10{,}000(\mathbf{1.480244285})$

Complete the multiplication:

\$14,802.44

As we did with other exponential growth and functions, a coordinate graph can make it easy to see how money grows over time. Notice how this graph gives us a picture for how a $10,000 investment will grow at a 4% yearly interest rate that's compounded yearly.

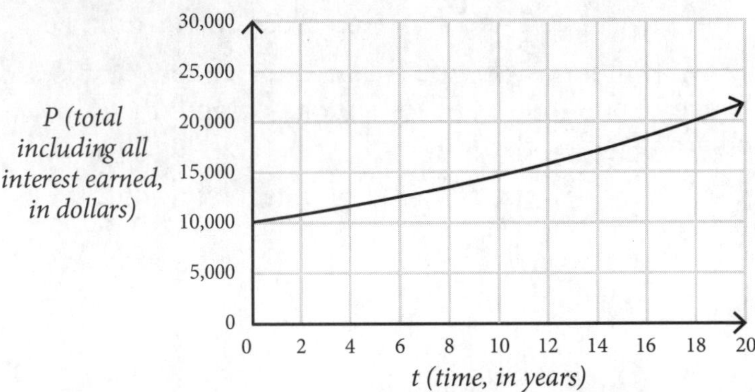

$$P = \$10{,}000(1 + 0.04)^t$$

> When referring specifically to interest rates, you'll often see the exponential growth formula rewritten using different letters. For example, you might be given this formula instead:
>
> $$A = P(1 + r)^t$$
>
> Notice that this is the same relationship, only different letters have been used. Don't let different letters confuse you. Both $P = P_0(1 + r)^t$ and $A = P(1 + r)^t$ represent the same relationship.

Example: Find the balance of an initial investment of $300 after 24 months if it is invested at a 0.08% monthly interest rate and the interest is compounded monthly.

Formula:

$$P = P_0(1 + r)^t$$

Substitute known numbers:

$$P = \mathbf{\$300}(1 + \mathbf{0.0008})^{\mathbf{24}}$$

Simplify inside the parentheses:

$$P = \$300(\mathbf{1.0008})^{24}$$

Simplify the 1.0008^{24} using the calculator's exponent button:

$$P = \$300(\mathbf{1.019377681})$$

Complete the multiplication:

$$P = \mathbf{\$305.81}$$

Notice that 0.08% converts to 0.0008 — be careful when solving interest problems to make sure you convert the percent to a decimal appropriately.

Growing Debt

While the examples showed interest earned on investments, the same principles apply to interest *owed* for money borrowed. Just as the bank pays interest when they receive money, they *charge* interest when they loan money. And that interest can add up quickly!

Ask the person with mounds of credit card debt or some other loan they can't afford, and they'll understand the proverb that "the borrower is servant to the lender."

> *The rich ruleth over the poor, and the borrower is servant to the lender (Proverbs 22:7).*

Keeping Perspective

In this lesson, we looked at **compound interest**, using the mathematic notations and tools you've learned to help calculate the growth of money earning interest. Compound interest is one example of how some of the skills we've been looking at can help with real-life tasks.

As we'll be exploring applications dealing with money in this chapter, it's worth pointing out that while math can help us assess financial decisions (and compare bank accounts), we always need to watch that money doesn't become our master. Treasure in heaven is the treasure that reaps eternal rewards — everything else is temporal. May we live each day with eternity in view.

> *"Do not lay up for yourselves treasures on earth, where moth and rust destroy and where thieves break in and steal; but lay up for yourselves treasures in heaven, where neither moth nor rust destroys and where thieves do not break in and steal. For where your treasure is, there your heart will be also. . . . No one can serve two masters; for either he will hate the one and love the other, or else he will be loyal to the one and despise the other. You cannot serve God and [money]" (Matthew 6:19–24; NKJV).*

20.2 Using the Correct Time and Rate

Throughout this course, we've looked at a lot of different formulas, from geometry to physics to finance. In this lesson, it's time to examine once again the importance of substituting the *correct* values into the formula. After all, a formula only gives the correct result *if* we input the correct information.

As you seek to use math to help make consumer decisions, you'll need to be careful to substitute correct values into the formulas. While we'll focus on the formula for calculating compound interest we looked at in the last lesson, know that this principle of being careful to use the correct numbers in formulas applies to any formula you're using.

Understanding the t in the Formula

Let's explore the t in $P = P_0(1 + r)^t$. The t represents the *number of compound periods*. After all, it's telling us how many times to multiply $(1 + r)$ . . . which we only want to do the number of times the interest has been compounded.

While in the last lesson, we always gave you the time you needed to insert into the formula, sometimes you'll need to think through *how many times the interest is compounded.*

For example, if interest is compounded *monthly* and you want to find the interest earned after 4 *years*, the interest will be compounded 4 • 12, or 48, times. Thus, 48 is the number to use in the formula, *not* 4.

Example: Find the value after 5 years if a 0.0032877% daily interest rate is compounded daily on a $1,000 investment.

Notice that the interest rate is compounded daily. So we have to find the number of days in 5 years.

The number of days in 5 years (i.e., the number of times the interest is actually compounded):

$$t = 5 \bullet 365 = 1{,}825$$

Now we have the appropriate time to use in the formula.

Formula:

$$P = P_0(1 + r)^t$$

Substitute known values:

$$P = \mathbf{\$1{,}000}(1+ \mathbf{0.000032877})^{\mathbf{1{,}825}}$$

Simplify inside the parentheses:

$$P = \$1{,}000(\mathbf{1.000032877})^{1{,}825}$$

Simplify $1.000032877^{1{,}825}$ using the calculator's exponent button:

$$P = \$1{,}000(\mathbf{1.061836057})$$

Complete the multiplication:

$$P = \mathbf{\$1{,}061.84}$$

In finance, 360 is often used as the number of days in a year rather than 365; you can check with the bank in question to see how many days in a year they use. In this book, we'll use 365 unless otherwise specified.

Understanding the r in the Formula

Let's think about the r in $P = P_0(1 + r)^t$ for a minute. We have to make sure the interest rate we use for r is the rate *per compound period.* While that sounds obvious, banks will often give the interest rate as an annual rate even if the interest is compounded daily or monthly.

The annual rate is the rate per compound period multiplied by the number of compound periods in a year. We could represent this relationship like this:

annual rate = rate per compound period • number of compound periods in a year

or

$$a = rp$$

In the last lesson, we gave you the rate per compound period, so you could easily substitute it into the formula. Now it's time to learn to find this rate when given an annual rate. Any ideas on how you could do this?

Look at *annual rate = rate per compound period • number of compound periods in a year* (i.e., $a = rp$) for a minute. How would you find the rate per compound period (r)? Let's solve the equation for r and see.

$$a = rp$$

$$\frac{a}{p} = \frac{r\cancel{p}}{\cancel{p}}$$

$$\frac{a}{p} = r \text{ or } r = \frac{a}{p}$$

We find the rate per compound period (r) by dividing the annual rate by the number of compound periods in a year.

For example, if an interest rate is given as 4% compounded monthly, you'd need to divide 4% by 12 to find the rate per compound period.

$$r = \frac{0.04}{12} = 0.00333333333$$

On the other hand, if an interest rate is given as 4% compounded daily, divide 4% by 365 to find the rate per compound period.

$$r = \frac{0.04}{365} = 0.000109589$$

From now on, if you're given an interest rate and it doesn't specify otherwise, assume it's the annual rate (a). If you need the rate per compound period (r), use the relationship $r = \frac{a}{p}$ to find it.

Example: What will the ending balance of $1,000 earning 5% compound interest be after 6 months if the interest is compounded monthly?

We can't substitute 5% into the formula, as it's not the rate that would be used each month. We have to first divide it by 12 to find the rate per compound period.

Notice that we assumed the 5% was an annual rate.

$$r = \frac{0.05}{12} = 0.004166667$$

Now we can solve to find the ending balance.

Formula:

$$P = P_0(1 + r)^t$$

Substitute known values:

$P = \mathbf{\$1,000}(1 + \mathbf{0.004166667})^6$

Simplify inside the parentheses:

$P = \$1,000(\mathbf{1.004166667})^6$

Simplify 1.004166667^6 using the calculator's exponent button:

$P = \$1,000(\mathbf{1.02526187})$

Complete the multiplication:

$P = \mathbf{\$1,025.26}$

Again, when using the formula $P = P_0(1 + r)^t$ to describe compound interest, make sure that the value for r you use is the rate per compound period, and that the value for t is the number of compound periods.

Keeping Perspective

Remember to pay attention when using a formula. Formulas only work if we substitute the correct values (otherwise, we're not accurately expressing the real-life relationship).

Your math worksheets will give you more practice with interest rates. Whether you ever invest money in a bank or not, use the practice to get comfortable with applying formulas to various wordings and situations. This will help prepare you to use math correctly in different settings the Lord might bring your way, whether personally or on a job.

20.3 Simple Interest

So far, we've been looking at **compound interest** — interest that gets added to the balance. Compound interest results in exponential growth, as every time the interest is calculated, it's based on the initial investment *plus* all the previous interest. For example, the chart shows the growth of $10,000 earning 4% interest, if that interest is compounded each year.

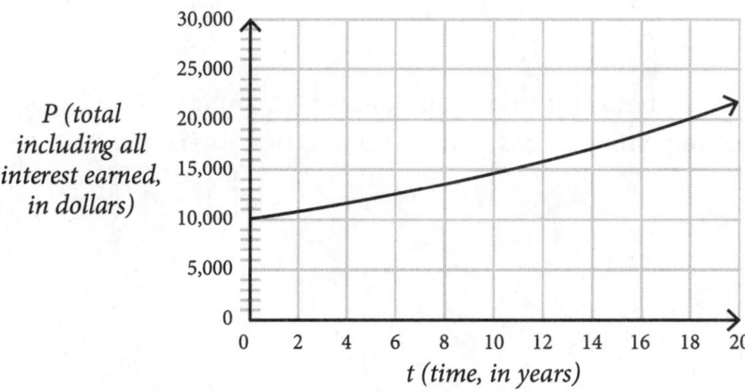

$P = \mathbf{\$10,000(1 + 0.04)^t}$

Not all interest grows exponentially like compound interest. Sometimes, the interest is calculated off the initial investment every time rather than off the initial investment plus all the previous interest. Interest calculated off the initial investment only is what we call **simple interest**.

Many bonds are an example of simple interest. In many bonds, the interest is paid periodically to the bond owner rather than added to a balance.

For example, if $10,000 earns 4% simple interest a year, the total interest after 1 year will be 0.4 • $10,000, or $400. The next year, rather than earning interest on the $10,000 *plus* the $400, the interest will again be calculated off the $10,000, making it $400 again.

Since the interest is calculated off the initial investment every time, growth invested at simple interest is linear — that is, it forms a straight line when graphed. The graph shows the growth of $10,000 invested at 4% simple interest. At the end of each year, the balance grows by the same amount ($400).

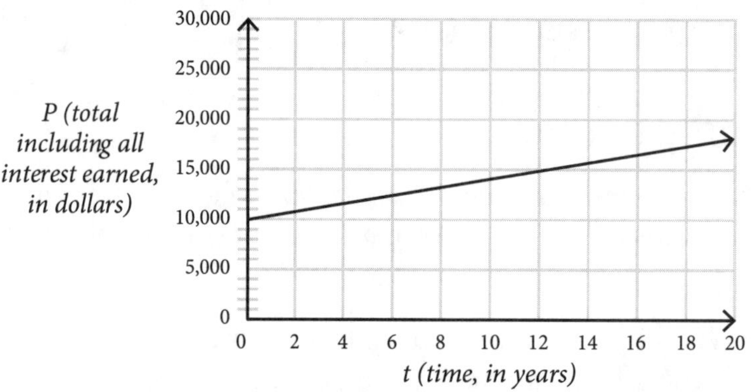

Any guesses on what equation we could use to describe the growth graphed above? Well, rather than telling you, Worksheet 20.3 will help you use what you know about coordinate graphing to describe the line mathematically.

Making Compound Interest Simple — APYs

It can get tricky trying to compare compound interest rates. After all, which earns more, 1% compounded monthly, or 1.2% compounded yearly?

In order to make compound interest rates simpler to compare, banks will list a rate called the **annual percentage yield**, abbreviated **APY**. The APY shares the overall effect over the course of a year *as a simple interest rate*. So a 4% APY means that, over the course of a year, a starting balance of $1,000 will earn 0.04 • $10,000, or $400, in interest.

An APY reduces compound interest to a simple interest calculation: multiply the interest rate by the starting balance, and you'll find the total interest earned for 1 year.

Example: If you invest $4,000, how much more will you earn the first year at an APY of 5% than at an APY of 1%?

earnings at 5% = 0.05 • $4,000 = $200

earnings at 1% = 0.01 • $4,000 = $40

difference between earnings at 5% and earnings at 1% = $200 – $40 = $160

You would earn $160 more the first year.

It's important to note that APYs express compound interest as simple interest for a *period of 1 year*. While they can help us compare accounts, they can't tell us what the ending balance will be for periods other than 1 year, as they only take into account the compounding for 1 year.

Keeping Perspective

If you'd seen a rate listed as 5% APY without knowing what APY meant, it might seem intimidating. Yet, as we saw in this lesson, **APYs (annual percentage yields)** give us an *easy* way to compare interest rates. Which brings us to an important point: as you apply math in everyday situations, you may need to do a little searching to find the meaning of an unfamiliar abbreviation or term. Don't let the abbreviations or terms scare you into thinking the math is hard.

20.4 Budgeting

While we're on the topic of consumer math and handling money, let's talk about budgets. A **budget** is "an itemized summary of probable expenditures and income for a given period, usually embodying a systematic plan for meeting expenses,"[5] or more simply put, a budget is a plan on how you will spend your income so as to cover all your expenses.

While there are whole courses written on the topic of budgeting and numerous different ways one can keep track of a budget, the basic principless of budgeting are both simple and universal.

Understanding a Budget

To develop a budget, you need to know

- what you expect the income to be for a specific period of time and
- what you expect the expenses (including ones that might not come until a later period of time, but for which you need to plan — such as a quarterly bill) to be for that same period of time.

While some expenses are recurring (like a cell phone bill), others might be big-ticket items you save up for (like a car or a vacation). Expenses can also include savings you want to set aside for the future and money you want to give away to your church, ministries, missions, etc.

You might wonder why you need a budget. Won't your expenses be obvious? Not always. Expenses tend to come at different times and from different sources. Your car insurance might be due every six months, your cell phone bill each month, and your property taxes once a year. If you don't know a bill will be due soon, it could surprise you, and you might have spent the money you needed to pay that bill elsewhere.

Figuring Out Income and Expenses

None of the math involved in budgeting is difficult, but the math will be different for every budget. You can develop a budget for different periods of time (a week, month, year, etc.) depending on your need. But whatever period of time you're budgeting for, you'll want to estimate your income and expenses for that period of time. To do that, you'll use basic addition, subtraction, multiplication, and division. A few examples are shown.

Example: If you make \$320 a week after taxes, what will your monthly income be? Use 4.35 weeks per month.

The monthly income will equal the weekly income times the number of weeks per month. We were told to use 4.35 weeks as the number of weeks per month. Thus we need to multiply 4.35 by \$320.

$4.35 \bullet \$320 = \$1{,}392$

Your monthly income will be \$1,392.

Example: If you spend \$600 every 6 months on car insurance, how much should you set aside every month for car insurance?

You know the expense per 6 months, and you need to find the expense per month. So you need to divide \$600 by 6.

$\frac{\$600}{6} = \$100$

You need to set aside \$100 a month for car insurance.

Example: Suppose someone is considering buying a house. They've talked with the realtor and homeowners, and decided that they need to set aside \$100 a month for home repairs, \$700 a year for property tax, and \$300 a month for utilities. If the mortgage would be \$1,200 a month, how much altogether would it cost per month to buy the house?

We're trying to find the cost of the home per *month*, so we need to first make sure all of the expenses are listed per *month*, and then add them together. We were told the property tax is estimated to be \$700 a *year*, so we need to divide \$700 by 12 to find the monthly cost.

$\frac{\$700}{12} = \$58.33$

Now we can add all the expenses together to find the estimated cost per month.

$58.33 + $100 + $300 + $1,200 = $1,658.33

Vacation Budgets

Budgets apply in a lot more ways than you might think! You can even use a budget to help plan for a vacation. In that case, the total you've set aside for the vacation will be the "income."

Example: Suppose a family is heading on vacation. They've set aside $700 for the trip. They need to make that amount cover hotels, gas, meals, and any souvenirs they want to buy or activities they want to do. They're staying 3 nights at a hotel that costs $65 plus a 10% tax. They'll be traveling 300 miles in a car that gets 40 miles per gallon; they're planning on an average price per gas of $2.50 a gallon. They plan to eat out meals, and expect it to cost $15 for breakfast, $30 for lunch, and $45 for dinner. They'll be eating meals out 4 days. How much of the $700 do they have left to spend on souvenirs, activities, or other expenses that arise?

To answer the question, we have to first find the total expenses for hotels, gas, and meals.

Let's start with the hotel expenses, multiplying the cost per night by 1.10 to find the cost with the tax and then multiplying that by the number of nights.

$$\textit{total hotel expenses} = 3(\$65 \bullet 1.10) = \$214.50$$

Now let's find the gas expenses. We need to divide the total miles by the miles we get per gallon to find the total gallons needed, and then multiply that by the cost per gallon.

$$\textit{total gas expenses} = \left(\frac{300 \text{ mi}}{40 \text{ mi}}\right)\$2.50 = \$18.75$$

Now let's find the total meal expenses. We need to find the cost per day, and then multiply that cost by the number of days (4).

$$\textit{total meal expenses} = 4(\$15 + \$30 + \$45) = \$360$$

Now we can add up all the expenses and see how much will be left from the $700.

$$\textit{total expenses} = \$214.50 + \$18.75 + \$360 = \$593.25$$

$$\textit{amount left after expenses} = \$700 - \$593.25 = \$106.75$$

They have $106.75 to spend on souvenirs, activities, or other expenses.

Keeping Perspective

This lesson was a broad picture of budgeting. Again, there are a lot of resources available that can walk you through budgeting details. A budget can help us live within the income God has provided. That way, we don't end up halfway through a vacation and totally out of money . . . or having spent money that should have been set aside for an upcoming bill . . . or unable to give to someone in need.

It is my prayer that you will use any budgets you develop as servants to help you serve God, without letting them become your master. A budget can help you avoid giving into a fleshly whim and spending money you don't really have or that you need to spend elsewhere. But it can also easily become a cruel master, keeping you from listening to the Lord's leading and trusting Him for provision. There are many true stories of how missionaries didn't know where their next meal would come from — we don't always know what's coming next. God can send ravens to feed us, as He did with Elijah (1 Kings 17:4). As you look at budgeting, ask the Lord to show you how to live with your money surrendered to Him.

20.5 Chapter Synopsis

While we only looked at a few aspects of consumer math, I hope you were encouraged that you have the tools to use math in your daily lives. You know how to use formulas. You know how to find unknowns. You know how to learn new terms. Whether you're exploring interest rates and budgets or a completely different aspect of consumer math we didn't cover, you have the skills you need.

And when you apply math in your own life, remember to praise God for the ability to use math, to guard yourself against the love of money, and to seek God with your whole heart. When this life is said and done, trusting Jesus and letting Him love and live through us is what's going to matter, not how much money we accumulated.

> *Seek the LORD, and his strength: seek his face evermore (Psalm 105:4).*

Review

21.1 Algebra Synopsis

As we near the end of our journey together, it's time to take a step back and look at the big picture. Although we avoided the word *algebra*, we nevertheless looked at a lot of the basic principles of algebra. Algebra is simply "the part of mathematics in which letters and other general symbols are used to represent numbers and quantities in formulae and equations"[1] or "the science which teaches how to determine unknown quantities by means of those that are known."[2]

Let's briefly review both of these key aspects of algebra.

Using Letters and Symbols for Unknowns

We learned early on that we can use letters and symbols as placeholders to stand for unknown quantities, which we refer to as unknowns. By doing so, we're able to describe, not just *one* situation, but relationships that hold true for *many* situations.

For example, we looked at the relationship between distance, time, and speed; the relationship between the rate, base, and percentage; the relationship between angles in right triangles and the ratios between the lengths of their sides; the relationship between an ending balance and the number of compound periods; and many others.

And why are there real-life relationships in the first place? Because God has created and sustains a consistent universe! As we explore mathematical relationships, we're really exploring His handiwork — something we can only do because He gave us minds capable of doing so. At every level, math depends on God.

Finding an Unknown's Value

We saw over and over again that we can perform the *same operation* (using the same quantity) to *both sides* of the equation without changing the equality. It doesn't matter if we know the value of a quantity or not — we know that whatever the value is, addition, subtraction, multiplication, and division will operate according to the "ordinances" God created and sustains.

> *Thus saith the LORD; If my covenant be not with day and night, and if I have not appointed the ordinances of heaven and earth; Then will I cast away the seed of Jacob and David my servant, so that I will not take any of his seed to be rulers over the seed of Abraham, Isaac, and Jacob: for I will cause their captivity to return, and have mercy on them (Jeremiah 33:25–26).*

Algebra is a continual reminder to us that God is faithful. The same God who holds the consistency of creation together, thus making algebra possible, is the same God in control of every detail of our lives. Wow! Let's trust Him and rely on His strength.

> *For ever, O LORD, thy word is settled in heaven. Thy faithfulness is unto all generations: thou hast established the earth, and it abideth. They continue this day according to thine ordinances: for all are thy servants (Psalm 119:89–91).*

21.2 Statistics, Probability, Trigonometry, and Consumer Math Synopsis

Throughout this course, we touched on the basic principles of several different branches of math besides algebra, including these:

- **Statistics** — In statistics, we use math to collect, organize, and interpret data.[3] Understanding the statistical process helps us discern through the stats we encounter in life.
- **Probability** — In probability, we explore the likelihood of something happening. Probability and related concepts help us make educated decisions about the weather, understand the amazing way God causes traits to pass down from generation to generation, explore the number of phone numbers possible using a certain number of digits — the list could go on. As we use probability, we do so knowing that God is the One in charge of each outcome.
- **Trigonometry** — In trigonometry, we use math to explore the ratios in right triangles, which in turn end up helping us describe angles we find all throughout God's creation. In fact, trigonometry even helps us explore parts of creation that don't seem to have anything to do with triangles at all, such as sound waves.

- **Consumer Math** — In consumer math, we use math to answer everyday questions, such as what bank account will earn the most interest.

Hopefully our brief look at these different branches of math gave you a glimpse of how math does indeed apply outside of a textbook. As you use math in your own life, remember to let biblical principles guide you and to praise the Creator of all.

21.3 Course Review

I hope the principles of mathematics we've covered in this course have excited you and equipped you to continue using math to explore God's creation and serve Him. No matter how much we learn, there's more left to learn — we'll never exhaust the depth of God's creation!

As we finish, let's take one final "big picture" look at math.

The Main Elements

In math, we keep encountering the same basic elements over and over again.

1. **Notations, Symbols, Terms, and Conventions** — A lot of our explorations together have focused on learning the language we use to describe the quantities and consistencies God created and sustains. From the order of operations to multiplication to inequalities to functions to domains to exponents, we looked at notations, symbols, terms, and conventions that help us describe God's creation.

2. **Operations** — Throughout the course, we revisited the basic operations (addition, subtraction, multiplication, and division) many times. Whether finding the base number of which a percent was taken or finding the height of a building using trigonometry, we added, subtracted, multiplied, and divided many times. Remember, though, that we can only rely on these operations to hold true *because* of God's faithfulness in holding all things together.

3. **Algorithms** — From simplifying fractions and expressions containing unknowns to cross-multiplying to find the missing number in a proportion to converting to and from scientific notation, we saw that we could follow step-by-step processes to find a solution. It's only because of the consistency God created and sustains that we can reduce math to algorithms, or rules.

Moving Forward

Whatever math course you take next, you're going to find yourself learning notations, applying operations, and exploring algorithms. As you do, keep remembering that math is a way of describing the quantities and consistencies

God created and sustains. As such, it points us to God, and is a real-life tool we can use to serve Him.

Parting Thought

Math itself only works outside of a textbook because creation is consistent, and creation is only so consistent because God is so consistent. As we use math to explore creation, we see design and order everywhere we look. All of creation is shouting out at us to trust the Creator — the question is, are we?

Ever since Adam partook of the forbidden fruit back in the Garden of Eden, mankind has been going its own way. The Bible tells us that even our righteous deeds are as filthy rags in God's eyes.

> *But we are all as an unclean thing, and all our righteousnesses are as filthy rags; and we all do fade as a leaf; and our iniquities, like the wind, have taken us away (Isaiah 64:6).*
>
> *They are all gone out of the way, they are together become unprofitable; there is none that doeth good, no, not one (Romans 3:12).*

Yet Jesus came to take the punishment our sin deserves that we might have everlasting life.

> *For God so loved the world, that he gave his only begotten Son, that whosoever believeth in him should not perish, but have everlasting life (John 3:16).*
>
> *He came unto his own, and his own received him not. But as many as received him, to them gave he power to become the sons of God, even to them that believe on his name (John 1:11–12).*

As we conclude our math explorations, take some time to think seriously about where you stand before God. The God who holds every aspect of creation together knows the innermost thoughts of your heart. We can't fool Him. He knows our sin — yet knowing it all, He chose to die in our place so He could give us His righteousness.

Have you responded to His great gift? Have you bowed your knees to the Creator, acknowledging Him as your Lord and accepting the salvation offered through Jesus? If not, don't put it off. Let today be the day of salvation (2 Corinthians 6:2). And if you have responded to God's gift, live in and share the joy of His salvation.

> *Behold, God is my salvation; I will trust, and not be afraid: for the Lord Jehovah is my strength and my song; he also is become my salvation. Therefore with joy shall ye draw water out of the wells of salvation. And in that day shall ye say, Praise the Lord, call upon his name, declare his doings among the people, make mention that his name is exalted (Isaiah 12:2–4).*

Appendix A: Reference

Polygon

(closed, two-dimensional figure with straight lines)

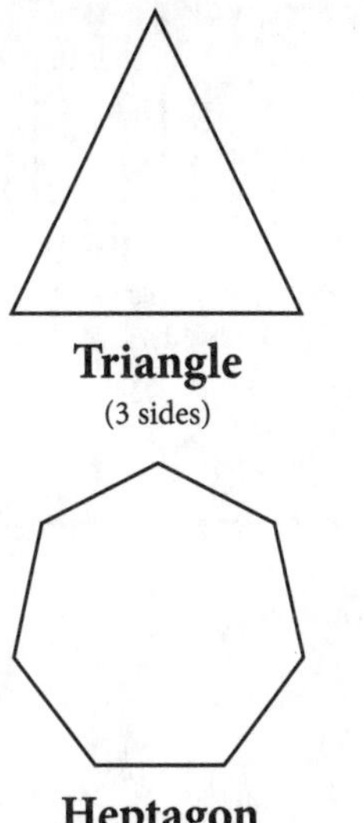

Triangle
(3 sides)

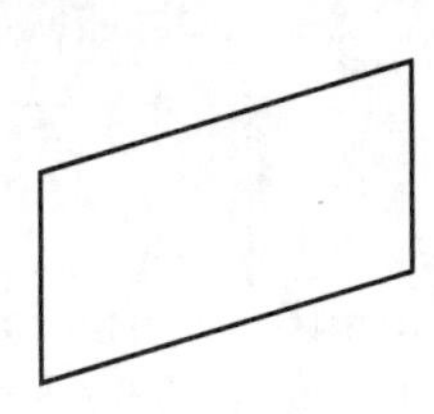

Quadrilateral
(4 sides)

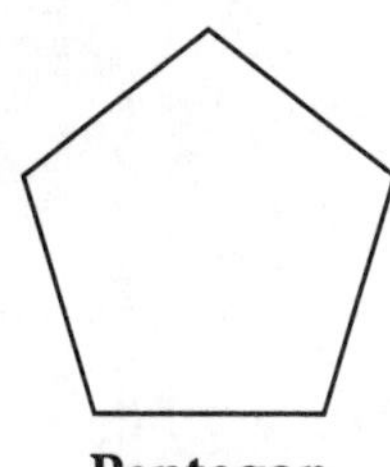

Pentagon
(5 sides)

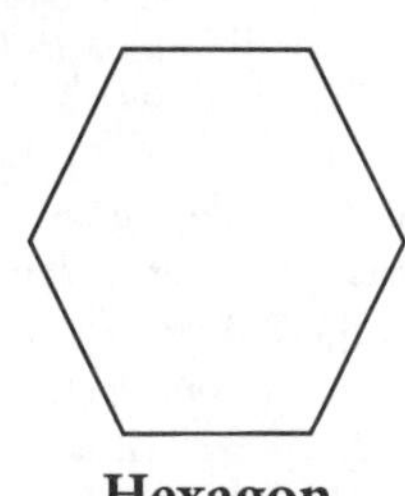

Hexagon
(6 sides)

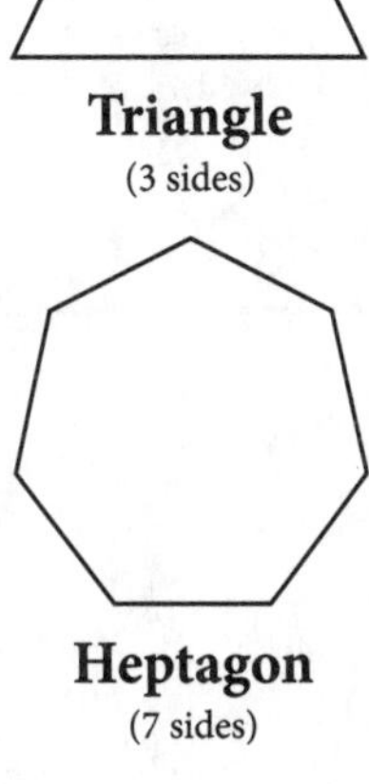

Heptagon
(7 sides)

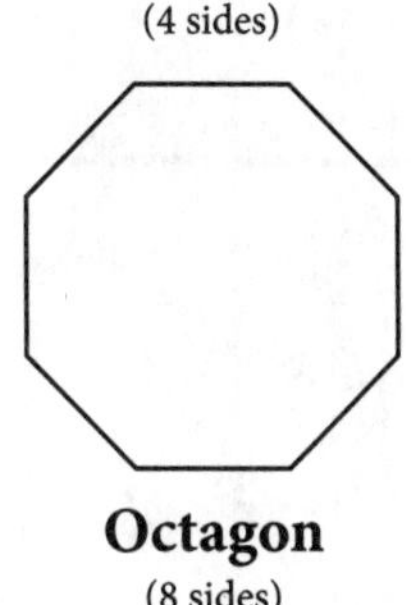

Octagon
(8 sides)

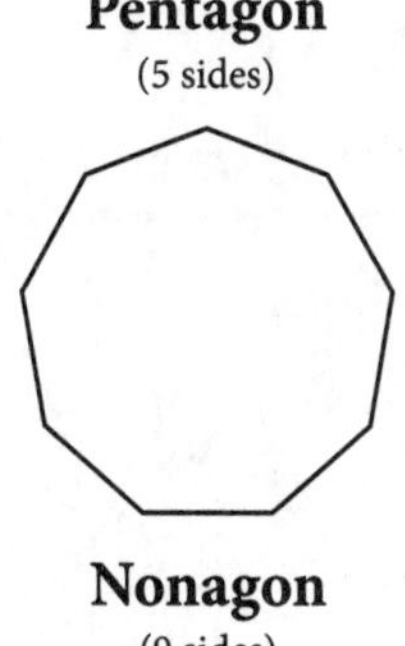

Nonagon
(9 sides)

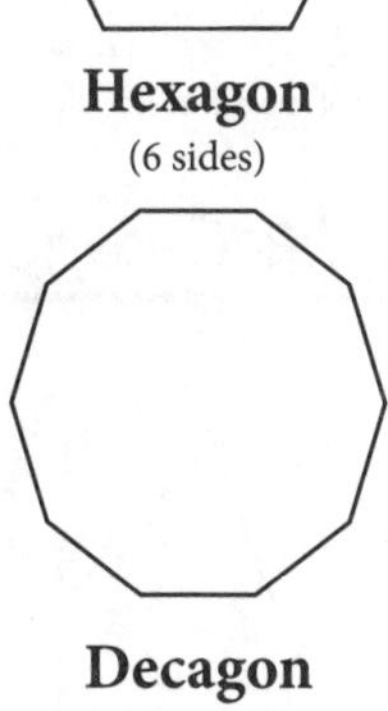

Decagon
(10 sides)

Regular Polygon

(All sides are equal; all edges would touch a circle drawn around the figure, as all angles are the same.)

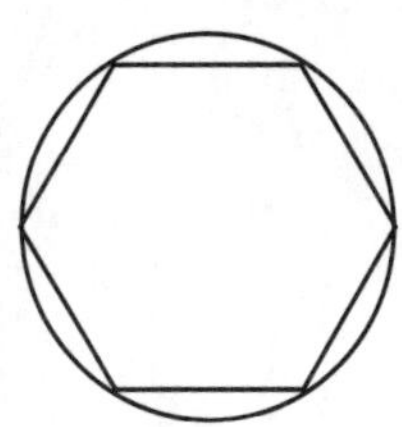

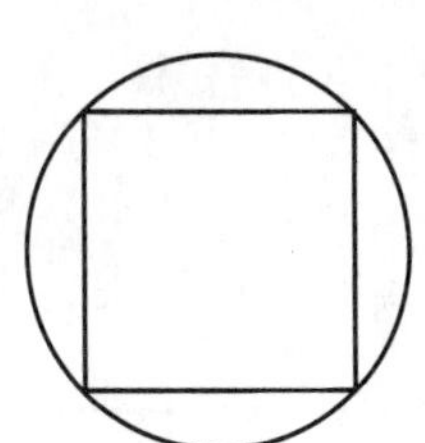

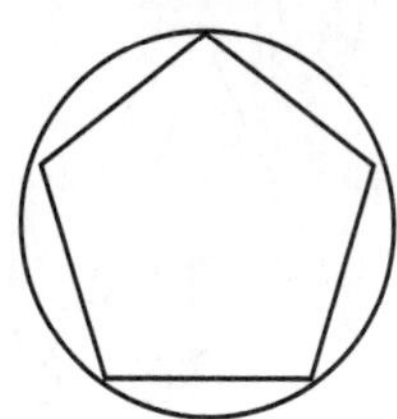

Irregular Polygon

(Polygons that are not regular.)

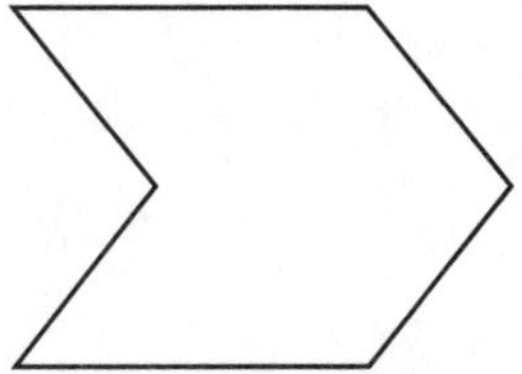

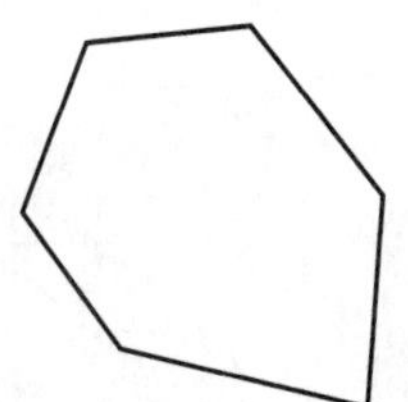

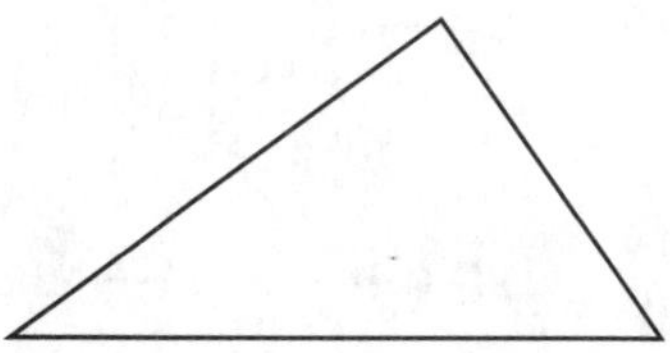

Specific Quadrilaterals

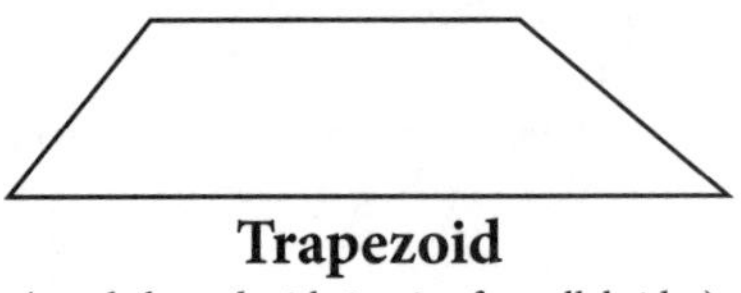

Trapezoid
(quadrilateral with 1 pair of parallel sides)

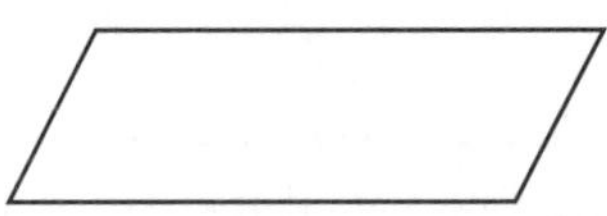

Parallelogram
(quadrilateral with both pairs of opposite sides parallel)

Some books define a trapezoid as a quadrilateral with 1, and only 1, pair of parallel sides, while others as a quadrilateral with 1 (or more) pair of parallel sides. Likewise, some define a rhombus/diamond differently than listed here. Always remember that definitions can — and do — vary!

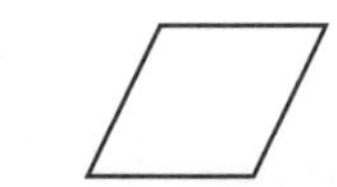

Rhombus/Diamond
(parallelogram with equal-length sides)

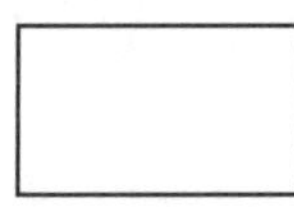

Rectangle
(parallelogram with right angles)

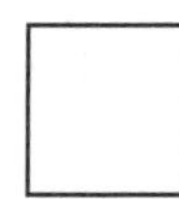

Square
(parallelogram with equal-length sides *and* right angles)

Triangles Categorized by Length of Sides

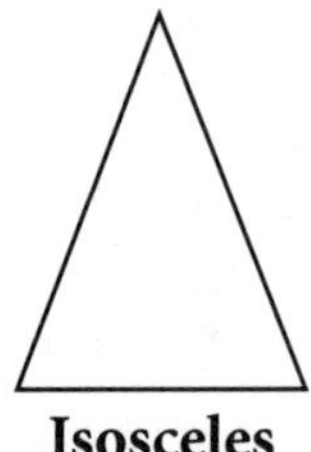

Isosceles
(two equal sides)

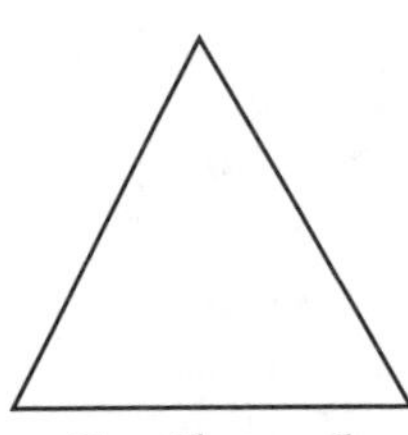

Equilateral
(all equal sides)

Scalene
(no equal sides)

Triangles Categorized by Angles

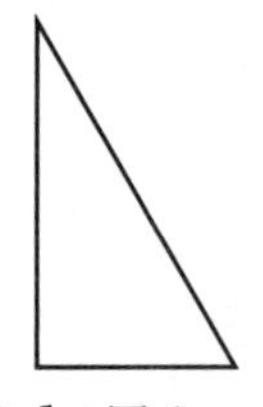

Right Triangle
(a right angle)

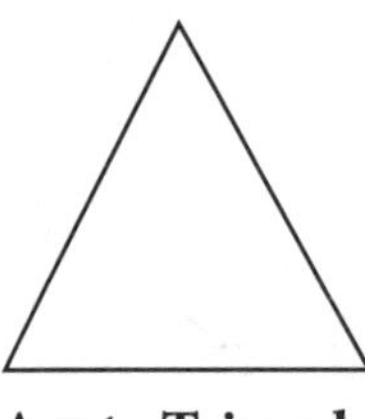

Acute Triangle
(all acute angles)

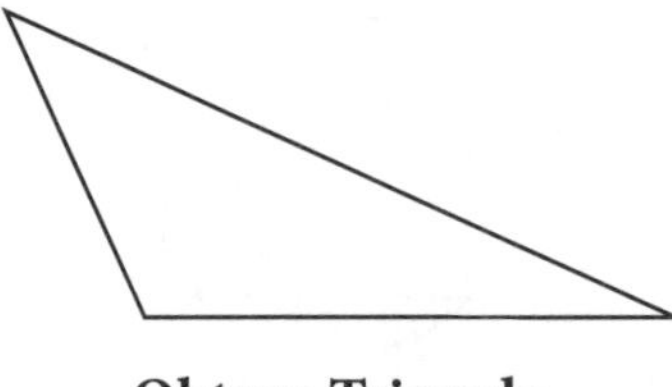

Obtuse Triangle
(an obtuse angle)

Circle

(closed two-dimensional figure; each part of the edge is equally distant from the center)

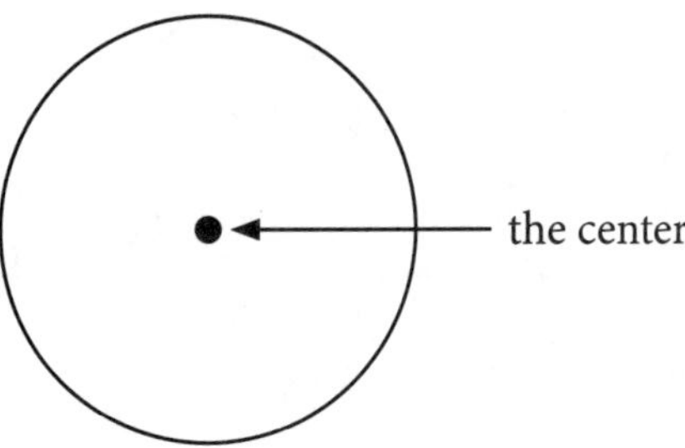

Prism

(A solid with two bases that are parallel polygons, and faces [sides] that are parallelograms; the prism is named after the shape of the bases.)

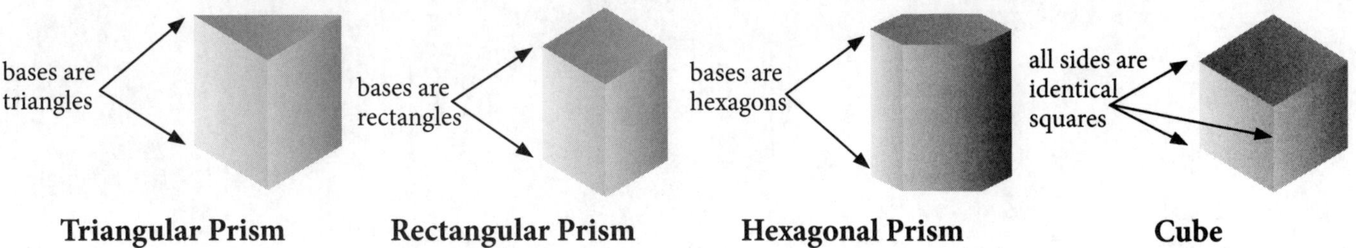

Cylinder

(A solid with two bases that are equal parallel circles, having an equal diameter in any parallel plane between them.)

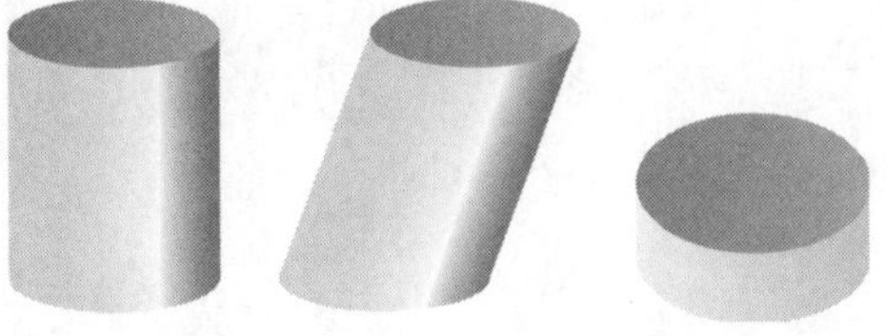

Prism and cylinder definitions were based on *Ray's New Higher Arithmetic*, Revised (Cincinnati: Van Antwerp, Bragg & Co., 1880), p. 390.

Formulas

Shape Name	Type of Shape	Perimeter	Area
Polygons		***P = sum of the lengths of each side*** *or* $P = s_1 + s_2 \ldots s_n$	View as multiple triangles or other shapes.
Regular Polygon	s	***P = (number of sides) • (length of a side)*** *or* $P = n \bullet s$ *or* $P = n(s)$ *or* $P = ns$	View as multiple triangles or other shapes.
Rectangle	w ℓ	***P = (2 • length) + (2 • width)*** *or* $P = 2 \bullet \ell + 2 \bullet w$ *or* $P = 2(\ell) + 2(w)$ *or* $P = 2\ell + 2w$	***A = length • width*** *or* $A = \ell \bullet w$ *or* $A = \ell(w)$ *or* $A = \ell w$
Square	s	***P = 4 • side*** *or* $P = 4 \bullet s$ *or* $P = 4(s)$ *or* $P = 4s$	***A = side • side*** *or* $A = s \bullet s$ *or* $A = s(s)$ *or* $A = s^2$
Parallelogram	s h b	***P = (2 • base) + (2 • side)*** *or* $P = 2 \bullet b + 2 \bullet s$ *or* $P = 2(b) + 2(s)$ *or* $P = 2b + 2s$	***A = base • height*** *or* $A = b \bullet h$ *or* $A = b(h)$ *or* $A = bh$
Triangle	h b	***Perimeter = sum of the lengths of each side*** *or* $P = s_1 + s_2 + s_3$	$A = \frac{1}{2} \bullet \text{base} \bullet \text{height}$ *or* $A = \frac{\text{base} \bullet \text{height}}{2}$ $A = \frac{1}{2} \bullet b \bullet h$ *or* $A = \frac{1}{2}bh$ *or* $A = \frac{b \bullet h}{2}$ *or* $A = \frac{bh}{2}$

A = Area
B = area of the base
b = base
C = circumference
d = diameter
h = height
ℓ = length
n = number of sides
P = Perimeter
π = 3.14
r = radius
s = side
V = Volume
w = width (or height)

Shape Name	Type of Shape	Circumference	Area
Circle		***Circumference*** $= \pi \bullet$ ***diameter*** *or* $C = \pi \bullet d$ *or* $C = \pi(d)$ *or* $C = \pi d$ ***Circumference*** $= 2 \bullet \pi \bullet$ ***radius*** *or* $C = 2 \bullet \pi \bullet r$ *or* $C = 2(\pi)(r)$ *or* $C = 2\pi r$	***Area*** $= \pi \bullet$ ***radius*** $\bullet$ ***radius*** *or* $A = \pi \bullet r^2$ *or* $A = \pi(r^2)$ *or* $A = \pi r^2$
		diameter $= 2 \bullet$ ***radius*** *or* $d = 2 \bullet r$ *or* $d = 2r$ ***radius*** $= \frac{1}{2} \bullet$ ***diameter*** *or* $r = \frac{1}{2} \bullet d$ *or* $r = \frac{1}{2}d$	

Shape Name	Type of Shape	Volume	Area
Prism		***Volume = area of base*** $\bullet$ ***height*** *or* $V = B \bullet h$ *or* $V = Bh$	***Total surface area = area of all the sides (i.e., surfaces) of a solid object***
Cylinder		***Volume = area of base*** $\bullet$ ***height*** *or* $V = B \bullet h$ *or* $V = Bh$	did not cover
Pyramid		***Volume*** $= \frac{1}{3} \bullet$ ***area of base*** $\bullet$ ***height*** *or* $V = \frac{1}{3} \bullet B \bullet h$ *or* $V = \frac{1}{3}Bh$	did not cover
Sphere		***Volume*** $= \frac{4}{3} \bullet \pi \bullet$ ***radius***^{3} *or* $V = \frac{4}{3} \bullet \pi \bullet r^3$ *or* $V = \frac{4}{3}\pi r^3$	did not cover

A = Area
B = area of the base
b = base
C = circumference
d = diameter
h = height
ℓ = length
n = number of sides
P = Perimeter
π = 3.14
r = radius
s = side
V = Volume
w = width (or height)

Units of Measure

Distance

Distance – U.S. Customary

12 inches (in) = 1 foot (ft)
3 feet / 36 inches = 1 yard (yd)
1,760 yard / 5,280 feet = 1 mile (mi)

Conversion Between Systems

1 inches (in) = 2.54 centimeter (cm)
1 foot (ft) = 30.48 centimeter (cm)
1 yard (yd) = 0.9144 meter (m)
1 mile (mi) = 1.609344 kilometer (km)

Distance – Metric/SI

10 millimeters (mm) = 1 centimeter (cm)
10 centimeters = 1 decimeter (dm)
10 decimeters / 100 centimeters / 1,000 millimeters = 1 meter (m)
10 meters = 1 decameters (dam)
10 decameters = 1 hectometer (hm)
10 hectometers / 1,000 meters = 1 kilometer (km)

Time

60 seconds (s) = 1 minute (min)
60 minutes = 1 hour (hr)
24 hours = 1 day (d)
7 days = 1 week (wk)
365 days = 1 year (yr *or* y)

Liquid Capacity

U.S. Customary

3 teaspoons (tsp) = 1 tablespoon (Tbsp)
16 tablespoons = 1 cup (c)
2 cups = 1 pint (pt)
2 pints = 1 quart (qt)
4 quarts = 1 gallon (gal)

2 tablespoons (Tbsp) ≈ 1 fluid ounce (fl oz)
8 fl oz = 1 cup (c)
16 fl oz = 1 pint (pt)
32 fl oz = 1 quart (qt)
128 fl oz = 1 gallon (gal)

Conversion Between Systems

1 teaspoon ≈ 5 milliliters
1 gallon = 3.78541 liters

1 pint = 28.875 in^3
1 quart = 57.75 in^3
1 gallon = 231 in^3

Metric

10 milliliters (ml *or* mL) = 1 centiliter (cl *or* cL)
10 centiliter / 100 milliliter = 1 deciliter (dl *or* dL)
10 deciliter / 100 centiliter / 1,000 milliliter = 1 liter (*l or* L)
10 liters = 1 dekaliter (dal *or* daL)
10 dekaliter = 1 hectoliter (hl *or* hL)
10 hectoliter / 1,000 liters = 1 kiloliter (kl *or* kL)

Dry Capacity

U.S. Customary

2 pints (pt) = 1 quart (qt)
8 quart = 1 peck (pk)
4 peck = 1 bushel (bu) / 32 quarts (qt)

Conversion Between Systems

1 quart = 67.2006 inches^3
1 bushel = 2,150.42 inches^3

Note: The pint and quart here represent a larger capacity than the ones measuring liquid—they should not be used interchangeably. Unless the problem specifically states otherwise, you can assume pint and quart in this course refer to the liquid units.

Mass

U.S. Customary

16 ounces (oz) = 1 pound (lb)
2,000 pounds = 1 ton (called a "short ton")

Conversion Between Systems

1 ounce = 28.3495 grams
1 pound = 453.592 grams
1 U.S. ton (called a short ton) = 0.907185 metric tons

Note: These ounces are different than the fluid ounces listed under liquid capacity.

Metric

10 milligrams (mg) = 1 centigram (cg)
10 centigrams / 100 milligrams = 1 decigram (dg)
10 decigrams / 100 centigrams / 1,000 milligrams = 1 gram (g)
10 grams = 1 dekagram (dag)
10 dekagrams = 1 hectogram (hg)
10 hectograms / 1,000 grams = 1 kilogram (kg)

For more unit details, see the official standards given in Tina Butcher, Linda Crown, Rick Harshman, and Juana Williams, eds. *NIST Handbook 44: 97th National Conference on Weights and Measures 2012*, 2013 ed. (Washington: U. S. Department of Commerce, 2012), Appendix C. Found on http://www.nist.gov/pml/wmd/pubs/h44-13.cfm, accessed 10/6/2014.

Important Mathematical Relationships

Distance Problems *See Lessons 3.5, 3.7, and 5.3.*

$d = s \bullet t$ or $d = st$

distance = speed • time

Altitude (or Height) Problems *See Lesson 3.7.*

$a = r \bullet t + a_i$

altitude (or height) = rate of change in altitude (or height) • time + initial altitude (or height)

Percent Problems *See Lesson 6.3.*

$R \bullet B = P$ or $RB = P$

Rate • Base = Percentage

Think: The rate *of* the base *equals* the percentage.

Probability *See Chapter 12.*

$$\textit{probability of an event} = \frac{\textit{outcomes that produce event}}{\textit{total possible outcomes}}$$

$$\textit{odds for} = \frac{\textit{outcomes that produce event}}{\textit{outcomes that do not produce event}}$$

$$\textit{odds against} = \frac{\textit{outcomes that do not produce event}}{\textit{outcomes that produce event}}$$

Pythagorean Theorem *See Lessons 17.5–17.7.*

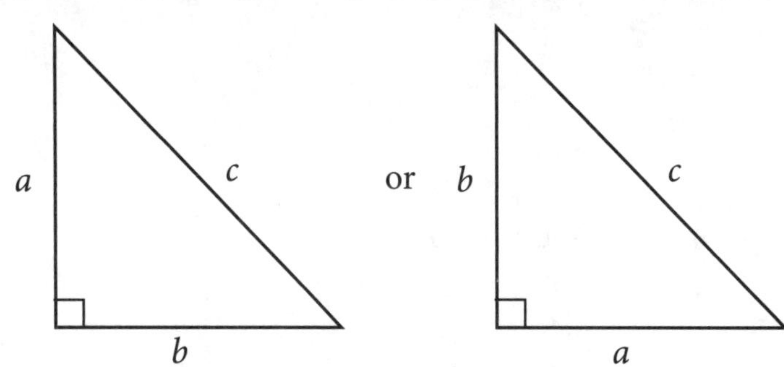

$a^2 + b^2 = c^2$

where c stands for the length of the hypotenuse of a right triangle, and a and b stand for the length of the two legs of the same right triangle

Trigonometry *See Chapter 18.*

Tangent of an angle — The ratio between the opposite and adjacent leg of either non-right angle in a right triangle.

$$\textit{tangent of an angle} = \frac{\textbf{opposite leg}}{\textbf{adjacent leg}}$$

opposite leg
hypotenuse
adjacent leg

adjacent leg
hypotenuse
opposite leg

Sine of an angle — The ratio between the opposite leg of either non-right angle in a right triangle and the hypotenuse.

$$\textit{sine of an angle} = \frac{\textbf{opposite leg}}{\textbf{hypotenuse}}$$

Cosine of an angle — The ratio between the adjacent leg of either non-right angle in a right triangle and the hypotenuse.

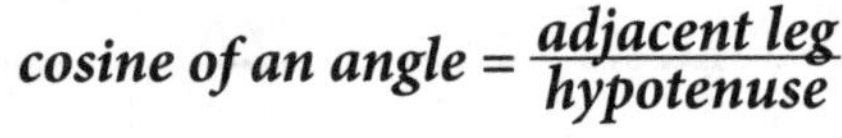

$$\textit{cosine of an angle} = \frac{\textbf{adjacent leg}}{\textbf{hypotenuse}}$$

Exponential Growth and Decay (Applies to Compound Interest Too) *See Lessons 15.5–15.7 and Lessons 20.1–20.2.*

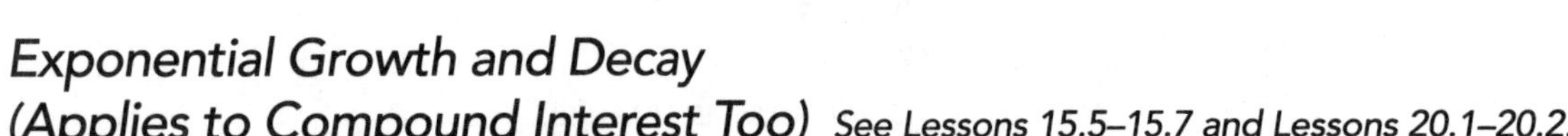

$$P = P_0(1 + r)^t$$

where

P = final amount after growth or decay
P_0 = initial amount before growth or decay
r = rate of growth or decay over a specified period of time
t = the number of specified periods of time that have passed

Mathematical Relationships *See Lesson 13.2–13.5 and 14.1 for an explanation.*

Important Terms

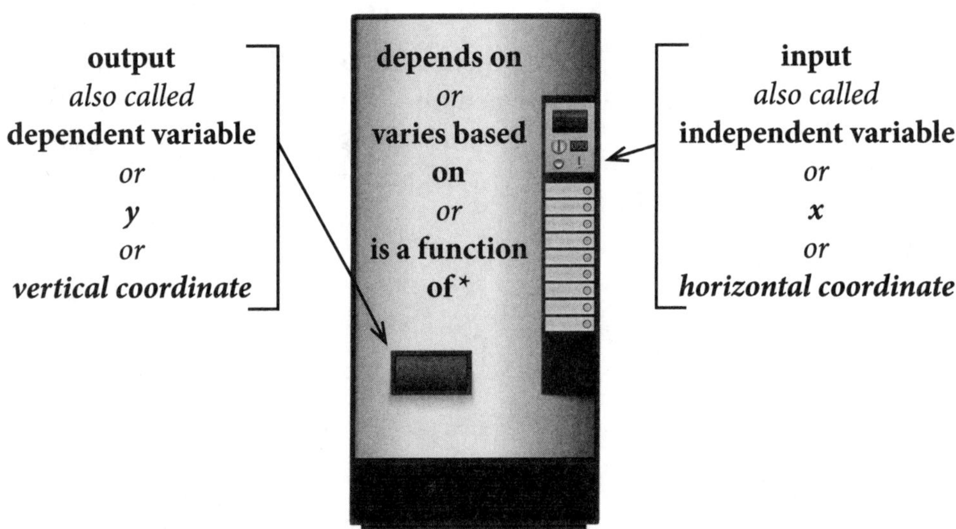

*The term *is a function of* is only used if we know there's only one output for every input.

Appendix B: Mathematical Relationships: Graphs and Functions

It's very easy to tell on a graph if the relationship between an input and output is a function or not. Remember, a function means that for every input there's one output. When you look at a graph, you can easily see if for every *x* value (i.e., every input), there's only one *y* value (i.e., one output). How? Well, using your finger, trace the *x*-axis horizontally. At any point does the line(s) or curve have two different vertical values? If it does, then it is not a function, as not every input has only one output.

Not a Function

(As we travel across the graph horizontally, there is *not* only one vertical value for *every* horizontal value. Thus, *each* input does not only have *one* output.)

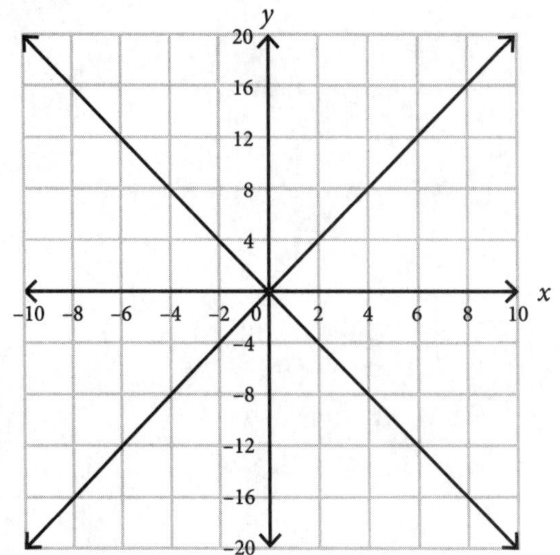

Function

(As we travel across the graph horizontally, there's only one vertical value for every horizontal position along the line or curve. There is only one output for each input.)

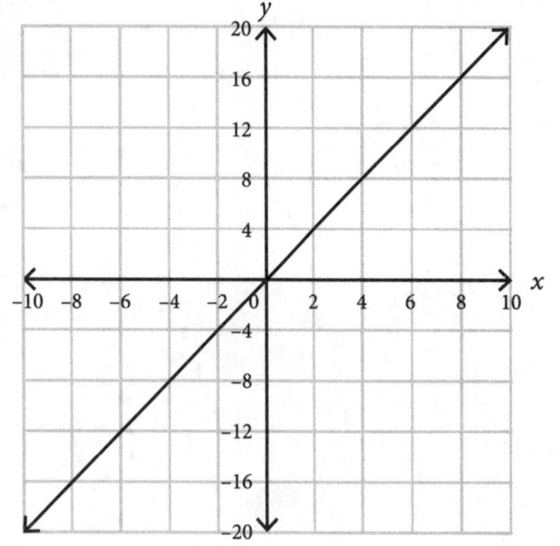

[ENDNOTES]

Chapter 1. The Big Picture

1 David A. Noebel, *Understanding the Times: The Collision of Today's Competing Worldviews*, rev. 2nd ed. (Manitou Springs, CO: Summit Press, 2006), p. 16.

2 Freeman J. Dyson, *The Mathematical Sciences: A Collection of Essays* (Cambridge, MA: Massachusetts Institute of Technology, 1969), p. 101–102.

3 See Morris Kline's discussion of Hermann von Helmhotz. Morris Kline, *Mathematics: The Loss of Certainty* (New York: Oxford University Press, 1980), p. 92.

4 *New Oxford American Dictionary*, 3rd ed. (Oxford University Press, 2012), Version 2.2.1 (156) (Apple, 2011), s.v., "expression."

5 Ibid. s.v., "equation."

6 Symbols based on those presented in Florian Cajori, *A History of Mathematical Notations: Two Volumes Bound As One* (Mineola, NY: Dover Publications, 1993), 1:2–45.

7 *New Oxford American Dictionary*, s.v., "notation."

8 We'll review in the next chapter that we can complete division by multiplying by the multiplicative inverse instead. So $2 \div 1$ means $2 \bullet \frac{1}{1}$, which simplifies to $2 \bullet 1$.

9 John H. Saxon Jr., *Algebra 2: An Incremental Development*, 2d ed. (Norman, OK: Saxon Publishers, 1997), p. 8.

10 Walter W. Sawyer, *Mathematician's Delight* (Harmondsworth Middlesex: Penguin, 1943), p. 10, quoted in James D. Nickel, rev. ed., *Mathematics: Is God Silent?* (Vallecito, CA: Ross House Books, 2001), p. 290.

11 John C. Stone and James F. Millis, *A Secondary Arithmetic: Commercial and Industrial for High, Industrial, Commercial, Normal Schools, and Academies* (Boston, MA: Benj. H. Sanborn & Co., 1908), http://books.google.com/books?id=RtYGAAAAYAAJ, p. 205–206.

12 *New Oxford American Dictionary*, s.v., "formula."

Chapter 2. Mastering Fractions and Negative Numbers

1 Euclid, "Euclid's Elements: Book 1, Definitions, Definition 2," found in David E. Joyce, *Euclid's Elements*, Department of Mathematics and Computer Science, Clark University, http://aleph0.clarku.edu/~djoyce/java/elements/bookI/bookI.html, accessed 10/04/14.

2 Longitude and latitude values vary slightly depending on where in the city they are describing. We used the values listed on David B. Zwiefelhofer, Find Latitude and Longitude, www.findlatitudeandlongitude.com, accessed 12/01/15, rounded to the nearest hundredth.

3 John Hudson Tiner, *Exploring the World of Mathematics* (Green Forest, AR: Master Books, 2004), chapters 1 and 2.

4 Also spelled Roemer.

Chapter 3. Exploring Unknowns and Equations

1 *New Oxford American Dictionary*, 3rd ed. (Oxford University Press, 2012), Version 2.2.1 (156) (Apple, 2011), s.v., "unknown."

2 See David Eugene Smith, *History of Mathematics*, vol. 2, *Special Topics of Elementary Mathematics* (New York: Dover Publications, 1958), p. 422, 430; Florian Cajori, *A History of Mathematical Notations: Two Volumes Bound As One* (Mineola, NY: Dover Publications, 1993), p. 71, 75, 379, and 380.

3 *New Oxford American Dictionary*, s.v., "equality."

4 *The American Heritage Dictionary of the English Language*, 1980 new college ed., s.v., "altitude."

5 *New Oxford American Dictionary*, s.v., "unknown."

6 Stuart Hollingdale, *Makers of Mathematics* (New York: Penguin Books, 1994), p. 275.

7 Ibid.

8 E.T. Bell, *Men of Mathematics* (New York: Simon and Schuster, 1965), p. 139.

9 Hollingdale, *Makers of Mathematics*, p. 278.

10 See JOC/EFR, "Leonhard Euler" (September 1998), http://www-history.mcs.st-and.ac.uk/Biographies/Euler.html, accessed 06/23/15.

11 William DunHam, *Journey Through Genius: The Great Theorems of Mathematics* (New York: John Wiley and Sons, 1990), p. 210.

12 See Augustus De Morgan, *A Budget of Paradoxes* (London: Longmans, Green, and Co., 1872), https://books.google.com/books?id=zvXv-oZ5TEQC&pg=PR3#v=onepage&q&f=false, p. 250.

13 De Morgan (*Budget of Paradoxes*), as quoted in Bell, *Men of Mathematics*, p. 147.

Chapter 4. Fractions, Unknowns, and Equations

1. Denis Guedj, *Numbers: The Universal Language* (New York: Harry N. Abrams, 1996), p. 74.

2. Book: Dr. Jason Lisle, *The Ultimate Proof of Creation* (Green Forest, AR: Master Books, 2009). Video: Dr. Jason Lisle, *The Ultimate Proof of Creation* (Petersburg, KY: Answers in Genesis, 2009), currently available free at http://www.answersingenesis.org/media/video/ondemand/ultimate-proof-of-creation/ultimate-proof, accessed 06/23/2015.

Chapter 5. Ratios, Proportions, and Unknowns

1 *New Oxford American Dictionary*, 3rd ed. (Oxford University Press, 2012), Version 2.2.1 (156) (Apple, 2011), s.v., "congruent."

2 John C. Stone and James F. Millis, *A Secondary Arithmetic: Commercial and Industrial for High, Industrial, Commercial, Normal Schools, and Academies* (Boston, MA: Benj. H. Sanborn & Co., 1908). Available on Google Books, http://books.google.com/books?id=RtYGAAAAYAAJ&pg=PP1#v=onepage&q&f=false, p. 193.

3 Charles Riborg Mann and George Ransom Twiss, *Physics*, rev. ed. (New York: Scott, Foresman & Company, 1910), http://books.google.com/books?id=8FERAAAAYAAJ&pg=PA316&dq#v=onepage&q&f=false, accessed 3/22/13, p. 17.

4 *New Oxford American Dictionary*, s.v., "lever."

5 David Halliday, Robert Resnick, and Jearl Walker, *Fundamentals of Physics*, 7th ed. (Chichester, England: John Wilely & Sons, 2005), p. 88.

6 Florian Cajori, *A History of Mathematics*, 2nd ed., rev. and enlarged. (New York: Macmillan, 1919), https://books.google.com/books?id=bBoPAAAAIAAJ&vq=archimedes&pg=PR3#v=onepage&q&f=false, p. 37.

7 Ibid., p. 34.

8 Sir Thomas Heath, "Archimedes." Found in *Pioneers of Progress: Men of Science* (New York: Macmillan, 1920), https://books.google.com/books?id=Ycxp9rbO2-0C&pg=PP5#v=onepage&q&f=false, p. 2.

9 This paragraph is based on and paraphrased from Walter W. Rouse Ball, *A Short Account of the History of Mathematics* (New York: Macmillan, 1888), http://www.google.com/books?id=U9zuAAAAMAAJ&q, p. 60–61.

Chapter 6. Percents, Unknowns, and Rearranging Equations

1 David Halliday, Robert Resnick, and Jearl Walker, *Fundamentals of Physics*, 7th ed. (Chichester, England: John Wilely & Sons, 2005), p. 88.

2 Stephen Hawking, ed., *On the Shoulders of Giants: The Great Works of Physics and Astronomy* (Philadelphia, PA: Running Press Book Publishers, 2002), p. 1157.

3 You'll sometimes see Newton's birth year listed as 1643 instead of 1642. His birth year depends on the calendar used. His birth date was December 25, 1642, in the Old Style and January 4, 1643, in the New Style. Search online for "old and new style dates" to learn more.

4 Stephen Hawking, ed., *On the Shoulders of Giants*, p. 1158.

5 E.F. King, *A Biographical Sketch of Sir Isaac Newton, to Which Are Added Authorized Reports of the Oration of Lord Brougham (with His Lordship's Notes)* . . . 2nd ed. (London: Simpkin, Marshall, & Co., 1858), http://books.google.com/books?id=2UwBAAAAQAAJ&printsec=frontcover&dq=newton&hl=en&sa=X&ei=B911UY3KMKyP0QHGlIGwAw&ved=0CGUQ6AEwCA, p. 18–22.

6 As quoted in Stuart Hollingdale, *Makers of Mathematics* (New York: Penguin Books, 1994), p. 171.

Chapter 7. Simplifying Expressions

1 *New Oxford American Dictionary*, 3rd ed. (Oxford University Press, 2012), Version 2.2.1 (156) (Apple, 2011), s.v., "expression."

2 Joseph Victor Collins, *Practical Algebra: First Year Course* (New York: American Book Co., 1910), http://google.com/books?id=hNdHAAAAIAAJ&pg=PP1#v=onepage&q&f=false, p. 25.

3 Found in Ron Aharoni, *Arithmetic for Parents: A Book for Grownups about Children's Mathematics*, trans. Danna Reisner (El Cerrito, CA: Sumizdat, 2007), p. 9.

4 *New Oxford American Dictionary*, 3rd ed., s.v., "term."

5 Joseph Victor Collins, *Practical Algebra: First Year Course* (New York: American Book Co., 1910), http://google.com/books?id=hNdHAAAAIAAJ&pg=PP1#v=onepage&q&f=false, p. 27. Note: Collins's actual definition has the adjective "algebraical" before expression (i.e., "an algebraical expression"). We omitted this word to avoid confusion.

6 Information based on Sir Thomas Heath, "Archimedes." Found in *Pioneers of Progress: Men of Science* (New York: Macmillan, 1920), https://books.google.com/books?id=Ycxp9rbO2-0C&pg=PP5#v=onepage&q&f=false, p. 1–6; Elmer Ellsworth Burns, *The Story of Great Inventions* (New York: Harper & Brothers, 1910), https://books.google.com/books?id=q8cNAAAAYAAJ&pg=PP1#v=onepage&q&f=false, p. 1–8; Florian Cajori, *A History of Mathematics*, 2nd ed., rev. and enlarged (New York: Macmillan, 1919), https://books.google.com/books?id=bBoPAAAAIAAJ&vq=archimedes&pg=PR3#v=onepage&q&f=false, p. 34–38. Walter W. Rouse Ball, *A Short Account of the History of Mathematics* (New York: Macmillan, 1888), https://books.google.com/books?id=U9zuAAAAMAAJ&q, p. 59–70; Vitruvius, *The Ten Books on Architecture*, trans. Morris Hicky Morgan (Cambridge: Harvard University Press, 1914), http://www.gutenberg.org/files/20239/20239-h/29239-h.htm, p. 254.

7 *New Oxford American Dictionary*, s.v., "Eureka."

Chapter 8. Negative Numbers and Unknowns

1 *The American Heritage Dictionary of the English Language*, 1980 New College ed., s.v., "evaluate."

Chapter 9. Parentheses, the Distributive Property, and Unknowns

1 Many authors used a line as a grouping symbol; the comma is from G. W. Leibniz, *Acta eruditorum* (1702), p. 212. Referenced in Florian Cajori, *A History of Mathematical Notations: Two Volumes Bound As One* (Mineola, NY: Dover Publications, 1993), 1:390. See *A History of Mathematical Notations* for further information on the history of grouping symbols.

2 Joseph Victor Collins, *Practical Algebra: First Year Course* (New York: American Book Co., 1910), http://google.com/books?id=hNdHAAAAIAAJ&pg=PP1#v=onepage&q&f=false, p. 39.

3 Technically, we could also view the multiplier of –2 as (–1)(2) and distribute the –1 and the 2 separately. The idea is that we have to distribute the negative sign in order to preserve the intended meaning.

4 *New Oxford American Dictionary*, 3rd ed. (Oxford University Press, 2012), Version 2.2.1 (156) (Apple, 2011), s.v., "algebra."

5 Leonard Euler, *Elements of Algebra, by Leonard Euler, Translated from the French; with the Additions of La Grange, and the Notes of the French Translator* (London: J. Johnson and Co., 1810), https://books.google.com/books?id=hqI-AAAAYAAJ&pg=PR1#v=onepage&q&f=false, p. 270.

Chapter 10. Inequalities

1 *New Oxford American Dictionary*, 3rd ed. (Oxford University Press, 2012), Version 2.2.1 (156) (Apple, 2011), s.v., "equation."

2 Symbols based on those presented in Florian Cajori, *A History of Mathematical Notations: Two Volumes Bound As One* (Mineola, NY: Dover Publications, 1993), 2:115–119.

Chapter 11. Statistics

1 *The American Heritage Dictionary of the English Language*, 1980 new college ed., s.v., "statistics."

2 Ibid.

3 *American Heritage Dictionary of the English Language*, 5th ed. (Boston, MA: Houghton Mifflin Harcourt Publishing Company, 2011), http://www.thefreedictionary.com/data, accessed 08/18/15, s.v., "data."

4 Eric W. Weisstein, "Sampling," from *MathWorld* — A Wolfram Web Resource, http://mathworld.wolfram.com/Sampling.html, accessed 9/27/14.

5 "In this table [referring to a frequency distribution shown], the word 'frequency' indicates how often (how frequently) that outcome (number of teenagers) occurred. A frequency distribution is a count of like outcomes." Marlene A. Smith, *The Data Analysis Handbook* (University of Colorado at Denver, 1997), p. 65.

6 For helpful information on when to use what graph, see National Center for Education Statistics, Kids' Zone, "Graphing Tutorial," http://nces.ed.gov/nceskids/pdf/graph_tutorial.pdf, p. 5, and Centers for Disease Control and Prevention (CDC), Department of Health and Human Services, "Using Graphs and Charts to Illustrate Quantitative Data," *Evaluation ETA: Evaluation Briefs*, No. 12 (July 2008): 2, http://www.cdc.gov/healthyyouth/evaluation/pdf/brief12.pdf

7 *New Oxford American Dictionary*, 3rd ed. (Oxford University Press, 2012), Version 2.2.1 (156) (Apple, 2011), s.v., "coordinate."

8 Ibid., s.v., "axis."

9 "When smaller changes exist, line graphs are better to use than bar graphs. Line graphs can also be used to compare changes over the same period of time for more than one group." National Center for Education Statistics, Kids' Zone, "Graphing Tutorial," http://nces.ed.gov/nceskids/pdf/graph_tutorial.pdf, accessed 10/14/14, p. 5.

10 *The American Heritage Dictionary of the English Language*, 1980 ed., s.v., "trend."

11 *New Oxford American Dictionary*, s.v., "correlation."

12 John C. Stone and James F. Millis, *A Secondary Arithmetic: Commercial and Industrial for High, Industrial, Commercial, Normal Schools, and Academies* (Boston, MA: Benj. H. Sanborn & Co., 1908), http://books.google.com/books?id=RtYGAAAAYAAJ, p. 201.

13 *The American Heritage Dictionary of the English Language*, 1980 new college ed., s.v., "statistics."

14 Carl B. Boyer, *A History of Mathematics*, 2nd ed., vol. 2, rev. by Uta C. Merzbach (New York: John Wiley and Sons, 1991), p. 434.

15 Ernst R. Breslich, *Second-Year Mathematics for Secondary Schools* (London: Forgotten Books, 2013, originally published in 1916), http://www.forgottenbooks.com/readbook_text/Second-Year_Mathematics_for_Secondary_Schools_1000031195/321, p. 321.

16 Walter W. Rouse Ball, *A Short Account of the History of Mathematics* (New York: Macmillan, 1888), http://www.google.com/books?id=U9zuAAAAMAAJ&q=archimedes#v=snippet&q=archimedes&f=false, p. 449.

17 Quoted in E.T. Bell, *Men of Mathematics* (New York: Simon and Schuster, 1965), p. 254.

Chapter 12. Probability

1 *The American Heritage Dictionary of the English Language*, 1980 new college ed., s.v., "probable."

2 Ibid., s.v. "event."

3 David Halliday, Robert Resnick, and Jearl Walker, *Fundamentals of Physics*, 7th ed. (England: John Wiley & Sons, 2005), p.1024.

4 Statistics is, "The mathematics of the collection, organization, and interpretation of numerical data; especially, the analysis of population characteristics by inference from sampling." *The American Heritage Dictionary of the English Language*, 1980 new college ed., s.v., "statistics."

5 *New Oxford American Dictionary*, 3rd ed. (Oxford University Press, 2012), Version 2.2.1 (156) (Apple, 2011), s.v., "factorial." The word "positive" was added because we defined integers differently than this dictionary.

6 D.A. Bradbury, "Reply to Landau and Landau," *Creation/Evolution*, 13, no. 2 (1993), p. 48–49.

7 Don Batten, "Cheating With Chance," first published in *Creation*, 17, no. 2 (March 1995), http://creation.com/cheating-with-chance, p. 14–15.

8 Ken Ham, with Cindy Malott, *The Answers Book for Kids*, vol. 3, (Green Forest, AR: Master Books, 2009), p. 35.

9 NANPA, "About the North American Numbering Plan" (Neustar), http://www.nanpa.com/about_us/abt_nanp.html, accessed 08/25/15.

10 Virginia Lottery, "Mega Jackpots . . . Mega Game!" https://www.valottery.com, accessed 9/04/15.

11 If we're wrong and they really meant the odds, the probability of winning would be $\frac{1}{258,890,851}$. The slight difference would be negligible.

12 Emily Haisley, Romel Mostafa, and George Loewenstein, "Myopic Risk-seeking: The Impact of Narrow Decision Bracketing on Lottery Play," *Journal of Risk and Uncertainty*, 37, no. 1 (August 2008), p. 57–75. As quoted in many papers and websites, including Geoff Williams, "Poor people spend 9% of income on lottery tickets; here's why" (*Daily Finance*, 05/31/10), http://www.dailyfinance.com/2010/05/31/poor-people-spend-9-of-income-on-lottery-tickets-heres-why/

13 "The Gross Annual Wager of the United States: 2006," Christiansen Capital Advisors, LLC., 2007, quoted in Chad Hill, "Frequently Asked Questions: Gambling in the United States" (Citizen Link, Revised: 6-11-2010), http://www.citizenlink.com/2010/06/14/frequently-asked-questions-gambling-in-the-united-states/, accessed 7/10/14.

14 Michael Windelspecht, *Genetics 101* (Westport, CT: Greenwood Press, 2007), p. 11, emphasis added.

15 Gary Parker, *Building Blocks in Life Science: From Genes & Genesis to Science & Scripture* (Green Forest, AR: Master Books, 2011), p. 7.

16 For more information on genes and a biblical worldview, check out "Genes and Genesis" in *Building Blocks in Life Sciences: From Genesis & Genes to Science & Scripture* by Gary Parker; the "Genes and Genesis" section is currently available to read for free at www.MasterBooks.com (search for *Building Blocks in Life Sciences* and download the preview).

You might also want to visit www.AnswersinGenesis.org and read an article or watch a video on natural selection, origin of the races, fitting the animals on the ark, or mutations (a related topic we didn't have time to explore).

17 Ken Ham and A. Charles Ware, *One Race One Blood: A Biblical Answer to Racism* (Green Forest, AR: Master Books, 2007), p. 67.

18 *New Oxford American Dictionary*, s.v. "factorial." The word "positive" was added because we defined integers differently than this dictionary.

Chapter 13. Exploring Mathematical Relationships

1 *New Oxford American Dictionary*, 3rd ed. (Oxford University Press, 2012), Version 2.2.1 (156) (Apple, 2011), s.v., "relation"

2 Christopher Stover, "Independent Variable," from *MathWorld*—A Wolfram Web Resource, created by Eric W. Weisstein, http://mathworld.wolfram.com/IndependentVariable.html.

3 Christopher Stover, "Dependent Variable," from MathWorld—A Wolfram Web Resource, created by Eric W. Weisstein, http://mathworld.wolfram.com/DependentVariable.html

4 *New Oxford American Dictionary*, s.v., "displacement."

5 Stover, "Independent Variable."

6 Stover, "Dependent Variable."

Chapter 14. Graphing Mathematical Relationships

1 Dictionary.com, *Dictionary.com Unabridged* (Random House, Inc.), http://dictionary.reference.com/browse/linear, accessed 09/02/15, s.v. "linear."

2 Morris Kline, *Calculus: An Intuitive and Physical Approach*, 2nd ed. (New York: Dover Publications, 1977), p. 63.

3 If you'd like to see how some other countries represent slope-intercept form, take a look at the list at the bottom of this Math is Fun webpage: MathIsFun.com, "Equation of a Straight Line," http://www.mathsisfun.com/equation_of_line.html, accessed 08/27/15.

4 Completely horizontal lines can still be thought of as functions. For example $y = 8$ could be written as $y = 0x + 8$. For every input we could pick for x, we'd still get one and only one value for y.

5 John C. Stone and James F. Millis, *A Secondary Arithmetic: Commercial and Industrial for High, Industrial, Commercial, Normal Schools, and Academies* (Boston, MA: Benj. H. Sanborn & Co., 1908), http://books.google.com/books?id=RtYGAAAAYAAJ, p. 203–204.

6 *New Oxford American Dictionary*, 3rd ed. (Oxford University Press, 2012), Version 2.2.1 (156) (Apple, 2011), s.v., "Descartes, René."

7 David Eugene Smith, *History of Mathematics*, Vol. 2, *Special Topics of Elementary Mathematics* (New York: Dover Publications, 1958), p. 322.

8 Elizabeth Sanderson Haldane, *Descartes: His Life and Times*, (London: n.p., 1905), https://books.google.com/books?id=PXkNAQAAIAAJ&dq=descartes&pg=PR8#v=onepage&q=descartes&f=false, p. 137.

9 Ibid., p. 143.

10 René Descartes, *A Discourse on Method, etc.*, John Veitch, trans. (New York: E.P. Dutton, 1916), https://books.google.com/books?id=-aRGAQAAMAAJ&pg=PP5#v=onepage&q&f=false, p. 27.

11 Dr. Jason Lisle, *The Ultimate Proof of Creation: Resolving the Origins Debate* (Green Forest, AR: Master Books, 2009), p. 62.

Chapter 15. Exponents and Unknowns

1 Leonard Euler, *Elements of Algebra, by Leonard Euler, Translated from the French; with the Additions of La Grange*, 2nd ed., vol. 1 (London: J. Johnson and Co., 1810), https://books.google.com/books?id=hqI-AAAAYAAJ&pg=PR1#v=onepage&q&f=false, p. 71.

2 See the "Power or Exponent?" article on The Math Forum for a thoughtful explanation of the different ways power is used. Dr. Peterson, "Power or Exponent?" The Math Forum: Ask Dr. Math, Questions & Answers from our Archives (The Math Forum @ Drexel, 2003), http://mathforum.org/library/drmath/view/64570.html

3 See Monty White, "Billions of People in Thousands of Years?" *Answers Magazine* (9/5/06), https://answersingenesis.org/evidence-against-evolution/billions-of-people-in-thousands-of-years/, and "The Race to Seven Billion," Perspective, *Answers Magazine* (04/01/12), https://answersingenesis.org/evidence-against-evolution/the-race-to-seven-billion/

The 4,400 years ago date for the Flood is a rounded estimate. For a more precise estimate, see David Wright, "Timeline for the Flood,"(Answers in Genesis, 03/09/12), https://answersingenesis.org/bible-timeline/timeline-for-the-flood/

4 Don Batten, Ken Ham, Jonathan Sarfati, and Carl Wieland, *The Revised and Expanded Answers Book: The 20 Most-Asked Questions About Creation, Evolution, & the Book of Genesis Answered!* rev. ed. (Green Forest, AR: Master Books, 2000), p. 81. See also Dr. Andrew A. Snelling, "Radiometric Dating: Problems with the Assumptions," *Answers Magazine* (September 2, 2009; last featured August 4, 2010), https://answersingenesis.org/geology/radiometric-dating/radiometric-dating-problems-with-the-assumptions/

5 Keith Swenson, "Radio-Dating in Rubble: The Lava Dome at Mount St. Helens Debunks Dating Methods," (Answers in Genesis, 06/01/01), https://answersingenesis.org/geology/radiometric-dating/radio-dating-in-rubble/, originally published in *Creation*, 23, no. 3, (June 2001), p. 23–25.

6 Batten, et al., *The Revised and Expanded Answers Book*, p. 83.

7 Formula based on one given in William Spence, Suart A. Sipkin, and George L. Choy, "Measuring the Size of an Earthquake: Energy, E," *Earthquakes and Volcanoes*, 21, no. 1 (1989), as seen on U.S. Geological Survey, http://earthquake.usgs.gov/learn/topics/measure.php

8 A shortcut for writing exponents known as logarithms is typically used when expressing this formula. Using logarithms, the same formula would be written like this: $\log_{10}E = 11.8 + 1.5M$. Also, the M in the formula stands for magnitude calculated a specific way (there is more than one way to calculate it). See Spence, Sipkin, and Choy, "Measuring the Size of an Earthquake: Energy, *E*," for more details.

Chapter 16. More with Exponents

1 Vivian Shaw Groza, *A Survey of Mathematics: Elementary Concepts and Their Historical Development* (New York: Holt, Rinehart, and Winston, 1968), p. 251.

2 You might wonder why the symbolic algebra lists $4x + 5$ rather than $5 + 4x$. Since addition is commutative, both mean the same thing. However, the convention is to list terms with variables before terms without any variables.

Chapter 17. Square Roots and Unknowns

1 Dimensions based on those given by the Federation Internationale de Football Association in "Regulations FIFA U-20 World Cup New Zealand 2015," FIFI.com, http://resources.fifa.com/mm/document/tournament/competition/02/45/23/69/regulationsfu20wc2015newzealand_e_011014_neutral.pdf, accessed 12/16/14, p. 28.

2 *The American Heritage Dictionary of the English Language*, 1980 new college ed., s.v., "radicand."

3 Information on Pythagoras based primarily on Walter W. Rouse Ball, *A Short Account of the History of Mathematics* (New York: Macmillan, 1888), https://books.google.com/books?id=U9zuAAAAMAAJ&q, p. 18–27; Florian Cajori, *A History of Mathematics*, 2nd ed. rev. and enlarged (New York: Macmillan, 1919), https://books.google.com/books?id=bBoPAAAAIAAJ&vq=archimedes&pg=PR3#v=onepage&q&f=false, p. 17–20; James D. Nickel, *Mathematics: Is God Silent?* rev. ed. (Vallecito, CA: Ross House Books, 2001), p. 21–24.

4 Definitions vary slightly as to how Pythagoreans is defined. See Ball, *A Short Account of the History of Mathematics*, p. 18.

5 Nickel, *Mathematics: Is God Silent?* p. 22. The creedal confession is referenced as being cited in Stanley L. Jaki, *The Relevance of Physics* (Edinburgh: Scottish Academic Press, [1966] 1992), p. 136.

6 Ball, *A Short Account of the History of Mathematics*, p. 18.

7 For more information on Pythagoras's worldview and its crumbling, see Nickel, *Mathematics: Is God Silent?* p. 21–24.

Chapter 18. Glimpses of Trigonometry

1 *New Oxford American Dictionary*, 3rd ed. (Oxford University Press, 2012), Version 2.2.1 (156) (Apple, 2011), s.v., "congruent."

2 For more information on how the biblical worldview makes sense of our ability to reason while other worldviews do not explain it, see Dr. Jason Lisle, *The Ultimate Proof of Creation: Resolving the Origins Debate* (Green Forest, AR: Master Books, 2009).

3 If you're curious about the unit circle, you can find more information online. Math Is Fun currently has a visual interactive unit circle at https://www.mathsisfun.com/algebra/trig-interactive-unit-circle.html

4 See Leon Harkleroad, *The Math Behind the Music* (New York: Cambridge University Press, 2006), p. 18–19.

Chapter 19. Sets, Sequences, Symbols, and Unknowns

1 *New Oxford American Dictionary*, 3rd ed. (Oxford University Press, 2012), Version 2.2.1 (156) (Apple, 2011), s.v., "element."

2 *The American Heritage Dictionary of the English Language*, 1980 new college ed., s.v., "sequence."

3 Ibid., emphasis added.

4 More technical details of mathematics and sound can be found online. I also found these two resources helpful in my research: Gareth Loy, *Musimathics: The Mathematical Foundations of Music*, vol. 1 (Cambridge, MA: The MIT Press, 2006) and Harvey E. White and Donald H. White, *Physics and Music: The Science of Musical Sound* (Philadelphia, PA: Saunders College, 1980).

5 Eric W. Weisstein, "Boolean Algebra," from *MathWorld*—A Wolfram Web Resource, http://mathworld.wolfram.com/BooleanAlgebra.html

Chapter 20. Glimpses of Consumer Math

1 *New Oxford American Dictionary*, 3rd ed. (Oxford University Press, 2012), Version 2.2.1 (156) (Apple, 2011), s.v., "consumer."

2 Eric W. Weisstein, "Interest," from *MathWorld*—A Wolfram Web Resource, http://mathworld.wolfram.com/Interest.html, (bolding added).

3 Dictionary.com, *Dictionary.com Unabridged* (Random House, Inc.), http://dictionary.reference.com/browse/compound, accessed 09/09/15, s.v., "compound."

4 *Farlex Financial Dictionary*, http://financial-dictionary.thefreedictionary.com/compounding+period, accessed 09/10/15, s.v. "compounding period."

5 *The American Heritage Dictionary of the English Language*, 1980 new college ed., s.v., "budget."

Chapter 21. Review

1 *New Oxford American Dictionary*, 3rd ed. (Oxford University Press, 2012), Version 2.2.1 (156) (Apple, 2011), s.v., "algebra."

2 Leonard Euler, *Elements of Algebra, by Leonard Euler, Translated from the French; with the Additions of La Grange, and the Notes of the French Translator* (London: J. Johnson and Co., 1810), https://books.google.com/books?id=hqI-AAAAYAAJ&pg=PR1#v=onepage&q&f=false, p. 270.

3 Statistics is "the mathematics of the collection, organization and interpretation of numerical data; especially, the analysis of population characteristics by inference from sampling." *The American Heritage Dictionary of the English Language*, 1980 new college ed., s.v., "statistics."

Additional Endnotes

Over the course of writing this curriculum, hundreds of websites and books were consulted, along with various learning standards, tests, and other curriculums. Below are a few additional resources not yet included in the endnotes or text that I want to acknowledge.

Barker, Eugene Henry. *Applied Mathematics for Junior High Schools and High Schools.* (Boston, MA: Allyn and Bacon, 1920). Available on Google Books, http://books.google.com/books?id=-t5EAAAAIAAJ&vq=3427&pg=PR2#v=onepage&q&f=false

Bennett, Jeffrey O., and William L. Briggs. *Using and Understanding Mathematics: A Quantitative Reasoning Approach.* 2nd ed. Boston, MA: Addison Wesley, 2002.

Collins, Joseph Victor. *Practical Algebra: First Year Course.* New York: American Book Co., 1910). Available on Google Books, http://google.com/books?id=hNdHAAAAIAAJ&pg=PP1#v=onepage&q&f=false

COMAP. *For All Practical Purposes: Mathematical Literacy in Today's World.* 6th ed. New York: W.H. Freeman, 2003.

Groza, Vivian Shaw. *A Survey of Mathematics: Elementary Concepts and Their Historical Development.* New York: Holt, Rinehart, and Winston, 1968.

Halliday, David, Robert Resnick, and Jearl Walker. *Fundamentals of Physics.* 7th ed. England: John Wiley & Sons, 2005.

Johnson, David B., and Thomas A. Mowry. *Mathematics: A Practical Odyssey.* 2nd ed. Boston, MA: PWS Publishing, 1995.

Stone, John C., and James F. Millis. *A Secondary Arithmetic: Commercial and Industrial for High, Industrial, Commercial, Normal Schools, and Academies.* (Boston, MA: Benj. H. Sanborn & Co., 1908). Available on Google Books, http://books.google.com/books?id=RtYGAAAAYAAJ&pg=PP1#v=onepage&q&f=false

For links to helpful resources, curriculum reviews, and other information to guide further study, please see my website, www.ChristianPerspective.net

Bolded references are to definitions.